Principles of European Law on
Benevolent Intervention in Another's Affairs
(PEL Ben. Int.)

Principles of European Law
Study Group on a European Civil Code

Benevolent Intervention in Another's Affairs
(PEL Ben. Int.)

prepared by
Professor **Christian v. Bar**, Osnabrück
Chairman of the Working Team on Extra-contractual Obligations

with advice from the Advisory Council
approved by the Co-ordinating Group

Particular advice on the drafting of the Articles from
Professor **Eric Clive**, Edinburgh, and Dr. **Stephen Swann**, Osnabrück

Translation: Dr. **Stephen Swann** and Dr. **Mary-Rose McGuire**, Osnabrück

OXFORD
UNIVERSITY PRESS

OXFORD
UNIVERSITY PRESS

Great Clarendon Street, Oxford OX2 6DP

Oxford University Press is a department of the University of Oxford.
It furthers the University's objective of excellence in research, scholarship,
and education by publishing worldwide in

Oxford New York

Auckland Cape Town Dar es Salaam Hong Kong Karachi
Kuala Lumpur Madrid Melbourne Mexico City Nairobi
New Delhi Shanghai Taipei Toronto

With offices in

Argentina Austria Brazil Chile Czech Republic France Greece
Guatemala Hungary Italy Japan Poland Portugal Singapore
South Korea Switzerland Thailand Turkey Ukraine Vietnam

Published in the United States
by Oxford University Press Inc., New York

First published 2006

British Library Cataloguing in Publication Data

Data available

Library of Congress Cataloging in Publication Data

Data available

Printed in Great Britain
on acid-free paper by
Biddles Ltd., King's Lynn

ISBN 0–19–929601–4 978–0–19–929601–9

10 9 8 7 6 5 4 3 2 1

The Osnabrück Working Team

Begoña Alfonso de la Riva (Spanish Law, August 1999-August 2003), Dr. *Erwin Beysen* (Belgian, French and Luxembourgian Law), Dr. *Evlalia Eleftheriadou* (Greek Law), *Silvia Fedrizzi* (Italian Law, August 1999-October 2000), Dr. *Andreas Fötschl* (Austrian Law, August 1999-April 2005), Dr. *Caterina Gozzi* (Italian Law, since February 2001), *Lodewijk Gualthérie van Weezel* (Dutch Law, February 2001-August 2002), *Annamaria Herpai* (Hungarian Law, since October 2003), Dr. *Matthias Hünert* (German Law), *Stefan Kettler* (Irish Law, November 1999-August 2001), *Ina El Kobbia* (Scottish Law; organisation and minutes for the Co-ordinating Group and the Advisory Council), Dr. *María Ángeles Martín Vida* (Spanish Law, since September 2003), Dr. *Mary-Rose McGuire* (translation, since May 2004), *Franz Nieper* (Dutch Law, November 1999-October 2000), *Rosalie Koolhoven* (Dutch Law, since March 2003), *José Carlos de Medeiros Nóbrega* (Portuguese Law), *Sandra Rohlfing* (Working Team rapporteur), *Johan Sandstedt* (Nordic Laws, since April 2001), *Mårten Schultz* (Nordic Laws, January 2000-March 2001) and Dr. *Stephen Swann* (Common Law).

The Advisory Council on Unjustified Enrichment Law and the Law on Benevolent Intervention in Another's Affairs

Professor *Eric Clive* (Edinburgh), Professor *Júlio Manuel Vieira Gomes* (Oporto), Justitierådet Professor *Torgny Håstad* (Stockholm), Professor *Ewan McKendrick* (Oxford), Professor *Peter Schlechtriem* (Freiburg i. Br.) and Dr. *Kristina Süg* (Aarhus).

The Co-ordinating Group

Professor *Guido Alpa* (Genua/Rome), Professor *Kaspars Balodis* (Riga, since December 2004), Professor *Christian v. Bar* (Osnabrück), Professor *Maurits Barendrecht* (Tilburg), Professor *Hugh Beale* (London), Professor *Michael Joachim Bonell* (Rome), Professor *Mifsud G. Bonnici* (Valetta, since December 2004), Professor *Carlo Castronovo* (Milan), Professor *Eric Clive* (Edinburgh), Professor *Ulrich Drobnig* (Hamburg), Professor *Bénédicte Fauvarque-Cosson* (Paris), Professor *Marcel Fontaine* (Leuven, until December 2003), Professor *Andreas Furrer* (Luzern, since December 2003), Professor *Jacques Ghestin* (Paris), Professor Sir *Roy Goode* (Oxford, until December 2002), Professor *Viggo Hagstrøm* (Oslo, since June 2002), Professor *Arthur Hartkamp* (The Hague), Justitierådet Professor *Torgny Håstad* (Stockholm), Professor *Johnny Herre* (Stockholm), Professor *Martijn Hesselink* (Amsterdam), Professor *Ewoud Hondius* (Utrecht), Professor *Giovanni Iudica* (Milan, since June 2004), Professor *Konstantinos Kerameus* (Athens), Professor *Ole Lando* (Copenhagen), Professor *Kåre Lilleholt* (Bergen, since June 2003), Professor *Brigitta Lurger* (Graz), Professor *Hector MacQueen* (Edinburgh), Professor *Denis Mazeaud* (Paris, since June 2005), Professor *Ewan McKendrick* (Oxford), Professor *Valentinas Mikelenas* (Vilnius, since December 2004), Dr. *Niamh Moloney* (Belfast, since December 2003), Professor *Eoin O'Dell* (Dublin), Professor *Edgar du Perron* (Amsterdam), Professor *Denis Philippe* (Leuven, since June 2004), Professor *Johannes Rainer* (Salzburg), Professor *Jerzy Rajski* (Warsaw), Professor *Christina Ramberg* (Gothenburg), Professor *Philippe Rémy* (Poitiers), Judge Professor *Encarna Roca y Trias* (Madrid/Barcelona), Professor *Peter Schlechtriem* (Freiburg i. Br.), Professor *Martin Schmidt-Kessel* (Osnabrück, since December 2004), Professor *Jorge Sinde Monteiro* (Coimbra), Professor *Lena Sisula-Tulokas* (Helsinki), Professor *Sophie Stijns* (Leuven), Professor *Matthias Storme* (Leuven), Professor *Jan Svidron* (Trnava, since June 2005), Dr. *Stephen Swann* (Osnabrück),

Professor *Luboš Tichý* (Prague, since June 2005), Professor *Verica Trstenjak* (Maribor), Professor *Paul Varul* (Tartu, since June 2003), Professor *Lajos Vékás* (Budapest), Professor *Anna Veneziano* (Rome).

Further Members of the Study Group's Advisory Councils

Professor *John W. Blackie* (Strathclyde, Tort Law), Professor *Michael G. Bridge* (London, Property Law and Securities), Professor *Angel Carrasco* (Toledo, Securities), Professor *Pierre Crocq* (Paris, Securities), Dr. *Eugenie Dacoronia* (Athens, Tort Law and Renting Contracts), Professor *Marie Goré* (Paris, Structure), Professor *Helmut Grothe* (Berlin, Renting Contracts), Professor *Jérôme Huet* (Paris, Sales, Services, Agency, Franchise and Distribution Contracts), Professor *Jan Kleineman* (Stockholm, Tort Law), Docent Dr. *Irene Kull* (Tartu, Renting Contracts), Professor *Guillermo Palao Moreno* (Valencia, Tort Law), Professor *Antoni Vaquer Aloy* (Lleida, Renting Contracts), Professor *Alain Verbeke* (Leuven, Renting Contracts), Professor *Anders Victorin* (Stockholm, Renting Contracts), Professor *Sarah Worthington* (London, Renting Contracts).

Volume 1

To be cited as: PEL/*von Bar*, Ben Int, Introduction, A, 1
PEL/*von Bar*, Ben Int, Chapter I, Article 1: 101, Comments, A, 1
PEL/*von Bar*, Ben Int, Chapter I, Article 1: 101, Notes, I, 1

Foreword

The Study Group on a European Civil Code has taken upon itself the task of drafting common European principles for the most important aspects of the law of obligations and for certain parts of the law of property in movables which are especially relevant for the functioning of the common market. It was founded in 1999 as a successor body to the Commission on European Contract Law, on whose work the Study Group is building.

The two groups pursue identical aims. However, the Study Group has a more far-reaching focus in terms of subject-matter and as an ultimate goal it aspires to a consolidated composite text of the material worked out by itself and the Commission on European Contract Law. Both groups have undertaken to ascertain and formulate European standards of 'patrimonial' law for the Member States of the European Union. The Commission on European Contract has already achieved this for the field of general contract law (*Lando and Beale* [eds.], Principles of European Contract Law, Parts I and II combined and revised, The Hague, 2000; *Lando/Clive/Prüm/Zimmermann* [eds.], Principles of European Contract Law Part III, The Hague, 2003). These Principles of European Contract Law (PECL) are being adopted by the Study Group on a European Civil Code with adjustments taking account of new developments and input from its research partners. The Study Group is dovetailing its principles with those of the PECL, extending their encapsulation of standards of patrimonial law in three directions: (i) by developing rules for specific types of contracts; (ii) by developing rules for extra-contractual obligations, i. e. the law of tort/delict, the law of unjustified enrichment, and the law of benevolent intervention in another's affairs (*negotiorum gestio*); and (iii) by developing rules for fundamental questions in the law on mobile assets – in particular transfer of ownership and security for credit.

Like the Commission on European Contract Law's Principles of European Contract Law, the results of the research conducted by the Study Group on a European Civil Code seek to advance the process of Europeanisation of private law. We have undertaken this endeavour on our own personal initiative and merely present the results of a pan-European research project. It is a study in comparative law in so far as we have always taken care to identify the legal position in the Member States of the European Union and to set out the results of this research in the introductions and notes. That of course does not mean that we have only been concerned with documenting the pool of shared legal values or that we simply adopted the majority position among the legal systems where common ground was missing. Rather we have consistently striven to draw up "sound and fitting" principles, that is to say, we have also recurrently developed proposals and concepts for the further development of private law in Europe.

The working methods of the Commission on European Contract Law and the Study Group on a European Civil Code are or were likewise quite similar. The Study Group, however, has had the benefit of Working (or Research) Teams – groups of younger legal scholars under the supervision of a senior member of the Group (a Team Leader) which undertook the basic comparative legal research, developed the drafts for discussion and assembled the extensive material required for the notes. Furthermore, to each Working Team was allocated a consultative body – an Advisory Council. These bodies – deliberately kept small in the interests of efficiency – were formed from leading experts in the relevant field of law who are representative of the major European legal systems. The proposals drafted by the Working Teams and critically scrutinised and improved in a series of meetings by the respective Advisory Council were submitted for discussion on a revolving basis to the actual decision-making body of the Study Group on a European Civil Code, the Co-ordinating Group. Until June 2004 the Co-ordinating Group consisted of representatives from all the jurisdictions belonging to the EU immediately prior to its enlargement in Spring 2004 and in addition legal scholars from Estonia, Hungary, Norway, Poland, Slovenia and Switzerland. Representatives from the Czech Republic, Malta, Latvia, Lithuania and the Slovak Republic joined us after the June meeting 2004 in Warsaw. However, due to reasons of time and capacity, it was only occasionally possible to summarise in the notes the current legal position in the new Member States of the EU. We are keen to fill the outstanding gaps (of which we are only too painfully aware) at a later point in time.

Besides its permanent members, other participants in the Co-ordinating Group with voting rights included all the Team Leaders and – when the relevant material was up for discussion – the members of the Advisory Council concerned. The results of the deliberations during the week-long sitting of the Co-ordinating Group were incorporated into the text of the articles and the commentaries which returned to the agenda for the next meeting of the Co-ordinating Group (or the next but one depending on the work load of the the Group and the Team affected). Each part of the project was the subject of debate on manifold occasions, some stretching over many years. Where a unanimous opinion could not be achieved, majority votes were taken. As far as possible the Articles drafted in English were translated into the other languages either by members of the Team or third parties commissioned for the purpose. The number of languages into which the Articles could be translated admittedly varies considerably from volume to volume. That is in part a consequence of the fact that not all Working Teams were equipped with the same measure of financial support. We also had to resign ourselves to the absence of a perfectly uniform editorial style. Our editing guidelines provided a common basis for scholarly publication, but at the margin had to accommodate preferences of individual teams. However, this should not cause the reader any problems in comprehension.

Work on these Principles had begun long before the European Commission published its Communication on European Contract Law (in 2001), its Action Plan for a more coherent European contract law (in 2003), and its follow-up Communication "European Contract Law and the revision of the *acquis*: the way forward" (in 2004). (All of these documents concerning European contract law are available on the Commission's website: http://europe.eu.int/comm/consumers/cons_int/safe_shop/fair_bus_pract/cont_law/index_en.htm). These documents for their part were published before we formed the Network of Excellence, together with other European research groups and institutions, which will collaborate in the preparation of an academic Common Frame of Reference with the support of funds from the European Community's Sixth Framework Programme. The texts laid before the public by the Study Group on a European Civil Code are therefore not necessarily identical with those which the Network of Excellence will propose to the European Commission for adoption in the

Common Frame of Reference. Rather they represent for the time being texts which the Study Group considers should serve as the starting point for the comprehensive process of discussion and consultation envisaged for the coming years. Whether that process will require any changes to our texts (and, if so, which changes) is something which will have to be weighed up carefully in a spirit of academic independence after a review of the arguments. The political domain can then determine at a later date which of our proposals, if any, it wishes to take up.

In order to leave no room for misunderstanding, it is important to stress that these Principles have been prepared by impartial and independent-minded scholars whose sole interest has been a devotion to the subject-matter. None of us have been rewarded for taking part or mandated to do so. None of us would want to give the impression that we claim any political legitimation for promoting harmonisation of the law. Our legitimation is confined to curiosity and an interest in Europe. In other words, the volumes in this series are to be understood exclusively as the results of scholarly legal research within large international teams. Like every other scholarly legal work, they restate the current law and introduce possible models for its further development; no less, but also no more. We are not a homogenous group whose every member is an advocate of the idea of a European Civil Code. We are, after all, only a *Study* Group. The question whether a European Civil Code is or is not desirable is a political one to which each member can only express an individual view.

Osnabrück, November 2005 *Christian v. Bar*

Our Sponsors

The project of the Study Group on a European Civil Code represents a research endeavour in legal science of extraordinary magnitude. Without the generous financial support of many organisations its realisation would not have been possible.

Our thanks go first of all to the *Deutsche Forschungsgemeinschaft (DFG)*, which has supplied the lion's share of the financing including the salaries of the Working Teams based in Germany and the direct travel costs for the meetings of the Coordinating Group and the numerous Advisory Councils. The work of the Dutch Working Teams was financed by the *Nederlandse Organisatie voor Wetenschappelijk Onderzoek (NWO)* and by the *Universiteit van Amsterdam*. Further personnel costs were met by the Flemish *Fonds voor Wetenschappelijk Onderzoek-Vlaanderen (FWO)*, the *Onassis-Foundation*, the Austrian *Fonds zur Förderung der wissenschaftlichen Forschung* and the *Fundação Calouste Gulbenkian*.

In addition we have consistently been able to fall back on funds made available to the respective organisers of the week long sittings of the Coordinating Group by the relevant university or other sources within the country concerned. It is therefore with the deepest gratitude that I must also mention the *Consiglio nazionale forense* (Rome) and the *Istituto di diritto privato* of the *Università di Roma La Sapienza*, which co-financed the meeting in Rome (June 2000). The session in Salzburg (December 2000) was supported by the Austrian *Bundesministerium für Bildung, Wissenschaft und Kultur*, the *Universität Salzburg* and the *Institut für Rechtspolitik* of the *Universität Salzburg*. The discussions in Stockholm (June 2001) were assisted by the *Department of Law, Stockholm University*, the *Supreme Court Justice Edward Cassel's Foundation* and *Stiftelsen Juridisk Fakultetslitteratur (SJF)*. The meeting in Oxford (December 2001) had the support of *Shearman & Sterling*, the *Hulme Trust*, *Berwin Leighton Paisner* and the *Oxford University Press (OUP)*. The session in Valencia (June 2002) was made possible by the *Asociación Nacional de Registradores de la Propiedad, Mercantil y Bienes Muebles*, the *Universitat de València*, the *Ministerio Español de Ciencia y Tecnología*, the *Facultad de Derecho* of the *Universitat de València*, the *Departamento de Derecho Internacional*, *Departamento de Derecho Civil* and the *Departamento de Derecho Mercantil "Manuel Broseta Pont"* of the *Universitat de València*, the law firm *Cuatrecasas*, the *Generalitat Valenciana*, the *Corts Valencianes*, the *Diputación Provincial de Valencia*, the *Ayuntamiento de Valencia*, the *Colegio de Abogados de Valencia* and *Aranzadi Publishing Company*. The subsequent meeting in Oporto (December 2002) was substantially assisted by the *Universidade Católica Portuguesa – Centro Regional do Porto*. For the week long session in Helsinki (June 2003) we were able to rely on funds from *Suomen Kultuurirahasto* (Finnish Cultural Foundation), the *Niilo Helanderin Säätiö* (Niilo Helander Foundation), the *Suomalainen Lakimeisyhdistys* (Finnish Lawyers Association), the Ministry of Justice and the Ministry for Foreign Affairs, the *Nordea Bank*, *Roschier Holmberg* Attorneys Ltd., *Hannes Snellman* Attorneys Ltd., the *Department of Private Law* and the *Institute of International Commercial Law (KATTI) of Helsinki University*. The session in Leuven (December 2003) was supported by *Katholieke Universiteit Leuven, Faculteit Rechtsgeleerdheid*, and the *FWO*

Vlaanderen Fonds voor Wetenschappelijk Onderzoek (Flanders Scientific Research Fund). The meeting of the Group in Warsaw (June 2004) was substantially assisted by the *Fundacja Fundusz Wspolpracy* (The Cooperation Fund) and the Faculty of Law and Administration of Warsaw University. The meeting in Milan (December 2004) was supported by the *Università Bocconi* and its *Istituto di diritto comparato*, by the Milan *Camera di Commercio*, by the *Associazione Civilisti Italiani* and by the *Comune di Milano*. The meeting in Berlin (June 2005) was made possible by *PricewaterhouseCoopers Deutschland AG*, Frankfurt/Berlin, *Sievert AG & Co.*, Osnabrück, by *Deutscher Sparkassen- und Giroverband*, Berlin, and by *Verband deutscher Hypothekenbanken e. V.*, Berlin. We thank all of these organisations and institutions for the funds which they made available to us and for the extraordinary warmth of hospitality with which our hosts received us.

Preface to this volume

The following text on the law of (justified) benevolent intervention in another's affairs, hereby presented to the interested public, has been deliberated by the Co-ordinating Group of the Study Group on a European Civil Code during its week-long meetings in Utrecht (December 1999), Rome (June 2000), Stockholm (June 2001) and finally in Valencia (June 2002). (Whereas the meetings in Salzburg (December 2000) and Oxford (December 2001) were not dedicated to this matter). In preparation of the respective meetings thorough deliberations with the Advisory Council of the Working Team have taken place. This Working Team in turn has under my supervision composed the first draft of these Principles and has integrated the amendments which had been proposed by the different councils and in some instances had been decided by vote. On this basis I have drawn up the comparative introduction, the comments and the notes. The material for this work again had been provided by the Members of the Osnabrück Working Team. They have carried the main burden of this research endeavour; without their contribution this Book could not have been realized.

Perhaps it may not appear as the most fortunate choice that one of the first publications of the Study Group on a European Civil Code of all subjects is dedicated to the law of benevolent intervention in another's affairs (*negotiorum gestio*). For it concerns a subject matter which accounts for a comparatively small area of law and which in addition from a systematic viewpoint is not even recognised as a separate private law concept under the Common Law. However, the work on this project could be concluded earlier than that of others and it did not seem appropriate to artificially hold back the results until all other parts of the project similarly have reached a stage for publication.

Legislation, case law and doctrine have been stated as of January 2005. Shortly before publication this text was circulated to stakeholders under the CFR net exercise as part of the European Commission's contract law programme.

Osnabrück, November 2005 *Christian v. Bar*

Short Table of Contents

Table of Contents

Principles of European Law on Benevolent Intervention in Another's Affairs

Introduction

Chapter 2: Duties of Intervener

Article 2:101: Duties during Intervention

Comments

Notes

Article 2:102: Duties after Intervention

Comments

Notes

Article 2:103: Reparation for Damage Caused by Breach of Duty

Comments

Article 3:106: Authority of Intervener to Act in the Name of the Principal

Comments

Annexes

Text of Articles

English
Benevolent Intervention in Another's Affairs

Chapter 1:
Scope of Application

Article 1:101: Intervention to Benefit Another

(1) This Book applies where a person (the intervener) acts with the predominant intention of benefiting another (the principal); and
 (a) the intervener has a reasonable ground for acting; or
 (b) the principal approves the act without such undue delay as would adversely affect the intervener.

(2) The intervener does not have a reasonable ground for acting if the intervener:
 (a) has a reasonable opportunity to discover the principal's wishes but does not do so; or
 (b) knows or ought to know that the intervention is against the principal's wishes.

Article 1:102: Intervention to Perform Another's Duty

Where an intervener acts to perform another person's duty, the performance of which is due and urgently required as a matter of overriding public interest, and the intervener acts with the predominant intention of benefiting the recipient of the performance, the person whose duty the intervener acts to perform is a principal to whom this Book applies.

Article 1:103: Exclusions

This Book does not apply where the intervener:
(a) is authorised to act under a contractual or other duty to the principal;
(b) is authorised, other than under this Book, to act independently of the principal's consent or
(c) is under a duty to a third party to act.

Chapter 2:
Duties of Intervener

Article 2:101: Duties during Intervention

(1) During the intervention, the intervener must
 (a) act with reasonable care;
 (b) except in relation to a principal within Article 1:102, act in a manner which the intervener knows or ought reasonably to assume accords with the principal's wishes; and
 (c) so far as possible and reasonable, inform the principal about the intervention and seek the principal's consent to further acts.

(2) The intervention may not be discontinued without good reason.

Article 2:102: Duties after Intervention

(1) After intervening the intervener must without undue delay report and account to the principal and hand over anything obtained as a result of the intervention.

(2) If at the time of intervening the intervener lacks full legal capacity, the duty to hand over is subject to the defences which would be available in the law of unjustified enrichment (PEL Unjust.Enr.).

Article 2:103: Reparation for Damage Caused by Breach of Duty

(1) The intervener is liable to make reparation to the principal for damage caused by breach of a duty set out in this Book if the damage resulted from a risk which the intervener created, increased or intentionally perpetuated.

(2) The intervener's liability is reduced or excluded in so far as this is fair and reasonable, having regard to, among other things, the intervener's reasons for acting.

(3) An intervener who at the time of intervening lacks full legal capacity is liable to make reparation only in so far as that intervener is also liable to make reparation under the law of non-contractual obligations arising out of damage caused to another (PEL Liab.Dam.).

Chapter 3:
Rights and Authority of Intervener

Article 3:101: Right to Indemnification or Reimbursement

The intervener has a right against the principal for indemnification or, as the case may be, reimbursement in respect of an obligation or expenditure (whether of money or other assets) in so far as reasonably incurred for the purposes of the intervention.

Article 3:102: Right to Remuneration

(1) The intervener has a right to remuneration in so far as the intervention is reasonable and undertaken in the course of the intervener's profession or trade.

(2) The remuneration due is the amount, so far as reasonable, which is ordinarily paid at the time and place of intervention in order to obtain a performance of the kind undertaken.

Article 3:103: Right to Reparation

An intervener who acts to protect the principal, or the principal's property or interests, against danger has a right against the principal for reparation for loss caused as a result of personal injury or property damage, suffered in acting, if:

(a) the intervention created or significantly increased the risk of such injury or damage; and
(b) that risk, so far as foreseeable, was in reasonable proportion to the risk to the principal.

Article 3:104: Reduction or Exclusion of Intervener's Rights

(1) The intervener's rights are reduced or excluded in so far as the intervener at the time of acting did not want to demand indemnification, reimbursement, remuneration or reparation, as the case may be.

(2) These rights are also reduced or excluded in so far as this is fair and reasonable, having regard among other things to whether the intervener acted to protect the principal in a situation of joint danger, whether the liability of the principal would be excessive and whether the intervener could reasonably be expected to obtain appropriate redress from another.

Article 3:105: Obligation of Third Person to Indemnify or Reimburse the Principal

If the intervener acts to protect the principal from damage, a person who would be accountable under PEL Liab.Dam. for the causation of such damage to the principal is obliged to indemnify or, as the case may be, reimburse the principal's liability to the intervener.

Article 3:106: Authority of Intervener to Act in the Name of the Principal

(1) The intervener may conclude legal transactions or perform other juridical acts in the name of the principal in so far as this is reasonable to benefit the principal.

(2) However, a unilateral juridical act by the intervener in the name of the principal has no effect if a third person to whom it is addressed rejects the act without undue delay.

Danish[1]
Godgørende indgriben i en andens anliggender

Kapitel 1:
Anvendelsesområde

Artikel 1:101: Intervention til fordel for en anden

(1) Denne bog finder anvendelse når en person (intervenøren) handler i den overvejende hensigt at gavne en anden (principalen), og
  (a) intervenøren har en rimelig grund til at handle, eller
  (b) principalen godkender handlingen uden en sådan forsinkelse, at forsinkelsen kan skade intervenøren.

(2) Intervenøren har ikke en rimelig grund til at handle, hvis han
  (a) har rimelig anledning til at fastslå principalens ønsker, men undlader dette, eller
  (b) ved eller burde vide, at interventionen er imod principalens ønsker.

Artikel 1:102: Intervention for at opfylde en andens forpligtelse

Når en intervenør handler for at opfylde en andens forpligtelse, der er forfalden og hvis opfyldelse er strengt påkrævet grundet hensynet til en overordnet offentlig interesse, og intervenøren handler i den overvejende hensigt at gavne den, til hvem forpligtelsen var skyldig, er den person, hvis forpligtelse intervenøren handlede for at opfylde, en principal, på hvem denne bogs bestemmelser finder anvendelse.

Artikel 1:103: Undtagelser

Denne bog finder ikke anvendelse, hvis intervenøren
(a) er bemyndiget til at handle på grund af en kontraktuel eller anden forpligtelse overfor principalen,
(b) er bemyndiget, bortset fra efter reglerne i denne bog, til at handle uafhængigt af principalens samtykke, eller
(c) er forpligtet overfor en tredjemand til at handle.

Kapitel 2:
Intervenørens forpligtelser

Artikel 2:101: Forpligtelser under interventionen

(1) Under interventionen må intervenøren
  (a) udvise tilbørlig omhu,
  (b) handle på en måde, som intervenøren ved, eller rimeligvis må antage, er i overensstemmelse med principalens ønsker, bortset fra i relation til en principal, der er omfattet af 1:102, og

---

[1] Translated by Dr. *Kristina Süg* (Aarhus).

(c) i det omfang, det er rimeligt og muligt, informere principalen om interventionen og søge principalens samtykke til yderligere handlinger.

(2) En intervenør må ikke ophøre med interventionen uden gyldig grund.

Artikel 2:102: Forpligtelser efter interventionen

(1) Efter interventionen skal intervenøren uden unødigt ophold afrapportere og afregne overfor principalen, og overdrage alt, hvad intervenøren har oppebåret som følge af interventionen.

(2) Hvis intervenøren på tidspunktet for interventionen er umyndig eller under værgemål, behandles forpligtelsen til at overdrage det, intervenøren har oppebåret som følge af interventionen, efter reglerne om uberettiget berigelse (PEL Unjust.Enr.).

Artikel 2:103: Erstatning for pligtbrud

(1) Intervenøren er erstatningspligtig overfor principalen for tab eller personskade, opstået som følge af, at intervenøren ikke har opfyldt de forpligtelser, der følger af denne bog, hvis tabet eller personskaden var en følge af en risiko, som intervenøren skabte, forøgede eller forsætligt forlængede.

(2) Intervenørens ansvar kan nedsættes helt eller delvist, for så vidt dette er rimeligt under hensyntagen til for eksempel intervenørens bevæggrunde for at handle.

(3) En intervenør, som på tidspunktet for interventionen er umyndig eller under værgemål, er kun forpligtet til at yde erstatning i det omfang, denne også ville være forpligtet til at yde erstatning efter reglerne om erstatning udenfor kontraktforhold (PEL Liab.Dam.).

Kapitel 3: Intervenørens rettigheder og bemyndigelse

Artikel 3:101: Ret til skadesløsholdelse eller kompensation

Intervenøren har ret til at kræve, at principalen skadesløsholder eller kompenserer intervenøren for forpligtelser eller udgifter (i form af penge eller andre aktiver), for så vidt som sådanne i rimeligt omfang er stiftet med henblik på interventionen.

Artikel 3:102: Ret til vederlag

(1) Intervenøren har ret til vederlag for så vidt som interventionen er rimelig og påtaget som et led i intervenørens profession eller erhverv.

(2) Vederlaget udgør, i det omfang dette er rimeligt, det beløb, som normalt betales for en præstation som den udførte på tiden og stedet for interventionen.

Artikel 3:103: Ret til godtgørelse

En intervenør, som handler for at beskytte principalen eller principalens ejendom eller interesser mod fare, har ret til at kræve godtgørelse af principalen for tab som følge af personskade eller tingsskade, intervenøren måtte have lidt som følge af handlingen, hvis

(a) interventionen skabte eller væsentligt forøgede risikoen for sådan skade, og

(b) risikoen for skaden, i det omfang dette kunne forudses, stod i rimeligt forhold til den risiko, der truede principalens ejendom eller interesser.

Artikel 3:104: Reduktion eller udelukkelse af intervenørens rettigheder

(1) Intervenørens rettigheder reduceres eller udelukkes i det omfang intervenøren på tidspunktet for handlingen ikke ønskede at kræve henholdsvis skadesløsholdelse, kompensation, vederlag eller godtgørelse.

(2) Disse rettigheder reduceres eller udelukkes også i det omfang, dette er rimeligt når henses til, blandt andet, om intervenøren handlede for at beskytte principalen fra en fælles fare, om principalens ansvar vil være uforholdsmæssigt og om intervenøren rimeligvis kunne forventes at få rimelig dækning af en anden.

Artikel 3:105: Tredjemands pligt til at skadesløsholde eller kompensere principalen

Hvis intervenøren handler for at beskytte principalen fra skade eller tab, er den person, som i forhold til principalen ville have været ansvarlig for skaden eller tabet ifølge reglerne om erstatning udenfor kontrakt, forpligtet til at skadesløsholde henholdsvis kompensere principalen for det ansvar, denne er ifaldet i forhold til intervenøren.

Artikel 3:106: Intervenørens bemyndigelse til at handle i principalens navn

(1) Intervenøren må kan indgå retshandler i principalens navn, for så vidt som dette er rimeligt for at gavne principalens interesser.

(2) En ensidig retshandel udført af intervenøren er dog uden effekt, hvis modtageren afviser retshandlen uden unødigt ophold.

Dutch[2]
Zaakwaarneming

Hoofdstuk 1:
Toepassingsgebied

Artikel 1:101: Waarneming in het belang van een ander

(1) Dit Boek is van toepassing indien een persoon (de zaakwaarnemer) hoofdzakelijk met de bedoeling handelt om een ander (de belanghebbende) te begunstigen en
  (a) de zaakwaarnemer een redelijke grond heeft om te handelen, of
  (b) de belanghebbende de handeling goedkeurt zonder onnodig en de zaakwaarnemer benadelend uitstel.

(2) De zaakwaarnemer heeft geen redelijke grond om te handelen indien de zaakwaarnemer:
  (a) redelijkerwijze de mogelijkheid heeft om de wil van de belanghebbende te achterhalen maar dit niet doet, of
  (b) weet of dient te weten dat de waarneming indruist tegen de wil van de belanghebbende.

Artikel 1:102: Waarneming om de plicht van een ander te vervullen

Handelt de zaakwaarnemer om een plicht van een ander te vervullen, waarbij de vervulling ervan opeisbaar is en de onmiddellijke nakoming ervan een zaak van zwaarwegend maatschappelijk belang vormt, en de zaakwaarnemer hoofdzakelijk met de bedoeling handelt om de ontvanger van de prestatie te begunstigen, dan is de persoon wiens plicht de zaakwaarnemer met zijn handelen wil vervullen een belanghebbende op wie dit boek van toepassing is.

Artikel 1:103: Uitzonderingen

Dit boek is niet van toepassing indien de zaakwaarnemer:
(a) krachtens een contractuele of andere plicht jegens de belanghebbende gerechtigd is om te handelen;
(b) krachtens een elders dan in dit Boek geregelde bevoegdheid gerechtigd is om onafhankelijk van de toestemming van de belanghebbende te handelen of
(c) jegens een derde verplicht is om te handelen.

---

2 Translated by Dr. *Erwin Beysen* (Osnabrück) and *Lodewijk Gualthérie van Weezel* (Osnabrück) in collaboration with Professor *Sophie Stijns* (Leuven), Professor *Matthias Storme* (Leuven) and *Rosalie Koolhoven* (Osnabrück).

Hoofdstuk 2:
Plichten van de zaakwaarnemer

Artikel 2:101: Plichten tijdens de waarneming

(1) Tijdens de waarneming moet de zaakwaarnemer
  (a) met redelijke zorg handelen,
  (b) behalve ten aanzien van een belanghebbende in de zin van artikel 1:102, op een wijze handelen waarvan de zaakwaarnemer weet of redelijkerwijze kan aannemen dat deze met de wil van de belanghebbende overeenstemt en
  (c) voor zover dit mogelijk en redelijk is, de belanghebbende over de waarneming informeren en diens toestemming voor verdere handelingen vragen.

(2) De waarneming mag niet zonder goede grond worden afgebroken.

Artikel 2:102: Plichten na de waarneming

(1) Na de waarneming moet de zaakwaarnemer zonder onnodig uitstel bij de belanghebbende verslag uitbrengen en rekening en verantwoording doen en al hetgeen ingevolge de waarneming verworven werd, afgeven.

(2) Is de zaakwaarnemer ten tijde van de waarneming niet volledig handelingsbekwaam, dan zijn de verweermiddelen die geput kunnen worden uit het recht der ongegronde verrijking (PEL Unjust.Enr.) van toepassing op de plicht tot afgifte.

Artikel 2:103: Vergoeding voor schade veroorzaakt door plichtsverzuim

(1) De zaakwaarnemer is ertoe gehouden de belanghebbende de schade veroorzaakt door de schending van een in dit Boek voorgeschreven plichte vergoeden, indien de schade veroorzaakt is door een risico dat de zaakwaarnemer deed ontstaan, toenemen of opzettelijk bestendigde.

(2) De aansprakelijkheid van de zaakwaarnemer wordt gematigd of volledig uitgesloten voor zover dit billijk en redelijk is, gelet op, onder andere, de beweegredenen van de zaakwaarnemer.

(3) De zaakwaarnemer die op het tijdstip van de waarneming niet volledig handelingsbekwaam is, is slechts tot schadevergoeding gehouden voor zover de zaakwaarnemer krachtens de „regeling inzake de buitencontractuele aansprakelijkheid voor schade die aan een ander berokkend werd“ (PEL Liab.Dam.) eveneens tot schadevergoeding verplicht is.

Hoofdstuk 3:
Rechten en bevoegdheden van de zaakwaarnemer

Artikel 3:101: Recht op vrijwaring en op vergoeding van de uitgaven

De zaakwaarnemer heeft tegenover de belanghebbende een recht op vrijwaring voor de aangegane verbintenissen en op vergoeding van de uitgaven en onkosten (in geld of andere vermogenswaarden) voor zover deze redelijkerwijze voor de doeleinden van de waarneming aangegaan dan wel opgelopen werden.

Artikel 3:102: Recht op loon

(1) De zaakwaarnemer heeft recht op een loon voor zover de waarneming redelijk is en geschiedt in de uitoefening van het beroep of bedrijf van de zaakwaarnemer.

(2) Het verschuldigde loon is, voor zover dit redelijk is, het bedrag dat op de plaats en het tijdstip van de waarneming gewoonlijk voor een dergelijke prestatie wordt gerekend.

Artikel 3:103: Recht op schadevergoeding

Een zaakwaarnemer die handelt om de belanghebbende, diens eigendom of andere belangen tegen een gevaar te beschermen, heeft jegens de belanghebbende een recht op vergoeding van de schade die voortvloeit uit een lichamelijk letsel of van de zaakschade die tijdens de handeling ontstond, indien

(a) de waarneming het risico op dergelijk letsel of dergelijke schade deed ontstaan of aanzienlijk deed toenemen, en

(b) dat risico, voor zover voorzienbaar, in een redelijke verhouding stond tot het risico van de belanghebbende.

Artikel 3:104: Matiging of uitsluiting van de rechten van de zaakwaarnemer

(1) De rechten van de zaakwaarnemer worden gematigd of uitgesloten voor zover de zaakwaarnemer, afhankelijk van het zich voordoende geval, op het tijdstip van de handeling geen vrijwaring voor de aangegane verbintenissen, vergoeding van de uitgaven, loon of schadevergoeding wilde vragen.

(2) Deze rechten worden eveneens gematigd of uitgesloten voor zover dit billijk en redelijk is, waarbij onder andere in aanmerking wordt genomen of de zaakwaarnemer handelde om de belanghebbende te beschermen in een situatie van gemeenschappelijk gevaar, of de aansprakelijkheid van de belanghebbende buitensporig zwaar zou zijn en of er redelijkerwijze van uitgegaan kan worden, dat de zaakwaarnemer een gepaste vergoeding van een ander verkrijgt.

Artikel 3:105: Verplichting van een derde om de belanghebbende te vrijwaren of te vergoeden voor uitgaven

Handelt de zaakwaarnemer om de belanghebbende voor schade te behoeden, dan is de persoon, aan wie de veroorzaking van deze schade krachtens de PEL Liab.Dam. wordt toegerekend, verplicht om, afhankelijk van het zich voordoende geval, de belanghebbende voor diens aansprakelijkheid tegenover de zaakwaarnemer te vrijwaren of de uitgaven te vergoeden.

Artikel 3:106: Bevoegdheid van de zaakwaarnemer om in naam van de belanghebbende te handelen

(1) De zaakwaarnemer is bevoegd om in naam van de belanghebbende rechtshandelingen (of andere juridische handelingen) te verrichten, voor zover dit gepast is om de belanghebbende een voordeel te verschaffen.

(2) Een eenzijdige rechtshandeling die door de zaakwaarnemer in naam van de belanghebbende verricht wordt, blijft evenwel zonder gevolg, indien de derde tot wie deze rechtshandeling gericht is deze zonder onnodig uitstel verwerpt.

Estonian[3]
Käsundita Asjaajamine

Peatükk 1:
Rakendamisvaldkond

Artikkel 1:101: Käsundita asjaajamine teise isiku soodustamiseks

(1) Käesoleva Seaduse sätteid kohaldatakse, kui isik (käsundita asjaajaja) tegutseb peamiselt kavatsusega soodustada teist isikut (soodustatu); ja
- (a) käsundita asjaajaja tegutsemine on mõistlik; või
- (b) soodustatu kiidab tegutsemise heaks sellise viivituseta, mis kahjustaks käsundita asjaajajat.

(2) Käsundita asjaajaja tegutsemine ei ole mõistlik, kui ta:
- (a) vaatamata mõistlikule võimalusele saada teada soodustatu tahe, ei ole seda teinud; või
- (b) teab või peab teadma, et asjaajamine ei vasta soodustatu tahtele.

Artikkel 1:102: Käsundita asjaajamine teise isiku kohustuse täitmiseks

Kui käsundita asjaajaja tegutseb eesmärgiga täita teise isiku kohustus, mille täitmise tähtaeg on saabunud ning mille täitmine on olulisest avalikust huvist tulenevalt tingimata vajalik, ning kui käsundita asjaajaja tegutseb peamiselt kavatsusega soodustada isikut, kellele kohustus täidetakse, on see isik, kelle kohustuse käsundita asjaajaja täidab, soodustatu ning tema suhtes kohaldatakse käesoleva Seaduse sätteid.

Artikkel 1:103: Välistavad asjaolud

Käesoleva Seaduse sätteid ei kohaldata, kui käsundita asjaajajal:
- (a) on lepingulisest või muust kohustusest tulenevalt õigus tegutseda soodustatu huvides;
- (b) on sõltumata soodustatu nõusolekust õigus tegutseda muul kui käesolevas Seaduses sätestatud õiguslikul alusel, või
- (c) on kohustus tegutseda kolmanda isiku ees.

Peatükk 2:
Käsundita asjaajaja kohustused

Artikkel 2:101: Kohustused käsundita asjaajamise kestel

(1) Käsundita asjaajamise kestel on käsundita asjaajaja kohustatud:
- (a) tegutsema mõistliku hoolsusega;
- (b) tegutsema viisil, mille kohta käsundita asjaajaja teab või peaks mõistlikult eeldama, et see vastab soodustatu tahtele, välja arvatud soodustatu suhtes artikli 1:102 kohaselt; ja

---

[3] Translated by Professor *Paul Varul* (Tartu).

(c) teavitama soodustatut asjaajamisest ning taotlema tema nõusolekut edasiste tegude tegemiseks, kuivõrd see on võimalik ja mõistlik

(2) Asjaajamist ei tohi ilma olulise põhjuseta katkestada.

Artikkel 2:102: Kohustused pärast asjaajamist

(1) Pärast asjaajamist on käsundita asjaajaja kohustatud põhjendamatu viivituseta soodustatut teavitama ja talle aru andma, samuti andma välja kogu asjaajamise tulemusena saadu.

(2) Kui käsundita asjaajaja ei ole asjaajamise ajal täielikult teovõimeline, kohaldatakse väljaandmise kohustusele alusetu rikastumise sätteid (PEL Unjust.Enr.).

Artikkel 2:103: Kahju hüvitamine kohustuse rikkumise tõttu

(1) Käsundita asjaajaja peab hüvitama soodustatule kahju, mis on tekkinud käesolevas Seaduses sätestatud kohustuse rikkumise tõttu, kui kahju tekkis riski realiseerumise tagajärjel, mille käsundita asjaajaja lõi, mida ta suurendas või tahtlikult hoidis.

(2) Käsundita asjaajaja vastutus on vähendatud või välistatud, kui see on mõistlik ja õiglane, arvestades muu hulgas käsundita asjaajaja tegutsemise ajendeid.

(3) Käsundita asjaajaja, kes asjaajamise ajal ei ole täielikult teovõimeline, on vastutav kahju tekitamise eest niivõrd, kuivõrd ta on vastutav ka kahju tekitamise eest teisele isikule lepinguväliselt tekitatud kahju hüvitamise sätete alusel (PEL Liab.Dam.).

Peatükk 3:
Käsundita asjaajaja õigused ja esindusõigus

Artikkel 3:101: Õigus kohustusest vabastamisele ja kulutuste hüvitamisele

Käsundita asjaajajal on õigus nõuda soodustatult asjaajamisel võetud kohustusest vabastamist ja tema poolt tehtud kulutuste (raha või muu varalise väärtuse) hüvitamist niivõrd, kuivõrd need on asjaajamise eesmärgil mõistlikult võetud või tehtud.

Artikkel 3:102: Õigus tasule

(1) Käsundita asjaajajal on õigus saada tasu niivõrd, kuivõrd asjaajamine on mõistlik ning toimub asjaajaja kutse- või majandustegevuse raames.

(2) Tasu on õigus saada summas, mida asjaajamise ajal ja kohas seda liiki täitmise eest tavaliselt makstakse, niivõrd, kuivõrd see on mõistlik

Artikkel: 3:103: Õigus kahju hüvitamisele

Käsundita asjaajaja, kes tegutseb soodustatut, tema omandit või muid huve ähvardava ohu tõrjumise eesmärgil, võib nõuda soodustatult asjaajamise ajal kantud kahju hüvitamist, mis tekkis kehavigastuse või asja kahjustamise tagajärjel, kui:

(a) asjaajamine lõi sellise kehavigastuse tekkimise või asja kahjustamise riski või oluliselt suurendas seda; ja

(b) nimetatud risk, kui see oli ettenähtav, oli mõistlikus suhtes soodustatut ähvardanud riskiga.

Artikkel 3:104: Käsundita asjaajaja õiguste vähendamine või välistamine

(1) Käsundita asjaajaja õiguseid vähendatakse või need välistatakse, kui käsundita asjaajaja, sõltuvalt asjaoludest, ei soovinud tegutsemise ajal nõuda asjaajamisel võetavast kohustusest vabastamist, tasu maksmist, kulutuste või kahju hüvitamist.

(2) Nimetatud nõudeid vähendatakse või need välistatakse ka sellisel juhul, kui see on õiglane ja mõistlik, võttes muuhulgas arvesse asjaolu, kas käsundita asjaajaja tegutses soodustatu kaitsmise eesmärgil neid mõlemaid ühiselt ähvardava ohu olukorras, kas soodustatu vastutus oleks ülemäärane või kas käsundita asjaajaja võis mõistlikult eeldada, et ta saab kohase hüvituse teiselt isikult.

Artikkel 3:105: Kolmanda isiku kohustus vabastada soodustatu vastutusest või hüvitada talle kulutused

Kui käsundita asjaajaja tegutseb eesmärgiga kaitsta soodustatut kahju eest, siis see isik, kes PEL Liab.Dam. sätete kohaselt vastutaks soodustatu ees sellise kahju tekitamise eest, on kohustatud vabastama soodustatu vastutusest käsundita asjaajaja ees või vastavalt asjaoludele hüvitama soodustatule kulutused.

Artikkel 3:106: Käsundita asjaajaja esindusõigus soodustatu nimel tegutsemiseks

(1) Käsundita asjaajajal on õigus teha soodustatu nimel tehinguid või muid õigus- toiminguid, kui see on soodustatu soodustamiseks mõistlik.

(2) Käsundita asjaajaja poolt soodustatu nimel tehtud ühepoolne õigustoiming, mis on suunatud kolmandale isikule, on kehtetu, kui kolmas isik lükkab selle põhjendamatu viivituseta tagasi.

Finnish[4]
Asiainhuolto

1. Luku:
Soveltamisala

Artikla 1:101: Asiainhuolto toisen hyväksi

(1) Tämän kirjan säännöksiä sovelletaan, milloin asiainhuoltotoimeen ryhtyneen henkilön (asiainhuoltajan) pääasiallisena tarkoituksena on toisen henkilön (päämiehen) etujen edistäminen; ja

(a) asiainhuoltajalla on kohtuudella hyväksyttävä peruste toimeen ryhtymiseen; tai

(b) päämies hyväksyy toimen ilman sellaista aiheetonta viivytystä, josta voisi koitua haittaa asiainhuoltajalle.

(2) Asiainhuoltotoimeen ryhtymiselle ei ole kohtuudella hyväksyttävää perustetta, jos:

(a) asiainhuoltajalla on mahdollisuus ilman kohtuutonta vaikeutta selvittää päämiehen tahto, mutta hän ei sitä tee; tai jos

(b) asiainhuoltaja tietää tai hänen pitäisi tietää toimen olevan vastoin päämiehen tahtoa.

Artikla 1:102: Asiainhuolto toisen henkilön velvoitteen täyttämiseksi

Milloin asiainhuoltotoimen kohteena on sellainen toisen henkilön erääntynyt velvoite, jonka pikaista täyttämistä vaatii erittäin tärkeä yleinen etu, ja asiainhuoltaja toimii pääasiallisena tarkoituksenaan edistää suorituksen vastaanottajan etua, tämän kirjan säännöksissä tarkoitettuna päämiehenä pidetään sitä, jonka velvoitteen täyttämisestä on kysymys.

Artikla 1:103: Soveltamisalan rajoitukset

Tämän kirjan säännöksiä ei sovelleta, milloin toimeen ryhtyminen perustuu:

(a) sopimus- tai muuhun velvoitteeseen päämiestä kohtaan;

(b) muihin kuin tämän kirjan säännöksiin, jotka oikeuttavat toimimaan riippumatta päämiehen suostumuksesta, tai

(c) toimimisvelvollisuuteen kolmatta henkilöä kohtaan.

2. Luku:
Asiainhuoltajan velvoitteet

Artikla 2:101: Velvoitteet asiainhuollon aikana

(1) Asiainhuollon aikana asiainhuoltajan tulee

(a) noudattaa häneltä kohtuudella edellytettävää huolellisuutta;

(b) menetellä, artiklassa 1:102 tarkoitettuja tilanteita lukuun ottamatta, tavalla, jonka hän tietää tai voi kohtuudella arvioida vastaavan päämiehen tahtoa; ja

---

4 Translated by Professor *Lena Sisula-Tulokas* (Helsinki).

(c) sikäli kuin on mahdollista ja voidaan kohtuudella edellyttää, tiedottaa päämiehelle asiainhuoltotoimeen ryhtymisestä ja pyrkiä saamaan päämiehen suostumus jatkotoimiin.

(2) Asiainhuoltaja ei saa keskeyttää asiainhuoltoa ilman pätevää syytä.

Artikla 2:102: Velvoitteet asiainhuollon jälkeen

(1) Asiainhuoltajan tulee toimen päätyttyä ilman aiheetonta viivytystä antaa päämiehelle selvitys ja tehdä tili sekä luovuttaa päämiehelle, mitä asiainhuollolla on saavutettu.

(2) Jos asiainhuoltajan oikeustoimikyky on ollut vajavainen, luovutusvelvollisuuden osalta voidaan vedota samoihin perusteisiin, joita sovelletaan perusteettoman edun palauttamiseen (PEL Unjust.Enr.).

Artikla 2:103: Korvaus velvoitteen rikkomisesta

(1) Asiainhuoltaja on velvollinen korvaamaan päämiehelle vahingon, joka on seurausta tämän kirjan säännöksiin perustuvan velvoitteen rikkomisesta, mikäli menetys johtui asiainhuoltajan aiheuttamasta, lisäämästä tai tarkoituksellisesti ylläpitämästä vahingonvaarasta.

(2) Asiainhuoltaja voidaan vapauttaa vastuusta tai vastuuta vähentää, jos se on kohtuullista ottaen huomioon asiainhuoltoon ryhtymisen syyt ja muut seikat.

(3) Asiainhuoltaja, jolla on ollut vajavainen oikeustoimikyky, on korvausvelvollinen vain siinä määrin kuin tällainen velvollisuus seuraa myös sopimussuhteiden ulkopuolella noudatettavista vahingonkorvaussäännöistä (PEL Liab.Dam.).

3. Luku: Asiainhuoltajan oikeudet ja toimivalta

Artikla 3:101: Oikeus velvoitteista vapauttamiseen ja kustannusten korvaukseen

Asiainhuoltajalla on oikeus vaatia, että päämies vapauttaa hänet velvoitteista tai korvaa suoritukset (rahat tai muut kulut), jotka ovat olleet asiainhuollon kannalta tarpeen.

Artikla 3:102: Oikeus palkkioon

(1) Asiainhuoltajalla on oikeus palkkioon sikäli kuin asiainhuolto on ollut hyväksyttävää ja se on liittynyt asiainhuoltajan ammatti- tai liiketoimintaan.

(2) Palkkion tulee, sikäli kuin se on kohtuullista, vastata sitä, mitä samanlaisissa olosuhteissa olisi normaalisti maksettu vastaavan suorituksen hankkimisesta.

Artikla 3:103: Oikeus korvaukseen

Asiainhuoltajalla on oikeus saada korvaus päämieheltä henkilö- ja esinevahinkojen seurauksena aiheutuneista menetyksistä, joita hänelle on aiheutunut suojellessaan vaaralta päämiestä tai tämän omaisuutta ja etuja, jos

(a) asiainhuolto aiheutti vahingonvaaran tai lisäsi sitä merkittävästi; ja

(b) tuo vahingonvaara, sikäli kuin se oli ennalta nähtävissä, oli järkevässä suhteessa päämiestä uhanneeseen vahingonvaaraan.

Artikla 3:104: Sovittelu ja oikeuden epääminen

(1) Oikeus velvoituksesta vapautumiseen, korvaukseen, suoritukseen tai palkkioon voidaan alentaa tai kokonaan evätä, jos asiainhuoltaja toimeen ryhtyessään ei halunnut tällaista oikeutta vaatia.

(2) Samoin voidaan menetellä, sikäli kuin se on kohtuullista ja hyväksyttävää, ottaen huomioon muiden seikkojen ohella, suojeliko asiainhuoltaja päämiestä yhteiseltä vaaralta, muodostuisiko päämiehen vastuu ylivoimaiseksi, sekä voidaanko asiainhuoltajan kohtuudella odottaa saavan asianmukaisen korvauksen tai hyvityksen muulta henkilöltä.

Artikla 3:105: Päämiehen oikeus velvoituksesta vapautumiseen, korvaukseen tai suoritukseen kolmannelta

Jos asiainhuoltaja ryhtyy toimeen suojellakseen päämiestä
vahingolta tai tappiolta, sellaisen vahingon tai tappion aiheuttamisesta lain mukaan (PEL Liab.Dam.) korvausvelvollisen henkilön tulee korvata tai suorittaa päämiehelle se, mistä päämies on vastuussa asiainhuoltajalle.

Artikla 3:106: Asiainhuoltajan valtuus toimia päämiehen nimissä

(1) Asiainhuoltaja saa solmia oikeustoimia tai ryhtyä muihin oikeudellisiin toimenpiteisiin sikäli kuin sitä on pidettävä hyväksyttävänä päämiehen edun edistämiseksi.

(2) Asiainhuoltajan yksipuolisella toimella päämiehen nimissä ei kuitenkaan ole vaikutusta, jos kolmas henkilö, johon toimi on kohdistettu, sen hylkää ilman aiheetonta viivästystä.

French[5]
Gestion d'affaires d'autrui

Chapitre 1:
Domaine d'application

Article 1:101: Gestion d'affaires au bénéfice d'autrui

(1) Les dispositions de ce livre s'appliquent quand une personne (le gérant d'affaires) agit dans l'intention principale de faire bénéficier une autre (le maître d'affaires) de quelque chose ; et
  (a) que le gérant d'affaires a un motif raisonnable d'agir ; ou
  (b) que le maître d'affaires autorise l'action sans retard, de façon à ne pas nuire au gérant d'affaires.

(2) Le gérant d'affaires n'a pas un motif raisonnable d'agir, quand il :
  (a) avait une opportunité raisonnable de connaître la volonté du maître d'affaires mais n'en a pas usé, ou
  (b) savait ou aurait dû savoir, que la gestion d'affaires était contraire à la volonté du maître d'affaires.

Article 1:102: Exécution de l'obligation d'autrui

Quand un gérant d'affaires agit pour exécuter l'obligation d'autrui, due et requise de façon urgente pour une raison d'intérêt public supérieur, et que l'intention principale de ce gérant d'affaires est d'agir au profit du bénéficiaire de cette exécution, le débiteur, dont le gérant d'affaires exécute l'obligation, est un maître d'affaires, auquel les dispositions de ce livre s'appliquent.

Article 1:103: Exclusions

Les dispositions de ce livre ne s'appliquent pas, quand le gérant d'affaires :
(a) est autorisé à agir en exécution d'une obligation contractuelle ou autre envers le maître d'affaires ;
(b) est autorisé, en dehors de l'application d'une disposition de ce livre, à agir sans le consentement du maître d'affaires ;
(c) est tenu d'agir en exécution d'une obligation envers un tiers.

Chapitre 2:
Obligations du gérant d'affaires

Article 2:101: Obligations pendant la gestion d'affaires

(1) Pendant la gestion d'affaires, le gérant d'affaires est tenu
  (a) d'agir avec une diligence raisonnable;

---

5 Translated by Professor *Jacques Ghestin* (Paris); first draft by *Judith Hauck* (Hamburg).

(b) d'agir, excepté dans les rapports avec le maître d'affaires régis par l'article 1:102, conformément à ce qu'il sait ou doit raisonnablement supposer être la volonté du maître d'affaires ;
(c) dans la mesure du possible et du raisonnable, d'informer le maître d'affaires sur la gestion d'affaires et de rechercher son consentement pour des actions ultérieures.

(2) La gestion d'affaires ne doit pas être interrompue sans justes motifs.

Article 2:102: Obligations après la gestion d'affaires

(1) Après la gestion d'affaires, le gérant d'affaires doit, sans retard excessif, informer le maître d'affaires et lui rendre compte ainsi que lui restituer tout ce qui résulte de sa gestion.
(2) Si le gérant d'affaires n'a pas la pleine capacité de contracter au moment de la gestion d'affaires, les obligations de restitution sont soumises au régime des défenses résultant du droit de l'enrichissement sans cause (PEL Unjust.Enr.).

Article 2:103: Réparation des dommages résultant de l'inexécution des obligations du gérant d'affaires

(1) Le gérant d'affaires est tenu de réparer les dommages causés au maître d'affaires par la violation d'une obligation prévue dans ce livre, quand ils résultent d'un risque que le gérant d'affaires a créé, augmenté ou intentionnellement prolongé.
(2) La responsabilité du gérant d'affaires est diminuée ou exclue dans la mesure où cela est juste et raisonnable, en prenant en considération, notamment, les raisons d'agir du gérant d'affaires.
(3) Un gérant d'affaires, qui, au moment de la gestion d'affaires, n'a pas la pleine capacité de contracter, n'engage sa responsabilité que dans la mesure où il engagerait celle-ci selon le droit de la responsabilité extra-contractuelle régissant les dommages causés à autrui (PEL Liab.Dam.).

Chapitre 3: Droits et pouvoirs du gérant d'affaires

Article 3:101: Droit à indemnisation et remboursement

Le gérant d'affaires a le droit d'exiger du maître d'affaires d'être indemnisé de ses engagements ou, le cas échéant, remboursé de ses dépenses (en argent ou autres biens) dans la mesure où les uns et les autres ont été raisonnablement assumés aux fins de la gestion d'affaires.

Article 3:102: Droit à rémunération

(1) Le gérant d'affaires a droit à une rémunération dans la mesure où la gestion d'affaires est raisonnable et réalisée dans l'exercice de son activité professionnelle.
(2) Le montant de la rémunération due est, dans la mesure du raisonnable, celui qui est habituellement payé au lieu et au moment de la gestion d'affaires pour des prestations du même genre.

Article 3:103: Droit à réparation

Un gérant d'affaires qui agit pour écarter un danger menaçant le maître d'affaires, ses biens ou ses intérêts, peut exiger de ce dernier la réparation d'un préjudice corporel ou matériel subi du fait de son intervention, si :

(a) la gestion d'affaires a créé ou augmenté de façon considérable le risque d'un tel préjudice ; et
(b) ce risque, dans la mesure du prévisible, était raisonnablement proportionné à celui du maître d'affaires.

Article 3:104: Diminution ou exclusion des droits du gérant d'affaires

(1) Les droits du gérant d'affaires sont réduits ou exclus dans la mesure où, au moment de son intervention, il n'entendait pas demander, selon les cas, une indemnisation, un remboursement, une rémunération ou une réparation.
(2) Ces droits sont également réduits ou exclus dans la mesure où cela est juste et raisonnable, en tenant compte, entre autres circonstances, de ce que le gérant d'affaires a agi pour protéger le maître d'affaires dans une situation de danger commun, de ce que la responsabilité du maître d'affaires serait excessive ou de ce que l'on pouvait raisonnablement s'attendre à ce que le gérant d'affaires recoive d'autrui un dédommagement approprié.

Article 3:105: Obligation pesant sur un tiers d'indemniser ou de rembourser le maître d'affaires

Si le gérant d'affaires agit afin d'éviter un dommage au maître d'affaires, le tiers, qui serait responsable de celui-ci en application des PEL Liab.Dam., est tenu d'assumer la responsabilité du maître d'affaires envers le gérant d'affaires ou, le cas échéant, de rembourser les sommes payées à ce dernier par le maître d'affaires en raison de cette responsabilité.

Article 3:106: Pouvoir du gérant d'affaires d'agir au nom du maître d'affaires

(1) Le gérant d'affaires peut conclure des contrats ou accomplir d'autres actes juridiques au nom du maître d'affaires dans la mesure où cela est raisonnable.
(2) Cependant un acte juridique unilatéral accompli par le gérant d'affaires au nom du maître d'affaires est dépourvu d'effet si le tiers auquel il est adressé a rejeté cet acte sans retard excessif.

German[6]
Besorgung fremder Angelegenheiten

Kapitel 1:
Anwendungsbereich

Artikel 1:101: Handeln in Begünstigungsabsicht

(1) Dieses Buch findet Anwendung, wenn eine Person (der Geschäftsführer) mit der überwiegenden Absicht handelt, einen anderen (den Geschäftsherrn) zu begünstigen; und
 (a) der Geschäftsführer aus vernünftigem Grund handelt; oder
 (b) der Geschäftsherr die Handlung ohne eine vermeidbare Verzögerung, die den Geschäftsführer benachteiligt, genehmigt.

(2) Der Geschäftsführer handelt nicht aus vernünftigem Grund, wenn er:
 (a) trotz angemessener Gelegenheit, den Willen des Geschäftsherrn zu ermitteln, dies nicht getan hat; oder
 (b) weiß oder wissen muss, dass die Besorgung der Angelegenheit dem Willen des Geschäftsherrn widerspricht.

Artikel 1:102: Erfüllung der Pflicht eines anderen

Handelt der Geschäftsführer, um die Pflicht eines anderen zu erfüllen, und ist die Erfüllung dieser Pflicht fällig und aus höherrangigem öffentlichen Interesse dringend erforderlich, und handelt der Geschäftsführer mit der überwiegenden Absicht, den Empfänger der Leistung zu begünstigen, ist die Person, deren Pflicht der Geschäftsführer erfüllt, ein Geschäftsherr, auf den dieses Buch Anwendung findet.

Artikel 1:103: Ausschlüsse

Dieses Buch findet keine Anwendung, wenn der Geschäftsführer:
(a) aufgrund einer vertraglichen oder anderen Pflicht dem Geschäftsherren gegenüber zu handeln berechtigt ist;
(b) aufgrund einer Befugnis außerhalb dieses Buchs berechtigt ist, unabhängig von der Zustimmung des Geschäftsherren zu handeln, oder
(c) einer dritten Partei gegenüber zu handeln verpflichtet ist.

Kapitel 2:
Pflichten des Geschäftsführers

Artikel 2:101: Pflichten während der Besorgung der Angelegenheit

(1) Während der Besorgung der Angelegenheit hat der Geschäftsführer
 (a) mit angemessener Sorgfalt zu handeln;

---

6 Translated by *Sandra Rohlfing* (Osnabrück).

(b) außer im Verhältnis zu einem Geschäftsherren nach Artikel 1:102 in einer Art und Weise zu handeln, von der der Geschäftsführer weiß oder vernünftigerweise annehmen muss, dass sie dem Willen des Geschäftsherren entspricht; und

(c) soweit möglich und angemessen den Geschäftsherren über die Besorgung seiner Angelegenheit zu informieren und seine Zustimmung zu weiteren Handlungen einzuholen.

(2) Die Besorgung der Angelegenheit darf nicht ohne guten Grund abgebrochen werden.

Artikel 2:102: Pflichten nach der Besorgung der Angelegenheit

(1) Nach der Besorgung der Angelegenheit hat der Geschäftsführer dem Geschäftsherren ohne vermeidbare Verzögerung Auskunft zu erteilen und Rechenschaft abzulegen sowie alles herauszugeben, was der Geschäftsführer aus der Geschäftsführung erlangt hat.

(2) Ist der Geschäftsführer im Zeitpunkt der Besorgung der Angelegenheit nicht voll geschäftsfähig, finden auf die Pflicht zur Herausgabe die Vorschriften über die Verteidigungsgründe im Recht der ungerechtfertigten Bereicherung (PEL Unjust.Enr.) Anwendung.

Artikel 2:103: Schadenersatz wegen Pflichtverletzung

(1) Der Geschäftsführer haftet dem Geschäftsherren auf Ersatz des Schadens, der durch die Verletzung einer in diesem Buch bestimmten Pflicht verursacht worden ist, wenn der Schaden aus einem Risiko resultiert, das der Geschäftsführer geschaffen, erhöht oder absichtlich aufrechterhalten hat.

(2) Die Haftung des Geschäftsführers ist insoweit gemindert oder ausgeschlossen, als dies unter Berücksichtigung unter anderem der Gründe, aus denen der Geschäftsführer gehandelt hat, billig ist.

(3) Ein Geschäftsführer, der im Zeitpunkt der Besorgung der Angelegenheit nicht voll geschäftsfähig ist, haftet auf Schadenersatz nur insoweit, als er auch nach dem Recht der außervertraglichen Haftung, die sich aus dem einem anderen verursachten Schaden ergibt (PEL Liab.Dam.), haftet.

Kapitel 3:
Ansprüche und Befugnis des Geschäftsführers

Artikel 3:101: Anspruch auf Freistellung und Aufwendungsersatz

Der Geschäftsführer hat gegen den Geschäftsherren Anspruch auf Freistellung von einer eingegangenen Verbindlichkeit und auf Ersatz seiner Aufwendungen (von Geld oder von anderen Vermögenswerten) insoweit sie für die Zwecke der Besorgung der Angelegenheit vernünftigerweise eingegangen oder getätigt worden sind.

Artikel 3:102: Anspruch auf Vergütung

(1) Der Geschäftsführer hat insoweit Anspruch auf Vergütung, wie die Besorgung der Angelegenheit angemessen ist und im Rahmen seines Berufes oder Gewerbes erfolgt.

(2) Geschuldet ist, soweit dies angemessen ist, die Vergütung, die üblicherweise zur Zeit und am Ort der Besorgung der Angelegenheit für eine Leistung dieser Art zu zahlen ist.

Artikel 3:103: Anspruch auf Schadenersatz

Ein Geschäftsführer, der zur Abwendung einer Gefahr für den Geschäftsherrn, dessen Eigentum oder dessen andere Interessen handelt, hat gegen den Geschäftsherrn Anspruch auf Ersatz des Verlustes, der aus einer Verletzung des Körpers oder der Gesundheit oder aus der Beschädigung einer Sache des Geschäftsführers resultiert und den er bei der Besorgung der Angelegenheit erlitten hat, wenn:

(a) die Besorgung der Angelegenheit das Risiko einer solchen Verletzung geschaffen oder wesentlich erhöht hat; und

(b) dieses Risiko, soweit vorhersehbar, in angemessenem Verhältnis zu dem Risiko des Geschäftsherrn stand.

Artikel 3:104: Minderung oder Ausschluss der Ansprüche des Geschäftsführers

(1) Die Ansprüche des Geschäftsführers sind insoweit gemindert oder ausgeschlossen, als der Geschäftsführer zum Zeitpunkt der Handlung, je nach Lage des Falles, Freistellung, Aufwendungsersatz, Vergütung oder Schadenersatz nicht verlangen wollte.

(2) Diese Ansprüche sind auch gemindert oder ausgeschlossen, insoweit dies billig ist, wobei unter anderem zu berücksichtigen ist, ob der Geschäftsführer in einer gemeinsamen Gefahrenlage zum Schutze des Geschäftsherren handelte, ob die Haftung des Geschäftsherrn übermäßig wäre oder ob vernünftigerweise erwartet werden kann, dass der Geschäftsführer eine gebührende Entschädigung von einem anderen erhält.

Artikel 3:105: Freistellungs- oder Ausgleichspflicht einer dritten Person

Handelt der Geschäftsführer zum Schutze des Geschäftsherren vor Schaden, so ist diejenige Person, der nach den PEL Liab.Dam. die Verursachung dieses Schadens des Geschäftsherren zuzurechnen wäre, verpflichtet, den Geschäftsherren von seiner Haftung gegenüber dem Geschäftsführer freizustellen bzw. dem Geschäftsherrn Ersatz für das in Erfüllung dieser Haftung Geleistete zu gewähren.

Artikel 3:106: Vertretungsmacht des Geschäftsführers, im Namen des Geschäftsherren zu handeln

(1) Der Geschäftsführer ist berechtigt, Rechtsgeschäfte oder ähnliche rechtliche Handlungen im Namen des Geschäftsherren vorzunehmen, soweit dies angemessen ist, um den Geschäftsherren zu begünstigen.

(2) Einseitige rechtliche Handlungen, die vom Geschäftsführer gegenüber einer dritten Person und im Namen des Geschäftsherren vorgenommen wurden, sind unwirksam, wenn sie von der dritten Person ohne vermeidbare Verzögerung zurückgewiesen werden.

Greek[7]
Διοίκηση αλλοτρίων

Κεφάλαιο 1:
Πεδίο εφαρμογής

Άρθρο 1:101: Επέμβαση για να ευνοηθεί κάποιος άλλος

(1) Το παρόν βιβλίο βρίσκει εφαρμογή όταν ένα πρόσωπο (ο διοικητής αλλοτρίων) ενεργεί προεχόντως με την πρόθεση να ευνοήσει κάποιον άλλο (τον κύριο της υπόθεσης) και
  α. ο διοικητής αλλοτρίων έχει εύλογο κίνητρο για να ενεργήσει ή
  β. ο κύριος της υπόθεσης εγκρίνει την ενέργεια χωρίς υπαίτια καθυστέρηση που επιβαρύνει τον διοικητή

(2) Ο διοικητής αλλοτρίων δεν ενεργεί με εύλογο κίνητρο όταν
  α. παραλείπει παρά την ύπαρξη κατάλληλης ευκαιρίας να διερευνήσει την βούληση του κυρίου ή
  β. γνωρίζει ή όφειλε να γνωρίζει ότι η διοίκηση της υπόθεσης αντίκειται στην θέληση του κυρίου

Άρθρο 1:102: Εκπλήρωση της υποχρέωσης ενός άλλου

Εάν ο διοικητής αλλοτρίων ενεργεί για να εκπληρώσει την υποχρέωση ενός άλλου και εάν η εκπλήρωση της υποχρέωσης αυτής είναι απαιτητή και για λόγους ανωτέρου δημοσίου συμφέροντος επειγόντως αναγκαία και εφόσον ο διοικητής ενεργεί κυρίως με την πρόθεση να ευνοήσει τον αποδέκτη της παροχής τότε είναι το πρόσωπο του οποίου την υποχρέωση εκπληρώνει ο διοικητής κύριος της υπόθεσης ως προς τον οποίο βρίσκει εφαρμογή το παρόν βιβλίο.

Άρθρο 1:103: Εξαιρέσεις (από το πεδίο εφαρμογής)

Το παρόν βιβλίο δεν βρίσκει εφαρμογή εάν ο διοικητής αλλοτρίων

a. βάσει συμβατικής ή άλλης υποχρέωσης έναντι του κυρίου της υπόθεσης δικαιούται να προβεί στην ενέργεια
β. βάσει νομιμοποιητικού λόγου μη κειμένου στο παρόν βιβλίο δικαιούται να ενεργεί ανεξαρτήτως της συγκατάθεσης του κυρίου της υπόθεσης
γ. έχει υποχρέωση έναντι τρίτου προσώπου να προβεί στην ενέργεια

Κεφάλαιο 2:
Υποχρεώσεις του διοικητή

Άρθρο 2:101: Υποχρεώσεις κατά την διοίκηση της υπόθεσης

(1) Κατά τη διοίκηση της υπόθεσης οφείλει ο διοικητής
  (α) να ενεργεί με την προσήκουσα επιμέλεια

[7] Translated by Dr. *Evlalia Eleftheriadou* (Osnabrück).

(β) εξαιρουμένης της σχέσης του προς έναν κύριο σύμφωνα με το άρθρο 1:102 να ενεργεί κατά τρόπο που γνωρίζει ή δικαιολογημένα μπορεί να υποθέσει ότι ανταποκρίνεται στην θέληση του κυρίου της υπόθεσης
(γ) εφόσον είναι δυνατό και εύλογο να πληροφορήσει τον κύριο για την διοίκηση της υπόθεσης του και να ζητήσει την συγκατάθεση του για περαιτέρω ενέργειες.
(2) Η διοίκηση της υπόθεσης δεν επιτρέπεται να διακοπεί χωρίς σημαντικό λόγο.

Άρθρο 2:102: Υποχρεώσεις μετά την διοίκηση της υπόθεσης

(1) Μετά την διοίκηση της υπόθεσης οφείλει ο διοικητής χωρίς υπαίτια καθυστέρηση να παράσχει πληροφορίες στον κύριο της υπόθεσης και να λογοδοτήσει όπως και να αποδώσει οτιδήποτε απέκτησε από την διοίκηση.
(2) Εάν ο διοικητής δεν είχε πλήρη δικαιοπρακτική ικανότητα κατά το χρόνο της διοίκησης εφαρμόζονται ως προς την υποχρέωση απόδοσης οι διατάξεις για τους λόγους απαλλαγής στο δίκαιο του αδικαιολόγητου πλουτισμού.

Άρθρο 2:103: Αποζημίωση λόγω παράβασης υποχρέωσης

(1) Ο διοικητής ευθύνεται έναντι του κυρίου σε αποζημίωση για την ζημία που προκλήθηκε από την παράβαση κάποιας από τις ρυθμιζόμενες στο παρόν βιβλίο υποχρεώσεις εάν η ζημία απορρέει από έναν κίνδυνο τον οποίο δημιούργησε, επαύξησε ή εκ προθέσεως διατήρησε ο διοικητής.
(2) Η ευθύνη του διοικητή μπορεί να μειωθεί ή και να αποκλειστεί εφόσον αυτό εμφανίζεται ως δίκαιο και προσήκον λαμβανομένων υπόψιν μεταξύ άλλων περιστάσεων και των λόγων για τους οποίους ενήργησε ο διοικητής.
(3) Ο διοικητής ο οποίος δεν είχε πλήρη δικαιοπρακτική ικανότητα κατά το χρόνο της διοίκησης ευθύνεται σε αποζημίωση μόνο εφόσον θα ευθυνόταν και κατά το δίκαιο της εξωσυμβατικής ευθύνης που προκύπτει από την πρόκληση ζημίας σε κάποιον άλλο.

Κεφάλαιο 3:
Αξιώσεις και δικαίωμα του διοικητή

Άρθρο 3:101: Αξίωση για απελευθέρωση και για απόδοση δαπανών

Ο διοικητής έχει απέναντι στον κύριο αξίωση για απελευθέρωση από αναληφθείσες υποχρεώσεις και για απόδοση των δαπανών του (χρηματικών ή άλλων περιουσιακών στοιχείων) εφόσον αυτές δικαιολογημένα αναλήφθησαν ή τελέστηκαν για τους σκοπούς της διοίκησης.

Άρθρο 3:102: Αξίωση για αμοιβή

(1) Ο διοικητής έχει αξίωση για αμοιβή εφόσον η διοίκηση της υπόθεσης ήταν προσήκουσα και έλαβε χώρα στα πλαίσια του επαγγέλματος ή του επιτηδεύματος του.
(2) Οφείλεται εφόσον αυτό είναι προσήκον η αμοιβή ή οποία στο τόπο και κατά το χρόνο της διοίκησης συνηθίζεται για μια παροχή όπως αυτή που έλαβε χώρα.

Άρθρο 3:103: Αξίωση για αποζημίωση

Ο διοικητής που ενεργεί για να προστατεύσει τον κύριο ή την κυριότητα ή άλλα συμφέροντα του κυρίου από κίνδυνο έχει έναντι του κυρίου αξίωση για αποκατάσταση της ζημίας που απορρέει από σωματική βλάβη του διοικητή ή από φθορά ιδιοκτησίας του και την οποία υπέστη κατά την διοίκηση, εφόσον

(α) η διοίκηση ή επαύξησε ουσιωδώς τον κίνδυνο μιας τέτοιας προσβολής ή ζημίας και

(β) ο κίνδυνος αυτός καθόσον προβλέψιμο βρισκόταν σε ανάλογη σχέση με τον κίνδυνο που απειλούσε τον κύριο.

Άρθρο 3:104: Μείωση ή αποκλεισμός των αξιώσεων του διοικητή

(1) Οι αξιώσεις του διοικητή μειώνονται ή αποκλείονται εφόσον ο διοικητής κατά τον χρόνο της διοίκησης και κατά τις περιστάσεις κάθε περίπτωσης δεν σκόπευε να ζητήσει απελευθέρωση από αναληφθείσες υποχρεώσεις, απόδοση δαπανών, αμοιβή ή αποζημίωση.

(2) Οι αξιώσεις αυτές επίσης μειώνονται ή αποκλείονται εφόσον αυτό είναι δίκαιο και προσήκον αφού ληφθεί υπόψιν μεταξύ άλλων και το γεγονός ότι ο διοικητής ενήργησε για να προστατεύσει τον κύριο σε κατάσταση κοινού κινδύνου ή ότι η ευθύνη του κυρίου θα ήταν υπερβολικά μεγάλη ή ότι είναι ευλόγως αναμενόμενο να λάβει ο διοικητής προσήκουσα αποζημίωση από κάποιον άλλο.

Άρθρο 3:105: Υποχρέωση ενός τρίτου προσώπου προς απελευθέρωση ή αποζημίωση

Ενεργεί ο διοικητής για να προστατεύσει τον κύριο από ζημία, τότε υποχρεούται το πρόσωπο στο οποίο θα καταλογιζόταν σύμφωνα με τις PEL Liab.Dam. η πρόκληση αυτής της ζημίας του κυρίου της υπόθεσης να απελευθερώσει τον κύριο από την ευθύνη του απέναντι στον διοικητή ή να καταβάλλει στον κύριο τα καταβληθέντα από αυτόν προς εκπλήρωση της ευθύνης του.

Άρθρο 3:106: Αντιπροσωπευτική εξουσία του διοικητή να ενεργεί στο όνομα του κυρίου

(1) Ο διοικητής δικαιούται να διενεργεί δικαιοπραξίες ή παρόμοιες νομικές πράξεις στο όνομα του κυρίου της υπόθεσης εφόσον αυτό είναι εύλογο για να ευνοηθεί ο κύριος της υπόθεσης.

(2) Μονομερείς νομικές πράξεις που διενεργούνται από τον διοικητή στο όνομα του κυρίου της υπόθεσης είναι ανίσχυρες εφόσον το τρίτο πρόσωπο προς το οποίο απευθύνονται τις απορρίπτει χωρίς υπαίτια καθυστέρηση.

Hungarian[8]
Megbízás nélküli ügyvitel

1. Fejezet
Alkalmazási terület

1:101. cikk. Beavatkozás egy másik személy javára

(1) E Könyv szabályait kell alkalmazni, ha egy személy (a megbízás nélküli ügyvivő) egy másik személy (az ügy ura) javára történő cselekvés szándékával jár el, és

(a) erre ésszerű oka van (helyénvaló eljárás), vagy

(b) az ügy ura a megbízás nélküli ügyvivő számára hátránnyal nem járó késedelem nélkül jóváhagyja az eljárást.

(2) A megbízás nélküli ügyvivő eljárása nem helyénvaló, ha

(a) megismerhetné az ügy urának akaratát, de nem teszi azt, vagy

(b) tudja, vagy tudnia kellene, hogy a beavatkozás az ügy urának akarata ellen történik.

1:102. cikk. Beavatkozás egy másik személy kötelezettségének teljesítése érdekében

Megbízás nélküli ügyvivőnek kell tekinteni, és a jelen Könyv szabályai szerint kell megítélni azt a személyt is, aki egy másik személy olyan lejárt kötelezettségét teljesíti, amelynek halaszthatatlan teljesítését fontos közérdek kívánja meg, és a beavatkozás a szolgáltatás jogosultjának javára való cselekvés szándékával történik.

1:103. cikk. A szabályok alkalmazásának kizárása

Nem a jelen Könyv szabályait kell alkalmazni abban az esetben, ha a beavatkozás

(a) az ügy urával szemben fennálló szerződéses vagy egyéb kötelezettség alapján történik;

(b) jelen Könyv szabályaitól függetlenül, az ügy urának hozzájárulása nélkül jogszerűen történik; vagy

(c) harmadik személlyel szemben fennálló kötelezettség alapján történik.

2. Fejezet
A megbízás nélküli ügyvivő kötelezettségei

2:101. cikk. Kötelezettségek a beavatkozás során

(1) A megbízás nélküli ügyvivő köteles

(a) kellő gondossággal eljárni,

(b) az 1:102. cikkben szabályozott eset kivételével úgy eljárni, ahogy tudomása vagy indokolt feltevése szerint az ügy urának akarata megkívánja, és

(c) indokolatlan késlekedés nélkül értesíteni az ügy urát a beavatkozásról, és hozzájárulását kérni a jövőbeni eljáráshoz.

(2) A beavatkozást kellő indok nélkül nem lehet megszakítani.

---

8 Translated by Professor *Lajos Vékás* (Budapest).

2:102. cikk. Kötelezettségek a beavatkozás után

(1) A beavatkozás után a megbízás nélküli ügyvivő indokolatlan késlekedés nélkül köteles az ügy urának jelentést tenni, számadást adni és kiadni neki mindazt, amihez a beavatkozás folytán hozzájutott.

(2) Ha a megbízás nélküli ügyvivő a beavatkozás időpontjában nem teljesen cselekvőképes, kiadási kötelezettsége a jogalap nélküli gazdagodás szabályai (PEL Unjust.Enr.) szerint megállapítható mértékre korlátozódik.

2:103. cikk. A kötelezettségszegés által okozott károk megtérítése

(1) A megbízás nélküli ügyvivő köteles az ügy urának megtéríteni azt a kárt, amelyet a jelen Könyvben megállapított kötelezettségének megszegésével okozott, ha a kár az általa előidézett, növelt, vagy szándékosan fenntartott kockázat eredménye.

(2) A megbízás nélküli ügyvivő felelősségét mérsékelni lehet, vagy annak megállapításától el is lehet tekinteni, amennyiben ez a méltányosságnak megfelel, különös tekintettel a beavatkozás indokára.

(3) Ha a megbízás nélküli ügyvivő a beavatkozás időpontjában nem teljesen cselekvőképes, csak a szerződésen kívüli kártérítési felelősség szabályai (PEL Liab.Dam.) szerint köteles az ügy urának kárát megtéríteni.

3. Fejezet
A megbízás nélküli ügyvivő jogai és képviseleti jogosultsága

3:101. cikk. Kárpótlás vagy költségtérítés

A megbízás nélküli ügyvivő az ügy urától kárpótlást igényelhet, vagy az eset körülményeitől függően követelheti tőle a beavatkozással összefüggésben indokoltan felmerült pénzbeni vagy természetbeni kiadásainak megtérítését.

3:102. cikk. Díjazás

(1) A megbízás nélküli ügyvivőnek díjhoz van joga, ha beavatkozása helyénvaló volt, és arra önálló szakmai vagy gazdasági tevékenysége körében került sor.

(2) A díjat a beavatkozás helyén és idején hasonló tevékenységért szokásos ellenszolgáltatásnak megfelelő mértékben kell meghatározni.

3:103. cikk. Kártalanítás

A megbízás nélküli ügyvivő követelheti az ügy urától az ő személyét, vagyonát vagy érdekeit veszélytől óvó beavatkozás során elszenvedett kárának megtérítését, ha

(a) a károsodás kockázatát a beavatkozás idézte elő, vagy azt számottevően növelte, és

(b) a károsodás kockázata, amennyiben előrelátható volt, arányban állt az ügy urát fenyegető kockázattal.

3:104. cikk. A megbízás nélküli ügyvivő jogainak korlátozása vagy kizárása

(1) A megbízás nélküli ügyvivő jogai az eset körülményeitől függően korlátozottak vagy kizártak, ha ő a beavatkozás időpontjában nem tartott igényt kárpótlásra, költségtérítésre, díjra vagy kártalanításra.

(2) Korlátozottak vagy kizártak a megbízás nélküli ügyvivő jogai akkor is, ha ez a méltányosságnak megfelel, különös tekintettel arra, hogy a megbízás nélküli ügyvivő az ügy urát közös veszélytől kívánta óvni, az ügy urának helytállása túlzott volna, és a megbízás nélküli ügyvivő okkal számolhat azzal, hogy más személytől megfelelő elégtételt kap.

3:105. cikk. Harmadik személy kötelezettsége az ügy urának kárpótlására vagy költségeinek megtérítésére

Ha a megbízás nélküli ügyvivő az ügy urának kártól való megóvása érdekében avatkozik be, a károkozásért a szerződésen kívüli kártérítés szabályai (PEL Liab.Dam.) szerint felelős személy köteles az ügy urát a megbízás nélküli ügyvivővel szemben terhelő helytállásért kárpótolni, vagy az eset körülményeitől függően költségtérítésben részesíteni.

3:106. cikk. A megbízás nélküli ügyvivő képviseleti jogosultsága

(1) A megbízás nélküli ügyvivő jogosult az ügy urának nevében jogügyletet kötni, vagy egyéb jognyilatkozatot tenni, ha ezzel az ügy urának javát szolgálja.

(2) A megbízás nélküli ügyvivőnek az ügy ura nevében tett egyoldalú nyilatkozata nem hatályos, ha a címzett harmadik személy indokolatlan késlekedés nélkül visszautasítja azt.

Italian[9]
Gestione d'Affari Altrui

Capitolo 1:
Ambito di applicazione

Articolo 1:101: Ingerenza al fine di arrecare vantaggio ad altri

(1) Questo libro si applica nei casi in cui una persona (il gestore) agisca con l'intenzione prevalente di arrecare vantaggio ad un' altra (l'interessato) e
  (a) il gestore abbia un motivo ragionevole per agire; o
  (b) l'interessato approvi la gestione senza un ingiustificato ritardo che possa pregiudicare il gestore.

(2) Il gestore non ha un motivo ragionevole per agire se:
  (a) ha una ragionevole possibilità di accertarsi della volontà dell'interessato e non lo fa
  (b) sa o dovrebbe sapere che l'ingerenza è contraria alla volontà dell'interessato.

Articolo 1:102: Ingerenza al fine di adempiere un obbligo altrui

Quando il gestore agisce per l'adempimento dell'obbligo di un'altra persona, adempimento che è dovuto e preteso senza ritardo per essere una questione di primario interesse pubblico, e il gestore agisce con l'intenzione prevalente di arrecare vantaggio a chi riceve la prestazione, la persona, i cui obblighi il gestore adempie, è un interessato ai sensi e per gli effetti di questo Libro.

Articolo 1:103: Esclusioni

Questo Libro non si applica quando il gestore:

(a) è legittimato ad agire in forza di un obbligo contrattuale o di diversa natura nei confronti dell'interessato;
(b) è legittimato ad agire a prescindere dal consenso dell'interessato in forza di una norma non compresa in questo libro o
(c) ha nei confronti di un terzo l'obbligo di agire.

Capitolo 2:
Doveri del gestore

Articolo 2:101: Doveri durante la gestione

(1) Durante la gestione il gestore deve
  (a) agire con ragionevole diligenza;
  (b) ad eccezione dei casi in cui intercorre con l'interessato una relazione del tipo di quella enunciata nell'art. 1:102, agire in un modo che il gestore sappia o possa ragionevolmente ritenere che corrisponda alla volontà dell'interessato e

---

9 Translated by Dr. *Caterina Gozzi* (Osnabrück).

(c) in quanto sia possibile e ragionevole, informare l'interessato della gestione e procurare di ottenere il consenso di questi per atti ulteriori.

(2) La gestione non può essere interrotta senza una buona ragione.

Articolo 2:102: Doveri al termine della gestione

(1) Al termine della gestione, il gestore deve senza ingiustificato ritardo riferire sulla gestione, rendere conto del suo operato all'interessato e consegnare tutto ciò che ha ottenuto quale risultato della gestione.

(2) Se al tempo della gestione il gestore non è pienamente capace, l'obbligo di consegna è soggetto alle eccezioni previste dalle norme sull'arricchimento senza causa (PEL Unjust.Enr.).

Articolo 2:103: Risarcimento del danno cagionato dalla violazione di un obbligo

(1) Il gestore è tenuto nei confronti dell'interessato risarcimento del danno cagionato dalla violazione di un obbligo previsto in questo Libro, se il danno risulta da un rischio che il gestore ha creato, aggravato o intenzionalmente fatto perdurare.

(2) La responsabilità del gestore è ridotta o esclusa in quanto sia equo e ragionevole, avendo riguardo, tra l'altro, ai motivi per cui il gestore ha intrapreso la gestione.

(3) Il gestore non pienamente capace al tempo della gestione risponde del risarcimento del danno solo in quanto il gestore risponda del risarcimento anche secondo il diritto delle obbligazioni extracontrattuali sorte da un danno cagionato ad un altro (PEL Liab.Dam.).

Capitolo 3:
Diritti e potere di rappresentanza del gestore

Articolo 3:101: Diritto ad essere tenuto indenne o rimborsato

Il gestore ha diritto nei confronti dell'interessato ad essere tenuto indenne o, a seconda dei casi, ad essere rimborsato per un' obbligazione che abbia contratto o per l'impiego di denaro o di altri beni, in quanto abbia agito ragionevolmente per gli scopi della gestione.

Articolo 3:102: Diritto ad un compenso

(1) Il gestore ha diritto ad un compenso in quanto la gestione sia ragionevole ed intrapresa nell'ambito della professione o dell'attività commerciale del gestore.

(2) Il compenso dovuto corrisponde, in quanto sia ragionevole, alla somma che è ordinariamente pagata nel tempo e nel luogo della gestione al fine di ottenere una prestazione del tipo di quella effettuata.

Articolo 3:103: Diritto al risarcimento

Il gestore, il quale agisce per difendere l'interessato o la proprietà o gli interessi dell'interessato da un pericolo, ha diritto nei confronti dell'interessato stesso al risarcimento delle perdite cagionate da una lesione personale o da un danno alla proprietà sofferti durante la gestione se:

(a) la gestione ha creato o ha sensibilmente aggravato il rischio di tale lesione o danno e

(b) il rischio, per quanto prevedibile, era ragionevolmente proporzionale al rischio corso dall'interessato.

Articolo 3:104: Riduzione o esclusione dei diritti del gestore

(1) I diritti del gestore sono limitati od esclusi in quanto il gestore al tempo della gestione non abbia voluto essere tenuto indenne, rimborsato, compensato o risarcito, a seconda dei casi.

(2) I suddetti diritti sono inoltre limitati od esclusi in quanto sia equo e ragionevole, avendo riguardo, tra l'altro, al fatto che il gestore abbia agito per difendere l'interessato in una situazione di comune pericolo, al fatto che la responsabilità dell'interessato sarebbe altrimenti eccessiva ed al fatto che si possa ragionevolmente ritenere che l'interessato ottenga conveniente riparazione da altri.

Articolo 3:105: Obbligazione di un terzo di tenere indenne o rimborsare l'interessato

Se il gestore agisce per evitare un danno all'interessato, la persona che sarebbe responsabile in base alle norme dei PEL Liab.Dam. per aver cagionato tale danno all'interessato è obbligata a tenere indenne o, a seconda dei casi, a rimborsare l'interessato in relazione alla sua responsabilità nei confronti del gestore.

Articolo 3:106: Potere del gestore di agire in nome dell'interessato

(1) Il gestore può stipulare negozi giuridici o compiere altri atti giuridici in nome dell'interessato in quanto sia ragionevole per arrecare vantaggio all'interessato.

(2) Tuttavia, un atto giuridico unilaterale compiuto dal gestore in nome dell'interessato non ha effetto se una terza persona a cui l'atto sia indirizzato rifiuti l'atto senza ritardo.

Latvian[10]
Neuzdota lietvedība

1. Nodaļa:
Piemērošanas joma

1:101.Pants: Lietu vešana cita labā

(1) Šī sadaļa tiek piemērota gadījumos, kad persona (lietvedis) apzināti rīkojas citas personas (pārstāvamā) interesēs, un
   (a) lietveža rīcībai ir saprātīgs pamats; un
   (b) pārstāvamais apstiprina rīcību bez nepamatotas kavēšanās, kas varētu negatīvi ietekmēt lietvedi.

(2) Lietveža rīcībai nav saprātīga pamata, ja:
   (a) lietvedim ir pietiekama iespēja noskaidrot pārstāvamā gribu, bet viņš to nedara; vai
   (b) lietvedis zina vai viņam vajadzētu zināt, ka lietu vešana neatbilst pārstāvamā gribai.

1:102.Pants: Lietu vešana cita pienākumu izpildei

Ja lietvedis rīkojas, lai izpildītu citas personas pienākumu, kura izpilde ir steidzami nepieciešama nozīmīgu sabiedrības interešu dēļ un lietveža galvenais nolūks ir rīkoties izpildījuma saņēmēja labā, tad persona, kuras pienākumu lietvedis ar savu rīcību izpilda, ir uzskatāma par pārstāvamo šīs sadaļas izpratnē.

1:103.Pants: Izņēmumi

Šī sadaļa netiek piemērota, ja lietvedis:
(a) ir pilnvarots rīkoties saskaņā ar līgumsaistībām vai citiem pienākumiem pret pārstāvamo;
(b) ir pilnvarots rīkoties bez pārstāvamā atļaujas apstākļos, kas nav paredzēti šajā sadaļā; vai
(c) rīkojas, izpildot pienākumu, kuru ir uzņēmies attiecībā pret trešo personu.

2. Nodaļa:
Lietveža pienākumi

2:101.Pants: Pienākumi lietu vešanas laikā

(1) Lietu vešanas laikā lietvedim
   (a) jārīkojas ar saprātīgu rūpību;
   (b) izņemot 1:102. pantā aprakstīto pārstāvības gadījumu, jārīkojas veidā, kas saskaņā ar lietvedim pieejamo informāciju vai saprātīgiem pieņēmumiem atbilst pārstāvamā gribai; un
   (c) ciktāl tas ir iespējams un saprātīgi pieņemams, jāinformē pārstāvamais par lietu vešanu un jālūdz pārstāvamā atļauja turpmāku darbību veikšanai.

(2) Lietu vešanu nedrīkst pārtraukt bez svarīga iemesla.

---

10 Translated by Professor *Kaspars Balodis* (Riga).

2:102.Pants: Pienākumi pēc lietu vešanas

(1) Pēc lietu vešanas lietvedim bez nepamatotas kavēšanās jāsniedz ziņojums un jāatskaitās pārstāvamajam, un jānodod tam viss, kas iegūts lietu vešanas rezultātā.

(2) Ja lietu vešanas laikā lietvedim nav pilnas rīcībspējas, iegūtā nodošanas pienākums ir spēkā tiktāl, ciktāl to neierobežo noteikumi par netaisnu iedzīvošanos (PEL Unjust.Enr.).

2:103.Pants: Pienākumu neizpildes dēļ nodarīto zaudējumu atlīdzināšana

(1) Lietvedim ir pienākums atlīdzināt pārstāvamajam zaudējumus, kurus izraisījusi šajā sadaļā noteikto pienākumu neizpilde, ja zaudējumu cēlonis ir lietveža radītais, veicinātais vai tīši turpinātais risks.

(2) Lietveža atbildība tiek samazināta vai izslēgta, ciktāl tas ir taisnīgi un saprātīgi, cita starpā, ņemot vērā lietveža iemeslus lietu vešanas uzsākšanai.

(3) Lietvedim, kuram lietu vešanas laikā nav pilnas rīcībspējas, ir pienākums atlīdzināt zaudējumus tikai tiktāl, ciktāl šāds pienākums viņam rodas, pamatojoties uz noteikumiem par zaudējumu nodarīšanu citai personai ārpuslīgumiskās attiecībās (PEL Liab.Dam.).

3. Nodaļa:
Lietveža tiesības un pilnvaras

3:101.Pants: Tiesības uz kompensāciju vai izdevumu atlīdzību

Lietvedim ir tiesības saņemt kompensāciju vai, atkarībā no apstākļiem, atlīdzību no pārstāvamā par saistībām vai izdevumiem (naudu vai citām vērtībām), ciktāl tādi saprātīgi radušies lietu vešanas nolūkā.

3:102.Pants: Tiesības uz samaksu

(1) Lietvedim ir tiesības uz samaksu par lietu vešanu, ciktāl lietu vešanas uzsākšana ir saprātīga un veikta saistībā ar lietveža profesiju vai arodu.

(2) Samaksas apmēru nosaka atbilstoši summai, kādu parasti maksā, lai saņemtu šādu pakalpojumu lietu vešanas laikā un vietā.

3:103.Pants: Tiesības uz zaudējumu atlīdzību

Lietvedim, kas rīkojas, lai aizsargātu pārstāvamo, pārstāvamā īpašumu vai intereses no apdraudējuma, ir tiesības saņemt no pārstāvamā atlīdzību par zaudējumiem, ko lietu vešanas laikā lietvedis cietis miesas bojājuma vai mantai nodarīta bojājuma rezultātā, ja:

(a) lietu vešana radījusi vai būtiski palielinājusi šādu bojājumu nodarīšanas risku; un

(b) paredzamais risks bijis samērīgi proporcionāls pārstāvamā riskam.

3:104.Pants: Lietveža tiesību samazināšana vai izslēgšana.

(1) Lietveža tiesības tiek samazinātas vai izslēgtas tiktāl, ciktāl lietu vešanas laikā lietvedis atbilstoši apstākļiem nav gribējis pieprasīt kompensāciju, izdevumu atlīdzību, samaksu vai zaudējumu atlīdzību.

(2) Šīs tiesības tiek samazinātas vai izslēgtas arī tiktāl, ciktāl tas ir taisnīgi un pamatoti, cita starpā ievērojot, vai lietvedis rīkojies, lai aizstāvētu pārstāvamo kopīga apdraudējuma situācijā, vai pārstāvamā atbildība būtu pārmērīga un vai lietvedim būtu pamats saņemt atbilstošu atlīdzību no citām personām.

3:105.Pants: Trešo personu kompensācijas vai atlīdzības pienākums pret pārstāvamo

Ja lietvedis rīkojas, lai pasargātu pārstāvamo no zaudējumiem, personai, kas saskaņā ar PEL Liab.Dam. būtu atbildīga par šādu zaudējumu nodarīšanu pārstāvamajam, ir pienākums pārstāvamā vietā sniegt kompensāciju vai, atbilstoši situācijai, atlīdzību lietvedim par pārstāvamā saistībām.

3:106.Pants: Lietveža pilnvaras rīkoties pārstāvamā vārdā

(1) Lietvedis ir tiesīgs slēgt tiesiskus darījumus vai veikt citas juridiskas darbības pārstāvamā vārdā, ciktāl ir pamats uzskatīt, ka tas ir pārstāvamā interesēs.

(2) Tomēr vienpusēja juridiska darbība, kuru lietvedis veicis pārstāvamā vārdā, nav spēkā, ja trešā persona, kurai darbība adresēta, to noraida bez nepamatotas kavēšanās.

Lithuanian[11]
Kito Asmens Reikalų Tvarkymas to Asmens Interesais

1 Skyrius:
Taikymo apimtis

1:101 Straipsnis. Kito asmens reikalų tvarkymas

(1) Šios Knygos nuostatos taikomos tais atvejais, kai asmuo (tvarkytojas) veikia turėdamas ketinimą veikti kito asmens (naudos gavėjas) interesais, jeigu
  (a) tvarkytojas tokiam veikimui turi protingą pagrindą arba
  (b) naudos gavėjas patvirtina tuos veiksmus be tokio neprotingo delsimo, kuris turėtų nepalankių padarinių tvarkytojui.

(2) Tvarkytojas neturi protingo pagrindo veikti, jeigu jis:
  (a) turėjo protingą galimybę išsiaiškinti naudos gavėjo valią, bet to nepadarė; arba
  (b) žino arba turi žinoti, kad veikia kito asmens interesais prieš šio valią.

1:102 Straipsnis. Reikalų tvarkymas, pasireiškiantis naudos gavėjo pareigos atlikimu

Jeigu tvarkytojas veikia vykdydamas kito asmens pareigą, kuri yra neatidėliotinai vykdytina ginant pažeistą viešą interesą, ir kai tvarkytojas veikia turėdamas tikslą duoti naudą asmeniui, gaunančiam įvykdymą, asmuo, kurio pareigą vykdo tvarkytojas, yra naudos gavėjas, kurio atžvilgiu taikomos šios Knygos nuostatos.

1:103 Straipsnis. Išimtys

Šios Knygos nuostatos netaikomos, jeigu tvarkytojas:
(a) yra įgaliotas sutartimi arba turi kitokią pareigą naudos gavėjui;
(b) kitokiu, nei numato ši Knyga, būdu yra įgaliotas veikti nepriklausomai nuo asmens, kurio interesais veikia, sutikimo; arba
(c) turi pareigą tretiesiems asmenims veikti kito asmens interesais.

2 Skyrius.
Tvarkytojo pareigos

2:101 Straipsnis. Pareigos kito asmens reikalų tvarkymo metu

(1) Tvarkydamas kito asmens reikalus tvarkytojas privalo:
  (a) veikti protingai rūpestingai;
  (b) veikti tokiu būdu, kurį tvarkytojas žino ar turėtų protingai žinoti atitinkant asmens, kurio interesais veikiama, valią, išskyrus tuos atvejus, kuriuos naudos gavėjo atžvilgiu nustato 1:102 straipsnis; ir

[11] Translated by Professor *Valentinas Mikelenas* (Vilnius).

(c) tiek, kiek tai įmanoma ir protinga, informuoti naudos gavėją apie reikalų tvarkymą ir siekti jo sutikimo tolimesniems veiksmams.

(2) Kito asmens reikalų tvarkymas negali būti nutrauktas be pakankamos priežasties.

2:102 Straipsnis. Pareigos pasibaigus kito asmens reikalų tvarkymui

(1) Pabaigęs kito asmens reikalų tvarkymą, tvarkytojas privalo nelestinai nedelsdamas pranešti apie tai naudos gavėjui ir atsiskaityti jam, taip pat perduoti jam viską, ką gavo tvarkydamas šio reikalus.

(2) Jeigu tuo metu, kai veikė kito asmens interesais, tvarkytojas nebuvo pilnai veiksnus, teisė reikalauti grąžinti viską, ką tvarkytojas gavo tvarkydamas kito asmens reikalus, gali būti ginama remiantis nepagrįsto praturtėjimo instituto normomis.

2:103 Straipsnis. Žalos, padarytos pareigos pažeidimu, atlyginimas

(1) Tvarkytojas privalo asmeniui, kurio reikalus tvarkė, atlyginti žalą, atsiradusią dėl šioje knygoje nustatytos pareigos pažeidimo, jeigu žala atsirado dėl rizikos, kurią sukūrė, padidino ar tyčia palaikė pats tvarkytojas.

(2) Tvarkytojo atsakomybė mažinama arba ji visai neatsiranda, jeigu tai yra sąžininga ir protinga, tarp kitų veiksnių atsižvelgus ir į tvarkytojo turėtas priežastis veikti kito asmens interesais.

(3) Tvarkytojo, kuris veikdamas kito asmens interesais nebuvo pilnai veiksnus, atsakomybė už žalos atlyginimą kyla tokiu laipsniu, kokiu tas tvarkytojas atsako pagal nesutartines prievoles už kitam padarytą žalą.

3 Skyrius.
Tvarkytojo teisės ir įgalinimai

3:101 Straipsnis. Teisė į atlyginimą arba išlaidų padengimą

Tvarkytojas turi teisę reikalauti iš naudos gavėjo atlyginimo, arba, reikalui esant, išlaidų atlyginimo, turėtų pinigais ar kitu turtu, tiek, kiek protingai tai buvo sąlygota tvarkant kito asmens reikalus.

3:102 Straipsnis. Teisė į atlyginimą

(1) Tvarkytojas turi teisę į tokį atlyginimą, kiek kito asmens reikalų tvarkymas yra protingas ir atliktas tvarkytojui ir atliktas tvarkytojui vykdant savo profesinę ar verslo veiklą.

(2) Mokėtinas atlyginimas yra protingo dydžio suma, kuri paprastai mokama tuo metu ir toje vietoje, kada ir kur buvo tvarkomi kito asmens reikalai, siekiant atitinkamo įvykdymo rezultato.

3:103 Straipsnis. Teisė į nuostolių atlyginimą

Tvarkytojas, kuris veikė siekdamas apginti nuo pavojaus naudos gavėją, jo turtą ar interesus, turi teisę reikalauti iš naudos gavėjo atlyginti jam veikiant patirtus nuostolius, pasireiškiančius sveikatos ar turto sužalojimu, jeigu:

(a) kito asmens reikalų tvarkymas sukėlė arba žymiai padidino tokio sužalojimo arba žalos riziką; ir

(b) ta rizika, tiek, kiek ją galima buvo numatyti, buvo protingai proporcinga rizikai, kylančiai asmeniui, kurio interesais veikiama.

3:104 Straipsnis. Tvarkytojo teisių susiaurinimas ar panaikinimas

(1) Tvarkytojo teisės yra susiaurinamos ar panaikinamos tiek, kiek tvarkytojas tuo metu, kai veikė kito asmens interesais, nenorėjo reikalauti atlyginimo, išlaidų kompensavimo, atlyginimo už darbą ar nuostolių atlyginimo, priklausomai nuo aplinkybių.

(2) Šios teisės taip pat susiaurinamos ar panaikinamos tuomet, kai tai yra sąžininga ir protinga, tarp kitų veiksnių atsižvelgiant ir į tai, ar tvarkytojas veikė siekdamas apsaugoti naudos gavėją bendro pavojaus situacijoje, taip pat į tai, ar naudos gavėjo atsakomybė nebūtų pernelyg didelė ir tvarkytojui galima buvo protingai tikėtis, kad šis gaus atitinkamą kompensaciją iš naudos gavėjo.

3:105 Straipsnis. Trečiojo asmens pareiga kompensuoti ar atlyginti asmeniui, kurio reikalai buvo tvarkomi

Jeigu tvarkytojas veikia turėdamas tikslą apsaugoti naudos gavėją nuo žalos, asmuo, kuris būtų atsakingas pagal PEL Liab.Dam. dėl žalos atsiradimo naudos gavėjui, turi pareigą kompensuoti tvarkytojui arba tam tikru atveju atlyginti naudos gavėjo išlaidas, turėtas atsakant prieš tvarkytoją.

3:106 Straipsnis. Tvarkytojo įgalinimai veikti asmens, kurio reikalus tvarko, vardu

(1) Tvarkytojas gali sudaryti sandorius ar atlikti kitus teisinius veiksmus asmens, kurio reikalus tvarko, vardu tiek, kiek tai protingai atitinka šio asmens interesus.

(2) Tačiau naudos gavėjo vardu tvarkytojo sudarytas vienašalis sandoris negalioja, jeigu trečiasis asmuo, į kurį šis sandoris nukreiptas, nepagrįstai nedelsdamas nepripažįsta šio sandorio.

Portuguese[12]
Gestão de Assuntos Alheios

Capítulo 1:
Âmbito de aplicação

Artigo 1:101: Intervenção em benefício de outrem

(1) Aplica-se o presente Livro quando uma pessoa (o gestor) age com a intenção predominante de beneficiar outrem (o interessado) desde que:
   (a) O gestor tenha um motivo razoável para agir ou
   (b) O interessado aprove o acto sem demora injustificada que possa prejudicar o gestor.

(2) O gestor não tem um motivo razoável para agir se:
   (a) Tendo uma oportunidade razoável para descobrir a vontade do interessado não o faz, ou
   (b) Sabe ou devia saber que a gestão é contrária à vontade do interessado.

Artigo 1:102: Gestão em cumprimento de um dever alheio

Quando o gestor age para cumprir um dever de outra pessoa, cujo cumprimento é exigível e urgentemente necessário por ser uma questão de interesse público primordial, agindo o gestor com a intenção predominante de beneficiar aquele que recebe a prestação, então a pessoa cujo dever o gestor cumpriu será o interessado, aplicando-se as disposições do presente Livro.

Artigo 1:103: Exclusões

Não se aplica o presente Livro quando o gestor:

(a) Estiver habilitado, por contrato ou por outro dever em relação ao interessado, a agir;
(b) Estiver autorizado, além dos termos do presente Livro, a agir independentemente do consentimento do interessado; ou
(c) Estiver obrigado, relativamente a um terceiro, a agir.

Capítulo 2:
Deveres do gestor

Artigo 2:101: Deveres durante a gestão

(1) Durante a gestão, o gestor deve:
   (a) Agir com a diligência razoável;
   (b) Excepto em relação a um interessado nos termos do artigo 1:102, agir de uma maneira tal, que o gestor saiba ou possa razoavelmente presumir estar em conformidade com a vontade do interessado; e

---

12 Translated by *José Carlos de Medeiros Nóbrega* (Osnabrück), agreed with Professor *Júlio Manuel Vieira Gomes* (Oporto).

(c) Logo que seja possível e razoável, informar o interessado sobre a gestão e procurar obter do interessado consentimento para acções posteriores.

(2) A gestão não pode ser interrompida sem uma boa razão.

Artigo 2:102: Deveres após a gestão

(1) Após a gestão, o gestor deve, sem demora injustificada, prestar tanto informações como contas ao interessado, e entregar-lhe tudo o que tenha obtido como resultado da gestão.

(2) Se, no momento da gestão, o gestor não tinha plena capacidade jurídica, são aplicáveis, quanto ao dever de entrega, os meios de defesa previstos nas regras do enriquecimento sem causa (PEL Unjust.Enr.).

Artigo 2:103: Reparação de dano causado pelo não cumprimento de um dever

(1) O gestor responde pela reparação, frente ao interessado, do dano causado pela falta de cumprimento de um dever disposto no presente Livro, se tal dano for resultante de um risco que o gestor criou, aumentou ou intencionalmente manteve.

(2) Desde que seja justo e razoável, a responsabilidade do gestor pode ser reduzida ou excluída, tendo em consideração, entre outras coisas, as razões do gestor para agir.

(3) Um gestor que, no momento da intervenção, não tinha plena capacidade jurídica, apenas é obrigado à reparação se este gestor também for obrigado à reparação de acordo com as regras da responsabilidade extracontratual por danos causados a outrem (PEL Liab.Dam.).

Capítulo 3:
Direitos e poder de representação

Artigo 3:101: Direito à liberação ou ao reembolso

O gestor tem, face ao interessado, direito a ser liberado das obrigações contraídas ou, conforme o caso, direito ao reembolso de despesas (em dinheiro ou em outros bens patrimoniais), desde que tenha sido razoável, para os fins da gestão, contrair obrigações ou efectuar despesas.

Artigo 3:102: Direito à remuneração

(1) O gestor tem direito à remuneração, desde que a gestão seja razoável e corresponda ao exercício da actividade profissional ou comercial do gestor.

(2) A remuneração devida corresponde ao valor que normalmente se paga, na medida em que for razoável, no momento e local da gestão, para obter uma prestação do género da que foi efectuada.

Artigo 3:103: Direito à reparação

O gestor que age para proteger o interessado, o seu património ou os seus interesses, de um perigo, tem direito à reparação, relativamente ao interessado, pelo prejuízo resultante de uma lesão corporal ou dano patrimonial sofridos durante a sua actuação se:

(a) A gestão criou ou significativamente aumentou o risco de tais lesões ou danos; e se

(b) O risco a que o gestor se expôs, tanto quanto se podia prever, era razoavelmente proporcionado ao risco do interessado.

Artigo 3:104: Limitação ou exclusão dos direitos do gestor

(1) Os direitos do gestor serão limitados ou excluídos, desde que este, no momento da actuação, não tivesse a intenção de exigir a liberação de uma obrigação, o reembolso, a remuneração ou a reparação, consoante o caso.

(2) Esses direitos também serão limitados ou excluídos, na medida do que for justo e razoável, tendo em consideração, entre outras circunstâncias, se o gestor agiu para proteger o interessado numa situação de perigo comum, se o montante da responsabilidade para o interessado for excessivo, bem como se fosse razoável esperar que o gestor pudesse obter de outrem uma indemnização adequada.

Artigo 3:105: Obrigação de uma terceira pessoa de liberar ou de reembolsar o interessado

Se o gestor age para proteger o interessado de um dano, a pessoa, a quem, segundo o disposto nos PEL Liab.Dam., a causa desse dano ao interessado seria imputável, será então obrigada, no que respeita à responsabilidade do interessado face ao gestor, a liberar o interessado ou, consoante o caso, a reembolsá-lo.

Artigo 3:106: Poder do gestor para agir no nome do interessado

(1) O gestor pode celebrar negócios jurídicos ou realizar outros actos jurídicos em nome do interessado, na medida em que tal se revele razoável como modo de beneficiar o interessado.

(2) No entanto, um acto jurídico unilateral realizado pelo gestor em nome do interessado não produzirá efeitos se o terceiro, seu destinatário, rejeitar o acto sem demora injustificada.

Slovenian[13]
Poslovodstvo Tujih Zadev

1. poglavje:
Obseg uporabe

Člen 1:101: Poslovodstvo v. korist drugega

(1) Ta knjiga se uporablja, kadar nekdo (poslovodja) ukrepa pretežno z namenom, drugemu (principalu) koristiti, in
   (a) ima poslovodja utemeljen razlog za ukrepanje, ali
   (b) principal odobri poslovodstvo brez neupravičenega odlašanja, ki bi prizadelo poslovodjo.

(2) Poslovodja nima utemeljenega razloga za ukrepanje, če
   (a) ima razumno možnosti ugotoviti principalove želje, pa tega ne stori, ali
   (b) ve oziroma bi moral vedeti, da je ukrep v. nasprotju s principalovimi željami.

Člen 1:102: Poslovodstvo z namenom izpolniti obveznost drugega

Kadar poslovodja ukrepa z namenom, da izpolni zapadlo obveznost koga drugega, ki je nujno potrebna zaradi prednostnega javnega interesa, in poslovodja ukrepa pretežno z namenom, da ima od tega korist upravičenec izpolnitve, je oseba, katere obveznost poslovodja izpolnjuje, principal, na katerega se nanaša ta knjiga.

Člen 1:103: Izključitve

Ta knjiga se ne uporablja, kadar je poslovodja:
(a) pooblaščen, da ukrepa na podlagi pogodbene ali druge obveznosti do principala;
(b) pooblaščen po pravilih, ki jih ta knjiga ne ureja, da ukrepa neodvisno od principalove privolitve, ali
(c) ga k ukrepanju zavezuje obveznost do tretje osebe.

2. poglavje:
Obveznosti poslovodje

Člen 2:101: Obveznosti tekom poslovodstva

(1) Med poslovodstvom mora poslovodja
   (a) ukrepati z razumno skrbnostjo,
   (b) razen v. zvezi s principalom v. smislu člena 1:102, ravnati na način, za katerega poslovodja ve ali bi moral razumno predvidevati, da je v. skladu s principalovimi željami, in

---

13 Translated by Judge Professor *Verica Trstenjak* (Luxemburg/Maribor).

(c) kolikor je mogoče in razumno, obvestiti principala o poslovodstvu in dobiti od njega soglasje za nadaljnje ukrepanje.

(2) Poslovodstvo se ne sme prekiniti brez utemeljenega razloga.

Člen 2:102: Obveznosti po končanem poslovodstvu

(1) Po končanem poslovodstvu mora poslovodja brez neprimernega odlašanja principalu podati poročilo in račun ter mu izročiti vse, kar je pridobil na račun poslovodstva.

(2) Če med poslovodstvom poslovodja nima popolne poslovne sposobnosti, veljajo glede obveznosti izročitve vsi ugovori, ki bi bili na voljo po pravu neupravičene obogatitve (PEL Unjust.Enr.).

Člen 2:103: Povrnitev škode, povzročene s kršitvijo obveznosti

(1) Poslovodja je dolžan principalu povrniti škodo, ki mu je bila povzročena s kršitvijo obveznosti, kakor je urejena v. tej knjigi, če je škoda nastala zaradi tveganja, ki ga je povzročil, povečal ali namerno ohranjal poslovodja.

(2) Odgovornost poslovodje se omeji ali izključi, kolikor je to pošteno in razumno, ob upoštevanju, med drugim, razlogov, ki jih je imel poslovodja za ukrepanje.

(3) Poslovodja, ki med poslovodstvom nima popolne poslovne sposobnosti, je dolžan povrniti škodo samo do te mere, kolikor je poslovodja dolžan povrniti drugemu povzročeno škodo tudi po pravilih o nepogodbenih obveznostih (PEL Liab.Dam.).

3. Poglavje:
Pravice in pooblastila poslovodje

Člen 3:101: Pravica do oprostitve ali povračila

Poslovodja ima pravico od principala zahtevati oprostitev, ali v. drugih primerih, povračilo za prevzete obveznosti ali izdatke (v denarju ali drugem premoženju), kolikor so razumno nastali z namenom ukrepanja.

Člen 3:102: Pravica do denarnega nadomestila

(1) Poslovodja ima pravico do denarnega nadomestila, kolikor je poslovodstvo razumno in opravljeno v. okviru njegovega poklica ali stroke.

(2) Dolguje se nadomestilo, kolikor je to razumno, ki se običajno plača v. času in kraju opravljenega poslovodstva za takšno vrsto izpolnitve.

Člen 3:103: Pravica do povračila škode

Poslovodja, ki ukrepa, da bi pred nevarnostjo zaščitil principala ali principalovo premoženje ali interese, ima pravico od principala zahtevati povračilo za izgubo, ki jo je utrpel med ukrepanjem kot posledico poškodbe osebe ali škode na premoženju, če:

(a) je poslovodstvo povzročilo ali znatno povečalo tveganje za takšno poškodbo ali škodo, in

(b) je bilo to tveganje, v. mejah predvidljivosti, v. razumnem razmerju do tveganja za principala.

Člen 3:104: Omejitev ali izključitev pravic poslovodje

(1) Pravice poslovodje se zmanjšajo ali izključijo, kolikor poslovodja tekom ukrepanja ni želel zahtevati oprostitve, povračila, denarnega nadomestila ali povračila škode, kakor izhaja iz okoliščin.

(2) Te pravice se tudi zmanjšajo ali izključijo, če je to pošteno in razumno, upoštevajoč med drugim, ali je poslovodja ukrepal zato, da bi zavaroval principala v. položaju skupne nevarnosti, ali bi bila odgovornost principala pretirana in ali bi se od poslovodje lahko razumno pričakovalo, da bo dobil ustrezno nadomestilo od druge osebe.

Člen 3:105: Obveznost tretje osebe do oprostitve ali povračila principalu

Če poslovodja ukrepa, da bi principala zavaroval pred škodo, je oseba, ki bi bila odgovorna po PEL Liab.Dam. za povzročitev take škode principalu, dolžna principala oprostiti odgovornosti do poslovodje ali, če je to primerno, mu povrniti s tem povezane izdatke.

Člen 3:106: Pooblastilo poslovodji, da ukrepa v. imenu principala

(1) Poslovodja lahko sklepa pravne posle ali opravlja druga pravna opravila v. imenu principala, kolikor to razumno v. korist principala.

(2) Vendar pa enostransko pravno opravilo poslovodje v. principalovem imenu nima učinka, če tretja oseba, na katero je naslovljeno, to opravilo brez neupravičenega zavlačevanja zavrne.

Spanish[14]
Gestión de Asuntos Ajenos

Capítulo 1:
Ámbito de aplicación

Artículo 1:101: Intervención en beneficio ajeno

(1) El presente libro se aplicará cuando una persona (el gestor) actúe con la intención predominante de beneficiar a otra (el interesado), y
- (a) el gestor tenga un motivo razonable para actuar; o
- (b) el interesado apruebe el acto sin una demora injustificada que pudiera perjudicar al gestor.

(2) El gestor no tiene un motivo razonable para actuar si éste:
- (a) tiene una oportunidad razonable de descubrir la voluntad del interesado pero no lo hace, o
- (b) sabe o debería saber que la gestión es contraria a la voluntad del interesado.

Artículo 1:102: Gestión en cumplimiento de un deber ajeno

Cuando un gestor actúe para cumplir el deber de otra persona, cuyo cumplimiento es debido, urgente y necesario por ser un asunto de interés público superior, y actúe con la intención predominante de beneficiar al receptor de esa prestación, la persona en cumplimiento de cuyo deber actúa el gestor será el interesado en el sentido del presente Libro.

Artículo 1:103: Exclusiones

El presente Libro no se aplicará cuando el gestor:
- (a) esté autorizado para actuar según un deber contractual o de otra índole frente al interesado,
- (b) esté autorizado, fuera del presente Libro, para actuar independientemente del consentimiento del interesado, o
- (c) esté sujeto a la obligación de actuar frente a un tercero.

Capítulo 2:
Deberes del gestor

Artículo 2:101: Deberes durante la gestión

(1) Durante la gestión, el gestor deberá
- (a) actuar con diligencia razonable;
- (b) excepto en relación al interesado descrito en el Artículo 1:102, actuar de un modo que el gestor sabe o debería presumir razonablemente que está en conformidad con la voluntad del interesado, y

[14] Translated by *Begoña Alfonso de la Riva* (Osnabrück) in collaboration with Professor *Guillermo Palao Moreno* (Valencia) and Dr. *María Ángeles Martín Vida* (Osnabrück).

(c) en tanto que sea posible y razonable, informar al interesado sobre la gestión y solicitar al interesado su consentimiento para posteriores acciones.

(2) La gestión no podrá ser interrumpida sin una buena razón.

Artículo 2:102: Deberes tras la gestión

(1) Tras la gestión el gestor deberá informar y rendir cuentas al interesado sin demora injustificada así como entregar cualquier cosa obtenida a través de la gestión.

(2) Si al tiempo de la gestión el gestor careciese de plena capacidad legal, el deber de entrega estará sujeto a las excepciones previstas en las normas sobre enriquecimiento injusto (PEL Unjust.Enr.).

Artículo 2:103: Reparación del daño causado por la violación de un deber

(1) El gestor será responsable de la reparación de los daños causados por la violación de un deber previsto en el presente Libro si el daño resultase de un riesgo que el gestor creó, aumentó o mantuvo intencionadamente.

(2) La responsabilidad del gestor se reducirá o excluirá en la medida en que sea justo y razonable, teniendo en cuenta, entre otras cosas, los motivos que le llevaron a actuar.

(3) El gestor que al tiempo de la gestión carezca de plena capacidad legal será responsable de la reparación sólo en la medida en que sea también responsable según las normas de las obligaciones no contractuales nacidas del daño causado a otro (PEL Liab.Dam.).

Capítulo 3:
Derechos y poder de representación del gestor

Artículo 3:101: Derecho a liberación o reembolso

El gestor tendrá frente al interesado el derecho a la liberación de las obligaciones contraídas o, en su caso, al reembolso de los gastos (ya fuesen en dinero u otros bienes patrimoniales), si fue razonable para los fines de la gestión contraer esas obligaciones o incurrir en esos gastos.

Artículo 3:102: Derecho a remuneración

(1) El gestor tendrá derecho a remuneración en la medida en que la gestión sea razonable y llevada a cabo en el curso del oficio o industria del gestor.

(2) La remuneración debida será la cantidad que, siendo razonable, habitualmente se paga en el momento y el lugar de la gestión para obtener una prestación del tipo de la llevada a cabo.

Artículo 3:103: Derecho a reparación

El gestor que actúe para proteger al interesado o la propiedad o intereses del interesado frente a un peligro tendrá frente al interesado el derecho a la reparación de las pérdidas sufridas como resultado de una lesión corporal o daño patrimonial padecido durante la actuación, si:

(a) la gestión creó o aumentó significativamente el riesgo de tal lesión o daño; y

(b) tal riesgo, siendo previsible, era razonablemente proporcional al riesgo del interesado.

Artículo 3:104: Reducción o exclusión de los derechos del gestor

(1) Los derechos del gestor se reducirán o excluirán si el gestor en el momento de actuar no tuvo la intención de pedir liberación, reembolso, remuneración o reparación, según el caso.

(2) Estos derechos también se reducirán o excluirán, si es justo y razonable, teniendo en cuenta entre otras cosas si el gestor pretendía proteger al interesado en una situación de peligro conjunto, si la responsabilidad del interesado resultaría excesiva, y si cabe esperar razonablemente que el gestor obtenga una indemnización apropiada de otra persona.

Artículo 3:105: Obligación de una tercera persona de liberar o reembolsar al interesado

Si el gestor actúa para proteger al interesado de un daño, la persona a la que, en base a las normas de los PEL Liab.Dam., le sería imputable la causa de dicho daño al interesado estará obligada, en el marco de la responsabilidad del interesado frente al gestor, a liberar al interesado de las obligaciones contraídas, o según el caso, reembolsarle los gastos en que haya incurrido.

Artículo 3:106: Poder del gestor para actuar en nombre del interesado

(1) El gestor podrá concluir negocios jurídicos o realizar otros actos jurídicos en nombre del interesado en la medida en que sea razonable para beneficiar al interesado.

(2) No obstante, un acto jurídico unilateral realizado por el gestor en nombre del interesado no tendrá efecto si la tercera persona a quien se dirige rechaza el acto sin una demora injustificada.

Swedish[15]
Tjänster utan uppdrag

Kapitel 1:
Tillämpningsområde

Artikel 1:101: Ingripande för att gynna annan

(1) Denna bok tillämpas när en person (sysslomannen) handlar med den huvudsakliga avsikten att gynna en annan (huvudmannen), och
(a) sysslomannen har rimlig grund att handla, eller
(b) huvudmannen godkänner handlandet utan ett till sysslomannens nackdel oskäligt dröjsmål.

(2) Sysslomannen har inte rimlig grund att handla om sysslomannen
(a) har en rimlig möjlighet att utröna huvudmannens vilja men inte gör detta, eller
(b) vet eller borde veta att ingripandet strider mot huvudmannens vilja.

Artikel 1:102: Ingripande för att fullgöra en annans förpliktelse

Handlar sysslomannen för att fullgöra en annans förfallna förpliktelse, vars fullgörande är omedelbart påkallat av ett överordnat offentligt intresse, med den huvudsakliga avsikten att gynna mottagaren av prestationen, är den förpliktade personen en huvudman i denna boks mening.

Artikel 1:103: Undantag

Denna bok tillämpas inte när sysslomannen
(a) är befogad att handla på grund av en kontraktuell eller annan förpliktelse mot huvudmannen,
(b) är befogad med stöd av regler vid sidan av denna bok att handla oberoende av huvudmannens samtycke, eller
(c) är förpliktad mot tredje man att handla.

Kapitel 2:
Sysslomannens plikter

Artikel 2:101: Plikter under ingripandet

(1) Under ingripandet skall sysslomannen
(a) handla med rimlig omsorg,
(b) utom i förhållande till en huvudman enligt artikel 1:102, handla på ett sätt som sysslomannen vet eller skäligen borde anta överensstämmer med huvudmannens vilja, och

15 Translated by *Johan Sandstedt* (Osnabrück).

(c) i den mån det är möjligt och lämpligt informera huvudmannen om ingripandet samt söka huvudmannens samtycke till fortsatta handlingar.

(2) Ingripandet får inte avbrytas utan goda skäl.

Artikel 2:102: Plikter efter ingripandet

(1) Efter ingripandet skall sysslomannen utan oskäligt dröjsmål till huvudmannen lämna information och redovisning samt utge allt som uppnåtts på grund av ingripandet.

(2) Om sysslomannen vid ingripandet saknar fullständig rättshandlingsförmåga, är plikten att utge det som uppnåtts på grund av ingripandet beroende av att sysslomannen inte har rätt att göra en invändning enligt reglerna om obehörig vinst (PEL Unjust.Enr.).

Artikel 2:103: Gottgörelse vid åsidosättande av plikt

(1) Sysslomannen ansvarar för gottgörelse av huvudmannen för skada som orsakats av att sysslomannen åsidosatt en i denna bok angiven plikt, om skadan är en följd av en risk som sysslomannen skapade, ökade eller uppsåtligen vidmakthöll.

(2) Sysslomannens ansvar jämkas eller utesluts i den mån det är skäligt med hänsyn till bland annat sysslomannens skäl att handla.

(3) En syssloman som vid tidpunkten för ingripandet saknar fullständig rättshandlingsförmåga ansvarar endast för gottgörelse i den mån detta även gäller enligt reglerna om utomkontraktuellt ansvar för skador som orsakats annan (PEL Liab.Dam.).

Kapitel 3:
Sysslomannens rättigheter och behörighet

Artikel 3:101: Rätt till befrielse från förpliktelser och till ersättning för uppoffringar

Sysslomannen har mot huvudmannen en rätt att bli befriad från förpliktelser eller att få ersättning för uppoffringar, vare sig dessa avsett pengar eller annan egendom, i den mån förpliktelsen respektive uppoffringen varit rimlig med hänsyn till syftet med ingripandet.

Artikel 3:102: Rätt till arvode

(1) Sysslomannen har rätt till arvode så vitt ingripandet är rimligt och företas inom sysslomannens yrke eller näringsverksamhet.

(2) I den mån det är skäligt skall arvodet uppgå till det belopp som vid tiden och platsen för ingripandet normalt betalas för en prestation av ifrågavarande slag.

Artikel 3:103: Rätt till gottgörelse

En syssloman, som handlar för att skydda huvudmannen eller dennes egendom eller intressen mot fara, har mot huvudmannen en rätt till gottgörelse för förlust på grund av personskada eller sakskada som lidits vid handlandet, om

(a) ingripandet skapade eller väsentligt utökade risken för sådan skada, och

(b) denna risk, så långt den var synbar, stod i rimligt förhållande till risken för huvudmannen.

Artikel 3:104: Jämkning eller uteslutning av sysslomannens rättigheter

(1) Sysslomannens rättigheter jämkas eller utesluts i den mån han vid tidpunkten för handlandet inte ville befrias från sin förpliktelse, kräva ersättning för sina uppoffringar, arvode eller gottgörelse.

(2) Dessa rättigheter jämkas eller utesluts också i den mån det är skäligt med hänsyn till bland annat om sysslomannen handlade för att skydda huvudmannen mot en gemensam fara, om huvudmannens ansvar skulle bli omåttligt eller om sysslomannen kan förväntas erhålla lämplig täckning från någon annan.

Artikel 3:105: Skyldighet för tredje man att befria huvudmannen från förpliktelser eller att utge ersättning för uppoffringar

Handlar sysslomannen för att skydda huvudmannen mot skada, är den som orsakandet av skadan av huvudmannen enligt PEL Liab.Dam. skulle ha tillskrivits, skyldig att befria huvudmannen från hans förpliktelse mot sysslomannen eller, i förekommande fall, ersätta huvudmannen för hans utgifter till sysslomannen.

Artikel 3:106: Sysslomannens behörighet att handla i huvudmannens namn

(1) Sysslomannen får företa rättshandlingar i huvudmannens namn i den mån detta är lämpligt för att gynna huvudmannen.

(2) En ensidig rättshandling av sysslomannen i huvudmannens namn är dock utan effekt, om den tredje man, mot vilken handlingen är riktad, avvisar rättshandlingen utan oskäligt dröjsmål.

Principles of European Law on
Benevolent Intervention in Another's Affairs

Introduction

A. General

1. Legal obligations complementary to contract law and tort law In all legal systems of the European Union the law of contract and the law of tort form the main pillars of the law of obligations. Legal history and comparative law show, however, that it is not possible to get along with these two bodies of legal rules alone – even if their scope of application is generously conceived. For that reason the Study Group on a European Civil Code has decided it is essential to draft Principles covering those parts of the law of obligations which to some extent lie 'between' the law of contract and the law of tort and which fill the gaps that those areas of the law leave behind. To be counted in among those 'gap fillers', as the Study Group sees it, in addition to the law of unjustified enrichment is the law relating to the unsolicited and voluntary undertaking of another's affairs on the basis of a reasonable ground for intervention. It is to that latter field of law that this Book is devoted.

2. Traditional Latin nomenclature In the continental European legal systems the law on voluntary management of another's affairs developed out of the Roman law concept of *negotiorum gestio*. Although the concept in its contemporary form is in many regards distinguishable from its historical origin, the Latin nomenclature has nonetheless remained current in legal usage for many lawyers in continental Europe (and Scotland). Consistent with that, the Latin term likewise features in this introduction, in the comments and in the notes, both as an umbrella term for the currently applicable national sets of rules and as a collective label for the European Principles set out and explained in the following text. It has been necessary, however, to give thought – on a purely linguistic level as well as a substantive one – to the fact that the English and Irish Common Law does not recognise an independent relationship of legal obligations derived from a (beneficial) voluntary and benevolent intervention in another's affairs. There one finds only functional equivalents which are scattered over a series of diverse legal constructs (see below *J58-76*).

3. An English term for negotiorum gestio As a result, the English legal language does not yet possess a native description for the legal obligation, addressed in this Book, which arises by operation of law out of the management of another's affairs. Since the working language of the Study Group is English and Principles are formulated in the first instance in English it has been necessary to develop a suitable English description. The Study Group has settled for "Benevolent Intervention in Another's Affairs". No practical consequences result from that, however, save that in the English version of the articles the person acting is called an "intervener", rather than the *gestor*.

4. Problems of traditional terminology in the other languages of the EU Quite apart from this the Study Group was additionally conscious of the fact that in the other languages of the EU the relevant term of art for the law of "*negotiorum gestio*" / "benevolent intervention in another's affairs" was no longer necessarily apposite in all regards from the point of view of the current substance of the law. The national terms of art (e. g. *Asianhuolto*, *Dioikisi allotrion*, *Berechtigte Geschäftsführung ohne Auftrag*, *Gestion d'affaires*, *Gestione di affari altrui*, *Gestión de asuntos ajenos*, *Gestão de assuntos alheios*, *Megbízás nélküli ügyvitel*, *Negotiorum gestio*, *Tjänster utan uppdrag*, *Uanmodet forretningsførelse*, *Zaakwaarneming*) are distinguishable not just at the surface level of language. Some of them also encapsulate a notion of the content of "benevolent intervention in another's affairs" which does not fully correspond either with the contemporary scope of application of this area of the law or with these Principles. (Among those discrepancies, for example, we might list the employment of terms – such as the German word "*Geschäfts*führung", the Portuguese "*negócios*" and the Spanish "*negocios*" – which like the historic formula "*negotiorum* gestio" tend to imply that one is concerned exclusively with safeguarding another's *economic* interests. Occasionally, moreover, the legal systems use terms which are at least misleading abbreviations of a lengthier formula – as in the German qualification "*ohne Auftrag*" and the similar usages of the Austrian, Greek and Spanish civil codes.) In other words, even among the continental European legal languages it would seem that here and there some modernisation is appropriate, at any rate in regard to the description of the area of law as a whole and in some cases also for the labels given to the persons who are parties to the legal relationship. However, the respective *termini technici* are so deeply rooted within the various legal languages of the European Union that, despite the reservations mentioned, we have only made moderate changes.

5. The concept of benevolent intervention in another's affairs What in essence the law of benevolent intervention in another's affairs is about is most easily recognised if one takes as a starting point both of the (only) legal definitions which exist in the current laws within the European Union, namely in Portuguese CC art. 464 and in Dutch CC art. 6:198. Port. CC art. 464 reads as follows: "There is a *gestão de negócios* when, without being authorised to do so, a person assumes the direction of another's business in the interest and for the account of the principal concerned." Dutch CC art. 6:198 articulates almost the same concept in a more modern form of expression; it reads: "*Zaakwaarneming* is the intervention in the furtherance of another's interest, wilfully and knowingly and with reasonable ground, without deriving the authority to do so from a legal transaction or a legal relationship subsisting elsewhere in the law." The other civil codes have not expressly defined *negotiorum gestio*. However, it is possible to derive from the individual rules alone, taken as a whole, the same or at any rate a quite similar underlying basic concept.

6. The spread of the concept of negotiorum gestio in the continental jurisdictions of the EU The concept of *negotiorum gestio* is a solid component part of the codified civil law systems of continental Europe which have adopted it from Roman law and continued its legal development. Among those jurisdictions there are admittedly a number of differences at the margins. That is in part attributable to the fact that the boundary to contract law is not drawn universally according to identical criteria. Some of these jurisdictions, furthermore, have demarcated the borderlines between the law of *negotiorum gestio* on the one hand and the law of tort and the law of unjustified enrichment on the other differently in response to particular issues. However, as regards the core questions of the law of benevolent intervention in another's affairs there is predominantly more common ground by far than there are points of difference.

7. **Scotland and Scandinavia** Scottish law also knows the institution of *negotiorum gestio* (see below *H51-52*). In the Scandinavian systems, by contrast, its profile is significantly less sharply pronounced (below *I53-57*).

8. **England and Ireland** As regards the English and Irish Common Law it is often maintained, as already mentioned, that it does not recognise a law of *negotiorum gestio*. That is true in so far as the Common Law orders the substance of the law from the standpoint of different perspectives and in some groups of cases even reaches results which differ in part from those of most other European legal systems. However, those differences are often overestimated. Ultimately they are hardly any greater than the differences encountered in those jurisdictions which do feature an independent legal relationship of *negotiorum gestio* as a solid component of its private law (below *J58-76*).

9. ***Negotiorum gestio* and the doctrine of quasi-contracts** The law of *negotiorum gestio* historically considered is closely related to the doctrine of quasi-contracts. That doctrine (which despite some still perceptible repercussions may nowadays be regarded as having fundamentally outgrown its usefulness) was based in classical times on the notion that a contractual relation existed between *gestor* and principal – not, admittedly, as a matter of fact, but fictitiously so to speak – when the former undertook for the benefit of the latter an act which the principal would probably have agreed to if he could have been asked at the time. This manner of approaching the law of *negotiorum gestio* was also promoted by its proximity to the concept of so-called "real contracts" and the phenotypical affinity between measures taken to look after another on the one side and *mandatum* on the other. In classical times the benevolent intervener in another's affairs was conceived as someone who, when the principal was not personally able to look after his affairs, jumped into the breach not because of a contractual bond, but on account of what in everyday life was not uncommonly a similarly compelling social obligation. Today it is hardly disputed that the strength of the doctrine of quasi-contracts in erecting a sound system of rules is too limited and in any case is no model for the future (see below at *L85*). At the same time the possibility cannot be ruled out that some aspects of the modern law are still rooted in a given connection to that doctrine. A possible example would be the fact (barely explicable solely in terms of the formulation of the relevant legislative provisions) that *de facto* the main focus of the law of benevolent intervention in another's affairs has remained intervention for the sake of another's patrimonial interests and not rescue from some personal emergency. The diverse ways of looking at the question whether an intervener has a power by operation of law to conclude contracts with third parties may also originate more from dogmatic rather than practical considerations: legal systems which do not distinguish between mandate (*Auftrag*) and agency (*Vollmacht*) usually confer on an intervener a power of representation whereas those which have established a distinction opt for the converse position.

10. Quasi-contracts and the Common Law A particular variant of the doctrine of quasi-contracts prevailed for a long time in the Common Law. It was finally dispelled only with the recognition of a systematically independent law of restitution in the early years of the last decade of the twentieth century. Hitherto enrichment claims for reversal of (or recompense for) benefits conferred were based on an "implied contract" which for its part was a result of the medieval English forms of action which, simply put, recognised *in personam* claims only on the basis of contract or tort. In cases of "benevolent intervention in another's affairs" (i. e., in cases which continental European jurisdictions solve by means of the concept of *negotiorum gestio*) the Common Law has always proceeded in a similar way. It has relied on a legal relationship – as it were, a quasi-contract – subsisting between the intervener and the 'principal' before the former has rendered his assistance. As a prerequisite for claims for reimbursement of expenditure it has insisted upon (and – according to the authorities at least – continues to demand until this day) the pre-existence of a legal relationship, even if that is established without particular rigour. In contrast to the law of restitution, where the doctrine of implied contracts has become part of legal history, a comparable process of liberation from the past has not yet taken place in the development of the law of benevolent intervention in another's affairs.

B. The Sources of Law on Benevolent Intervention in Another's Affairs (*negotiorum gestio*) in the Codified Systems of the EU

11. The sources in overview All the codifications of the states which currently belong to the EU contain, as already indicated, an independent law on the unsolicited and unobligated undertaking of another's affairs, though the designation for that law varies. The codifications have either a dedicated sub-division for *negotiorum gestio* or else they at least expressly regulate the topic with a series of connected articles. The most important statutory sources for the law of *negotiorum gestio* in these countries are at present the following: Austria: CC §§ 1035-1040; Belgium: CC arts. 1372-1375; Czech Republic: CC arts. 742-746; Estonia; CC §§ 1018-1023; France: CC arts. 1372-1375; Germany: CC §§ 677-687; Greece: CC arts. 730-740; Hungary: CC §§ 484-487; Italy: CC arts. 2028-2032; Lithuania: CC arts. 6:229-6:236; Luxembourg: CC arts. 1372-1375; Malta: CC §§ 1013-1020; the Netherlands: CC arts. 6:198-202; Poland: CC arts. 752-757; Portugal: CC arts. 464-472; Slovakia: CC arts. 742-746; Slovenia: CC (Code of Obligations) arts. 199-206; Spain: CC arts. 1888-1894 (and also various devolved laws, e. g. Ley 560 and 561 of the collection of laws of the Assembly of Navarra). In addition to these provisions there is admittedly also a multitude of regulations which point to a close relation to the law of *negotiorum gestio* either because they provide a concretisation of that law for specified situations or because they touch upon substantially congruent value judgments. As to these so-called "applied" laws of *negotiorum gestio* see below at *D30-38*.

12. The location of negotiorum gestio within the overall private law system The European codifications have placed the law of *negotiorum gestio* at quite different locations within their systems of private law. In Germany and in Greece *negotiorum gestio* is regulated in the special part of the second Book (law of obligations) and more particularly (as a mere matter of its place in the sequence of provisions) in the middle of the law of "special contracts" directly after the law on contracts of mandate. (The contract of mandate is itself conceived in these legal systems as a contract directed towards the gratuitous undertaking of another's affairs.) The Hungarian Civil Code (as in force at the moment) as well as the Polish Civil Code have likewise regulated the law of *negotiorum gestio* immediately after the law on contracts of mandate. The Hungarian Civil Code even combines these two areas within a single section under the heading of 'special contracts'. The Code Napoléon placed *gestion d'affaires* in its third Book ("Of the different manners by which one acquires property") and more specifically in the First Chapter ("Of quasi-contracts") of the Fourth Title (extra-contractual obligations). In the Spanish CC *negotiorum gestio* is to be found in the fourth Book ("Of obligations and contracts"), Title 16 ("Of obligations which are incurred without agreement"), Chapter 1 ("Of quasi-contracts"). The Austrian CC (which is divided into three Parts) places *negotiorum gestio* in its second Part ("Of the law of patrimony"), Second Division ("Of the personal patrimonial rights"), Chapter 22 ("Of agency and other modes of management"). The Italian CC devotes the Sixth Title of the Fourth Book ("Obligations") to the subject. Portugal likewise places *negotiorum gestio* in the law of obligations (Book Two), but in this case in the general part, in the first title of the Book. In the most recent western European codification, the Dutch CC, *zaakwaarneming* is equally located in the general law of obligations (Sixth Book) – in the First Section of the Fourth Title ("Obligations from another source than delict or contract").

13. **The essential content of the rules** More important of course than the question *where* within their system the codifications have placed the law on benevolent intervention in another's affairs is the question *what* those codes regard or have regarded as calling for statutory provision. One notices at a glance that the depth of regulation and the associated scope of the provisions reveal substantial differences. Continental Europe looks back on a history of two hundred years of codification in which the balance and focus of concern has moved through a range of nuances. One can add that taken as a whole there is hardly a codification which expressly addresses all the relevant questions of this area of the law; only when the civil codes of continental Europe are superimposed in a pile does one obtain a halfway complete picture of the essential problematic areas of the law of *negotiorum gestio*.

14. **Fixing the scope of application (definition)** A first point concerns the ascertainment of the scope of application for the law of benevolent intervention in another's affairs. (For special rules on the so-called unjustified management of another's affairs see below at C26-29.) As already stated, a genuine legal definition is only found in Portugal (CC art. 464) and the Netherlands (CC art. 6:198; see above at A5). The *Code Napoléon* in art. 1372 speaks merely of "someone who voluntarily manages the affair of another". The Austrian CC (§ 1035) presupposes someone who intervenes in the affair of another without authority. Formulated more precisely is Spanish CC art. 1888 ("One who voluntarily undertakes the agency or administration of the business of another, without their mandate ..."). The German CC fleshes out its basic norm (§ 677) with further details: "Whoever takes care of the business of another without being mandated by him or otherwise entitled to do so in relation to him". The Hungarian CC § 484 ("If a person acts in an affair of another, without being entitled to that on the basis of mandate or

otherwise, is obliged to act according to the interests and presumed wishes of the person for whose benefit he intervenes") and Polish CC art. 752 provide rules similar in all relevant points. Downright bare is the listing of essential elements formulated in Greek CC art. 730 ("One who undertakes the affair of another without mandate"), and the same goes for Italian CC art. 2028 ("Whoever, without being obliged to, knowingly assumes the management of the affair of another ...").

15. Provisions on the persons brought together in the legal relationship There are always (at least) two participants in the legal relationship of benevolent intervention or *negotiorum gestio*. In the following text they are referred to as the "intervener" and the "principal". The codifications (which, on account of their different dates of origin, employ quite diverse expressions) have not given the matter of their precise ascertainment special consideration. Only in Estonian CC § 1019 and in German CC § 686, for example, does one come across the clarification that a mistake of the intervener about the true identity of the principal is immaterial in establishing who the principal is. Provisions about multiple principals are missing from all the codes; as regards multiple interveners there are provisions only in Portugal (CC art. 467) and Spain (CC art. 1890 para (2)), namely touching upon their joint liability to the principal. Problems which result from the deficient legal capacity of the intervener, on the other hand, have only been addressed by the Estonian (CC § 1021 (2)), German (CC § 682), Greek (CC art. 735) and Italian (CC art. 2029) civil codes. Nowhere are there special provisions for the benefit of principals who are minors or otherwise not of full legal capacity.

16. Indirect clarifications Indirectly, however, those rules which are concerned with provision of maintenance to persons who have been neglected by those liable to maintain them (see Spanish CC art. 1894, Greek CC art. 738, German CC § 679 (final limb)) contribute for their sphere of application a clarification of the issue who is to be regarded as the principal. Whether in these cases the person who receives the benefit is also a principal depends on the circumstances of the particular case. In any event the person who was primarily obliged is a principal. Only in relation to the recipient of a gift do Greek CC art. 738 (2) and German CC § 685 (2) provide the rule of construction in a case of doubt that for payments of maintenance between persons who are related in the direct line (Germany) or, additionally, between siblings (Greece) one must presume a waiver of repayment. Spanish CC art. 1894 (2) even contains a special rule derived from Roman law for expenditure on funeral costs in management of another's affairs. Such costs are to be reimbursed by those who in the lifetime of the deceased would have been obliged to maintain him or her, and those persons remain principals even if the deceased has died without leaving any assets. Austrian law provides for a comparable rule in CC § 549, which according to recent doctrine, however, is considered to be part of the law on unjustified enrichment (see below *D32*). One may also say that those norms too which enable a *gestor* for reasons of public interest to disregard the contrary will of the *dominus* (Estonian CC § 1018 (1) (iii), Greek CC art. 730 (2), German CC § 679, Hungarian CC § 485 (2), Polish CC art. 755, Portuguese CC art. 465 (a) (at the end), Italian CC art. 2031 (2) (at the end)) also simultaneously contribute something towards his identification.

17. **Clarification of the intervener's duties** In the main the duties of the justified intervener are governed by more detailed rules. In essence they consist everywhere in duties of care and to surrender proceeds, while breach of those duties entitles the principal concerned to reparation. The latter principle is admittedly only expressly declared in Greek CC art. 731, Portuguese CC art. 466 (1) and Spanish CC art. 1889, but it is silently assumed in the other codifications.

18. **Duty of care** The duties of care concern the correct assumption of the intervention and/or its correct execution (cf. Belgian, French and Luxembourg CC arts. 1374 (1); Greek CC art. 731 (1); Dutch CC art. 6:199 (1); Portuguese CC art. 466 (1); Italian CC art. 2030 (1) (referring to the law of mandate) and Spanish CC art. 1889). The person rendering emergency aid enjoys certain privileges. Either he or she is liable only for intentional or grossly negligent causation of damage (German CC § 680 and Greek CC art. 732), or the quantum of his or her liability can be reduced to an amount which is equitable in the circumstances (Spanish CC art. 1889 (2); Italian CC art. 2030 (2); Belgian, French and Luxembourg CC art. 1374 (2); Dutch CC art. 6:109). Admittedly for the Belgian, French and Luxembourg CC art. 1374 (2) only the altruistic attitude of the intervener is decisive; the case of rendering emergency aid is not the only possible application of this provision.

19. **Duty to continue the intervention** In the context of the duty of care some of the codifications also include the duty to continue a management of another's affairs which the *gestor* (the intervener) has begun until the principal (or in case of his death, the heir) is able to look after his affairs himself (cf. Austrian CC § 1039; Belgian, French and Luxembourg CC arts. 1372 and 1373; Maltese CC arts. 1013 and 1014; Spanish CC art. 1888; Collection of Civil Laws of the Assembly of Navarra Ley 560; Portuguese CC art. 466; Italian CC art. 2028 and – in a modernised formulation – Dutch CC art. 6:199 (1)). The German and the Greek CC, by contrast, do not recognise a duty to continue an intervention in their wording.

20. **Informing the principal** The information related duties of the intervener are either directed towards ascertainment of the real wishes of the principal (in which case, in so far as compliance with those wishes is not a precondition for the existence of a justified benevolent intervention, they are subsumed within the requirement of care in the execution of the measure undertaken), or else they serve (in the form of a duty to give an account) to shore up the duty of the intervener to surrender any proceeds of his intervention. The duty at every stage of an on-going intervention, so far as that is reasonable in the circumstances, to inform the principal about what has been begun and to ascertain whether he is opposed to further measures be undertaken is expressly contained (as a particularisation of the general duty of care) in many of the codes: Austrian CC § 1037 sent. 1, Czech CC § 743 (1), Dutch CC art. 199 (2), Estonian CC § 1020, German CC § 681 sent. 1, Greek CC art. 733, Hungarian CC § 486 (1), Italian CC art. 2030 in conjunction with art. 1712, Polish CC art. 753, Portuguese CC art. 465 limb b-d.

21. **Giving an account and surrender of proceeds** The duty to provide an account – and of course the duty to hand over to the principal what has been obtained in the course of

the intervention – are to be found in practically all codifications (e. g. Austrian CC § 1039; Belgian, French and Luxembourg CC art. 1372 (2) in conjunction with art. 1993; Estonian CC § 1021 (1), German CC § 681 sentence 2 in conjunction with § 667; Italian CC art. 2030 (1) in conjunction with art. 1713 (1); Dutch CC art. 6:199 (2); Polish CC art. 753 (2), Portuguese CC art. 465 limbs c-e; Collection of Civil Laws of the Assembly of Navarra Ley 560). In all systems this duty to surrender belongs to the core elements of the law of benevolent intervention in another's affairs.

22. **Clarification of the intervener's rights** Equally the focus of rules in all the European codifications are of course the rights of the intervener (which, admittedly, sometimes are phrased as duties of the principal). Despite the fact that on this point too the depth of rules in the codes is varied (for instance, of all the rules of the Belgian, French and Luxembourg CC only art. 1375 touches on the rights of the *gestor*, all other provisions dealing with his duties), there is agreement nowadays on this aspect of the *negotiorum gestio* regime.

23. **Reimbursement of expenditure** By far the most important right of the justified intervener is the claim to reimbursement of expenditure. The claim is expressly mentioned in all the continental European codifications (Austrian CC §§ 1036 and 1037; Belgian, French and Luxembourg CC art. 1375; Czech CC § 742; Dutch CC art. 6:200 (1); Estonian CC § 1023; German CC § 683 sentence 1; Greek CC art. 734; Hungarian CC § 486 (2); Italian CC art. 2031; Maltese CC art. 1018; Polish CC art. 757; Portuguese CC art. 468 (1); Spanish CC art. 1893; Collection of Civil Laws of the Assembly of Navarra Ley 560). Together with the intervener's duty to surrender proceeds this claim constitutes what in the last resort is the decisive reason why it has come about in these legal systems that the unsolicited management of another's affairs has been conceived as an independent area of the law. The claim to reimbursement of expenditure, however, may depend in some countries on whether the intervention was in the end successful, if, rather than help rendered in an emergency, it consisted only of less urgent measures (Austrian CC § 1037, Polish CC art. 757, and Spanish CC art. 1893).

24. **Further claims which are expressly governed** In contrast to the claim for reimbursement of expenditure the additional rights of the intervener (or *gestor*) are by no means expressly mentioned everywhere. They must be gathered together, as it were, from the European codifications. Firstly, there is the claim of the intervener for (statutory) interest on his outlay (German CC § 256; Greek CC art. 301 (1); Italian CC art. 2031 (1); Portuguese CC art. 468 sentence 1). Then there is his right to indemnification in respect of obligations which the intervener has incurred in the principal's interest (Belgian, French and Luxembourg CC art. 1375; Estonian CC § 1023 (1); German CC § 257; Italian CC art. 2031 (1); Maltese CC art. 1018; Spanish CC art. 1893). Furthermore, persons who undertake a benevolent intervention in exercise of their profession or trade have, under some jurisdictions, claims for remuneration. Such claims to remuneration are, however, only expressly envisaged by three European civil codes (namely in Estonian CC § 1023 (2), in Dutch CC art. 6:200 (2) and in Portuguese CC art. 470 in conjunction with art. 1158 (2)). They represent an exceptional case which in terms of legal policy has remained contested to today. The omission of such claims from the text of other codes may (but need not) mean that they are also not in fact granted

by modern case law. On the other hand, the principle that the intervener has an independent claim for reparation of damage suffered in the course of his intervention is provided for in Estonian CC § 1025; Greek CC art. 736; Dutch CC art. 6:200 (1); Portuguese CC art. 468 (1) (at the end) and in Spanish CC art. 1893 (1). However, the ancient rule that someone who acts with an *animus donandi* (a donative intent) has no claim to the extent that intent featured at the time of acting is now to be found expressly stipulated in the current codes only in Estonian CC § 1023 (3), in Greek CC art. 738 and in German CC § 685 (1).

25. **Intervener's power of representation** As already mentioned above at A9, the question whether the law of benevolent intervention should also grant to the intervener a statutory power of representation is not answered uniformly by the European codifications. In Belgium, France and Luxembourg such a right is affirmed by CC art. 1375. The same is true for Italy, if the benevolent intervention has been "usefully" undertaken (CC art. 2031). In the Netherlands too a *gestor* is "authorised to carry out legal transactions in the name of the person concerned, in so far as the latter's interest is duly furthered thereby" (Dutch CC art. 6:201). In all other legal systems in continental Europe, by contrast, a justified intervener acts as an agent without a power of representation if he acts in the name of the principal without an agreed power of attorney and the subsequent ratification (*ratificação*) of the principal is not forthcoming, albeit that this is only expressly set out in statute in Portugal (CC art. 471 sent. 1 in conjunction with art. 268).

C. Provisions in the Codifications concerning (i) Benevolent, but Officious Intervention and (ii) Management of Another's Affairs for One's Own Benefit.

26. **Restriction of the law on negotiorum gestio to justified management of another's affairs** The European codifications of civil law can be divided into two groups according to whether they are confined to justified management of another's affairs or whether they also cover unjustified intervention. If the more restricted scope is adopted, then the latter (in its various manifestations) is tacitly understood to belong exclusively to the law on non-contractual liability for damage or unjustified enrichment law. True unsolicited management of another's affairs which is *justified* is, as indicated already, the deliberate undertaking of the interest of another with the intention to benefit that person (hence 'true' benevolent intervention) and with reasonable grounds (which justify the intervention). If we put aside provisions enabling a principal to approve acts which the intervener undertook in order to benefit the principal, but which were rash and without reasonable grounds (and which consequently only qualify as justified as a result of subsequent approval), we may say that the Civil Codes of Belgium, France, Italy, Luxembourg, Malta, the Netherlands and Spain (but see here CC art. 1891) belong to the first group. The legitimate management of another's affairs is regarded as the sole subject of the law of *negotiorum gestio*. Illegitimate intervention in these legal systems is left to the law on non-contractual liability for damage or, depending on the circum-

stances of the particular case, unjustified enrichment law.[1] The same holds true for Scotland.[2]

27. Inclusion of unjustified management of another's affairs The other codifications go further. Thus a person who interferes in another's affairs with the intention to benefit that other, but on an unjustified basis (i. e. without reasonable grounds), is dealt with in the Austrian CC not only in the law on non-contractual liability for damage (CC §§ 1311 sent. 2; 1312) but also within the law on *negotiorum gestio* (CC §§ 1035 and 1040). However, the Austrian Civil Code (as is also the case for Hungarian CC § 486 (3)) tackles the unjustified management of another's affairs only from the standpoint of liability for damages (cf. CC § 1039) and reimbursement of expenditure.[3] In principle only *negotiorum gestio* according to CC § 1036 (rendering emergency aid) is justified, while all other forms of *negotiorum gestio* are by contrast considered as unjustified.[4] The German Civil Code, enacted almost a century after the Austrian, has a similar starting point as it also contains rules on the unjustified management of another's affairs (CC §§ 678; 684 sentences 1 and 2). It has gone a step further based on the proposition that a principal confronted with a tortfeasor should not be placed in a worse position than a principal who is asserting his or her rights against a justified intervener. The unjustified (true) intervener (i. e. someone who acts 'on behalf' of another, but contrary to the principal's wishes or interest) is in general subjected to the same rules relating to 'accessory duties' as the justified intervener (CC §§ 681 sentences 1 and 2 in conjunction with § 667). In other words, under German law too the unjustified intervener is subject to the rules of *negotiorum gestio*.[5] (The Greek CC art. 737 likewise contains rules on unjustified *negotiorum gestio*, but by way of cross-reference to another legal regime (*Rechtsgrundverweisung*), namely the law on unjustified enrichment.[6] It does not create a legal relationship similar to agency. The same holds true for Estonian CC § 1024).

28. Arrogated management of another's affairs The German Civil Code in § 687 (2) additionally provides for yet another variation of *impure gestio*, namely the so-called "*angemaßte Eigengeschäftsführung*" (arrogated management of another's affairs). This is

---

1 See for instance on French law JClCiv (*-Bout*), Art. 1372-1375, V° Quasi-Contrats. Gestion d'affaires – Conditions d'existence, Fasc. 10 no. 99; for Italy *Breccia*, La gestione d'affari, 708 and *Aru*, Gestione d'affari, 9; and for Spain *Sánchez Jordán*, Gestión de negocios, 115. But compare Spanish CC art. 1891.

2 See further Stair (*-Whitty*), vol. 15, para 137 (in the case of an 'impure gestio' only claims in unjustified enrichment can be considered – for which claims the expenditure incurred provides a ceiling; there is no firm authority for the concept of "impure gestio" in Scotland).

3 For further details *Meissel*, GoA, 110 et seq.

4 *Meissel*, GoA, 119, 135; Schwimann (*-Apathy*), ABGB V² § 1035 no. 2; Rummel (*-Rummel*), ABGB I³ § 1035 no. 1, § 1036 no. 2, § 1037 no. 2.

5 This view, which is the prevailing opinion (Palandt [*-Sprau*], BGB⁶³, Introd. to § 677, no. 5; MünchKomm [*-Seiler*], BGB³, Vor § 677, no. 15, 12, § 677, no. 43, § 681, no. 2; Soergel [*-Beuthien*], BGB¹², Vor § 677, no. 3), has not, however, gone undisputed; it has been rejected, by (among others) *Gursky*, Schuldrecht BT⁴, 170; Staudinger (*-Wittmann*), BGB¹³, § 681, no. 2 and *Larenz*, Schuldrecht BT II/1¹³, § 57 II a.

6 Georgiades/Stathopoulos (*-Papanikolaou*), Art. 737, no. 4.

the situation where someone "*manages another's affairs as his own, even though he knows that he is not entitled to do so*". The person acting thus intermeddles in the legal affairs or sphere of interests of another person in pursuance of his own advantage. In other words he commits (as a general rule) a tort. Nonetheless one aspect of this extra-contractual liability has been dealt with as a part of the law on *negotiorum gestio*. The main purpose of CC § 687 (2) is to ensure that the principal can obtain a disgorging of profits – in particular from an "*Eigengeschäftsführer*" (an intervener acting in his own interest), who is pursuing his own benefit (CC § 687 (2) in conjunction with §§ 681 sentence 2 and 667). The more recent codifications, however, have only occasionally adopted this approach. (The concept is of course not known to the Codes enacted prior to the German Code.) In particular the Dutch CC has dealt with the problem of disgorgement of profits *en bloc* within the law on liability for damages rather than the law on *negotiorum gestio* (CC art. 6:104). The Greek CC on the other hand – like the German CC – distinguishes between justified 'true' *negotiorum gestio* (CC arts. 730 and 736), unjustified 'true' *negotiorum gestio* (CC art. 737) and arrogated 'false' management of another's affairs (i. e. performed without the intention to act on another's behalf) (CC art. 739). However, it is open to debate whether or not the unjustified true *negotiorum gestio* triggers the same ancillary obligations as the justified *negotiorum gestio* does (see the conclusion to C27 above). The arrogated management of another's affair (the false *negotiorum gestio* referred to in CC art. 739) is characterised by statute as a tort, though one for which the *gestor* is (also) liable according to the rules of contract law (CC arts. 739, 734, 718-720). The reason given for this solution (as in Germany) is the desire to confer on the principal a right to disgorgement of profits.[7] Influenced by German law, it is a point of controversy in Austrian doctrine whether or not Austrian CC § 1039 (concerning the duty to render an account and to surrender profits) is applicable in a case of arrogated 'false' management of another's affair.[8] The Supreme Court has answered this question in the negative in respect of claims for delivery up; to that extent the matter rests exclusively on the remedies available under the law on unjustified enrichment.[9] A similar controversy can be found in Portugal, where the discussion concerns the question whether or not the *gestor*'s duty to render an account and to surrender proceeds (CC art. 465 limb (c) and (e)) is applicable to arrogated management of another's affair (*gestão imprópria de negócio* or *gestão de um negócio como próprio sabendo que é alheio*) inspite of the fact that this is not explicitly provided for by statute.[10] However, a provision resembling German CC § 687 (2) may be found in Estonian CC § 1026 (2), as well as in Hungarian CC § 487.

29. Management of another's affair in the mistaken belief it is one's own Only Italy (CC art. 2032 (at the end)) and Portugal (CC art. 472 (1)) have enacted a rule according to which even a person who intermeddles with another's affairs in the erroneous belief that

---

7 Georgiades/Stathopoulos (*-Papanikolaou*), Art. 739, no. 1; Erm.AK (*-Sakketas*), Art. 739, no. 1.

8 See further Rummel (*-Rummel*), ABGB I^3, § 1039 no. 7.

9 OGH 4 December 1968, JBl 1969, 272; confirmed by OGH 18 March 1997, SZ 70/48.

10 Arguing in favour *Menezes Leitão*, Responsabilidade do gestor, 233 and *Antunes Varela*, Obrigações em Geral I^{10}, 454, fn. 2; against this view and in favour of the law on unjustified enrichment is *Pereira Coelho*, Enriquecimento e o dano, 85. See also CA Coimbra 22 March 2000, BolMinJus 495 (2000) 366.

he acts on his own behalf is within the scope of *negotiorum gestio*, if the principal ratifies the act. The German (CC § 687 (1)), Estonian (CC § 1026 (1)) and Greek (CC art. 740) Civil Codes have expressly rejected this concept; they have completely detached this emanation of 'false' management of another's affairs from the law of *negotiorum gestio*. The other European jurisdictions have no explicit provision of this type, but they too deal with these questions solely under the law of non-contractual liability for damage and the law of unjustified enrichment. For Hungarian law, for example, this follows implicitly from CC § 484, which requires that the intervener acts "on behalf of another person".

D. 'Applied' *negotiorum gestio*

30. **General** The sources mentioned above in *B11* constitute the core of the law on *negotiorum gestio*, but they are not exhaustive. A functional approach to the various jurisdictions, by contrast, shows that each of them contain a variety of special provisions which for conceptual reasons have been set in different contexts, but to a great extent follow the same fundamental ideas as the law on *negotiorum gestio*. In both Austria and Germany the term 'applied *negotiorum gestio*' ('*angewandte Geschäftsführung ohne Auftrag*') has emerged as the accepted label for these bundles of rules. The term is barely known in other jurisdictions, but in substance the phenomonen is widespread and to be found there too.

31. **Manifestations** The rules on the so-called 'applied' *negotiorum gestio* have in common an extension of the typical remedies of the law of *negotiorum gestio* to situations in which it is at least questionable whether or not all requirements for a remedy under the general rules of *negotiorum gestio* are fulfilled. Without exception they relate to cases in which a claim (in particular a claim to reimbursement) ought not to fail on the ground that it is doubtful whether or not the intervener has acted with the intention to benefit another. From a formal viewpoint a subgroup of these cases is beyond the scope of *negotiorum gestio* for an additional reason – namely, because the remedy provided for is assigned by statute (for whatever reason) to a more specific and therefore overriding regime of duties (in particular the law of contract), although the underlying values supporting the remedy are practically identical to those of the law of *negotiorum gestio*. More concretely, it is reimbursement of expenditure incurred for the preservation or improvement of goods belonging to another which is primarily at stake here.

32. **Family and inheritance law** References to the law in *negotiorum gestio* are to be found in rules of family law and succession law. Examples may be found in French CC art. 219 (power of one spouse to represent the other where the latter is not in a position to express his or her wishes) and CC art. 815-4 (power of one heir to represent a co-heir who is not in a position to express his or her wishes) respectively. Austrian CC § 549 (claim for reimbursement of funeral costs) might also have fallen into this category.[11]

---

[11] This at any rate was the opinion of *v. Zeiller* II § 549 p. 409. According to current academic analysis CC § 549 is considered to be a provision relating to unjustified enrichment (Rummel [-*Welser*], ABGB I^3, § 549 no. 5).

Spanish CC art. 1386 relates to urgent and necessary expenditure by one spouse for the benefit of the matrimonial property of both spouses. Portuguese CC art. 1679 in conjunction with art. 1678 (2) lit. f concerns the authority of one spouse to take precautionary measures in administration of the assets of the other spouse where the latter is not themselves in a position to take measures in time to avert damage. As regards German law, one can point to CC § 1959 (1) in respect of the rights and duties of an heir who disclaims his interest in the estate vis-à-vis the person who in consequence becomes heir. A rule of similar structure may also be found in CC § 1978 (1) and (3). Apart from the intention to benefit another (*Fremdgeschäftsführungswille*), all the requirements of CC § 683 sentence 1 still have to be met in order to establish a claim for reimbursement of expenditure. Most of the provisions which point to the law on *negotiorum gestio*, however, are to be found in Scandinavian family law and succession law. This is due to the fact that there is practically no general law of *negotiorum gestio* in Scandinavian law (see below *I53-57*).

33. **Property law** Property law rights to claim reimbursement of expenditure on goods belonging to another are widespread. A first group of rules relate to finders of lost property. These entitle the finder to recover costs from the owner (e.g. Dutch CC art. 5:10 (1); German CC § 970; Greek CC art. 1085; Italian CC art. 929 (2)[12]; Portuguese CC art. 1323 (3); Spanish CC art. 615 and Austrian CC § 392[13]). A second group embraces rules of the law on the legal relationship between proprietor and possessor. These envisage a duty of the proprietor to compensate the person who is in possession without authority. At least some European jurisdictions invoke a reference to the law on *negotiorum gestio* to address the problem of compensation for expenses incurred for the benefit of the owner's property by a person who is in possession or detention in bad faith (or while an action for restitution of the property is pending): see for instance Austrian CC §§ 336[14], 418[15], 517[16] and 1097[17]; Italian CC art. 1150 (1)[18]; German CC § 994 (2); Spanish CC art. 446 et seq. and Portuguese CC art. 1273 (albeit that the latter two provisions do not explicitly refer to the rules on *negotiorum gestio*).

34. **Right of recourse** Closely connected to the law on *negotiorum gestio* are, furthermore, a variety of specially regulated rights of recourse. Under Greek CC art. 286 sent. 2 a person who is liable to make reparation to a third party for damage caused by an act of necessity may "claim compensation by way of recourse from the person who has benefited from the act in accordance with the provisions on the management of an-

---

12 See on this and further points of Italian law on the finding of lost property that have a bearing on the law on negotiorum gestio *Sirena*, Gestione di affari, 254-255.

13 Cf. *v. Zeiller* II § 391 no. 2 p. 172 and Rummel (*-Rummel*), ABGB I³, § 1035 no. 8.

14 According to this rule the unjustified possessor is to be treated in the same manner as a *gestor*.

15 Cf. OGH 27 February 1996, SZ 69/50 (building on another's land).

16 Claim of the usufructuary for reimbursement of expenses incurred for the improvement of the goods according to the rules on *negotiorum gestio*.

17 Cf. OGH 4 April 1984, SZ 57/71 (lease of land; expenditure by the tenant which the landlord ought to have made).

18 On this see *Sacco*, Il possesso, 365. The rule in CC art. 1150 (1) concerns extraordinary improvements; an explicit reference to the law on *negotiorum gestio* is not provided for.

other's affairs". Similarly in Austria analogous application of Austrian CC § 1043 (common danger) is envisaged in a case of interference with another person's goods which is prompted by necessity.[19] Under Dutch law CC art. 6:30 (payment of another person's debts) and CC arts. 7:850 (2) and 7:870 (assumption of a guarantee without knowledge of the primary debtor) are characterised as instances of *negotiorum gestio*, albeit ones specially regulated by statute.[20]

35. **Contract law** Practically all legal systems in the Member States of the EU contain numerous rules of contract law which relate to the general notion of the law on *negotiorum gestio*. Technically speaking these provisions do *not* belong to the law on *negotiorum gestio*: either the relevant act is considered as a matter of obligation under a contract or it is assumed that a contract is concluded by the act itself. This by itself does not of course mean that contract law does not call upon values very similar to those in the law on *negotiorum gestio*. Rules of contract law which give expression to such similar values may be conceived as a manifestation of the law on 'applied *negotiorum gestio*'. For instance, Greek CC art. 528 sent. 2 (but compare also Italian CC arts. 1514[21] and 1207 (3)) deals with the situation where a vendor who is still in possession of goods after risk has passed (beneficially) incurs expenses in respect of the goods. The vendor obtains on account of the expenditure a claim for reimbursement against the purchaser. In Austria, while there is no provision to that effect in the CC, the courts have repeatedly affirmed the application of the rules of *negotiorum gestio* to the case where a vendor has had to continue to feed an animal because the purchaser (without justification) has purported to exercise rights resulting from an alleged breach of warranty[22] or the purchaser has had to feed the animal after a (justified) rescission of the sale contract.[23] Closely related to these rules are provisions which grant the debtor a claim for reimbursement of additional expenses incurred in the preservation of goods where the creditor is in default of acceptance of those goods and, as a result of this breach of contract, the debtor is forced to take measures to preserve the goods destined for the creditor (e. g. as in Portuguese CC art. 816). Such a claim for reimbursement of expenses is also provided for in the Principles of European Contract Law (PECL art. 7:110 (4)). As the debtor in these cases is by contract law obliged to preserve the goods, he does not act above and beyond the limits of his contractual duties and accordingly cannot be considered to act as an intervener. On the other hand, the acts of the debtor are only within the scope of the contractual obligations precisely because the debtor is assured a claim for reimbursement of his additional expenses. Austrian case law thus assumes that a debtor in such cases acts on his own behalf[24]; academic writing, however, has voiced another view

19 *Gschnitzer*, Schuldrecht Besonderer Teil^2, 286; Rummel (*-Rummel*), ABGB I^3, § 1043 no. 1.

20 Asser (*-Hartkamp*), Verbintenissenrecht III^{10}, no. 292, p. 308; *Schrage*, Verbintenissen uit andere bron, no. 3-6, p. 3-5; *Jehoram*, WPNR 1968, no. 5014, p. 447-448.

21 This provision concerns the case in which the purchaser does 'not appear for the purposes of receiving the goods bought'; here the vendor is permitted to deposit the goods at the expense of the purchaser at a public depository.

22 OGH 14 December 1875, GlU 5941.

23 OGH 8 February 1928, SZ 10/30.

24 OGH 4 July 1923, SZ 5/188. However, this decision is a matter of controversy in the current debate: see *Meissel*, GoA, 92.

according to which this case is one of applied *negotiorum gestio*.[25] Similarly the case of a (re-)sale on default (*Selbsthilfeverkauf*) of perishable goods may be considered a *negotiorum gestio*.[26]

36. Further examples Provisions of this type are not confined to sales law or general rules on non-performance. They may also be found within the law of landlord and tenant, e. g. the rules on reimbursement of expenditure which the tenant incurs for the benefit of the leased property (see for instance Austrian CC § 1097 [according to which the tenant may be regarded as a *gestor*, if he incurs expenses which the landlord was obliged to expend (CC § 1036) or the expenditure is useful (CC § 1037)]; German CC §§ 539 (1) and 581 (2) [reimbursement of tenant's expenditure in remedying defects under the rules on *negotiorum gestio* if the landlord was in default]; for similar rules also see Italian CC art. 1577 (2) and Portuguese CC art. 1036; also compare Spanish CC art. 1573 in conjunction with art. 487). In cases of this nature residual elements of an intention to benefit another can be divined where the tenant knows that the benefit of his expenditure on the property will pass to the landlord (at the very latest) on the termination of the contract. Closely related to these provisions is a spectrum of rules in the law governing contracts for gratuitous hire (Austrian CC § 981; German CC § 601 (2); Italian CC art. 1808 (2)) and deposit (e. g. Austrian CC § 967; Belgian, French and Luxembourgian CC art. 1947; Portuguese CC art. 1199 limb (b); Italian CC arts. 1789 (1) [storage in public warehouses; sale of deposited goods] and 1690 (2) [obstacles to delivery under contracts of carriage]). Further impressive examples of (in practical terms almost inconsequential) adjustments to the boundary between the law of contract, on the one hand, and the law of *negotiorum gestio*, on the other, may be found in the law on contracts of mandate. Numerous provisions permit an agent to deviate from the original instructions of the principal in a situation where the agent is unable to confer with the principal and may presume that his action will accord with the interests of the principal (e. g. Austrian CC § 1009 sent. 2; Italian CC art. 1711 (2) in conjunction with 1710 (2); Portuguese CC art. 1162). If the relevant legal system considers the agent to be under a contractual *duty* to act on these deviations from the original instructions (as for instance the Austrian[27], Italian[28] and Portuguese Codes do, the latter for both the law on contracts of mandate as well as for the law on contracts of deposit, CC arts. 1161, 1162, 1187 and 1190), the boundary between the law of *negotiorum gestio* and contract law is apparent. By contrast, if these rules only provide a ground of justification for departing from the original instructions (without also imposing a duty to do so), they fall to be considered as in substance part of the law of *negotiorum gestio*. The same also holds true for situations where the *gestor* goes beyond limits imposed by the principal with intention of benefiting the latter.

37. *Conventions d'assistance* An further arguable manifestation of 'applied *negotiorum gestio*' is the French construction of *convention* (or *contrat*) *d'assistance* which is based on a wide approach to the provisions on formation of contract. The *contrat d'assistance* is an

---

25 For further details and references see *Meissel*, GoA, 93.

26 OGH 12 April 1950, SZ 23/95.

27 Rummel (*-Strasser*), ABGB I³, § 1009 no. 16.

28 Cass. 14 July 1954 no. 2471, Rep.Giur.it. 1954, voce Mandato, no. 56.

innominate contract (*un contrat innommé*) developed by case law. The purpose of this construction is to grant a person who helps another out of kindness, but in doing so himself suffers damage, a contractual remedy against the person in need. The *cause célèbre* is Cass.civ. 27 May 1959.[29] (In this case a contract of assistance, *une convention d'assistance*, was held to have been concluded between a truck driver who got stuck in the mud and a farmer who rushed to help him; under the contract the farmer had a claim (independent of any fault) against the employer of the truck driver on account of the eye injury the farmer suffered while providing assistance.) It is assumed that the *Cour de Cassation* in this decision implicitly relied on French CC art. 1135, as the corresponding case law in Luxembourg also indicates.[30] However, the French courts also apply the concept of a *contrat d'assistance* to cases of assistance to a person in physical distress.[31] Whether or not the *convention d'assistance* is restricted to compensation for bodily injury of the person providing aid is not clear from existing case law.[32] In academic writing this notion of an implicit contract of assistance continues to be the object of fierce criticism.[33]

38. **Emergency medical treatment** Finally, another particular manifestation of management on another's behalf without authority may be found in Dutch CC art. 7:464. According to this article, the statutory provisions on contracts of medical treatment also apply to medical treatment provided without a contract – for instance, treatment of an unconscious person. Dutch CC art. 7:466 also includes a special regime for emergency treatment of persons incapable of deciding for themselves where there is insufficient time to obtain the consent of the patient's representative. There is no time to ask for consent if immediate action is necessary to prevent serious disadvantage to the patient (para (1) sentence 2). These provisions of Dutch law incidentally find a distant echo in the United Kingdom Road Traffic Act 1988 ss. 157-159 (see below *J60*).

E. The Range of Acts within the Scope of the Law on *negotiorum gestio*

39. **General** The law on *negotiorum gestio* has its historical origin in acts undertaken for the benefit of another, often a neighbour absent from his property, in relation to legal proceedings or which, like the service of a notice, have legal effects (juridical acts).[34] The legal terminology still in use to date in some jurisdictions provides evidence of this: that the principal in some statutory provisions is referred to as "owner" (*eigenaar*, *propriétaire*) or the intervention is described as conduct of "transactions" (*Geschäftsführung*) may serve as examples. From this point of departure the thrust of modern law has shifted considerably: the law on *negotiorum gestio* today includes acts of all kinds; as a matter of principle only strictly personal rights – legal acts which cannot be performed

---

29 JCP 1959 no. 11187, note *Paul Esmein*.

30 *Douchy*, Notion de quasi-contrat, no. 115, p. 260. See also CA Luxembourg 27 June 2001, Pas.lux. 2002, 154.

31 Cass.civ. 1 December 1969, JCP 1970, II, no. 16445, note *J. L. Aubert*.

32 *le Tourneau/Cadiet*, Droit de la responsabilité (2004/2005) no. 1954 p. 465.

33 *Malaurie and Aynès*, Contrats et quasi-contrats, no. 49 p. 56.

34 *Zimmermann*, Law of Obligations, 435-436.

by a representative – remain excluded. Meanwhile the question whether or not acts undertaken in the name of the principal in relation to proceedings can be the object of a benevolent intervention has almost universally been shifted to the law of procedure.[35] The matter is therefore as a rule now resolved in procedural law and not in substantive law.

40. **Juridical acts and mere conduct** It is now no longer in doubt that not only juridical acts (legal transactions and related acts having legal effects such as making payments and serving notices), but also mere conduct can be the object of *negotiorum gestio*. Italian law is no exception. Certainly Italian CC art. 2029 states that "the *gestor* … must have the capacity to conclude contracts" (as does the similar provision in Maltese CC art. 1013). However, this provision according to the prevailing understanding of the rule only applies to cases in which the benevolent intervention involves the *gestor* in incurring an obligation by means of a legal transaction. In other words, CC art. 2029 is not intended to exclude from the scope of possible acts of benevolent intervention *atti materiali* (purely physical acts, such as extinguishing the fire in a burning house).[36]

41. **Conduct for the protection of a person** The overwhelming view of European academic writing is that besides acts to protect the property of the principal acts that serve to protect the principal's *person* fall within the scope of application of the law on *negotiorum gestio*.[37] Admittedly cases of this type have only occupied the courts on comparatively rare occasions and consequently some residual doubt remains as to whether or not absolutely all European jurisdictions subscribe to this statement.[38] It is also true that cases concerning emergency medical treatment raise a variety of special problems. For these cases it is important that special insurance cover is available (see below at *L87*). However, that does not alter the fact that, from a pan-European perspective, the inclusion of *de facto* acts within the law on *negotiorum gestio* is now beyond question.

---

35 A different approach is taken by Belgian law, according to which the question whether or not procedural acts can be considered as *negotiorum gestio* is consistently dealt with in the context of substantive law and from this perspective is largely answered in the affirmative, as long as it does not concern a strictly personal claim such as divorce proceedings, cf. *de Page*, Droit civil belge II^3 no. 1076; *Van Ommeslaghe*, Droit des Obligations II^2, 385; CFI Leuven 17 June 1916, Pas. belge 1915-1916, III, 336 und CA Bruxelles 3 March 1964, Pas. belge 1965, II, 96. On recent contrasting Dutch case law compare CRvB 20 August 1996, LJN-No: ZB6325, 95/2421, www.rechtspraak.nl.

36 *Sirena*, Gestione di affari, 422; Enciclopedia giuridica Treccani (*-Vela*), XV, Gestione di affari, I, p. 6.

37 For extensive references on European case law see *v. Bar*, Festschrift Schlechtriem (2003), 609-719.

38 This qualification has to be made especially in the case of Scotland. But as far as Italy is concerned too the legal situation seems not yet to be finally clarified. Both in Greece and Spain decisions of the Supreme Courts which explicitly apply the law on negotiorum gestio to emergency aid in favour of a person are still missing. For further details see *v. Bar* loc.cit.

42. **Acts contrary to law or bonos mores** It has often been asserted that illegal acts or acts contrary to *bonos mores* cannot be the object of benevolent intervention.[39] Indeed the Spanish CC art. 1887 explicitly states this. This approach, however, is not self-evident. The contrary position, adopted by German case law in particular, is that whether the intervention in question offends legal policy or morality is of no importance for the concept of '*Geschäftsbesorgung*' as used in the German Civil Code. The necessary correction should instead be introduced when considering the question whether or not the intervener was justified in regarding the measure taken and the expenses thereby incurred as "necessary". It is that condition which the intervener who acts contrary to law or *bonos mores* will typically fail to satisfy.[40]

43. **Long-term measures and omissions** Measures of benevolent intervention are only intended to bridge the gap arising when the principal is unable to attend to his affairs himself, which is why they are often only of a provisional nature. Nonetheless there is no rule stating that benevolent intervention is necessarily restricted to one-off acts or short time activities. On the contrary, it may consist of a bundle of measures and last for considerable time. The legal position as far as omissions are concerned, however, is unclear. In academic writing it has often been stated that omissions cannot constitute benevolent intervention. European case law, by contrast, contains a series of decisions in which mere omissions have been treated as amounting to benevolent intervention.[41]

F. The Position of the Law on Benevolent Intervention within the Legal System

44. **The subsidiarity of the law of benevolent intervention: general** The law of benevolent intervention can be regarded as a subsidiary regime within the law of obligations in so far as it does not apply where the rights and duties of the parties are conclusively governed by another branch of law. This subsidiarity, however, should not be understood as a matter of concurrence of actions (like, for instance, the principle of *non-cumul des responsabilités* in the French tort law or the subsidiarity in the French rules on *enrichissement sans cause*), but rather as an integral ingredient of the law on benevolent intervention in another's affairs which has exclusionary effect. The phrases adopted in the

---

39 For further references see *v. Bar* loc.cit.

40 BGH 25 June 1962, BGHZ 37, 258, 263; BGH 31 May 1990, BGHZ 111, 308, 311; BGH 30 April 1992, BGHZ 118, 142, 150.

41 CA Rome 3 May 1983, Temi rom. 1983y (a notary did not transfer money because he was informed that the municipal tax which the money was meant to pay would shortly cease to apply); *Bank of Scotland* v. *McLeod Paxton Woolard* SLT 1998, 258 (Bank withholding money paid into a fund in the interest of the victims); HR 10 December 1948, NedJur 1949 no. 122 p. 225 (garage deliberately leaving a car unserviced in order to save it from being seized by the German occupying power). Compare as well CFI Paris 21 October 1970, GazPal 1971, I, 28 (proprietor of a parking space tolerating a car parked on his property by a thief. The court negated the application of *negotiorum gestio*, but not for the reason that it was a mere ommision or toleration, but on the basis amongst others that the proprietor acted on a contract with the thief.).

Civil Codes for this negative prerequisite vary greatly (e. g. Austrian CC § 1035: "*ohne vertragliche, gerichtliche oder gesetzliche Befugnis*"; German CC § 677: "*ohne beauftragt oder sonst dazu berechtigt zu sein*"; Italian CC art. 2028: "*senza esservi obbligato*"; French CC art. 1372: "*lorsque volontairement on gère l'affaire d'autrui*"). The substance of all these rules is the same. Differences in their construction may be encountered, if at all, in cases in which the intervener discharges a statutory duty to render aid.

45. **The relationship to contract law** Of particular importance is the principle that there is no room for the concept of benevolent intervention to the extent that the rights and duties of the parties are governed by contract. The width of the contractual regime thus indirectly also determines the ambit of the law on benevolent intervention. There is only room for the latter in a case where a party to a contract renders performance to another if that performance is neither owed nor barred by the contract. Examples for the demarcation between contract law and the extra-contractual law of benevolent intervention have already been given above at *D34-38*.

46. **The relationship to tort law** By contrast there is no scope for a subsidiarity of the law on benevolent intervention in relation to the other extra-contractual legal relationships, – in particular in the relationship to tort law and unjustified enrichment law. Tort law and law of benevolent intervention connect at various points. In the first place, benevolent intervention in another's affairs constitutes a defence against claims of the principal, in particular in respect of damage to property and personal injury.[42] In some legal systems the person rendering assistance in an emergency has the further protection of a special standard of care (Estonian CC § 1022 (2), German CC § 680, Greek CC art. 732), which also restricts his liability in tort law. (Other legal systems provide relief in the form of a clause on reduction of liability.[43]) In addition the law on benevolent intervention in some jurisdictions provides for a claim for reparation for an intervener who has endangered himself against the principal – regardless of fault – although, of course, this claim is not granted everywhere and it may be the subject of a *convention d'assistance*: see above at *D37* and below at Article 3:103 (Right to Reparation) and the notes to that article. Even expenses incurred in order to prevent impending damage are compensated in particular situations under the rules of the law of benevolent intervention rather than under tort law.[44] However, it is widely appreciated within Europe that

---

42 See PEL Liab.Dam. Article 5:202 (2) (Self-Defence, Benevolent Intervention and Necessity) and the respective Notes.

43 Cf. in particular Belgian, French and Luxembourgian CC art. 1374, Italian Cc Art. 2030 (2) and Maltese CC art. 1017. Portugese commentators have suggested to give the delictual clause on reduction of liability (Port. CC art. 494) a wide scope of application, e. g. to apply it to a *gestor* who acts in order to avoid an immediate danger (*Menezes Leitão*, Responsabilidade do gestor, 280-281).

44 This holds true in particular for Austrian law. In general expenses incurred to prevent impending damage is compensated under tort law (see in particular OGH 8 March 1994, SZ 67/35 and *Koziol*, Haftpflichtrecht I³ no. 2/21), because the expenses incurred for the prevention of impending damage is qualified as actual damage ("*positiver Schaden*"). The reasonable expenses incurred for prevention will be compensated (OGH 10 February 1960, EvBl 1960/161 p. 297; OGH 30 August 1988, JBl 1989, 46). By contrast the law on *negotiorum gestio* is not

this claim should rather be regarded as a part of tort law, and that view is shared by these Principles. Accordingly that claim is integrated into the tort law rules relating to prevention of damage (PEL Liab.Dam. art. 6:302 (Liability for Loss Averting Damage)). Finally, manifold points of contact and overlaps with the law of torts emerge where the law of benevolent intervention is applied to unjustified intervention in another's affairs (*impure gestio*) or arrogated management of another's affair: on this point see above at C26-29. If the *gestor* in the course of his intervention causes damage to a third party, the claims of the third party will find their legal basis only in tort law.[45] However, contrary to what has sometimes been suggested, there seems to be no convincing reason why the question whether or not a tortious duty has been breached should be answered by reference to whether or not the defender has also violated a duty arising from the *negotiorum gestio*.[46]

47. **The relationship to the law of unjustified enrichment** As far as its relationship to the law of unjustified enrichment (understood in a broad sense – as is the basis of the PEL Unjust.Enr.), the law of benevolent intervention is not only not subsidiary; it has priority. The legal obligation arising from benevolent intervention in another's affairs may claim priority because it provides a legal basis for the services and benefits provided by the intervener to the principal or the principal to the intervener respectively. This too similarly seems to be widely accepted throughout Europe.[47]

---

applied to the so-called 'reserve vehicle cases' which are of some importance. Typically at issue here is compensation for a proportion of the costs incurred in respect of a vehicle (e. g. a bus of a local transport provider) which has been bought solely in case of an accident to a vehicle in service: see *Fötschl*, ZVR 2003, 220-234; *Koziol* loc.cit. 3/20 and OGH 7 December 1972, SZ 45/137.

45 For examples see OGH 9 December 1971, SZ 44/187 (the local authority undertook to remove snow and keep the pavement clear for some of the owners of property adjacent to public streets, but it did not discharge this duty properly; a passer-by was injured). See also the considerations of Advocaat-Generaal *Spier* in HR 12 September 2003, no. C02/132 HR, www.juriforum.nl (note in NJ 2003, afl. 40, p. 4357) (in spite of the generally accepted duty to continue an intervention once started, it would be wrong to jump to the conclusion that the animal rescue service becomes the keeper of the animal; the duty to continue an interverntion started is a duty owed only to the principal and not with resprect to third parties).

46 See CFI Utrecht 1 October 2004, LJN-number AN7871, www.rechtspraak.nl.

47 Cf. for Germany BGH 30 September 1993, NJW 1993, 3196; as to Portugal *Menezes Leitão*, Enriquecimento sem causa, 821; Italy CC art. 2042 (subsidiarity of the law of unjustified enrichment; by constrast the demarcation between the law of benevolent intervention on the one hand and the law of payment of a non-existing debt is so sharply drawn by means of different pre-requisites that overlaps only rarely occur, cf. *Aru*, Gestione d'affari, 19-20); for Spain (here the claim for unjustified enrichment is no longer regarded as a subsidiary remedy) *Pasquau Liaño*, Gestión de negocios, 419. With regard to Belgian, French and Luxembourg law one must similarly distinguish between *paiement de l'indu* and *enrichissement sans cause*. As far as the *paiement de l'indu* is concerned this will only apply if there is no *obligation, civile ou naturelle* between *solvens* and *accipiens* (*Mazeaud and Chabas*, Obligations[9], no. 655) or if the payment has no cause for the person rendering payment (*Dirix/Van Oevelen*, RW 1992-93, p. 1249 [1259], no. 93). The *enrichissement sans cause* may find its legal basis in either an *acte juridique*,

G. The Practical Relevance of the Law of Benevolent Intervention in the Codified Systems of Continental Europe

48. **Different starting points** The practical relevance of the modern law of benevolent intervention varies greatly within the codified systems of the European Union. This is a result of the legal systems' different starting points set out above. The different lines of demarcation between contract law and the law of benevolent intervention are of particular importance in this respect. Equally significant is the fact that the courts of some jurisdictions apply *negotiorum gestio* solely to juridical acts even though the underlying principles can consistently be applied to *de facto* acts where a party renders assistance to a person in an emergency situation (see above *E41*). It seems that there is a reluctance even within the codified systems of continental Europe to make use of the mechanisms of the legal concepts of benevolent intervention.

49. **Empirical material** The impression that the law of benevolent intervention has varied relevance is confirmed by the difference in the numbers of reported cases concerning benevolent intervention – the only empirical material that is at our disposal. The concept is widely employed by Austrian, German, and, albeit apparently with greater reluctance, Dutch and French courts. By contrast the number of decisions in this area of the law is strikingly low in Greece, Italy, Portugal, Scotland and Spain. The same holds true for the Scandinavian jurisdictions (below *I53-57*).

50. **Social relevance** Of course it should be borne in mind, that the limited number of litigious disputes in this area of law may not be a compelling indicator of its social relevance. After all, the acts that fall within the scope of the law of benevolent intervention more often than not will be acts which can be described as manifestations of neighbourly solidarity. The participants therefore may regard their respective rights and obligations as self-evident – so much so that they have no cause for quarrelling, let alone contesting the point in court.

H. Scotland

51. **Negotiorum gestio a recognised institution** It is uniformly accepted that Scots law too recognises *negotiorum gestio* as a distinct legal institution. However, the Scots law of *negotiorum gestio* has remained particularly faithful to its historic model in Roman law. It embraces 'true' justified (lawful) intervention on behalf of another, but also includes

a *fait juridique*, a statutory provision or a legal custom (*Starck/Roland/Boyer*, Les obligations II[6], no. 2198, p. 772). A claim for unjustified enrichment is therefore barred if the transfer of assets is supported by a legal, economic or moral justification (*Stijns/Van Gerven/Wéry*, JT 1996 p. 689 [699] no. 28). In Austria too the question is discussed as to whether or to what extent an unsolicited management of another's affairs can also consitute a legal basis for an enrichment (within unjustified enrichment law): see in particular *Meissel*, GoA, 223-224 and Rummel (*-Rummel*), ABGB I[3] § 1035 no. 6 as well as § 1041 no. 9. However, an unequivocal judicial statement is still awaited. In the Scandinavian legal systems this issue seems not to have been discussed yet (as is also of course the case within the Common Law jurisdictions).

other forms and in particular the *unjustified* intervention in another's affairs.[48] This seems to be related to an extraordinary particularity of Scots law, namely the fact that it has not yet been resolved whether intervention within the scope of *negotiorum gestio* may only consist of a juridical act for the benefit of another person's assets, or whether it might also consist of acts to save the life or health of another. There are as yet no reported judicial decisions indicating that an intervention rendering such aid to a person in an emergency is within the scope of the law of benevolent intervention, but equally there seesms to be no decision explicitly to the contrary.[49] In *Lord Advocate* v. *Rodgers* expenses incurred in order to prevent impending damage arising from a tortious act have been held to be due compensation according to the rules of tort law and not according to the law of *negotiorum gestio*.[50]

52. **Agency of necessity** Contemporary scholarship has emphasised the close relationship to the Common Law institution of *agency of necessity*[51] (as to which see below at *J66-70*). An intervener has on principle the same rights and obligations as a contracted agent.[52]

I. Scandinavia

53. **General** In contrast to the continental European codified systems of civil law, the three Nordic jurisdictions which are Member States of the European Union do not possess a general statutory body of law on *negotiorum gestio* with an overarching structure and at a conceptual level more abstract than that of the particular case. The concept of *negotiorum gestio* itself is well-known, but decisions that explicitly refer to this area of law are very rare. This holds true for Sweden and Finland in particular, whereas the situation in Denmark is more similar to Scotland. However, in Denmark – in contrast to Scotland – it seems to be regarded as self-evident that acts of benevolent intervention may be directed towards saving the life and preserving the health of another.[53]

54. **Specific basis and reasoning by analogy** To assess whether a valid claim has arisen as a result of the altruistic furtherance of another's interest the Scandinavian jurisdic-

---

48 *Leslie*, JuridRev 1983, 15; Stair (-*Whitty*), Vol. 15, no. 137, fn. 6.

49 For details see Stair (-*Whitty*), Vol. 15, no. 102.

50 *Lord Advocate* v. *Rodgers* (1978) SLT (Sh.Ct) 31.

51 *Walker*, Principles of Scottish Private Law, Vol. II, Book IV[4], 218; *Marshall*, Scots Mercantile Law[3],13, paras 1-28; Stair (-*Whitty*), Vol. 15, no. 94.

52 *Gloag and Henderson*, The Law of Scotland[10], 373; *Walker*, loc.cit., chapter 4.14; Stair (-Whitty), Vol. 15, no. 91; *Leslie*, loc.cit. 23.

53 This may be deduced indirectly from the fact that the concept of *negotiorum gestio* is accepted as a general ground of justification in Danish tort law (see inter alia *von Eyben/Nørgaard/Vagner*, Lærebog i erstatningsret[3], 49; *Jørgensen*, Kontraktsret, Bind 2, 152 f; *Vinding Kruse*, Erstatningsretten[5], 48 ff). Cf. also HD 8 February 1961, UfR 1961, 344 (an employee was killed during his attempt to calm horses running wild; the claim of the employee's relatives against the accident insurer was upheld on considerations similar to those of the law of benevolent intervention).

tions as a rule rely on specific regimes which either explicitly govern the problem or serve as a basis for analogy. In comparison to continental legal systems little importance is attached to an unambiguous systematic classification of the legal rule which is derived. Accordingly, the boundary with contract law in particular remains fluid. However, the platform for an analogy may also be found in other areas of the law such as the law of persons, family law, the law of succession or property law.[54] At least as far as Finland and Sweden are concerned a discrete profile of the law of benevolent intervention is hardly discernible.

55. Commercial Code Chapter 18 § 10 and the Scandinavian consumer protection statutes Amongst the provisions which – taking a functional approach – bear reference to the law of *negotiorum gestio* Chapter 18 § 10 Commercial Code 1734 ought perhaps to rank first, it being overwhelmingly assumed that the provision remains in force.[55] This rule provides that if a person is absent and not in a position to authorize someone to take care of his affairs, a relative or a friend of the relative may 'speak and answer' for the absent person. However, the rule immediately adds that if the absent person does not approve the transaction the agent is liable for all losses caused by his intervention. Attention should also be drawn to the Swedish *konsumenttjänstlagen* 1985:716 (Consumer Services Act) § 8. It provides that a person rendering services in defined circumstances is authorized to provide services which have not been ordered and may claim remuneration for them according to § 38. A prerequisite for the application of this provision is that the instructions of the consumer could not be obtained in time, that the price for this additional service is insignificant in proportion to the services ordered, or that the person rendering the service had a particular reason to assume that the consumer wanted the additional service. A provision similar in all material regards may also be found in Chapter 8 § 6 Finnish Consumer Protection Law [*Konsumentskyddslag*] of 20 January 1978/38.

56. Further examples of rules which may serve as a basis for analogy In addition some rules of the law on commission agency may form part of the context of benevolent intervention – at least in relation to 'applied' *negotiorum gestio* (see above at *D30-38*). Of particular interest are the rules which oblige the commission agent to attend to the interests of the principal when the agent is unable to obtain in time instructions from the principal (Swedish and Danish Commission Act § 8[56]). Further particular questions are governed by rules in the law concerning lost property (reimbursement of expenses and finder's reward, e. g. Swedish Act Concerning Lost Property § 3[57] [Sweden, however, has enacted further special rules concerning lost property], Danish Lost Property Act § 3[58] and Finnish Lost Property Act § 10[59]) and by provisions on emergency assistance to preserve joint property either in joint ownership or part ownership[60] (see

54 *Håstad*, Tjänster utan uppdrag, Chapter VI.

55 For details see *Håstad* loc.cit. 285-286.

56 *Lag* (1914:45) *om kommission; kommissionslov* (*lovbekendtgørelse* of 15 September 1986 no. 636).

57 *Lag* (1938:121) *om hittegods*.

58 *Lovbekendtgørelse om hittegods* of 1 September 1986 no. 591.

59 *Hittegodslag* of 26 August 1988 no. 778.

60 This compilation follows *Håstad*, loc.cit. 71 ff.

for Sweden §§ 5 and 48 of the former Act on Commercial Companies and Trading Partnerships[61] or Ch. 2 § 3 and Ch. 4 § 3 of the recent Act on Commercial Companies and Trading Partnerships,[62] for Finland Ch. 2 §§ 2 and 7 Act on General Partnership and Partnership Limited by Shares;[63] also Swedish Act on Joint Ownership § 2[64] and the similar provision in § 4 of the Finish Act on Certain Community Property;[65] cf. further Swedish Act on Succession Ch. 18 §§ 1-2[66]). Similarly the Swedish Sales Act [*köplag* (1990:931)] §§ 72-78 (relating to the duty of safekeeping, the right to sell uncollected goods and the compensation of costs between the parties to a contract in case of default in performance or restitution of goods) as well as a range of provisions of the Commercial Code [*handelsbalk*], in particular Ch. 11 § 3 (relating to the claim for compensation of the borrower of goods in respect of necessary expense for maintenance) and Ch. 12 § 8 (necessary expenses incurred for maintenance by the person keeping goods safe) are considered to be a proper basis for an analogy. Attention should also be drawn to the Act on Real Property [*jordabalk* (1970:994)] Ch. 5 § 3 (compensation of necessary expense for maintenance where the property has to be returned by a non-entitled acquirer) and the Insolvency Act [*konkurslag* (1987:672)] Ch. 4 § 15 (3) (claim for compensation of necessary or useful expenses incurred by the person in possession of goods obliged to restore them to the bankrupt's estate in case of rescission by the trustee in bankruptcy). Numerous provisions of contract law (in particular in respect of leases) grant the lessee a self-help right to remedy defects where the landlord does not do so: Swedish Land Code [*jordabalk*] Ch. 9 § 17 (2) and (3), Kap 12 § 11 Nr. 1 and § 17, Finnish Act on Renting of Flats [*lag om hyra av bostadslägenhet*] of 31 March 1995 no. 481 § 20 (2) and (3) and Danish Lease Act [*lejelov*] of 14 May 2001 Nr. 347 § 11 (1). Even the Swedish law on suretyship bears a reference to the *negotiorum gestio* of continental European law, as it distinguishes between a 'requested' and an 'unrequested' suretyship. It is assumed that a suretyship is requested even though there is no contract between guarantor and principal debtor if the conduct of the principal debtor indicates that he agrees to the assumption of a suretyship (*Lehrberg*, Borgen, 143; *Walin*, Borgen och tredjemanspant^3, 200). Accordingly, there is hardly any room left for the concept of 'unrequested' suretyship (which is closer to benevolent intervention) (*Walin*, loc.cit. 203). Finally, numerous provisions with some relationship to the notion of benevolent intervention may be found in the Inheritance Code [*ärvdabalk* (1958:637)]. Chapter 18 §§ 1 and 2 contain extensive provisions on the rights and duties of spouses, unmarried couples and other persons (e. g. a member of the household or even, as the case may be, a landlord), who may attend to the deceased's estate until the persons entitled can take possession and may even be under a duty to do so. Furthermore, in Ch. 25 § 7 the Code even contains such details as a claim for compensation for necessary or (if the heir is bona fide) useful expenditure on the property of a missing person assumed to have died, but subsequently reappearing. Quite similar rules may be found in the Finnish Succession Act [*ärvdabalk*] of 5 February 1965 no. 40 Ch. 18 §§ 2-4 (whereas the Danish Act

61 *Lag om handelsbolag och enkla bolag* of 28 June 1895,

62 *Lag* (1980:1102) *om handelsbolag och enkla bolag*.

63 *Lag om öppna bolag och kommanditbolag* of 29 April 1988 no. 389.

64 *Lag* (1904:48 s. 1) *om samäganderätt*.

65 *Lag om vissa samäganderättsförhållanden* of 25 April 1958 no. 180.

66 *Ärvdabalk* (1958:637).

on the Disposition of a Deceased's Estate [*lov om skifte af dødsboer*] of 22 May 1996 no. 383 § 8 has adopted thoroughly independent solutions, inter alia, imposing a duty on hospitals to take care of the deceased's belongings). It is possible to draw a general analogy from these specific provisions to justify the proposition that in appropriate cases a person who attends to the property of another may claim compensation for the expenses incurred even though this specific situation has not explicitly been considered by the legislator.

57. **Power of representation between spouses** With some oversimplification it can be said that Finnish and Swedish law essentially rely on analogies drawn from the specific instances of 'applied' benevolent intervention provided by statute. Thus they abstain from a clear-cut demarcation between contractual and extra-contractual relationships. As regards the law on representation regards must also be had to provisions which grant a spouse the authority to administer the affairs of the other spouse where the latter, due to illness or absence, is unable to attend to them himself or herself and a custodian has not been appointed by the court and could not be obtained in time.[67] This is also a case of 'applied' intervention in another's affairs. Of course, the general provisions of the law of benevolent intervention are not applicable (because the spouse is authorized by specific provisions to do exactly what he or she does), but the only reason why they are not applicable is that there is a specific rule which solves this situation exhaustively.

J. England and Ireland

58. **The lack of a discrete concept of a legal relationship arising from benevolent intervention in another's affairs** The Common Law approach in England and Ireland is even more remote from the codified systems of continental Europe than the Scandinavian, as the Common Law has never developed a discrete concept of a legal relationship arising from benevolent intervention in another's affairs.[68] The social potential for conflict, which the Codes of continental Europe address by means of the concept of *negotiorum gestio*, is resolved by a variety of completely different legal instruments in the Common Law. This in turn is due to the fact that the general rule is shaped differently: whereas the systems of continental Europe in general accept that expenses incurred in another's interest are due compensation even though there was no duty to perform and try to keep this general rule within reasonable limits, the Common Law has chosen the opposite starting point. As a general rule expenses incurred in the interest of another, but where there is no underlying duty to perform, do not give rise to a claim to compensation.[69]

67 Swedish Marriage Act [*äktenskapsbalk* (1987:230)] Ch. 6 § 4, Danish Proclamation of Law on the Legal Effects of Marriage [*Lovbekendtgørelse om ægteskabets retsvirkninger*] of 5 May 1995 no. 37 § 13. These provisions of matrimonial law also apply to unmarried couples, Ch. 3 § 1 Swedish Registered Partnership Act [*lag* (1994:1117) *om registrerat partnerskap*]. The same also holds true for Danish law (Karnov [*-Nielsen*], Retsvirkningslov § 13 no 20), while no similar provision is contained in the Finnish Marriage Act [*äktenskapslag*] of 16 April 1987 no. 411.

68 For details (and articulate criticism of this situation) see *Birks*, 24 (1971) CurrLegProbl 110-132.

69 *Falcke v. Scottish Imperial Insurance Co.* (1887) 34 ChD 234; *In re Cleadon Trust, Limited* [1939]

Accordingly the main focus is on the exceptions to this rule. Here the comparison between Civil Law and Common Law reveals two overlapping circles, the area of overlap being so remarkably large that the differences seem to be rather a matter of presentation and not a matter of substance.

59. **Exceptions from the general rule that expenses incurred for the interests of another are not compensable if there is no underlying duty to perform** The acknowledged exceptions to this general rule are supposed to fit (and largely do fit) into a structure whereby the claim for compensation of the 'intervener' is restricted to cases where a legal relationship of proximity (whatever the nature of this relationship) between the parties is already established at the time of performance. (By contrast the legal relationship between the parties according to the theoretical concept of *negotiorum gestio* is established through the act itself.) Accordingly there is no consistent body of law on benevolent intervention in another's affairs. Rather the separate elements of this legal concept, which are only considered as parts of an overarching concept from the point of view of continental European law, are spread over a variety of separate areas of law, which are not considered as parts of the same structure.

60. **Statute law** In addition to this exceptions from the general rule mentioned above there are some few specific provisions of statute law as well as trust law. As far as the former in England and Wales are concerned, attention has to be drawn in particular to the Road Traffic Act 1988 secs. 157-159 which grant both a doctor and the hospital a fixed amount of compensation for expenses incurred and the assistance provided in case of treatment arising out of a road accident. The debtor (e. g. the user or owner of the vehicle; the motor vehicle insurance) is set out by statute. This statute, however, is restricted to emergency situations arising from road traffic accidents and cannot be applied by means of analogy to comparable situations (such as accidents caused by a train or aircraft or in the course of sport).

61. **Trust law** A person who as a trustee properly incurs expenses in the administration of the trust estate is entitled to recoup them from the trust funds (for England and Wales, see the Trustee Act 2000, sec. 31(1), superseding the Trustee Act 1925 sec. 30(2)). This also includes emergency expenses.[70] The courts have the authority to grant the trustee a remuneration not provided for by the trust terms (or an increase of the agreed amount of compensation) if the trustee renders additional services which were not contemplated at the time the trust was created.[71] It may be argued that this also includes emergency assistance provided in person.[72]

62. **The instruments of Common Law** The functional equivalents of the concept of *negotiorum gestio* developed by Common Law are to be found primarily within the law

1 Ch 286; approved by *Crantrave Ltd. v. Lloyds Bank plc* [2000] 3 WLR 877 (CA). For details see *v. Bar*, Festschrift Werner Lorenz (2001), 441-461.

70 *Re Smith's Estate* [1937] Ch 636.

71 *Re Duke of Norfolk's Settlement Trusts* [1983] 1 All ER 220.

72 *Tettenborn*, Restitution^2, 182 (§ 9-09).

on gratuitous agents, in the law of bailment and the law of restitution (law of unjustified enrichment).

63. **Gratuitous agents** By contrast to a *contractual* agent who, as the term indicates, acts for another on a contractual basis, the *gratuitous agent* is under no obligation to render any services. In addition to this, another feature common to both the gratuitous agent and the benevolent intervener is this: if the gratuitous agent has once decided to attend to the affairs of another then he has to do so diligently and may not terminate his commitment prematurely.[73] In the event of breach of this duty the agent will be liable according to tort law rules.[74] The duty of care as regards this tortious liability is established by an analogy to the duty of care within the frame of a bailment relationship.[75] As the gratuitous agent is an agent, he is in general (of course with the exception of the duty to act at all) subject to the same duties as a contractual agent.[76] In this respect too the resemblance to the concepts of the continental European law of benevolent intervention in another's affairs and the law of agency are quite obvious.

64. **The duties of an agent** The duties of an agent have their origin partly in Common Law and partly in Equity. The latter include *fiduciary* duties; their breach too leads to claims for compensation (in equity). An agent may not prefer his own interests over those of his client.[77] If the agent passes up the opportunity to realize profits for the principal, even though he could have done so without difficulty, he will be personally liable.[78] In particular the agent has to hand over everything he has obtained in his capacity as agent to his client.[79] For this duty to be established it will be sufficient that the agent has gained the opportunity of profit in the course of his agency; whether or not he has acted within or beyond his competence is of no consequence.[80] According to the maxim "equity looks upon as done that which ought to be done", the principal acquires in equity ownership of the property that is to be handed over, even before it has

---

73 *Gomer* v. *Pitt & Scott* (1922) 12 Ll. L.Rep. 115, 116 (*Warrington* LJ); *Bromley LB* v. *Ellis* [1971] 1 Lloyd's Rep 97, 99 (Lord *Denning* MR) (an estate agent who in relation to the plaintiff was not a *contractual* agent [this must be the meaning of Lord *Denning's* comment that the defendant was not an agent for the plaintiff] but was undoubtedly a *gratuitous* agent had at first acted properly, but then failed to continue diligently what he had begun as he did not forward to the plaintiff information of importance to him).

74 Which tort is applicable depends on the circumstances of the case. In case of doubt negligence seems appropriate, but others may also be considered, in particular trespass and conversion.

75 *Grill* v. *General Iron Screw Collier Co.* (1866) LR 1 CP 600, 612 (*Willes* J).

76 *Fridman*, Agency[5], 140; Bowstead (*-Reynold/Graziadei*), Agency[16], Article 44.

77 Bowstead (*-Reynold/Graziadei*) loc.cit. Article 45.

78 *Re Waterman's W. T.* [1952] 2 All ER 1054 (*Harman* J); also see *Wallersteiner* v. *Moir (No. 2)* [1975] QB 373 (the director misappropriated moneys belonging to his company; he was held liable also for interest).

79 *De Bussche* v. *Alt* (1878) 8 ChD 286, 304 (*Hall* V-C).

80 *Attorney-General for Hong Kong* v. *Reid* [1994] 1 AC 324 (PC).

actually come into his possession; a trust is established between client and agent.[81] In general the agent may not demand remuneration for his services. This may, as a rule, be different if the agent has made extraordinary efforts to obtain the acquisition for the principal[82] or if the principal has confirmed the acts with the intention of affording the agent recompense. The latter case will though be within the ambit of the law of restitution (*quantum meruit*). The same applies to expenses incurred by the agent within the scope of his authority.[83] In respect of all three categories, the contractual agent[84], the fiduciary agent[85] and in particular the agent of necessity[86] the distinctive feature must be born in mind, that the claim for compensation does not depend on whether or not the service was advantageous for the principal; it will be sufficient that it was reasonable in the circumstances to act as the agent has.

65. **Agency by agreement and agency by ratification** According to the Common Law an agency-relationship outside of contract can be established by three different means, namely an agreement without consideration (agency by agreement), a ratification (agency by ratification) and necessity (agency of necessity). These agreements which, due to the doctrine of consideration, fall outside the scope of contract law under the Common law, would be characterised as gratuitous contracts by the other European jurisdictions. From this perspective an agency by agreement will virtually always fall outside the scope of the law of benevolent intervention. However, as an exception, an agency-relationship can also be established without an agreement of the parties. One of these exceptions is the retrospective ratification by the principal (*agency by ratification*). This ratification – and current academic writing still supports this view – has retroactive effect.[87] This both constitutes a waiver by the principal of any claim against the agent for compensation on the ground of interference with the principal's affairs[88] and provides the agent with the claims for recompense which he would have had if he had acted under a valid contract from the outset.[89]

66. **Agency of necessity** A third basis from which an agency relationship may arise is particularly close to the idea of *negotiorum gestio*: necessity.[90] Moreover, agency of

---

81 *Attorney-General for Hong Kong* v. *Reid* loc.cit.

82 *Boardman* v. *Phipps* [1967] 2 AC 46 (HL).

83 Expenses which an agent incurs ultra vires are not compensable: *Falcke* v. *Scottish Imperial Insurance Co*. (1887) 34 ChD 234.

84 *John Koch Ltd*. v. *C. & H. Products Ltd*. [1956] 2 Lloyd's Rep 59.

85 *Wallersteiner* v. *Moir (No. 2)* [1975] QB 373, 396 G-H (Lord *Denning* MR), 403 F (*Buckley* LJ) and 407 B-C (*Scarman* LJ).

86 *Gaudet* v. *Brown* (1872) LR 5 PC 134, 165 (PC, Sir *Montague Smith*); *China Pacific SA* v. *Food Corporation of India* [1982] AC 939, 965 D-F (Lord *Simon*, obiter).

87 *Bolton Partners* v. *Lambert* (1888) 41 ChD 295, 301 (*Kekewich* J); 306 (*Cotton* LJ), 309 (*Lindley* LJ) and 309-310 (*Lopes* LJ). But compare on the other hand the critical comments on *Bolton* by Lord *Lindley* in *Fleming* v. *Bank of New Zealand* [1900] AC 577, 587 (PC).

88 *Verschures Creameries Ltd*. v. *Hull & Netherlands SS Co.Ltd*. [1921] 2 KB 608; *United Australia Ltd*. v. *Barclays Bank Ltd*. [1941] AC 1, 31 (Lord *Atkin*, PC).

89 *Keay* v. *Fenwick* (1876) 1 CPD 745; *Hartas* v. *Ribbens* (1889) 22 QBD 254.

90 As to the requirement of *necessity* (not necessarily: *emergency*) and the similarities with the law

necessity does not require a contractual basis.[91] As a rule an agent of necessity who acts reasonably has a claim for compensation of expenses and in addition as a security for this compensation is granted a possessory lien with respect to his principal's property in his possession.[92] The first essential requirement of an agency of necessity is that it is virtually impossible for the agent to contact the client and to communicate with him.[93] For precisely this reason the agency of necessity has been pushed to the back shelves in our modern information society. An agent who under present circumstances cannot expect to receive an answer in time does not even have to try to venture his inquiry;[94] by contrast, an agent who is only temporarily unable to reach a contact person has to try again, or if he acts for a company must try to contact someone else.[95]

67. **Necessity** A further requirement is that the intervention is necessary, according to a standard of reasonableness, in the interests of the principal. An example may be to call at a harbour of refuge and subsequently steer the damaged ship to a port, where it can be repaired for a reasonable price.[96] A sale of perishable goods[97] or goods which are likely to be stolen[98] is necessary, whereas to sell commodities suitable for storage in general is not.[99] An intervention may also not be necessary because in the circumstances it would have been more appropriate to inform the relevant public authority and to leave to their judgment the decision as to what has to be done.[100] All depends on whether or not the agent "adopts the course which, to the judgment of a wise and

---

of benevolent intervention see the striking statement of Lord *Goff* in *In re F. (Mental Patient: Sterilisation)* [1990] 2 AC 1, 74-75.

91 *Petrinovic & Co.Ltd.* v. *Mission Française des Transports des Maritimes* [1941] 71 Ll. L.Rep. 208, 223 (*Atkinson* J).

92 Loc.cit. 222 (*Atkinson* J).

93 *Australasian Steam Navigation Co.* v. *Morse* (1872) LR 4 PC 222; *Gwilliam* v. *Twist* [1895] 2 QB 84, 87 (Lord *Esher* MR); *Prager* v. *Blatspiel, Stamp & Heacock Ltd.* [1924] 1 KB 566, 571 (*McCardie* J). See further *Springer* v. *Great Western Railway Co.* [1921] 1 KB 257 (CA): the defendant was transporting the plaintiff's tomatoes from Jersey to London. Bad weather and a strike at the harbour delayed carriage. The tomatoes were threatening to spoil and the defendant therefore sold them directly at the port. The court considered this to be a breach of duty, because the defendant could have obtained instructions from the plaintiff and he was accordingly obliged to do so.

94 *Australasian Steam Navigation Co.* v. *Morse* loc.cit. 232 (Sir *Montague Smith*); *Tetley & Co.* v. *British Trade Corporation* 10 (1922) 10 Ll. L.Rep. 678; *Petrinovic & Co.Ltd.* v. *Mission Française des Transports des Maritimes* 71 (1941) Ll. L.Rep. 208.

95 *John Koch Ltd.* v. *C. & H. Products Ltd.* [1956] 2 Ll. L.Rep. 59.

96 *Phelps, James & Co.* v. *Hill* [1891] 1 QB 605 (where it was impossible to communicate with the owner of the ship).

97 Cf. *Springer* v. *Great Western Railway Co.* loc.cit.

98 *Sachs* v. *Miklos* [1948] 2 KB 23, 34-36 (*Goddard* LJ).

99 *Prager* v. *Blatspiel, Stamp & Heacock Ltd.* loc.cit. (this concerned furs, which could have been stored in a cold-house).

100 *Flannery* v. *Dean* [1995] 2 ILRM 393 (*Castello* P) (the defendant had brought a stallion into his possession, which the claimant had neglected, and looked after it; he should have informed the local authority, which would have taken care of the animal).

prudent man, is apparently the best for the interest of the persons for whom he acts in a given emergency." Then and only then "may [it] properly be said of the course so taken, that it was, in a mercantile sense, necessary to take it."[101] If these requirements are met then the principal will have to bear the risk of an economic failure of the intervention, not the agent.[102] It goes without saying that the agent has to act in the interests of the principal,[103] a requirement that may be absent for instance where someone acts or pretends to act in fulfilment of a contractual duty, whether this duty actually exists or is merely supposed to exist.[104]

68. **Restriction of the scope of application to specific categories of cases** These general requirements of an agency of necessity are quite similar to those of the rules on benevolent intervention of continental European law. Yet there are considerable differences too, in particular because the scope of application of the concept of agency of necessity is far more narrowly determined in comparison with the scope of application of *negotiorum gestio*. It is of particular importance that claims of the agent for compensation of both expenses incurred as well as remuneration are subject to the further requirement that they fall within one of the recognized categories of cases.[105] Furthermore the concept of agency still seems to rely on a relationship including three persons: a person who renders assistance to an unconscious adult only attends to the adult and for this reason alone is not considered to be an agent. A person who attends to an unconscious child may well act in the interests of the parents, but he will not be granted a claim for compensation against the parents as this act does not fall within the scope of a recognized category of cases. By contrast a claim for compensation of necessary expenses in arranging a funeral is recognized, a continuing consequence of the Roman law *actio funeraria*.[106] Another recognized case of agency of necessity is where a manager in the name of his company provides medical assistance to an injured employee of the same company.[107]

69. **Matters of carriage** The cases of practical relevance either concern matters of carriage or the slight excess of a contractual agency already existing. Firstly, the special

---

101 *Australasian Steam Navigation Co.* v. *Morse* (1872) LR 4 PC 222, 230 (Sir *Montague Smith*).

102 *Tetley & Co.* v. *British Trade Corporation* loc.cit.

103 *Sachs* v. *Miklos* [1948 2 KB 23, 29 (*Goddard* LJ).

104 *Jebara* v. *Ottoman Bank* [1927] 2 KB 254, 264 (*Bankes* LJ).

105 In English case law – though these are not exactly recent cases – *dicta* may be found which argue against broadening the scope to cases not covered: see for example *Guilliam* v. *Twist* [1895] 2 QB 84, 87 (Lord *Esher* MR) and *Jebara* v. *Ottoman Bank* loc. cit. (unaffected by the fact that this decision was reversed by the House of Lords: [1928] AC 269). However, *obiter dicta* by *McCardie* J in *Prager* v. *Blatspiel, Stamp & Heacock Ltd.* [1924] 1 KB 566, 570 as well as in *Sachs* v. *Miklos* [1948] 2 KB 23, 35-36 (*Goddard* LJ) point in the opposite direction.

106 *Rees* v. *Hughes* [1946] KB 517; *Jenkins* v. *Tucker* (1788) 1 HBl 90; *Rogers* v. *Price* (1829) Y & J. 28. On the *actio funeraria* cf. further D. 11. 7. 14. 12-13 and D. 11. 7. 16 (Ulp. 25 ad edict). As a subsidiary claim the *actio funeraria* was also granted in spite of the contrary preference of the person responsible for the burial (for details *Seiler*, Negotiorum gestio im römischen Recht 86-89). It has been incorporated into English law presumably via the ecclesiastical courts.

107 *Walker* v. *GWR Co.* (1867) LR 2 Ex 228 (Court of Exchequer).

authority of a captain should be mentioned. If necessary, he may sell or mortgage the ship[108], conclude a contract on remuneration for salvage[109], sell the cargo[110] as well as pledge it[111] or take any measure to avert damage to the goods.[112] The legal position of the carrier by land is quite similar.[113] Of course, almost all decisions on this subject which are the basis of the legal rules set out, are quite stale. They have lost their significance due to the continuous improvement of modern communication technologies. The genuine question today therefore is, whether or not a 'general principle' may be derived from these decisions so that every possessor of property belonging to another – in contrast to the restriction to possessors of cargo belonging to another[114] – may act as an agent in an emergency. A statement of Lord *Simon* dating from 1982[115] points in this direction, and there are other indications that this view of the matter may be correct,[116] but the whole area remains uncertain.[117]

70. Excess of authority There is a second group of cases, which overlaps with the cases of possession of cargo mentioned above, and in which the application of an agency of necessity is generally acknowledged. This group concerns situations where a (contractual) agency already exists but the particular act of intervention is not covered by that contract. Predominantly the scope of the contract is widened by reference to an implied authorization.[118] Hence necessity can lead to the situation that the agent may take out a

---

108 *The Karnack* (1869) LR 2 PC 505.

109 *The Renpor* (1883) 8 PD 115; *The Unique Mariner* [1978] 1 Lloyd's Rep 438. Cf. *China Pacific SA* v. *Food Corporation of India* [1982] AC 939 (HL).

110 *Australasian Steam Navigation Co.* v. *Morse* (1872) LR 4 PC 222, 228 (Sir *Montague Smith*).

111 *The Onward* (1873) LR 4 A & E38.

112 Where the necessity arises, the captain is not only authorized to do so, but also under a duty: see *Australasian SN* loc.cit. and *Hingston* v. *Wendt* (1876) 1 QBD 367, 372 (*Blackburn* J) as well as *Notara* v. *Henderson* (1872) LR 7 QB 225, 235 (*Willes* J).

113 *Great Northern Railway Co.* v. *Swaffield* (1874) LR 9 Ex 132; *Sims* v. *Midland Railway Co.Ltd.* [1913] 1 KB 103. Cf. further *Springer* v. *Great Western Railway Co.* [1921] 1 KB 257.

114 The possessor of another's cargo may always act as an agent of necessity: *Petrinovic & Co.Ltd.* v. *Mission Française des Transports des Maritimes* (1941) 71 Ll. L.Rep. 208, 220 (*Atkinson* J).

115 In *China Pacific SA* v. *Food Corporation of India* [1982] AC 939, 965 A-C.

116 See in particular *Tetley & Co.* v. *British Trade Corporation* (1922) 10 Ll. L.Rep. 678 (*Bailhache* J) and *Petrinovic & Co.Ltd.* v. *Mission Française des Transports des Maritimes* (1941) 71 Ll. L.Rep. 208, 223 (*Atkinson* J).

117 A precedent which relies on the crucial reasoning that an agency of necessity may find its basis in the mere possession of another's goods is still awaited. The same holds true for the opposite, as in *Munro* v. *Willmott* [1949] 1 KB 295, 297 *Lynsky* J only answered this point by way of *obiter dictum*.

118 *De Bussche* v. *Alt* (1878) 8 ChD 286, 310-311 (*Thesiger* LJ). That agency of necessity operates primarily as a widening of existing authority can be seen perhaps in the context of a captain's implied authority in a case of necessity to mortgage or even sell the ship, at any rate if Scottish authority is to be followed. Such power will only operate in relation to the captain's (pre-existing) principal; if a third party is the ship's owner, the captain will not effect a transfer of title to or create proprietary rights in favour of the purchaser or creditor: cf. *Miller & Co v*

loan even higher than 'in fact' approved by the client.[119] or that the agent may take measures for the preservation of his employer's assets.[120] Of course in all these cases it is crucial that an agency-relationship had already been established before the emergency measure was undertaken. A stranger may rely on necessity in order to avoid liability for damages for tortious acts (i. e. personal injury or damage to property)[121] but will not enjoy a claim for reimbursement or even remuneration.[122] In these cases only two other basis for claims can be considered: either the construction of an implied contract[123] or by means of the – to some extent related – concept of *quantum meruit* within the context of unjustified enrichment.

71. **Bailment** According to the general rule – though manifold questions are still a matter of dispute – a bailment-relationship (from French *bailler* to hand over) arises where a bailee voluntarily takes another's (the bailor's) goods into custody. Such a consensual taking of possession establishes a bundle of rights and duties between bailor and bailee and may or may not be based on a contract.[124] In exceptional cases the bailor need not even have agreed to the transfer of possession. This may be the case if the bailor believes that the relationship of bailment would improve his position and therefore subsequently authorizes the taking of custody and thereby retroactively makes the

---

Potter, Wilson & Co 1875 R 105, 112-113 (Lord *Gifford*) and at 116 (Lord Justice-Clerk *Moncrieff*).

119 *Montaignac* v. *Shitta* (1890) 15 App.Cas. 357, 362 (Lord *Herschell*, PC).

120 *Poland* v. *John Parr & Sons* [1927] 1 KB 236, 240 (*Bankes* LJ), 243-245 (*Scrutton* LJ) and 244-245 (*Atkin* LJ); *Walker* v. *GWR Co.* (1867) LR 2 Ex 228 (Court of Exchequer).

121 *In re F. (Mental Patient: Sterilisation)* [1990] 2 AC 1, 74 (Lord *Goff*).

122 See in this context also *Macclesfield Corporation* v. *Great Central Railway* [1911] 2 KB 528 (CA): the defendant, a railway company, had also operated a canal and in this capacity was obliged to take care of the bridges which crossed it. This notwithstanding the company refused to undertake urgently needed road work with respect to one of these bridges. Nor did the company act according to the requests issued by the public authority, whereupon the local authority finally itself arranged for the necessary work to be carried out. Its claim was dismissed, as it had voluntarily discharged the duty of another. There is however an unusual earlier Irish case, *Re Pike* (1889) 23 LRIr 9. The Dublin police had found an old woman destitute in her house and had taken her to a hospital. The police subsequently monitored the empty house until they had successfully contacted relatives of the woman, who soon passed away. In order to secure the costs incurred the court granted the police a lien with respect to the house. It will hardly be possible to state that by monitoring the house the police has furnished 'necessaries' to the old woman, nor does this case fit into the doctrine of salvage. Rather it seems that this is a singular decision, that is to use the words of *Tettenborn*, Restitution[2], 186, "a case of pure necessity".

123 But compare *Upton RDC* v. *Powell* [1952] 1 All ER 1265 (*Vaisey* J). This case concerned a fire which occurred on a farm in the area of the Pershoe fire brigade, which would accordingly have had to fight the fire at no charge. All parties concerned, including the police, however, believed that the Upton fire brigade was responsible for extinguishing this fire and therefore called upon the latter to assist. Their claim for payment against the owner of the farm was granted on the basis of an 'implied contract'.

124 *Morris* v. *C. W. Martin & Sons Ltd.* [1966] 1 QB 716, 731 E-G (*Diplock* LJ).

custodian a bailee – with the result that even if the bailee has changed his mind in the meantime this does not affect either the existence or the continuation of the bailment relationship.[125] On the other hand in a number of cases a person is authorized by law to take possession of another's properties. In such cases the possessor will also become a baillee by law – with all its consequences.[126] This group includes the finder of lost property[127] and, most notably, all persons who (according to continental-European terminology) take custody of property of another after they have saved it from damage or loss by justified intervention.[128]

72. The legal position of the bailee The legal position of a (gratuitous) bailee in all important features resembles the position of a *gestor* in relation to his principal.[129] The bailee is under a primary obligation to treat the goods carefully and to hand them over to the bailor, as soon as the latter requests restitution.[130] The bailee is therefore under no duty to bring about a guaranteed outcome;[131] moreover, a breach of the duty of care must be causative of the loss of or damage to the goods.[132] The counterpart of these duties is that the bailee is granted a claim against the bailor for reimbursement of expenses. The bailor must cover the costs the bailee has incurred in the course of

---

125 *Bell*, Personal Property, 90; *Johnson Matthey Ltd.* v. *Constantine Terminals Ltd.* [1976] 2 Lloyd's Rep 215, 222 (*Donaldson* J).

126 The question whether the duty of care of the gratuitous bailee in comparison to a bailee for reward is a reduced one (to this effect: *Morris* v. *C. W. Martin & Sons* [1966] 1 QB 716, 725 E-F [Lord *Denning* MR] and 737 B-C [*Diplock* LJ]), or whether it is to be judged according to the general standards of tort law (so held by the majority of judges in *Houghland* v. *R. R. Low (Luxury Coaches) Ltd.* [1962] 1 QB 694, and further *Salmon* LJ in *Morris*, loc. cit., p. 738 A-B) is a matter of dispute. Whether or not this question is of practical relevance is difficult to decide, in particular because the determination of the standard of care depends on the circumstances of each separate case and may take into account the fact that the act was conducted gratouitous and for another's benefit.

127 v. Bar (-*Middleton*), Sachenrecht in Europa, England, 111.

128 Examples given by *Bell*, Personal Property, 91: A person takes a thing away from a drunken person in order to keep it safe; for like reasons the jewellery of an unconscious or mentally disabled person is locked away by the hospital; a person saves things from his neighbour's house which has caught fire and stores them in his house.

129 Whether the legal positions of *gestor* and bailee are similar also with respect to third parties is a matter of property law and cannot be dealt with in the present context. It depends not on the characterisation of the *gestor* under the law of obligations, but on the fact that the latter is considered to be a possessor within the meaning of property law.

130 *Mitchell* v. *Ealing LBC* [1979] QB 1, 6C (*O'Connor* J) (concerning gratuitous bailment).

131 *Houghland* v. *R. R. Low (Luxury Coaches) Ltd.* [1962] 1 QB 694, 699 (*Omerod* LJ) (no liability for the theft of goods by a third party which occurred without negligence on the part of the bailee).

132 Besides *Houghland* see also *Lilley* v. *Doubleday* (1881) 7 QBD 510 and *Mitchell* v. *Ealing LBC* loc.cit. (in this case the bailee had not handed over the goods to the bailor when due and *for this reason* was liable for the theft, for which in normal circumstances he would not have been held liable as he did not himself act negligently).

fulfilment of his duties.[133] From the point of view of an agent of necessity, who at the same time is a bailee, it may be more favourable to rely on the latter position. As mentioned above he would have to show and, should the situation arise, prove that it would have been impossible or unacceptable to contact the principal in advance. By contrast there is no such requirement in bailment;[134] it is sufficient that the act constitutes an emergency measure to prevent damage.[135]

73. **Unjustified enrichment** The third area of Common Law that concerns cases which continental European systems analyze under the aspect of benevolent intervention is restitution (or unjustified enrichment law, as it increasingly tends to be renamed now). Two heads of claims merit particular mention: *quantum meruit* and *money paid to the defendant's use*.

74. **Quantum meruit** *Quantum meruit* is a head of claim which has been transferred from the law on agreements for services into English 'enrichment' law by means of the concept of implied contracts. Under Common Law a claim for the 'quantity, which the claimant deserves' is also granted for a service[136] rendered without an underlying contractual obligation, if and only if (i) the plaintiff has voluntarily accepted it and (ii) he knew or should have known that the claimant expects a remuneration for his services.

75. **Relation to the law of negotiorum gestio** A close link between this approach, which of course primarily relates to unjustified enrichment law, and the law of benevolent intervention appears under three aspects. First, a service rendered, which is accepted for one's own benefit without objection, even though a reasonable person who does not want this service would have objected, constitutes without any further requirements a benefit within unjustified enrichment law.[137] Secondly, it is important to realize that many successful claims have been litigated in the context of contracts for services which were ineffective, void or where conclusion of the contract failed.[138] In this situation a row of continental-European courts instead of applying unjustified enrichment law have fallen back on the law of benevolent intervention in another's affairs. Under the law of benevolent intervention the person who has acted in another's interest may not only claim compensation for expenses incurred, but may also be

---

133 *China Pacific SA* v. *Food Corporation of India* [1982] AC 939, 960 F-G (Lord *Diplock*) (concerning warehouse charges of the salvor).

134 *The Winson* [1979] 2 All ER 35 (HL) (the intervener had undertaken to take care of the preservation of a quantity of wheat, which had been saved from a stranded ship. The House of Lords upheld a claim for expenses incurred, as it was obviously impossible to find out whom the batch belonged to and therefore to contact the owner).

135 *Tettenborn*, Restitution², 182 (§ 9-07).

136 Where it is not services rendered but goods provided which are in issue – although this will rarely occur in the context of benevolent intervention, it does not make any difference in principle – this is not referred to as *quantum meruit* but as *quantum valebat*.

137 *BP Exploration Co. (Libya) Ltd.* v. *Hunt (No. 2)* [1979] 1 WLR 783, 803 (*Goff* J); *Brenner* v. *First Artists' Management Pty.Ltd.* [1993] 2 VR 221, 258 (*Byrne* J); *Goff and Jones*, Restitution⁵, 21.

138 E. g. *Way* v. *Latilla* [1937] 3 All ER 759, 765 (Lord *Wright*, HL) and *William Lacey (Hounslow) Ltd.* v. *Davis* [1957] 1 WLR 932, 934 (*Barry* J).

granted a claim for remuneration. Thirdly, there is an ongoing discussion as to whether or not a person who has rendered services in an emergency situation to save a person (or another's property) should be granted a claim on the basis of *quantum meruit*. Some influential English authors argue that under certain additional prerequisites it should be possible to hold the defendant to be enriched even though he has not 'voluntarily accepted' the services rendered, notwithstanding that the intervention of the claimant has been reasonable but unsuccessful in the end. In this case of a not voluntarily accepted yet incontrovertible benefit these authors opt for compensation of expenses incurred by volunteers, while those acting within their professional sphere of activity might also claim recompense for the services rendered.[139] However, recent case law adopting this approach is lacking and even the chance that it will be adopted in the future is not very high at present,[140] though with the decision in *Re Pike* there is at least one older Irish authority which points towards this direction.[141]

76. Money paid to the defendant's use The modern approach holding expenses incurred for another in an emergency situation to be compensable by virtue of the law of unjustified enrichment (now also referred to by this term in England) may also rely on a second line of authorities. *Goff and Jones*[142] for example point to a decision from 1795, *Waters* v. *Weigall*.[143] In this case the lessee was granted the right to offset his claim for compensation of expenses incurred for the repair of damage of the rented property caused by a storm against the lessor's claim for rent. It was held to constitute "money paid to the landlord's use". A similar reasoning may be found in *Gebhardt* v. *Saunders* from 1892.[144] The plaintiff had been ordered by the local authority to repair a defective waste water sewage system, although the plaintiff as the lessee was not responsible, whereas the defendant (the owner) was. Again it was held that the expenses incurred were "money paid for the defendant's use". The plaintiff's claim for compensation of costs of repair incurred was allowed. In a more recent case a firm deployed its crane equipment, at the request of the police, to free a lorry that was jammed under a bridge. The County Court granted the firm a claim against the owner for a reasonable payment for its services because it had acted as agent of necessity.[145] Similarly noteworthy is the case of *Owen* v. *Tate*.[146] The plaintiff had furnished a guarantee on his own accord and asserted he did so, because this had been the only possibility to save the plaintiff from great damage to his ship already under arrest. Although the claim – for other factual reasons – failed, *Scarman* LJ took the opportunity to give his opinion on "the true

139 This is argued in particular by *Goff and Jones*, Restitution⁵, 25-26 and 471-474 and *Virgo*, Restitution, 312-315. Cf. further *Burrows and McKendrick*, Cases and Materials, 473-475.

140 In *The Goring* [1987] QB 687 the claim for compensation for services rendered was denied (cf. in particular 708 per *Gibson* LJ); however this should neither exclude the compensation for expenses incurred nor the related right of a professional rescuer to claim compensation for services rendered (*Goff and Jones* loc.cit 470, fn. 81).

141 *Re Pike* (1889) 23 LRIr 9.

142 *Goff and Jones*, Restitution⁵, 25-26 and 471-474.

143 (1795) 2 Anst 575.

144 *Gebhardt* v. *Saunders* [1892] 2 QB 452.

145 *White (J. D.) v. Troups Transports* [1976] C. L. Y. 33 (*Goff and Jones* loc.cit).

146 [1976] QB 402 (CA). See *Virgo*, Restitution, 311.

principle of the matter": "If without an antecedent request a person assumes an obligation or makes a payment for the benefit of another, the law will, as a general rule, refuse him a right of indemnity. But if he can show that in the particular circumstances of the case there was some necessity for the obligation to be assumed, then the law will grant him a right of reimbursement if in all the circumstances it is just and reasonable to do so."[147] In other words, a person who incurs expenses or debts for the benefit of another will have a claim for indemnity arising also under Common Law. The remaining difference between Common Law and the continental-European jurisdictions is firstly, that this notion is implemented by means of the law on unjustified enrichment rather than by the law of benevolent intervention and secondly, that greater reservation is exercised before such an act is held to be reasonable.

K. International Law and European Law

77. **Admiralty law** Bodies of rules which in terms of function and values form part of the wider context of the law of *negotiorum gestio* can be found not just in national law, but also in international treaties and standard contract terms generally used in international settings. The most important area in this respect is maritime law and more especially the law of salvage and the law of general average.

78. **Salvage** Thirteen Member States of the European Union have so far ratified the London International Convention on Salvage of 28 April 1989,[148] which has already partly superseded the Convention for the Unification of Certain Rules of Law relating to Assistance and Salvage at Sea of 23 September 1910 (which still applies to those EU Member States which have not yet ratified the 1989 Convention) and which is intended to supersede it entirely. The basic principle of the law of salvage of a ship and its cargo from distress is "no cure, no pay" (International Convention on Salvage, art. 12). The law of salvage therefore partly involves an aspect of unjustified enrichment law. Particular rules, however, apply to efforts to rescue a ship carrying environmentally hazardous cargo (International Convention on Salvage, art. 14). No provision is made for the legal consequences of a rescue of persons (or an unsuccessful attempt to rescue persons). This matter was left to the national jurisdictions to decide. Where the law on salvage and the law on benevolent intervention overlap, the former will prevail as this is *lex specialis*. Dutch CC art. 8:577 states this explicitly. This precedence over the law of benevolent intervention is of practical relevance in particular because a duty to continue an act of benevolent intervention on the high seas may prove inappropriate.[149]

79. **General average** As regards the law of general average, current general practice is largely orientated by general terms and conditions of contract, namely the York Ant-

---

[147] Loc.cit. 411H-412A.

[148] Namely Belgium, Denmark, Estonia, France, Germany, Greece, Ireland, Italy, Latvia, Lithuania, the Netherlands, Sweden and the United Kingdom. The text of the conventions may be found in UNTS vol. 1954 (1996) no. I-33479, p. 166 or at http://www.jus.uio.no/lm/imo.salvage.convention.1989/doc.html.

[149] MvT, Parl. Gesch. VIII, 613.

werp Rules (YAR). They concern the sacrifice of property in a ship and/or cargo to salvage the rest in the face of a common danger (such as water damage to part of the cargo caused by extinguishing a fire). "There is a general average act when, and only when, any extraordinary sacrifice or expenditure is intentionally and reasonably made or incurred for the common safety for the purpose of preserving from peril the property involved in a common maritime adventure" (YAR Rule A). If the rescue is successful, the expenses incurred and the damages are divided between the parties involved in proportion to their interests in the cargo and the ship.

80. **European Community law** The law of the European Union to date does not contain any rules which specifically address the law of benevolent intervention. However, the Directive on Protection of Consumers in Respect of Distance Contracts (97/7/EC of 20 May 1997)[150] in art. 9 contains a provision – not amenable to easy interpretation – according to which the Member States have to take the necessary measures to (i) "prohibit the supply of goods or services to a consumer without their being ordered by the consumer beforehand, where such supply involves a demand for payment", and (ii) to "exempt the consumer from the provision of any consideration in cases of unsolicited supply, the absence of a response not constituting consent". According to a strict literal interpretation of this provision no *gestor* could ever claim indemnification (compensation for expenses incurred or services rendered) from a consumer (as opposed to a business) arising from benevolent intervention. This would of course go to the heart of the concept of benevolent intervention in another's affairs as the term 'unsolicited supplies' of services covers a considerable range of the acts which fall within the scope of this area of the law. However, such a construction would fall short of the true meaning of the provision of the EC directive. The aim of the directive is to prevent certain unfair commercial practices and not to abandon the law of benevolent intervention with respect to consumers. This can be seen from the fact that a differentiation between businesses and consumers is not a feature of the law of benevolent intervention. Moreover, the directive aims at abolishing a systematic commercial strategy, whereas the law of benevolent intervention typically concerns a spontaneous act of relief. The better view, therefore, is that art. 9 of the Distance Selling Directive does not, as a general rule, affect the law of benevolent intervention. Of course this does not preclude taking account of the rationale of that provision when deciding whether a *gestor* has in fact acted with reasonable cause or whether his act is mere rash intermeddling. In other words, art. 9 narrows the intervener's scope for establishing grounds for intervention; it has not abolished the law of benevolent intervention altogether by an (incautious) stroke of the pen.

L. The Basic Tenor of the Following Principles

81. **A unitary approach** The following draft proceeds on the basis that it is both expedient and necessary to construct the law of benevolent intervention in another's affairs in a systematically discrete section and to formulate it in principles. There are in essence only two approaches: the approach of continental European law, on the one

150 OJ L 144, 4/6/1997, p. 19.

hand, and the Common Law approach, on the other. The latter does not recommend itself for the nascent European private law. This is the case in particular because the Common Law approach is in part based on a number of concepts which either are specifically English and therefore cannot be 'Europeanized' or which (such as bailment) are not subject matter within the the Study Group on a European Civil Code's fields of work. From this point of view there was no alternative to the unitary approach chosen.

82. **Necessary amendments of contract and unjustified enrichment law** The manifold functions which the law of benevolent intervention in another's affairs performs (and which, in the cause of justice, it must perform) cannot be adequately mastered by means of the "ordinary" instruments of the law of obligations, in particular contract law and the law of unjustified enrichment. As a general rule there is no contract between the intervener and the principal. The basic situation in which a legitimate intervention in another's affairs takes place is precisely the case where the intervener cannot ask the principal whether or not he wants the intervention. Even if the requirements for the conclusion of a contract under PECL were to be diluted (for which the Study Group can see no reason), there would still remain a variety of situations which could not be mastered by means of the fiction of a conclusion of contract between intervener and principal.

83. **Incentive to act out of neighbourly solidarity** It would be wrong to judge every type of intervention in another's affairs as fundamentally socially undesirable without having regard to the circumstances – in particular, the principal's need for help and the intervener's willingness to render assistance. A society which is built upon notions of solidarity and shared responsibility for common welfare cannot reward an attitude of 'looking the other way'; quite the opposite, so far as justifiable and to an extent which respects the principal's freedom such a society ought to provide an incentive to act. The instrument of private law to achieve this goal is the law of benevolent intervention in another's affairs. At the same time, it is the only means by which effect can be given to the basic value judgment that (in contrast to the law of unjustified enrichment) it is not decisive whether or not the intervention in the end has been successful. To establish a legal relationship it should suffice that a reasonable person, acting in like circumstances, would have similarly tried to render assistance. The rationale of this concept is that on the basis of all criteria and information available at the material time it appears that the principal, if he could have been asked, would himself have 'ventured the attempt'. Moreover unjustified enrichment law is restricted in its possibilities; it is solely designed to reverse an unjustified movement of patrimony. Because its task is so restricted, it cannot reproduce the composite array of rights and obligations between intervener and principal required.

84. **European Community law** As already mentioned, the draft proceeds on the footing that the EC Directive on the Protection of Consumers in Respect of Distance Contracts[151] has left the substance of the law of benevolent intervention in another's affairs (*negotiorum gestio*) unaffected despite the fact that the directive provides for particular consumer protection in respect of unsolicited services (and not merely unsolicited goods). The reasons for this view are set out above at *K80*.

---

151 See previous fn.

85. No resuscitation of the law of quasi-contracts For reasons likewise explained already (above at *A9-10*) these Principles do not attempt a revitalisation of the Roman law concept of quasi-contracts. This was from the very beginning a stopgap and has caused more obscurities than it was able to solve. Even within the European jurisdictions which have adopted this concept in their Civil Codes the concept of quasi-contracts has long since come in for fierce criticism. For more than 100 years no codification has incorporated this concept[152] (and in the meantime the Common Law has similarly consigned it to legal history). From today's perspective at any rate it does not seem appropriate to merge under one heading the law of benevolent intervention, the law of the *condictio indebiti*, and the remaining law of unjustified enrichment (which for the most part has been a more recent development historically). The notion of a quasi-contract satisfies only on the surface: even the notion that it concerns situations which are 'as good as' a contract cannot brush aside the fact that there is no such contract. It is true that the French *Cour de Cassation* has recently ruled that certain unfair commercial practices can be counteracted by a recourse to French CC art. 1371 (the general definition of quasi-contracts).[153] The subject matter of these judgments were ostensible notifications to consumers that they had won lottery prizes. The *Cour de Cassation* has held that such communications may establish a quasi-contract between the sender and the addressee. However, this new type of quasi-contract does not have much in common with the law of *gestion d'affaires*. Rather it appears to be a construction *sui generis* between the law of contract and tort law and seems more closely related to the law of *culpa in contrahendo* (itself often interpreted as a quasi-contractual construction, giving a completely different meaning to the term) than it does to the law of quasi-contracts in the traditional meaning of the concept derived from Roman origin. Other EU Member States have in the meantime adopted specific provisions on incorrect or misleading promotional communications of this type (Austrian Consumer Protection Act § 5j[154], German CC § 661a, Portuguese Código da Publicidade art. 11[155]).

---

152 This at any rate holds true for substantive law. In the context of private international law Belgium in 2004 adopted a new provision into the Code de droit international privé, art. 104, which relates to the law applicable to *obligations quasi contractuelles* (BS 27 July 2004, p. 57344, 57366).

153 Cass. ch. mixte 6 September 2002, Bull.civ. (Ch. mixte) 2002, no. 4 p. 9; D. 2002, 2531, note *Lienhard*; D. 2002, 2963, note *Denis Mazeaud*; RTD civ 2003, 94, note *Mestre and Fages*; JCP 2002 éd. G, II, 10173 (2e arrêt), note *Reifegerste*; JCP 2002 éd. G, I, 186, no. 1, note *Viney*; JCP 2002 éd. E (1er arrêt), 1869, note *Viney*; Def. 2002, 37644, note *Savaux* (*arrêt Bossa*); approved by Cass.civ. 18 March 2003, Bull.civ. 2003, I, no. 85 p. 64; D. 2003, 1009. But compare also Cass.ch.mixte 6 September 2002, D. 2002, 2531; Bull.civ. (Ch. mixte) 2002, no. 5 p. 10; JCP 2002 éd. G, II, 10173 (1er arrêt), note *Reifegerste*; and JCP 2002 éd. E (2e arrêt), 1869, note *Viney* (*arrêt Marchewka*; tort law solution).

154 For the perspective of international jurisdiction see in particular ECJ 11 July 2002, C-96/00 (*Gabriel*), ecolex 2002, 574 note *Klauser* (=NJW 2002, 2697 = RIS-Justiz RS 0113168) and OGH 19 December 2001, SZ 74/203 (=RIS-Justiz RS 0116104).

155 Decreto-Lei no. 330/90 of 23 October 1990, amended by Decreto-Lei no. 275/98 of 9 September 1998. In contrast to Austrian and German law, the Portuguese statute does not provide for a right to specific performance. It merely provides for a fine to be paid by those responsible for the advertisement.

86. Exclusion of public law In many countries there are special statutes which govern assistance provided by public bodies. The claims of public bodies or persons acting in exercise of public functions which arise out of such intervention are not the subject matter of the following rules. That principle is implicit in the following text because public institutions are "authorised to act" (see Article 1:103 (b) (Exclusions)), but for the sake of avoiding any ambiguity on the point it also needs to be spelled out in this introduction. The following Principles thus have no impact on the consequences for patrimonial law of, for example, intervention by the police or the fire service which is undertaken in discharge of public functions. In that regard it makes no difference whether a fire service extinguishes a fire caused by a third party (e. g. a forest set alight by sparks from a passing train, the fire service demands reimbursement of its costs from the railway company) or whether the situation is one in which nothing points to the responsibility of a third party (e. g. a house fire resulting from a lightening strike). The position is correspondingly the same when the police service responds to a traffic accident. The legal nature of their activity is always of a different kind from that of a private citizen who intervenes as *gestor* because they act under powers of intervention which a private *gestor* necessarily lacks. A multitude of further state activities likewise fall within this category (e. g. the work of bomb disposal units, the maintenance of public roads and state provision of health services). However, none of this excludes the possibility that individual statutes in public law (assuming that is the qualification placed on the legislation in the relevant jurisdiction) may refer to the remedies (as opposed to the prerequisites) contained in the law of *negotiorum gestio* in order to resolve the legal issues generated by public intervention. Moreover, it remains a matter of national law whether or not the Principles of the following draft are to be applicable to legal relationships between various holders of public authority – for example, in those situations where one holder of public authority undertakes another's functions, as in the case where one public fire service extinguishes a fire arising in an area for which another fire service is responsible because at the time in question the latter is either unable or unwilling to discharge its function. Finally, the question whether (and, if so, in which circumstances) a private citizen who intervenes as a *gestor* and thereby discharges a duty of the state or another public authority may establish a claim against the public body is likewise outside the scope of application of these Principles.

87. Public insurance schemes Some European jurisdictions have extended their insurance schemes for accidents sustained at work (which as a rule are governed by public law) to the protection of persons rendering emergency aid and cover in such cases is provided even if the accident does not occur in the context of the employment relationship. This is the case for Austria (Austrian General Social Insurance Act [ASVG] § 176 (1) no. 2[156]), Denmark (Danish Act on Workplace Indemnity Insurance § 3 no. 4[157]), Finland (Act on Indemnity Against Accidents in the Course of Emergency Assistance § 1[158]) and Germany (German Social Security Code, Book VII (*SGB*) § 2 (1)

156 On its relationship to the law of benevolent intervention see further *Meissel*, GoA, 189-190.
157 *Lov om arbejdskadesikring* of 20 May 1992 no. 390 (as amended).
158 *Lag om skadestånd för olycksfall vid räddning av människoliv of* 12 April 1935, no. 158.

no. 13[159]). According to Art. 115 of the Spanish General Social Insurance Act[160] the term 'industrial accident' covers all personal injury which an employee suffers due to or as a result of work rendered on behalf of another. As expressly provided for in Art. 115 (2) limb (d) this includes accidents which occur as a result of rendering emergency assistance. In contrast to the other schemes mentioned above, however, this is restricted to acting in an emergency which is connected with employment. According to § 1 (1) in conjunction with § 2 of the Swedish Regulation on Refund and Reward Granted to a Person who Renders Assistance to the Police[161] any person who intervenes in order to assist a policeman or a 'guard' is granted compensation from the state for personal injury, property damage and pure economic loss. § 1 (2) of the same Act contains a similar rule for acts of self defence or acts preventing an offender absconding before the police arrive. In addition § 5a grants any person who comes to the rescue of a victim of a crime a claim against the state for adequate compensation. A person who has acted with particular resoluteness may even count on a public reward (§ 10). In Belgium the Act of 24 October 2001 has introduced a new art 42 § 2, 9° as well as a new art. 42 § 4*bis* into the "Act of 1 August 1985 with regard to fiscal law and other provisions". Prior to this amendment art. 42 comprised a rule on possible further compensation for non-pecuniary damage incurred by policemen or other public servants in circumstances particularised in the Act. These circumstances include, inter alia, the rescue of persons whose life is endangered. By the amendment of 24 October 2001 another provision has been inserted in Art. 42 on so-called *sauveteurs occasionnels*, that is to say, for private citizens who intervene in order to save the life of another. These 'occasional rescuers' can apply to the minister of justice for a compensation; the decision of the latter is a matter for discretion. The maximum amount of the 'symbolic reward' amounts to 62,500 Euro. There is no public insurance provision. The same holds true for Portugal. Neither the Act of 13 September 1997 on workplace accidents (Act no. 100/97), *Regime jurídico dos acidentes de trabalho e das doenças profissionais*, nor the *Bases da Segurança Social* (Framework Law of Social Security, Act no. 32/2002 of 20 December 2002[162]) grants insurance cover for rescuers in an emergency.

88. Right of recourse and reduction of claim The Principles set out below leave open the question whether and under which circumstances claims of an insured rescuer are subrogated to the insurance company and equally whether by virtue of other provisions the accident insurance or the relevant public body (as the case may be) has a claim for recourse against the person who caused the danger. However, Article 3:104(2) (Reduction or Exclusion of Intervener's Rights) does take account of possible insurance solutions in so far as the claim of the rescuer against the person injured may be reduced or

---

159 SGB VII § 13 provides in addition to an insurance for personal injury of the rescuer for insurance coverage of his property damage and for expenses incurred which the rescuer was entitled to regard as necessary. Claims of the rescuer against third parties are subrogated to the insurance company (SGB X § 116 (1)).

160 *Real Decreto Legislativo 1/1994, de 20 de junio, por el que se aprueba el Texto Refundido de la Ley General de la Seguridad Social*, BOE of 29 June 1994, no. 154 (with later amendments).

161 *Förordning (1988:842) om ersättning och belöning åt den som hjälper polisen.*

162 An English translation of this Act may be found at *http://www.msst.gov.pt/doc/lei_bases_seg_social_ingles.pdf*.

excluded on equitable principles to the extent that the rescuer can claim compensation under the insurance. This of course may also affect a right of recourse inasmuch as the latter is based on subrogation or an assignment of the claim by operation of law: the claim passing to or taken over by the insurer is the claim which has been reduced or (in the case of a 100% reduction) excluded.

89. **Limitation to justified interventions in another's affairs** These Principles address only justified *negotiorum gestio*, i. e. benevolent interventions in another's affairs for a reasonable purpose. The matters dealt with in some European jurisdictions by certain particular forms of the law of *negotiorum gestio* – unlawful management of another's affairs (above at *C26-27*) and various forms of "impure *gestio*" (above at *C28-29*) – can be freely subsumed within the law of tort and the law of unjustified enrichment.

90. **The priority of contract law** Consistent with the conclusion drawn from comparative law set out above at *D35-38* and *F45*, the law on benevolent intervention in another's affairs as provided for in these Principles is understood as a means of compensation within the law of obligations but subsidiary to contract law. Accordingly it only comes into play when the regime of contract law does not provide for a solution. This follows from Article 1:103(a) (Exclusions). Where a person acts in discharge of a contractual duty owed to the principal, he is "authorised to act under a contract" within the meaning of that provision. Whether such contract has been concluded by the parties and which duties it comprises, by contrast, is to be decided according to the PECL together with any relevant Principles on specific contracts. Likewise if during the course of performance one party does something which is not provided for by the agreement, it must first be decided whether that amounts to a breach of contract. Once again it is the regime governing the contract which applies. If, for example, an independent contractor or other service provider renders services beyond the scope of his duty, the question whether he may claim payment for these services has to be decided according to the principles of contract law. This follows from the fact that the contractor who renders additional services will presumably do so in order to serve his own interests and not those of the client. Where a party acts contrary to the agreement there will only rarely be room for a legitimate benevolent intervention; an example of the exceptional case would be where an agent deliberately exceeds his authority in order to avert danger for the principal which could not otherwise be prevented. The rules on benevolent intervention then may operate as a justification for the breach of contract and grant the agent a claim for compensation of expenses incurred.

91. **Relationship to unjustified enrichment law and tort law** In keeping with the results of the comparative analysis (above at *F46-47*) these Principles assume that benefits which one party renders to another on the basis of a benevolent intervention, are, as a general rule, justified within the meaning of unjustified enrichment law. With respect to tort law, a legitimate intervention in another's interest constitutes a defence to extracontractual liability (PEL Liab.Dam. art. 5:202 (2) (Self-Defence, Benevolent Intervention and Necessity)). For tortious liability and liability arising from benevolent intervention there is as a general rule concurrence of actions. Specific mention should be made of Article 3:103 (Right to Reparation), which grants the intervener a claim for indemnification regardless of fault on the part of the principal, thus extending to cases

where the principal is not liable to the intervener under tort law. As already set out above at F46, expenses incurred in order to prevent what under tort law amounts to a legally relevant damage are exclusively covered by PEL Liab.Dam. art. 6:302 (Liability for Loss Averting Damage); they are not governed by these PEL Ben.Int.

92. **Contribution between joint debtors; property law** As with contract law, the law on contribution between joint debtors is understood as constituting a set of specific rules which has priority over the law on benevolent intervention. Under these Principles, therefore, this matter rests with the PECL. Moreover, until such time as the law of property has its own set of Principles it is not possible to determine whether or to what extent it would be expedient for rules there (for instance with respect to finding of lost property or the relationship between an owner and a possessor) to refer to the remedies furnished by the PEL Ben.Int. These questions can only be solved at a later point in time.

93. **Agency rules of PECL and intervener's authority under Article 3:106** PECL art. 3:102(1) invokes the rules on direct representation (that is PECL arts. 3:201-3:209) where an agent acts in the name of the principal. The rules on agency comprised in the PECL, however, are restricted to cases where the power of representation finds its basis in a voluntary grant of authority. PECL Chapter 3 "does not govern an agent's authority bestowed by law" (PECL art. 3:101(2)). This, however, is precisely the nature of benevolent intervention. Article 3:106 of these PEL Ben.Int. does not operate on the basis of an authority granted by legal act, but on the basis of an authority bestowed by law. This authority is additional to any voluntary grant of authority and it remains subject to its own rules. If, for example, a person is authorized by a juridical act to conduct contract negotiations, but is not authorized to conclude the contract as such, or if the agent is only authorized to conclude a contract within a certain limit the application of Article 3:106 remains possible where the agent concludes the contract (in the first case) or concludes it outside the permitted limit (in the latter). This of course is subject to the essential condition that the excess of authority was in the circumstances 'reasonable to benefit the principal'. This will only be so in rare exceptional cases. In the unexceptional case the agent will be personally liable. With respect to this personal liability of the agent PECL art. 3:204 lends itself to analogous application. A secondary liability according to PEL Liab.Dam. art. 1:101, however, is excluded by PEL Liab.Dam. art. 1:103 (b). The liability of a *falsus procurator* under PECL is more restricted than the comparable liability would be under tort law. In the long run, however, it will have to be considered whether PECL Chapter 3 should not be explicitly extended to certain cases of authority bestowed by law.

94. **The requisite balance between the interests of the gestor and the protection of the principal from officious intermeddling** The main challenge of the law of benevolent intervention is to find a reasonable balance between the interests of the principal and those of the *gestor*. The rules on benevolent intervention ought not to lead to a restriction of the freedom of the principal. As a matter of principle he should not be burdened by duties he has not accepted from the outset. On the other hand, a modern private law cannot be erected on a principle of social isolation. It should therefore promote interventions in favour of helpless or absent persons if such intervention would

be considered reasonable, according to the judgment of an objective observer at the material time, and, considering all information available to the intervener at the time, the intervener has accorded to the (presumed) wishes of the principal. A misinterpretation of the principal's presumed wishes in any particular case admittedly remains possible and in such a case the principal suffers the consequences under the distribution of risks made by these Principles. Such cases, however, will remain a rare exception and from the point of view of an adequate balance of interests serve to protect the *gestor*. The *gestor* must have a reasonable ground for intervening and must exhaust all possible means available to assure himself that he does not interfere with the principal's affairs against the principal's wishes (cf. further on this point infra *L97-98*). It is only under such conditions that these Principles aspire to provide an incentive to action.

95. **The structure of these Principles** The Principles set out below are divided into three chapters. Chapter 1 determines the scope of application; it defines what is to be understood by the term benevolent intervention in another's affairs. Chapter 2 then sets out the duties of the *gestor* and Chapter 3 regulates his rights and powers. This structure (which to some extent has a parallel in the Greek Civil Code) has been adopted in the interests of intelligibility and to assist understanding. The Principles do not in general distinguish (as for instance the Austrian and Spanish CC do) between intervention in case of emergency (irrespective of success) and intervention which is only legitimate if it is to the principal's benefit. Whether *ex post facto* the intervention is beneficial is not a prerequisite of a legitimate benevolent intervention in another's affairs without authority. In fact the assessment *ex post facto* is a concept or rather a value determinant to be found in the context of the law of unjustified enrichment. The expectation that the intervention will be beneficial is in general sufficient and not only with regard to intervention in a case of personal danger. More often than not, a clear distinction cannot be drawn between intervention in favour of the life or health of another and intervention in favour of the property of another.

96. **Acts within the purview of negotiorum gestio** The draft accords with what is by far the predominant majority of European jurisdictions (above at *E39-43*) in generally permitting all kinds of acts to be the possible subject of an intervention. There is neither a restriction to juridical acts for the protection of the property of another, nor a general restriction to juridical acts. The only exception concerns strictly personal acts. This is understood to be self-evident and for this reason is not specifically spelled out in Articles 1:101 and 1:103; it follows indirectly from Article 3:106 (Authority of Intervener to Act in the Name of the Principal). Whether or not this exception of strictly personal acts also includes the conduct of legal proceedings or whether legal proceedings, at least for a restricted time-period (and perhaps subject to leave of the court), may be undertaken as benevolent intervention in the name of the principal is a question which is left unanswered by these Principles. This question is considered to be a matter of procedural law, which is outside the scope of these Principles.

97. **Required subjective elements** Subject to the specific provisions of Article 1:102 (Intervention to Perform Another's Duty) and Article 1:103 (Exclusions), a justified intervention with the intention to benefit another according to these Principles has in general two requirements. First it requires a subjective element: the intervener must

have acted with the 'predominant intention of benefiting another', Article 1:101 (1) (Intervention to Benefit Another). The details as to this requirement may be found in the comments on that provision. Article 1:102 (Intervention to Perform Another's Duty) supplements and extends this basic concept. The intervener must still have acted with the predominant intention of benefiting another, but in this case the benefited party and the principal may be different persons. The reason for this provision may be found in the urgency of performance required by an overriding public interest. In contrast, a person who discharges a contractual duty – be it under a contract with the principal or a contract with a third party – will not be a *gestor* even if the aim was predominantly to serve another's interest. The same applies where the intervener is entitled to act irrespective of the wishes of the principal (Article 1:103 (Exclusions)).

98. Required objective elements The mere endeavour to act in the interests of another does not of course suffice to safeguard the latter from officious intermeddling by strangers. A further requirement is therefore that there was a reasonable ground for the intervention (Article 1:101(1)(a)). The draft has adopted this criterion from Dutch CC art. 6:198 (see above at A5). Alternatively the reasonable ground may be substituted by the subsequent approval of the principal (Article 1:101(1)(b)). Article 1:101(2) elaborates on the concept of the reasonable ground and makes clear that a reasonable ground is not present if the intervener could have asked the principal in time and has omitted to do so (in which case he will be dependent on an after-the-fact approval of the principal) or, if he could not reach the principal, he knew or should have known that the principal would not agree to the chosen mode of proceeding.

99. The affair 'of another' Both between and within a number of European legal systems there is disagreement as to whether the application of *negotiorum gestio* law requires that the intervener manages 'another's' affair. The text of German CC § 677 for instance does not contain such requirement; it only demands that the intervener acts 'for another'. Dutch CC art. 6:198 invokes the criterion that the intervener 'looks after the interest of another'. Italian CC art. 2028 has the precondition of knowingly undertaking *un affare altrui* and French CC art. 1372 similarly requires that a person voluntarily performs *l'affaire d'autrui*. Greek CC art. 730 requires the management of 'another's affair'. Austrian CC §§ 1036 and 1037 similarly rely on the requirement of 'another's affair'. Portuguese CC art. 464 contains the term 'affair of another' and Spanish CC art. 1888 refers to *agencia o administración de los negocios de otro*. However, all jurisdictions which operate on the basis of this requirement that the management must concern 'another's' affair have brought upon themselves a considerable difficulty as regards both interpretation and demarcation (for details see notes *III 26-37* under Article 1:101 (Intervention to benefit Another) below). The requirement of managing 'another's' affair is only satisfied unambiguously where the act of intervention actually interferes with the other's rights. This will often not be the case. Yet the prevailing opinion is that this does not necessarily preclude other acts from constituting benevolent intervention. We only have to refer to cases such as the rescue of an unconscious person from danger, the intervener's sacrifice of his own goods, his exposure to danger in the interest of the principal or the conclusion of contracts in his own name. The requirement of the management of 'another's' affair is the consequence of a quasi-delictual conception of benevolent intervention: according to this view, whatever the *gestor* does is in general perceived as a tortious act, which is justified only by exception – that is, if the requirements of benevolent intervention are met. This is not the underlying concept of benevolent intervention as set out in this Book. Of course it includes interference with another's legal responsibilities. However, depending on the respective circumstances of the case, such interference is nothing more than an indicator for the existence of a predominant intention to benefit another. Beyond this, the element of 'another's affair' is of no significance. Instead it is sufficient and conclusive that the intervener has reasonable grounds for acting and has a predominant intention of benefiting another. Nor do the terms 'intervener' or 'intervention in another's affairs' alter this result. They only stand for the fact that somebody interferes in order to promote the well-being of another. Which form this interference takes and whether or not it results in a violation of another's rights is, as a general rule, without relevance for the scope of application of benevolent intervention. This question only becomes relevant in the context of tort law and unjustified enrichment law. In the law on benevolent intervention everything depends on the intention to benefit another – a requirement which at the same time answers the question who is the principal. An incongruity between the intention of the intervener and the determination of the principal only occurs in the context of Article 1:102 (Intervention to Perform Another's Duty). This, however, is a genuine exception and is characterised as such. Whereas Article 1:103 (b) (Exclusions) in the main concerns cases of interference with another's sphere of legal responsibility, this is not without exception: parents who rescue their child from danger are not excluded from the scope of benevolent intervention because they do not undertake 'another's' affair. They are excluded instead because they do not depend on their child's consent. The requirement of managing an affair objectively another's, that is to say, the interference with another's sphere of legal responsibility, is therefore not reintroduced into the draft concept via Article 1:103 (b) on the general prerequisites for the application of benevolent intervention. Accordingly Article 1:101 (Intervention to Benefit Another) does not comprise this requirement.

100. Duties of the intervener These Principles collate the duties of the intervener in Chapter 2. A distinction is made between duties during the intervention (Article 2:101) (the question whether the intervention was permissible at all is in contrast a matter for Chapter 1), duties which arise after termination of the intervention (Article 2:102), and the general duty to make reparation for damage caused by misfeasance in the course of the intervention (Article 2:103). During the intervention the intervener is under a duty of care; he has to undertake the intervenetion in accordance with the known – or failing that the presumed – wishes of the principal; he must try to contact the principal; and he may not discontinue the intervention prematurely. Once the intervention is terminated, the intervener must account to the principal as soon as reasonably possible, and surrender to the principal all that he (the intervener) has received in the course of the intervention. If the intervener breaches his duties he is liable to make reparation to the principal. However, the intervener is only liable for the damage for which he is responsible. Moreover, his liability may be reduced by the proviso to Article 2:103 (2). This makes allowance for the fact that the intervener has acted with a benevolent intention. An intervener who lacks full legal capacity deserves even greater protection (Articles 2:102 (2) and 2:103 (3)).

101. Rights of the intervener The rights of the intervener (which at the same time constitute the duties of the principal) are comprised in Articles 3:101-3:104. In the first place, the intervener has a right against the principal for indemnification or, as the circumstances of the case dictate, a right to reimbursement of expenses incurred (Article 3:101 (Right to Indemnification or Reimbursement)). The *gestor* who spontaneously renders assistance that is within the field of his profession or trade also has a right to remuneration for the services rendered (Article 3:102 (Right to Remuneration)). This right for remuneration is still disputed as a matter of policy within some of the national jurisdictions (see the notes to Article 3:102), but from the perspective of this draft it is indispensable. An intervener who is not a professional may instruct a person who is to undertake (as a rule provisional) work and accordingly will be liable to pay the latter his full contractual remuneration, for which the intervener may in turn claim reimbursement from the principal. Against this background it does not seem convincing to deny a professional intervener a right to reimbursement for services rendered for the mere reason that he has not instructed a third party to act, but instead has acted of his own accord. Finally an intervener who in the course of undertaking (or attempting to undertake) emergency measures suffers personal injury may claim reparation from the principal under Article 3:103 (Right to Reparation), subject to the restrictive requirements of that provision.

102. Articles 3:104 and 3:105 Article 3:104 (Reduction or Exclusion of Intervener's Rights) limits the rights of the intervener. These provisions concern not just the right to reparation, but rather all rights of the intervener. Article 3:104 (1) sets out the principle that a person who acted with *animus donandi*, although a *gestor*, cannot claim those rights which at the time of acting he did not intend to assert in the future. Paragraph (2) contains a reduction clause, which is likewise not confined to reparation. Only Article 3:105 (Obligation of Third Party to Indemnify or Reimburse the Principal) is restricted to reparation. It is not self-evident that the right granted could also be derived from the tort law system as drafted by the Study Group. For that reason this clarification appeared to be necessary. Although this provision may appear at first glance to be inappropriate in this context since it contains a right of the principal to claim reimbursement from a third party, the rule has been included into the law of benevolent intervention because, from an economic perspective, it results in a reduction of the principal's liability as against the intervener.

103. Authority of the intervener Article 3:106 (Authority of Intervener to Act in the Name of the Principal) comprises a privilege of the intervener rather than a right in the strict sense. The draft in this respect is again modelled on the Dutch law (Dutch CC art. 6:201). The relationship of this provision and the provisions on the right of agency are set out above at *L93*.

104. Burden of proof As far as the burden of proof is concerned the general rules apply. Each party has to assert the facts which support their case and corroborate them if they are disputed (see the comments to Article 1:101 (Intervention to Benefit Another)).

105. Applied negotiorum gestio These Principles do not affect the rules on applied *negotiorum gestio* (above at *D30-38*); they are only of relevance in so far as specific provisions explicitly refer to the rights and duties of the intervener or principal.

Chapter 1: Scope of Application

Article 1:101: Intervention to Benefit Another

(1) This Book applies where a person (the intervener) acts with the predominant intention of benefiting another (the principal); and
  (a) the intervener has a reasonable ground for acting; or
  (b) the principal approves the act without such undue delay as would adversely affect the intervener.

(2) The intervener does not have a reasonable ground for acting if the intervener:
  (a) has a reasonable opportunity to discover the principal's wishes but does not do so; or
  (b) knows or ought to know that the intervention is against the principal's wishes.

Comments

A. General

1. **Terminology** The provisions of this Chapter contain rules regulating the legal relationship between two persons where one party, either for good reasons or with the subsequent approval of the other, has taken it upon himself to intervene in the other's affairs for the furtherance of the latter's interests. This law of benevolent intervention in another's affairs or *negotiorum gestio* thus governs the rights and duties of the party acting (in the various laws of the Member States presently termed, *inter alia, dioikitis allotrion, forretningsfører, gérant, Geschäftsführer, gestor, gestore, megbízás nélküli ügyvivo,o, zaakwaarnemer*) and the party to be benefited (the *belanghebbende, dominus, dono do negócio, dueño, forretningsherre, géré, Geschäftsherr, huvudman, interesado, interessato, kyrios, maître de l'affaire, ügy ura*). In the English version of these Articles, the *dominus* is referred to as the "principal". The active party is referred to as the "intervener".

2. **Requirements of negotiorum gestio** According to Article 1:101 (1) and Article 1:103 (Exclusions), *negotiorum gestio* has two positive requirements (Article 1:101 (1) (a)) and three negative requirements (Article 1:103 (a), (b) and (c)). There must be (i) an act which is undertaken with the predominant intention of benefiting another (the principal) and (ii) a reasonable ground for this intervention. Additionally the party acting must not be either (iii) obliged or (iv) otherwise authorised under other rules of the legal system (that is to say, rules outside the law of *negotiorum gestio*) to act in relation to the benefited party, or (v) under a duty to act in relation to a third party. In addition limb (b) of Article 1:101 para (1) makes it clear that the provisions of this Chapter also apply if the *gestor* intervenes without reasonable ground in the affairs of the principal, but his activity is approved by the latter without such undue delay as would adversely affect the intervener. The approval by the principal substitutes, in other

words, for the (missing) reasonable ground for acting in the principal's sphere of interest. There is no further requirement in Article 1:101 that the intervener must manage an affair which from an objective perspective is the affair of another (that is to say, an extraneous affair in relation to the intervener); the single decisive element is that the intervener acts with the predominant intention to benefit the other. It is the intention to benefit another, acted upon on the basis of a reasonable ground, which attributes the act to the principal.

Illustration 1
G is the owner of a very ugly factory site. In order to save his neighbours the awful sight of the buildings, G, acting on his own initiative, plants a row of trees along the property boundaries. G may have acted with the predominant intention to benefit his neighbour, but he is not an intervener because he has not acted upon his intention to benefit another on the basis of a reasonable ground. He has imposed an enrichment on his neighbour.

Illustration 2
In order to apply an emergency bandage on a badly injured pedestrian, P, a passer-by G uses dressing material. G will qualify as an intervener in relation to P irrespective of whether he uses his own dressing material or if he smashes the window of a car belonging to a third party in order to get hold of dressing material lying on the back seat. In relation to the third party, this act qualifies as a justified act of emergency with in the meaning of PEL Liab.Dam. Article 5:202 (2) (Self-Defence, Benevolent Intervention and Necessity) for which G is liable to provide reasonable compensation.

3. **Protection of the principal against officious intermeddling in his affairs** In order to protect the principal from officious intermeddling by others paragraph (2) makes the clear demand that in acting the intervener must orientate himself as far as possible in the circumstances according to the wishes of the principal, so far as the intervener is in a position to identify them. Para (2) is an ancillary norm serving as a particularisation of para (1)(a).

4. **Special forms of the law of negotiorum gestio are not within this regime** As already noted in the introduction, the provisions of this Chapter have as their subject matter only the so-called justified management of another's affairs and the rights and duties of the intervener and the principal which arise out of that. If someone interferes in the affairs of another without reasonable ground and that other is not moved to approve the intervention, then the rights and duties of the parties remain subject to other areas of the law – in particular the law of tort and the law of unjustified enrichment – and not the law of *negotiorum gestio*. The same correspondingly holds true where a person intermeddles in the affairs of another in order to pursue his own interests, and that is so irrespective of whether this happens intentionally or by mistake (for example, because that person meant to advance his own interest, but has actually furthered another's interests). Contrastingly, the provisions of this Chapter are applicable where the intervention is justified, but the intervener infringes a duty which arises out of the

justified management of another's affairs. See for more detail Chapter 2 (Duties of Intervener).

5. **Negotiorum gestio as a defence within the framework of the law of tort** Justified benevolent intervention in advancement of another's interests constitutes a ground of defence in respect of an extra-contractual liability in damages which would otherwise be imposed. That is expressly set out in PEL Liab.Dam. Article 5:202 (2) (Self-Defence, Benevolent Intervention and Necessity).

Illustration 3
As a result of a traffic accident P is rendered unconscious and locked in in his car. G smashes a car window in order to be able to unlock the door from the inside and pull P out of the car. G is not liable to P under the law of tort for the damage caused to the car.

6. **Burden of proof** These Principles regard rules on burden of proof as belonging to substantive law. Rules on burden of proof are applicable when it is not possible to clearly establish the circumstances of the case. Within the law of *negotiorum gestio* the general principle applies whereby each party must make out the circumstances favourable to its case and in case of dispute prove them. When a given party is not able to do that, the decision in the case must be adverse to them.

Illustration 4
The facts are the same as in illustration 3, save that in smashing in the window G is injured. Both parties claim compensation – P in tort law on account of property damage and G in *negotiorum gestio* under Article 3:103 (Right to Reparation) on account of the personal injury suffered in acting as intervener. If it is disputed and cannot be established whether G really acted for the purpose of rescuing P, then P's claim to compensation will succeed, while G's claim will fail.

7. **Proof** By contrast, all questions which are related to the problem whether a given fact is to be regarded as proven are part of the law of procedure. They are therefore not the subject matter of these Principles.

Illustration 5
The facts are again the same as in illustration 3. However, P later maintains that G smashed the window only (or at least primarily) for opportunistic reasons, meaning to steal the camera lying on the passenger seat of P's car. (National) procedural law determines under what conditions and to what extent G's case is supported by presumptions triggered by a *prima facie* case. (For example, G might prove that P was in fact subsequently liberated from the car by G, from which it may *prima facie* follow that when he struck the glass beforehand G was acting predominantly with the intention of rescuing P.) The same goes for the question as to what concrete circumstances place upon P an onus of introducing evidence to rebut a *prima facie* case. (For example, P might seek to show that G was later found with the camera in his possession and unable to offer a convincing explanation for his custody and that G had made no serious venture to free P from his plight.)

B. The Activities Covered

8. **'Acting' for another** Article 1:101 (1) states that the provisions of this Part apply where a person 'acts' for another. The type of act required is not further qualified. It follows that every type of act may be considered a *negotiorum gestio* – services as much as making things (or money) available for use or paying another's debt. This wide scope of application embraces acts having legal effects as well as acts merely changing the physical state of affairs. A *negotiorum gestio* may consist in the conclusion of a contract or giving notice to terminate a legal relationship just as much as it may consist in effecting repairs, making a telephone call, keeping property safe, giving a warning, removing a vehicle, cutting back trees overhanging into the public thoroughfare, feeding (or, in a case of emergency, killing) animals, and so forth. All of these are 'acts' within the meaning of that term in Article 1:101. That of course does not exclude the possibility that certain of the following provisions of this Book may be entirely or at any rate predominantly directed towards one form of acting rather than another, be it acts having legal effects or acts of a merely physical import. A case in point where it is the former rather than the latter which is in focus is Article 3:106 relating to the power of representation of an intervener and thus necessarily only concerning 'juridical acts'. By contrast, Article 3:103 concerning reparation in cases of damage suffered by the intervener will as a rule only come into play in respect of acts of a merely physical significance.

9. **Acts to protect another's person are included** Furthermore, it is unmistakeable that the concept of benevolent intervention in another's affairs as understood in these Principles is in no way limited just to acts for the protection of another's patrimonial interests. Instead it includes within its compass acts for the protection of another's person and hence such acts as bandaging the wounded, bringing the injured to hospital and saving someone from an ill-boding predicament (as in illustration 3 above).

10. **One-off activities and long-term undertakings** The 'act' can consist in an isolated, one-off act as much as an enduring matrix of activities such as the administration of a bank deposit or the management of another's farm or business. To cater in particular for such longer term activities the provision in Article 2:101 (c) (concerning the on-going duty of the intervener to provide information) has been devised; for activities which start and finish in a momentary act that provision will not come into play.

11. **Omissions** It is theoretically conceivable that a benevolent intervention might even consist in an omission. Practically speaking, however, that can rarely be the case, not least because the commonest situations in which the outward appearance of a person's conduct would lend itself to a *negotiorum gestio* will often be absorbed by the law of contract and in such circumstances, in accordance with Article 1:103(a) (Exclusions), the rules of contract law will claim priority over the law of benevolent intervention in another's affairs.

Illustration 6
A notary, acting contrary to instructions, does not forward his client's money to the tax authority because he has learned in the meantime of a change to the taxing statutes whereby tax is no longer payable. A garage, acting in the interest of a customer, does not repair the car he brought to be repaired in order to save it from the grasp of an occupying power. One will normally construe this conduct as discharging a contractual duty and one is therefore outside the law of benevolent intervention in another's affairs from the very outset.

12. **Actions contrary to law or public policy** Acts of an intervener which are unlawful or contrary to public policy are not *per se* excluded by the Articles from their scope of application. Such a rule does not appear necessary and, moreover, it would be dangerous to introduce one because in defined circumstances it could be the cause of misunderstanding. Certainly, under normal circumstances the act of the intervener must not be either prohibited by law or contrary to public policy. However, that follows from the fact that in both of those cases the reasonable ground for intervention would usually be missing.

Illustration 7
P, a member of a band of thieves, is ill. Disproving the adage that there is no honour among thieves, P's friend G undertakes P's "workload" on P's behalf. Under the law of benevolent intervention P can have no claim against G to the money stolen from third parties by G on P's behalf (and correspondingly G has no claims against P).

13. **Emergency situations** However, it is conceivable that in situations of emergency even otherwise illegal conduct might, in special circumstances, be reasonable. The emergency might compel an intervener to action prohibited by law or what, under normal circumstances, would be regarded as contrary to public policy.

Illustration 8
A person is only able to obtain the release of a travelling companion, who is being wrongfully held in custody in a corrupt foreign state, by paying bribes. Although bribery is prohibited and although the legal system to which the intervener and the principal are subject (be it by reason of common nationality or habitual residence) would also usually disapprove of the bribery of foreign officials, in such extreme conditions the act of bribery might still be reasonable in relation to the principal. The intervener can consequently demand reimbursement of the expenditure incurred in making the bribes: see Article 3:101 (Right to Indemnification or Reimbursement).

14. **Disallowed interventions** It may nonetheless be the case that even after considering the situation of emergency, a given conduct is regarded by a legal system as prohibited for reasons of overriding significance. In that event it is unreasonable for the purposes of the law of *negotiorum gestio* to disregard the prohibition.

Illustration 9
Under the law of a Member State it is prohibited on the basis of a particular statutory provision to pay a ransom to a kidnapper. A son who ransoms his father from the clutches of his captors has no claim against his father for reimbursement on the basis of *negotiorum gestio*. The son has no reasonable ground to intervene in this manner.

15. **Acts of a personal nature excluded** Only acts of a personal nature are by their very nature excluded. That is not expressly stated in Article 1:101, but should be understood as inherent and can be inferred from Article 3:106 which under certain conditions confers on the intervener the authority to act in the name of the principal so as to act in a way which binds and favours the principal directly in relation to third parties. Acts which cannot permissibly form the subject-matter of an agency relationship cannot permissibly be made the subject-matter of a benevolent intervention in another's affairs. In so far as the law of succession does not allow a person to execute a will for another, it will not be possible for an intervener to undertake such an act as *gestor* for the testator. A similar point can be made in relation to a legal transaction which purports to change another's marital status or parental responsibility or to alter an individual's name. However, a person is also precluded from putting forward a particular philosophical or political viewpoint on behalf of another – for example election publicity as benevolent intervener for a political party.

16. **Conducting litigation as a benevolent intervener** An act within the meaning of the law of benevolent intervention in another's affairs can also consist in conducting litigation. In that case, however, one must distinguish between two fundamentally different situations, namely conducting litigation in one's own name and conducting litigation in the name of the principal. The first situation, in which the intervener litigates against a third party in the principal's interest but in the intervener's own name (for example, in pursuing through the courts a claim to the purchase price where in a case of necessity the intervener has sold, in his own name, goods belonging to the principal), does not throw up any special issues. The intervener may even be obliged to take such action in defence of the principal's interests (in consequence of prior acts) as part of his duty to continue his intervention within the bounds set out in Article 2:101 (2) (Duties during Intervention). More difficult, by contrast, is the problem of whether and under what conditions an intervener may litigate in the name of the principal if the latter is hindered personally from attending to his affairs. A case in point would be, for example, an attempt by an intervener to commence legal proceedings in order to prevent a statutory limitation of the principal's claim to an unpaid purchase price which threatens to become time-barred. Whether such a form of undertaking the affairs of another is possible or whether the matter remains reserved to the principal as something which can only be carried out personally is not determined by these Principles. Rather they presuppose, in keeping with most jurisdictions of the EU, that one is concerned here with a question of procedural law which must be resolved by the applicable law of procedure. The position adopted in the majority of national procedural laws appears to be that an intervener will be permitted by a court to conduct litigation on a provisional basis up to a certain point in time, determined by the court,

when a power of attorney must be filed, in default of which the action will be dismissed as not maintainable.

C. The Intention Predominantly to Benefit Another (Para (1))

17. Meaning of 'benefiting' As regards the positive requirements of benevolent intervention in another's affairs, as stated already the text operates with one subjective element (intention to benefit) and one objective element (reasonable ground). As a first essential, the intervener must act with the intention of *benefiting* another. The word 'benefiting' is to be understood in this context as having a wide significance; in particular it does not relate merely to benefits of a type falling within patrimonial law in the sense of an enrichment. That follows already from the explanation in paras. 8-9 above of the concept of an 'act'. See also illustration 3 above.

18. The success of the venture is not essential Furthermore, it is important to recognise that it is the *intention* of benefiting another that matters, not an actual benefit as such. This intention turns only on the *prospective* utility which, at the time of acting, might be anticipated and not the *resultant* usefulness which may or may not have emerged after the act has been completed or stopped. The intervener must therefore have acted with the intention to manage another's affairs for their benefit, assessed at the time he is active, but as a fundamental principle this good intention is sufficient. Whether or not the act was ultimately successful (the resultant benefit) is not a criterion and is immaterial. In this way the law of benevolent intervention in another's affairs is distinguishable from the law of unjustified enrichment.

> *Illustration 10*
> P suddenly loses consciousness behind the wheel of her car. Her car comes to rest over a sheer drop; she is rescued and taken to hospital. P's car threatens to run down the slope. G, who operates a breakdown service and has been informed of the situation by a third party, resolves to tow the car back onto the road using a winch and bring it on to P's house. Due to a latent defect in the material, the steel cable snaps; the car tumbles down into the void. G acted with the intention of benefiting P. That his intervention ultimately resulted in more harm than good does not alter the matter.

19. Benefiting another, not intending to pursue one's own interests The intervener must have acted with the intention of benefiting *another*. A person who pursues their own interests is not a *gestor*. Moreover, merely having in fact undertaken another's affairs will also not suffice if that was done inadvertently or unwittingly. Someone who assumes they are discharging their own obligation and acts accordingly, in reality discharging another's obligation, is not acting as a *gestor*. A case in point would be a married man who maintains a child of his wife in the assumption that he is the father, though in reality another man is the biological father of the child. In the absence of a special statutory regime (in this case, in family law), such cases remain to be dealt with within the law of unjustified enrichment.

Illustration 11
From a vague report provided by children G takes it that his son has broken a neighbour's window pane with a ball. On that basis G pays for the damage. Later it emerges that a different boy was responsible. G does not act as intervener for either the boy responsible or (so far as they would be vicariously liable for the property damage caused by their son) the boy's parents. Any claim for reimbursement of the payment made can be made only in accordance with the law of unjustified enrichment. It will be for the law of unjustified enrichment to determine whether G has a claim against the other boy, or the parents of the other boy, or whether instead he can demand a repayment from the neighbour.

Illustration 12
A music publishing company continues to make use of publishing rights, assigned to the company for its use for a limited time only, after the death of the composer in the erroneous supposition that the rights had fallen into the public domain. The publishing company cannot set off against the claim of the composer's successors for surrender of the proceeds a claim based in *negotiorum gestio* for remuneration for its commercial activity in marketing the music. The company had not intended to benefit the composer's successors.

20. **No possibility of approval for acts undertaken for own benefit** In contrast to the element of reasonable ground (para (1) limb (a) in conjunction with para (2)), the subjective requirement of an intention to benefit another cannot be replaced by a timeous approval of the act by way of ratification. The justification for the possibility of an approval of an intermeddler's act is based on the assumption that the intermeddler was acting for the person subsequently giving their approval for what has been done, so that there is, as it were, in retrospect a meeting of minds between the parties. According to the rules of benevolent intervention in another's affairs an approval by the principal is not therefore an option if the intervener has been acting mainly in his own interest and if he happened to have a secondary aim of benefiting the principal. That, however, does not preclude the possible application of the rules on representation. Under PECL art. 3:207 (Ratification by Principal) a principal can ratify a transaction which a person acting in his name, but without his authority, has concluded with a third party. In this context it does not matter whether the *falsus procurator* has acted with the intention of benefiting the principal or for his own benefit.

21. **'Predominant' intention of benefiting another** In order to evade the problem arising where an intervener acts with a mixture of interests in mind – that is, the problem that hardly anybody ever acts exclusively in another's interest – para (1) requires that the intervener must intend *predominantly* to benefit the principal. Where the pursuit of another's interest and the pursuit of one's own interest have been combined together, it is sufficient that the former is, at the margin, uppermost. This excludes all argument that an intervener will have a right to reimbursement when in substance he has been acting for his own advantage merely because some lesser part of his intention was to benefit the principal.

Illustration 13
A genealogist (G) makes his living by, among other things, responding to public announcements of apparently 'heirless' estates. Such publications arise where a person dies leaving an estate and the court responsible for matters relating to intestate succession to the estate is compelled according to the tenor of the documentation before the court to assume that the deceased died without relatives entitled to succeed to the estate. If such relatives do not identify themselves within a given time limit, the estate will pass to the public exchequer. G is successful in seeking out such relatives. He offers, in exchange for a reward amounting to 20% of the estate, to provide them with requisite details and to conduct the process of winding up the estate. To demonstrate his seriousness, he reveals to them preliminary information of a rudimentary kind. However, that information turns out to be sufficient for the relatives to locate the court with responsibility for the succession and to press their claims to the inheritance. G has only collaterally sought to advance the interests of the relatives. His main concern was the conclusion of a contract into which, however, the relatives did not in fact enter. G has no claim against the relatives and in particular none arising out of Article 3:102 (Right to Remuneration). A second reason to deny such a claim for remuneration would be that under Art. 9 of the Directive 97/7 on protection of consumers in respect of distance contracts no consumer is compelled to pay for unsolicited services. As already noted in the introduction, this provision does not mean that European Community law has completely abolished claims for expenditure in respect of unsolicited services, but it does mean that its value judgments must be reflected by the law of *negotiorum gestio*.

Illustration 14
Farmer F notices that following a storm in his locality a tree in the highway has fallen down and is lying across the street. Being a weekend, nobody can be contacted at the local authority, which is responsible for the tree and the safety of the street, who will be able to react promptly. If the farmer pulls the tree trunk out of the road with the aid of his tractor, he acts as intervener for the local authority (Article 1:102 (Intervention to Perform Another's Duty)). That remains the case irrespective of the fact that a collateral benefit of his activity is to enable the farmer himself to reach part of his estates which could otherwise only be reached by making a detour.

Illustration 15
Grown up children discharge their father's unpaid tax liability in order to prevent the Revenue from impounding some valuable pictures belonging to their father. It is no objection to recognising the existence of a benevolent intervention that the children in making the payment also had in mind their prospective inheritance of the pictures on their father's eventual death.

Illustration 16
The majority of the owners of land on an industrial estate make a request to the responsible local authority for the construction of a spur to connect with a nearby dual carriageway. The local authority consents on the basis that the land owners

make a substantial contribution to the costs of construction. Land owners A and B are agreeable. C agrees too in principle, but makes it clear from the outset that he is not prepared under any circumstances to pay more than € 100,000. A and B (but not C) subsequently conclude a contract with the authority to make a contribution to the construction costs; the authority undertakes to construct the road. The resultant costs amount to € 770,000. Quite independent of the fact that C expressly ruled out a greater contribution to the costs of construction, A and B have no claim against C in *negotiorum gestio* because they did not act "predominantly" with the purpose of benefiting C.

22. **Acting in pursuance of a void contract** A special case (which is not the subject of an explicit rule) in which an intention *predominantly* to benefit another is missing is when a person undertakes an act in the erroneous assumption that they are discharging a contractual duty which they believe they have incurred to the principal. Typical cases concern performances rendered on the basis of contracts which are void for illegality, want of required form, or because the parties are not truly *ad idem*. These Principles proceed on the basis that claims in respect of such performances rendered fall within the domain of the law of unjustified enrichment and not within the law of benevolent intervention in another's affairs. Illustrative cases involve the repair of another's automobile pursuant to a void contract for services or the acquisition of property in one's own name in supposed discharge of a void mandate. A few of the higher courts in Europe admittedly judge these latter cases differently at present, but within those countries their solution is anything but undisputed. Speaking in favour of the solution chosen here is the fact that someone who acts on the basis of a void contract is certainly, from a technical point of view, acting 'without authority' (see Article 1:103 (a) (Exclusions)), but they also act without the intention "predominantly" of benefiting another, seeking rather to advance their own interest by executing the concluded bargain.

23. **Similar cases** The position is no different when a person discharges a debt as a result of a misapprehension as to the legal situation – for example, where a person mistakenly assumes that they are obliged on account of a supposed unjustified enrichment or tort to make a monetary payment. Here too an intention predominantly to benefit another is missing and consequently there is no benevolent intervention. Distinguishable, however, is the case of discharge of an obligation to render assistance arising under criminal law (on which see further comment *B11* under Article 1:103 (Exclusions)). Moreover, one who erroneously supposes that a person in need has a right to assistance nonetheless acts predominantly with the intention of benefiting that person. The (unfounded) concern of the rescuer that they may otherwise be subject to a claim for damages blends into the background in a real life situation.

24. **Collateral advancement of a subordinate personal interest can affect the quantum of the intervener's claim** It not uncommonly transpires that an intervener is predominantly acting to advance the interests of the principal, but at the same time he has the advancement of his own objectives at the back of his mind. As stated above, that will not exclude the application of the rules on benevolent intervention in another's affairs. The (subordinate) collateral advancement of one's own purposes may call for consid-

eration, however, in determining the legal consequences of the intervention – in particular in assessing the quantum of damages or reimbursement of expenditure to which the intervener is entitled. That is the case primarily where the intervener and principal were exposed to a common danger (see Article 3:104 (Reduction or Exclusion of Intervener's Rights)).

Illustration 17
Adjacent plots of land belonging to G and P respectively are situated on a slope in the hills, G's land lying immediately below that of P. After heavy rainfall and especially when settled snow melts, the stream which flows down the hill and along both plots of land overflows and floods the land. G knows from experience that when the water has reached P's house it will flood into P's kitchen if nothing is done. When the water levels upstream by P's land once more rise ominously high, G commissions a contractor to deal with the problem, P being away from the scene and not reachable by telephone. G has a claim against P for reimbursement in respect of the costs arising from commissioning the contractor. That claim will be reduced under Article 3:104 (2), however, if and so far as G's house would similarly have been flooded had he not commissioned the contractor to prevent the flooding of P's house.

25. **Intervener and principal: general observations** Fundamentally anybody can be an intervener or a principal. That applies to legal persons as much as to natural ones. In many cases it will be not-for-profit organisations, formed as legal persons, which intervene as *gestors* (though this does not exclude the possibility that in the circumstances of the case they may often fall to be regarded for the purposes of Article 3:104 (1) (Reduction or Exclusion of Intervener's Rights) as having manifested an intention at the time of their intervention not to assert their rights as intervener). Equally children may act as intervener or be a principal (but see also the rules for their protection in Article 2:102 (2) (Duties after Intervention), Article 2:103 (3) (Reparation for Damage Caused by Breach of Duty) and Article 3:104 (2) (Reduction or Exclusion of Intervener's Rights)). Whether mentally disabled persons are capable of acting as an intervener depends essentially on whether they are capable of mustering sufficient powers of comprehension so as to be able to resolve to intervene predominantly with the intention of benefiting another. It is even conceivable that a benevolent intervener may act for a person not yet in existence (e. g. a foetus), though here the general rule must be observed that a person can only be subject to legal obligations if they obtain legal capacity (i. e., in this case, if they are born and survive the birth).

26. **Multiple interveners** Where multiple interveners act, it will depend on the circumstances of the individual case whether or not they are to be regarded as solidary debtors. According to general rules, they will usually be solidary debtors if (but only if) they carry out one and the same undertaking. They will be independent debtors however if they are pursuing different tasks.

Illustration 18
For lack of expertise, A is not in a position to put right certain damage to water pipes in the home of his neighbour N. A calls a plumber and, in his own name,

commissions the plumber to undertake the repairs. If the repairs are carried out unprofessionally, A will not be vicariously liable to N. However, under Article 2:102(1) (Duties after Intervention) A is obliged to assign to N his claim for damages under the contract he made with the plumber which will entitle N to claim damages from the plumber.

Illustration 19
The facts are as in illustration 18, except that instead of engaging the plumber in his own name, A merely alerts the plumber to the burst pipe and leaves to him the decision whether or not he, the plumber, will intervene. If the plumber does intervene, then both A (because of his alerting the plumber) and the plumber himself constitute *gestors*. As regards the defective execution of the repairs, however, they do not constitute solidary debtors; in relation to that activity, A was not a *gestor* at all.

27. **PECL Part III, Chapter 10** Where interveners are liable as solidary debtors, their obligations towards the creditor principal to settle their liabilities will follow, by means of analogy, the rules of Part III, Chapter 10 of the PECL.

28. **Identifying the principal** The intervener is the person who has acted for another (and not primarily for himself); the principal is generally the person whose interests the intervener sought to look after. There can only be one principal or class of co-principals whom the *gestor* intends to benefit *predominantly* – i. e. to benefit above all others. The approach by which the principal is defined is thus a subjective one. It depends according to the basic rule on the intentions of the intervener. In the circumstances circumscribed by Article 1:102 (Intervention to Perform Another's Duty) however, there is an exceptional case in which an "objective" approach supplements the core "subjective" one.

Illustration 20
In the immediate aftermath of a railway disaster which has resulted in a large number of victims, some private individuals in the vicinity of the accident rush to give assistance. Two of the helpers injure themselves when breaking the window of an overturned carriage, supposing there are survivors inside. There are in fact five survivors whom it is possible to rescue. Those five survivors, as well as the railway company (see Article 1:102 (Intervention to Perform Another's Duty)), are principals in relation to the rescuers. As between the railway company and the rescued victims, however, the railway company alone will be accountable if it is liable vis-à-vis its passengers: Article 3:105 (Obligation of Third Party to Indemnify or Reimburse the Principal).

29. **The determinability of the principal at the moment of intervention** The intention of the intervener to benefit another must relate to the principal. That does not mean that the intervener must have known the principal personally or by name; nor does it even mean that he must have had a specific person in mind whom he wished to benefit. It does mean, however, that at the moment of intervention the principal must at least have been ascertainable. Unless that requirement is satisfied there can be no benevolent intervention "for another".

Illustration 21

A company which runs a bus passenger service and as a precaution in case of accident keeps one or two vehicles in reserve in its depot does not act on behalf of someone who is responsible for a subsequent accident and causes damage to its fleet when it keeps those maintained vehicles on stand-by. Consequently, the company cannot under the rules of benevolent intervention in another's affairs demand from the person causing the accident a proportion of the costs of keeping the vehicles in reserve. That person was not identifiable at the time the decision was taken to establish a reserve fleet. (Quite aside from this the company may have acted predominantly to pursue its own interests. That is because such vehicles are not primarily held in reserve in anticipation of an accident. Rather they are maintained first and foremost in order to provide undisrupted service to customers in the contingency that a vehicle has to be taken out of service due to a breakdown).

Illustration 22

A water leakage occurs in a coal mine. The responsible authority prohibits the owner of the mine from pumping out the water, because it fears damage to the water table in summer. The costs of pumping out the mine later are considerably higher than if the measure had been undertaken immediately; in addition the owner suffers loss of earnings as a result of this delay. He is not a *gestor*, however, in delaying the draining of the mine because an indeterminate number of people benefits from his omission: a spa, hotels and bed and breakfast accommodation, retailers, other residents of the town and even traders in the towns through which the guests of the health resort, who would otherwise have stayed away, have to travel.

30. **Where the principal is unknown to the intervener** As already indicated, it is not necessary that the *gestor* should know the principal personally. An intervener acting to benefit an unknown person is, without more, quite permissible. Someone who is on the point of rescuing a stranger's property does not need to know who the owner is or which other persons, if any, have proprietary entitlements in respect of the property in order to be able to act as intervener in relation to them. The general intention to aid those who have some patrimonial interest in the property suffices. To that extent the 'subjective' method of identifying the principal also subsumes certain 'objective' elements within it. Moreover, in situations of emergency which require a rapid response it is quite unrealistic to expect of the intervener that he should entertain precise thoughts about who exactly it is that he is benefiting. In such cases the principal is that person whom the intervener would reasonably have contemplated as the object of his assistance had he been able to give the matter full consideration at his leisure. In this context it is also possible to bring into focus considerations of what is customarily the case. Someone who protects a small child from the dangers of road traffic, for example, might intend in a case of doubt to act also for the child's parents.

31. **Mistake about the person benefited** It is correspondingly not fatal to the existence of a benevolent intervention in another's affairs that the intervener is mistaken as to the person who is in fact benefited by the intervention. In the case of a change in the

supposed benefited persons, identification of the legally relevant parties turns on the material rather than the personal intentions of the intervener.

Illustration 23
Someone who intends to pull out of the ditch a car which he supposes belongs to X, but later learns is in fact owned by Y, acts with the intention of furthering the interests of Y: they act with the intention of benefiting the owner of the car, albeit that this is coupled with a mistaken assumption as to the identity of the owner. The same applies even if it later turns out that the car actually belongs to the person who has pulled it out. However, in this case he has acted on his own behalf and not 'for another'; because of this congruence of the person acting and the person benefited this case falls outside the scope of benevolent intervention.

32. **Indirect beneficiaries are not principals within the sense of Article 1:101** On the other hand, the boundary is reached when the intervener obviously intended to benefit a particular person and it subsequently emerges that third parties have also profited from the intervention (or would have profited, had the intervention been successful). Third parties of that type, in the ordinary course of life, are not within the intervener's contemplated class of beneficiaries. Such third party beneficiaries come into consideration as principals at most in the special circumstances of Article 1:102 (Intervention to Perform Another's Duty) (on which see the comments to that Article).

Illustration 24
A person who protects his neighbour's house from a fire does not generally act for the purpose of benefiting the insurance company with whom the neighbour has a fire insurance policy and who would otherwise incur a financial liability. Someone who endeavours to free a person from a glass window frame which has fallen on their head during the injured party's course of employment would not have a claim to compensation under Article 1:101, in conjunction with Article 3:103 (Right to Reparation), against the employee's insurer against industrial accidents if the rescuer himself is injured in the process. Someone who intends to save another's life does not act for the benefit of their life insurance company or their employer, etc.

Illustration 25
At one o'clock in the morning G hears a woman's cry for help from a derelict site. He hurries over to it, but before he is able to reach the injured woman within he is struck on the back of the head with a hammer by a maniac. When he comes to, G manages to drag himself out into the street and alert passers-by to the plight of the injured woman (who has likewise been attacked by the maniac with the hammer); the injured woman is then immediately brought to a hospital. G will only have a claim against the woman's health insurer for compensation for the loss of income suffered as a result of his injury (Article 3:103 (Right to Reparation)) if the insurer is to be regarded as the principal in accordance with Article 1:102 (Intervention to Perform Another's Duty). It would not follow from Article 1:101 that the insurer is a principal.

33. **Multiple principals** It is, however, possible to act for multiple principals simultaneously. Someone who takes care of another's young child (for example by driving the child to hospital) may act on behalf of both parents; someone who takes care of a house belonging to various co-owners will act for all of them, etc. In their relation to the intervener multiple principals are liable according to the general rules governing solidary liabilities.

D. A Reasonable Ground (Para (1)(a))

34. **General** In the absence of an approval by the principal (cf. para (1) limb (b)), the rules on benevolent intervention in another's affairs are only applicable if the intervener has a reasonable ground for taking care of the principal's affairs (para (1)(a)). Whether a party intervening in the affairs of another acts with reasonable grounds must be assessed objectively – from the point of view of a reasonable intervener; a reasonable belief in the existence of a justification for intervention can itself constitute a reasonable ground. What is decisive is whether a reasonable person in the actual situation in which the intervener finds himself would consider that there was cause for intervening by means of a measure of the type undertaken. Hence a person who takes measures to rescue the principal's property will act with reasonable ground if a reasonable person, placed in the circumstances confronting the intervener, would consider the property to be endangered and that intervention to protect it was necessary, even if (for reasons which the intervener could not know) the property was not in fact at risk.

35. **Defective and deficient performance of the intervention** However, a justified intervention in another's affairs is excluded, if the person intervening makes an irrational assessment as to the existence of a sound reason for acting. On the other hand, someone who does have a reasonable ground for intervention, but merely makes a mistake in carrying out the measures he takes, remains a (justified) *gestor*. In such a case the intervener has simply breached his duty of care and is answerable for that in accordance with the rules in Article 2:103 (Reparation for Breach of Duty); he does not forego his status as a *gestor*.

> *Illustration 26*
> Someone notices that a water pipe in a neighbour's house has burst and (acting in his own name) engages a plumber to make temporary repairs. If a bad choice of plumber is made, this may constitute a breach of the duty of care, but that does not alter the fact that there was a reasonable ground for intervention. Only in the unlikely event that the commission for the job went to a plumber to whom the neighbour would never have entrusted the repairs, even at the price of considerable water damage in his home, and the intervener knew or ought to have known this, would the required 'reasonable ground' for the intervention fall away because, to the intervener's knowledge, the act of commissioning the objectionable plumber contradicts the wishes of the principal (para (2)(b)). The situation is also different if the water damage threatens to spread to other buildings. In that case the contrary wishes of the principal do not stand in the way of acting as a justified *gestor* (Article 1:102 (Intervention to Perform Another's Duty)).

36. No requirement of pre-existing legal relationship Since it is one purpose of the law of benevolent intervention in another's affairs to provide an incentive towards socially desirable intervention, there is no call for setting down strict standards to be satisfied when posing the question why this particular intervener undertook the measure (instead of leaving the matter to another). It is not necessary that the intervener and the principal should stand in a particular close pre-existing legal or personal relationship to one another. In fact, if the latter is the case, there will often be cause for Article 3:104 (1) (Reduction or Exclusion of Intervener's Rights) ("*animus donandi*") to come into play. Equally conceivable are cases in which a reasonable ground for intervention is excluded from the outset because in the circumstances there was no reasonable solution for the difficulty which the intervener sought to eradicate. In that case one is concerned not with a mere defective mode of conducting the intervention, but with the absence of reasonable ground for the intervention. The distinction between the two (which is occasionally difficult and in the last resort must be drawn by the courts in the particular circumstances of the case) will depend on whether a reasonable person would have considered that there was cause for intervention of the sort undertaken by the intervener.

Illustration 27
A stranger in an unfamiliar town sees a window in a building blown in by a strong wind. He has no reasonable ground for intervening: he should take into account in particular the fact that the owner of the dwelling will not want to have a complete stranger enter his home and destroy his door just because such a comparatively minor problem has arisen.

Illustration 28
A fire breaks out in a chemical factory. If a private individual notifies the fire service he acts with reasonable grounds. If, on the other hand, he attempts to extinguish the fire himself after the fire brigade has arrived on the scene, he does not act with reasonable grounds. If he makes an attempt to extinguish the fire before the fire service arrives, it will depend on the circumstances of the case whether there were reasonable grounds. If an enormous blaze has already developed it would be perfectly senseless for a private individual to make any attempt to extinguish the fire. Were the fire to be a small one, however, it could possibly be sensible to tackle it oneself.

37. A 'reasonable' ground A definition of the concept of 'reasonableness' for the purposes of contract law can be found in PECL art. 1:302: "Under these Principles reasonableness is to be judged by what persons acting in good faith and in the same situation as the parties would consider to be reasonable. In particular, in assessing what is reasonable the nature and purpose of the contract, the circumstances of the case and the usages and practices of the trade or professions involved should be taken into account." It is possible to fall back on this definition, at least in part, within the realm of benevolent intervention in another's affairs because a reasonable ground for such an intervention is broadly on a par with a contract of mandate. Allowance only has to be made for the fact that PECL art. 1:302 is geared towards both parties to the contract, whereas in the situation under discussion here one is concerned with an intervener acting without contractual authority. Instead of 'contract' one has to read the word 'act' in order to focus PECL art. 1:302 on the intervener's perspective.

38. **Some guidance in the following rules** Beyond this general rule, and unaffected by the rule in para (2), the following provisions offer some additional particularised guidance as to when a person acts as an intervener with reasonable ground. In particular, rendering assistance in a case of emergency is (as a rule) regarded as a justified intervention. That emerges automatically from Article 3:103 (Right to Reparation), the provisions of which are of direct application only to the right to reparation, but can also be enlisted for another purpose as a concrete illustration of the concept of "reasonable ground". The Article envisages that the intervener may be "acting to protect the principal, or the principal's property or interests, against danger". Equally, it may be, for example, that a reasonable ground for stepping in arises only when the acting party has learned on inquiry that the principal, although obliged to act due to some overriding public interest, nonetheless intends to remain passive: see Article 1:102 (Intervention to Perform Another's Duty).

E. Want of Respect for the Principal's Wishes (Para (2))

39. **Reasonable ground to act absent** Putting to one side the exceptional situations designated in Article 1:101 (1)(b) (approval) and Article 1:102 (overriding public interest), a person does not act as a justified intervener if they rashly meddle in the affairs of another. Such is the case when it has been made known to the intermeddler that his interference is against the wishes of the person assisted or the intermeddler would have recognised this if he had taken the care required in the circumstances. This last possibility arises when the intervener could have asked the principal whether he was agreeable to the intervention, but failed to pose that question. In such a situation the intermeddler, according to the rules in para (2)(a), acts without a reasonable ground. Should he cause legally relevant damage to the other party as a result of his intervention, he may be liable for a tort. The same applies if the intervener could not ask the principal but for other reasons knew or should have known that the principal was not inclined to such intervention in the matter at hand (para (2) limb (b)).

40. **Where the wishes of the principal are not binding** There are, however, exceptional situations in which the intervener acts with reasonable ground, although the principal has made it manifest that he is not agreeable to an intervention. Leaving to one side those cases in which the principal behaves in bad faith in a way which contradicts what he is saying (so that the latter does not truly represent his wishes), one is concerned here as a rule with situations in which the intervener is acting for the benefit of a principal whose wishes an intervener acting responsibly and with due care would not heed. This is not to be regarded as a case of giving insufficient respect to another's right to free determination of their will. Rather the wishes of persons who by reason of mental disability, the influence of drugs or alcohol, or their minority are unable to express themselves in a way which would carry any weight with a reasonable intervener are not fundamentally opposed to a justified management of another's affairs. That goes for limb (a) as much as for limb (b) of para (2). The wishes of someone intent on committing

suicide are also as a general rule not binding on an intervener – at any rate not when (as is often the case) his desire to take his own life is the consequence of a psychiatric condition ('the balance of his mind is disturbed') or some other disturbance of his capacity for self-determination. Where devotees of a particular religious community are fundamentally opposed to blood transfusion on religious grounds, that wish should be respected as a matter of principle. The matter is different, however, as regards their wish as parents to allow their child to die in preference to undergoing a medically warranted blood transfusion. This wish is one which is not to be heeded if the circumstances are such that there is not enough time for taking blood from the child himself or herself for later use when needed. That is because the wishes of parents to deny their children, for religious reasons, a medical treatment involving a comparatively slim risk to health does not generate an obligation to respect them.

41. **Overriding public interest** A further special situation in which the wishes of the principal are not opposed to a justified benevolent intervention is the subject matter of Article 1:102 (Intervention to Perform Another's Duty). In such a case (as a matter of law) the third party is to be regarded as principal, whether or not the recipient is also principal. See as to this special situation the comments to Article 1:102 and to Article 2:101 (1)(b) (Duties during Intervention).

42. **Priority of the principal's free determination of their will** In all legal systems of the EU the intervener is subject to the duty (regarded as self-evident) to indicate to the principal the business being managed (which business the latter may then take over). This is likewise the fundamental position adopted in these Articles (Article 2:101(1)(c)) (Duties during Intervention). In contrast to that provision (which is focused on enduring measures undertaken by the intervener), and also in contrast to Article 2:102(1) (Duties after Intervention) (which concerns the information provided by the *gestor* at the conclusion of his intervention) Article 1:101 (2) is not concerned with the correct discharge of a benevolent intervention in another's affairs which has been rightfully begun. Article 1:101 (2) is concerned instead with the *prerequisites* for commencement of a justified benevolent intervention. Limb (a), just like limb (b), is an ancillary norm for interpretation of the requirement of 'reasonable ground' contained in Article 1:101 (1)(a).

43. **Para (2) limb (a)** Article 1:101 (2)(a) expresses the rule that a person who in the circumstances of the case has a reasonable opportunity of asking the principal whether he wants help and fails to use it only acts as a justified intervener if the principal later approves his act (para (1) limb (b)). For these purposes a reasonable opportunity of contacting the principal suffices. One can imagine a multitude of situations in which the principal would be pleased about the assistance rendered by an intermeddler, but (quite rightly) filled with indignation at the fact that he had not been contacted despite the fact that it had been possible to do so. In such cases the rights of independence and self-determination deserve priority over the protection provided by a well-meaning, but rashly intermeddling fellow citizen. The requirement for and the possibility of a subsequent approval give due expression to those basic values. Only the approval of the act done creates in such cases the relationship of intervener and principal with its preferential legal position for the intervener and a legal position for the

principal which differs clearly from that of an enriched party under the law of unjustified enrichment.

> *Illustration 29*
> One Saturday afternoon, G trims his garden hedge. Out of pure neighbourliness he goes on to cut the hedge belonging to his absent next door neighbour without bothering to ask him for permission. G is not a *gestor.*

44. The intervener is unable to contact the principal However, it would be wrong to infer from limb (a) the converse conclusion that a reasonable ground for intervention will always exist when the intervener is not able to contact the principal. In this instance too it remains of course the case that there must be reasonable cause for intervention by the intervener having regard to all the other circumstances of the case.

> *Illustration 30*
> A knows from his friend B that B has always longed to acquire a particular rare (and correspondingly expensive) stamp to augment his collection. While on holiday A suddenly notices that this stamp is on sale and, on the spur of the moment, buys it then and there. A has entered into this transaction at his own risk, even if he had no opportunity to reach B by telephone before deciding whether to buy. That is because an action of this type could have been postponed, or in other words it was unreasonable to act *without a mandate*. Should B have changed his mind in the meantime and accordingly chooses not to approve the purchase (Article 1:101 (1)(b)), he is not obliged either to take the stamp off A's hands or to reimburse A for the sum he expended in purchase.

> *Illustration 31*
> A's neighbour, N, has failed to pay his telephone bill with due punctuality. That in itself is not a reasonable ground for A to pay the bill in N's stead. However, the matter might be different if the telephone company threatened to disconnect and A knew that N is dependent on maintaining his telephone connection in tact. Only in this latter situation does the matter turn on the additional requirement in para (2)(a).

45. Positive steps required The *gestor* must go so far as to undertake positive steps to discover what the wishes of the principal are or would be if this is something which, according to the wording of the Article, he had "a reasonable opportunity to discover". In view of the modern possibilities of communication (not least, nowadays, the ever increasing availability of mobile telecommunication and electronic mail), the field of application for the law of *negotiorum gestio* has come to occupy a considerably shrunken domain. The easier it is to get in contact with the principal, the lower the probability that a justified *negotiorum gestio* will occur if no attempt to communicate is made.

46. Reasonable opportunity to discover the principal's wishes The effort which must be expended in order to ascertain the actual wishes of the principal depends on the circumstances of the particular case. There must be a reasonable relationship between the significance and urgency of the measure on the one hand and the time and cost expended in seeking out the principal on the other hand. Everything turns on a sense of proportion. There are cases in which the measure called for by the situation is so pressing that no time remains even to pose the question; there are also cases in which it would be unreasonable to waste an hour telephoning the other side of the world in order to obtain permission for effecting provisional repairs; and there are contrasting cases in which one can simply wait.

47. **Contacting the principal can in itself amount to a justified negotiorum gestio** The attempt to reach the principal and to solicit his decision (an endeavour which in some circumstances might be very cost intensive in itself) will as a general rule amount to an act capable of constituting benevolent intervention in another's affairs. If it was reasonable in the circumstances to search for the principal (Article 1:101 (1)(a)) and if the expenditure sustained in making the attempt is incurred reasonably within the meaning of Article 3:101 (Right to Indemnification or Reimbursement), then a claim to reimbursement arises, irrespective of whether in the end it proved possible to reach the principal (or, if he could be reached, to get his approval). That demonstrates, on the other hand, that as a rule, in the absence of special circumstances, one may not proceed to undertake the substantive act of assistance before making that attempt to obtain the principal's instructions where such an attempt is sensible in the circumstances. Of course an attempt to solicit information which, on a reasonable estimation, would appear at the outset to be pointless need not be commenced (or, as the case may turn out, repeated). That is because the costs of such an attempt would not be incurred reasonably within the meaning of Article 3:101 (Right to Indemnification or Reimbursement) and no liability on the part of the principal to reimburse would arise.

48. **Negotiorum gestio or contract?** Whether a contract comes into being between intervener and principal if the principal requests the intervener, in response to the latter's inquiry, to commence (or continue) his undertaking is to be determined in accordance with the Principles of European Contract Law (PECL); it does not need to be decided here. Should a contract be concluded, the rules of benevolent intervention in another's affairs will not of course apply from this point in time because the intervener will be contractually obliged to provide the service (Article 1:103 (a) (Exclusions)). It is also possible that the terms of the contract might extend to the act carried out (as a benevolent intervention) before the contract was concluded – thus substituting, for example, a contractual right to reimbursement of expenditure for that contained in Article 3:101 (Right to Indemnification or Reimbursement) in respect of the intervention preceding the conclusion of the contract. Presumably, unless such an agreement can be inferred from the context, something more than a mere request to continue the act would be required in order that the contractual agreement should have such an extensive effect.

49. **Para (2) limb (b)** Even if the intervener had no reasonable opportunity in the circumstances to contact the principal, the intervener must do what is possible to satisfy the known wishes or probable wishes of the principal. This is the rule contained in para (2) limb (b).

50. **Actual knowledge of the contrary wishes of the principal** It follows as a fundamental principle that a person does not act as a justified intervener if they disregard contrary wishes of the principal of which they know. Whether or not those wishes are 'reasonable' plays no role. Every person is entitled to live their life as they choose within the bounds of what is allowed. One is not obliged to kowtow to judgements volunteered by others – even if one's own viewpoint is skew-whiff.

> *Illustration 32*
> The industrial injuries insurer and the liability insurer fall into a dispute over who will bear responsibility to indemnify in respect of the damage resulting from an accident. There is much in favour of the view that it is a case for a claim under the liability insurance. The industrial injuries insurer therefore demands that payment be made to the entitled injured party. The liability insurer issues a written refusal to do so, insisting (albeit, from the point of view of a neutral observer, somewhat obstinately) that there must be a further scrutiny of the facts of the case. The industrial injuries insurer thereupon pays the injured person. That insurer cannot turn to the liabilities insurer for payment with a claim founded on the notion that they have managed the affairs of the liability insurer. The problem here is one of settlement of liabilities which falls under the law of unjustified enrichment and not the law of benevolent intervention in another's affairs.

51. **Negligent failure to appreciate the principal's wishes** A justified intervention is not only excluded when the intervener positively knows that in acting he would be contradicting the wishes of the principal. The *gestor* must also contemplate ("ought to know") what might represent the presumed wishes of the principal. The significance of this rule, when set against the background of limb (a) (i. e. the obligation to take positive steps to discover the principal's wishes), is perhaps not especially great, but as part of the overall picture is not to be overlooked. When the principal cannot be contacted, the intervener must (still) consider what a reasonable person in his situation would undertake in order to do justice to the principal's wishes.

52. **Standard of care** The standard of care is an objective one (as in the law of tort). There may admittedly be circumstances, of course, in which a quiet consideration of the matter in hand is made decidedly difficult. The same problem arises when it comes to determining whether an intervener has acted with care (Article 2:101(a)) (Duties during Intervention) (which assumes that there *is* a benevolent intervention in another's affairs and resolves the subordinate question whether the intervener is in breach of his duty in the manner in which he has performed). The degree of care required depends on the circumstances; in particular, in emergency cases account must be taken of the fact that the intervener will most likely have had hardly any time for reflection before making a decision. On the other hand, an individual's personal ignorance of matters of general knowledge (which it is legitimate to expect a would-be intervener to know) will not provide an excuse.

> *Illustration 33*
> An armed robbery takes place in the foyer of a bank. A customer leaps into action and attempts to disarm the bank robber. In the struggle a shot is fired and the

bullet lodges in the customer's knee. He has not acted as a justified intervener for the benefit of the bank, because he ought to have known that the bank would have instructed its employees not to defend its stock of cash at the risk of life and limb.

53. **Acting in ignorance of the principal's wishes, but without negligent failure to heed them** The *gestor* does not act without reasonable grounds merely because he does not enjoy the real consent of the principal to act. Para (1) proceeds essentially on the basis that a reasonable ground to act is unaffected by the absence of actual consent as such and, indeed, is to be assessed given an absence of actual consent. The purpose of para (2) is to preclude the existence of a reasonable ground where the wishes of the principal are disregarded, not properly considered or knowingly contradicted. What is decisive is whether the intervener knew, should have known or in the circumstances should have ascertained the principal's contrary wishes. Where the intervener had no reasonable opportunity to inquire as to the principal's wishes, however, and neither knew nor ought to have known that the principal did not want the intervention, the intervener nevertheless acts lawfully if according to the standard of para (1) there was a reasonable ground for intervening. In those (infrequent) cases the principal's wishes, though they are in fact contrary to the act undertaken, do not preclude a justified benevolent intervention in his or her affairs. If the principal subsequently disapproves of the intervention, which according to the information obtainable for the intervener at the material time was adequate and reasonable, this retrospective disapproval does not alter the fact that the benevolent intervention is justified. If this were otherwise almost every principal could free himself of a duty to compensate which has already arisen.

F. Approval by the Principal (para (1)(b))

54. **Significance and consequences of an approval by the principal** Limb (b) of para (1) effects the rule that an approval by the principal transforms an originally unreasonable (and therefore unjustified) intervention into a justified benevolent intervention in another's affairs. An approval can be effected by any express or implied unilateral manifestation of an intention on the part of the principal that legal relations with the intervener in respect of his act be governed by the rules of *negotiorum gestio* – in other words, that the legal rights and duties between the parties should be those which would have existed had there been at the outset a reasonable ground for acting. All that is required, therefore, is an indication by the principal that he intends to be bound by the act. The requirement remains, however, that the intervener acted with a view predominantly to benefit another. If this condition is missing, because the active party pursued his own interest when he intermeddled in another's affairs, the rights and duties of the participants fall to be determined by the law of tort and the law of unjustified enrichment.

55. **Legal nature of the approval** The approval by the principal is a statement of intention. The rules of PECL apply correspondingly to this manifestation of intention. That is the case in particular in relation to PECL art. 1:303 (Notice).

56. An important case An important case, perhaps even the most frequent one, in which the rule on approval applies is the situation in which, before acting, the intervener could have asked the principal and therefore ought to have done so. If the intervener in such a case has in fact acted in a way that accords with the principal's wishes, approval under para (1)(b) at the principal's election is only possible if the intervener has acted with the predominant intention to benefit the principal. The circumstance that the intervener intended to act for the principal's benefit must assume some external manifestation susceptible to proof.

57. Approval without such undue delay as would adversely affect the intervener As a matter of principle, approval is not restricted to a precise period of time. It is important only that the principal approves the act without such undue delay as would adversely affect the intervener. The person whom the intervener intended to benefit has the opportunity of deciding for himself whether the intervener had a good ground for intervening. However, that right can only subsist for an indefinite period of time if (i) the principal was satisfied with the act, *and* (ii) approval at the time when it is given would still be to the benefit of the intervener. If the latter is not the case, the right to approval has expired. It should have been exercised (if at all) promptly, that is to say, without what in the circumstances of the case would amount to an unreasonable delay. The underlying policy of the rule, in other words, is to protect the intervener from legal uncertainty. He is entitled to know where he stands.

Illustration 34
The facts are the same as in illustration 30. When A offers B the stamp and B refuses to reimburse the purchase price, A is free to sell the stamp to a third party. He is equally free to add it to his own stamp collection, if he has one. B no longer has the (inchoate) right to demand the stamp from A. From this point on, if B changes his mind, B can procure the stamp only on the same basis as any third party – by negotiating for purchase of the stamp a contractual price agreeable to both parties.

58. Approval and contract The provisions of this Book are not concerned with whether the approval has contractual effect as between intervener and principal. It might be possible to construe the act of the intervener as an offer (in performance) made to the principal which the principal accepts by approval. Whether that analysis is apt must be determined in the context of particular facts. The question is the same as that which arises in the context of para (2)(a) when an intervener asks the principal what he wants. The general rule always applies that if a contract comes into existence between the parties, the rules of the law of *negotiorum gestio* are ousted so far as the contract extends. See Article 1:103(a) (Exclusions).

59. Approval does not, as a rule, create a contract It is clear at least that in many cases an approval could not create a valid contract. That might be because the intervener, while he intended to benefit the principal, lacked the requisite intention to be legally bound when he performed his act, and the principal when he approves may mean to bind himself but may not mean to do so *by way of contract* (cf. PECL art. 2:102 (Intention)). Equally the intervener may lack the requisite legal capacity to conclude a binding contract. For these reasons some provision within the rules of *negotiorum gestio* itself is necessary as a rule of general application. It does not preclude the possibility that the parties might regulate their relationship by contractual agreement and thus displace the default rule that approval effects a retrospective creation of an intervener-principal relationship.

60. All other requirements of para (1) remain unaffected. All other requirements of para (1) must of course be satisfied in order for approval to create an intervener-principal relationship (see comment *F54* above). Actions carried out for one's own benefit are only susceptible to approval within the law of agency and not within the law of benevolent intervention in another's affairs. Someone who has acted for another, on the other hand, must accept that they can be held to that altruistic intention. It follows, therefore, that he has to surrender to the benefited party everything which he (the active party) has acquired due to the benevolent intervention if the principal ratifies the undertaking. If he chooses to ratify it, the principal must of course bear the associated burdens.

Notes

I. Prevalence and Notion of the Law of Negotiorum Gestio *in General*

1. A treatment of the prevalence of the *negotiorum gestio* concept within the jurisdictions of the European Union has already been given in the introduction above. This includes in particular the different approach of the Common Law in ENGLAND and IRELAND (see Introduction *J58-76*). The absence of a free-standing and cohesive law of *negotiorum gestio* or necessitous intervention in the Common Law has not passed without criticism (see, e. g., *Diamond*, Contract and Tort, 70) and there is not yet a clear consensus about the extent to which the law provides comparable legal redress for the intervener, although the trend seems to favour a more expansive restitutionary liability than the case law has hitherto acknowledged (see *Allen*, 40 (1931) Yale LJ 331, 374 (no equivalent); *Williston*, 22 (1944) Can. Bar Rev. 492, 508 (English law has not adopted *negotiorum gestio* in its entirety, but is not hostile to it in principle); *Marasinghe*, 8 (1976) Ottawa L Rev 573, 574 and 587 (English law has always recognized the doctrine under one heading or another; there is a right to restitution in cases where civilians would grant *actio negotiorum gestorum contraria*); *McCamus*, 11 (1979) Ottawa L Rev 297, 297 ("it seems to have been accepted as a general principle that one who, being an appropriate person to do so, responds to another's emergency by supplying (or by arranging at this own expense for the supply of) needed goods, services, or money, is entitled to restitution for the value of these benefits, provided that their conferral was not intended as a gift"); *Goff and Jones*, Restitution[6], para. 17-026, regretting that a general doctrine of necessitous intervention has not yet developed). Moreover, even where the Common Law does not recognise rights to reimbursement or remuneration, a reasonable ground for action (typically formulated enigmatically in terms of 'necessity') does at least render what is done lawful in relation to the affected party: cf. *Sorrell v. Paget* [1950] 1 KB 252 (CA) (farmer taking in a neighbouring farmer's heifer, which had strayed onto an adjacent railway line, did not commit a tort in taking possession as

he acted in the interest of the owner and the railway company), and Children Act 1989, s. 3(5), which provides that a person without parental resonsibility, but having care of a child may do what is reasonable to safeguard or promote the child's welfare.

2. Those jurisdictions which recognise a distinct legal relationship arising from the justified management of another's affairs formulate the requirements for its existence by and large in similar fashion. The most recent definition may be found in the ESTONIAN Code of Obligations (CC) § 1018 (Definition of *negotiorum gestio*). It reads: "(1) If a person (*negotiorum gestor*) acts for the benefit of another person (principal) without being granted the right or obligated by the principal to perform the act, the *negotiorum gestor* has the rights and obligations provided in §§ 1019-1023 of this Act if: (i) the principal approves of the act; (ii) the act corresponds to the interests and actual or presumed wishes of the principal; (iii) in the case of failure to act, the principal's obligation arising from law to maintain a third party would not be performed in a timely manner or the act is essential in the public interests for another reason. (2) A case where a person has no desire to act for the benefit of another person is not deemed to be *negotiorum gestio*." (This definition is unusual in requiring that the intervention has in fact resulted in benefit to the principal). DUTCH CC art. 6:198 defines *negotiorum gestio (zaakwaarneming)* as "the intentional undertaking of an interest of another, with knowledge and on reasonable grounds, without authority derived under a transaction or under a legal relationship provided for elsewhere in the law" (translation by *Haanappel* et al., Netherlands Business Legislation). PORTUGUESE CC art. 464 reads: "There is a *gestão de negócios* when, without being authorised to do so, a person assumes the direction of another's business in the interest and for the account of the principal concerned". Here too *gestão de negócios* is recognised as a source of a legal relationship (*fontes das obrigações*).

3. Closely related to Portuguese law is Italian law. According to ITALIAN CC art. 1173 ("Sources of Obligations") obligations may arise from contracts, unlawful acts or any other conduct or fact which according to law is apt to give rise to an obligation. This includes benevolent intervention (CC art. 2028 et seq.). The provisions are applicable subject to two requirements: (i) the absence of a pre-existing obligation (so-called *spontaneità*) and (ii) the link to another's sphere of interest (so-called *alienità dell'affare*). Further requirements are *absentia et inscientia domini*, *utiliter coeptum* and an *animus aliena negotia gerendi* (*Breccia*, La gestione d'affari[2], 857-860).

4. GREEK law defines benevolent intervention as the management of another's affairs without an authority or duty on the part of the intervener. As a general rule, such acts constitute undesired interference with the rights and interests of another (Georgiades and Stathopoulos [-*Papanikolaou*] Introduction to Artt. 730-740, no. 1). Exceptionally, however, they may be the emanation of an altruistic commitment for a fellow human being. In this case they fall within the scope of application of Greek CC arts. 730-740 on benevolent intervention. This is an *ex lege* legal relationship: it arises by operation of law and not from a contract. Attempts to construe the law of benevolent intervention as 'quasi-contractual' (see, for example, *Filios*, Enochiko Dikaio I/2, 192) have been rejected in the main as unnecessary, because interveners lacking legal capacity or restricted in their legal capacity are already sufficiently protected by Greek CC art. 735. The location of the law of benevolent intervention, as a matter of systematics, within contract law is justified by reference to substantive similarity with the law of mandate –

in particular as regards the legal consequences (Georgiades and Stathopoulos [-*Papanikolaou*], Introduction to Artt. 730-740, no. 12).

5. The GERMAN CC sets out the law of benevolent intervention in its second book in §§ 677-687. As expressed in CC § 677 an act qualifies as benevolent intervention in another's affairs if a person (the intervener) takes care of some matter for another (the principal) without having been authorized by him or being otherwise entitled to do so in relation to him. An unauthorized management of another's affair is in general determined by the fact that a person attends to another's interest without request, whereby the expenses are incurred by the intervener and the benefit obtained by the principal. A balancing of interests seems to dictate protection for the principal against officious intermeddling or acts serving an intermeddler's own interests (CC §§ 677-681), but equally to grant an intervener whose act constitutes an emanation of community spirit legal security (CC §§ 683-686).

6. The relevant rules of the SPANISH CC which originates from almost the same time, may be found in arts. 1888 ff. In addition provisions on the law of benevolent intervention are comprised in the provincial law of the Foral Community of Navarra (*Fuero Nuevo de Navarra*, Ley 560 and 561 [Act 1/1973 of 1 March, which has adopted the *Compilación del Derecho Civil Foral de Navarra*]). There is no concise definition as there is in Estonian, Dutch and Portuguese law. The introductory phrase of SPANISH CC art. 1888 reads: "A person who consciously undertakes to manage or administer the affairs of another without being authorized by this other person, is obliged ..." and ley 560 of the *Fuero Nuevo de Navarra* states: "If a person undertakes the management of another's affairs in the interest of that other without being authorized, it is obliged ...". The *Tribunal Supremo* in its case law relies on a very narrow concept of benevolent intervention. Benevolent intervention is held to require "that the acts, which aim at the management of another's neglected affairs must be undertaken spontaneously, without authorization or knowledge of the principal and therefore without either explicit or tacit approval and without his objection, with an intention free of interest but without the aim of conferring a pure gift and without the intention to profit" (TS 2 February 1954, RAJ 1954 no. 322 p. 198). Spanish legal writing has voiced the criticism that the case law only very reluctantly resorts to the law of benevolent intervention (*Pasquau Liaño*, La gestión de negocios ajenos, 297). It is therefore of very limited practical importance. The *Tribunal Supremo* prefers the application of other concepts (*Pasquau Liaño*, loc.cit. 301). It is important to state in this context that the ratification of an unauthorized benevolent intervention results in the application of the law of mandate (CC art. 1892). Since the courts are comparatively eager to accept that an intervention has been approved, the law of mandate remains a focal point.

7. The BELGIAN, FRENCH and LUXEMBOURG CC regulate the concept of benevolent intervention in arts. 1372–1375. The *Code Napoléon* does not provide for a comprehensive definition of *gestion d'affaires*. An extensive range of similar definitions may be found in legal commentaries. For BELGIAN law, for example, it is maintained that '*zaakwaarneming*' is a voluntary act – which is not intended to be a benefaction and is not self-interested – in taking care of the interests of another without being under a statutory duty, a duty arising by operation of law, or a contractual duty to do so; it may be with or without the knowledge of the other provided the *zaakwaarnemer* might reasonably assume that the other would have acted in a similar way (*Van Gerven*, Verbintenissenrecht II^{7}, 214). According to *de Page*, Droit Civil Belge II^{3}, no. 1069

p. 1129, it is an act of *gestion d'affaires* if a person who, without being under a contractual, statutory or other duty, intervenes in the affairs of another and acts, or effects a juridcal act, on that other's behalf and in his interest so as to confer benefit. The intervention at its outset must be carried out without the prior knowledge of the principal. For FRENCH law a similar definition is put forward: a benevolent intervention takes place where a person spontaneously and in a reasonable way intervenes in the affairs of another in order to manage them in the interest of that other (JClCiv [*-Bout*], Art. 1372-1375, V° Quasi-Contrats. Gestion d'affaires – Conditions d'existence, Fasc. 10 no. 1). The MALTESE CC follows the French model (CC art. 1013).

8. Like all other early European codifications the AUSTRIAN CC does not contain any statutory definition. According to Klang (*-Stanzl*), ABGB IV/1^2, 890 the prerequisites of a benevolent intervention are as follows: (i) it must concern another's affairs, (ii) there must be an absence of authority to intervene and (iii) there must be an intention to act on another's behalf. In more recent literature the following definition is offered: benevolent intervention is an act at one's own instigation whereby the intervener undertakes to manage another's affair with the intention to advance that other's interests (Schwimann [*-Apathy*] ABGB V^2, § 1035 no. 1; *Koziol and Welser*, Grundriss II^{12}, 364). HUNGARIAN CC § 484 expresses the same concept in these words: "A person proceeding in a matter on behalf of another person without being authorized thereto by agency or otherwise shall be obliged to handle the matter as required by the interest and probable intent of the person in whose favour he has intervened". SLOVENIAN Code of Obligations art. 199 states that the unsolicited intervention in the affairs of another is only permissible if it could not be postponed without the other suffering serious damage or foregoing an obvious advantage. Thus necessity or usefulness belong to the prerequisites for a justified benevolent intervention.

9. This in turn comes close to the classical definitions of *negotiorum gestio* in SCOTTISH law: "The management of the affairs of one who is absent or incapacitated from attending his affairs, spontaneously undertaken without his knowledge, and on the presumption that he would, if aware of the circumstances, have given a mandate for such interference" (*Bell*, Rule 540). *Erskine* 323 in 1816 wrote: "*Negotiorum gestio* forms those obligations which arise from the management of a person's affairs in his absence, by another without a mandate." And *Stair* (Book I Title 8 § 3) wrote in 1693: "Likewise the obligation betwixt negotiators and these, to whose behalf they negotiate, ties to recompense what others (without our command, knowledge, or presence), have necessarily or profitably done for carrying on of our affairs, l. 2.ff neg. gest." [D. 3. 5. 2]).

10. As already mentioned in the introduction the NORDIC COUNTRIES not only lack a general statutory regime for the law of benevolent intervention (see Introduction *I53-57*); the concept hardly plays any role in their contemporary court practice. The starting point for SWEDEN and FINLAND is Ccom Ch. 18 § 10. In DANISH law not even such provisions exist. The (mainly) older Danish literature therefore as a rule bases itself on the Roman law concept of *negotiorum gestio* (*Lassen*, Handlinger paa fremmed formueretsomraade i romersk og dansk ret, 1880, 279-319; *idem*, Haandbog i obligationsretten, Speciel del, 1897, 851-872; *idem*, Lærebog i obligationsrettens specielle del, 1912, 422-439; cf. *Håstad*, Tjänster utan uppdrag, 36 et seq.). In older Swedish literature too the view is maintained on a number of occasions that a self-standing concept of benevolent intervention exists in addition to the specific rules, mentioned earlier, which are to be found in the Commercial Code (for references see

Håstad, loc.cit. 40 et seq.). In contemporary scholarship *Håstad's* influential monograph is of major importance. It demonstrates that the law of benevolent intervention could be inferred from general principles of law by means of analogy. Essentially three groups of cases fall to be distinguished in which the principal is not in a position to attend to his own affairs, namely – as *Håstad* labels them – 'joint interest cases', 'trust cases' and 'possession cases'.

II. *The Activities Covered*

11. In the continental European legal systems it has been stressed time and again that the law of benevolent intervention covers a broad field of activities. Fundamentally it is only strictly personal acts which are excluded. The subject-matter of benevolent intervention under PORTUGUESE law can accordingly be either juridical acts or physical acts. It is not a necessary requirement that the act serves to protect the principal's assets; his interest may also be of a 'moral or spiritual nature' (as it is expressed) such as, for example, his health, his reputation or life and limb (*Antunes Varela*, Obrigações[10], 452). Juridical acts include juridical acts in a strict sense (*negócios jurídicos em sentido estrito*) and unilateral juridical acts which are not legal transactions (*actos jurídicos não negociais*), such as acceptance of payment or collection and discharge of debts (*Almeida Costa*, Obrigações[9], 433; *Antunes Varela*, loc.cit. 451).

12. The field of application of the law of benevolent intervention under GERMAN law is equally broad. The concept of *Geschäftsbesorgung* (CC § 677) covers all acts, whether of a juridical or physical nature and whether economic or non-economic in nature (Staudinger [-*Wittmann*], BGB[13], Introduction to §§ 677 ff, no. 20), which do not merely consist of an omission. The intervener need not undertake the act personally; he may instruct his own employees or third parties (BGH 25 November 1976, BGHZ 67, 368; Palandt [-*Sprau*], BGB[63], § 677, no. 2). Acts of a very short duration may also be considered (*Kropholler*, Studienkommentar BGB[6], § 677, no. 4). Examples are turning a steering wheel to effect a swerve (BGH 27 November 1962, BGHZ 38, 270, 275), giving medical assistance to an unconscious accident victim or making efforts to procure necessary medical assistance for the injured person (BGH 7 November 1960, BGHZ 33, 251), halting a motor vehicle in order to draw the driver's attention to the dangerous condition of the vehicle (BGH 16 March 1965, BGHZ 43, 188), and hindering unlawful interference with another's property (BGH 22 March 1966, NJW 1966, 1360). According to the case law of the BGH it is even the case that 'where a legal transaction is void due to infringement of a statutory prohibition or because it is contrary to *bonos mores* resort may be had to the law of benevolent intervention' (BGH 20 October 1996, NJW 1997, 47 with numerous further references). The intervener in this case, however, is not entitled to reimbursement of expenses (BGH loc.cit.).

13. In GREEK law too it is generally considered that the concept of undertaking (another's) business is to be understood in a wide sense (Georgiades and Stathopoulos [-*Papanikolaou*], Art. 730, no. 2; ErmAK [-*Sakketas*], Art. 730, no. 14). It covers all types of activities and therefore, besides juridical acts, includes rendering services and other acts (*Papanikolaou* and *Sakketas* loc.cit.), such as for instance transporting an injured person to hospital (*Kavkas and Kavkas*, Enochikon Dikaion II/2, 7). Undertaking (another's business) may take the form of an intervener (who is not himself at fault) placing himself in peril in road traffic to prevent an impending accident (*Papanikolaou*

loc.cit. Art. 736 nos. 2 and 11). On the other hand, mere omissions are excluded (*Papanikolaou* loc.cit. no. 3; *Sakketas* loc.cit. no. 15), as are acts which are contrary to law or *bonos mores* (*Papanikolaou* loc.cit. no. 12; *Bosdas*, NoB 18/1970, 769, 772; *Sakketas* loc.cit. no. 24; *Kavkas and Kavkas* loc.cit. 8) and strictly personal acts, i. e. those which do not allow for representation (*Kavkas and Kavkas* loc.cit.). The latter includes acts relating to proceedings (instituting legal proceedings and replying to a statement of claim in another's name) (CA Thessaloniki 2823/1990 EllDik 33/1992, p. 1226; CA Athens 1210/1987 EllDik 29/1988, p. 1606; CA Athens 202/1975 NoB 23/1975, p. 504; CA Thessaloniki 258/1977 Arm 31/1977, p. 385; however, the contrary was held in Areopag 28/1977, NoB 25/1977, p. 959 and as to outcome likewise Areopag 981/1973 NoB 22/1974, p. 509).

14. As regards AUSTRIAN law it is undisputed that both juridical acts and physical acts can be the subject-matter of benevolent intervention (Schwimann [-*Apathy*], ABGB V^2, § 1035 no. 4; Rummel [-*Rummel*], ABGB I^3, § 1035 no. 2. *Meissel*, GoA, 58). Case law supplies a variety of examples (conclusion of a sale contract: OGH 17 May 1950, SZ 23/159; giving a guarantee: OGH 5 March 1963, EvBl 1963/309; OGH 19 October 1976, SZ 49/121; conduct of litigation by a solidary debtor: OGH 24 November 1997, SZ 70/241 [see for details on this problem *Pochmarski/Strauss*. JBl 2002, 353-374]; self-help remedy of sale of perishable goods: OGH 12 April 1950, SZ 23/95; snow clearance: OGH 9 December 1971, JBl 1972, 324; killing an injured dog: OGH 4 November 1981, EvBl 1982/83). According to Klang (-*Stanzl*), ABGB $IV/1^2$, 890, however, the act must be lawful. The discharge of debts of the principal may also be an act of benevolent intervention. If the intervener pays in his own name, the provisions of benevolent intervention supplement the rules on both assignment by operation of law (CC § 1358) and the discharge of another's debt (CC § 1422) (Rummel [-*Rummel*], ABGB I^3 § 1035 no. 3). Acts to protect the principal's person were regarded by the drafters of the ABGB as naturally falling within the scope of benevolent intervention (*v. Zeiller* III § 1036 no. 2 p. 318).

15. In FRANCE, BELGIUM and LUXEMBOURG similar basic principles are accepted. The intervention here may consist either of juridical acts (*actes juridiques*) or physical acts (*actes matériels*) (*Flour/Aubert/Savaux*, Le fait juridique[10], no. 8 p. 10-11; *de Page*, Droit Civil Belge II^3, no. 1076 p. 1143). However, mere omissions (*abstentions*) are excluded from the scope of application (*le Tourneau*, RépDrCiv, VI, v° Gestion d'affaires [2002], no. 50) as are acts which require the principal personally to act or make an evaluation (*Marty and Raynaud*, Obligations I^2, no. 381 p. 394-395 and respectively *Paulus*, Zaakwaarneming, no. 34 p. 33-34 [with the common example of marriage]). The discharge of another's debts too is considered to be within the category of *actes juridiques* (cf. for FRANCE Cass.civ. 11 February 1986, Bull.civ. 1986, I, no. 23 and for BELGIUM Cass. 2 July 1948, Pas. 1948, I, p. 422), and *actes matériels* include acts for the protection of the principal's person (*Flour/Aubert/Savaux*, loc.cit. no. 8 p. 11; CA Liège 26 October 1992, JLMB 1993, 798).

16. The SPANISH CC does not explicitly set out which activities are covered by the law of benevolent intervention. Although the law of mandate, which is often applied by analogy, in SPANISH CC art. 1713 is confined to administrative acts, the *Tribunal Supremo* has not extended this restriction to the law of benevolent intervention. The latter has been held to have a wider scope of application (TS 16 October 1978, RAJ 1978 (2) no. 3076 p. 2606), since it covers not only juridical acts (such as the collec-

tion of debts), but also activities of a purely economic nature and even simple physical activities (TS 2 February 1954, RAJ 1954 no. 322 p. 198). The matter of discharge of another's debt is elaborately provided for in SPANISH CC arts. 1158 et seq. The provision in CC art. 1158 reads: "A person who discharges a debt for another may claim from the debtor what he has rendered, provided he has not done so against the express will of the debtor. In that case he may only claim from the debtor to the extent the performance has been useful for the debtor." The person who discharges the debt with an *animus solvendi* must have neither a contractual nor a personal close relationship to the debtor (TS 8 May 1992, RAJ 1992 (2) no. 3892 p. 5113). An overlap with the law of benevolent intervention is therefore conceivable, but this is by no means always clearly analysed in the case law (contrast TS 8 May 1992 loc.cit. [where only CC art. 1158 was applied] with TS 25 June 1992, RAJ 1992 (3) no. 5474 p. 7160 [where it is expressly stated that a third party, who pays a debt for another in his own name and for his own account, is a benevolent intervener, but not under a duty to continue his intervention]). Although the CC only refers to 'dealings' and 'assets' of the principal, there appears to be unanimity both in academic writing (*Sánchez Jordán*, Gestión de negocios, 106; Paz-Ares/Diez-Picazo/Bercovitz/Salvador [*-Lasarte*], Código Civil I², 1953; Paz-Ares/Díez-Picazo/Bercovitz/Salvador [*-Díez-Picazo*], Código Civil II, 1944) and case law (TS 2 February 1954, RAJ 1954 no. 322 p. 198) that the activities covered by benevolent intervention may also include acts for the personal protection of the principal. Case law on such activities is extremely rare. However, strictly personal acts (in other words, those for which representation is not possible) are excluded under Spanish law from the scope of application of *negotiorum gestio* (*Lacruz Berdejo*, Rev.Crít.Der.Inm. 1975, 249; *Puig Brutau*, Compendio II, 599; *Lete del Río*, Obligaciones II³, 160; *Pasquau Liaño*, La gestión de negocios ajenos, 117).

17. Under ITALIAN law it is undisputed that benevolent intervention may also take the form of a juridical act. Examples are the discharge of another's duty to provide maintenance (Cass. 9 August 1988, no. 4883, Rep.Giur.it. 1988, voce Alimenti, no. 2), the placing of a professional order (Cass. 13 March 1964, no. 550, Foro it. 1965, I, 866), the conclusion of a tenancy agreement (Cass. 23 May 1984, no. 3143, Rep.Giur.it. 1984, voce Gestione d'affari, no. 1), services rendered by a lawyer without instruction (Cass. 13 February 1996, no. 1085, Rep.Giur.it. 1996, voce Avv. e proc., no. 131) and the payment of a share of a several liability which another is due to discharge (Cass. 9 August 1988, no. 4883, in Rep.Giur.it. 1988, voce Alimenti no. 2). The act must be permissible and of a patrimonial character (Cass. 29 May 1952, no. 1555, Foro it. 1953, I, 33). This includes dispositions and extraordinary administrative measures (*Breccia*, La gestione d'affari², 876-877; Cass. 23 July 1960, no. 2122, Giur. it. 1962, I, 1, 92; Cass. 3 March 1954, no. 607, Giur. it. 1954, I, 1, 596; CA Firenze 16 August 1955, Foro it. 1956, I, 93). Conducting litigation in another's name is excluded (Cass. 30 July 1973, no. 2229, Giur. it. 1974, I, 1, 1212) as are other strictly personal acts (such as for example conferring generous benefits from the property of the principal [*Breccia*, loc.cit. 874] or the acceptance of an inheritance [Cass. 10 June 1954, no. 1933, Rep. Giur. it. 1954, voce Successione no. 25]). According to case law, physical acts are also eligible for consideration, including, for example, the pursuit of a stolen motor vehicle in the intervener's own car in order to assist the owner to regain possession (Cass. 23 October 1956, no. 3843, Rep.Giur.it. 1956, voce Gestione d'affari no. 1). It has also been held that a woman who paid the medical expenses and funeral expenses for the

man with whom she cohabited has acted as *gestor* for the heirs (Cass. 28 June 1975, no. 2557, Rep.Giur.it. 1975, voce Gestione d'affari no. 2). However, there do not appear to be any reported decisions in which rescue from imminent danger of personal injury has been characterised as a benevolent intervention.

18. As regards the determination of the scope of application of *zaakwaarneming* under DUTCH Law the distinction between juridical acts and physical acts is likewise of no consequence. Examples of physical acts drawn from Dutch case law include preventing a ship from sinking (CFI Rotterdam 7 March 1939, NedJur 1940 no. 1017 p. 1515), towing a car away (CA s'-Hertogenbosch 8 November 1966, NedJur 1967 no. 368 p. 974 and President Rechtbank Amsterdam 19 December 1991, KG 1992, 50), maintenance of another's animal (HR 20 November 1924, NedJur 1925 p. 153) and maintaing the child of an acquaintance (HR 27 March 1924, NedJur 1924 p. 656). The right to discharge another's debts is the subject matter of a separate provision: CC art. 6:30. As is the case elsewhere, Dutch law follows the principle that strictly personal acts do not come within the law of benevolent intervention. The rule is explained on the basis that in such cases a reasonable ground to act is missing. The *travaux préparatoires* of the CC give the example of conclusion of a contract of employment; that is normally a strictly personal act. Only in the exceptional case where the intervener has actual knowledge of the principal's wishes might a reasonable ground exist (T. M. Parlementaire Geschiedenis Book 6, p. 791). HR 20 September 2002, RvdW 2002 no. 142 concerned the question under which conditions the claim for damages for pain and suffering of the deceased will pass to the heirs. According to Dutch CC art. 6:106 (2) this requires that the deceased informed the other party in his lifetime that he intended to assert the claim for damages. In contrast to the courts of lower instance and the Advocate-General, the Hoge Raad did not discuss the question whether or not that communication might also be undertaken as a benevolent intervention (by the relatives). Instead it was inferred from the circumstances of the case that the patient had the 'presumed intention' to assert his claim for non-economic loss and for that reason the claim devolved on the heirs. The fact that as a consequence of serious injuries the deceased has not been conscious of his condition was held not to be relevant.

19. In SCOTLAND it is similarly understood that the law of *negotiorum gestio* relates to both juridical acts and physical acts (Stair [-*Whitty*], Vol. 15, para 96). However Scots law has not yet extended the doctrine of *negotiorum gestio* to cases where the principal's life or personal safety is endangered. It is argued that the rescuer typically has no intent to charge for his expenses and outlays. Such an extension would impose strict liability on rescued persons, undermining the general rule of the law of delict that a rescuer can only obtain damages for personal injuries sustained in rescuing a person from danger if the defender had negligently created the danger. Finally, it is argued that the compensation of rescuers for their injuries would be more appropriately achieved by other means, such as social insurance or discretionary payments out of public funds (*Whitty* loc.cit., para 102; *Stoljar*, IECL X 17, 141, 149, 150).

20. In the light of the different starting point (see Introduction *I53-57*) it is far more difficult to summarize the situation in the NORDIC COUNTRIES. According to SWEDISH and FINNISH Ccom Ch. 18 § 10 the intervener may 'speak and answer' for the principal. The question what is to be understood by this phrase 'speak and answer' has in the past found three different answers: some have argued that the

subject matter is an authorization to conduct legal proceedings for another, others consider that it includes in addition juridical acts of all types, and the third view contends that besides the authority to conduct litigation the terms only cover (unilateral) juridical acts which are binding on the recipient of the declaration (such as termination of a contract or the interruption of a limitation period) (*Håstad*, Tjänster utan uppdrag, 34 with fn 2-4). The scope of application has likewise not yet been properly resolved. It may be assumed that the question of authority to conduct litigation in another's name is solved by specific provisions of other statutes (SWEDISH Code of Judicial Procedure [*rättegångsbalk* (1942:740)] Chapter 12 §§ 9, 20 and 23 and FINNISH Code of Judicial Procedure [*rättegångsbalk*] of 31 December 1734 Ch. 15 § 4) and therefore Ccom Ch. 18 § 10 according to current understanding at most covers the unilateral juridical acts just mentioned, whereas the conclusion of contracts in the name of another and more especially purely physical acts in the interest of another are excluded. The latter are subject to the general rules (see below note 22). As far as DANISH law is concerned it has been held in HD 19 January 1912, UfR 1912 p. 239 that the conclusion of a compromise settlement between a life insurance company and the surviving dependants of the insured whose cause of death, it seems, was probably suicide can constitute a justified benevolent intervention with respect to the reinsurance company.

21. There are special statutory regimes dealing with a number of particular problems. One of these provides that a bank may accept gifts for the donee without the donee's authorisation (SWEDISH Gifts Act [*lag (1936:83) angående vissa utfästelser om gåva*] § 4; cf. further *Walin*, Lagen om skuldebrev m. m.[2], 241; *Håstad* loc.cit. 225). The provision was restricted to banks as these are subject to special supervision and therefore seem suited to attend as *gestor* to the interests of the donee (*Walin*, loc.cit. 242). Notwithstanding this reasoning, *Håstad* loc.cit. 225-226 considers the provision can be extended by analogy. Case law, however, is largely silent on the issue. SWEDISH HD 28 December 1961, NJA 1961 p. 673 and HD 2 July 1962, NJA 1962 p. 428 held that in principle a private individual's acceptance of a gift for another is possible, although in the first of these two cases the intention to act for another (a child) was absent. FINNISH law has a rule similar to that in the Swedish statute in the Act no. 625 on promises to make a gift (*lag om gåvoutfästelser*) of 31 July 1947 (§ 4). By contrast there is no comparable provision under Danish law.

22. Both the DANISH and the SWEDISH case law contain examples of physical acts of benevolent intervention for another (see in particular DANISH HD 28 November 1976, UfR 1977, 183 [reimbursement of the costs of a fire brigade under the rules of the law of *negotiorum gestio*; a defective pump in a factory pumped oil into the soil and a river; an immediate intervention was necessary, because the defendant had neither sufficient professional competence nor a sufficient number of employees at his disposal] and SWEDISH HD 9 March 1972, NJA 1972, 88 [a fire brigade eliminated the danger created by roof sheeting which had been almost stripped away by a strong wind; however, the firemen did not contact the owner of the house, who was at home; for this reason, and also because the repair had been effected unskilfully, the owner was not held to be obliged to compensate]; see also SWEDISH Hovrätten 24 June 1991, RH 1991:56 [where custody of another's goods is dealt with under the keyword "*negotiorum gestio*"; HD 8 February 1993, NJA 1993, 13, however, seems to prefer a solution invoking the rules of unjustified enrichment law and HD 6 October 1999, NJA

1999, 617 even resorts to landlord and tenant law]). Compensation for expenses incurred in intervention of a physical nature is also the subject matter of some more specific statutes, such as the SWEDISH Act on Proceeding with Abandoned Property and Lost Property etc [*Lag (1974:1066) om förfarande med förverkad egendom och hittegods m. m.*]. The Act on Certain Stolen Goods etc [*Lag (1974:1065) om visst stöldgods m. m.*] obliges the owner who claims recovery of the asset from the person with custody of it to compensate for costs incurred for its improvement and repair (§ 7): see further *Lennander*, Återvinning i konkurs[2], 356; *Hellner*, Om obehörig vinst, 374; *Håstad*, loc.cit. 80. Besides this, *negotiorum gestio* is dealt with in particular in DANISH legal literature in the context of tort law (and treated as a defence) (*von Eyben and Isager*, Lærebog i erstatningsret[5], 51; *Jørgensen*, Kontraktsret, Bind 2, 152; *Vinding Kruse*, Erstatningsretten[5], 48). A similar analysis can be made in SWEDISH and FINNISH law. At the same time, it is maintained that as a matter of principle an intervener without authority cannot be granted more rights than a custodian appointed by a court would enjoy (*Håstad*, loc.cit. 53).

23. The discharge of debts of the principal in general only gives rise to a claim against the principal if he has consented to this beforehand (*Håstad* loc.cit. 109; *Hellner* loc.cit. 378; SWEDISH HD 23 November 1910, NJA 1910 p. 622 [where the payment was made against the debtor's wishes]; HD 28 April 1920, NJA 1920 p. 234; HD 29 December 1945, NJA 1945 p. 728; HD 21 May 1973, NJA 1973 p. 286; see, drawing the dividing line, HD 12 January 1979, NJA 1979 p. 51 [a haulage contractor, importing goods for another business and obliged by statute in such circumstances to discharge that business' debts in respect of custom duties and taxes, performed that duty]). In other words a claim for reimbursement of expenses incurred is not recognised if the payment is made in the knowledge there is neither an authority nor a duty to do so (*Håstad* loc.cit. 133), unless specific rules providing otherwise apply.

24. The COMMON LAW rules of agency and in particular the rules on agency of necessity have already been outlined in the Introduction *J63-70* (in particular *J66-70*). As in other jurisdictions a general restriction to juridical acts does not seem to exist: there may be agency of necessity, for example, in conduct – including omitting to do something: see, for instance, *The San Roman* (1872) LR 3 A & E 583, 593 (Sir *Robert Phillimore*: ship's captain has authority in the interests of the owners of the ship and the cargo to interrupt a journey, delay its continuation and remain in port until danger [here: seizure by foreign naval forces] passed). However, the scope of application of agency of necessity is arguably restricted to specific narrow categories of cases. According to a traditional view an agency of necessity can only arise out of a pre-existing agency: *Hanbury*, Agency[2], 42. More modern judicial decisions (albeit only at County Court level) have not adopted this restriction: see *Palmer v Stear* (1963) 113 LJ 420; *White v J. D. Troups Transport* [1976] CLY 33. Moreover, even in the older cases there are indications that a stranger may have authority implied by law to act for another in a case of emergency: see, for instance, the *dictum* in *Beard v London General Omnibus Co* [1900] 2 QB 530, 532 (*Smith* LJ). The remaining gaps typically have to be bridged by falling back on bailment law (Introduction *J71-72*), unjustified enrichment law (Introduction *J73-76*) and trust law (Introduction *J61*). A case in point is where a legal action is maintained in the interests of one who, by reason of their lack of full capacity, is in need of protection; this may likewise constitute necessitous intervention entitling reimbursement of costs: see *Re Meares* (1879) 10 Ch D 552 (CA).

25. Of course an agent cannot undertake a strictly personal act. However, the demarcation of acts falling within the category of strictly personal acts may differ significantly between Civil Law and Common Law. The most important example may be the execution of a will. Under ENGLISH law (Wills Act 1837, sec. 9) and IRISH law (Succession Act 1965, sec. 78 rule 1) it is possible for someone other than the testator to sign a testamentary instrument on the testator's behalf, provided this is done at the testator's direction and in his presence. If the signature is not rendered by the testator's nominee under a contractual duty to the testator (e. g. as legal adviser to the testator), this act will remain within the scope of this Book. A mere authorisation to act (without a contractual or non-contractual duty to do so) is not excluded by Article 1:103 (a).

III. *Act on 'Another's Behalf' and the Intention to Benefit Another*

26. As already mentioned in the Introduction above at *L99*, many European jurisdictions have a double requirement in their law on benevolent intervention, namely that the *gestor* intervenes (i) in the affairs of 'another' and that he does so (ii) 'on another's behalf'. The second requirement (the intention to act on another's behalf) is universally undisputed, whereas the question whether or not the first requirement (that the intervention must concern the affairs of another – extraneous affairs) is necessary and expedient is the subject matter of a controversial debate in many jurisdictions. Nowhere does there appear to be any marked practical relevance in the sense that the requirement of furtherance *of another's affairs* actually excludes from the scope of benevolent intervention some precisely identifiable category of cases. As set out above in comment A2, Article 1:101 therefore proceeds on the basis that, as a matter of principle, it is only the intention of the *gestor* which converts the matter being taken care of into an 'extraneous affair'.

27. This corresponds to the wording of GERMAN CC § 677. The terms of that provision likewise do not set out an additional requirement that the affair taken care of 'on behalf of another' must also qualify as an extraneous affair with respect to the *gestor* – that is to say, an affair which from an objective perspective would be considered to be the principal's. It is nonetheless often asserted in Germany that an act 'for another' must also be objectively extraneous and that the intervener must know it is extraneous. For example it is not an objectively extraneous affair for a hirer of goods to hire them out to another unlawfully (BGH 13 December 1995, BGHZ 131, 297). The intervener must have both the intention and knowledge that he is taking care of (or at least *also* taking care of) another's affairs. The intervener must thus recognize that the matter attended to is not his own (awareness of the extraneous nature of the business as a cognitive element) and he must act with the intention of serving the interest of another (intention to further another's affairs in a narrow sense, as a purpose-orientated voluntary element) (see to this effect: Soergel [-*Mühl*], BGB[11], § 677, no. 3; MünchKomm [-*Seiler*], BGB[3], § 677, no. 5; *Larenz/Canaris*, Schuldrecht BT II/1[13], p. 438; for further references see also Staudinger [-*Wittmann*], BGB[13], Introduction §§ 677 ff, no. 21). A strong movement within legal writing, however, regards this separate test of 'extraneous nature' as dispensable (as Article 1:101 does); an 'extraneous' affair is always present when an intervener acts with the intention to benefit another (Soergel [-*Beuthien*], BGB[12], § 677 no. 3; *Gursky*, AcP 185 [1985] 13-45;

Wittmann, Begriff und Funktionen der Geschäftsführung ohne Auftrag [1981], passim). Moreover, the requirement of an intention to act for another arises not just from CC § 677 (*"für einen anderen"*), but also from CC § 687 (1) and (2): if a person takes care of another's affair in the mistaken belief it is his own (subsection 1: putative management of one's own affairs [*vermeintliche Eigengeschäftsführung*]), the legal consequences of benevolent intervention do not apply; if a person takes care of another's affair as if it were his own, but knowing it is not (subsection 2: arrogated management of one's own affairs [*angemaßte Eigengeschäftsführung*]), they will not apply without further conditions being satisfied. The prevailing opinion which sticks to the requirement of an 'extraneous affair' defines these 'objectively' extraneous affairs as those affairs which a neutral observer would readily identify as belonging to the legal sphere of someone other than the intervener. According to case law, the mere fact that the objectively extraneous affair has been taken care of creates a (rebuttable) presumption that there was an intention to act on another's behalf; an outward manifestation of the intention is not necessary. In contrast 'neutral' affairs (where an objective observer cannot identify whether they were managed 'for another') qualify as extraneous affairs only if the intervener's intention to act for another becomes discernable for third parties (BGH 20 June 1963, BGHZ 40, 28, 31; MünchKomm [-*Seiler*], BGB^3, § 677, no. 5). The textbook example for a 'neutral' affair is the acquisition of an asset or the conclusion of a contract for services to be rendered in the intervener's own name but for the account of the principal. By contrast, where a health insurer provides benefits in kind to an injured person it is not to be supposed that the insurer is attending to the affairs of a tortfeasor who is liable to compensate the injured person (BGH 8 July 2003, NJW 2003, 3193). ESTONIAN CC § 1018 (1) similarly dispenses with the requirement of an extraneous affair. The intention to benefit another is decisive. § 1018 (2) accordingly provides the clarification that 'a case where a person has no intention to act for the benefit of another is not deemed to be *negotiorum gestio*.'

28. GREEK law requires both the awareness of the intervener that he or she is managing an extraneous affair and the intention to manage it as another's affair. That emerges from a juxtaposition of CC arts. 730, 736 (which do not expressly mention the requirement to act with the intention of benefiting another) with CC arts. 739, 740 (which exclude from the scope of application of justified benevolent intervention acts which are not managed with the intention of benefiting another) (Georgiades and Stathopoulos [-*Papanikolaou*], Art. 730, no. 13). The intention to manage another's affairs does not presuppose legal capacity; in fact this intention need not be declared expressly provided it is manifest (*Papanikolaou* loc.cit. no. 14-15). Besides this, CC art. 730 explicitly requires that the matter taken care of be an 'extraneous affair'. The prevailing opinion is that an affair is extraneous if it concerns another's sphere of interest. A distinction is drawn between affairs objectively extraneous and affairs subjectively extraneous. An affair is objectively extraneous if its apparent substance is such that it belongs to another's legal sphere, because it is the exercise of another's right or the discharge of another's duty. By contrast a subjectively extraneous affair appears neutral from an objective perspective, but by means of the intervener's intention to manage another's affair takes on an extraneous nature. The prime example in Greece too is the acquisition of an asset for another (Georgiades and Stathopoulos [-*Papanikolaou*], Art. 730, no. 4).

29. Likewise PORTUGUESE law contains an *animus aliena negotia gerendi* as a requirement for the application of the rules on justified benevolent intervention: only a person acting with "*intenção de gerir para outrem*" – that is to say, a person who intends to act in the interest of and for the account of another (*Vaz Serra*, BolMinJus 66 [1957] 95) – will qualify as a *gestor* (CC art. 464). Portuguese law has also held on to the traditional requirement of *negotium alienum*. *Vaz Serra*, on whose draft (see art. 1, no. 4 of the draft) the wording of the law is based, did not further expound on the problem of this criterion; he considered it would not accord with the rationale of the law of benevolent intervention to restrict the application to the management of extraneous affairs (loc.cit. 69).

30. AUSTRIAN law similarly requires a *Fremdgeschäftsführungswillen* (i. e. the intention to act on another's behalf) on the part of the intervener (Schwimann [-*Apathy*], ABGB V^{2}, § 1035 no. 6; *Koziol and Welser*, Grundriss II^{12}, 364; *Meissel*, GoA, 79 et seq.; OGH 19 November 1974, SZ 47/130; OGH 11 July 2001, RIS-Justiz RS0085741 [no benevolent intervention if a pretender to the inheritance operates a kiosk against the express wishes of the actual heir]; but see for a critical discussion *Fötschl*, ERPL 2002, 550, 570). Austrian CC § 1036 (intervention in order to prevent impending damage) does not expressly set out the requirement of an intention to act on another's behalf, but it will usually be a feature of such cases (*Meissel*, GoA, 79). Emergency actions undertaken in the face of a common danger are dealt with by the law of unjustified enrichment (CC § 1043). Intervention other than in a situation of emergency must be beneficial for the principal (CC § 1037). Besides the requirement of an intention to act on another's behalf, CC §§ 1036 and 1037 expressly require that the intervener manages an 'extraneous affair'. OGH 11 November 1987, SZ 60/235, for instance, dismissed a claim in a case where a person erradicated damage to the ground water on his own property which had been caused by an oil supplier because it was not another's affair. Austrian CC regards "intermeddling with the affairs of another" (CC § 1035) as a rule as constituting an infringement of rights. However, the boundary between an 'extraneous' affair and an itnervener's 'own' affair is bedevilled with numerous problems of demarcation; it is also acknowledged that the 'extraneous' nature of an affair may be derived from the intention of the intervener alone (*Meissel*, GoA, 65). SLOVENIAN law produces the same outcome (*Cigoj*, Teorija obligacij, 245).

31. In both FRANCE and BELGIUM scholarly writing unanimously takes the view that a *gestion d'affaires* requires an intention to act on another's behalf (see, for France, *Mazeaud and Chabas*, Leçons de droit civil II,1^{9}, no. 675 p. 808-809; for Belgium, *Stijns/Van Gerven/Wéry*, JT 1996, no. 17 p. 696). Where a person manages the affairs of another in the firm belief that they are his own, the conduct does not constitute benevolent intervention (French Cass.civ. 25 June 1919, D. 1923, I, 223; S. 1921, I, 12). (See also for MALTA CC art. 1019: "Where the agent was under the impression that he was managing his own affairs, he shall not be entitled to any indemnity beyond the benefit which the party interested may have actually derived"). BELGIAN and FRENCH CC art. 1372 ("*lorsque volontairement on gère l'affaire d'autrui*") combines the requirements of an extraneous affair and the intervener's intention to act on another's behalf in a more or less inseparable fashion. Both elements likewise coalesce in scholarly treatment of the subject (see, for example, for Belgium *Paulus*, Zaakwaarneming, no. 33 p. 33 and B. H.Verb. [-*Roodhooft*] Hdst. V, De quasi-contracten, no. 2239; for

France *Mazeaud and Chabas*, Obligations[9], no. 675 p. 808). Some French authors even set out the *intention de gérer les affaires d'autrui* and the *utilité* of the intervention as the sole requirements of benevolent intervention (e. g. JClCiv [-*Bout*], Art. 1372-1375, V° Quasi-Contrats. Gestion d'affaires – Conditions d'existence (1996), Fasc. 10, no. 19 et seq.). The intention to act on another's behalf may be missing, for example, where two persons who have provided negotiable instruments as security obtain a release of the instruments from a creditor of the bankrupt borrower by repaying the outstanding loan; this act has been held to be undertaken in the sole interest of those who provided the security, even though it may lead to a third provider of security regaining his negotiable instruments (CFI Hasselt 25 June 1990, RW 1991-92, 925). A further example of lack of intention to act on another's behalf is where a son-in-law equips and furnishes a flat in a part of his father-in-law's house (CA Rouen 15 January 1992, Juris Data 1992-040373). Recent French legal writing introduces a further distinction, namely between benevolent intervention with an altruistic intention (so-called *gestion d'affaires désintéressée*) and benevolent intervention without an altruistic intention of the intervener (so-called *gestion d'affaires intéressée*); in the latter case the objective characterization of an intervention as being undertaken 'on another's behalf' merges into the requirement of *utilité*, which is assessed from an objective perspective. As regards *gestion d'affaires désintéressée*, this appears to turn solely on the altruistic intention of the intervener; there is no scrutiny of whether the affair managed is objectively extraneous (see, in particular, Cass.civ. 16 November 1955, J. C. P. 1956 II no. 9087, note *Esmein;* RTD civ 1956, p. 356, obs. *Mazeaud*: the rescue of an unconscious driver by a passenger, who himself sustained bad injuries as a result of the rescue, was considered a benevolent intervention on behalf of the insurance company with whom the car was insured, although the driver as a member of the policy holder's family was not himself insured).

32. By contrast SPANISH CC art. 1888 only refers to an extraneous act (*alieneidad*), in other words interference with the legal sphere of the principal (*Pasquau Liaño*, La gestión de negocios ajenos, 110) as a requirement for the application of the law of benevolent intervention. Yet under Spanish law too it is undisputed that the *animus aliena negotia gerendi* represents an indispensable requirement of a benevolent intervention in another's affairs. Only a person acting with an altruistic intention will qualify as a *gestor* (*Pasquau Liaño*, loc.cit. 61), or, as the Supreme Court has put it, acts "with a disinterested intention, but without the purpose of making a donation, and without the intention to make a profit" (TS 2 February 1954, RAJ 1954 no. 322 p. 198). Essential elements are the intervener's actual knowledge that the interest concerned is extraneous and the intervener's disinterested wish to protect it (*Puig Brutau*, Compendio II, 599; *Sánchez Jordán*, Gestión de negocios, 151). Consequently, the management of another's affairs in the mistaken belief they are one's own is exclusively governed by unjustified enrichment law or, depending on the facts, tort law (*Lacruz Berdejo*, Rev.Crít.Der.Inm. 1975, 253).

33. ITALIAN law likewise has a requirement that the affair managed be extraneous (*"alienità" dell'affare*). This can be inferred from CC art. 2028 (*gestione di un affare* "altrui"). The prevailing view is that whether an act relates to another's affair is to be assessed in line with an objective standard (*Aru*, Gestione d'affari, 8; *Fane*, Solidarietà sociale e gestione di affari altrui, 78; Cass. 5 April 1971, no. 976, Rep.Giur.it. 1971, voce Gestione d'affari, c. 1537). It is said to be a prerequisite that the management concerns another's legal sphere (*Breccia*, La gestione di affari[2], 858-859) or property (*Cercone*,

Codice civile a cura di Rescigno, sub. Art. 2028 CC). However, it is accepted that if there is no inherent objective connection to another's sphere, the issue will depend on the intention of the intervener; Italian law thus also recognizes the category of acts which are extraneous merely from a subjective point of view (*negozi soggettivamente altrui*). The details are a matter of dispute. Legal writing resolves the issue in disparate fashion. A growing body of opinion now equates an 'extraneous affair' with the pursuit of another's interest (*Pane*, loc.cit. 77-80), which effectively reconciles the objective and the subjective perspective (*Sirena*, Gestione di affari, 236-237). It is undisputed that from the onset of his action the intervener must act with the intention to act on behalf of the principal (*Aru* loc.cit. 13). This intention need not necessarily be explicitly stated; it may also be inferred form the circumstances (Cass. 13 March 1964, no. 550, Foro it. 1965, I, 866). The intention to benefit another was affirmed, for example, in a case where an heir incurred expenses in administering the deceased's estate, which administration benefited co-heirs (Cass. 30 January 2002, Foro it. Mass. 1222). By contrast the intention to benefit another was held to be absent where a seller of real estate sold the property to a second purchaser after it had already been sold under a written contract (Cass. 4 November 1995, no. 11519, Giur.it. 1996, I, 1, 902).

34. A *zaakwaarneming* under DUTCH CC art. 6:198 requires that a person voluntarily, knowingly and with a reasonable ground attends to the interest of another (*eens anders belang*). Activities covered by benevolent intervention may be acts which aim at the protection, preservation or the augmentation of legal interests (*rechtsgoederen*) of another (Asser [-*Hartkamp*], Verbintenissenrecht III^{10}, no. 291). Surprisingly few particulars can be found neither in case law nor legal writing as to when a person is to be regarded as attending to "*een anders belang*". Instead the focus is on the existence of an intention to act on another's behalf, which is understood to be the crucial prerequisite of *zaakwaarneming* (see for instance HR 10 April 1953, NedJur 1953, 630; CFI Almelo 24 November 1954, NedJur 1955, 753 and CFI Maastricht 7 April 2004, LJN-number AP4483, www.rechtspraak.nl).

35. SCOTTISH law likewise relies on the category of an extraneous affair: see above note no. 9.

36. Within the SCANDINAVIAN legal systems there appears to be no discussion in detail of the concept of an 'extraneous' affair or the intention to act on another's behalf. However, it may nonetheless be inferred from HD 28 December 1961, NJA 1961 p. 673 that according to SWEDISH law a benevolent intervention may only be recognised if the *gestor* acts with the intention of interfering in another's legal sphere. As regards DANISH case law, one might point to HD 18 May 1995, UfR 1995 p. 691, a case where it may be doubted whether the *gestor* acted with the intention to act on another's behalf. The case concerned a contract for the sale of land which ostensibly had been concluded. The putative purchaser had made an advance payment to the estate agent, but could not claim it back from the estate agent because of the latter's bankruptcy. According to trade practice, the broker's commission would be met by the seller. The court therefore granted the buyer a claim for compensation against the seller, as he (the seller) was 'closer' to bearing the risk of repayment. However, a further claim of the putative buyer to recover the wasted costs of enforcement which was likewise founded on the law of benevolent intervention was dismissed.

37. For agency of necessity the COMMON LAW requires that the agent acts in the interest of his principal. Of necessity this excludes acts which are a collusion with or otherwise

manifestly intended to benefit third parties, rather than the principal. So, for example, there can be no question of a ship's captain having authority to create a security interest in his principal's property (the ship) if the purpose of the transaction is merely to benefit an existing creditor: *The Empire of Peace* (1869) 39 LJ (N. S.) Adm 12 (Sir *R. J. Phillimore*) (bottomry bond, which was intended simply to enhance the security of a pre-existing debt owed by the principal without advantage procured for the principal was ineffective as debt already secured). The same applies where a captain enters into a contract of salvage with the aim of benefiting the salvor rather than in good faith in the interests of the principal whose property is to be salvaged: *The Theodore* (1858) Swab 351, 166 ER 1163 (Dr *Lushington*). (See also *Prager v. Blatspiel, Stamp & Heacock Ltd* [1924] 1 KB 566, 572-573 where *McCardie* J indicates as one ground of his decision (albeit without elaborating the point) that the agent must act in good faith.) A professed intention to act on behalf of another may render a person a self-appointed agent and liable to account for benefits obtained: see Chapter 2, Art. 2:102, Notes I, 22. Where the intervener has caused loss to the putative principal, however, an agency will be denied if the intervener has acted exclusively or predominantly in their own interest: cf. *Sachs v. Miklos* [1948] 2 KB 23, 29 (Lord *Goddard* CJ), where the defendant had sold the plaintiff's furniture solely in order to use the room which the furniture occupied, followed in *Anderson v. Anderson* [1980] CLY 133 (*Fay* J) (defence of sale through agency of necessity unavailable), and see also *Beaman v. ARTS Ltd* [1948] 2 All ER 89, 94E (*Denning* J), holding that a person who stores things for an absent friend who cannot be contacted and then gives them away because they have decayed or have little value and the storage takes up space or costs money commits the tort of conversion – but see now also the statutory power of sale in the Torts (Interference with Goods) Act 1977, sec. 12, which protects an involuntary bailee. Equally, one reason for the common law's unwillingness to recognise a right to a reward for the finder of another's property may be that preservation of property by a finder is deemed to be in one's own (finder's) interest – a preserving for oneself rather than the 'true' owner – because in the event that the owner does not or cannot claim it, title being relative, the finder is an owner subject only to the claims of one who is better entitled (i.e, the finder's title becomes impregnable when the true owner's claim in tort is time-barred): cf. *Sutton v. Buck* (1810) 2 Taunt 302 at 312, 129 ER 1094 at 1098 (Lord *Mansfield* CJ: salvaging, so far from being a duty to benefit the owner, is a mode of entitling oneself to the property in case the owner does not claim it), which case, however, only lays down the principle that there is no *duty* on a stranger to intervene to salvage wreck from navigable river.

IV. *The Preponderance of the Intention to Benefit Another; Simultaneous Pursuit of One's Own Interests*

38. None of the European concepts of the law of benevolent intervention requires that a person acts *exclusively* for altruistic reasons. This, as is generally accepted, would be unrealistic, because the intervener will often also be pursuing his or her own interests at the same time. Consequently, benevolent intervention is only held to be inapplicable if the relationship between the intention to benefit another and the intention to serve one's own interests is reversed, the intervener predominantly attending to his own interests and only secondarily attending to another's interests. However, no na-

tional legal system contains a clear provision which states with clarity that the intervener must act with the 'predominant' intention to benefit another (as Article 1:101(1) does).

39. GERMAN case law has always emphasized that an intention to benefit another is not excluded by the fact the intervener has also acted in pursuit of own interests (BGH 24 October 1974, BGHZ 63, 167; BGH 8 March 1990, BGHZ 110, 313). Such cases are referred to as cases involving 'affairs which are also another's' (*auch fremde Geschäfte*). The (rebuttable) presumption of intention to benefit another also applies to these cases (BGH 18 September 1986, BGHZ 98, 235, 240; *Palandt* [-*Sprau*], BGB[63]2, § 677, no. 6; see, however, *Medicus*, Schuldrecht II BT[12], nos. 620, 630).

40. Under GREEK law it is similarly universally accepted that benevolent intervention is not excluded by the intervener serving his own interests as well as those of another. However, such coexistence of interests may make it more difficult to fulfill the requirement of the intention to act on another's behalf (Georgiades and Stathopoulos [-*Papanikolaou*], Art. 730, no. 10; CA Athens 2896/1977, NoB 26/1978 p. 223 [where in a case of discharge of another's debt the court took the view that there was no *animus aliena negotia gerendi*] and ErmAK [-*Sakketas*], Art. 730, no. 22 [if an affair is partly another's interest and partly the intervener's own, benevolent intervention can apply, but if the intervener acts solely to further his own interests benevolent intervention will not apply even if the act is also beneficial for other persons]).

41. This accords with the position under PORTUGUESE law. The application of the provisions on benevolent interventions remains possible where the intervener acts on behalf of another and on his own behalf at the same time, as long as he acts with the intention to benefit another in regard to the extraneous affair (*Vaz Serra*, BolMinJus 66 [1957], 97). Typical cases of coexistence of interests concern interveners who act in the course of their profession or trade (as, for instance, in STJ 22 April 1986, BolMinJus 356 [1986], 352).

42. Likewise in AUSTRIA the law on benevolent intervention in general remains applicable even if the intervention for another also serves the *gestor's* own interests at the same time. Both case law (OGH 7 December 1972, SZ 45/137; OGH 8 November 1984, JBl 1985, 421, 423; OGH 3 October 1996 RdW 1997, 275) and academic writing (Rummel [-*Rummel*], ABGB I^3, § 1035 no. 5, Schwimann [-*Apathy*], ABGB V^2, § 1035 no. 5, *Meissel*, GoA, 66 et seq.) recognise the concept which in Austria too is termed 'affairs which are also another's' (*auch fremde Geschäfte*). Older case law had required an intervention for another free of self-interest (for references see *Rummel* and *Meissel* loc.cit), and phrases which point in this direction reappear in some more recent judgments (e.g. OGH 28 January 1997,WBl 1997, 214 [full text in RIS-Justiz RS0085741] and OGH 27 November 2001, RIS-Justiz RS0023484). However, this does not seem to indicate a general change of the established practice of the courts as set out in the leading case OGH 7 December 1972, SZ 45/137. The terms of Article 1:101 seem to be in line with the current state of Austrian law.

43. Under BELGIAN law the question whether and, if so, to what extent an intervener may also pursue his own interests without loosing his status of benevolent intervener is still a matter of dispute (for details see *Stijns/Van Gerven/Wéry*, JT 1996, no. 17 p. 697). As far as FRENCH law is concerned, it is accepted that the law of benevolent intervention may apply although the intervener does not act solely with the intention to further another's interests, acting partly in his own interest (*Mazeaud and Chabas*,

Leçons de droit civil II,1[9] no. 675 p. 808-809). Some authors even consider that a tendency can be discerned in recent case law to the effect that benevolent intervention will be recognized even if the intervener lacks any altruistic intention. This is explained by the development of a distinction between 'classic' benevolent intervention (acting with an altruistic motive – *gestion d'affaires désintéressée* –) and benevolent intervention without an altruistic motive (the so-called *gestion d'affaires intéressée*). As a result, a dualistic system of the law of benevolent intervention has emerged. A *gestion d'affaires désintéressée* only requires that from the subjective perspective of the intervener the act appeared at the outset to be beneficial, whereas the *gestion d'affaires intéressée* requires that from an objective perspective the act must ultimately prove to be beneficial (JClCiv [-*Bout*], Art. 1372-1375, V° Quasi-Contrats. Gestion d'affaires – Conditions d'existence, Fasc. 10, no. 19 et seq.). In at least one instance French case law has adopted this terminological distinction (CA Orléons 14 September 1993, Juris Data 1993-045124).

44. SPANISH legal writing unanimously maintains that a benevolent intervention will only be precluded if the intervener places the principal's interest second to his own interests (*Lacruz Berdejo*, Rev.Crít.Der.Inm. 1975, 257; *Sánchez Jordán*, La gestión de negocios ajenos, 151; *Díez-Picazo and Gullón*, Sistema II, 567). Although there is no elaborate doctrine on 'affairs which are also another's', the approach taken is in substance quite similar to that of German law (*Sánchez Jordán*, loc.cit. 156). One justification may be an argument *e contrario* from CC art. 1891, according to which the intervener is liable for accidental risks if he has put the interest of the principal second. In case law it has been held that a co-owner who, acting in his own name, had a second elevator built into an apartment house and in so doing (also) pursued his own interests might act with *animus aliena negotia gerendi* (CA Las Palmas 6 November 1985, La Ley 86 [1] no. 6091 p. 540); similarly this was also held to apply where one of several joint heirs fed animals forming part of the deceased's estate before the estate was distributed (TS 3 January 1962, RAJ 1962 [1] no. 265 p. 165; for details see *Pasquau Liaño*, La gestión de negocios ajenos, 237).

45. The rule contained in Article 1:101 also states the position of ITALIAN law. The *gestor* need not act exclusively in the interests of the principal, but he or she must act predominantly in the principal's interests (judged from an objective perspective) (Cass. 13 March 1964, no. 550, Foro it. 1965, I, 866). Where a part of the activity which concerns the intervener's own interests can clearly be distinguished from those parts of the activity which serve another's interests, the rules on benevolent intervention apply only to those activities which serve the interest of another (*Aru*, Gestione d'affari, 8). Benevolent intervention comes into play where one parent provides maintenances also on behalf of the other parent (Cass. 5 December 1996, no. 10849, Rep.Giur.it. 1997, voce Filiazione, no. 38) or where a *gestor* attends to the interests of multiple owners or heirs when he himself is one of them (Cass. 11 July 1978, no. 3479, Giur. it. 1979, I, 1,820; Cass. 4 May 1985, no. 2795, Rep.Giur.it. 1985, voce Responsabilità no. 154).

46. DUTCH law recognises the principle that a *gestor* may attend to own interests alongside the interests of the principal. The son who arranges for the provisional administration of his father's estate after the latter's death is *gestor* for his siblings even though he acts on his own behalf at the same time. An intervener may attend to the interests of another and at the same time pursue his personal interests. The concept of

an affair which is 'also another's' is thus recognized (T. M. Parlementaire Geschiedenis VI, 790; Asser [-*Hartkamp*], Verbintenissenrecht III[10], no. 293, p. 308; Verbintenissenrecht [-*Heisterkamp*], Art. 6:198 BW, note 11; see also HR 24 January 1902, W 7714 and HR 26 June 1959, NedJur 1959 no. 586, p. 1284).

47. Under SCOTS law too the pursuit of one's own interests alongside an intention to advance another's interest does not fundamentally preclude the existence of a relationship of *negotiorum gestio* (*Kolbin & Sons v. William Kinnear & Co.* 1931 SLT (HL) 464; *SMT Sales & Services Co. Ltd.* 1954 SLT (ShCt) 107). However, it is not yet completely resolved what the balance must be between one's own interest and the interest of another. The boundary line seems to be drawn where a person acts selfishly, that is to say, with the predominant intention of advancing his own interests. In such instances the case is one for the law of unjustified enrichment or tort law (Stair [-*Whitty*], vol. 15, no. 138; see, however, *Gretton*, SLT 1978, 145). As a general rule compensation under the law of benevolent intervention is available only for expenses which have not been incurred to advance one's own interest (*Leslie*, SLT 1981, 259, 260; *idem*, Jur.Rev. 1983, 32, 33).

48. Within SCANDINAVIAN case law too there are cases in which the intervener has pursued his own interest as well as another's. In DANISH HD 3 December 1936, UfR 1937, 357, the Danish Ministry of Foreign Affairs arranged at the expense of the Danish charterer for the return of Danish seamen who had missed the departure of their vessel from a Columbian port and could not remain in Columbia for want of visa. The shipping company had been informed in advance, but although obliged to do so had refused to come to the seamen's assistance. The charterer was granted a claim against the shipping company for reimbursement of expenses incurred, although in effecting return carriage the chraterer had also acted in his own interest. Danish HD 19 January 1912, UfR 1912, 239 concerned compensation between several reinsurance companies as a result of a compromise settlement concluded by one of the reinsurance companies on behalf of them all. SWEDISH HD 28 December 1961, NJA 1961, 673 dismissed a claim alleged to have arisen out of *negotiorum gestio* for the reason that the defendant had not accepted the gift in dispute either for herself or for the claimant child.

49. The COMMON LAW on this point aspires to ensure the principal is fully protected. Agency by ratification is not precluded by the fact that the agent is (subjectively) also acting in furtherance of his own interests provided the agent is (objectively) demonstrably acting on behalf of the principal: *Re Tiedemann and Ledermann Frères* [1899] 2 QB 66. Moreover, where the agent is only ostensibly acting on the principal's behalf the principal is nonetheless able to obtain from the agent the fruits of an unauthorised venture (so precluding the agent from profiting from his breach of duty). On the other hand, if the agent acts exclusively in their own interest, though in the principal's name, there will be no agency of necessity to the detriment of the principal (i. e. by recognising a burdensome transaction of the agent with a third party and holding the principal bound by it, or where the 'agency' would be at the principal's expense): cf. *The Alexander* (1842) 1 W Rob 346 at 355-356, 166 ER 602 at 606 (Dr *Lushington*). Notwithstanding this there is some doubtful indication in more modern case law that the performance of a 'duty' which is no more than a matter of self-interest (i. e., its non-performance does not entitle the other party to any redress, but merely excludes or restricts a possible claim of the 'obliged' party) does not preclude the party performing

the 'duty' from also acting as an agent of necessity for the other party. It has been held (though only at County Court level) that a buyer of 'eating' strawberries to whom the seller delivers a proportion which are unfit for eating (but who apparently cannot or does not reject and return them, but instead claims a diminution in price) acts as agent of necessity in selling them to a jam-maker: see (1932) 76 SJ 663. (Until 1995, when the Sale and Supply of Goods Act 1994, sec. 3(1), inserted a new sec. 35A into the Sale of Goods Act 1979 – which replaced the Sale of Goods Act 1893 – the buyer had no right to reject part only of the goods supplied under an inseverable contract of sale since partial acceptance precluded repudiation for breach of condition: see secs. 11(4) and 53(1) of the 1979 Act; the former section and thus also indirectly the latter are now subject to s. 35A.) The proposition seems doubtful, however, because it is difficult to see how in such circumstances the agent is acting on behalf of anyone but himself. Where the breach of contract relates to the quality of the goods, the reduction in the price for the accepted goods which the buyer may set up against the purchaser for breach of warranty is *prima facie* determined by the difference between the value the goods would have had if they had fulfilled the warranty and the market value of the actual goods supplied: Sale of Goods Act 1979, s. 53(3). Moreover, where the buyer resells the goods at a time proximate to delivery and to a purchaser with knowledge of the (inferior) quality, that resale price provides strong evidence of their actual value: see Benjamin (*-Harris*), Sale of Goods[6], § 17-052. Thus on a claim for the contract price by the unpaid seller, the buyer was liable to pay that price less the difference between the market value of 'eating' strawberries and the price that could have been obtained (and in this case was obtained) by a sub-sale to a jam-maker. Assuming (as the judge did) that the contract price reflected the market value of 'eating' strawberries, the defendant buyer was in all events liable under the Sale of Goods Act to pay the realisable value of the strawberries supplied. Sale to the jam maker did not affect the seller's position, but merely ensured that the buyer obtained the value of the inferior strawberries which he would in any case have to pay to the seller. The application of "agency of necessity" principles was entirely unnecessary to achieve the judgment outcome. Indeed, so far as it implied that the buyer was acting in the seller's interest and would be liable to account to the seller for the sub-sale, the application of the doctrine seems profoundly misleading. Academic literature supports the view that an individual who acts predominantly in their own interests is not conducting a "necessitous intervention": see *McCamus*, 11 (1979) Ottawa L Rev 297, 253 n 12, explaining *Falcke v. Scottish Imperial Insurance Co* (1886) 34 Ch D 234 on the basis that the benefit of another was merely incidental to the pursuit of one's own interests. See also *Re Leslie* (1883) 23 Ch D 552, where the husband, who paid premimums on an insurance policy taken out by his wife, had himself an interest in the policy, and the claim of his personal representatives for a lien on the policy failed. Any redress for expenditure made to safeguard one's own interest and benefiting another will be referable to other principles such as those governing contribution or subrogation. That the intervener has *some* interest in the matter, however, does not of itself preclude a restitutionary claim and the case law is not entirely clear on the exact boundary line: cf. *Williams v. Wentworth* (1842) 5 Beav 325, 49 ER 603 (Lord *Langdale* MR) (where a creditor could obtain reimbursement of the costs of litigation for the protection of his debtor).

V. *In Particular: Performance on the Basis of a Void Contract for Services*

50. A problem much discussed in many legal systems is whether services rendered under a void contract for services can constitute a benevolent intervention, or whether this question must be answered in the negative because the requirement to act with the intention to benefit another is absent. GERMAN law in such cases applies the law of benevolent intervention (see for instance BGH 31 January 1963, BGHZ 39, 87, 90; BGH 24 September 1987, BGHZ 101, 393, 399; BGH 30 September 1993, NJW 1993, 3196; BGH 10 October 1996, NJW 1997, 47, 48; BGH 20 October 1996, NJW 1997, 47 and (where the contract was void because administrative consent was withheld) BGH 4 December 2003, BGHZ 157, 168; see also BGH 4 November 2004, RIW 2005, 144 where the contract was void for want of the required formality). The justification given is that an erroneous belief in an obligation to perform does not preclude benevolent intervention. However, a growing body of opinion holds this approach to be wrong because by this means provisions which specifically address such situations are circumvented. This relates in particular to the statutory provisions on reversal of transactions in CC §§ 812 ff (unjustified enrichment law) and in particular CC §§ 814, 817 sentence 2 and 818 (3) (so, *inter alia*, *Medicus*, Schuldrecht II BT[12], no. 622; MünchKomm [*-Seiler*], BGB[3], § 677, no. 41).

51. GREEK case law has held the law of benevolent intervention applicable to cases of void contracts of mandate for the purchase of land. (At the time those cases were decided it was assumed that the contract of mandate – like the main contract itself – was subject to the requirement of a notarised deed. However, the line of authority to that effect was abandoned in 1975; since then it has been held that the mandate does not require any specific form: Areopag 104/1975 NoB 23/1975, p. 653; affirmed by Areopag 1489/1982 NoB 31/1983, p. 1353). The acquisition of the land which was effected in accordance with the void contract of mandate was categorised as a subjectively extraneous affair if the agent implicitly indicated the intention to acquire the land for another. In such instances the courts have in consequence applied the law of benevolent intervention (Areopag 161/1974 NoB 22/1974 p. 1048). However, in the case of a void bilateral contract, the application of the rules on benevolent intervention seems doubtful. Greek legal writing assumes that if the contract is void there is no mandate in the sense of CC art. 730 (Georgiades and Stathopoulos [*-Papanikolaou*], Art. 730, no. 21; ErmAK [*-Sakettas*], Art. 730, no. 31), but the additional requirement of an intention to benefit another is considered to be missing (*Papanikolaou*, loc.cit. no. 23).

52. PORTUGUESE legal writing (case law on this point seems to be non-existent) likewise argues in favour of the application of the law on benevolent intervention where services are rendered on the basis of a void contract – at any rate if the person acting did not know that the contract was void. The absence of an 'authority' is accordingly to be assessed objectively (*Vieira Gomes*, Gestão de negócios, 66 and *Vaz Serra*, BolMinJus 66 [1957], 104-105).

53. The starting point for AUSTRIAN law is different. Here (in agreement with the solution adopted by this draft) the view is taken that a service rendered under a contract which (unknown to the parties) is void is rendered without the intention to benefit another (OGH 19 November 1974, SZ 47/130; OGH 17 January 1979, SZ 52/

9; for further case law see RIS-Justiz RS 0019735). Legal writing endorses that view (Schwimann [-*Apathy*], ABGB V², § 1035 no. 6; *Meissel*, GoA, 82 f; 215 ff; Rummel [-*Rummel*], ABGB, I³ § 1035 no. 6 [though differing in respect of gratuitous mandates]). Exceptions from this principle are occasionally made in cases where the grant of a power of representation was more apparent than real (*Meissel* loc.cit. 216 and OGH 26 January 1995, SZ 68/21 [concerning a tax adviser]).

54. Despite pointers to the contrary in FRENCH legal writing (in particular JClCiv [-*Bout*], Art. 1372-1375, V° Quasi-Contrats. Gestion d'affaires – Conditions d'existence, Fasc. 10 no. 78), there appears to be no cases in which the courts have treated a party rendering services as agreed under a void contract to be an intervener in relation to the other contracting party. In BELGIUM this question has not even be addressed in the legal literature; equally there is no case law in which the law of benevolent intervention has been applied to the reversal of void contracts. The same holds true for ITALY.

55. SPANISH legal writing clearly identifies the *animus aliena negotia gerendi* as the crux of the issue (*Sánchez Jordán*, Gestión de negocios, 95, *Lacruz Berdejo*, Rev.Crít.Der.Inm. 1975, 253). Older case law assumed that if the intervener at the time of performance believed he was obliged to perform, an intention to manage another's affairs was absent (TS 26 November 1926, reported by *Pasquau Liaño*, La gestión de negocios ajenos, 253 and *Lacruz Berdejo*, loc.cit.). The current position of the *Tribunal Supremo* is contradictory. The Fourth Division of the court (then competent in matters of administrative law) has repeatedly applied the law of benevolent intervention to void contracts between private individuals and local authorities (TS 11 October 1979, RAJ 1979 [2] no. 3448 p. 2814; TS 29 October 1980, RAJ 1980 [2] no. 3964 p. 3213; TS 8 March 1984, RAJ 1984 [1] no. 1384 p. 1052 [Third Division, competent for contentious administrative proceedings]; TS 22 January 1975, RAJ 1975 [1] no. 8 p. 20). However, the First Division (competent in private law) has declined to apply the law of benevolent intervention to reverse void contracts (TS 9 April 1980, RAJ 1980 [1] no. 1373 p. 1045; TS 28 September 1960, RAJ 1960 no. 3149 p. 2031). The more recent academic view seems rather to tend towards the approach of the administrative division, which for its part accords with the approach taken by the German BGH (*Lacruz Berdejo*, loc.cit.; *idem*, Elementos II [2] 418).

56. DUTCH case law has apparently not yet had opportunity since the coming into force of the new BW to consider the application of the law of benevolent intervention to cases of performance under a void contract assumed to be valid. The question is disputed in the literature (favouring the application of the law of benevolent intervention see in particular Verbintenissenrecht [-*Heisterkamp*], Art. 6:198 BW, no. 14 with reference to Rb Dordrecht 30 December 1953, NedJur 1954 no 618 p. 1148; for a contrary opinion, see *Schoordijk*, Zaakwaarneming een onderbelichte bron van verbintenis, 12-13). As a matter of principle, however, the reversal of contracts which are void or avoided (on the latter see also CC art. 3:53 (2)) is a natural subject for the rules on prestations conferred without obligation (CC art. 6:203).

57. Unambiguous authority on the application of the law of benevolent intervention to reverse void contracts is also missing from SCOTS law. However it may be assumed that this question is to be answered in the negative. Use is made of the law of benevolent intervention only very restrictively (*Schneiderhan*, Der Quasi-Contract im schottischen und englischen Recht, 135-136; Stair [-*Whitty*], vol. 15, paras 106, 108; *Leslie*, Jur.Rev. 1983, 13, 16, 18). Furthermore, the formative altruistic element is

lacking in a case of performance in accordance with an obligation assumed to be valid. In addition the principal will have knowledge of the activity of the intervener. Scholarly treatment of the reversal of contracts which are void or avoided features only under the heading of the law of unjustified enrichment (e.g. *McBryde*, The Law of Contract in Scotland, 325-327; *Laura J Macgregor*, Edinburgh LRev 2000, 19; *MacQueen*, JuridRev 1994, 137; *Gloag and Henderson*, The Law of Scotland[10], ch. 29).

58. As far as SCANDINAVIAN legal systems are concerned it seems that the application of the law of *negotiorum gestio* to reverse transactions is considered out of the question. Such a construction would be perceived as unnatural. Neither case law nor academic writing show any inclination for such a solution.

59. Since agency in the COMMON LAW is not dependent on the existence of a contract, there is nothing which intrinsically excludes the operation of agency principles between the parties once an agreement is reached, even though, for some reason, that agreement is not (as the parties intended) valid as a contract. While an agent cannot be obliged to carry through the agreement (in the absence of a contractually binding obligation), an agent will be obliged to surrender any profits obtained if the agent nonetheless performs: cf. *Boston Deep Sea Fishing and Ice Co v. Farnham* [1957] 1 WLR 1051 (*Harman* J) (where reasons of illegality prevented agency by ratification, but the self-appointed agent was nonetheless liable to surrender the profits made on the principal's behalf). However, there can be no agency where the principal lacks capacity and in such cases (as in other cases of intervention by strangers) it is the law of restitution which applies based on the principal's unjustified enrichment. The provision or financing the provision of food, clothing, accommodation and other necessaries to a person lacking capacity to conclude a contract so as to maintain and protect that person has long been recognised as entitling the provider to payment for the (necessary) goods or services rendered: see *Wentworth v. Tubb* (1841) 1 Y & C CC 171, 62 ER 840 (*Knight Bruce* VC), affirmed (1842) 12 LJ Ch (N. S.) 61 (Lord *Lyndhurst* LC) (claim against recipient's successors); *Re Gibson* (1871) LR 7 Ch App 52 (CA in Chancery) (claim in respect of maintenance of mentally ill sister in a private institution for recoupment out of her estate); *Re Rhodes* (1890) 44 Ch D 94, 102 (*Kay* J), 105 (*Cotton* LJ), *107 (Lindley* LJ) and 108 (*Lopes* LJ), where the requirements of the claim were not satisfied; *Re Clabdon* [1904] 2 Ch 465 (*Farwell* J) (minor); *Re J* [1909] 1 Ch 574, 576 (*Cozens-Hardy* MR); *Guardians of the Poor of St Mary Islington v. Biggenden* [1910] 1 KB 105, 111 (*Bray* J: minors). The principle extends to the payment of or provision of legal services for the protection of the individual concerned, independently of the success of the litigation, provided it was necessary: see *Ex parte Price* (1751) 2 Ves Sen 407, 28 ER 260 (Lord *Hardwicke* LC); *Sherwood v. Sanderson* (1815) 19 Ves Jun 280, 34 ER 521 (Lord *Eldon* LC); *Williams v. Wentworth* (1842) 5 Beav 325, 49 ER 603 (Lord *Langdale* MR); *Wentworth v. Tubb* (1843) 2 Y & C CC 537, 63 ER 241 (*Knight Bruce* VC); *Nelson v. Duncombe* (1846) 9 Beav 211, 50 ER 323 (Lord *Langdale* MR); *Tayler v. Tayler* (1851) 3 Mac & G 426, 42 ER 325 (Lord *Truro* LC); *Chester v. Rolfe* (1853) 4 De G M & G 798, 43 ER 720 (CA in Chancery); *Re Meares* (1879) 10 Ch D 552 (CA). The claim in respect of necessaries provided is a personal one – historically based on the notion of a contract implied by law and now more properly recognised simply as one of restitution: see *Wentworth v. Tubb* loc. cit. at 173-174 (842) (*Knight Bruce* VC); *Williams v. Wentworth* loc. cit. at 329 (605) (Lord *Langdale* MR); *Re Gibson* loc. cit., 53 (*Mellish* LJ); *Re Rhodes* loc. cit., 97 (*Kay* J); *Re J* loc. cit. 577 (*Fletcher Moulton* LJ) – though the point

was left open by *Cozens-Hardy* MR (loc. cit., 576) and see also *Re Weaver* (1882) 21 Ch D 615, 619 (*Jessel* MR: possibly a discretionary claim in Equity) and 620 (*Cotton* LJ: open question where claim arises at common law. *Brett* LJ: reseving the question whether an implied contract). The concept of an implied contract was particularly unsuitable in a context where the enriched person could never have concluded an express contract: *Re Rhodes* loc. cit., 105 (*Cotton* LJ: for that reason an erroneous and very unfortunate expression), 107 (*Lindley* LJ, pointing to "the unfortunate terminology of our law, owing to which the expression 'implied contract' has been used to denote not only a genuine contract established by inference, but also an obligation which does not arise from any real contract, but which can be enforced as if it had a contractual origin [i. e.] *quasi ex contractu*"). The principle has been given statutory effect: see the Mental Capacity Act 2005, sec. 7, which, when it comes into effect, will supersede (except as to supplies of goods sold and delivered to minors and drunks) the Sale of Goods Act 1979, sec. 3. The restitutionary claim does not give rise to a proprietary security in the form of a charge over that person's assets: *Re Marman's Trust* (1878) 8 Ch D 256, 259 (*James* LJ).

VI. *The Principal*

60. The question who is to be considered the principal is decided under GERMAN law, according to the prevailing opinion, in line with the (unwritten, see Introduction *L99*) requirement that the intervention must concern the affair of 'another'. An affair is considered to be that of another if it concerns the legal sphere or sphere of interest of another. However, this definition only relates to 'objectively extraneous affairs' (those affairs which according to their nature, content or outward appearance belong to another's sphere of interest) whereas in the case of a subjectively extraneous affair (where the outward appearance does not permit a clear-cut attribution) the existence of a principal and determination of the principal's identity is inferred by reference to the intention of the intervener. Examples are BGH 16 March 1965, BGHZ 43, 188 (where a car was stopped on a dark road in order to draw the driver's attention to a defective rear light and the danger of a collission from behind; this was held to constitute an intervention for the driver and the road users behind who were at risk of an accident); BGH 7 November 1960, BGHZ 33, 251 (a person who procures necessary medical assistance for an injured person acts on behalf of the health insurer with whom the injured person is insured); BGH 20 June 1968, BB 1969, 194 (a person who discharges another's debt is held as a general rule to act on behalf of the debtor); BGH 20 June 1963, BGHZ 40, 28 (a fire brigade extinguishing a fire intervenes on behalf of both the arsonist and the owner of the property on fire). Any natural or legal person may be a principal; according to BGH 25 June 2003, NJW 2003, 3268 this extends to a community of heirs.

61. According to the prevailing opinion in GREECE the principal is whose affair is managed. Again this falls back on the distinction between an objectively extraneous affair and a subjectively extraneous affair (see above note 28). The 'extraneous' quality of an affair where the affair is subjectively extraneous is inferred from the intervener's intention to benefit another. That intention pinpoints the principal (Georgiades and Stathopoulos [-*Papanikolaou*], Art. 730, no. 4). It is not a requirement that the intervener should know exactly who the principal is. Where the intervener is mistaken as

to his identity, it will be the principal who is actually affected by the intervention who will obtain the rights and incur the duties arising from the benevolent intervention (*Papanikolaou*, loc.cit. no. 17; ErmAK [-*Sakketas*], Art. 730, no. 12). An act of benevolent intervention may concern multiple principals. Problems may arise where other persons besides the directly affected principal have an (indirect) interest in the intervention. For instance, where assistance is rendered to an unconscious accident victim, the injred person's health insurance will have an indirect interest. The question whether or not persons who only benefit indirectly from the intervention are also to be regarded as principals is usually answered in the negative in Greek legal literature. It is argued that the scope of application of benevolent intervention would otherwise become too broad (*Papanikolaou*, loc.cit. no. 9; see, however, *Filios*, Enochiko Dikaio I/2, 194, who in this case considers the health insurance to be a principal). Both natural and legal persons may be principals (ErmAK [-*Sakketas*], Art. 730, no. 10); the same applies to an unborn child and a legal person which has not yet been established (*Sakketas* loc.cit.).

62. PORTUGUESE academic treatment of the subject likewise emphasizes that both natural and legal persons as well as persons not yet in existence (such as an unborn child or a legal person not yet established) can be a principal. It is not required that the intervener should personally know the principal. It is of no consequence if the intervener is mistaken about the true identity of the principal; only the 'true' principal will be relevant. It is of importance that the intervener acts *for* another, but it is irrelevant *who* this other person is (*Vaz Serra*, BolMinJus 66 [1957] 99).

63. As far as AUSTRIAN law is concerned it is undisputed that the principal need not have legal capacity (Schwimann [-*Apathy*], ABGB V^2, § 1035 no. 7), unless (as in the case of ratification) some statement of intention is essential (Rummel [-*Rummel*], ABGB I^3, § 1035 no. 7). It is possible to act on behalf of a (legal) person which is not yet in existence (Klang [-*Stanzl*], ABGB $IV/1^2$, 892; *Ehrenzweig*, System $II/1^2$, 715). The principal is the person with whose legal sphere the intervener interferes and for whom he intends to act (Schwimann [-*Apathy*], ABGB V^2, § 1035 no. 7; Rummel [-*Rummel*], ABGB I^3, § 1035 no. 3; *Meissel*, GoA, 59 ff). A determination of the principal's identity may depend on the intention of the intervener (*Meissel*, loc.cit. 65). However, an error of the intervener concerning the identity of the principal is without consequence (*Ehrenzweig*, System $II/1^2$, 715; Klang [-*Stanzl*], loc.cit. 892; Schwimann [-*Apathy*], loc.cit. no. 6). Instead an objective determination as to whose affair is concerned will be decisive (*Meissel*, GoA, 82). If the intervener believes that there is a principal when in fact there is none, there can be no benevolent intervention (*Meissel*, loc.cit. 109 giving the example of a search following an avalanche without the certain knowledge whether or not any person had been buried by the avalanche). The intervener need not know the principal personally (*Koziol and Welser*, Grundriss II^{12}, 364). It must merely be possible to ascertain the principal at the material time, that is to say at the onset of the intervention (Schwimann [-*Apathy*], ABGB V^2, § 1035 no. 6; Klang [-*Stanzl*], ABGB $IV/1^2$, 892). Case law from time to time adopts a rather generous approach to this requirement of 'ascertainability' (e. g. OGH 23 February 1995, ZVR 1995/129; OGH 27 June 1996, ecolex 1997, 81 and OGH 6 December 2001, RIS-Justiz RS0019810, all relating to compensation for costs incurred in maintaining vehicles held in reserve in case a third party causes an accident to those in operation). A person who merely draws indirect benefit from an intervention is not considered a

principal (*Meissel*, GoA, 60). However, it is possible for more than one person to be a principal (OGH 8 November 1984, JBl 1985, 421: several co-owners of a house held to be principals).

64. Similarly, both natural and legal persons can be principals under FRENCH law (JClCiv [-*Bout*], Art. 1372-1375, V° Quasi-Contrats. Gestion d'affaires – Conditions d'existence, Fasc. 10, no. 27). The *Cour de Cassation* has even held a legal person under public law to be the principal in a case of benevolent intervention (Cass.civ. 8 July 1918, S. 1921, I, 5, note *Achille Mestre*), although it has never referred to this decision since. Whether or not a benevolent intervention is possible in favour of a legal person in the course of incorporation cannot be clearly stated. The *Cour de Cassation* has held (though without precise reference to the law of benevolent intervention) that a company cannot incur obligations by virtue of acts performed before its establishment (Cass.civ. 1 July 1971, D. 1972, 436, note *Larroumet*). However, academic treatment of such cases usually considers benevolent intervention to be applicable (for references see *Bout* loc.cit. no. 27). Moreover, persons who lack legal capacity may be principals (*le Tourneau*, RépDrCiv, VI, v° Gestion d'affaires [2002] no. 30). In general the legal position in BELGIUM is the same. It is, however, a matter of dispute both in case law and legal literature whether a private citizen can intervene benevolently for the benefit of a public authority (see for further details *Paulus*, Zaakwaarneming, nos. 27-28 p. 29-30; this has been affirmed by CA Liège 2 March 1967, JT 1967, 632 and CFI Zinnik 10 June 1992, TAgrR 1993, 202; but rejected in Cass. 13 October 1898, Pas. 1898, I, 301, *concl. Mesdach de ter Kiele*). It is clear at any rate that the law of benevolent intervention may apply where one legal person constituted under public law acts in favour of another legal person constituted under public law (CA Brussel 7 February 1964, Pas. 1965, II, 70: where the fire brigade of town A extinguished a fire within a district coming under the responsibility of the neighbouring local authority B).

65. By contrast, the problem how to determine the principal has only rarely been considered in FRENCH and BELGIAN law. The principal is the person in whose affairs the intervener spontaneously and beneficially interferes (JClCiv [-*Bout*], Art. 1372-1375, V° Quasi-Contrats. Gestion d'affaires – Conditions d'existence, Fasc. 10 no. 1) or whose affairs are attended to (*de Page*, Droit Civil Belge II[3], no. 1069 p. 1130). Apparently objective criteria (the sphere of interests concerned) are decisive. However, in respect of *gestion d'affaires désintéressée* some French case law has held a person to be the principal even though – from an objective perspective – his affairs were not concerned at all (Cass.civ. 16 November 1955, JCP 1956 II no. 9087, note *Esmein*; Rev.trim.dr.civ. 1956, 356, *obs. Mazeaud*: in this case of benevolent intervention by a rescuer who pulled an unconscious driver from a burning car, the insurer of the car owner was held to be the principal although the insurance cover did not extend to the driver). If the intervener is mistaken about the identity of the principal all depends on the actual person whose interests are concerned (*Bout* loc.cit. no. 24-25). The same approach is taken in Belgium (*Paulus*, Zaakwaarneming, no. 33 p. 33). Where several persons qualify as principal, there is no solidary liability – either in France or in Belgium – notwithstanding that the contrary solution is adopted in the law of mandate (CC art. 2002): JClCiv [-*Bout*], Art. 1372-1375, V° Quasi-Contrats. Gestion d'affaires – effets, Fasc. 20 no. 86 and *Paulus* loc.cit. no. 92 p. 53.

66. SPANISH law refers to the principal as *dueño de los negocios, dueño* or *propietario*. However, the principal may not only be the owner of property; he or she may be any person who has an interest in having the matter addressed (*Pasquau Liaño*, La gestión de negocios ajenos, 86). The principal may be either a natural or a legal person (and in the latter case constituted under either private or public law). Spanish legal writing in general accepts that an unborn child or a legal person not yet established may be the principal in a benevolent intervention (*Pasquau Liaño*, loc.cit. 87). Likewise a benevolent intervention for the benefit of an unknown principal is accepted (TS 18 January 1908, cited according to *Pasquau Liaño*, loc.cit. 225). The principal need not have legal capacity (TS 2 February 1954, RAJ 1954 no. 322 p. 198); legal capacity is only required with respect to ratification (*Lacruz Berdejo*, Rev.Crít.Der.Inm. 1975, 262). The question who is a principal is usually decided by reference to the notion of the extraneous affair. The concept of a subjectively extraneous affair, however, is treated with great reservation (*Sánchez Jordán*, La gestión de negocios ajenos, 80). It is possible for an act of benevolent intervention to serve the interest of several principals, but if so they are not subject to the rules on joint liability under CC art. 1731, only the general rules (*Lacruz Berdejo*, loc.cit. 268). There are no statutory provisions on resolving the problem of an intervener's mistake as to the identity of the principal, nor is there any case law on the point.

67. Under ITALIAN law any person who can benefit from the acts of the intervener can be a principal. Thus under Italian law too it is not necessary that the principal has a proprietary right affected by the intervention (*Pane*, Solidarietà sociale e gestione d'affari altrui, 84). A mistake concerning the identity of the principal is without consequence (Cass. 23 July 1960, no. 2122, Giur. it. 1962, I, 1, 92; *Aru*, Gestione d'affari, 15). However, the person of the principal must be ascertainable (*Breccia*, La gestione d'affari[2], 871). Accordingly, acts in the interest of a person not yet in existence are in principle excluded; as soon as the affected person obtains legal capacity, however, he or she may ratify the act (Cass. 27 February 1971, no. 495, Foro it. 1971, I, 1945). Legal capacity on the part of the principal is not required (Corte dei Conti, Sez. giur. Sardegna, 3 November 1986, no. 384, Inf. prev. 1987, 469; *Bianca*, Diritto civile, 3, Il contratto[2], 143); in a case of complete lack of legal capacity, however, the legal representative may be regarded as the principal (*Aru*, loc.cit. 53). The co-existence of several principals is possible; they will be liable as joint debtors (CC art. 1294), but enjoy their rights as creditors on a several basis (*Sirena*, Gestione di affari, 296). The co-owners of common property may serve as an example (Cass. 15 October 1963, no. 2757, Foro it. 1964, I, 580 and Cass. 11 July 1978, no. 3479, Giur. it. 1979, I, 1, 820).

68. For DUTCH law too it is not necessary for the intervener to know the identity of the principal; it is precisely in those cases where it is most in the interest of another that someone takes action that the intervener will more often than not lack that knowledge (Asser [-*Hartkamp*], Verbintenissenrecht III[10] no. 298 p. 312; *Verburg*, De vrijwillige zaakwaarneming, no. 39 p. 67-68). Intervention on behalf of several principals is possible: for example, the admission of a child to hospital is an intervention both on behalf of the child and on behalf of the parents (CA Amsterdam 16 November 1984, NedJur 1985 no. 778 p. 2542; Verbintenissenrecht [-*Heisterkamp*], no. 11. 1; *Verburg*, loc.cit. no. 40, p. 68-69). Intervention in favour of a *dominus negotii* not yet existing (such as a foundation yet to be constituted [HR 20 November 1981, NedJur 1982

no. 568 p. 1974], an association yet to be incorporated [HR 8 January 1982, NedJur 1982 no. 333 p. 1227], or a foetus) has been held to be possible.

69. Under SCOTS law the principal is determined by reference to the intention of the intervener. An error concerning the identity of the principal is of no consequence; it will only preclude a benevolent intervention if the would-be *gestor* acts in the mistaken belief that the affair attended to is his own, or if he erroneously assumes he is acting for another, but is in reality taking care of his own affair (Stair [-*Whitty*], vol. 15, paras 103, 110 and 140; *Leslie*, JuridRev 1983, 14).

70. SCANDINAVIAN legal literature does not explain in detail how the principal is to be ascertained. The SWEDISH Act on Parents [*Föräldrabalk* (1949:381; republished in SFS 1995:974)] Ch. 11 § 3 contains a provision on caring for strangers; FINNISH Debt Enforcement Act [*utsökningslag*] of 3 December 1895 Ch. 4 § 25 touches upon the risk that the debtor's land might be wasted or buildings destroyed. In such a case the court may authorize an 'agent' who will attend to the property at the expense of the creditors, which may not (yet) necessarily be known. Of course, technically speaking this agent is not a benevolent intervener since he is authorized by the court.

71. Under ENGLISH LAW, agency by ratification presupposes that the agent's intention to act on behalf of the principal was made manifest. Ratification is not possible if the agent has acted in his own name: the prospective agent must have acted in the name of the prospective principal; there can be no ratification of the acts of an unauthorised agent by an *undisclosed* principal: *Brook v. Hook* (1871) LR 6 Exch 89, 91 (*Kelly* CB); *Keighley, Maxstead & Co v. Durant* [1901] AC 240 (third party unable to obtain damages from principal for breach of contract concluded by agent, despite ratification, as the agent had acted beyond his authority with the undisclosed intention to act on behalf of the principal). However, while the agent must disclose that he is acting on behalf of another, it is not necessary for the principal to be personally identified, at any rate if the identity of the principal is ascertainable at the time of the agent's intervention. An agent is thus able to act on behalf of a deceased's successors 'whoever they might be', since they are legally ascertainable at the time of death: *Lyell v. Kennedy* (1889) 14 App Cas 437, 456 *per* Lord *Selborne*. The question of for whom an agent of necessity acts has been disputed in the case where, due to necessity, a ship's captain pledges, disposes or otherwise deals with the cargo. A strong line of authority holds that the captain, who is ordinarily the agent of the ship owner who engaged him, acts in such a case as the agent of necessity of the owners of the cargo: *The Gratitudine* (1801) 3 C. Rob 240 at 257-258 and 260, 165 ER 450 at 456 and 457 (Sir W. *Scott*) approved by Dr *Lushington* in *The James Seddon* (1866) LR 1 A & E 62, 65, and Sir *Robert Phillimore* in *The Lizzie* (1868) LR 2 A & E 254, 258-259; *Freeman v. East India Co* (1822) 5 B & Ald 617 at 621, 106 ER 1316 at 1318 (*Bayley* J) (where, however, necessity was not proven); *The Hamburg* (1863) 2 Moore PC (N. S.) 289, 321 (Lord *Kingsdown*: "The master is invested by presumption of law with authority to give directions on this ground – that the owners have no means of expressing their wishes.) See also *The Lizzie*, loc. cit., 259 (Sir *Robert Phillimore*: "If there be an opportunity for the owners to express their will ... with respect to their cargo, the master, who is the agent of necessity and not of their choice, has no right to deprive them of this opportunity, and therefore must communicate with them if it be reasonably within his power to do so"); *The Karnak* (1868) LR 2 A & E 289, 299 and 309 (Sir *Robert Phillimore*); *The Onward* (1873) LR 4 A & E 38, 51 (Sir *Robert Phillimore*); *Metcalfe v.*

Britannia Ironworks Co (1876) 1 QBD 613, 626 (*Cockburn* CJ); and *Atlantic Mutual Insurance Co v. Huth* (1880) 16 Ch D 474, 481 (*Cotton* LJ). It may be, however, that this is in substance a short of hand for a chain of relationships. According to *Parke* B in *Vlierboom v. Chapman* (1844) 13 M & W 230 at 239-240, 153 ER 96 at 99-100, a captain who sells the cargo in a case of necessity acts in the interests of the ship owner and exercises the ship owner's powers vis-à-vis the owners of the cargo and does not act as an agent of the owners of the cargo (though in that case *Parke* B also considered that, even if a direct agency were accepted, it would not have generated the right to remuneration contended for). See also *The Gaetano and Maria* (1882) 7 PD 137, 145 (*Brett* LJ), where English law was not applicable, but it was doubted by way of *obiter dicta* that a captain is ever an agent for the owner of cargo.

VII. *The Concept of Reasonable Ground and its Equivalents*

72. As far as the concept of a reasonable ground is concerned, Article 1:101 has largely drawn on the DUTCH CC art. 6:198 as its source of inspiration. The Dutch legislator intended the requirement of a reasonable ground to exclude improper and unlawful intermeddling with another's affairs (Asser [-*Hartkamp*], Verbintenissenrecht III[10], no. 299 p. 313). This criterion thus marks off justified intervention from an unlawful act in the sense of tort law. The existence of a reasonable ground does not depend on the result of the intervention, but rather from the circumstances which provide the incentive for the *gestor* to intervene in another's legal sphere. The court thus has to balance various factors. Within that framework the questions whether or to what extent the principal himself was capable of acting and whether the intervention accorded with the actual or presumed wishes of the principal are of particular importance (T. M. Parlementaire Geschiedenis VI, 791; Verbintenissenrecht [-*Heisterkamp*], Art. 6:198 BW no. 12-12. 3; Asser [-*Hartkamp*], Verbintenissenrecht III[10], no. 299-302 p. 312-315; T & C [-*Hijma*], Art. 6:198, no. 2). If the intervener takes action without prior consultation of the principal despite the fact that he could have easily contacted him, there is no reasonable ground for the intervention (so held by HR 31 October 1952, NedJur 1953 no 477 p. 756; CFI Zwolle 24 April 1957, NedJur 1957 no. 569 p. 1137). Exceptionally the intention to save time, effort and costs may serve as a sufficient justification (T. M. Parlementaire Geschiedenis loc.cit.; Asser [-*Hartkamp*] loc.cit. no. 300, p. 314; Verbintenissenrecht [-*Heisterkamp*], Art. 6:198 BW, no. 12. 1). A reasonable ground will also be absent if the intervener acts contrary to the intention of the person concerned unless the latter is unable to state his mind in a manner which binds him (Parlementaire Geschiedenis loc.cit.; HR 8 January 1982, NedJur 1982 no. 333 p. 1227). Otherwise contrary wishes may only be disregarded in extraordinary circumstances (HR 19 April 1996, NedJur 1997 no. 24 p. 101 [*Delta Lloyd/Interlloyd*]). The prime example for such cases is the prevention of suicide by someone professedly weary of life (Asser [-*Hartkamp*] loc.cit. no. 295 p. 310; *Schoordijk*, Zaakwaarneming een onderbelichte bron van verbintenis, 34; HR 23 February 1996, NedJur 1997 no. 276 p. 1465).

73. The formula 'the intervener must have a reasonable ground for intervening' is largely unfamiliar to other jurisdictions of the European Union, but this only relates to the phrase itself, not to its substance. Similar considerations are reflected in all the jurisdictions. According to GERMAN CC § 677 the act is to be undertaken in accordance

with the interests of the principal and with regard to his actual or presumed intention. Whereas in CC § 677 both these criteria (interest and intention) relate to the manner of carrying out the intervention, CC § 683 takes up these requirements in relation to the fact of intervention as such. A corresponding distinction is drawn between justified and unjustified benevolent intervention. Taking the principle of private autonomy into account, the question of justification is to be answered first and foremost in accordance with the actual wishes of the principal – even if that intention might run contrary to his objective interests. In the absence of actual wishes, reference must be had to the principal's presumed intention. Only at this stage does the objective interest of the principal come into play where it may be an important indicator of the principal's presumed intention; the details are a matter of dispute (for further details see *Medicus*, Schuldrecht II BT[12], no. 624, 627; MünchKomm [-*Seiler*], BGB[3], § 677, no. 45; § 683, no. 13; Palandt [-*Sprau*], BGB[63], § 677, no. 13; § 683, no. 6). Under CC § 679 contrary wishes of the principal are irrelevant if a duty of the principal whose discharge is required as a matter of public interest (for example, removal of dangerous obstruction from traffic road: BGH 4 December 1975, BGHZ 65, 354), or a duty to furnish maintenance, would not be performed in time without intervention. In setting out this requirement of a reasonable ground ESTONIAN CC § 1018 (1) uses the classic phrase that the "intervention has to correspond to the interests and actual or presumed intention of the principal".

74. Under GREEK law it is one of the requirements of a justified legitimate benevolent intervention that intervention accords with the interest and the wishes of the principal (CC art. 736). Only if this requirement is satisfied does a legal relationship comparable to mandate arise. The actual wishes of the principal have to be heeded so far as this is discernable, that is to say, so far as expressed or implicit. Where an actual intention is established, this will be the sole criterion for assessing whether it was correct to intervene. There is no control of reasonableness; actual intention will prevail over objective interest, unless the further requirements of CC art. 730 (2) (principal's wishes contrary to statute or morality) apply, cf. *Bosdas*, NoB 18/1970, 769, 774 and CA Thessaloniki 693/1993, EllDik 34/1993 p. 1507). If the actual wishes of the principal cannot be ascertained, the presumed intention will be decisive instead. In determining what was the principal's presumed intention all the circumstances of the case are taken into account, including the principal's subjective considerations. The presumed intention does not necessarily correspond with the principal's objective interest (*Papanikolaou*, loc.cit. no. 34). An intervention will be in the objective interest of the principal if it is beneficial; a non-economic interest will suffice.

75. PORTUGUESE CC art. 464 likewise adheres to the principle that the intervener must act in the interest of the principal and in accordance with his or her wishes. CC art. 340 (3) confirms this general rule (*Menezes Leitão*, Responsabilidade do *gestor*, 189). The Portuguese CC does not distinguish between useful and urgent interventions. Neither is it required that the intervention is necessary. Apparent utility at the time of intervention will suffice.

76. The equivalent concept of 'reasonable ground' under AUSTRIAN law may be found in CC § 1036 (intervention in order to prevent an impending damage; benevolent intervention in a case of emergency). Where intervention serves to eliminate a common danger, regard must also be had to CC § 1043 (which contains elements of unjustified enrichment law) (Rummel [-*Rummel*], ABGB I[3], § 1043 no. 1 and no. 7). As far as an

emergency is concerned, the intervener will only have a claim if the activity proves to be useful from the subjective perspective of the principal, CC § 1037. Thus in such cases the presence of a reasonable ground for the intervention is determined by the success of the intervention.

77. A similar approach is taken by SPANISH CC art. 1893. The wording requires the intervention to be successful: the principle must have appropriated the fruits of the intervention, even though a profit in the sense of an economic advantage is not a prerequisite (*Díez-Picazo and Gullón*, Sistema II, 569). The criterion of usefulness assessed from an ex ante perspective is a point of discussion within legal literature; the intervention must have been undertaken in order to achieve an advantageous result for the principal (*Sánchez Jordán*, Gestión de negocios, 197; *Puig Brutau*, Compendio II, 559-560; *Lete del Río*, Obligaciones II, 126). The case law of the Tribunal Supremo has sent mixed messages (*Pasquau Liaño*, La gestión de negocios ajenos, 75). TS 27 April 1945, RAJ 1945 no. 685 p. 417, for instance, held that an assessment of utility at the material time of action is decisive, not the utility which results from it. TS 3 February 1965, RAJ 1965 (1) no. 525 p. 326, however, seems to proceed on the basis of some sort of ratification in the case where intervention has proved to be ultimately successful. Little clarity is provided by the proposition that while some advantage for the principal must arise from the intervention, that advantage may be present at any time and that it is therefore not necessary to examine the consequences of the intervention in more depth (TS 26 June 1946, RAJ 1946 no. 839 p. 549). CC art. 1893 (2) dispenses with the requirement of a resultant usefulness where the intervention is undertaken to prevent 'impending damage of an obvious nature'. In other words, in this case it exceptionally suffices according to the literal terms of the provisions that at the time of action it appears the intervention will be useful (*Sánchez Jordán*, loc.cit. 234). The provincial law of the Foral Community of Navarra, by contrast, relies generally only on the concept of an apparent usefulness at the time of intervention (*Sánchez Jordán*, loc.cit. p. 234, fn. 67; *Pasquau Liaño*, loc.cit. 75). Ley 560 of the *Compilación Navarra* only requires that the intervention was reasonably 'undertaken and continued' (*razonablemente asumida y realizada*).

78. The ITALIAN law of benevolent intervention builds on the concept of solidarity. CC art. 2031 therefore requires that it was useful for the intervention to be commenced (*qualora la gestione sia stata utilmente iniziata*). The material time is that of the first act of intervention (Cass. 4 July 1964, no. 1750, Giur. it. 1964, I, 1, 1129). By contrast, it is irrelevant whether or not the outcome of the intervention is beneficial for the principal (*Aru*, Gestione d'affari, 44-45). The usefulness of the intervention will be assessed according to the presumed wishes of the principal, which are inferred from objective factors (*Breccia*, La gestione d'affari[2], 878; Cass. 13 October 1951, no. 2634, Foro it. 1952, I, 201). Regard is also had to how a *bonus pater familias* would have acted in the circumstances (Cass. 13 March 1964, no. 550, Foro it. 1965, I, 866). The usefulness of the intervention is presumed if the intervener undertakes something which the principal was under a duty to do (Cass. 15 October 1963, no. 2757, Foro it. 1964, I, 580) or if the principal's omission to act threatens to have a detrimental impact on inalienable rights of a third party. In that case, moreover, a *prohibitio domini* is to be disregarded (CC art. 2031 (2); Cass. 17 July 1969, no. 2636, Foro it. 1971, I, 713).

79. Although in older FRENCH legal literature some authors have argued that the intervention must be necessary (see, for instance, *Vasseur*, Urgence en droit civil, Rev. trim. dr. civ. 1954, no. 8-9 p. 415-420), recent legal literature prefers a test of usefulness of the intervention (*utilité de la gestion*) to one of necessity (*Mazeaud and Chabas*, Leçons de droit civil II (1)[9] no. 683 p. 811). According to French case law (as it is interpreted in French legal literature, at least), how that usefulness is to be assessed depends on whether or not the intervener acted with an altruistic intention (JClCiv [-*Bout*], Art. 1372-1375, V° Quasi-Contrats. Gestion d'affaires – Conditions d'existence, Fasc. 10 nos. 98 et seq.). In a case of *gestion d'affaires désintéressée* the matter turns on whether in the circumstances the intervener might permissibly assume that the intervention would be beneficial to the principal. Thus in a case of *gestion d'affaires désintéressée* it suffices if the intervention appears promising at the outset; whether or not the principal has been ultimately enriched is not critical. Where assistance is rendered in an emergency situation, but to no avail, the usefulness will be assessed according to the expected outcome, not the actual outcome. By contrast, in a case of *gestion d'affaires intéressée* the usefulness of a benevolent intervention *is* determined by whether or not the principal has actually profited as a result. However, according to the prevailing legal opinion in BELGIUM, benevolent intervention only arises if the intervention by the *gestor* was necessary (*de Page*, Droit Civil Belge II[3], no. 1074 p. 1138-1139). Moreover, the intervention must be beneficial for the principal, although usefulness at the outset of the intervention will suffice (Cass. 12 November 1998, De Verz 1999, 208). Belgian law does not follow the distinction between *gestion d'affaires désintéressée* and *gestion d'affaires intéressée.*

80. The SCOTTISH Institutional Writers echo the distinction set out above in the context of Austrian law and Spanish law, namely between an intervention in a case of emergency and a useful intervention. *Stair* states that "a negotiater cannot begin any new business, but only carry on that which is begun, and they must be necessarily or profitably done, otherwise he hath his labour for his pains" (The Institutions of the Law of Scotland, Book I / Title 8 § 3). *Erskine* elaborates on 'necessity' mainly in the context of the intervener's liability (Institutes of the Law of Scotland Book III § 53: "Where the *gestor*, from friendship, and the necessity of the case, takes upon him the direction of an affair which requires immediate execution, he is accountable only for gross omissions"). Modern legal literature likewise demands a certain urgency and necessity for the intervention (*Walker*, Principles of Scottish Private Law, II[4], 513-514). The predominant view is that an initial utility at the outset of the intervention – determined in the context of the presumed wishes of the principal – is decisive. An acute emergency is not required (*Leslie*, Jur.Rev. 1983, 28, 29; Stair [-*Whitty*], vol. 15, paras 117, 120; *Marshall*, General Principles of Scots Law[5], para 12-11). The same approach is taken in the case law: *Fernie v. Robertson* (1871) 9 M 437; *Dunbar v. Wilson and Dunlop's Trustee* (1887) 15 R 210.

81. Similarly, in the SCANDINAVIAN countries the basic idea that a claim may only arise in favour of the intervener if he has acted with 'reasonable grounds' is widely received, though the phrase itself is not contained in any of the statutory provisions. Since an overarching concept of benevolent intervention is largely unknown, resort must be had as far as possible to specific statutory provisions. They are referred to in the introduction to this Book (see *I53-57*).

82. ENGLISH law draws on a notion of reasonable necessity for the measure undertaken as a fundamental requirement for agency of necessity: there must be a necessity that the agent act without instructions in order to safeguard the property or interests of the principal which are in danger. The notion of what is necessary is recognised to be question-begging (cf. *Gunn v. Roberts* (1874) LR 9 CP 331, 332 (*Brett* J)), but the requirement is of long-standing and seemingly entrenched: see *East India Co v. Ekins* (1718) 2 Bro PC 382, 1 ER 1011 (HL), affirming *Ekins v. East India Co* (1717) 1 P Wms 395, 24 ER 441 (Lord *Cowper* LC); *The Alexander* (1842) 1 W Rob 346, 166 ER 602 (Dr *Lushington*); *Lindsay v. Leathley* (1863) 3 F & F 902 at 937, 176 ER 410 at 427 (*Cockburn* CJ); *The Pontida* (1884) 9 PD 102, 104 (Butt J). The necessity must relate both to the situation and the means adopted to remedy it. (As to the latter, see also Chapter 3, Art. 3:106, Notes, 11.) There can be no necessity to act if the principal is himself on the scene and capable of acting: see *Arthur v. Barton* (1840) 6 M & W 138, 142 (*Alderson* B) and 143 (Lord *Abinger* CB); *Beldon v. Campbell* (1851) 6 Exch 886, 890-891 (*Parke* B); *Gunn v. Roberts* loc. cit., 331, 332 and 337 (*Brett* J) and 338 (*Denman* J) – all confirming the absence of necessity for conclusion of a loan contract by a ship's captain in his principal's name at a port where the principal or his representatives are themselves able to procure required finance – and see also *Nelson v. Duncombe* (1846) 9 Beav 211 at 233, 50 ER 323 at 332 (Lord *Langdale* MR) (a restitutionary claim in respect of provision of necessaries to a person lacking capacity presupposes that that person is not able to cater for themselves) and, from the same context, *Pontypridd Union v. Drew* [1927] 1 KB 214, 218 (*Bankes* LJ: "there is no pretence for applying principles or doctrines of agency of necessity to relief given to a person of full age and capacity to contract"). Moreover, an intervener has no authority to act (e.g by selling property of the principal) merely because this would be of benefit to the principal: *Cammell v. Sewell* (1858) 3 H & N 617 at 635, 157 ER 615 at 623 (*Martin* B). Nor does it suffice that an agent considers the measure would be beneficial if the measure was not manifestly necessary: *Robertson v. Clark* (1824) 1 Bing 445, 450 (Lord *Gifford* CJ); *Ewbank v. Nutting* (1849) 7 CB 797, 137 ER 316; *Tronson v. Dent* (1853) 8 Moore PC 419, 452 (Sir *John Patteson* for the PC); *The Segredo* (1853) 1 Spinks Ecc & Ad 36 at 48, 164 ER 22 at 28 (Dr *Lushington*); *The Australia* (1859) 13 Moore PC 132, 144 (Dr *Lushington* for the PC); *Lindsay v. Leathley*, loc. cit. 938 (427) (*Cockburn* CJ), and see also *Atlantic Mutual Insurance Co v. Huth* (1880) 16 Ch D 474, 481 (*Cotton* LJ). The intervention must be a response which is called for in the circumstances and proportionate to the problem, cf. *Wilson v. Millar* (1816) 2 Stark 1 at 4, 171 ER 553 at 554 (Lord *Ellenborough* CJ: sale of entire cargo unauthorised as a mere pledge would have sufficed). A touchstone is whether a prudent person with clear knowledge of the circumstances of the case would have no doubt as to how he should proceed: *Somes v. Sugrue* (1830) 4 Car & P 276 at 282, 172 ER 703 at 706 (*Tindal* CJ). What is done or obtained must be necessary and it must be necessary that it be done or procured at the time it is done or supplied: cf. *Pocahontas Fuel Co (Incorporated) v. Ambatielos* (1922) 27 Com Cas 148, 153 (*McCardie* J), where, however, there was a "course of dealings" between the parties from which, besides considerations of necessity, authority for the transaction could be inferred, and in the same sense *The Sophie* (1842) 1 W Rob 368, 369, 166 ER 610 at 611 (Dr *Lushington*). In particular the problem must be so pressing that the agent is entitled to act without (fresh) instructions from the principal: see *Freeman v. East India Co* (1822) 5 B & Ald 617 at 624, 106 ER 1316

at 1319 (*Best* J: captain should have awaited owner's instructions because the cargo was not threatening to deteriorate); *Cammell v. Sewell*, loc. cit., 635 (623) and 644 (626) (*Martin* B), where the sale of cargo was unnecessary because it was not perishable, and consider also *Harris v. Fiat Motors Ltd* (1906) 22 TLR 556 (defendant's employee, whom the defendants had instructed to drive the plaintiff's car personally, had no power to delegate the driving to a non-employee passenger (whose driving damaged the car) in order to investigate noise at the back of the car – so as to make the defendants vicariously liable for the driver's negligence – because there was no necessity to keep the vehicle moving). The necessity is to be assessed objectively, based on what a reasonable and prudent person would contemplate in the circumstances; the fact that the intervener considered intervention justified is not sufficient. An interference with another's property may be justified, for example, where there is a risk of its loss or damage because it is exposed to bad weather or theives: *Sachs v. Miklos* [1948] 2 KB 23, 34-36 (Lord *Goddard* CJ). Although there is authority for the view that the reasonable necessity must amount to a real emergency (*Sachs v. Miklos*, loc. cit., 34-36 (Lord *Goddard* CJ), approved in *John Koch Ltd v. C & H Products Ltd* [1956] 2 Lloyd's LLR 59, 60 and similarly at 65 (*Singleton* LJ), other formulations of the requirement are broader and more flexible, requiring only that the circumstances determine the course which a person ought to take: *Australasian Steam Navigation Co v. Morse* (1872) LR 4 PC 222, 230 *per* Sir *Montague Smith* ("[W]hen by the force of circumstances a man has the duty cast upon him of taking some action for another, and under that obligation, adopts the course which, to the judgment of a wise and prudent man, is apparently the best for the interest of the persons for whom he acts in a given emergency, it may properly be said of the course so taken, that it was, in a mercantile sense, necessary to take it"). Possibly the correct test turns on whether the intervener is a stranger or a person who is already an agent to the principal and merely acting outside the scope of his authority, the requirement of "emergency" being confined to the former case: in *Palmer v. Stear* (1963) 113 LJ 420, which was a case of intervention by a stranger, it was successfully argued for the vet that *in a case of emergency* one person might discharge another's legal duty; and in *Langan v. GWR Co* (1873) 30 L. T. (N. S.) 173, 176 *Cleasby* B considered that an employee of the rail company would be authorised to procure medical and other necessary assistance for persons injured in a rail accident, but (short of ratification) a stranger would not – a distinction presumably based on the assumption that if there are employees of the rail company on the scene there is no need for a stranger to usurp their responsibility. The measure ventured need not be ultimately successful, but the intervention must have been necessary as a prospective solution to the difficulty: see *The Lizzie* (1868) LR 2 A & E 254, 256 (Sir *Robert Phillimore*) (secured lending by a ship's captain valid becausse concluded by the agent honestly and with due care, notwithstanding that it resulted in no benefit to the principal); *Re Meares* (1879) 10 Ch D 552 (CA), upholding a right to reimbursement of legal costs incurred in maintaining an action to procure the appointment of administrators for the estate of a person without full mental capacity, in order to protect that person's property, despite the fact that the individual concerned died before administrators were appointed, and see similarly in resepect of litigation which was reasonable, though unsuccessful, *Sherwood v. Sanderson* (1815) 19 Ves Jun 280, 34 ER 521 (Lord *Eldon* LC), *Nelson v. Duncombe*, loc. cit. (Lord *Langdale* MR) and; *Phelps, James & Co v. Hill* [1891] 1 QB 605 (CA), where a ship transporting goods from Swansea to New York was damaged due to bad weather and put into Queenstown as a safe harbour and the defendant's decision to deviate from his instructions and make for Bristol, where the ship could be repaired the most economically, was "reasonably necessary" (*ibid*, 610-611 (*Lindley* LJ), 614 (*Lopes* LJ), 617 (*Kay* LJ)), although the ship subsequently sank; *Tetley & Co. v. British Trade Corporation* (1922) 10 Ll. L.Rep. 678, where the principal's goods were transported in order to safeguard them from probable serious public disturbances and then sold, but the cost of transportation exceeded the proceeds of sale.

VIII. *In Particular: the Duty to Ascertain the Principal's Wishes*

83. The draft deviates by a nuance from some of the national legal systems with its rule that an intervention is not justified if the intervener could have consulted the principal and failed to do so. Under GERMAN CC § 681 sentence 1, the intervener is obliged to notify the principal as soon as practicable of his intervention to manage the principal's affair and, unless delay would cause damage, to await the decision of the principal. In setting out these duties the legislator wanted to achieve clarity as regards the actual wishes of the principal (MünchKomm [-*Seiler*], BGB[3], § 681, no. 5; Prot II, 727). According to the case law of the BGH (BGH 4 December 1975, BGHZ 65, 354, 356) the duties arising from CC § 681 sentence 1 are only secondary obligations, which as a general rule presuppose the intervention (RGRK [-*Steffen*], BGB[12], § 681, no. 3). A violation of the duty of notification merely leads to a duty of the intervener to compensate for damage sustained by the principal as a result of the absence of or delay in notification (RGRK [-*Steffen*], BGB[12], § 681, no. 11; Staudinger [-*Wittmann*], BGB[13], § 681, no. 8; *Soergel* [-*Beuthien*], BGB[12], § 681, no. 4 and Erman [-*Ehmann*], BGB I[10], § 681, no. 4). The fact that the intervener has omitted to notify the principal does not of itself automtically preclude an intervener from claiming compensation for expenses incurred (CC § 683). As the duty to notify serves first and foremost to enable the actual wishes of the principal to be ascertained, it is only of minor importance in the context of CC § 679 (discharge of a duty of the principal which is of public interest) (Staudinger [-*Wittmann*], BGB[13], § 681, no. 3), though an intervener is not liberated from the duty even then since notification may induce the principal to change his mind (RGRK [-*Steffen*], BGB[12], § 681, no. 8). Furthermore, breach of the duty to notify does not imply that the intervener intended to serve his own interests rather than act on behalf of another (BGH 4 December 1975, loc.cit.). Notification is 'feasible' if, looking at the circumstances objectively, it is required in the interest of all persons concerned and the intervener can be expected to do it. This is to be assessed according to the circumstances of the individual case, whereby both the possibility to contact the principal and the significance of the intervention are of particular importance (RGRK [-*Steffen*], BGB[12], § 681, no. 4; MünchKomm [-*Seiler*], BGB[3], § 681, no. 5; Staudinger [-*Wittmann*], BGB[13], § 681, no. 3; CFI Stuttgart 7 January 1972, VersR 1973, 517). If it is easy to contact the principal, the intervener has to notify him at once (MünchKomm [-*Seiler*], BGB[3], § 681, no. 5). The intervener will then have to await the principal's decision, unless any delay would lead to (further) damage.

84. GREEK law to a large extent resembles German law in this respect, as it also extends the main duty of the intervener to act in accordance with the interest and wishes of the principal by absorbing secondary obligations drawn from the law of mandate, *inter alia* the duty of the intervener to notify the principal of the fact of intervention (CC

art. 733). The intervener should be compelled to ascertain the wishes of the principal (Georgiades and Stathopoulos [-*Papanikolaou*], Art. 733 no. 1). A violation of this duty to notify the principal gives rise to a liability for damages on the part of the intervener (*Papanikolaou*, loc.cit. no. 4); the lawfulness of intervention, however, remains unaffected (CA Patras 92/1955, NoB 4/1956, 96).

85. POLISH CC art. 753 (1) provides for a duty of the intervener to notify the principal as soon as possible. CZECH and SLOVAK CC art. 743 (1) require that the intervener notifies the principal of his intention to act and awaits the principal's decision, unless the intervention serves to prevent impending damage. By contrast PORTUGUESE CC does not explicitly provide for a duty to ascertain the principal's wishes. CC art. 465 limb (b) confines itself to imposing a duty on the intervener to inform the principal as soon as possible.

86. The AUSTRIAN OGH (21 April 1982, JBl 1984, 256) has held that the intervener must act in accordance with the interests of the principal, having regard to the principal's actual or presumed wishes. Consideration must be given to the probable wishes of the principal – in particular where the intervention involves expense where it cannot be taken for granted that the principal will be willing to bear the costs. A *gestor* intervening in case of emergency (CC § 1036) will not only lose his right to compensation if he acts contrary to the presumed wishes of the principal; he will also be held to have acted unlawfully (Schwimann [-*Apathy*], ABGB V^2, §§ 1036-1040 no. 11; *Meissel*, GoA, 118 et seq.). If the intervener does not make use of an opportunity to contact the principal, his acts will not constitute benevolent intervention under CC § 1036; they will (at most) amount to intervention under CC § 1037 (OGH 22 November 1984, SZ 57/167; OGH 26 November 1981, SZ 54/176). That is because it is not a case of emergency if there is sufficient time to contact the principal and ask for his consent (Schwimann [-*Apathy*], ABGB V^2, §§ 1036-1040 no. 1, *Meissel*, GoA, 30). There may also be an element of fault in not contacting the principal where the case falls under CC § 1037 (*Ehrenzweig*, System $II/1^2$, 714 fn. 5), which in turn may render the intervention unlawful (Rummel [-*Rummel*], ABGB I^3, § 1037 no. 2). If the intervener acts contrary to the express and legally binding wishes of the principal, a claim for compensation of expenses incurred is barred by CC § 1040 (Schwimann [-*Apathy*], ABGB V^2, §§ 1036-1040 no. 5). An exception is contained in CC § 1042 which allows for the discharge of debts contrary to the intention of the debtor (CC § 1042); in this case no overriding public interest is required (*Meissel*, GoA, 47 et seq.).

87. The intervener's duty to ascertain the wishes of the principal is hardly ever explicitly referred to in France or Belgium. As regards BELGIAN law, *Paulus*, Zaakwaarneming no. 48 p. 39, points out that only with great reservation could it be accepted that there was a 'necessity' for intervention if the intervener could have contacted the principal but failed to do so. In FRANCE it is said that the 'presence' of the party benefited is an indicator that the intervention was not necessary. The easier it was for the principal to act himself, the stronger the presumption that the intervener should not have acted (JClCiv [-*Bout*], Art. 1372-1375, V° Quasi-Contrats. Gestion d'affaires – Conditions d'existence, Fasc. 10 no. 105 ; see also *le Tourneau*, RépDrCiv, VI, v° Gestion d'affaires [2002], no. 60: if the measure was not urgent and the issue is open to doubt, it cannot have been appropriate to intervene without first contacting the principal). The opportunity to contact the principal prior to taking any measures does not, however, seem to preclude a justified intervention on another's behalf under all circumstances

(cf. CA Paris 3 May 1989, Juris Data 1989-022252). It is generally assumed that as a rule a measure taken is regarded as unlawful if the principal disapproves it (*Flour/Aubert/Savaux*, Le fait juridique[10], no. 5 p. 7). The only exception is if the principal's opposition is manifestly unlawful (Cass.civ. 11 February 1986, Bull.civ. 1986 I, no. 23).

88. Under SPANISH CC art. 1888 the intervener is 'obliged to continue measures undertaken until completion of the measures or ancillary matters or to request the person concerned to take over from the intervener when he [the principal] is in a position to undertake them on his own'. The duty arising under CC art. 1888 to contact the principal is not aiming at eliciting his intention; it is concerned instead with calling upon the principal to continue a measure already underway. A duty of the intervener to make enquiries as to the principal's wishes is not set out. The existence of such a duty is nonetheless recognised and may either be inferred from the requirement of *absentia domini* (*Pasquau Liaño*, La gestión de negocios ajenos, 93) or from CC art. 1189 which codifies the general standard of care of an intervener (*Sánchez Jordán*, Gestión de negocios, 498-501). If, when the intervener makes inquiry, the principal consents to the measure, this may constitute a contract of mandate (*Sánchez Jordán*, loc.cit. 502).

89. Similarly under ITALIAN law the view is maintained that a person who interferes with another's legal sphere is obliged to ascertain the wishes of the principal and to await his directions, at least as far as this is possible in the circumstances (*Sirena*, Gestione di affari, 320). If the principal gives his consent, this will constitute a contract of mandate under Italian law too (*Breccia*, La gestione d'affari[2], 879-880; with some reservation *Aru*, Gestione d'affari, 23). If the principal disapproves, the provisions on benevolent intervention will not apply (CC art. 2031 (2); Cass. 23 May 1984, no. 3143, Rep.Giur.it. 1984, voce Gestione d'affari, no. 1, c. 1299). Disapproval may also be inferred from consistent conduct of the principal (*Aru* loc.cit. 47). Of deciding importance is whether the intervener knew of the contrary wishes of the principal or would have known of them if he had exercised reasonable care (*Breccia* loc.cit. 878).

90. According to DUTCH law only a person who acts in accordance with the actual wishes – and in particular the expressed wishes – of the principal acts with reasonable grounds (see above note 72). Acts which do not correspond with the presumed (unexpressed) wishes of the principal may constitute a justified intervention in another's affair if the intervener has tried in vain to contact the principal (Verbintenissenrecht [-*Heisterkamp*], Art. 6:198 BW, comment 12. 2; Asser [-*Hartkamp*], Verbintenissenrecht III[10], no. 300 p. 314; HR 23 February 1996, NedJur 1997 no. 276 p. 1465). As a general rule a benevolent intervention contrary to the wishes of the *dominus negotii* is not permissible. However, exceptions are conceivable – for example, in preventing a suicide or overriding the wishes of a mentally disabled person (CA s'Gravenhage 28 November 1984, NedJur 1985 no. 863 p. 2831).

91. The legal position under SCOTS law is not quite clear. A justified benevolent intervener must abide by the presumed wishes of the principal. The main distinction between the law of *negotiorum gestio* on the one hand and mandate and implied mandate on the other is precisely that the principal has no knowledge of the action taken and has therefore not authorised it (*Gloag and Henderson*, The Law of Scotland[10], p. 373 no. 22. 31; *Walker*, Principles of Scottish Private Law, Volume II, Book 4: Obligations[4], 218). The Institutional Writers merely point out that an action contrary to the (express) wishes of the principal will in principle not found claims in *negotiorum gestio*; in this case it is at most claims on the basis of 'recompense' which can be

considered (e. g. *Erskine* § 53). Stair (-*Whitty*), vol. 15 para 122 holds that the requirement to act in accordance with the 'assumed wishes' of the principal is a necessary and appropriate corrective to protect the principal against unwelcome interference.

92. SWEDISH law puts great emphasis on the intervener's duty to make inquiries about the principal's wishes. A breach of this duty in principle excludes claims on the basis of *negotiorum gestio* (*Bengtsson/Victorin*, Hyra och annan nyttjanderätt till fast egendom[6], 198; see also HD 9 March 1972, NJA 1972, 88, summarised above in note 22). Exceptions to this general rule are in part set out in statute. The duty to preserve goods and keep them in safe custody arising in the context of sales law may serve as an example (Sale of Goods Act §§ 72-78; see for further details *Håstad*, Tjänster utan uppdrag, 79; *Hellner*, Speciell Avtalsrätt II (2)[3], ch. 29).

93. As the COMMON LAW largely integrates its cases of benevolent intervention into agency of necessity, it too emphasises the requirement that the intervener seek out and heed the principal's instructions, which is fundamental to agency in general. An agent may not act in contradiction of the principal's expressed or implicit wishes (if his instructions foresee the case at hand): see, for example, *Jones v. Simons* (1842) 2 QB 424, 114 ER 168, where the owner had instructed the captain to obtain necessary money only by selling cargo, but the captain obtained it by a loan from the claimant instead; *Acatos v. Burns* (1878) 3 Ex D 282, 290-291 (*Brett* LJ). Where the principal's wishes are unknown, there will be no agency of necessity as a rule unless it is impossible or practically impossible for the agent to contact the principal (and so obtain his authority to act): *Australasian Steam Navigation Co v. Morse* (1872) LR 4 PC 222; *Gwilliam v. Twist* [1895] 2 QB 84, 87; *Pontypridd Union v. Drew*[1927] 1 KB 214, 220 (*Scrutton* LJ); *Prager v. Blatspiel, Stamp & Heacock Ltd* [1924] 1 KB 566, 571. (Consider also *Palmer v. Stear* (1963) 113 LJ 420, where there was no means for the vet to identify the owner of the dog). As the extensive authorities relating to the powers of a ship's captain solidly demonstrate, if the principal can be contacted, then as a rule there is no scope for agency of necessity; the agent must obtain instructions and abide by them: see *Hayman v. Molton*, loc. cit. at 68 (740) (Lord *Ellenborough* CJ; *La Ysabel* (1812) 1 Dods 273 at 274, 165 ER 1308 at 1309 (Sir *W. Scott*); *Wilson v. Millar* (1816) 2 Stark 1 at 4, 171 ER 553 at 554 (Lord *Ellenborough* CJ: captain should have sought instructions before selling the cargo); *Freeman v. East India Co* (1822) 5 B & Ald 617 at 624, 106 ER 1316 at 1319 (Best J); *Stonehouse v. Gent* (1841) 2 QB 431n, 114 ER 170; *Jones v. Simons*, loc. cit. at 430 (170) (Lord *Denman* CJ); *The Lochiel* (1843) 2 W Rob 34 at 48, 166 ER 668 at 673 (Dr *Lushington*); *Beldon v. Campbell* (1851) 6 Exch 886, 889 (*Parke* B: no necessity for the ship's captain to create security rights in the ship because it had already reached a port from which the owner could be contacted); *The Segredo* (1853) 1 Spinks Ecc & Ad 36 at 62, 164 ER 22 at 36 (Dr *Lushington*); *The Royal Arch* (1857) Swab 269 at 282, 166 ER 1131 at 1139) (Dr *Lushington*); *Cammell v. Sewell* (1858) 3 H & N 617 at 635 and 644, 157 ER 615 at 623 and 626 (*Martin* B); *The Olivier* (1862) Lush 484 at 492, 167 ER 219 at 223-224 (Dr *Lushington*); *The Hamburg* (1863) 2 Moore PC (N. S.) 289 at 299 (Dr *Lushington*) and 321-322 (Lord *Kingsdown*, for the PC); *The Karnak* (1868) LR 2 A & E 289, 300 and 309 (Sir *Robert Phillimore*); *The Onward* (1873) LR 4 A & E 38, 51 (Sir *Robert Phillimore*: "[W]hen the circumstances permit the master must communicate with the owner before he does any acts which seriously affect the value of the ship ... or of of the cargo."); *Kleinwort, Cohen & Co v. The Cassa Marittima of Genoa* (1877) 2 App Cas 156, 157 (Sir *Montague Smith*, for the PC); *Acatos*

v. Burns loc. cit. at 286 and 290 (*Brett* LJ, implicitly) and 288 (*Bramwell* LJ); *Atlantic Mutual Insurance Co v. Huth* (1880) 16 Ch D 474, 481 (*Cotton* LJ); *The Gaetano and Maria* (1881) 7 PD 1, 4 (Sir *Robert Phillimore*) and, on appeal (where it was held, reversing the court below on the point, that English law was not applicable), (1882) 7 PD 137 at 143-144 (*Brett* LJ) and 148 (*Cotton* LJ). The mere fact that the owner of the property affected is insolvent does not provide an excuse for failing to contact the principal if that was practicable: *The Panama* (1870) LR 3 PC 203. The fact that the conduct is otherwise reasonable will not protect the agent if he had a reasonable opportunity to contact the principal and failed to do so: see *Springer v. Great Western Ry Co* [1921] 1 KB 257 (CA) (where tomatoes being transported from St. Helier to Covent Garden were held up by bad weather and a port strike and were sold before arrival because of their deterioration, but the court held the agent should have sought instructions). Whether there is a practical impossibility – a matter of time and opportunity – depends on the circumstances: *Australasian SN Co v. Morse*, loc. cit., 231 (Sir *Montague Smith*). Communication may be practically impossible where there is a multitude of principals who would have to be addressed: see, e. g., *Phelps, James & Co v. Hill* [1891] 1 QB 605 (where there were numerous owners of cargo being carried by the distressed ship). A further case of impracticality of communication is where the matter is of such urgency that, weighed up against the chances of a successful and prompt correspondence, the principal's interests are at risk if the agent delays until he can ascertain the principal's wishes: *The Hamburg.*, loc. cit., 299-300 (Dr *Lushington*), and for a clear application of this principle see *The Olivier*, loc. cit., 478-488 (221) and 492-493 (224) (Dr *Lushington*) and further confimration of the principle in *The Lizzie* (1868) LR 2 A & E 254, 256 (Sir *Robert Phillimore*). Thus even if communication with the principal is possible, a person nonetheless acts as an agent of necessity if that communication would involve such delay that it would be detrimental to the principal's interests to await the principal's instruction: see *Jones v.* Simons, loc. cit., 430 (170) (*Patteson* J); *Edwards v. Havill* (1853) 14 CB 107, 139 ER 45 (ship confined to harbour due to bad weather; captain borrowed a small sum – without communicating with the owner, because if he had to await a reply (by post) first the ship would have been held up for two further days until a reply arrived, whereas the weather might have improved in the meantime); *Cargo Ex Sultan* (1859) Swab 504 at 511-512, 166 ER 1235 at 1239) (Dr *Lushington*); *The Victor* (1865) 13 L. T. (N. S.) 21 (Dr *Lushington*) (where a master's sale of the ship was within the scope of his agency of necessity because communication to the principal would have involved a three month delay – during which time the ship might have been taken by creditors or, in view of its deterioration, lost to the elements); *Acatos v. Burns* (1878) 3 Ex D 282, 290 (Brett LJ) (to store goods while awaiting instructions would exceed their value and thus be uneconomical); and the IRISH case *The Staffordshire* (1871) 25 LT (N. S.) 137, 140 (*Townsend* J), affirmed *sub. nom. Smith v. Bank of New South Wales* (1872) LR 4 PC 194, 203 (*Mellish* LJ for the PC), where it would have been two or three months before a reply would have been received. Thus an attempt at communication can be dispensed with if the agent cannot receive or expect a reply 'in time': *Australasian SN Co v. Morse*, loc. cit., 232.

IX. *Ratification by the Principal*

94. As regards interventions which are commenced without a sufficient ground, four distinct questions arise: (i) is ratification possible, (ii) what conditions must ratification satisfy, (iii) when does the time period during which the principal may ratify the intervention expire, and (iv) what effects does ratification have? These questions are not addressed in all jurisdictions with equal thoroughness.

95. Under GERMAN CC § 684 sentence 2, the principal may ratify an unjustified intervention and thereby bring about the legal consequences of a justified benevolent intervention. The ratification must be declared vis-à-vis the intervener, either expressly or by implication. An implicit ratification may be inferred if the principal demands a surrender of proceeds under CC § 681 sentence 2 (in conjunction with § 667) (Palandt [-*Sprau*], BGB[63], § 684 no. 2). A ratification substitutes for the requirements set out in CC § 683, according to which the intervention must be in the interest of the principal and in keeping with the actual or presumed wishes of the principal (BGH 16 December 1994, BGHZ 128, 210, 213). It does not, however, supersede the requirements of CC § 677, i. e. the condition that the intervention must have been undertaken on another's behalf (MünchKomm [-*Seiler*], BGB[3], § 684 no. 14). Consequently a ratification is not possible in the case of management of another's affairs by mistake (CC § 687 (1)) or arrogated management of another's affairs (CC § 687 (2)) (Palandt [-*Sprau*], BGB[63], § 684 no. 2). The effect of ratification is that the intervention is justified *inter partes*, i. e. between principal and intervener, with retrospective effect. However, ratification alone does not give rise to a contract of mandate (CC § 662) (Palandt [-*Sprau*], BGB[63], § 684 no. 2). A ratification under CC § 684 is subject to the rules of CC §§ 182 et seq. (BGH 14 February 1989, NJW 1989, 1672), but no specific time limit is stipulated (CA Stuttgart 25 June 1953, NJW 1954, 36). However, it is conceivable that the underlying ethos of CC §§ 108 and 177 may be applicable by analogy with the result that a ratification is deemed to be refused if, after a request for ratification, the principal does not ratify within a reasonable time.

96. GREEK law likewise enables a principal to ratify an unjustified intervention. The ratification may be declared expressly or tacitly. An implied ratification is inferred, for example, if the principal discharges an obligation which the intervener incurred in relation to a third party. As in Germany, the main effect of a ratification is that the unjustified intervention will be transformed into a justified intervention with retroactive effect. This is justified by means of an analogous application of CC art. 238 (Georgiades and Stathopoulos [-*Papanikolaou*], Art. 738, no. 7). Ratification alone does not conclude a contract of mandate; Greek law does not follow the Roman law principle *ratihabitio mandato aequiparatur* (*Kavkas and Kavkas*, Enochikon Dikaion II/2, 28). A management of another's affairs in the mistaken belief they are one's own cannot be the subject of ratification (*Papanikolaou*, loc.cit. no. 5).

97. PORTUGUESE law draws a distinction between *aprovação* and *ratificação*. An *aprovação* (CC art. 469) is a general approval by the principal of the unauthorized intervention. An *aprovação* is only effective inter partes, that is to say between principal and intervener; if such an approval is given a justified *gestão de negócios* is created. By contrast a *ratificação* (CC art. 268) concerns juridical acts which the intervener has undertaken in relation to third parties; as a result of a ratification these transactions become valid retrospectively (for details see CA Evora 1 June 1999, CJ XXIV [1999-3]

270). An *aprovação* may be made manifest either expressly or implicitly (CC art. 217); it is not subject to any specific formal requirements or a time limit (CC art. 219). By contrast a *ratificação* must comply with the same formality requirements as are required for the grant of an authority (CC art. 268 (2)) to conclude the relevant transaction (CC art. 262 (2)); an implicit ratification will not suffice (STJ 17 February 1998, CJ(ST) VI [1998-1] 68). Moreover, for *ratificação* CC art. 268 (3) grants the third party who has contracted with the intervener the right to set a time limit in which to ratify; if ratification is not granted within the time limit it is deemed that the principal has refused to ratify. CC art. 469, read in conjunction with art. 468, sets out the legal consequences of an *aprovação* namely (i) the principal's waiver of any claim for damage negligently caused by the intervener and (ii) acceptance of the intervener's claims for compensation of expenses incurred and damage suffered. A *ratificação* pursuant to CC art. 268 (2) has retroactive effect and renders all contracts concluded by the intervener in the name of the principal effective (*eficácia retroactiva*). The limitation period, however, will only start to run *ex nunc* from the time of *ratificação* (CA Coimbra 2 March 1999, CJ XXIV [1999-2] 11). Special regulations on *ratificação* apply where a lawyer manages affairs relating to legal proceedings without authorization: for details see CCP art. 41 and CA Coimbra 4 January 1989, BolMinJus 383 (1989) 620 and STJ 15 February 1966, BolMinJus 154 (1966) 286.

98. Under AUSTRIAN law a ratification may be declared expressly or by implication (*v. Zeiller* III § 1039 no. 2 p. 324); an implied ratification is typically inferred in the case of CC § 1016 (conferring benefit) (Klang [-*Stanzl*], ABGB IV/1², 895; Schwimann [-*Apathy*], ABGB V², §§ 1035 no. 3). The question of a time limit for ratification does not seem to have been a topic of discussion. The effect of a ratification is a matter of dispute. Formerly the view was held that ratification transforms the relationship between principal and intervener into one of *Bevollmächtigung* (agency) authorized from the outset (*v. Zeiller* III § 1039 no. 2 p. 324; *Ehrenzweig*, System II/1², 714; similarly *Gschnitzer* Schuldrecht BT², 283 and Klang [-*Stanzl*], ABGB IV/1², 895 [where the intervener has concluded legal transactions, this would point towards the law on contracts of mandate; where the intervention consists of physical acts, it points towards a contract for services]). The current view is that ratification transforms the unjustified intervention into a justified benevolent intervention (Rummel [-*Rummel*], ABGB I³, § 1037 no. 2). What precisely a ratification covers is a matter of interpretation (Rummel [-*Rummel*], ABGB I³, § 1037 no. 2; Schwimann [-*Apathy*] ABGB V² § 1035 no. 3). However, an intervention may only be ratified as a whole; the principal may not pick and choose particular component acts to ratify (OGH 4 December 1968, JBl 1969, 272). The intervener is bound by a ratification even if this is contrary to his wishes (Klang [-*Stanzl*], ABGB IV/1², 895). Under SLOVENIAN law too the principal may ratify an unjustified intervention. The ratification results in the retroactive conclusion of a contract between the intervener and the principal (*Cigoj*, Komentar II, 878). ESTONIAN CC § 1018 (1) (i) provides three alternative criteria for a justification of a benevolent intervention and puts the ratification by the principal at the top of the list (the other options are agreement with the presumed and actual wishes of the principal and intervention required as a matter of overriding public interest).

99. FRENCH and BELGIAN authors point out that only a principal capable of acting may validly ratify (*ratifier*) a benevolent intervention (JClCiv [-*Bout*], Art. 1372-1375, V° Quasi-Contrats. Gestion d'affaires – Effets, Fasc. 20 no. 76; *Paulus*, Zaakwaarneming

no. 106 p. 60). The ratification does not require any specific formalities (*Bout* loc.cit. no. 72; de *Page*, Droit Civil Belge II[3], no. 1088*bis* p. 1153). It may be either express or tacit (*tacite*), provided that the wishes of the principal are free from doubt (Cass.com. 13 May 1980, Bull.civ. 1980 IV, no. 199 p. 159; *Paulus*, loc.cit. no. 106 p. 60); in particular the principal must have knowledge of all relevant circumstances (*Bout* loc.cit. no. 73). No time limits seem to apply to ratification (*Flour/Aubert/Savaux*, Le fait juridique[10], no. 13 p. 15). The effect of *ratification* is usually expressed as *ratihabitio mandato aequiparatur*: the relationship between intervener and principal is transformed into a contractual mandate with retroactive effect (*Mazeaud and Chabas*, Leçons de droit civil II, 1[9] no. 691 p. 815; *Paulus*, loc.cit. no. 103 p. 59).

100. The corresponding POLISH provision may be found in CC art. 756 ('If the principal ratifies the intervention the legal consequences of a mandate arise'). SPANISH CC art. 1892, which is quite similar, reads: "the ratification of the intervention by the principal brings about the effects of an express mandate." Unless the parties agree otherwise, the ratification of an intervention (which has been started or completed) results in the application of the law of mandate with retroactive effect and the exclusion of the law of benevolent intervention. In this way the intervener is freed from liability for damages caused without fault (Paz-Ares/Diez-Picazo/Bercovitz/Salvador [-*Lasarte*], Código Civil II, 1949). Ratification may be express or implicit (*Albaladejo*, Derecho civil II (2) 497; *Lasarte* loc.cit. 1950; *Puig Brutau*, Compendio II, 602; *Lete del Río*, Obligaciones II, 127); the formality requirements mirror those required for the legal transaction to be ratified. A tacit ratification may be inferred, for example, where the principal does not take over the management of affairs from the intervener despite a request by the intervener to do so (*Sánchez Jordán*, Gestión de negocios, 427; *Lacruz Berdejo*, Rev.Crít.Der.Inm. 1975, 265). Substantial problems of interpretation however arise in the context of CC art. 1893 (1), which reads: "even if he has not expressly ratified the intervention, the owner of goods or principal who takes advantage of the benefits of the intervention will be liable for the obligations ...". The meaning of the phrase 'not expressly ratified' is a matter of dispute, but of great importance for determining the scope of the law of benevolent intervention. A recent decision of the *Tribunal Supremo* construes this provision as meaning only that a tacit ratification may be inferred if the principal takes advantage of the benefits of the intervention. Thus CC art. 1892 relates to express ratification, while CC art. 1893 concerns tacit ratification, and a tacit ratification does not bring about the legal consequences of CC art. 1892 (TS 14 May 1991, RAJ 1991 [3] no. 3672 p. 4945). TS 21 October 1958, RAJ 1958 (2) no. 3109 p. 2055 (a case concerning remuneration for services provided by an architect) took a different approach and held the law of contracts of mandate and contracts for services applicable also to cases covered by CC art. 1893. This interpretation radically limits (or limited) the scope of application of the law of benevolent intervention (*Pasquau Liaño*, La gestión de negocios ajenos, 208), since it confines (or confined) benevolent intervention to the cases which do not call for ratification contained in CC art. 1893 (2) (prevention of an impending damage). Legal literature has thoroughly criticised both judgments of the *Tribunal Supremo* (e. g. *Lasarte* loc. cit. 1952; *Puig Brutau*, loc. cit. 602; *Albaladejo*, loc.cit. 497 and *Lete del Río* loc. cit. 127). The authors cited consider CC art. 1892 to be applicable both to express ratification and tacit ratification; both cases result in the conclusion of a contract of mandate. In contrast to the *Tribunal Supremo*, they maintain that there is no tacit ratification in the

mere fact of the principal taking advantage of the benefits provided by the intervention. Whether or not a ratification is subject to a specific time limit is not a topic of discussion. Finally, Ley 561 of the Fuero Nuevo de NAVARRA should be mentioned. It reads: "If a person in whose interest an intervention is undertaken ratifies such intervention, that person is bound like a mandator."

101. In ITALY CC art. 2032 provides that the principal may ratify an act undertaken by the intervener even if the latter has not acted with an *animus aliena negotia gerendi*. The ratification gives rise to the same effects which a mandate contract would have had. The Italian case law has taken the line that a ratification may replace every single prerequisite of a relationship of benevolent intervention (Cass. 23 July 1960, no. 2122, Giur. it. 1962, I, 1, 92; Cass. 3 March 1954, no. 607, Giur. it. 1954, I, 1, 596). However, legal writing has in part adopted a more narrow approach. The minimum requirement is that the affair is that of another and that it has been managed without any obligation to do so (*Breccia*, La gestione d'affari[2], 901-902; even more restrictive is *Aru*, Gestione d'affari, 56). Ratification in respect of a legal transaction must be declared vis-à-vis the affected third party (Cass. 24 January 1959, no. 193, Foro it. 1959, I, 979). A tacit ratification is possible. An example is enforcing rights arising from a contract concluded by the intervener (Cass. 23 July 1960, no. 2122, Giur. it. 1962, I, 1, 92). The formal requirements of the ratification depend on the requirements of the legal transaction which the intervener has concluded (*Breccia*, loc. cit. 903; contra *Aru*, loc. cit. 59). The law does not provide for a specific time limit for the ratification. The prevailing (but not undisputed) view is that ratification is subject to the general limitation period of ten years (*Aru*, loc.cit. 60). However, some authors have argued that the time limit under CC art. 1712 (2) (ratification without delay) should be applied (for details see *Breccia*, loc.cit. 904). Both the third party and the intervener may request the principal to ratify the intervention within a reasonable time. If there is no ratification in response, it will be presumed to have been withheld (Cass. 3 March 1954, no. 607, Giur. it. 1954, I, 1, 596). In that case the intervener is personally liable on all legal transactions which he has concluded in the name of the principal (Cass. 18 March 1957, no. 931, Rep.Giur.it. 1957, voce Gestione d'affari, no. 1; 6). A ratification has retroactive effect (Cass. 23 November 1954, no. 4297, Rep.Giur.it. 1954, voce Gestione d'affari no. 5; 12), but any rights acquired by third parties are not affected. If the intervener has acted in the name of the principal, the latter assumes the rights and duties arising. If the intervener has acted in his own name, the ratification only has effect for the internal relationship between principal and intervener (Cass. 11 July 1978, no. 3479, Giur. it. 1979, I, 1, 820; Cass. 25 January 1974, no. 199, Giur. it. 1975, I, 1, 1373, note *Stolfi*).

102. DUTCH CC art. 6:202 BW reads: "Where a person who has acted with a view to looking after the interest of another had done so without good reason or has not properly done so, the interested party may, by approving the acts, surrender the right to invoke the defect against the manager of his affairs (...)" (translation by *Haanappel* et al., Netherlands Business Legislation). The ratification is categorized as a juridical act. It replaces the reasonable ground to act and cures the intervener's breach of a duty of care within the meaning of CC art. 6:200. Where both a reasonable ground is absent and the intervener has breached his duty of care, the principal can choose which of these elements he wishes to eliminate by ratification. In case of doubt, his ratification will be regarded as remedying both defects (T. M. Parlementaire Geschiedenis VI, 801-

802; Asser [-*Hartkamp*], Verbintenissenrecht III[10], no. 306 p. 317-318; T & C Vermogensrecht [-*Hijma*], Art. 6:202 BW, no. 1). Furthermore, CC art. 6:202 provides that the principal may set a reasonable time limit (*redelijke termijn*) for a ratification. After expiry of this time limit ratification is no longer possible; claims may only arise under the provisions of unjustified enrichment law and tort law (T. M. Parlementaire Geschiedenis VI, 802; *Hartkamp* loc.cit. no. 306 p. 317-318; *Hijma* loc.cit. no. 3). If the intervener has acted without reasonable grounds for intervening, a ratification has the effect that the law of benevolent intervention remains applicable nonetheless (*Hartkamp*, loc.cit. no. 306 p. 318). A ratification restricted to the conduct of the intervention (breach of the duty of care) will only lead to a waiver by the principal of a claim for compensation. The principal himself remains liable to compensate the intervener under CC art. 6:200 (T. M. Parlementaire Geschiedenis VI, 801; *Hartkamp* loc.cit. no. 306 p. 318; *Hijma* loc.cit. no. 2).

103. Again the legal situation under SCOTS law is not quite clear. It seems that a ratification is considered the retroactive acceptance of an offer to conclude a contract, such as a contract of mandate or of agency; a tacit ratification is possible (for details see *Leslie*, JuridRev 1983, 34 and Stair [-*Whitty*], vol. 15, para 109).

104. According to SCANDINAVIAN law the rules on ratification under the statutes on contract law in general seem to be applied also in the context of benevolent intervention. A ratification may also be inferred from conduct, such as the use of the benefits obtained from the benevolent intervention. A principal may also be bound if in the circumstances he ought to have realised that the *gestor* was acting in his interest and expected a remuneration (*Håstad*, Tjänster utan uppdrag, 57; see also *Grönfors*, Avtalslagen[3], 158), or if (as in HD 15 July 1941, NJA 1941, 459) a principal pays a fine which has become due as a result of an act of the intervener conducted in the interest of the principal. A ratification leads to the application of the law of mandate (*Håstad* loc.cit. 57). In the context of the SWEDISH and FINNISH Commercial Code Ch. 18 § 3 *in fine* (principal bound as a consequence of his making use of the benefit of a contract concluded in excess of authority) it is a matter of discussion whether or not the third party has a direct contractual claim against the principal. This is arguably answered in the affirmative in Finland (*Chydenius and Hakulinen*, cited according to *Zackariasson*, Direktkrav, 100), but in the negative in Sweden. In Sweden only a claim of the third party against the principal arising from unjustified enrichment (*vinstanspråk*) is recognised (*Grönfors*, Ställningsfullmakt och bulvanskap, 115; *Hellner*, Om obehörig vinst, 324, 336; *Karlgren*. TfR 1951, 180; *Zackariasson*, Direktkrav, 103).

105. Agency by ratification in the COMMON LAW requires (a) an act on the part of the prospective agent demonstrably undertaken in the name of or on behalf of the prospective principal, (b) capacity of the principal at the time of the agent's act to ratify, and (c) a subsequent effective ratification of the act by the principal based either on complete knowledge of the act or an unqualified (i. e. unconditional) approval: see *Marsh v. Joseph* [1897] 1 Ch 213, 246-247 (Lord *Russell* CJ, for the CA); *Firth v. Staines* [1897] 2 QB 70, 75 (*Wright* J), approved in *Boston Deep Sea Fishing and Ice Co v. Farnham* [1957] 1 WLR 1051, 1057 (*Harman* J). As to (a), see further Chapter 1, Art. 1:101, Notes, VI, 71. As regards (b), the principal must have had been in existence and have had capacity to undertake the agent's act personally both at the time of the act and at the time of ratification. Consequently a corporation is not able to ratify an act undertaken before the corporation was created or (subject to statutory exceptions)

if it was outside the corporation's own powers for the corporation itself to undertake that act. If a person acting ostensibly as agent for a not yet existent corporation concludes a contract in the name of that corporation, the corporation cannot take over the rights and obligations arising out of that contract by ratifying its conclusion by the agent: *Kelner v. Baxter* (1866) LR 2 CP 174, 183 (*Erle* CJ), 184 (*Willes* J), 185-186 (*Byles* J). (In such cases the agent may be regarded – contrary to the wording of the contract – as himself a party to the contract and liable on it accordingly.) Subject to developments in the law of unjustified enrichment, a corporation may in principle retain the benefit of such work done on its behalf by its putative agent before its creation without liability. A bare promise by the corporation to reward the agent will not give rise to contractual liability because the agent's act is only past consideration for the corporation's promise, while the absence of an anterior request by the corporation for the service rendered precludes a quasi-contractual claim: see *Re English & Colonial Produce Co* [1906] 2 Ch 435; *Re Rotherham Alum & Chemical Co* (1883) 25 Ch D 103. (Equally a corporation is not liable for unsolicited services rendered on its behalf after its dissolution: see *Re Banque des Marchands de Moscou* [1952] 1 All ER 1269 (*Vaisey* J).) Furthermore, the principal cannot ratify in respect of acts which the principal could not have authorised or undertaken at the time the agent acted: see *Boston Deep Sea Fishing and Ice Co v. Farnham*, loc. cit. (French company could not ratify act of English company carrying on a fishing business in its name during world war two because, due to German occupation, the company had enemy status at the time of the agent's acts: it could not itself have lawfully conducted the fishing business at that time and the English company would have committed a criminal offence in accepting any mandate from the French company). However, where a self-appointed agency remains unauthorised, the agent will nonetheless remain liable to surrender any profit obtained: see Chapter 2, Art. 2.102, Notes II, 22. As regards (c), "ratification is the act of giving sanction and validity to something done by another.": *Brook v. Hook* (1871) LR 6 Exch 89, 95 (*Martin* B, giving a dissenting minority view in that case, but not affecting this point). This requires that the principal recognises and accepts the agent's act or in some other manner treats the act as authorised. Ratification may be either express or implied. The latter may take the form of acquiescence on the principal's part if that is unambiguous and expliciable only by reference to the agent's act (i. e., where there is an 'obligation' on the principal to make a different view manifest): *Phillips v. Homfray* (1871) LR 6 Ch App 770, 778 (Lord *Hatherley* LC) and consider in this context *Hunter v. Parker* (1840) 7 M & W 322 (ratification of unauthorised sale by receipt of the purchase price). If the client knows the essential details of the agent's act, he may recognise it by making use of the rights resulting from that act in order to raise an action against a third party or to defend such an action: *Verschures Creameries Ltd v. Hull & Netherlands SS Co Ltd* [1921] 2 KB 608, and see similarly *The Australia* (1859) 13 Moore PC 132, 158 (Dr *Lushington*). A prerequisite of any ratification is knowledge of the circumstances of the agent's act at the time of the act or omission alleged to constitute the ratification: *Gunn v. Roberts* (1874) LR 9 CP 331, 335 (*Brett* J). For IRISH law (in connection with a gratuitous agency) see, for example, *O'Beirne v. Cornwall* (1852) 3 Ir Ch Rep 130, 138 (*Blackburne* LC). (iii) An unnecessary delay in contesting the agent's act may in suitable circumstances constitute a ratification: *The Australia*, loc. cit., 158 (Dr *Lushington*) (where, however, necessity sufficed to justify the captain's sale of the ship). A factor limiting the time period for ratification is the requirement that in order to be effective the principal must ratify at a time when he himself might have undertaken the agent's act (e. g. exercised the right vis-à-vis some third party or concluded the contract with the third party): see *Dibbins v. Dibbins* [1896] 2 Ch 348, where the principal had an option to buy the share of a partner exerciseable by notifying the personal representatives of the partner within three months of the partner's death of an intention to buy, but the act of an unauthorised agent within that period signifying to the executors the principal's intention was not effectively ratified by the principal (who at the time was mentally unfit and lacked capacity) where the purported ratification took place after the three months period had expired. Ratification has retrospective effect so that the act of the agent is to be regarded from the outset as authorized: *Boston Deep Sea Fishing and Ice Co v. Farnham*, loc. cit., 1057 (*Harman* J); *Danish Mercantile Co Ltd v. Beaumont* [1951] Ch 680, 686 (*Jenkins* LJ). As a result, where a person acts without authority, but in the name of the potential principal, in order to conclude a contract between that principal and a third party, a withdrawal from the agreement by the third party before the principal has ratified the agent's act is ineffective, even though, assessed at the time the third party purported to withdraw, there was no contract binding the third party. The contract between the principal and the third party comes into being at the time of the principal's ratification, but with effect from the time the agreement was made by the agent. See *Bolton Partners v. Lambert* (1888) 41 Ch D 295, 301 (*Kekewich* J), and on appeal (where the decision was affirmed), 306 (*Cotton* LJ), 309 (*Lindley* LJ) and 309-310 (*Lopes* LJ). (However, the PC in *Fleming v. Bank of New Zealand* [1900] AC 577, 587 (Lord *Lindley*) expressly reserved the right to reconsider the proposition decided in *Bolton Partners*.) On the other hand, a third party may withdraw from the contract before ratification by the principal if that ratification is an express condition of the contract: *Watson v. James* [1931] 1 Ch 455. As a further exception to the principle of retrospective effect, the ratification by the principal does not set aside any cancellation of the agreement which the agent and third party have undertaken before the principal ratified: *Walter v. James* (1871) LR 6 Ex 124. Ratification retrospectively alters the legal position of agent and principal (their rights and obligations) as between them. As a result of the retrospective authorization conferred by ratification, the agent is generally not liable to the principal in respect of his intervention: *Verschures Creameries Ltd v. Hull & Netherlands SS Co Ltd*, loc. cit. (the legal action of the principal against a third party, wrongly supplied by the agent with goods, for payment of the purchase price operated to ratify the agent's supply so as to preclude the principal from suing the agent for damages in respect of the goods lost by the wrongful supply); *United Australia Ltd v. Barclays Bank Ltd* [1941] AC 1, 31 (Lord *Atkin*, for the PC). Moreover, the agent will have a claim for reimbursement of his expenditure: see *Bristow v. Whitmore* (1861) 9 HLC 391, 11 ER 781 (HL), especially Lord *Campbell* LC at pp. 400-402 (784) (where, however, the claim to a proprietary security in the form of a *lien* for the benefit of the agent was rejected). Ratification may likewise provide the agent with a claim to remuneration: if ratification was contractually agreed between the parties for the agent's performances under the contract, ratification of an act outside the terms of the contract may operate to bring the act within the terms of the remuneration clause. See *Keay v. Fenwick* (1876) 1 CPD 745; *Hartas v. Ribbons* (1889) 22 QBD 254.

X. *Burden of Proof*

106. Under GERMAN law the general rules on the allocation of the burden of proof apply: each party has to allege those circumstances which are favourable to its case and prove them if they are disputed. Consequently the party (whether principal or intervener) who asserts a claim arising from benevolent intervention will have to prove the requirements of that claim. Proof of an intention to act on another's behalf will as a general rule require objective indications. Otherwise a person intermeddling could render themselves an intervener in the sense of CC § 677 retrospectively. However, according to settled German case law the intention to act on another's behalf is rebuttably presumed in the case of an 'objectively extraneous affair' or an affair which is 'objectively also another's'. This presumption applies independently of whether it is the intervener or the principal who is asserting a claim: see above notes *27* and *39*.

107. Under GREEK law the intervener has to prove that he has conducted an affair of the principal and that this was in line with the interests of the principal. A principal seeking to set up a defence against claims arising from benevolent intervention must prove either that there was a mandate in the sense of CC art. 730, that the intervener did not act with the intention to act on the principal's behalf, or that the conduct of the intervention was irreconcilable with his wishes (Georgiades and Stathopoulos [-*Papanikolaou*], Art. 736, no. 15 and Art. 730, no. 16). As in Germany, it is said that the intention to act on another's behalf will be presumed in the case of an objectively extraneous affair, whereas the intervener will have to assert and prove that he acted on another's behalf in the case of a merely subjectively extraneous affair (*Papanikolaou* loc.cit. Art. 730, no. 5). However, the concept of a subjectively extraneous affair is nowadays severely criticised.

108. Under PORTUGUESE law too the general rule on the burden of proof applies to the law of benevolent intervention. Facts establishing a right fall to be proved by the person who invokes the right. As in Germany and Greece, the intention to act on another's behalf is presumed (but open to rebuttal) if the intervener knew that the affair managed was objectively extraneous (*Vaz Serra*, BolMinJus 66 [1957] 95-97). It is a matter of dispute who bears the burden of proving fault in the context of CC art. 466 (2), which provides that the intervener is at fault if his intervention does not accord with the interest or the actual or presumed wishes of the principal. The Supreme Court has placed the burden of proof on the person sustaining damage in line with CC art. 487 (1) and so applied the rules of tort law by analogy (STJ 22 April 1986, RLJ 121 [1988] 59 with a critical note by *Baptista Machado*; BolMinJus 356 [1986] 352). However, a growing body of academic opinion advocates application of the contract law rule in CC art. 799 (1), which contains a reversal of the burden or proof (*Menezes Leitão*, Responsabilidade do gestor, 292-297).

109. The AUSTRIAN OGH (12 December 1962, SZ 35/130), in a case concerning exceeding an authority, indicated that it does not favour a reversal of the burden of (dis)-proving the intervener's fault (as an application of CC § 1298 by analogy). However, the impact of this decision is a matter of controversy within Austrian legal literature. It is doubted whether it has general relevance for the law of benevolent intervention and whether it would not be more appropriate to distinguish between the different types of benevolent intervention recognised by Austrian law. That would imply that the bur-

den of proof as regards fault would remain with the principal within the context of CC § 1036, but in all other cases it would be shifted to the intervener (for details see *inter alia* Rummel [-*Rummel*], ABGB I^3, § 1036 no. 3 and § 1040 no. 4; Schwimann [-*Apathy*], ABGB V^2, §§ 1036-1040, no. 18-19; *Meissel*, GoA, 147-148 and Klang [-*Stanzl*], ABGB IV/1^2, 896). The debate does not yet seem to be over as far as the details of the various modes of explanation are concerned. In contrast to Germany, the question whether or not the intention to act on another's behalf may be presumed in respect of specific measures taken by the intervener has hardly been discussed in Austria. It would seem the burden of proof remains with the party who asserts that the intervener intended to manage another's affair (*Meissel*, loc.cit. 149).

110. In accordance with the principle *actori incumbit probatio* under BELGIAN law the intervener has to prove all the requirements of the claims arising from justified benevolent intervention which he asserts. This includes the negative requirements (lack of a contractual or other legal obligation to act; absence of contrary wishes of the principal; action without *animus donandi*). As regards the latter requirement, the judge may exercise discretion and reallocate the burden of proof (B. H.Verb. [-*Roodhooft*] Hdst. V, De quasi-contracten, no. 2260). Under FRENCH law too *faits juridiques* must be proven by the claimant, that is to say the party who relies on *un fait*, *un acte* or *un moyen quelconque* (*Malinvaud*, Droit des obligations^7, no. 197 p. 135). No more specific rules apply for the proof of 'mental elements' such as the intention to manage another's affair.

111. No indications can be found in SPANISH legal writing of specific rules on the allocation of the burden of proof in relation to the law of benevolent intervention. It is assumed that the general rules contained in CCP art. 217 apply. Of course the defendant will have to assert and corroborate any defence. Thus, for example, it will be for the principal to prove that the intervener acted with *animus donandi* (*Sánchez Jordán*, Gestión de negocios, 321; *Pasquau Liaño*, La gestión de negocios ajenos, 67). However, the *Tribunal Supremo* has ruled that *animus donandi* will be presumed (unless rebutted) if the intervener is related to the principal and provides the latter with maintenance (cf. CC art. 1894), (TS 25 September 1968, RAJ 1968 [2] no. 3959 p. 2657).

112. ITALIAN law too applies the principle (contained in CC art. 2697) that the party who asserts a right in judicial proceedings has to prove the facts on which the right is based, while one who controverts those facts or asserts they are not effective to establish the right, or claims the right has been altered or extinguished, must prove the facts on which the defence is based. It would seem that no exceptions from this general rule are discussed in the context of benevolent intervention.

113. Under DUTCH law it is assumed that the intention to manage another's affairs – the intention to attend to the affairs of another in the interests of that other – must be made manifest to third parties (Verbintenissenrecht [-*Heisterkamp*], Art. 6:198 BW, no. 11. 2; *Verburg*, De vrijwillige zaakwaarneming, no. 35 p. 63-64). The case law as a rule infers an intention to act on another's behalf from the nature of the act undertaken and from the circumstances of the case (inter alia CA Amsterdam 29 October 1936, NedJur 1937, no. 1035 p. 1455; CA Amsterdam 17 December 1947, NedJur 1948, no. 318 p. 545; CFI Almelo 24 November 1954, NedJur 1955, no. 753 p. 1347). If the intention to act on another's behalf is not convincingly evident, the burden of proof remains with the intervener (HR 24 April 1992, NedJur 1992, no. 688 p. 2955).

114. The legal position of SCOTS law seems to accord with that of SPAIN. Explicit discussion of the matter, however, is confined to the defence of acting with *animus donandi*: "The *gestor* may be able to rely on the presumption against donation to prove that he did not intend to donate his outlays. Where the *gestor* is a near relative of the dominus, this presumption may be displaced by a contrary presumption that the benefits are conferred out of a sense of family duty" (Stair [-*Whitty*], vol. 15, para 116).

115. A discussion bearing particular rules of allocation of the burden of proof with respect of the law of benevolent intervention are not apparent in the SCANDINAVIAN legal systems.

116. The ordinary rules of burden approach for private law claims apply in the COMMON LAW to claims arising out of benevolent intervention, whereby the legal burden of proof rests with the party seeking to establish the propositions on which their claim to legal redress or the defence rests. Hence if a third party asserts a personal or proprietary claim against the principal on the strength of a contract concluded by an agent of necessity on behalf of the principal, it will be for the third party to prove the necessity which provided the agent with authority to conclude the transaction: see *The Alexander* (1842) 1 W Rob 346, 166 ER 602, where the plaintiffs failed to discharge the burden.

Illustration 1 is taken from the conclusions of Advocaat-Generaal *Hartkamp* to HR 21 December 2001, no. R00/032HR (http:www.rechtspraak.nl) (published in part also in RvdW 2002 no. 5); **illustration 3** from Cass.civ. 16 November 1955, JCP 1956 II no. 9087, note *Esmein*; RTD civ 1956, 356, obs. *Mazeaud*; **illustration 6** (two examples) from CA Rome 3 May 1983, Temi rom. 1983, 327 and from HR 10 December 1948, NedJur 1949 no. 122 p. 225; **illustration 9** from CFI Torino 1 December 1986, Riv.Dir.Comm. 1987, 541; **illustration 10** from STJ 22 April 1986, BolMinJus 356 (1986) 352; RLJ 121 (1988) 59; **illustration 12** from Cass.civ. 25 June 1919, D. 1923, I, 223; S. 1921, I, 12; **illustration 13** from OGH 3 October 1996, RdW 1997, 275; NZ 1997, 290; EFSlg. 81.427; RIS-Justiz RS0019782; **illustration 14** from CFI Zinnik 10 June 1992, TAgrR 1993, 202; **illustration 16** from BGH 8 November 2001, MDR 2002, 270; **illustration 21** from OGH 7 December 1972, SZ 45/137; JBl 1973, 476 note *Koziol;* **illustration 22** from OGH 11 September 1885, GlU10.689 and OGH 6 February 1894, GlU15.008 (same facts; two different defendants); **illustration 24** (glass window frame) from CA Liège 3 April 1979, Pas. belge 1979, II, 88; RGAR 1980 no. 10195, obs. *Glansdorf*; **illustration 25** from BGH 7 November 1960, BGHZ 33, 251; **illustration 32** from HR 19 April 1996, NedJur 1997 no. 24 p. 101; **illustration 33** from Cass.civ. 26 January 1988, Bull.civ. 1988, I, no. 25, p. 16; JCP 1989 éd. G., no. 21217, obs. *Dagorne-Labbe*; RTD civ 1988, 539, obs. *Mestre*; D. 1989 Jur. 405, note *Martin*, and CA Karlsruhe 23 March 1977, VersR 1977, 936.

Article 1:102: Intervention to Perform Another's Duty

Where an intervener acts to perform another person's duty, the performance of which is due and urgently required as a matter of overriding public interest, and the intervener acts with the predominant intention of benefiting the recipient of the performance, the person whose duty the intervener acts to perform is a principal to whom this Book applies.

Comments

A. General

1. **Scope and purpose** Article 1:102 governs a special situation within the law of *negotiorum gestio*. It concerns the discharge of duties owed by another who has neglected them despite the fact that their performance is urgently required as a matter of overriding public interest. The provision states that, without prejudice to other possible principals (primarily the recipient beneficiaries) the person whose duty is discharged is to be regarded as a principal to whom this Book applies. If the *gestor*, when he acted, intended primarily to promote the interests of the party who owes the obligation, the latter's status as principal may be deduced from the application of Article 1:101; Article 1:102 is neither applicable nor necessary in this situation. The matter rests with the general requirements in Article 1:101. If, by contrast, the *gestor* acts primarily with the intention of benefiting the immediate recipient of the money paid or services rendered, the person primarily obliged to perform would not be considered a principal under Article 1:101. It is the aim of Article 1:102 to prevent this outcome. Provision to the effect that the third party "is a principal to whom this Book applies" at the same time clarifies that the subsequent rules, i. e. Article 1:103 (Exclusions) and Chapters 2 and 3 apply independently of whether the requirements of Article 1:101 are met. There is therefore no need to determine if the *gestor* has acted with reasonable ground (Article 1:101(1)(a) in conjunction with (2)). In other words, if the requirements of Article 1:102 are fulfilled, that in itself constitutes a reasonable ground to intervene. It follows that a justified *negotiorum gestio* in relation to such a principal is not excluded merely because that principal (who by his default is responsible for the situation) has forbidden intervention.

2. **Duties during intervention** Furthermore, it follows from Article 2:101(1)(b) and (c) (Duties during Intervention) that only to a very limited extent must the intervener have regard to the wishes of the principal in the course of the intervention. The *gestor* is not constrained by the contrary wishes of the principal – either within the context of 'whether' the *gestor* may intervene or in the matter of 'how' the undertaking should be carried out. The constraint of the principal's wishes is ousted to the extent that an overriding public interest displaces it.

3. **Need for a rule within the framework of negotiorum gestio** One question which can be posed is whether the special situations, which form the subject matter for Article 1:102, should not be taken out of the law of *negotiorum gestio* and addressed in the law of

unjustified enrichment instead. The answer is certainly not merely a matter of the aesthetics of codification. Quite apart from the consideration that the approach adopted here corresponds to the traditions of the civil law systems, this approach is supported by the notion that in this situation too the intervener ought to benefit from the privileges granted by the law of *negotiorum gestio*. Numbering among those in particular is the point that (in contrast with the law of unjustified enrichment) the intervener's claim turns only on the prospective usefulness assessed at the time the act was commenced; it is not decisive that as a result of the intervener's act the principal was actually saved expenditure and consequently enriched. Moreover, with the assistance of the approach chosen here, it is clear from the outset that the intervening *gestor* acts lawfully within the meaning of the law of tort. The situations covered will not infrequently involve acts of intervention for which Article 3:103 (Right to Reparation) is material.

B. Intervention Urgently Required in Overriding Public Interest

4. **Overriding public interest** The contrary wishes of the principal need not be heeded if the principal is not discharging his duty, the performance of which is due and urgently required as a matter of overriding public interest. This rule requires not merely that the intervener acts to discharge a duty of the principal, but also that the discharge of the duty is of overriding public interest. It relates to the discharge of duties which are founded in private law context, but are of such importance that their fulfilment is at the same time a matter of public interest. The question as to which circumstances generate an overriding public interest cannot be answered once and for all and perhaps the answer may not even be the same for all European jurisdictions. (The public attitude towards suicide, which differs from country to country, may serve as an example.) A minimum requirement for a 'public' interest, however, is that the discharge of the duty is not merely in the interest of a single person. The typical cases concern tort law based duties to secure safety at large, whereas the discharge of contractual obligations to perform will hardly ever be a matter of public interest.

5. **Performing another's maintenance obligations** The performance of obligations to maintain persons who are being left in the lurch by the provider of maintenance also falls under Article 1:102. Within the conception of this draft, such obligations of maintenance are not to be understood as confined to furtherance of a private interest only, at any rate so long and in so far as the social policy of the state follows the principle of subsidiarity. That is because an elementary public interest is contained within the advancement of a privately maintained community and the contingent relief of the public purse which that entails. A comparable case since time immemorial is the arrangement of a burial.

6. **Performance must be due** Performance of the neglected duty must of course be due. It will not suffice that a duty whose performance will become due at some future point of time will most likely not be discharged. An imminently dangerous situation must already subsist at the moment of intervention. The requirement that performance of the duty is due is otherwise not of particular importance since the discharge of a duty where performance is not yet due will hardly ever be a matter of overriding public interest.

7. Performance must be urgently required Not every duty that satisfies the requirement that its discharge is of overriding public interest may be enforced by a third party against the contrary wishes of the debtor. Performance must be urgently required. There must be a need for immediate action, which for its part will as a rule consist of a provisional measure to ensure safety. Examples would be measures taken to safeguard dangerous spots for other road users, or to extinguish a fire or remove the risk of water damage which threatens to encroach onto neighbouring premises. Further examples would be taking measures (which cannot be postponed) to prevent an environmental damage which is immediately threatening to occur.

Illustration 1
P has parked his car in front of the emergency access for the fire service at a student halls of residence. I notices that the halls of residence have caught fire. He may remove the car despite the protest of P, if the removal is necessary in order not to delay the efforts of the fire brigade which is already under way. If, by contrast, there are no signs that the building has caught fire and the obstruction of the emergency access by P's car presents a merely notional danger for the building and its residents, then the removal of the car, although in overriding public interest, does not require I to intervene personally. It would be sufficient to call the police

Illustration 2
A society for the prevention of cruelty to animals attends to a maltreated and injured pet lying in agony in the street. The owner may not counter a claim for compensation for the costs incurred by the society with the objection that he had informed the association that he does not consent to the emergency treatment. That would entail cruelty to the animal of a criminal nature.

Illustration 3
A warehouse, which P has rented from I in order to store large quantities of milk powder, catches fires. The warehouse is destroyed. Some of the milk powder has burned; the rest of it has mixed with the water from the fire fighting and threatens to pollute the ground water. The competent public authority instructs I to clean up the ground and remove the remains of the milk powder. I does not have to heed the contrary wishes of P, whose lease has terminated. He can claim compensation in respect of the costs incurred for the sum which P would in any case have had to bear in the case of a normal termination of the lease. The removal of the remaining milk powder was a matter of overriding public interest. The claim for compensation is not blocked by Article 1:103(c) (Exclusions), since the "duty to a third party to act" referred to in that Article only extends to a duty arising from a private law legal relationship (whereas I's obligation to follow the instructions of the public authority is a duty under public law).

C. Third Party to be Regarded as Principal

8. An exception to Article 1:101(1) The rule in Article 1:102 specifies that the third party who has not fulfilled his duty is to be regarded as a principal. This clarification is necessary because Article 1:101(1) looks to the direction in which the subjective aspiration of the intervener points and often (though, of course, not necessarily) the intervener will have the individual whose body or property he is in fact protecting from danger exclusively or at any rate predominantly in mind. However, the person who is responsible in law for the situation of danger should not be relieved from that responsibility. It follows, therefore, that in such a case he too is to be regarded as a principal and that must be so even though the person that the *gestor* predominantly intended to benefit was the beneficiary of the performance of the principal's duty. In other words, it must be decided from case to case on the basis of Article 1:101(1) whether the beneficiary is to be recognised as a principal too. Article 1:102, on the other hand, stipulates the general rule that in any case the person under the obligation to act is "a" principal (albeit not necessarily "the", i. e. the sole, principal). He is a principal even if the *gestor* never even thought of seeking to protect him from possible liability. On the other hand, it remains the case in situations of this type that the *gestor* must have intended to benefit *another* (as recipient of his performance). Just as with the basic situation covered by Article 1:101, there can be no *negotiorum gestio* in these circumstances if he discharges a duty of the principal which was owed to him, the *gestor*, intending thereby to benefit himself.

Illustration 4
The facts are the same as in illustration 25 to Article 1:101. The woman's health insurer established under public law is also regarded as a principal. The duty of such a health insurer to provide medical treatment is a matter of public interest.

Illustration 5
A woman, who is separated from her husband but dependent on maintenance payments received from him, has an adipoma removed from her back by a doctor. Prior to the operation her husband states that he will not cover the costs of the operation. If the woman cannot obtain her husband's financial support for the operation under the applicable provisions of family law, she will not be able to do so by virtue of the rules on benevolent intervention either, since the surgery performed is not of urgent necessity. The doctor therefore only has a claim against the woman who is exclusively liable.

D. Article 1:101(2) Inapplicable

9. Public interest overriding the contrary wishes of the principal For cases which satisfy Article 1:102, Article 1:101(2) can have no application. We are concerned here with situations in which an overriding public interest has priority over the otherwise constraining wishes of the principal. Often the situation will amount to precisely the opposite of a conventional *negotiorum gestio*; if the *gestor* has learned that the principal intends to default on his duties, he (the *gestor*) has a reasonable ground for his intervention.

Illustration 6
A toddler is badly injured by a car accident and is taken to a hospital in a state of unconsciousness. The doctor in charge is able to contact the parents by telephone, but the parents object to the emergency operation for religious reasons. There is no time to apply to a court. The emergency operation may be conducted despite the contrary wishes of the parents.

Notes

I. *General Requirements of a Lawful Management of Another's Affairs Contrary to the Principal's Wishes*

1. GERMAN CC § 679 provides that the contrary wishes of the principal may be disregarded, if without the management of the affair, a duty of the principal whose fulfilment is of public interest, or a statutory duty to provide maintenance, owed by the principal would not be fulfilled in due time. An example for the first alternative is a duty to ensure public safety by removing an obstacle which jeopardizes traffic on a public road (BGH 4 December 1975, BGHZ 65, 354). It is a matter of dispute whether CC § 679 can be applied to cases in which a person prevents the suicide of another. Some authors answer this question in the negative on the basis that objections to suicide are merely a matter of ethics (Soergel [-*Mühl*], BGB[12], § 679 no. 5). However, the prevailing opinion is that the contrary wishes of the person intending to commit suicide are to be disregarded; mere immorality suffices, as the duty to render aid under criminal law (on this point see further the notes under Article 1:103 [Exclusions]) according to case law (BGH 10 March 1954, BGHSt 6, 147) is effective also as against the person intent on suicide (Staudinger [-*Wittmann*], BGB[13], § 679 no. 10). Other authors have argued that the wishes of the suicide are insignificant because a person who intends to commit suicide lacks legal capacity (MünchKomm [-*Seiler*], BGB[3], § 679 no. 13; and with different emphasis also Erman [-*Ehmann*], BGB I[10], § 679 no. 4).
2. According to GREEK CC art. 730 (2) the contrary wishes of the principal are to be disregarded if these are either contrary to law or infringe principles of morality. A violation of law requires the infringement of a provision within the scope of CC art. 174 and hence a breach of the public order. This restrictive construction of the requirement of a provision within the meaning of art 174 is said to be necessary for the protection of the principal against interference with his affairs (Georgiades and Stathopoulos [-*Papanikolaou*], Art. 730, no. 31). It is of no concern, for example, if the principal refuses to comply with a statutory duty to furnish maintenance (infringement of CC art. 1476) or an obligation to repair a building which threatens to collapse (infringement of CC art. 925) (*Papanikolaou*, loc.cit.). The term 'principles of morality' conforms with the term contained in CC art. 178. A violation of *bonos mores* is made out for example where a person is intent on committing suicide (*Papanikolaou*, loc.cit. no. 32). POLISH CC art. 754 corresponds with Greek CC art. 730 (2). Under this provision the opposed wishes of the principal may be disregarded, if they are "contrary

to law or the fundamental principles of social coexistence". HUNGARIAN CC § 485 (2) formulates the matter in these terms: "Intervention is fitting and proper in order to avert life threatening situations even against the will of the person whose life is endangered, prevent or avert extensive potential hazards even against the will of the owner or another duly authorized person, or fulfil the obligation to provide support even against the will of a person who is obliged to provide support" (Official Translation, Hungarian Legal Norms in Force in three Languages, CompLex CD HMJ, 2004). ESTONIAN CC § 1018 (1) (iii) goes beyond Article 1:102 in so far as any act performed for another is deemed justified if it is essential and in the public interest.

3. In the PORTUGESE law of benevolent intervention an intervention contrary to the principal's wishes is lawful if the wishes are contrary to law, public order or *bonos mores* (CC art. 465 (a)). Such wishes need not be and should not be heeded by the intervener. Examples are a suicide who is saved against his will (*Menezes Leitão*, Responsabilidade do gestor, 194; *Vieira Gomes*, Gestão de negócios, 199) and assistance to a child abandoned by its parents (*Almeida Costa*, Obrigações^{9}, 438; *Pires de Lima/Antunes Varela*, Código Civil Anotado I^{4}, Art. 465 no. 2).

4. AUSTRIAN CC § 1040 denies the intervener a claim under CC § 1037 for compensation of costs incurred, if he has knowingly acted contrary to the legally effective explicit or implicit wishes of the principal (Schwimann [-*Apathy*], ABGB V^{2}, §§ 1036-1040 no. 5). CC § 1040 similarly excludes claims on the basis of unjustified enrichment (OGH 23 October 1973, RIS-Justiz RS0019806; Rummel [-*Rummel*] ABGB I^{3}, § 1040 no. 1). However, by virtue of CC § 1040 the intervener is granted the right to take back an outlay *in specie* (*Meissel*, GoA, 46). Monies paid are considered always recoverable (OGH 30 August 2000, RIS-Justiz RS0114088). A prohibition uttered by the principal is without significance, however, if it is contrary to law or good morals within the meaning of CC § 879 (OGH 26 November 1963, ÖJZ 1964, 429), if it adversely affects the rights of third parties in an impermissible manner or if the principal lacked legal capacity at the time of his statement (*Meissel*, GoA, 46). Older legal writing also maintains that a prohibition is ineffective if it is contrary to general safety or public order (*Ehrenzweig*, System II/1^{2}, 719-720 [prohibition by home owner against extinguishing a fire; prohibition against bury a deceased person or providing maintenance to a child]) or if it is contrary to a duty owed to the community (Klang [-*Stanzl*], ABGB IV/1^{2}, 907; *v. Zeiller* II § 549 p. 408). According to CC § 1042 the discharge of a valid debt or other obligation which has fallen due is permissible despite the contrary wishes of the principal (the debtor); there is no further requirement of a particular public interest in the discharge (*Meissel*, GoA, 47). However, it has been argued that a debtor in his capacity as principal must have the opportunity of recourse against the intervener, who has discharged the debt, if the principal has suffered any disadvantages from the payment (such as the loss of a right of retention or set-off: *Meissel*, loc.cit, 51).

5. FRENCH case law proceeds from the principle that someone who intermeddles in the affairs of the principal against the principal's wishes commits a *faute*, which in a case of damage establishes tortious liability (*Flour/Aubert/Savaux*, Le fait juridique^{10}, no. 5 p. 7). The case law indicates, however, that the relationship of benevolent intervention can also arise where the opposition of the principal to the intervention was manifestly unjustified (*manifestement injustifiée*). This may be the case, for example, if the principal does not discharge a statutory duty and the intervener does nothing more

than fulfil that duty (*Flour/Aubert/Savaux* loc.cit.). The cases of most practical relevance for this exception concern the discharge by a third party of one spouse's duty to provide maintenance and render assistance to the other spouse (JClCiv [-*Bout*], Art. 1372-1375, V° Quasi-Contrats. Gestion d'affaires – Conditions d'existence, Fasc. 10 no. 112). Similarly in BELGIAN legal literature the view has been voiced that the principal's opposition to intervention may be unlawful or socially unreasonable and in consequence may be disregarded (*Paulus*, Zaakwaarneming no. 53 p. 41).

6. The SPANISH CC does not contain any rule according to which, as an exception, a benevolent intervention may arise notwithstanding explicit contrary wishes of the principal; on the contrary, the case law has emphasized that the intervener has to respect the wishes of the principal (TS 2 February 1954, RAJ 1954 no. 322 p. 198). Note should be taken of CC art. 1158 according to which a person who "settles an account of a third party may claim from the debtor what he has contributed unless he has not acted against the express will of the debtor. In the latter case he may only claim compensation in so far as the performance was of benefit for the debtor." CC art. 1158 however is not considered as laying down a rule on benevolent intervention, but rather as a provision on unjustified enrichment (*Díez-Picazo*, Fundamentos II[4], 488). Despite this statutory starting point, Spanish legal literature considers that in some cases the rules on benevolent intervention may apply, even though the intervener has acted contrary to the wishes of the principal. These are situations in which the principal's wishes run contrary to statute or to a duty whose discharge is of public or social interest (*Sánchez Jordán*, Gestión de negocios, 290; *Pasquau Liaño*, La gestión de negocios ajenos, 456). According to *Lacruz Berdejo*, Rev.Crít.Der.Inm. 1975, 261 the principal's wishes may even be disregarded if they conflict with *bonos mores*. It is not evident how CC art. 1894 (1) is to be reconciled with this analysis. The provision contains the rule that if a stranger provides maintenance "without the knowledge" of the person obliged to provide it, the stranger has a right to demand the sum paid from the person obliged unless it is established that he provided maintenance "for charitable reasons and without the intention to claim compensation". CC art. 1894 is problematic on account of the opening phrase ('without the knowledge' of the person obliged) (*Puig Brutau*, Compendio II, 604). The phraseology has been criticized because it places the person who pays the maintenance in a worse position than any third party who discharges a debt of another under CC art. 1158. A more logical legal policy would lead to the opposite result (*Lacruz Berdejo* loc.cit. 270; *Sánchez Jordán* loc.cit. 292). Finally, the Collection of Civil Laws of the Assembly of NAVARRA Ley 561 reads: "If he [the principal] has previously forbidden intervention, he is not under a duty to compensate."

7. Under ITALIAN law too acting contrary to a prohibition of the principal generally cannot not constitute a benevolent intervention. Such conduct is not held to be 'beneficial'. However, a prohibition of the principal is nugatory if it is contrary to statute or fundamental principles of the legal system or *bonos mores* (CC art. 2031 (2); CA Genova 10 April 1954, Foro Pad. 1955, I, 76). In cases of this type there is no requirement that the principal could not attend to his affairs himself. For example, the prohibition of the principal against intervention may be disregarded if, without intervention, inalienable rights of third parties would be infringed or adversely affected (Cass. 17 July 1969, no. 2636, Foro it. 1971, I, 713: a third party provides maintenance to an estranged wife in lieu of the defaulting husband). Acts by which a duty of the

principal is discharged are in general held to be useful (Cass. 15 October 1963, no. 2757, Foro it. 1964, I, 580).

8. It is likewise the case under DUTCH law that benevolent intervention contrary to the wishes of the principal is generally not possible. In such a case a reasonable ground for intervening is missing. However, regard need only be given to the 'fully effective' wishes of the principal. Acts contrary to the wishes of a person who is mentally disabled are not necessarily wrongful and may even be necessary (T. M. Parlementaire Geschiedenis VI, 791; Asser [-*Hartkamp*], Verbintenissenrecht III[10], no. 301 p. 315; Verbintenissenrecht [-*Heisterkamp*], Art. 6:198 BW, no. 12. 2; *Schrage*, Verbintenissen uit andere bron, no. 16 p. 12-13). An intervention contrary to the wishes of the principal will otherwise only be reognized in extraordinary circumstances (T. M. Parlementaire Geschiedenis loc.cit.; HR 19 April 1996, *NedJur* 1997 no. 24, p. 101). The rescue of a person intending to commit suicide may serve as an example (Asser [-*Hartkamp*], Verbintenissenrecht III[10], no. 301 p. 314-315; *Verburg*, De vrijwillige zaakwaarneming, no. 55 p. 84-85). There is no statutory counterpart to German CC § 679. However, it has been accepted that as a matter of public interest the public authority might clean up land as an intervener against the contrary wishes of the person responsible (*Frenk/Messer*, NJB 1993, 48-49; Verbintenissenrecht [-*Heisterkamp*], Art. 6:198 BW, no. 12. 5).

9. The legal situation in SCOTLAND appears not to be resolved. Among the institutional writers only *Stair*, Institutions, Book I, title 8, 3 and *Erskine* (1828), Book III, Volume II, 53 address the issue and discuss a claim of the intervener for reimbursement of expenditures limited to the surviving enrichment of the principal. Stair (-Whitty) vol. 15 para 139 (1996), in reference to this, ventures the opinion that in extremely exceptional circumstances public interest may override the contrary wishes of the principal – at any rate where the latter is opposed to the discharge of his duty to provide maintenance. Whether the claim for reimbursement in this exceptional case is a matter of unjustified enrichment law or the law of benevolent intervention remains unclear.

10. In a case in which the fire brigade removed loose roof sheeting which a storm threatened to cast onto the street, the SWEDISH Supreme Court has held that the owner in general must suffer such an intervention (of the fire brigade or any third party) (HD 9 March 1972, NJA 1972, 88). HD 20 February 1952, NJA 1952, 63 has held the same in a case of maintenance of animals where the principal would otherwise render himself criminally liable for cruelty to animals.

11. In a case of emergency – at any rate where human or animal welfare is concerned – a person may have authority in ENGLAND AND WALES as an agent of necessity to act contrary to the wishes of the principal: cf. *Palmer v. Stear* (1963) 113 LJ 420 (Kingsbridge County Court), where a vet employed by the defendants destroyed a seriously injured dog belonging to the plaintiff in view of its condition and an action for damages for trespass failed because it would have caused suffering to the semi-conscious and dying dog not to have done so, the owner being under a legal duty to destroy or procure the destruction of the dog to prevent cruelty, and the vet had authority as agent of necessity to put the dog down. There is no requirement that an act in connection with the care or treatment of a person lacking capacity under sec. 5 of the Mental Capacity Act 2005 (which, when it comes into force, also provides for rights under sec. 8 for indemnification, to pledge that person's credit or to dispose of

money in their possession) correspond with that person's wishes, but it must be done in the reasonable belief it is in that person's best interests and (under sec. 6) there are further restrictions if the act is intended to restrain that person's liberty. In extreme cases a *duty* to act may arise. Where a husband acquiesces in the request of his gravely-ill wife not to summon a doctor to attend to her and the wife dies as a result, the husband may commit the crime of manslaughter based on the fatal consequences of the ommission to discharge a spouse's duty to care for the other spouse's health; the capacity of the wife to make rational decisions is a matter to be considered in determining whether there has been a "reckless disregard" of the duty to act: *R v. Smith* [1979] Crim LR 251. However, a person will not have authority to act contrary to the principal's wishes so as to interfere with the principal's right of self-determination if the principal is competent to act and makes his informed and free choice known: cf. Clerk and Lindsell (*-Jones*), Torts[18], para. 3-106. Nor will there be authority to act against the principal's wishes if the intervener can pass the matter to the public authorities who will have the necessary powers to intervene: cf. the IRISH case of *Flannery v. Dean* [1995] 2 ILRM 393, 397 (*Costello* J) (no right to retain possession of the owners horses against her consent, despite her neglect of them, because the defendant could have referred the matter to the local authority which had power to keep the animals in a local pound), and see to similar effect *Carter v. Thomas* [1893] 1 QB 673 (no right for volunteer to force his assistance where adequate fire brigade attending to fire). Where the claimant acts at the request of the public authorities in order to discharge a public duty for the defendant, performance of the duty being required urgently and the defendant being out of contact, the claimant will act as an agent of necessity: cf. *White v. J. D. Troups Transport* [1976] CLY 33 (Stockton-on-Tees County Court), where a business hiring out equipment acted as the defendant's agent of necessity when, at police request, it removed the defendant's vehicle which was stuck under a bridge on blocking a busy road before the rush hour.

II. *Specific Cases Subject to Particular Rules (Maintenance, Funeral Costs)*

12. ESTONIA, GERMANY and SPAIN have explicit rules on rights in respect of maintenance provided and funeral costs incurred. Estonian CC § 1018 (1) (iii) stipulates that an intervention contrary to the wishes of the principal is lawful if the principal does not discharge his statutory duty to pay maintenance when due. Similarly the German CC in § 679 declares the contrary wishes of the principal to be immaterial if these would lead to the principal's duty to pay maintenance not being discharged when due. Spanish CC art. 1894 (1) provides that a third party who discharges the duty of the party obliged 'without the knowledge' of the latter, may claim compensation unless he did not have any intention to claim compensation at the time he provided the benefit. CC art. 1894 (2) grants a claim for compensation of reasonable funeral costs incurred against the deceased's estate and, as a subsidiary claim, against the persons who were under a duty to maintain the deceased while he was alive. The notion of funeral costs is given a wide meaning (Paz-Ares/Diez-Picazo/Bercovitz/Salvador [*-Lasarte*], Código Civil II, 1955). The duty to reimburse funeral costs contained in AUSTRIAN CC § 549 was originally also regarded as part of the law on benevolent intervention (*v. Zeiller* II, § 549 p. 409), but is now characterised as a claim in unjustified enrichment law. (Rummel [*-Welser*], ABGB I[3], § 549 no. 5). CC § 1042 (for

whose application the provision of maintenance by a third party has always constituted a prime example) is likewise now seen as a provision of unjustified enrichment law. If a third party pays maintenance (provided for by statute) in the expectation of receiving compensation from the debtor under the maintenance obligation (and thus in absence of an *animus donandi*), that person has a claim for compensation under CC § 1042 (OGH [strengthened Division] 9 June 1988, SZ 61/143).

13. The GREEK Civil Code allows an intervention against the wishes of the principal if those wishes infringe statute or *bonos mores* (CC art. 730 (2)). Failure to pay maintenance (see above note 2) is an example of this. Apart from this rule CC art. 738 (2) only provides that in case of doubt a person is regarded as acting with *animus donandi* when they provide maintenance to a blood relation in the direct line or the second degree (by civil law reckoning) in the collateral line (i. e. brother and sister). PORTUGUESE law has no provision which explicitly provides for maintenance or funeral costs. Such cases will fall within the scope of CC art. 465 limb (a), a provision which has been drafted in wider terms than (for instance) German CC § 679 because (among other reasons) according to this provision an act may permissibly be undertaken in contravention of the principal's wishes if those wishes infringe *bonos mores* (*Menezes Leitão*, Responsabilidade do gestor, 194 (fn. 3)). As mentioned above (see note 5) FRENCH academic writing regards the discharge of an *obligation d'assistance et de sécours entre époux* as the textbook example of a legitimate intervention contrary to the wishes of the debtor of the maintenance obligation. On the claim for reimbursement of funeral costs under the rules on benevolent intervention see also CA Paris 3 May 1989, Juris Data 1989-022252. ITALIAN case law has repeatedly held that unless it is provided with an *animus donandi* payment of maintenance despite the contrary wishes of the defaulting principal can constitute benevolent intervention (Cass. 20 May 1961, no. 1196, Foro it. 1962, I, 1, 756; Cass. 17 July 1969, no. 2636, Foro it. 1971, I, 713; Cass. 9 August 1988, no. 4883, Rep.Giur.it. 1988, voce Alimenti, no. 2). The same holds true for meeting funeral expenses for the benefit of the heirs (Cass. 28 June 1975, no. 2557, Rep. Foro it. 1975, voce Gestione d'affari, no. 2; Trib. Milano, 13 July 1987, no. 6615 cited by *Rescigno*, Codice Civile, art. 2028 § 4). Under DUTCH law payment of maintenance for the benefit of neglected children likewise constitutes a recognized case of benevolent intervention which is justified despite the parents' contrary wishes (T. M. Parlementaire Geschiedenis VI, 791). It has also been held that necessary medical attendance provided by a hospital to a child who has fallen ill will be a legitimate benevolent intervention although the child's parents are opposed to treatment (CFI Rotterdam 20 August 1993, NedJur 1995 no. 18 p. 73).

14. In SCOTLAND it is argued that where a family member steps into the breach on behalf of another family member it may be assumed if there is nothing more to go on that that person has acted out of a sense of family loyalty and therefore with an *animus donandi*. A benevolent intervention or claims for 'recompense' will thus only be considered in exceptional circumstances (Stair [-*Whitty*], Vol. 15, paras 98, 116).

15. There appear to be no decisions yet in SWEDISH case law on claims for compensation in respect of maintenance provided not merely in place of the person liable to provide it, but also contrary to that person's wishes. The decided cases all concern claims for contribution between siblings where one of the siblings has carried the sole or disproportionate burden of providing for their parents (HD 19 November 1909, NJA 1909, 551; HD 13 November 1937, NJA 1937, 524; HD 16 September 1944, NJA

1944, 429), or claims where the reputed father has raised a child in the belief he is the biological parent (HD 29 April 1968, NJA 1968, 183; HD 5 June 1975, NJA 1975, 330; HD 29 March 1978, NJA 1978, 144). However, changes to family law have rendered this line of case law irrelevant. The claims of the Swedish state for compensation against parents whose duty to maintain the children has been discharged by the state are specifically regulated by statute in §§ 21-31 of the Maintenance Support Act.

16. ENGLISH law recognises a right to intervene at another's expense in order to discharge a duty of that other which is due and a matter of overriding public interest where a person arranges for the funeral of a deceased person, although that person may not themselves be under an obligation to do so. An intervener (whether an undertaker or a third party who pays the undertaker: *Ambrose v. Kerrison* (1851) 10 CB 776 at 779, 138 ER 307 at 308 (*Jervis* CJ)) has a claim to reimbursement of their expenses, provided these are reasonably incurred, i. e. that "no unnecessary expense is incurred" (*Rogers v. Price* (1829) 3 Y & J 28 at 37, 148 ER 1080 at 1083 (*Vaughan* B)). (As a rule, however, the reasonableness of the sum expended seems not to have been challenged: see, for instance, *Tugwell v. Heyman* (1812) 3 Camp 298, 170 ER 1389 and *Ambrose v. Kerrison*, loc. cit..) There is no requirement that the intervener act at the request of a person obliged to dispose of the body: *Jenkins v. Tucker* (1788) 1 H Bl 90 at 93, 126 ER 55 at 57 (Lord *Loughborough* CJ) (action supportable "though there was neither request nor assent on the part of the defendant"); *Rees v. Hughes* [1946] KB 517, 523 (*Scott* LJ), 527-528 (*Tucker* LJ, invoking the then commonplace legal fiction of a request implied by law) and for illustrations see *Tugwell v. Heyman*, loc. cit. (executor liable, though did not request burial). The basis for the exceptional rights of an intervener in this type of case (whose origins, if they lie in the case law of the ecclesiastical courts, may have been influenced by the Roman *actio funeria* through the channels of civil and canon law learning) is the public interest in discharge of the obligation to dispose of the body: see *Jenkins v. Tucker*, loc. cit., 93 (57) (Lord *Loughborough* CJ: "a duty which the defendant was under a strict legal necessity of [. . .] performing, and which common decency required"); *Shallcross v. Wright* (1850) 12 Beav 558 at 561, 50 ER 1174 at 1175 *per* Lord *Langdale* MR ("reasons of an important nature that the dead body should be buried without delay"), and similarly *Rogers v. Price*, loc. cit., 34 (1082) (*Garrow* B) and *Tugwell v. Heyman*, loc. cit., (where Lord *Ellenborough* CJ emphasises the necessity for intervention by a stranger). Traditionally the claim has been regarded as "quasi-contractual" (*Shallcross v. Wright*, loc. cit., 561 (1175) (Lord *Langdale* MR: "if this [burial] had been done by a stranger, there would have been a sufficient consideration, from which a contract to pay would have been implied") on the basis that in discharging the defendant's obligation the claimant has 'paid to the defendant's use' (*Jenkins v. Tucker*, loc. cit., 93 (57) (Lord *Loughborough* CJ)). In modern terminology it may be restated as a restitutionary claim based on unjustified enrichment arising from the discharge of another's liability, necessity providing the requisite unjust factor. The principle is obscured somewhat by unclarity in the law as to who or, rather, when a given person is obliged to bury the deceased, though the following statement of the law may be extracted from the authorities. (1) Since the expense will be met by the deceased's estate (see the Administration of Estates Act 1925, secs. 33(2) and 34(3)), the duty to arrange the funeral is placed in the first instance on the person lawfully entitled to its administration. The persons primarily responsible for arranging a funeral are thus the personal representatives: see *Williams v. Williams* (1882) 20 Ch D

659, 664 (*Kay* J: executors responsible for burial); *Holtham v. Arnold* (1986) 2 BMLR 123, 124-125 (*Hoffman* J) (the legal position of an administrator is no different from that of an executor and has the right and duty to arrange the funeral): *Grandison v. Nembhard* (1989) 4 BMLR 140 (*Vinelott* J) (executors); and see also *Dobson v. N. Tyneside Health Authority* [1996] 4 All ER 474, 478e (*Peter Gibson* LJ). (2) Where there are no personal representatives in a position to do so (e. g. because there is no will, or no appointment of an executor under a will, and no administrator has been appointed, or the deceased's estate is insufficient for the purposes), the duty of interring the body devolves on the parent, if the deceased is an infant child and the parent has the means: see *R v. Vann* (1851) 2 Den 325 at 326 and 300, 169 ER 523 at 524 and 525-526 (Lord *Campbell* CJ) (where, however, a criminal nuisance in failure to bury was not established because the impoverished parent was not obliged to take out a loan to finance burial), confirmed by *Bramwell* B in *Osborn v. Gillett* (1873) LR 8 Ex 88, 99, and applied by *Stephen* J in *R v. Price* (1884) 12 QBD 247, 254; *Bedwell v. Golding* (1902) 18 TLR 436 (*Phillimore* J); and *Clark v. London General Omnibus Co Ltd* [1906] 2 KB 648, 652, 655 and 659 (Lord *Alverstone* CJ) (but cf. 663, where *Farwell* LJ assumed the point without being satisfied of it), cited to this effect with approval in *Dobson v. N. Tyneside Health Authority* loc. cit., 478 f (*Peter Gibson* LJ); *R v. Gwynedd CC ex parte B* [1992] 3 All ER 317, 319j (*Balcombe* LJ); *Hume*, 2 (1956) Sydney L Rev 109, 112. If the deceased was married, the surviving spouse is under a like contingent liability to bury the deceased: see *Clark v. London General Omnibus Co Ltd* loc. cit., 663-664 (where *Farwell* LJ assumed this) as well as the cases cited below; *Hume*, 2 (1956) Sydney L Rev 109, 110-112. For the view that a child of the deceased, if of full age, is correspondingly bound to bury their parent, see *Hume*, loc. cit., 113. However, there appears to be no authority for a wider proposition that the next of kin as such are under a duty to bury the deceased: see *Dobson v. N. Tyneside Health Authority* loc. cit., 478 f (Peter Gibson LJ). (3) Failing someone responsible within the above categories, burial becomes the responsibility of the occupier in whose premises the deceased died (unless the householder does not have the requisite means): *R v. Stewart* (1840) 12 Ad & El 773 at 778, 113 ER 1009 (Lord *Denman* CJ) (deceased dying in hospital; husband of the deceased, who was in receipt of social assistance, was too poor to effect burial). (4) If no suitable arrangements are apparently being made for burial or cremation, the local authority for the area where the person has died or been found dead has a statutory obligation to bury or cremate the body: Public Health (Control of Diseases) Act 1984, sec. 46(1) (replacing the National Assistance Act 1948, sec. 50). (At common law there was no such duty on the authority: *R v. Stewart*, loc. cit. (disbursement for such purposes *ultra vires*; application for mandamus failed); *Woolwich Overseers v. Robertson* (1881) 6 QBD 654, 658 (*Lindley* LJ).) (On the rights and duties of local authorities in this matter, see further Chapter 1, Art. 1:103, Notes, IV, 30.) These rules set out a hierarchy of liabilities; a person liable to arrange burial has no right of contribution or indemnification from a person whose contingent liability is of lower degree: see *Rees v. Hughes*, loc. cit., where the claim of an executor against the husband of the deceased failed because of the primacy of the executor's liability. (*R v. Stewart*, loc. cit., where the application against the local authority was made on behalf of the hospital in which the pauper died, could also now be regarded as a decision to the same effect.) The claim of an intervener is in the first instance for reimbursement out of the deceased's estate, since the personal presentatives are primarily obliged to dispose of the body (and have a right of recourse to the deceased's estate for that purpose): *Tugwell v. Heyman*, loc. cit.; *Arlot v. Churchland* (1828) unreported (Court of Common Pleas) cited 3 Y & J 32-33, 148 ER 1081; *Rogers v. Price*, loc. cit.; *Ambrose v. Kerrison*, loc. cit., 777 and 779 (308) (*Jervis* CJ: "There can be no question that an undertaker who performs a funeral may recover from the executor of the deceased (having assets) the reasonable and necessary expenses of such funeral, without any specific contract"); *Sharp v. Lush* (1879) 10 Ch D 468, 472 (*Jessel* MR: an executor is liable even though he has not arranged the funeral); *Rees v. Hughes*, loc. cit., 524-525 (*Scott* LJ), 528 (*Tucker* LJ). Alternatively the intervener may himself apply part of the deceased's estate to effect the funeral and does not become an executor *de son tort* in doing so: *Rees v. Hughes*, loc. cit., 524 (*Scott* LJ). (Prior to reform of the law of succession, the intervener's claim against the personal representatives or right to use the deceased's assets could only touch upon the deceased's personal property; an heir or devisee to whom the deceased's real property passed was unaffected: *Carter v. Beard* (1839) 10 Sim 7, 59 ER 514.) Only when the deceased's estate is insufficient to satisfy the expenses incurred does the intervener have a claim against the relatives of the deceased or third parties who are (in the circumstances, by virtue of their contingent obligation) liable to effect the funeral. The legal position in such a case was left open in *Rees v. Hughes*, loc. cit., 527 (*Morton* LJ), but the proposition is supported by and explains earlier case law. Where the deceased was a married woman who by virtue of that status (prior to reforms in the late nineteenth century) largely lacked an independent personal estate, an action for reimbursement of funeral costs could be brought against the husband: *Jenkins v. Tucker*, loc. cit. (deceased's father arranging the funeral, the husband being abroad); *Ambrose v. Kerrison*, loc. cit., and *Bradshaw v. Beard* (1862) 12 CB (N. S.) 344, 142 ER 1175 (where in both cases the deceased and her husband were separated). It has been asserted that there is no requirement that the intervener first contact the person who is obliged to effect the funeral and will be liable to make reimbursement: see to this effect *Bradshaw v. Beard*, loc. cit., 348 (1177) (*Erle* CJ). Arguably, however, that this is confined to cases where the intervener is himself (contingently) obliged to effect a funeral and is merely seeking reimbursement from one who is primarily liable: in *Bradshaw v. Beard* itself the brother was obliged at common law to arrange burial because the deceased had died in his house (loc. cit., 348 *per Willes* J). There is no clear authority that the same rule applies where a stranger who is not under any obligation intervenes; in a number of cases communication was either impossible or impractical in the circumstances – see *Ambrose v. Kerrison*, .loc. cit (claimant did not know where the husband resided); *Jenkins v. Tucker*, loc. cit. (husband abroad); *Rogers v. Price*, loc. cit. (executor residing too far away for advance notification). In any case there is no claim to reimbursement if the intervener (e. g. by concealment) impedes the person primarily liable to arrange the funeral from doing so: *Bradshaw v. Beard*, loc. cit., 349 (*Willes* J). Moreover, an intervener may not act in contravention of the known wishes of the person (primarily) obliged if the latter (lawfully) refuses to bury the body at that point in time: *Rogers v. Price*, loc. cit., 36 (1083) (*Hullock* B). Statutory provisions enable public authorities providing social assistance or maintenance to recover expenses incurred from persons who were liable to provide maintenance to the person assisted: see National Assistance Act 1948, sec. 43; Children Act 1989, sec. 29 and Sch. 2, Part 3; Child Support Act 1991 (as amended by Part 1 of the Child Support, Pensions and Social Security Act 2000 and supplemented by the Child Support Act 1995).

Illustration 2 is taken from CFI Groningen 2 September 1999, Prg. 2000, 5375; **illustration 3** from BGH 8 March 1990, BGHZ 110, 313; **illustration 4** from BGH 7 November 1960, BGHZ 33, 251; **illustration 5** from CFI Toulouse 26 October 1932, D. 1933, 2, 107; **illustration 6** from CFI Rotterdam 20 August 1993, NedJur 1995 no. 18 p. 73.

Article 1:103: Exclusions

This Book does not apply where the intervener:
(a) is authorised to act under a contractual or other duty to the principal;
(b) is authorised, other than under this Book, to act independently of the principal's consent or
(c) is under a duty to a third party to act.

Comments

A. The Negative Requirements for the Applicability of the Law of negotiorum gestio

1. **Fundamentals** The provisions of Article 1:103 concern cases in which the law of *negotiorum gestio* is not applicable, despite the fact that the conditions of Articles 1:101 (Intervention to Benefit Another) or 1:102 (Intervention to Perform Another's Duty) are satisfied. Article 1:103 therefore touches upon the 'negative' requirements of a *negotiorum gestio*, namely (a) the absence of an authorisation (and duty) to act arising out of some contract or other legal ground, (b) the absence of a power to intervene which is independent of the wishes of the principal, and (c) the absence of a duty to act owed to a third party.

2. **Priority of special statutory regimes** The Article does not expressly state that the law of *negotiorum gestio* also yields priority to special statutory regimes which aim to provide a complete set of rules for the cases covered. That does not seem necessary because it is merely an instance of the general principle whereby in case of conflict more specialised statutory provisions oust the application of general provisions. Consequently, where the law provides for special and exhaustive rules governing the relationship between the intervener and the principal, those special rules have precedence over the Principles in this text. Examples are to be found in statutes on the provision of emergency aid by doctors.

B. Authority and Duty (limb (a))

3. **The principle** A person who is obliged to the principal to undertake the act in question does not act as an *intervener without authority*. This is a defining feature of this area of law, whose purpose is precisely to bridge the gap which may arise from the absence of a pre-existent duty under private law – in particular the absence of a contractual duty to act. Moreover, someone who is obliged to the benefited party to undertake the act in question is necessarily at the same time also authorised to act. That is the point of departure for the formulation adopted for limb (a) and is true both for contractual duties and duties imposed by law whose discharge the active party is obliged to the benefited party to undertake. The authority to act derives its foundation from the particular duty whose performance falls for consideration. Someone who is obliged to the principal to act is always also authorised to act (though conversely not everyone who is authorised to act is also obliged to act: see limb (b)).

4. **Precise identification of the duty** It is important, however, to identify the relevant duty precisely in the context of the particular case.

> *Illustration 1*
> A plumber who has been summoned by a home owner to repair the plumbing, but is not greeted by the owner on arrival at the house proceeds to repair the plumbing off his own bat. The plumber was obliged to make the repairs, but not authorised to enter the house without consent (unless the parties had agreed this). The apparent contradiction is resolved when it is accepted that the plumber was not obliged to convert his promise into action *in this way*. So considered it remains the case that one who is obliged to do an act is always also authorised to do it, while one who is authorised to do it is not thereby automatically obliged to do it.

5. **Acting under a contractual obligation towards the principal** A *negotiorum gestio* can only be made out if the parties do not stand in a legal relationship defined by an obligation between them which confers on the principal a right to conduct the affairs of the principal which are in fact managed. In particular, there is no *negotiorum gestio*, therefore, if the party acting was contractually obliged to the entitled party to undertake the act in question. Whether a contract between the parties has come into existence and, if so, what duties between them it establishes are questions which are exclusively for determination in the law of contract. Contract law thus has complete priority to this extent in relation to the law of *negotiorum gestio*. The latter comes into play only if the necessary contractual authority to act and a corresponding contractual duty cannot be found. In that case there remains room for the law of *negotiorum gestio* to operate between the parties.

Illustration 2
Where a party to a long-term contract suffers a heart attack during a business negotiation about termination of the contract and is brought to hospital by the other party, the latter acts as *gestor* in doing so. Ferrying the contractual partner to the hospital has nothing to do with the contractual relationship between the parties.

6. **Existence of a contract** The Article leaves to the law of contract all questions as to the existence of a contract and the rights and duties which arise out of it. It is for contract law to decide whether and in what circumstances a contract has come into existence between an intervener and a principal by which the former obtains the consent of the principal to intervene or, as the case may be, continue his intervention. The Article equally leaves it to contract law to decide whether an approval of an intervention (Article 1:101(1)(b)) leads in any given case to the conclusion of a contract (see comments *F58-59* to Article 1:101). Moreover, under the rules on benevolent intervention in another's affairs it is for the law of contract to determine whether and in what cases a contract comes into existence where someone intervenes at the request of another or in response to another's cry for help. Article 1:103(a) is accordingly silent on the particular issue of what conditions are necessary for a contractual duty to provide aid or the assumption of a contractual obligation to pay damages in favour of a saviour (a *convention d'assistance*). Presumably, under the PECL, as a rule, no contract to provide assistance or to pay damages comes into being between the injured party and the saviour he has bidden to help him, since neither the saviour nor the party calling for help will normally have the intention to bind themselves legally. Thus in such cases room is left for the application of the law of benevolent intervention. The same goes for courtesies and favours which do not entail the character of a legal obligation. However in case of such arrangements (such as for example being given a lift in another's car) it will often be assumed that the active party acts with an *animus donandi* (Article 3:104(1) (Reduction or Exclusion of Intervener's Rights)). A contractual relationship does come into existence, however, if someone promises another a reward for doing something specific; it is concluded at the moment that the promisee commences performance of that activity. Finally, so long as there is no European regime to determine under what circumstances a (valid and enforceable) contract is concluded with a person who lacks full legal capacity (e. g. a minor) this area too remains to be governed exclusively by the applicable law of contract or law of persons, as the case may be. In this context it may be that by virtue of a special statutory regime the relationship between doctor or hospital on the one hand and an unconscious patient on the other is configured on a contractual basis.

7. **Acting in pursuance of a void contract** Article 1:103 does not touch upon the question whether a person who supposes he is obliged to perform under a contract for services, but falls short of achieving that because the contract is void, may qualify as an intervener. This question falls to be decided instead under Article 1:101 (Intervention to Benefit Another) and must be answered in the negative due to the absence of an intention to benefit another (see comment *C22* under Article 1:101).

8. **Acting in breach of contract** There is equally no intervention without authority where a party to a contract acts in that capacity but in breach of his contractual duties. The fact that a party to the contract performs his duties under the contract poorly does not alter the fact that he was authorised to intervene.

9. **The priority of contract law rules of a quasi-negotiorum gestio nature** As already noted in the introduction (at *D30 ff*), the law of contract contains various rules which from a functional point of view show certain similarities to the law of *negotiorum gestio*. These rules too, of course, have priority and thus correspondingly exclude the law of *negotiorum gestio*. A case is provided by the obligation of a debtor whose creditor is in delay in accepting performance to safeguard or accept the subject matter of the performance (e. g. goods sold) in the interests of (but also at the expense of) the creditor (cf. PECL art. 7:110 (Property not Accepted)). Another example can be found in the extended rule of the law of mandate whereby in a case of unforeseen events the agent may depart from the instructions which have been given to him and, after a vain attempt to contact the principal, may make his own decision in the principal's interest. Where such a power arises out of contract law rules governing the relationship between the parties, the agent does not act as intervener. That is the case independently of whether he is also *bound* to deviate from his original instructions (i. e. to do what a reasonable agent would do to safeguard the principal's interest) (in which case Article 1:103(a) would apply); even if the applicable contract law regime merely authorises him to deviate from the principal's declared wishes, the intervener is entitled to act despite the absence of the principal's consent (Article 1:103(b)). Where, on the other hand, under the applicable contractual regime such a power founded on the law of contract is absent, then that very same act without more may constitute a *negotiorum gestio*. A conceivable case in point would be an agent who is compelled by a sudden and exceptional course of events in undertaking the interests of his principal to exceed a price limit set by the principal for good reason. If the applicable contract law does not contain its own rule for this situation, then the law of benevolent intervention applies (and the converse is also true). As regards the substantive result in cases of this type, however, it will not make any difference whether they are resolved on the basis of the law of contract or the law of benevolent intervention in another's affairs.

10. **Acting under another duty towards the principal** The performance of a contractual duty is only one case among many (albeit a particularly important one) in which intervention as *gestor* does not surface because vis-à-vis the principal the party acting *must* do so as a matter of private law, is correspondingly authorised to act and consequently is not dependent on the law of *negotiorum gestio* for a justification for his acting. The Article does not employ the criterion of the "voluntariness" of the act, which can be found in Romance legal systems. That has been done, however, primarily for technical reasons and not on account of any legal policy consideration. The criterion of "voluntariness" appears both on the one hand too imprecise and on the other hand too narrow. What should be decisive instead is whether the party acting was under a duty towards the principal. However, the matter does not turn on the source (statutory or contractual) of the obligation. Someone who discharges their statutory obligation to maintain their children, their spouse or their parents does not act as an intervener any more than someone who fulfils his duty under the law of unjustified enrichment to

return something in his possession or ownership. The discharge of an obligation arising, for example, from the initiation of expectations of a concluded contract ("*culpa in contrahendo*", cf. PECL arts. 2:302 and 2:302) or in consequence of a tort is likewise not an incidence of *negotiorum gestio*.

> *Illustration 3*
> A person does not act as *gestor* when he remedies a damage for which he is responsible, such as damage to ground water which he has caused by trying to refill an underground oil tank which in fact no longer exists.

11. **Moral duties** Only legal duties are relevant here; the discharge of a moral obligation will not suffice to exclude the application of the law of benevolent intervention in another's affairs.

12. **The duty to render assistance under criminal law** Many European legal systems contain a rule which renders a person liable to criminal sanctions when he sees a fellow human being in substantial peril to life or limb and fails to render assistance despite the fact that it would have been possible to do so without having to subordinate any significant interests of his (a criminal omission to render assistance). In some cases particular professional groups (especially doctors, but in given circumstances also vets too, for example) are subject to wide-ranging obligations to help and must reckon with the possibility of criminal punishment should they fail to fulfil them. Someone who acts appreciating the threat of punishment if they do not help may well not act "voluntarily", but there should be no doubt that such persons are afforded the (privileged) legal position of a *gestor*. The threat of punishment is meant to provide only a *further* 'incentive' for taking action; it should not have the counter-productive effect that interveners should be stripped of legal protection available under private law. In these Principles, therefore, it matters only whether the intervener is authorised to act under a private law duty *owed to the person assisted*. It is precisely that requirement which is not in fact satisfied in the case of acts taken under the impulse provided by a threat of punishment by criminal law. That is because in the first place such duties exist for the general public interest; they do not provide even a theoretical platform for a claim based in private law and, according to the overwhelmingly predominant European legal viewpoint, their breach does not found a claim for compensation for the person who was not assisted. Even if one were to decide that point differently (i. e. one would regard a claim to reparation for a tort as well-founded), the circumstance that (at least theoretically) the assisted person could at any time refuse assistance as an unwanted interference shows that the intervener is in fact a *gestor*. The duty to render assistance imposed by the criminal law does not provide the helper with authority to intervene which is independent of the principal's will. Correspondingly the duty to act does not exist, or cease to exist, when the principal rejects assistance as unwanted.

C. Acting under another Authority (limb (b))

13. **General** The second of the "negative" conditions for a justified benevolent intervention in another's affairs is the requirement that the acting party must not be au-

thorised in relation to the benefited party to do what he or she does independent of the latter's consent. This is the case where the authority to act stems from rules outside the law of *negotiorum gestio*. Where there are such special grounds justifying intervention, there will also be as a rule an independent – and in a case of doubt exhaustive – legal regime for the regulation of the rights of the participants. That in itself, however, is not the decisive consideration; what matters is whether either the person acting is entitled to act against the wishes of the person affected or, as the case may be, the person acting is himself the one who generates the affected person's legally binding will. In either case one is concerned with an authorisation for a person to interfere in the legal position of another; that circumstance precludes a *gestor*-principal relationship from arising between them.

14. **Examples in private law** Examples include a guardian in relation to his ward, parents in relation to their children, or the governing organs within a legal person in relation to the legal person itself. In relation to particular acts undertaken these persons will often also fall under the rule in limb (a); that is the case when they are fulfilling their existing (statutory) duties in relation to their 'principal'. However, even when that is not the case, by virtue of limb (b) they still do not act in relation to that person as intervener. Furthermore, a neighbour who is granted power by property law rules to lop overhanging branches encroaching from neighbouring land or to clean shared drains against the wishes of a co-owner does not act as a *gestor*. The same holds where a tenant exercises a power under his tenancy agreement to carry out necessary repairs at the landlord's expense and without his consent in the particularly pressing circumstances envisaged by the contract.

15. **Authority to act under public law** The situation is similar where someone is entitled to intervene under public law (a public fire service, the police etc.). The intervention of such services for the maintenance of public safety and order is referable to a special legal basis; it does not constitute a benevolent intervention in another's affairs. As a general point and for the avoidance of misunderstanding, it should be reiterated here that the draft only engages with questions of private law and does not address problems of reimbursement of costs or any other "quasi-*negotiorum gestio* issue" arising from the exercise of powers under public law. The power of an authority to intervene is of course an essential feature in the make up of a state or public prerogative.

Illustration 4
Other road users are obliged to stop when instructed to do so by a school crossing patrol; the patrol does not act as a *gestor* in relation to either the children nor the other road users.

Illustration 5
While a cattle truck is being unloaded an ox breaks free and escapes onto a dual carriageway, where it is shot by a policeman. The policeman suffers trauma as a result of the blast. This does not entitle him to compensation from the cattle dealer under Article 3:103 (Right to Reparation) in conjunction with Article 1:102 (Intervention to Perform Another's Duty); the officer was authorised under public law – independently of the cattle-dealer's consent – to shoot the animal in order to protect road users from the danger.

Illustration 6
On the other hand, someone who at the invitation of the revenue service informs on tax dodgers in return for a 'bounty' acts without special authority in his investigations and passing on details to the tax authorities. The informer acts outside the field of public law and is not a *gestor* (and thus cannot charge the tax authorities his costs) only because he acts predominantly in pursuit of his own interests – namely for the purpose of earning the reward on offer.

16. **"independently of the principal's consent"** As already mentioned, a benevolent intervention is out of question if the party acting does not depend on the consent of the principal for intervention in the principal's affairs and instead acts by virtue of his own authority. An express consent of the principal, on the other hand, excludes the application of the rules on *negotiorum gestio* only if as a result a contract is concluded between the *gestor* and the principal (see comment B6 above). Taken by itself, the consent of the principal does not constitute an authorisation because it can be revoked at any time prior to carrying out the measure in question. Moreover, no other outcome would be possible here because the *negotiorum gestio* concept revolves around protecting the active party who is entitled to set forth to comply with the wishes of the other party. If he does in fact comply with those wishes, that is obviously no reason to *deny* a benevolent intervention in that other's affairs.

Illustration 7
Following a road accident abroad, the holder of a third party insurance policy is arrested. At his pressing request the insurance company puts up the bail, although both parties know that according to the contract of insurance the insurance company is not obliged to do so. It is also clear to both sides that the insurance company has provided this additional service as a goodwill gesture. The insurance company acts as a *gestor*. It would not be correct to seek to deny the company that status on the basis that it had been "authorised to act". The insurance company's authority depends solely on the principal's consent.

D. Performing a Duty Towards a Third Party (limb (c))

17. **Significance** Someone who by his intervention discharges duties imposed on him under private law does not act as intervener even if the other requirements of para (1) are satisfied. In practice, however, it will seldom be the case that an intervention fails to qualify as a *negotiorum gestio* for this reason alone. The intervention will often be excluded from the law of benevolent intervention due to the basic requirements of Article 1:101, e. g. because performances which are rendered for the purpose of discharging a (real or imagined) duty are normally not undertaken with the intention *predominantly* of benefiting another. In particular, it follows from this that a person who mistakenly assumes that in acting they are fulfilling a contractual duty does not come under the regime of benevolent intervention in another's affairs; they must seek recompense instead within the law of unjustified enrichment.

18. Scope of application Even if the requirements of Article 1:101 are met as between the intervener and the benefited party, where the intervener is obliged to a third party to undertake the act done (the typical case involving a contractual duty) the intervener is not to be regarded as a *gestor* in relation to the party benefited. In such cases there is neither need nor sufficient ground for the creation of a *gestor*-principal relationship: the party acting (the 'intervener') is entitled only to look to his relationship with his contractual partner. A frequent case is where someone is commissioned to undertake repairs for the benefited party. (It is immaterial in that respect whether or not the person commissioning the repairs acts as a *gestor* in relation to the party benefited). In such situations it is occasionally the case that the person commissioned acts in relation to the party benefited with the intention of furthering the latter's interests – when (among other things) the contract is not the motive for intervening. It is the purpose of limb (c) to clarify that in those instances too there is no *negotiorum gestio*.

Illustration 8
R is commissioned by a landlord L to carry out repairs in the apartment let to the tenant T and carries these out. L is not a *gestor* in relation to T because L acts in relation to T in discharge of his duties as landlord and is thus authorised to act. R in turn is also not a *gestor*, either in relation to L because of the priority of the law of contract or in relation to T because of limb (c). The latter provision is necessary for the case where R acts under contract to L, but would have been willing to intervene even if he had not been commissioned by L (e. g. because R and T are neighbours on very good terms) and thus acted all along with a predominant intention to benefit T. (If, depending on the application of PECL art. 6:110, L and T concluded a contract for T's benefit, then R is no *gestor* in relation to T because of Article 1:103 (b)). If R carries out the repairs badly, he is liable under the contract to L (and, as the case may be, to T); but there is no liability to either L or T under the law of *negotiorum gestio*.

Illustration 9
A charitable organisation concludes a contract with a public authority whereby the charity is obliged to carry out certain rescue services for which the public authority, for its part, carries the cost. The charitable organisation in performing these services does not act as a *gestor* for the persons rescued.

19. Demarcation One should not confuse with this situation cases in which a *gestor* fulfils duties he incurred in his own name but on behalf of his principal in benevolent intervention.

Illustration 10
The facts are the same as in illustration 8, except that L is not the landlord of T but rather another friend of T who commissions R to deal with a broken pipe in T's apartment. L's act of commissioning R is in this case a benevolent intervention by L in T's affairs. The payment of R's bill by L remains a *negotiorum gestio* in relation to T, unaffected by the circumstance that L is contractually under a duty to R to pay: that obligation is merely the consequence of the intervention undertaken by L. It is not merely that L has a claim against T for reimbursement of

expenditure. It is also the case that (so far as this is reasonable in view of the circumstances) L must inform T that the debt to R will become due and provide him (T) with the possibility of paying R directly.

20. Precise analysis of the contractual duty What matters is whether the person acting is contractually obliged to a third party in regard to the activity which he undertakes. Such cases may call for close scrutiny of the contract between the person acting and the third party in order to determine whether the actor is or is not actually under an obligation to perform the act which benefits another.

Illustration 11
A ship's doctor attends to a suffering passenger who has lost consciousness. If the doctor has undertaken to the shipping company to provide medical services to passengers (most probably in return for a fee), then it is not him but rather the shipping company, with its employment of or arrangement with the doctor, that acts as *gestor* in relation to the patient. (This is assuming that the situation ought not rather to be analysed on the basis that the company for its part is merely discharging a contractual duty to the passenger – in which case, there would be no *gestor* at all.) On the other hand, if the doctor has merely agreed to be "on call" (e. g. because the shipping company merely wished to preclude any potential tortious liability to a passenger which might result if the passenger fell ill and no medical assistance was available on board ship), the doctor performs his contractual duty by being on the ship and accessible to those in medical need. Actual provision of medical treatment to any particular passenger who needs the doctor's assistance will exceed the doctor's contractual duty to the shipping company.

21. No limitation to contractual duties The provision in limb (c), however, is not limited to the discharge of *contractual* duties incurred to third parties. It will also cover the performance of subsisting duties to third parties arising under statute or by operation of law. Article 1:103(c), however, does not touch upon acts which are conducted in discharge of an obligation vis-à-vis the state, such obligations being duties under public law.

Illustration 12
Someone who complies with their subsisting duty *owed to their spouse* to contribute to the maintenance of stepchildren (i. e. to their spouses' children living in the same household) is not a *gestor* in relation to the children in making that contribution.

Illustration 13
I and P are co-owners of a joint gablewall which is in danger of collapsing. A supervisory authority for buildings orders I to pull down the wall on grounds of public safety. I may claim from P a proportionate contribution in respect of the costs: P cannot veto the demolition of the wall due to Article 1:102, and I does not act in compliance with a duty to a third party arising under private law.

Notes

I. The Precedence of Contract Law

1. The precedence of contract law over the law of benevolent intervention is recognized in all legal sytems of the Member States of the European Union. Under GERMAN law the intervener must not have been entrusted with authority by the principal nor otherwise be entitled to act (CC § 677); from this point of view the rules on benevolent intervention are subsidiary (*Medicus*, Schuldrecht II BT[12], no. 622). The only point of dispute in this respect is the situation of an intervener acting under a void contract for services (cf. on this point note V50 under Article 1:101) or where an authority conferred by contract is exceeded (for details see inter alia MünchKomm [-*Seiler*], BGB[3], § 677 no. 42; Soergel [-*Beuthien*], BGB[12], § 677 no. 17; Palandt [-*Sprau*], BGB[63], § 677, no. 11 and § 713 no. 11). Recent case law has dealt with such cases exclusively on the basis of a breach of contractual duty (see for example BGH 11 January 1988, DB 1988, 1377: the managing director of a company does not act without authority if he exceeds his competence; in this case no room remains for the application of the law of benevolent intervention; for the former approach to the contrary see RG 22 October 1938, RGZ 158, 302, 312 and BGH 7 January 1963, BGHZ 39, 1).
2. It is inferred from the requirement of 'without mandate' in GREEK CC art. 730 that managements of another's affair which find their basis in an already existing legal relationship do not come within the scope of application of the law of benevolent intervention. As in German law the term 'mandate' is not to be understood here in its technical meaning. Rather it indicates that there is no justification for or duty of the intervener to manage another's affair (Georgiades and Stathopoulos [-*Papanikolaou*], Art. 730, no. 20). The same holds true for ESTONIAN CC § 1018 (1) ("without being granted the right or obligated by the principal"), POLISH CC art. 752 ("without mandate") and HUNGARIAN CC § 484 ("without being authorised by mandate or otherwise"). According to Hungarian case law an intervention without authority may therefore only arise where the intervener provides more than he was contractually obliged to or continues to act on another's behalf after discharging his contractual duties (Legf.Bir. no. 564/1999, Bírósági Határozatok [Court Decisions] no. 12/1999). Under PORTUGUESE law the precedence of contract law is derived from CC art. 464: the intervention must have taken place without 'authorisation'. Should the intervention be founded on a contract, it will be left to contract law alone to decide on the rights and obligations of the participants (*Vaz Serra*, BolMinJus 66 [1957] 102-103). The concept of '*convention d'assistance*' is as foreign to Portuguese law as it is to German law.
3. Under AUSTRIAN CC § 1035 only an 'act without authority' can give rise to a benevolent intervention. 'Authority' may be conferred by a contract, a court order or by statute (for details see *Meissel*, GoA, 72 et seq. and *Fötschl*, ERPL 2002, 550, 562 (fn. 67)). A contractual agreement between principal and intervener consequently precludes the application of the law of benevolent intervention: contract law has priority. The scope of the contractual duties is to be determined by construction of the contractual agreement (OGH 25 April 1963, SZ 36/68; *Gschnitzer*, Schuldrecht BT[2], 279). For instance, the operator of an Austrian hospital had no claim for reimbursement in a

case where, because of its own shortage of resources to deal with the case itself, it flew a newly born child to a clinic in Zürich for treatment there: under Austrian social insurance law the parents had concluded a contract with the hospital and according to the terms of that contract no counter-performance was due as *quid pro quo* for the hospital's services (OGH 29 March 2001, ZVR 2002/36 p. 154). In some rare cases, however, the provisions of the law of benevolent intervention may have an impact on contract law. For example, the OGH applies the provisions of benevolent intervention in the context of determining the amount of compensation of a person who has contractually agreed to keep property in safe custody (OGH 12 November 1997, JBl 1998, 303). If the intervener acts in response to another's request for help, a contract may be concluded, though the emergency situation of the person requesting help calls for particular attention (OGH 13 July 1994, SZ 67/123), both with respect of a possible lack of an intention to be legally bound in the case of non-professional assistance and in the case of professional assistance under the aspect of usury (Rummel [-*Krejci*], ABGB I^3, § 879 no. 218). However, under Austrian law a benevolent intervention may be precluded not only by the existence of a contract but also in the case of a courtesy arrangement which is not legally binding. This follows from CC § 1036 and its requirement of an emergency situation, which may be held to be missing if the intervener had the possibility to obtain the principal's prior consent (OGH 22 November 1984, SZ 57/167; *Meissel*, GoA, 31). But it is also linked to the converse requirement of CC § 1037 that the intervener has not obtained the consent of the principal. If he has that consent, there is a 'courtesy-relationship' interposing between contract and benevolent intervention. Its legal consequences are yet to be determined and are a matter of academic debate.

4. In SPAIN too the law of benevolent intervention is considered a subsidiary instrument. From CC art. 1888 ("voluntary, without being mandated") or Fuero Nuevo de NAVARRA ley 560, as the case may be, it is inferred that the intervener must neither be obliged to act nor be entitled to do so by reason of some special legal basis (*Pasquau Liaño,* La gestión de negocios ajenos, 101); otherwise the rights and duties of the parties will be determined exclusively by that special legal relationship (*Sánchez Jordán*, Gestión de negocios, 93). The term 'mandate' in CC art. 1888 is not to be understood as a technical term (Paz-Ares/Díez-Picazo/Bercovitz/Salvador [-*Díez-Picazo*], Código Civil II, 1944; *Lacruz Berdejo*, Rev.Crít.Der.Inm. 1975, 252). The demarcation between contractual and extra-contractual rights and obligations is regarded as difficult. An agent may exceed the limitations of the mandate pursuant to CC art. 1715 if he can thereby obtain advantages for the principal beyond those he would have by conduct in conformity with the contract. However, the principal will only be bound by such an act in excess of contractual duty if he ratifies it (CC art. 1727). In this case the rules of benevolent intervention are superseded. Moreover, according to the case law of the Supreme Court they remain inapplicable if ratification is withheld (TS 8 January 1980, RAJ 1980 (1) no. 79 p. 64; TS 19 October 1993, RAJ 1993 (4) no. 7744 p. 9863). The French concept of a *convention d'assistance* is also completely unknown in Spain.

5. ITALIAN CC art. 2028 only counts subject of the law of benevolent intervention those acts which the intervener is not obliged to conduct, which (as it is often put) the intervener renders 'voluntarily' (Cass. 30 November 1988, no. 6499, Rep. Foro it. 1988, voce "Gestione d'affari", no. 1; *Breccia*, La gestione di affari[2], 857). If the intervention

finds a legal basis in either a contract or by operation of law itself this will render the law of benevolent intervention inapplicable. Even acts which are conducted in excess of a mandate (cf. CC art. 1711) do not constitute a benevolent intervention (Cass. 23 January 1953, no. 202, Rep.Giur.it. 1953, voce Appelo civile, no. 128; Cass. 14 July 1954, no. 2471, Rep.Giur.it. 1954, voce Mandato, no. 48-56, voce Obbligazioni e contratti, no. 262). Only where the intervention does not have any connection to the contract concluded by the parties will there be room for the application of benevolent intervention.

6. FRENCH and BELGIAN law as well as MALTESE law (CC art. 1013) require that the intervener has acted 'spontaneously' or as the case may be 'voluntarily'. Accordingly the law of benevolent intervention will not come into consideration if the intervener is obliged to act under a contract or statute (Cass. soc. 11 October 1984, Bull.civ. 1984, V, no. 369 p. 276; *Van Gerven*, Verbintenissenrecht II^7, 213-219). In case of performance beyond the contractual duties, however, it is held possible to resort to the law of benevolent intervention (*le Tourneau*, RépDrCiv, VI, v° Gestion d'affaires (2002) no. 37; *Paulus*, Zaakwaarneming, no. 39 p. 35). French case law, moreover, has held that an act may be characterised as 'spontaneous' or, as the case may be, 'voluntary' with respect to the relationship between intervener and principal, even though the intervener vis-à-vis a third party is under a contractual duty to act (Cass.civ. 24 May 1989, Bull.civ. 1989, I, no. 211 p. 141). A further distinctive feature of French law is the case law on so-called 'contracts for emergency assistance'. These concern the situation where a person has rendered emergency assistance to another without being obliged to do so and has themselves been injured in the course of acting. French courts have granted these rescuers a contractual claim for damages independent of fault against the person who has received the emergency assistance. A contract between the party rendering assistance and the party receiving assistance is held to arise with the term that the party receiving assistance is obliged to compensate the party rendering assistance for any personal injury suffered (leading decision Cass.civ. 27 May 1959, JCP 1959 no. 11187). This concept of a *convention d'assistance* has had a hostile reception from commentators (*Viney*, JCP 1998 éd. G, I. 144, no. 7, p. 1096), but the case law adheres to the concept. In Belgium the French example has not been followed, while LUXEMBOURG has adopted the concept of *convention d'assistance* (CA Luxembourg 27 June 2001, Pas. lux. 2002, 154).

7. DUTCH CC art. 6:198 excludes the relationship of *zaakwaarneming* if a contractual or statutory relationship already exists between the parties from which the authority to undertake the management of affairs may be derived. Typical examples are the employment contract, contract for services, and contract for work. Medical treatment rendered to unconscious patients in a case of emergency is regulated by CC arts. 7:465 and 466 on contracts governing medical treatment. If someone acts upon the express or implied request of another, it will depend on the circumstances of each case whether or not a contract is held to be concluded. More often than not it will be a spontaneous attendance to another's interests which, as the reaction to a cry for help of a drowning person, will fall under the law of benevolent intervention (for details see Verbintenissenrecht [-*Heisterkamp*], Art. 6:198 BW, note 12. 3).

8. As everywhere else the precedence of contract law over *negotiorum gestio* is also acknowledged in SCOTLAND. As soon as it is established that the principal was not unaware of the management of the affairs or that the intervener has acted upon a prior

expression of intent on the part of the principal then as a first step it will be ascertained whether or not this relationship is governed by a mandate (or an implied mandate, as the case may be) or whether (where the transaction is not gratuitous) a relationship of agency has been established (*Walker*, Principles of Scottish Private Law, II[4], Ch. 4. 14, p. 213-218; *Marshall*, Scots Mercantile Law[3], 31-41).

9. One reason why the law of benevolent intervention lacks a clear-cut concept under SCANDINAVIAN law is that numerous situations are governed by specific regulations, which in turn thrust a general concept aside. Furthermore, the law of contract is granted a broad scope of application with respect to cases on the boundary between contract law and the law of *negotiorum gestio* discussed here. This in part is achieved by the concept of a 'tacit promise' (see further on such *stiltiende løfte* under DANISH Law HD 23 October 2000, UfR 2001, 100) and also a consequence of the fact that even mere passivity may lead to the conclusion of a contract pursuant to Scandinavian Contract Act §§ 4 (2) and 6 (2). A further example for this approach giving precedence to contract law may be found in the SWEDISH Act on Consumer Service Contracts *[Konsumenttjänstlagen (1985:716)]* § 8 and the FINNISH Consumer Protection Act [*Konsumentskyddslag*] of 20 January 1978 no. 38 Ch. 8 § 6. Both provisions deal with remuneration for additional services rendered which had not been ordered and do so in a way which strongly resembles the general principles of the law of benevolent intervention. The underlying values of benevolent intervention may even be discerned in arbitral awards: these concern remuneration due for preparatory work which had not been ordered, but was necessary for the paintwork which was the subject matter of the service contract, as was pointed out to the principal, although he made no comment on the issue (*Andersson/Söderlund*, JT 2002-03, 14). Numerous other examples may be found in the introduction to this Book (*I53-57*).

10. In ENGLISH law agency of necessity, like any other form of agency, may or may not be contractual: *Petrinovic & Co Ltd v. Mission Francaise des Transports des Maritimes* (1941) 71 Ll L R 208, 223 (*Atkinson* J). It is thus no requirement of a valid agency of necessity that the agent act without contractual authority from the principal. Indeed the normal if not invariable case for the application of agency of necessity is where the necessity operates to enlarge or override pre-existing instructions from the principal (i. e. as a buttress to agency of agreement). For this reason an agent of necessity is often regarded as being both authorised *and bound* to act by reason of the emergency in order to protect his principal's interest: see further Chapter 2, Art. 2:101, Notes IV, 41. However, something of the same distinction arises through the requirement that in his dealings with third parties an agent of necessity must base his authority on the necessity and not on his (superseded) instructions or a purported mandate or another legal relationship altogether: see *Jebara v. Ottoman Bank* [1927] 2 KB 254, 264 (*Bankes* LJ), where the bank purported to act in accordance with the terms of the contract, rather than because of necessity not envisaged by the contract, and this was regarded as an additional ground (besides the absence of necessity) for dismissing the claim. Where the claim to recompense of an intervener is based on restitution, that will be excluded if the benefit is provided by the claimant to the defendant on the basis of a subsisting contract: cf. *Wentworth v. Tubb* (1841) 1 Y & C CC 171 at 173-174, 62 ER 840 at 841-842 (*Knight Bruce* VC) (in the context of provision of necessaries to a person without contractual capacity); *The Solway Prince* [1896] P 120, 128 (*Jeune* P, indicating that were the contract with a the owner instead of a third party there would

likewise be no claim on the basis of salvage for the same reason that the matter rested in contract).

II. Contributions Between Joint Debtors

11. A question not easily answered is the impact of the law of benevolent intervention on contributions between joint debtors (for instance joint debtors liable under a contract or liable under tort law) in favour of a joint debtor who has paid the creditor. By discharging the common debt he has also discharged the other joint debtors vis-à-vis the creditor. The prevailing opinion holds the rules on contribution between joint debtors (cf. PECL art. 10:106) to be an exhaustive special regime which has precedence over *negotiorum gestio* law. The reasons given in favour of this opinion vary, however, and from time to time even the rationale of this approach has been questioned.

12. Under GERMAN Law CC § 426 on contribution between joint debtors not only precludes the application of the law of justified enrichment, but also renders the law of benevolent intervention inapplicable. The justification for this approach is to be found either in the principle that the provisions are *leges specialis* and thus claim precedence (BGH 4 July 1963, NJW 1963, 2067; Erman [-*Ehmann*], BGB I[10], § 426, no. 15; *Esser and Weyers*, Schuldrecht II(2)[8], § 46 V), or in the argument that a joint debtor who renders performance beyond the amount he is obliged to pay according to the relationship *inter partes* between the joint debtors does not attend to another's affair. From the point of view of the other debtors, the effect is no more than a subrogation of creditors (*Medicus*, Bürgerliches Recht[19], no. 415).

13. So far as is apparent GREEK legal literature does not discuss the interaction between a joint debtor's right to contribution (CC arts. 487 and 488) and the law of benevolent intervention. However a claim arising from *negotiorum gestio* seems to be precluded because in such cases the requirement of an *animus aliena negotia gerendi* is not satisfied. The case law has even held that a person does not attend to another's affair if he discharged the debts of another on the basis of a settlement (CA Athens 2896/1977, NoB 26 [1978] 223).

14. The PORTUGUESE CC provides rules for joint debtors (*obrigações solidárias*) in arts. 512 et seq. The discharge of the entire debt by one of the joint debtors will satisfy the debts also for all other debtors (CC art. 523). A party who effects payment in excess of the amount he is obliged to bear according to the internal relationship of the joint debtors thereby acquires a *direito de regresso* vis-à-vis the co-debtors (CC art. 524). This right of recourse has no additional basis in the law of benevolent intervention: it may be doubted at the outset whether the joint debtor who effects payment attends to another's affair with the intention to benefit that other. In any case he acts, so it is said, with *autorização* (CC art. 464), which will render the law of benevolent intervention inapplicable (*Pires de Lima and Antunes Varela*, Código Civil Anotado I[4], 446). The sole point of discussion in legal literature therefore concerns the question whether or not CC arts. 490 and 497, which contain specific provisions on the contributions *inter partes* of joint tortfeasors, shall be applied to the particular case of liability of multiple interveners (*Menezes Leitão*, Responsabilidade do gestor, 299).

15. Earlier AUSTRIAN case law and doctrine have in part held that the legal basis of the claim for contribution by joint debtors (CC § 896) is to be found in CC § 1041 or in CC §§ 1042 et seq. (Rummel [-*Gamerith*], ABGB I[3], § 896 no. 1a). However recent case

law and legal literature no longer follow this approach; the prevailing view is that the claim for contribution *inter partes* by the joint debtor who has effected payment to the creditor is an independent right which is exhaustively regulated in CC § 896 (OGH 23 March 1987, SZ 60/55; Rummel [-*Rummel*], ABGB I[3], § 1042 no. 8). The law of benevolent intervention cannot apply because the requirement in CC § 1042 of 'expenses incurred for another' is not met: the joint debtor effecting payment is liable for the complete amount. However, CC § 1037 may be considered as far as reimbursement of litigation costs is concerned which one party has incurred as defendant after it has in vain requested the other joint debtor to intervene as a co-defendant in the dispute (OGH 24 November 1997, SZ 70/241); a number of other points of law in the context of the compensable nature of litigation costs as between several joint debtors are yet to be resolved (cf. OGH 26 February 2002, JBl 2002, 658; OGH 18 July 2002, RIS-Justiz RS 0109200 and more generally *Pochmarski/Strauss*, JBl 2002, 353 and *Fötschl*, ÖJZ 2004, 781).

16. FRENCH law draws a distinction between a *solidarité passive* of several debtors and their liability *in solidum*. A *solidarité passive* of multiple contract debtors according to CC art. 1202 as a general rule must form part of the agreement with the creditor; it is presumed only in relation to commercial transactions (*Flour and Aubert*, Le rapport d'obligation[3], no. 313 p. 195). *Inter partes* the debtors are liable according to their respective share. The debtor who has effected performance can rely on either an *action subrogatoire* pursuant to CC art. 1251-3 or an *action personnelle* for his right of recourse. The latter may find its legal basis either in a *mandat* (in the case of a contractual *solidarité passive*) or in the law of *gestions d'affaires* (in the case the *solidarité passive* arises by statute: *Mazeaud and Chabas*, Obligations[9], no. 1068 p. 1114-1115; *Flour and Aubert*, loc.cit. no. 325 p. 218-219). In any case the debtor can only claim payment of the relevant share in relation to each co-debtor (CC art. 1214). Because of CC art. 1202 and the fact that only in rare cases does statute provide for joint liability, legal literature and case law have developed the concept of an *obligation in solidum*. It plays an important role in the context of tort law. A debtor *in solidum* is similarly liable for the total amount in damages (*Flour and Aubert*, loc.cit. nos. 327-328 p. 219-220). A debtor who discharges the full amount may claim reimbursement from the other debtor or debtors, a claim which is usually held to arise under CC art. 1251-3 (*action subrogatoire*), though case law has often granted the debtor who has performed an *action personnelle* which appears to find its legal basis in CC art. 1214 (*Flour and Aubert*, loc.cit. no 329 p. 221; Cass. civ. 7 June 1977, Bull. civ. 1977, I, no. 266 p. 210). In legal literature, however, the view has also been advanced that an *action personnelle* of a debtor *in solidum* against the other co-debtors finds its legal basis, like a *solidarité passive*, in *gestion d'affaires* (*Terré/Simler/Lequette*, Les obligations[8], no. 1263 p. 1173, with fn. 2). The legal position in BELGIUM is the same. The legal basis for the claim for reimbursement is barely elaborated in more detail. *De Page* assumes that the joint debtor rendering performance to the creditor may invoke an *action de mandat*, an *action de gestion d'affaires* and a claim arising from a *subrogation légale* pursuant to CC art. 1251 (3) (*de Page*, Traité élémentaire de droit civil belge, Tome 3: Les obligations[3], no. 367 p. 350). Besides the *solidarité passive* (*passieve hoofdelijkheid*) the *obligation in solidum* (*verbintenis in solidum*) is also recognised in Belgium. A claim for contribution likewise exists between the joint debtors, which is assumed to find its legal basis either in CC arts. 1382-1383 (tort law) or a *subrogation légale* (*wettelijke sub-*

rogatie) under CC art. 1251 (3) (*Cornelis*, Algemene theorie van de verbintenis, no. 135 p. 171-172).

17. It would appear that the relationship between *derecho de regreso* pursuant to CC art. 1145 (2) and the law of benevolent intervention under SPANISH law is only discussed by *Díez-Picazo*, Fundamentos II[4], 215. He considers that the law of benevolent intervention is inapplicable for the reason that the joint debtor who discharges the entire debt acts in his own interest, namely to free himself from a liability. Thus the condition of an *animus aliena negotia gerendi* is not met. The right of contribution finds its underlying justification in a specific emanation of principles relating to unjustified enrichment, an interpretation which unsurprisingly is a matter of dispute (for further details see *Puig Brutau*, Compendio II[2], 43; *Albaladejo*, Derecho Civil II (1)[10], 97; *Lacruz Berdejo*, Elementos II (1), 45). As regards joint creditors, as a *gestión del crédito* under CC art. 1141 a joint creditor may undertake acts which are advantageous for all creditors but none that result in detriment to the other creditors. The statute (it is construed) presumes a tacit mandate between the joint creditors (*Lacruz Berdejo*, loc.cit. 46).

18. A joint debtor who discharges the entire debt will also not be considered as a benevolent intervener acting in the interest of the other debtors under ITALIAN law. This is explained on the basis that the joint debtor does not act voluntarily (*Rescigno*, Codice civile, sub art. 2028). Similarly DUTCH case law does not rely on the law of benevolent intervention for the claim for contribution of one joint debtor against the other debtors. The matter rests with a claim for compensation under CC art. 6:8 ascribed to the principle of good faith. The application of the law of *negotiorum gestio* is likewise excluded in SCOTLAND; it would appear this issue is not even a matter for discussion.

19. In contrast to the legal situation under Belgian and French law, multiple debtors in SCANDINAVIA will as a general rule be jointly and severally liable. This principle is derived inter alia from the Promissory Notes Act (which on this point is held to be a suitable basis for generalisation) (cf. for SWEDEN the Promissory Notes Act § 2 and *Mellqvist and Persson*, Fordran och skuld[6], 51 and 60). The joint debtor effecting payment has a claim for contribution in the amount of the relevant share against each joint debtor (para (2); for details see *Håstad*, Tjänster utan updrag, 110). No room is left for an independent claim for compensation arising from the law of benevolent intervention; it is not even discussed in extraordinary cases concerning contribution (compare for instance HD 29 December 2000, NJA 2000, 773).

20. Contribution as between co-debtors in the COMMON LAW, though forming part of the law of restitution, is not regarded as a matter of necessitous intervention. For details of the governing common law, equitable and statutory rules, see *Goff and Jones*, Restitution[6], Ch. 14.

III. *Statutory Duties to Provide Help*

21. In many Member States of the European Union it is a punishable offence not to render assistance to someone whose life or physical integrity is endangered, if such assistance could be rendered without suffering any significant disadvantage. The question arises whether or not the person who discharges this duty to provide help will still come within the scope of benevolent intervention. This draft as a general rule answers this

question (see above comment *B11*) in the affirmative. This accords with the legal position in GERMANY (Palandt [*-Sprau*], BGB[63], § 677, no. 11), GREECE (*Filios*, Enochiko Dikaio I/2, 197), PORTUGAL (*Menezes Leitão*, Responsabilidade do gestor, 201; *Vieira Gomes*, Gestão de negócios, 82), AUSTRIA (OGH 24 August 1995, SZ 68/142; cf. on the duty of a vet to provide aid arising out of the professional code of conduct OGH 18 June 1997, SZ 70/113) and THE NETHERLANDS (T. M. Parlementaire Geschiedenis VI, 792; Asser [*-Hartkamp*], Verbintenissenrecht III[10], no. 297, p. 311-312; Verbintenissenrecht [*-Heisterkamp*], Art. 6:198 BW, no. 13; T & C Vermogensrecht [*-Hijma*], Art. 6:198, no. 2).

22. By contrast in SPAIN it is assumed that acts which are undertaken to fulfil a duty to provide aid arising under criminal law (Spanish CP art. 195) are not performed 'voluntarily' and are therefore outside the scope of benevolent intervention. However, it is acknowledged that this outcome may contradict the rationale of the regime since the prerequisite of CP art. 195 is a 'manifest and serious danger' (*peligro manifiesto y grave*) while CC art. 1893 confers a claim for compensation of costs incurred and damages suffered on a person who renders assistance in a case of 'impending obvious danger' (*perjuicio inminente y manifiesto*). The latter is granted even if the action undertaken does not result in any benefit to the person threatened by danger. The problem is assumed to be resolved on the basis that if a saviour has suffered damage, that fact of damage indicates that he could not have acted without accepting a risk (which in turn is a requirement of the duty under CP art. 195); hence the rescuer remains within the scope of benevolent intervention (*Sánchez Jordán*, Gestión de negocios, 104). The prevailing view in ITALY likewise seems to hold that acts which fulfil a duty to provide help arising under criminal law (Italian CP art. 593) are not undertaken 'voluntarily' and therefore do not constitute an act of benevolent intervention without authority (*Sirena*, Gestione di affari, 162-163). Only if a person exerts himself beyond the extent demanded by criminal law will a benevolent intervention according to private law rules be constituted (*Bianca*, Diritto civile, V, La responsabilità, 669). To date there appears to be no case law on this question.

23. A line of argument similar to that in Spain may also be found in FRANCE. French legal literature points towards the fact that so far no claim arising from benevolent intervention has failed because the action was underpinned by a duty to provide help arising from criminal law. This may be explained by the fact that the duty to provide help under criminal law never obliges a person to put himself at risk of bodily injury, while it is exactly such cases which have been adjudicated upon by the courts (JClCiv [*-Bout*], Art. 1372-1375, V° Quasi-Contrats. Gestion d'affaires – Conditions d'existence, Fasc. 10 no. 57). By contrast BELGIAN legal literature does distinguish between a statutory *obligation générale* and a statutory *obligation spécifique*. The duty to provide help arising under criminal law (Belgian CP art. 422) merely represents an *obligation générale* which concerns all citizens and whose main feature is precisely that it does not preclude the application of benevolent intervention (*Van Gerven*, Verbintenissenrecht II[7], 219-220). The opposite is true of an *obligation spécifique* – for instance where a fire brigade in discharge of its statutory duty extinguishes a fire (CFI (commercial matters) Antwerp 30 June 1998, JPA 1998, 342).

24. In ENGLAND AND WALES this issue is of limited magnitude. That is because a failure to render aid to someone in peril is only exceptionally subject to sanctions under the criminal law: *Stone*, Offences against the Person, p. 16 (reciting the example of a

passer-by not assisting a drowning man). Where a by-stander is not himself the cause of the danger, an omission to act can form the *actus reus* of a criminal offence only if there is a specific duty to intervene; there are no general duties imposed on citizens to act: see *Ashworth*, Principles of Criminal Law[3], 48. Where there is neither a contractual duty to act nor a duty to act implied by law, non-feasance will not give rise to criminal liability: see *R v. Smith* (1826) 2 Car & P 449 at 457, 172 ER 203 at 207 (*Burrough* J) (where the accused failed to provide their mentally handicapped brother with adequate warmth, food, and other necessaries, but an indictment was unsupportable because the siblings were not obliged to care for their brother); *R v. Shepherd* (1862) Le & Ca 147, 169 ER 1340 (where the accused failed to call a midwife to attend her eighteen year old daughter, who died in labour, but conviction for manslaughter was quashed) – which cases, however, would be decided differently now precisely on the ground that an implied duty to act existed. Duties to intervene are often imposed by law for the furtherance of public law functions. An example is the criminal law duty of a citizen to comply with a constable's reasonable request to assist him in the execution of his duties in quelling a breach of the peace (*R v. Brown* (1841) Car & M 314, 174 ER 522 (*Alderson* B); *R v. Sherlock* (1866) LR 1 CCR 20), the discharge of which might operate to the benefit of a victim of physical attack or threats, but the ambit of this "uncertain" common law criminal liability does not as such extend to a duty to assist the police in rescuing those in peril (see *Nicholson*, Crim LR 1992, 611, 612). A further case is the duty of a water undertaker under the Water Industry Act 1991, sec. 57(1), to allow water to be taken for extinguishing fires. Criminal law duties to act also arise in relation to children: a parent has a duty to act for the welfare of his child and may be criminally liable at common law if the child suffers harm because of a failure to act: *R v. Bubb* (1850) 4 Cox CC 455, 460 (where the father was acquitted); *R v. Gibbins and Proctor* (1918) 13 Cr App Rep 134 (father's conviction for murder by neglect in starving his daughter to death upheld). At common law, any other person who fails to discharge a duty (contractual or otherwise) to provide necessaries such as food, clothing and lodging to a child of tender years (i. e., under sixteen years of age: *R v. Sloane* (1851) 15 JP 22) who is under that person's control and unable to fend for himself or herself, so as to injure that child, commits an offence: see *R v. Ridley* (1811) 2 Campb 650 at 652-653, 170 ER 1282 at 1283 (*Lawrence* J) (concerning a child servant, but where the indictment was defective); *R v. Friend* (1802) Russ & Ry 20, 168 ER 662 (failure to provide apprentice with necessaries); *R v. Bubb*, loc. cit., 459 (where the duty of the cohabitee of the child's father was self-imposed) and see also *R v. Lee and Parkes* (1917) 13 Cr App Rep 39 (where the conviction for manslaughter of a midwife, engaged to nurse an infant for whom she neglected to summon medical aid, was upheld). The common law principles in relation to children are given statutory effect in provisions stipulating that any person who has the custody, charge or care of a person under sixteen may commit an offence if the child is neglected or abandoned: see the Children and Young Person's Act 1933, sec. 1, and see also the Offences against the Person Act 1861, sec. 27 (for children under two). A general duty to act for the welfare of a person unable to fend for himself is imposed on a stranger under the criminal law only where that stranger has already assumed responsibility for the welfare of that other (whether expressly or impliedly, contractually or otherwise): see *R v. Marriott* (1838) 8 Car & P 425 at 433, 173 ER 559 at 563 (*Patteson* J); *R v. Bubb*, loc. cit., 459 (*Williams* J) (cohabitee convicted of manslaughter by neglect of partner's child); *R v. Instan* [1893] 1 QB 450 (where the accused neglected to feed and procure medical assistance for an aunt who was immobilised by gangrene and with whom she resided); *R v. Gibbins and Proctor*, loc. cit., 139 (*Darling* J, giving the opinion of the CCA) (where a cohabitee's conviction for murder in deliberately withholding food and medical care from her partner's daughter was upheld); *Stone*, Offences against the Person, p. 18. See also the National Assistance Act 1948, sec. 51 (failure to maintain a person who is provided as a result with accommodation by a local authority). All such offences presuppose a pre-existing relationship or involvement with the vulnerable person. In SCOTLAND a failure to render aid is likewise not as a rule punishable under criminal law; an offence will only be committed if there is a particularly close relationship between the victim and the person who fails to act (such as a family tie) (cf. Stair [-*Christie*], Vol. 7, Criminal Law, para 40); therefore the problem treated above does not arise. This corresponds with the legal position under SWEDISH law (*Håstad*, Tjänster utan uppdrag, 60 and 138). In DENMARK (CP § 253 [*Straffelov*], promulgation of 6. September 2000 Nr. 849) and in FINLAND (CP Ch. 21 § 15 [*Strafflag*] of 19. December 1889) the failure to provide aid is punishable, but discussions on the relationship between this offence and the law of *negotiorum gestio* are nowhere to be found.

IV. *Other Powers of Intervention*

25. For most legal systems of the European Union a matter is outwith the scope of benevolent intervention if the active party is entitled by some other legal authority (i. e., other than under a contract) to interfere with the affairs of another. Statutory powers to intervene recognised in GERMANY include, for instance, guardianship, curatorship, parental authority, administration in bankruptcy, position as executive of a legal person, and sovereign powers (MünchKomm [-*Seiler*]^3, § 677 BGB no. 36). It is similarly held in GREECE that a justification displacing the law of *negotiorum gestio* may arise from statute law. Guardianship, parenthood and administration in bankruptcy are mentioned as examples (Georgiades and Stathopoulos [-*Papanikolau*], Art. 730, no. 20; ErmAK [-*Sakketas*], Art. 730, no. 25). In PORTUGAL reference is made to the existence of a power of representation (CC arts. 262 et seq.), parental authority (*poder paternal* – CC arts. 1877 et seq.) and guardianship (*tutela* – CC arts. 1927 et seq.). In addition, according to STJ 8 July 1997, CJ(ST) V. (1997-2) 144 explicit consent of the person whose affairs are interfered constitutes an *autorização* and thus displaces the law of benevolent intervention; in such cases only unjustified enrichment law is held to be applicable. For DUTCH Law the standard examples or parental authority, guardianship and administration in bankruptcy are again taken as illustrations of statutory powers which render the law of benevolent intervention inapplicable (T. M. Parlementaire Geschiedenis VI, 791-792; Asser [-*Hartkamp*], Verbintenissenrecht III^{10}, no. 296-297, p. 310-312).

26. As mentioned above, a 'power' to interfere with the affairs of another precluding benevolent intervention under AUSTRIAN law may arise not only from contract but also from a statutory provision or a court decision (CC § 1034). The appointment of a curator by the court (CC § 273) or parental authority by operation of law (CC § 144) may serve as examples (Schwimann [-*Apathy*], ABGB V^2, §§ 1035 no. 4). Likewise the law of benevolent intervention will not apply if a public authority acts within its competences (OGH 11 February 1953, SZ 26/35); this does of course not exclude

public law from adopting some of the underlying thinking contained in the law of benevolent intervention (OGH 21 March 1999, SZ 72/47).

27. By contrast under FRENCH Law it is not the existence of a power to interfere but only the existence of a duty to interfere which will be decisive. However, this different nuance will only rarely lead to a different outcome. The execution of a power (*fonction*) in accordance with the statutory provisions is said not to preclude benevolent intervention. If the active party exceeds the duty imposed on him by law, that is if he renders performance in excess of the *obligation légale* then this leaves room for benevolent intervention (JClCiv [-*Bout*], Art. 1372-1375, V° Quasi-Contrats. Gestion d'affaires – Conditions d'existence, Fasc. 10 no. 58-60). The same holds true for BELGIUM, where again it is not the existence of a power but the existence or non-existence of a duty to act which will be decisive: see for instance CFI (in commercial matters) Antwerp 30 June 1998, JPA 1998, 342 and CA Brussels 7 February 1964, Pas. belge 1965, II, 70). For both countries it is therefore true that the existence of the active party's power to intervene will only preclude the application of benevolent intervention if this right coincides with a contractual or statutory duty to intervene. The mere fact that the principal was present during the intervention and has agreed to its execution does not necessarily preclude the existence of benevolent intervention (CA Paris 14 October 1997, Juris Data 1997-023144).

28. Under SPANISH law the rules of benevolent intervention are displaced if the active party is entitled to representation (TS 2 February 1954, RAJ 1954 no. 322 p. 198); the phrase 'without authority' also includes 'without authority to represent' (*Albaladejo*, Derecho civil II (2), 495). Any kind of entitlement, whether derived from the wishes of the principal or from operation of law is assumed to exclude the law of benevolent intervention (*Lacruz Berdejo*, Rev.Crít.Der.Inm. 1975, 252). Similarly a benevolent intervention cannot come into existence under ITALIAN Law if a (non-contractual) legal relationship between the parties already subsists (Cass. 30 November 1988, no. 6499, Rep.Giur.it. 1988, voce Gestione d'affari, no. 1). Hence, for example, a father who manages the assets of his son will not qualify as an intervener without authority (*Aru*, Gestione d'affari, 4).

29. As regards SWEDISH law *Håstad*, Tjänster utan updrag, 53, indicates that as a general rule a *gestor* may not be granted more power than a custodian appointed by court would obtain. Departing from the former legal position, recent amendments ensure a custodian can be granted authority with respect to personal (i. e. non-economic) interests of the person under curatorship, cf. HD 4 November 1999, NJA 1999, 691. The custodian himself, however, is not an intervener without authority. The same applies, for example, for the administrator which may be appointed by the court pursuant to FINNISH Enforcement Act [*utsökningslag*] of 3 December 1895 Ch. 4 § 25 in order to prevent dilipadation of the debtor's immovable property.

30. In ENGLISH LAW countless statutory regimes confer on a public authority a power or duty to intervene for necessary reasons and a right to recoup the expenses incurred from the beneficiary of that conduct or a person who was obliged to act. So, for example, a local authority in whose area a person has died or a dead body is found is under a statutory duty to make arrangements for disposal of the body if it appears to the authority that no such suitable arrangements are being made (see Chapter 1, Art. 1:102, Notes, II, 16) and a local authority has a statutory power to bury or cremate a deceased person whom that authority was providing with accommodation under

social assistance legislation (Public Health (Control of Disease) Act 1984, sec. 46(2)) or if the deceased is a child whom the authority was looking after (Children Act 1989, Sch. 2, para. 20, replacing the Child Care Act 1980, sec. 25). However, the latter power by contrast is exerciseable only with the consent "so far as it is reasonably practicable to obtain it" of every person who has personal responsibility for the child (para. 20(1)(c)). The duty and power to intervene under the 1984 Act are additional to those arising at common law (set out in Chapter 1, Art. 1:102, Notes, II, 16): see sec. 72 of that Act. Where an authority discharges the statutory duty or makes use of the statutory power under the 1984 Act, it may recover the expenses incurred as a civil debt from the deceased person's estate or from any person whom the relevant legislation regards as having been liable to maintain to the deceased (*ibid*, sec. 46(5),(6)), namely a spouse or (if the deceased is under 16) parent of the deceased (National Assistance Act 1948, sec. 42 (read in conjunction with sec. 64(1)). An authority may similarly recover as a civil debt from a parent of a deceased child who died aged under sixteen and was buried or cremated by the authority the expenses it has incurred in exercising its power: para. 20(4) of Sch. 2 of the 1989 Act. Subject to exceptions, a local authority is under a statutory duty to provide accommodation for a person who refuses or neglects to maintain himself and as a result needs care and attention not otherwise available to them (National Assistance Act 1948, sec. 21) and to recover some or all of the cost (sec. 22). Where, in that person's own interests or in order to prevent injury to health or a serious nuisance to others, a court orders a person to be detained in accommodation (other than a NHS hospital) because of that person's disease, infirmity, or the like, coupled with their inability to devote to themselves the proper care and attention which they are not receiving from others, the local authority (who in such circumstances is primarily liable to maintain the person: sec. 47(8)) may recover costs from that person, or someone liable under social assistance legislation to maintain that person: *ibid*, sec. 47(9). Equally, where a person is admitted to hospital, or moved into local authority accommodation (or other accommodation under the power in sec. 47), the council may recover from that person, or someone liable under social assistance legislation to maintain that person, the cost of any reasonable expenses incurred in discharging its duty to take reasonable steps to prevent or mitigate loss or damage to movable property of that person as a result of their inability to protect or deal with it: *ibid*, sec. 48. A local authority has power to cleanse and disinfect premises in order to prevent the spread of infectious disease if the occupier fails to take required steps and to recover from the occupier as a "simple contract debt" expenses reasonably incurred: Public Health (Control of Disease) Act 1984, s. 31. Where there is an authority to act, a restitutionary claim is as a rule not envisaged – not least because it may be assumed that in conferring power to intervene the legislature or a court will also address issues of compensation and costs: cf. *Wentworth v. Tubb* (1841) 1 Y & C CC 171 at 173-174, 62 ER 840 at 841-842 (*Knight Bruce* VC) (provider of necessaries to a person without contractual capacity must not be acting under a court order); *Pontypridd Union v. Drew* [1927] 1 KB 214, 219 (*Scrutton* LJ) (no right to repayment could be implied by law where the guardians acted under a statutory duty to afford relief, which *prima facie* negatives any condition for repayment). Conversely, the fact that the intervener is a public body is not precluded from relying on a common law claim to restitution if there is no statutory authority: cf. *West Ham Union v. Pearson* (1890) 62 LT (N.S.) 638 (reimbursement of cost of accommodation and supervision of a violent and dangerous alcoholic suffering from delerium tremens and incapable of protecting himself – though not, under menthal health legislation in force at the time, regarded as suffering from a mental illness so as to come within statutory rules). Powers to manage the property and affairs of a person suffering from mental incapacity, or to make arrangements affecting that person's welfare, may be granted in advance of mental decline under a 'lasting power of attorney' or are conferred by court order under a statutory regime: see the Mental Capacity Act 2005, which, when it comes into force, will supersede the Enduring Powers of Attorney Act 1985 and the statutory regime under the Mental Health Act 1983, Part VII.

V. *Acts Done to Discharge an Obligation to a Third Party*

31. A further issue is whether a benevolent intervention without authority is possible where the active party has done what that party was obliged to do under a contractual or statutory duty toward a third party. According to the prevailing view in GERMANY the application of the rules on benevolent intervention remains possible where it can be discerned that the intervener also intends to act for the principal (MünchKomm [-*Seiler*], BGB[3], § 677, no. 9). However recent case law notably inclines towards the basic position of these Principles. On that view a claim arising from benevolent intervention will be excluded if the issue of remuneration is comprehensively provided for in the contract concluded with the third party (BGH 21 October 2003, NJW-RR 2004, 81). BGH 15 April 2004, NJW-RR 2004, 956 asserts that "a claim against the 'principal' ... will be outside the scope of consideration if the duty the 'intervener' has discharged arises under a contract validly concluded which lays down the rights and obligations of the 'intervener' and in particular includes the issue of remuneration".

32. In GREEK law it is emphasized that in general only authority or duty vis-à-vis the principal will render the rules on benevolent intervention inapplicable. A duty of the intervener owed to a third party does not constitute a mandate within the meaning of CC art. 730 (Georgiades and Stathopoulos [-*Papanikolaou*], Art. 730, no. 24), though in such cases as a rule the basic requirement that the act is undertaken with the intention to benefit another will not be satisfied (*Papanikolaou*, loc.cit.). As a result the legal situation in Greece is also along the lines of these Principles.

33. As regards PORTUGUESE law it may again be assumed that acts which are undertaken in order to discharge an existing duty owed to a third party will not qualify as benevolent intervention (*Vieira Gomes*, Gestão de negócios, 73-79). The legal relationship between the parties is governed by the provisions on contracts in favour of a third party (*contrato a favor de terceiro;* CC arts. 443-451). The existence of a contractual relationship between the intervener and a third party under AUSTRIAN Law likewise excludes the application of benevolent intervention in relation to the act performed. One and the same act cannot qualify both as the discharge of a contractual duty to a third party and as a benevolent intervention for the benefit of the principal (*Meissel*, GoA, 75; OGH 15 December 1954, EvBl 1955/134, RIS-Justiz RS0019765).

34. By contrast the FRENCH *Cour de cassation* has held that an act may be 'spontaneous' and 'voluntary' as regards the relationship between intervener and principal although the intervener was under a contractual duty to a third party to do the act undertaken (Cass.civ. 24 May 1989, Bull.civ. 1989, I, no. 211 p. 141). By contrast, in BELGIUM scholarly commentators seem to incline towards the view that benevolent intervention

cannot apply if the active party has committed itself to that act vis-à-vis a third party. Thus, for example, a company operating a breakdown service which moves a vehicle on instruction by the police cannot rely on the rules of benevolent intervention as against the owner of the vehicle (B. H.Verb. [-*Roodhooft*] Hdst. V, De quasi-contracten, no. 2231). However, acts in compliance with a statutory duty (vis-à-vis the state) will exclude a benevolent intervention under French law (Cass.civ. 17 July 1996, Bull.Civ. 1996, I, no. 323 p. 225), whereas Belgium, as noted above in note 23, distinguishes between an *obligation légale spécifique* and an *obligation légale générale*.

35. This question has hardly even been discussed within SPANISH law. One author expresses the opinon that the application of benevolent intervention is possible where the active party acts in discharge of a contractual obligation vis-à-vis a third party and at the same time acts in the interest of the principal (*Sánchez Jordán*, Gestión de negocios, 90). TS 23 July 1999, RAJ 1999 (4) no. 6355 p. 9958 has not elaborated further on this point, as the principal *in casu* had not obtained any benefit from the intervention. According to ITALIAN law a benevolent intervention is in general excluded if the active party is under a duty towards a third party to undertake the acts performed. CA Rome 22 May 2002 (cited by *Baralis*, Riv.dir.comm. 2004, 211, 223, fn. 17) may well be understood as an affirmation of this traditional approach in the legal literature (which has only rarely been disputed). Certainly benevolent intervention is excluded if the intervener acts on the basis of a contract in favour of the 'principal' (CC art. 1411 (2)) (*Sirena*, Gestione di affari, 169-170). For DUTCH Law, by contrast, it is again maintained that benevolent intervention will only be excluded where the intervener is obliged vis-à-vis the *principal*, whether that obligation arises from a contract or a statutory provision, but not merely because he discharges a duty to a third party. A person, for example, who is obliged to his employer under an employment contract to attend to the interests of a third party may 'under certain conditions' be considered a benevolent intervener vis-à-vis the principal (T. M. Parlementaire Geschiedenis VI, 792; Verbintenissenrecht [-*Heisterkamp*], Art. 6:198 BW, no. 13. 1).

36. Where two parties contractually agree that one is to attend to the affair of a third party the view is maintained by some in SCOTLAND that the party obliged also has a direct claim against the benefited party on the basis of *negotiorum gestio*. This is supposedly the case in particular if someone instructs another to attend to the affairs of the principal. This is only the basis that the person acting is subrogated to the legal position of the original *gestor* (giving the instruction). In this way the principal retains the defences which he would have had in relation to the original or 'true' *gestor* (*SMT Sales & Services Co. Ltd.* v. *Motor and General Finance Co. Ltd.* 1954 SLT (Sh.Ct.) 107; Stair [-*Whitty*], vol. 15, para 142; *Whitty*, JuridRev 1994, 278, 279; see, however, *Leslie*, SLT 1981, 260, 261).

37. From all the SCANDINAVIAN jurisdictions only two DANISH judgments can be found which deal with a case where a *gestor* has acted in compliance with a duty arising under public law. That subsisting duty did not exclude a claim against the benefited party for compensation in respect of the expenditure incurred (HD 24 May 1937, UfR 1937, 697 and HD 3 December 1936, UfR 1937, 357).

38. In those exceptional types of case where ENGLISH law is prepared to recognise restitutionary liability towards a stranger who has intervened, it too refuses to sanction a claim for reimbursement or recompense if the expenditure was incurred or service provided on the basis of a contract with a third party: cf. *Barnesley v. Powell* (1750)

Amb 102, 27 ER 63 (Lord *Hardwicke* LC) (solicitor commissioned by third party to act in respect of person without full capacity must claim remuneration from third party); *Wentworth v. Tubb* (1841) 1 Y & C CC 171 at 173-174, 62 ER 840 at 841-842 (*Knight Bruce* VC) (in the context of provision of necessaries to a person without contractual capacity). Thus while a person may have a claim against the deceased's estate for reimbursement of expenditure in arranging the funeral where those obliged to do so have failed to act, a person paying funeral expenses is not automatically a creditor of the estate; if the payment is made at another's order, it is the person who gave the order who is responsible for reimbursement. A claim to reimbursement is not excluded by the mere fact the intervener acted at the request of a third party: *Arlot v. Churchland* (1828) unreported (Court of Common Pleas) cited 3 Y & J 32-33, 148 ER 1081 (action of undertaker acting at request of deceased's solicitor); *Rogers v. Price* (1829) 3 Y & J 28, 148 ER 1080 (action of undertaker acting at request of testator's brother); *Ambrose v. Kerrison* (1851) 10 CB 776, 138 ER 307 (request of a friend of the deceased), and consider also *Palmer v. Stear* (1963) 113 LJ 420 (vet alerted by a third party). If the acceptance of the request amounts to the conclusion of a contract, however, a restitutionary claim against the estate or relatives is apparently excluded: see *Rogers v. Price*, loc. cit., 35 and 37, where *Hullock* B emphasises that the claimant was not acting as agent of the deceased's brother, who was merely drawing his attention to the situation, and *Vaughan* B indicates that if the case were otherwise the claimant would have had no claim against the executor. Whether administration of the estate (entailing the right to payment out of the deceased's estate) will be granted to an undertaker on the basis he is a creditor of the estate will thus depend on whether another authorised the expense; if he has acted on another's order, the undertaker is simply an unsecured creditor of the person ordering the funeral: see *In the Goods of Fowler* (1852) 16 Jur 894 (Sir *J Dodson*), considered in *Newcombe v. Beloe* (1867) LR 1 P & D 314, 315 (Sir *J P Wilde*). The decision in *Re Leslie* (1883) 23 Ch D 552, where a husband paid the premiums on an insurance policy taken out by his wife, is also explicable on the narrow basis that the husband acted under an obligation to a third party (though the judgment itself only alludes to this point in its conclusion and is largely expressed in broader terms) because the husband had covenanted with trustees of a settlement to pay the premiums. Cf. also *Castellain v. Thompson* (1862) 13 CB (N. S.) 105, 143 ER 41 (as the claimant had concluded a contract with an insurer to retrieve cargo from the river bed, there could be no salvage type claim against the owner of the cargo), as explained in the similar case *The Solway Prince* [1896] P 120, 128 (*Jeune* P), where redress was sought from the owner because the insurer was insolvent. However, where the third party instigating another's intervention is regarded as themselves being an agent of the person benefited, the intervener may have a direct claim against the principal on the basis that the intermediary has exercised their power of representation so as to bind the principal to the intervener: see *Chester v. Rolfe* (1853) 4 De G M & G 798, 43 ER 720 (CA in Chancery) (solicitor able to claim from the estate of the person whom he represented at the instigation of the latter's wife) – and the same reasoning might explain the decision in *Brockwell v. Bullock* (1889) 22 QBD 567 (CA) that the claim for remuneration of a doctor instructed by a solicitor to examine the mental state of his client was wrongly stopped at first instance.

Illustration 3 is taken from OGH 11 November 1987, SZ 60/235; **illustration 5** from BGH 13 November 2003, BGHReport 2004, 305; **illustration 6** from OGH 4 April 1906, GlUNF 3374; **illustration 7** from STJ 8 July 1997, CJ(ST) v (1997-2) 144; **illustration 8** (with slightly changed facts) from OGH 15 December 1954, EvBl 1955/134 and from BGH 21 October 2003, NJW-RR 2004, 81; **illustration 9** from OGH 10 May 1989, SZ 62/87; and **illustration 13** from BGH 15 December 1954, BGHZ 16, 12.

Chapter 2: Duties of Intervener

Article 2:101: Duties during Intervention

(1) During the intervention, the intervener must
  (a) act with reasonable care;
  (b) except in relation to a principal within Article 1:102, act in a manner which the intervener knows or ought may reasonably to assume accords with the principal's wishes; and
  (c) so far as possible and reasonable, inform the principal about the intervention and seek the principal's consent to further acts.

(2) The intervention may not be discontinued without good reason.

Comments

A. The Duties of the Intervener in Overview

1. **Contents of the second Chapter** The provisions of the second Chapter of these Principles relate to the duties of the intervener to the principal. The subsequent Articles differentiate between the actual phase of intervention (Article 2:101) and the period after the conclusion of the intervention (Article 2:102). Finally Article 2:103 regulates liability for damages where the intervener breaches one of his duties arising from either Article 2:101 or 2:102.

2. **Duties during intervention** During the intervention a *gestor* is subject to (i) a general duty to act with reasonable care (Article 2:101(a)). He (ii) must orientate his conduct according to the actual or presumed wishes of the principal (limb (b)). Furthermore, an intervener is (iii) subject to a parallel duty to inform the principal of the intervention; as soon as he has succeeded in contacting the principal he may only continue his intervention if and only if he has sought the principal's consent (limb (c)). On the other hand the intervener may not (iv) discontinue the intervention without a reasonable ground. He may not discontinue at an inopportune time an intervention which he has already begun (para (2)).

3. **Duties after intervention** After conclusion of the act undertaken the *gestor* is subject to (v) a duty to report, (vi) account and (vii) deliver up any proceeds (Article 2:102(1)). In the case of an infringement of one of these duties and a liability for damages arising, the fact that the intervener has acted for reasons of human solidarity will have to be taken into account. Thus he may not be burdened with the entire risk of erroneous conduct during or subsequent to the intervention (Article 2:103(2)).

4. **The second Chapter's scope of application** The second Chapter concerns the duties of the acting party in the phase of carrying out the *negotiorum gestio*. It regulates the matter of 'how' another's affairs may be managed without their authority and how this management must be brought to an end, as opposed to 'whether' they may be conducted, which is addressed in Articles 1:101 (Intervention to Benefit Another) and 1:102 (Intervention to Perform Another's Duty). The application of Articles 2:101-2:103 thus presupposes that the requirements of Articles 1:101-1:102 are satisfied and that none of the exclusions of Article 1:103 applies. If one of these requirements is absent or an exclusion applies, then the rights and duties of the parties will be governed exclusively by other areas of the law – in particular, the laws of contract, tort and unjustified enrichment.

Illustration 1
The facts are the same as in illustration 9 of Article 1:103. A staff member of a charitable organisation giving emergency aid to an injured person makes a clinical error. Any liability of the organisation will be under the provisions of tort law. There is no scope for the application of Article 2:103(2) (Reparation for Damage Caused by Breach of Duty).

B. The General Duty to Act with Reasonable Care (Para (1) (a))

5. **General** Interventions for the benefit of another are only useful as a rule if the intervener acts with reasonable care. A person who temporarily manages the assets of another must act as a *bonus paterfamilias* would act; if someone instructs a workman to effect an emergency repair in his neighbour's house he will have to choose a qualified workman; a person who attends to a person injured in a traffic accident will have to secure the scene of the accident and if he brings the person to hospital will have to comply with the traffic regulations, etc. The requirements which reasonable care dictates are as manifold as life itself and thus cannot be elaborated in detail. As regards the management of affairs which interfere with interests protected by tort law recourse may be had to the definition of negligence in PEL Liab.Dam. art. 3:102 (Negligence). In accordance with that a definition an intervener may breach his duty of care by omitting to take a precautionary measure. This may occur for instance if he takes valuable goods into custody but fails to take out insurance cover.

6. **Standard of care of professionals** Conduct of a *gestor* who is acting in the course of his profession or trade is to be assessed against the standards of care expected of persons in that skilled group. That is in a way merely the flip side of his coin under Article 3:102 (Right to Remuneration), which entitles him to remuneration. Compare in this context also the comments to PECL art. 6:108 (Quality of Performance).

7. **Emergency measures** These Principles do not set out a specific standard of care applicable to emergency measures. For one thing, it did not seem necessary to do so. The general principles of the law of negligence lead to the result that, in determining whether the intervener is in breach of his duty to act with reasonable care in the course of acting, regard is to be had to the difficulty in judging a situation of danger and in

endeavouring to eliminate it. The text of this Article only refrains from spelling out this principle because it is assumed to be self-evident. Moreover, the situations concerned also require a distinction with regard to the applicable standard of care – for instance, between a professional rescuer and a private individual. Emergency (para)medics, sea rescue services and other comparable professional groups and organisations should be capable, even in serious cases, of exercising a greater degree of composure in decision-making in the stress of an emergency, as is expected of their profession and acquired through training. On the other hand the drafting of a specific standard of care for emergency situations also appeared to be dispensable in view of the reduction clause in Article 2:103(2). Under the latter the intervener's liability is reduced or excluded in so far as this is fair and reasonable, having regard to, among other things, the intervener's reasons for acting. This rule will be of great relevance in particular in cases of measures taken in an emergency.

C. Compliance with the Principal's Wishes (limb (b))

8. **Specification of the general duty of care** The law of *negotiorum gestio* has on the one hand the task of protecting the activities of persons who are active for another's benefit, but on the other hand it must check rash acts of intervention. Someone who takes it upon himself to look after the interests of other people must do so with care; if he is not prepared to do so, then he ought to stay out of the matter altogether. However, para (1) does not merely contain the general duty of care (limb (a)); it also specifies that duty from the point of view of *negotiorum gestio*. As part of the *gestor*'s duties of care, the *gestor* must comply so far as possible with the wishes of the principal in the carrying out of his duties (just as much as in determining under Article 1:101(2) (Intervention to Benefit Another) whether he has at the outset a reasonable ground to act as *gestor* at all). Only if those wishes are neither known nor ascertainable must the *gestor* take for orientation the notion of what, objectively understood, amounts to a reasonable *dominus*' wishes.

9. **Special information available to the intervener** The touchstone for the duty of care in such cases are therefore the wishes of a principal who takes reasonable care of his rights and interests. That is because the wishes of the *dominus* can take priority only in so far as they were known to the *gestor* or, if such care as was reasonable in the circumstances had been exercised, would have been known by him. Should the *gestor* have special information at his disposal which sheds light on the wishes of the principal, then the *gestor* must make use of that information.

10. **The exception in Article 1:102** Compliance with the contrary wishes of the *dominus* is not obligatory if he is set against the discharge of an obligation which he is obliged to a third party to fulfil as a matter of overriding public interest (Article 1:102 (Intervention to Perform Another's Duty)). The same consideration which applies in relation to taking up the *negotiorum gestio* activity applies also to the actual carrying out of that activity. This is expressed in the introductory phrase of limb (b). In this case too, though, all other duties continue to exist. This includes in particular the duty to inform in limb (c).

Illustration 2
On a rainy autumnal day, B's fleet of construction vehicles have left residues of earth and building materials on the road. There is a great danger of an accident occurring. A, a neighbour, instructs a firm to clean the street without first telephoning B because due to the weather conditions he could not decipher the name of B's firm displayed on the vehicles. A's intervention was with reasonable ground. However, this does not free A of his duty to contact B if in the meantime he (A) has learned about B's identity and telephone number – for instance, from an employee of the cleaning company instructed to clean the road. If A fails to contact B, B can set off against A's claim to reimbursement of his expenditure the fact that B would have been able to dispose of the material on premises available to it much more cheaply than the road cleaning firm, which deposited the material (in the absence of contrary instructions) on a public authority site. The difference between the actual expense expended by A and this hypothetical cost which B would have incurred is a loss which A must carry himself.

D. The Duty to Inform (limb (c))

11. **A continual duty** Whereas Article 1:101(2) (Intervention to Benefit Another) gives effect to the rule that someone who attends to others must first find out whether they in fact want that, Article 2:101(1)(c) clarifies that the duty to inform (and abide by the *gestor*'s decision to abstain from any further interference) is a continual one: the *gestor* is obliged to keep the principal informed, so far as this is practicable and appropriate. This applies in particular when the *gestor* was unable to contact the principal before commencing his intervention, but it is not confined to that situation alone. As circumstances change, it may be necessary for the *gestor* to return to the principal to report on developments which might materially affect the principal's instruction.

12. **"during the intervention"** All duties specified in this Article relate to the executory phase of a benevolent intervention. Clearly the nature of the continual duty to inform – or more precisely, the duty, so far as possible and reasonable, continually to make fresh attempts to reach the principal – is such that it can apply only in the case of benevolent interventions which endure for any length of time; it cannot apply to measures which consist only of an instantaneous act.

13. **An indicator of the intention to act for another** The performance of the duty to inform does not merely serve the interests of the principal. Informing the principal (or, depending on the circumstances, the attempt to contact the principal) also helps to reveal the *gestor*'s intention to conduct another's affairs (required by Article 1:101(1) (Intervention to Benefit Another)). Moreover, it points to the person for whom the *gestor* intends to act and helps identify the principal.

14. **Providing the information itself amounts to a negotiorum gestio** As stated before, the provision of information is in itself a *negotiorum gestio* and consequently, if it necessitates expenditure, it can give rise to a claim for reimbursement where the conditions in Articles 1:101 and 3:101 (Right to Indemnification or Reimbursement) are satisfied.

15. **Content of the information required** The issue of under what circumstances the *gestor* must make a fresh attempt to inform the principal and the question what he must tell the principal if he succeeds in contacting him are matters which turn on the circumstances of individual cases and cannot be answered in a statutory provision of general application. As a rule the *gestor* must inform the principal of the situation of danger which has arisen, the measures which have been attempted in order to eliminate it and what has happened in between. Above all it is essential that the *gestor* gives the principal the chance to forbid a further undertaking of his affairs.

16. **Consent and contract** However, the *gestor* is not bound by the wishes of the principal if the principal desires the continuation of an act of *negotiorum gestio* after its commencement. That is because no contract exists between the parties and there is consequently nothing out from which a claim to performance could be derived. The duty to continue the act is purely an obligation arising under this Book and it exists only under the conditions envisaged in para (2). Should the *gestor*, however, accept a request from the principal to continue an intervention he has begun or undertake a new one, then as a rule the matter will be governed from this point in time onwards by the contract arising between them. Moreover, one will mostly be able to proceed on the basis that such positive conduct of the principal denotes a conclusive statement of approval of the measures already undertaken.

E. The Duty not to Discontinue an Act after Commencement without Good Reason (Para (2))

17. **General** Whereas para (1) is concerned with the actual phase of acting in management of another's affairs, para (2) addresses the question when the intervener may discontinue an intervention once it has been started. The basic rule is that everyone is free to decide whether he wishes to attend to the affairs of another, but having once resolved to do so, one must in principle bring the matter to a conclusion. The purpose of the obligation to continue consists in the protection of the principal from the impetuous intermeddling of others. Potential *gestors* ought to appreciate that they will be assuming responsibility with their intervention. On the other hand, the duty to continue the intervention ought not to extend so far that an activity embarked upon as a non-contractual management of another's affairs ceases to be distinguishable from a specifically enforceable duty to perform an agreed contractual obligation. The law of *negotiorum gestio* should give well-meaning persons an incentive to look after their fellow citizens. For that reason it must remain possible for a *gestor* to venture the attempt to render assistance and to be able to give it up later if there is a good reason.

18. **Good reasons to discontinue the intervention** Para (2) deliberately does not list the "good reasons" for ending an activity in benevolent intervention; the matrix of possibilities in everyday life is too extensive. Without making claim to completeness, however, it is possible to compile the following list of four groups of cases: (i) achievement of the desired object, (ii) restoration of the principal's capacity to act for himself, (iii) the wish of the principal that the *gestor* desist from further measures, and (iv) reasons attributable either to the intervener's circumstances (e.g. continuance would require

unreasonable exertion) or the circumstances generally (e. g. uselessness of further exertion).

19. **Achievement of the desired object** As soon as the intervention has achieved its purpose, that is to say, when the problem on account of which the *gestor* intervened has been solved, the *gestor* is not merely allowed to bring his intervention to an end. As a rule he will also be obliged to refrain from other activity on behalf of the principal. (Whether further intervention would be justified or not has to be decided afresh in accordance with Article 1:101 (Intervention to Benefit Another.)) What remains at this stage are merely the duties to report, account and surrender anything acquired by reason of the intervention. These are regarded by Article 2:102 (Duties after Intervention) as independent duties consequential on the intervention and not as a mere part of a duty to continue an intervention.

20. **The principal can reasonably be expected to take over** The *gestor* also has a reasonable ground to end his intervention if he can legitimately expect the principal to resume the management of his own affairs. This will more often than not be the case as soon as the intervener draws the principal's attention to the existence of the dangerous situation.

21. **Actual or presumed contrary wishes of the principal** The intervener must discontinue his undertaking if he knows that the principal does not want it to be continued and the principal's wish is not (by way of exception to the general rule) non-binding. Moreover, the intervener is also obliged by para (1)(b) to orientate himself according to what may reasonably be supposed to be the wishes of the principal. Consequently the *gestor* must also desist from continuing his intervention if the circumstances are such that he ought reasonably to suppose that the principal would not want further measures to be undertaken. This is often the reason why a benevolent intervention is complete when it merely achieves a provisional 'shoring up' of the principal's affairs. The decision as to the manner and timing of any permanent securing of the principal's interest must as a rule remain reserved to the principal.

22. **Unreasonableness** The intervener also has a good ground for ending his management of the principal's affairs if it has become unreasonable for him to continue the intervention in the manner in which he had begun it. What passes for reasonable or unreasonable depends on the particular circumstances and can hardly be expressed in an abstract formula. The personal circumstances of the *gestor* (dangers he faces, pressure of time in regard to the discharge of other legal or social duties, the intensity of effort and time which has already been invested in the services rendered and would have to be invested in their continuation, etc) and the extent of the danger which cessation of the benevolent intervention would pose for the principal must be weighed up against one another. Within the boundaries of what is appropriate and reasonable the intervener is invested with a degree of discretion. As part of the balancing of interests, moreover, one must ascertain whether and (if so) in what way the intervener has adversely affected the interests of the principal by his intervention up to that point in time and whether he (the intervener) had the opportunity to secure the assistance of third parties. The test question in such cases is: would a careful person, placed in the intervener's situation and

conscious of the fact that they have assumed responsibility of their own free will for some affair of the principal, have done more?

Illustration 3
If a person helps someone and by doing so causes others, who would equally have helped, to go home, then he may not give up his assistance all of a sudden, since the injured party would now be completely helpless, whereas in the situation at the outset he might have counted on the (enduring) intervention of others. The person helping must at the very least see to it that the emergency medical services or the police are notified.

23. **Uselessness** Finally, a measure undertaken in benevolent intervention may be ended if it emerges after a first attempt that it will not meet with success. Here too, however, it is conceivable that the duty to continue an intervention may take on the form of a duty to secure the help of third parties, should it transpire that the intervention has in fact made the situation worse.

Illustration 4
A has embarked on repair of the roof on the house of his neighbour, B, and, in order to be able to penetrate through to the damaged part, he removes further tiles and roof battens. At this point it becomes clear to A that he will not be able to carry out the repairs by his own exertions after all. He must call in a professional roofer. Were it the case that A ought to have recognised at the outset that the required work would exceed his own capability, then A would have been in breach of the duty of care under para (1) and thus become liable for any additional damage to the building his intervention has caused.

24. **Termination of the benevolent intervention without good reason** It does not suffice, however, as a reason for abandoning the matter in hand that the intervener has simply lost interest. Moreover, that is so irrespective of whether the interim intervention has increased the risk of damage to the principal in some shape or form.

Illustration 5
Of his own free will, A looks after the landed estate belonging to his brother, who is lying in a coma in hospital. After one year has passed, A decides to move into the city. He does nothing towards the administration of the farm and does not undertake or arrange for the tilling of the fields that should be carried out at this time of the year. A is of course not obliged to look after the farm permanently. However, he has not brought his benevolent intervention to a conclusion because he has failed to arrange what in the given circumstances was a reasonable solution for the future care of the farm (which could have consisted of a lease of the farm or, if there were no other relatives, its sale). A is liable to B for the damage suffered by the growth of weeds.

Notes

I. *The General Duty to Take Reasonable Care*

1. The general duty to exercise reasonable care in the conduct of another's affair is essentially universal. That it has not been explicitly set out by the GERMAN CC may be explained by the fact that the intervener (both at the point of time he takes up the management of the affair as well as in the executory phase) is required to orientate his conduct by the principal's wishes or the principal's interests. No principal will have an interest that another attends to his affairs without the required caution and attention. AUSTRIAN CC § 1036 grants the intervener in an emergency a claim for reimbursement of expenditures even if his "efforts without his fault have remained unsuccessful". BELGIAN, FRENCH and LUXEMBOURGIAN CC art. 1372 subject an intervener without authority to all duties which would arise in a case of a *mandat exprès*. By this means CC art. 1992 (1), which provides for the liability of the agent for fault (i. e. wilful and negligent wrongdoing), also applies to the law of benevolent intervention. CC art. 1374 (1) confirms that the intervener will have to come up to the standard of care of a *bonus paterfamilias*. MALTESE CC art. 1015 subjects the "voluntary agent" to the high standard of care of a *bonus paterfamilias*. CC art. 1016 adds that this provision is to be applied "with the greatest strictness" if the intervener (a) acted in contravention of a prohibition by the principal, (b) the intervener by his intervention prevented a more skilled person from attending to the affair or (c) the "agent himself did not possess the requisite skill".
2. Similarly GREEK CC art. 731 sentence 1 makes it clear that the intervener will be liable "for any fault". POLISH CC art. 752 and ESTONIAN CC § 1022 demand from an intervener that he acts with requisite care. PORTUGUESE CC art. 466 sets out the rule that the intervener is liable to the principal for "damages, which he has caused by his fault during the intervention". Both formulas encompass a general duty of care. Portuguese CC art. 466 (2) adds that the intervener's management renders him liable if he does not act in accordance with the interest and the true or presumed wishes of the intervener. In contrast to tort law (CC art. 487 (2)) and contract law (CC art. 799 (2) in conjunction with art. 487 (2)) the law of benevolent intervention does not contain an explicit statement that fault will be determined according to the "standard of care a *bonus paterfamilias* would have taken with regard to the circumstances of the particular case". As a result the arguably prevailing opinion seems to be that within the law of benevolent intervention a *culpa in abstracto* will not suffice to give rise to liability and that a *culpa in concreto* or even a breach of the *diligentia quam in suis* is required instead (*Antunes Varela*, Obrigações em Geral I[10], 460-462; STJ 22 April 1986, BolMinJus 356 (1986) 352-357; *Ribeiro de Faria*, Obrigações I, 355-356; *Almeida Costa*, Obrigações[9], 442; but see for a distinct opinion *Galvão Telles*, Obrigações[7], 189-190; *Vaz Serra*, Gestão de negócios, 134 and 270, see also *Menezes Leitão*, Responsabilidade do gestor, 288 and *idem*, Direito das obrigações I, 439-440).
3. SPANISH CC art. 1889 demands that the intervener manage the affair with such care as a *bonus paterfamilias* would take. The standard is that of 'normal care of ordinary people' (Paz-Ares/Díez-Picazo/Bercovitz/Salvador [*-Díez-Picazo*], Código Civil II, 1946), and therefore as a general rule not such care as an expert in the field would be able to exercise, unless the *gestor* is such an expert (*Sánchez Jordán*, Gestión de

negocios, 448). The standard is determined by comparison with the standard of care a *bonus paterfamilias* would exercise with respect to his own affairs. This standard of care is intended to prevent a *gestor* from being liable in cases of mere *culpa levissima* or *culpa leve* (i. e. a slight or lesser degree of negligence) (*Díez-Picazo*, loc.cit.).

4. Under ITALIAN CC art. 2030 the intervener is subject to the same duties as would arise had a contract of mandate been concluded with the principal. CC art. 2030 thus points to CC art. 1710 (1). The same degree of care expected of the *bonus pater familias* provided for in the latter is demanded of an intervener in another's affairs (Cass. 4 May 1985, no. 2795, Rep.Giur.it. 1985, voce Divisione, no. 12; voce Responsabilità civile, no. 154). However, the second limb of CC art. 1710 (1), which provides that liability for negligence will be judged less strictly in the case of a gratuitous mandate, is not held to be invoked by CC art. 2030 (Cass. 4 October 1956, no. 3336, Rep.Giur.it. 1956, voce Gestione d'affari, nos. 8, 9, 12 and 13; Cass. 20 May 1953, no. 1472, Rep.Giur.it. 1953, voce Gestione d'affari, no. 5).

5. The SLOVENIAN Code of Obligations art. 210 requires that the intervener acts as a person exercising average care would act and that he heeds the true or presumed needs of the intervener. The same holds true for DUTCH Law. Under CC art. 6:199 the intervener has to exercise reasonable care while he manages the affair of another. The intervener has to attend to the interests of the principal with the same care which would be expected in that context from a reasonable and diligent intervener. Whether the intervener has satisfied this standard will be determined by the judge according to the circumstances of the particular case (T. M. Parlementaire Geschiedenis VI, 793; Asser [-*Hartkamp*], Verbintenissenrecht III[11], no. 307 p. 318-319; *Schrage*, Mon. Nieuw BW, no. 21 p. 15; T & C Vermogensrecht [-*Hijma*], Art. 6:199 BW, no. 2; Verbintenissenrecht [-*Scheltema*], Art. 6:199 BW, no. 2).

6. With regard to SCOTS law it was held in *AS Kolbin & Sons v. William Kinnear & Co.* SC(HL) 1931, 128 that an intervener is obliged to act according to the standard of care which a reasonable person would exercise in his own affairs. Particularities of the individual case are to be taken into account (*Walker*, Principles of Scottish Private Law[4], 513-514; *Leslie*, Jur.Rev. 1983, 27; Stair [-*Whitty*], vol. 15, para 136).

7. As regards SCANDINAVIAN jurisdictions it is said or at least has been said that the standard of care the intervener has to exercise also requires that the intervener does not act beyond the scope of necessary measures and thus as a general rule restricts himself to temporary measures. The *gestor* should in general confine himself to measures which prevent the aggravation of the state of affairs and not try to improve it, as the latter are not necessary (*Håstad*, Tjänster utan uppdrag, 36 with reference to earlier Danish literature as well as to *Vinding Kruse*, En nordisk lovbog, 6-14-1, p. 272 and 599; *idem*, A Nordic Draft Code, ch. 57, sec. 1437, p. 379). Of note as regards SWEDISH case law is HD 9 March 1972, NJA 1972, 88 (where the fire brigade during a storm removed roof sheeting which threatened to be swiped on the street. The claim for recompense has been dismissed on the ground that it would have been more skilful and more advantageous to pin down the roof sheeting).

8. In the COMMON LAW an agent of necessity is invariably regarded as being obliged at the very least to take ordinary (i.e reasonable) care, even where the agent acts gratuitously: cf. *Grill v. General Iron Screw Collier Co* (1866) LR 1 CP 600, 612 (*Willes* J); *Fridman*, Agency[5], p. 140. Where a pre-existing agency for reward is enlarged by necessity, the obligation (so far as not otherwise agreed by the parties) is one of best

endeavours in order to protect the principal's interests: cf. *The Onward* (1873) LR 4 A & E 38, 57 (Sir *Robert Phillimore*). For example, this includes a positive obligation on a ship's captain to protect cargo against further deterioration arising out of an accident for which he is not responsible and to store cargo, rather than simply leaving it, if it is not collected at the time of unloading: see *Notara v. Henderson* (1870) LR 5 QB 346, 353 (*Cockburn* CJ, for the Court of Queen's Bench), affirmed (1872) LR 7 QB 225, 235 (*Willes* J, for the Court of Exchequer Chamber), where the cargo (beans) became damp as a result of a collission, but the captain refused to unload it to enable it to be dried while the ship was being repaired and it deteriorated. Conversely, an agent of necessity is not burdened with strict liability (unless this is contractually agreed) and if he has discharged his obligations honestly and reasonably he will not be liable for damage resulting from his lawful management of the principal's affairs: see *The Lizzie* (1868) LR 2 A & E 254, 256 (Sir *Robert Phillimore*) (concerning use of a ship as security for a loan which, it transpired, exceeded the value of the assets and thus created a net indebtedness for the principal). See further Chapter 3, Art. 3:106, Notes 11.

II. *The Duty to Orientate the Exercise of Care According to the Principal's Wishes*

9. Similar to POLISH CC art. 752 and HUNGARIAN CC § 484, GERMAN CC § 677 too obliges the intervener to conduct the management of the affair in accordance with the principal's interests with regard to his actual or supposed wishes. The decisive criterion to assess the 'interests' (as opposed to the 'wishes') will be what from an objective perspective and according to a generally accepted view would be considered to benefit the principal. However, the actual wishes of the principal will always claim priority, whether or not they are reasonable ones. Thus the supposed wishes of the principal will only be decisive in a case where the actual wishes are not ascertainable or are not binding as being contrary to law or *bonos mores*. The question arises as to what according to an objective evaluation of all circumstances are to be regarded as the hypothetical wishes of the principal. If other pointers are lacking the supposed wishes will be ascertained according to the principal's objective interests (BGH 7 January 1971, NJW 1971, 609, 612). If in the exceptional case the principal's interests and wishes do not concur the question of an order of priority arises. Some commentatory, adhering to the wording of CC § 677 ("*mit Rücksicht auf*" – 'having regard to'), give priority to the principal's interests and therefore to an objective standard (Jauernig [-*Vollkommer*], § 677, no. 9; MünchKomm [-*Seiler*], BGB[3], § 677, no. 45; Palandt [-*Sprau*], BGB[63], § 677, no. 12 et seq.). Others disagree, arguing that this does not accord with the rationale of the law of benevolent intervention and that it conflicts with the principal's right to self-determination to allow or even promote unauthorized interventions which are well-meant and useful but not undesired by the principal (Soergel [-*Beuthien*], BGB[12], § 677, no. 19; Staudinger [-*Wittmann*], BGB[13], § 677, no. 4; *Esser and Weyers*, Schuldrecht BT II/2[8], § 46 II 4 b).

10. GREEK CC art. 730 determines the most important duty of the intervener: the duty to conduct the affair in accordance with the interest and the actual or presumed wishes of the principal. This duty will only arise if the requirements of a justified intervention without authority are met. An intervener acts contrary to his principal's interest if he in arranging for necessary repairs, for instance, instructs a contractor whose services are less reasonably priced than those of a competitor (*Kavkas and Kavkas*, Enochikon

Dikaion II/2, 25). The culpable breach of the duty to act in accord with the principal's interests or, as the case may be, the wishes of the principal does not transform a justified intervention into an unjustified intervention, but it may lead to the intervener's liability for damages. As regards the relation between the two criteria (interest and wishes of the principal), legal literature refers to the corresponding rule on taking over the management of another's affair (e. g. *Papanikolaou*, Art. 730, no. 40). Accordingly the principal's wishes will take priority over his objective interests. The latter will only be of relevance if the actual or supposed wishes are not ascertainable (ErmAK [-*Saketas*], Art. 730, no. 55 f; *Papanikolaou*, loc.cit. no. 35; but in part taking a different view, *Filios*, Enochiko Dikaio I/2, 200).

11. From PORTUGUESE CC art. 465 lit. a arises a duty of the intervener to have regard to the interests and the actual or supposed wishes of the principal, unless the latter are contrary to law or morality. According to the wording of CC art. 465 lit. a both the (objective) interest and the (subjective) wishes share the same priority. If (in exceptional circumstances) they differ the prevailing opinion holds the (legitimate) wishes of the principal to be decisive (*Antunes Varela*, Obrigações em Geral I[10], 462; *Menezes Leitão*, Responsabilidade do gestor, 218 ff). Others rate the objective interest to be of greater importance (*Vaz Serra*, Gestão de negócios, 122) and a third group considers that in such a case the *gestor* must abstain from acting altogether (*Menezes Cordeiro*, Obrigações II, 18).

12. AUSTRIAN CC § 1037 merely sets out a duty of the intervener to attempt to obtain the principal's consent. According to settled case law the intervener is nonetheless obliged to manage the affair in accordance with the principal's interest having regard to the latter's actual or supposed wishes. Regard is to be had to the probable intentions of the principal – in particular where the management involves expenses (OGH 21 April 1982, JBl 1984, 256). Observance of the supposed wishes of the principal is of great importance, as both the justification of the intervention (CC § 1036) and the claim for reparation depend on it (Schwimann [-*Apathy*], ABGB V[2], §§ 1036-1040 no. 11, *Meissel*, GoA, 118 et seq.). This also holds true for cases of intervention in an emergency (*Meissel*, loc.cit. 119).

13. The SLOVENIAN Code of Obligations art. 201 demands that in the course of his management the intervener acts in accordance with the actual or supposed wishes of the intervener. Art. 204 adds that the intervener must refrain from any action if the principal forbids it.

14. BELGIAN, FRENCH and LUXEMBOURGIAN CC do not explicitly provide that the duty of care is coupled to observance of the principal's wishes. CC art. 1374 (1) merely states that the intervener must take such care as a *bonus paterfamilias* would exercise. Whether or not the intervener's action is culpable will accordingly be assessed *in abstracto* (*Flour/Aubert/Savaux*, Le fait juridique[10], no. 14 p. 16; *De Page*, Droit Civil Belge II[3], no. 1082 p. 1147). Although the conclusion is only infrequently stated explicitly, the conclusion may be drawn from this obligation of careful management that the intervener has to heed the principal's wishes (*Paulus*, Zaakwaarneming, no. 67 p. 45-46). The starting position of MALTESE CC is quite similar (CC art. 1015). However, CC art. 1016 tightens the standard of care if the intervener does not comply with a prohibition by the principal.

15. The starting point of SPANISH law is the basic rule that benevolent intervention cannot be undertaken contrary to the express wishes of the principal (TS 2 February

1954, RAJ 1954, no. 322 p. 198). An intervention undertaken contrary to the wishes of the principal does not meet the requirement of usefulness, i. e. *utiliter coeptum* (Paz-Ares/Díez-Picazo/Bercovitz/Salvador [-*Díez-Picazo*], Código Civil II, 1944). Ley 561 of *Fuero Nuevo de* NAVARRA reads "If he (the principal) has previously forbidden the intervention, he is not obliged to pay compensation". In addition CC art. 1891 provides that the intervener will be liable for accidental loss in two cases, namely if he either undertakes a 'risky measure' which the principal does not usually engage in or if the intervener gives preference to his own interests over those of the principal. 'Risky measures' include, for instance, engaging in speculation on the stock exchange (*Díez-Picazo*, loc.cit. 1949).

16. In ITALY a determination whether the intervener has observed the required standard of care is likewise closely linked to the assessment of whether or not there is *utiliter coeptum*: the usefulness of a measure is to be assessed according to the standard whether or not it is in line with the presumed wishes of the principle or the principal's interest (Cass. 13 October 1951, no. 2634, Foro it. 1952, I, 201; *Breccia*, La gestione d'affari[2], 879). In addition the assessment follows objective criteria, i. e. regard is had to whether the intervener has acted as a *bonus paterfamilias* would have done in similar circumstances (Cass. 13 March 1964, no. 550, Foro it. 1965, I, 866).

17. Under DUTCH CC art. 6:200 claims of the intervener will depend on whether or not he has attended to the principal's interests properly. It is not only a pre-condition for the existence of a reasonable ground but also a requirement for satisfying the standard of care under CC art. 6:199 (1) that the management of the principal's affairs accords with the actual or presumed wishes of the principal. Thus fault in commencing an intervention in the first place and fault in its execution once begun hinge on the same criteria (T. M. Parlementaire Geschiedenis VI, 793; Asser [-*Hartkamp*], Verbintenissenrecht III[11], no. 307 p. 318-319; T & C Vermogensrecht [-*Hijma*], Art. 6:199 BW, no. 2; Verbintenissenrecht [-*Scheltema*], Art. 6:199 BW, no. 2).

18. Despite some problems which have their origin in the Roman legal sources and the paucity of useful observations among the institutional writers on this point, SCOTS law too seems to arrive at the same conclusion that the *gestor* is obliged to orientate his conduct according to the presumed wishes of the principal (Stair [-*Whitty*] vol. 15, para 122). A duty to ascertain the wishes of the principal can at least be indirectly inferred from the notion that a measure will only constitute a benevolent intervention if it benefits the principal in his particular circumstances (for details see *Leslie*, Jur.Rev. 1983, 25). Agency of necessity under the COMMON LAW requires that the agent act reasonably and in the interests of the principal and that what he does be 'necessary'; these requirements are satisfied in effect if the principal, conducting himself as prudent person, would himself have undertaken the measure in question: *Gunn v. Roberts* (1874) LR 9 CP 331, 337 (*Brett* J), and see further *Notara v. Henderson* (1870) LR 5 QB 346, 353 (*Cockburn* CJ, for the Court of Queen's Bench), affirmed (1872) LR 7 QB 225, 235 (*Willes* J, for the Court of Exchequer Chamber), where it is indicated that where a ship's captain is under an obligation (arising from necessity) to store unloaded cargo, he must store it at the place which, considering the matter carefully, he regards as the most convenient for the cargo owner. In similar manner a claim to restitution which is based on necessitous intervention (e. g. in maintaining a person without full legal capacity) presupposes that the benefit conferred was a necessity and that quality is to be determined by reference to the recipient's reasonable

needs and circumstances: cf. *Re Rhodes* (1890) 44 Ch D 94. 105 (*Cotton* LJ) and 109 (*Lopes* LJ).

19. In relation to the NORDIC Countries reference can be made to a small number of provisions of commercial law which all require that the active party act in accordance with 'the interest' of the other party. Under the DANISH and SWEDISH Factors Acts § 7 the commission agent has to take account of the interests of the principal and the same also applies under the SWEDISH Maritime Code *[sjölag* (1994:1009)] Kap 13 § 12 to the carrier of goods with regard to the interests of the owner of the goods. These rules may well be applied to the *gestor* by analogy.

III. *The Duty to Inform*

20. GERMAN CC § 681 sentence 2 refers to the law of mandate (which under German law is a gratuitous contract) and by this means subjects the intervener to the same duties as a contractual agent. The latter's duties according to CC § 666 also include the duty to inform and to give an account. Strictly speaking CC § 666 contains three separate duties of information, namely the duty to inform that an intervention is being conducted, the duty to provide information and the duty to provide an account. The duty to inform on the event of an intervention must be adhered to by the intervener on his own initiative, i. e. without a prior request from the principal; by contrast, the duty to provide information and to give an account will only arise as a consequence of a request by the principal. Though no clear line can or need be drawn between them, the duty to inform the principal that an intervention has occurred primarily relates to the circumstances which rendered the undertaking necessary, while the second duty to provide information concerns the state of the management of the affair as a whole.

21. GREEK law likewise extends the main duty of the intervener to act in accordance with the interest and wishes of the principal by accessory duties, which are drawn from the law of mandate. Setting out one accessory duty CC art. 733 states that the intervener must inform the principal of the commencement of the intervention and inquire as to the principal's wishes (Georgiades and Stathopoulos [-*Papanikolaou*], Art. 733, no. 1). Of course it must be possible to contact the principal, which in turn will depend on the circumstances of the individual case. A stricter standard is supposed to apply where intervener and principal reside at the same place or if the intervener is acquainted with the principal (*Papanikolaou*, loc.cit. no. 2). After informing the principal the intervener has to await further instructions. It is a matter of controversy, however, whether the continuation of the intervention in accordance with instructions given may be characterised as a performance under a contract. A violation of the duty to inform the principal results in a liability for damages, but it does not render the intervention unjustified as such (CA Patras 92/1955, NoB 4/1956 p. 96).

22. PORTUGUESE CC art. 465 lit. b obliges the intervener to inform the principal of the commencement of the intervention as soon as possible. An infringement of this duty supposedly may not only result in a liability for damages; it will have the effect that the management of the affair from this point in time is not justified (*Almeida Costa*, Obrigações[9], 438; *Pires de Lima and Antunes Varela*, Código Civil Anotado I[4], Art. 465 no. 3). If the duty to inform the principal is discharged, the intervener my continue the intervention until he receives instructions to the contrary. If the principal issues instructions approving the intervention, it has to be determined whether this con-

cludes a contract of mandate. Furthermore, CC art. 465 lit. d expressly obliges the intervener to make full disclosure to the principal as regards the intervention.

23. Similarly the SLOVENIAN Code of Obligations art. 200 obliges the *gestor* to inform the principal about the commencement of the intervention as soon as possible. CZECH and SLOVAKIAN CC art. 743 (1) contains a corresponding obligation. HUNGARIAN CC § 486 (1) even provides that "an impromptu agent shall *immediately* inform the person in whose favour he has intervened" (Official Translation, Hungarian Legal Norms in Force in three Languages, CompLex CD HMJ, 2004). ESTONIAN CC provides for the duty of information in § 1020.

24. The AUSTRIAN CC does not expressly provide for a duty of information. However, the existence of such a duty is recognised in the legal literature (*Koziol and Welser*, Grundriss II[12], 366 et seq.). An infringement of this duty will lead to liability for damages under general rules (Rummel [-*Rummel*] ABGB I[3] § 1039 no. 5).

25. Equally, the duty of the intervener to inform the principal about the commencement of the undertaking as soon as possible is not expressly provided for in the CODE NAPOLÉON. Even in legal literature that duty is only rarely mentioned. Only occasionally is it indicated that the duty to inform is one of the main duties of the intervener. Its main purpose is supposed to be that the intervener may receive instructions from the principal as a response and to enable the latter to resume attendance to his own affairs (*le Tourneau*, Rép. Dr. Civ., Bd. VI, V° Gestion d'affaires (2002), no. 68).

26. Similarly, the SPANISH CC does not explicitly set out a duty to inform, but it is acknowledged both in legal literature and in case law (TS 16 October 1978, RAJ 1978 (2) no. 3076 p. 2606). It is inferred from the general system of duties of an intervener and from the principle of good faith. So far as possible the principal must be informed both of the commencement of the intervention and of its continuation.

27. By contrast it is disputed whether under ITALIAN Law the intervener is obliged to inform the principal as soon as possible of the commencement of the intervention (*Aru*, Gestione d'affari, 30-31, for instance, has argued against such a duty.) Arguments in favour of the existence of such a duty are based on the general duty of fair conduct and the explicit duty in the law of mandate (CC art. 1712; see *Breccias*, La gestione d'affari[2], 897).

28. Under DUTCH Law the intervener must both try to contact the principal prior to the commencement of the intervention (a consequence of the requirement of a reasonable ground) and attempt to contact him as soon as possible during the executory phase of the intervention in order to enable the principal to attend himself to his affairs. This duty has not been explicitly provided for by statute for the mere reason that it is already considered as covered by the intervener's general duty of care (CC art. 6:199 (1)) (T.M. Parlementaire Geschiedenis VI, 793; Asser [-*Hartkamp*], Verbintenissenrecht III[11], no. 307 p. 319; *Schrage*, Mon. Nieuw BW, no. 22 p. 15-16).

29. Under SCOTS law a benevolent intervention without authority is only justified if the principal is unable to attend to the problem that has occurred because he is not aware of the situation. Against this background a duty to give notice of the commencement of the intervention or to inform about the intervention is considered to be irreconcilable with the concept of benevolent intervention; insofar as the principal is informed the rules on mandate will prevail over the law of benevolent intervention. However, even the effort to search out the principal may in itself be considered as a benevolent

intervention. Generally it is emphasized that the law of *negotiorum gestio* has become less important due to the improvement in communication technology (*Marshall*, General Principles of Scots Law[7], para 11-11).

30. With regard to the legal systems of SCANDINAVIA one can only point towards the provisions on duties to inform to be found in neighbouring areas of the law. Strict adherence is to be inferred, so far as they apply by anology, because the relationship in a case of a management of another's affairs without an underlying contractual agreement ordinarly lacks a voluntary entrustment of the affair to another. Compare in particular the SWEDISH Maritime Code [*sjölag* (1994:1009)] Ch. 13 § 16 (3) in conjunction with § 12 (duty to inform of the carrier if the goods are damaged or if the carrier feels constrained to undertake extraordinary measures) and DANISH and SWEDISH Act regarding Factors § 7 (Duty of the commission agent to inform the principal).

31. The position in ENGLISH law is comparable to that of SCOTS law on this point: since agency of necessity presupposes that contact with the principal is impossible, or impracticable in the circumstances, acts undertaken when it is possible (without detriment to the principal's interests) to await the principal's instructions may be regarded as unnecessary and outside the scope of the authority which necessity created. It is now recognised that seeking such instructions may itself be an act entitling an agent to reimbursement: see *Pocahontas Fuel Co (Incorporated) v. Ambatielos* (1922) 27 Com Cas 148, 156 (*McCardie* J), but contrast the (implied) view of Sir *Robert Phillimore* in *The St. Lawrence* (1880) 5 PD 250, 253.

IV. *Duty to Continue the Intervention*

32. GERMAN Law deviates from Article 2:101(2) in so far as the intervener is not obliged as a rule to continue an intervention which has been commenced (RG 10 May 1906, RGZ 63, 280, 283; however, an intervener who puts his own interests first and neglects those of the principal will be liable according to this judgement even for loss of profits, i. e. the 'positive' (expectation) interest, loc.cit. 287). The legislature (Mot. II, 858) assumed that the intervener must conduct the intervention in a way which accords with the care of a *bonus pater familias*. The question whether or not the intervener may give up an intervention once begun is assessed against the same standard. If the discontinuance of the intervention would result in damage which would have not occurred if the intervener had not interfered in the principal's affairs, then the intervener is under a duty to continue the intervention. Apart from this a particular duty to continue an intervention is not recognised. An agent may similarly terminate a mandate at any time (CC § 671). In special circumstances, however, there may exceptionally be a partial duty to continue the intervention. This duty in particular cases is derived from the principle of good faith and also from the fact that the intervener by commencing the intervention takes upon himself the duty to consider the principal's interests (RG 10 May 1906, loc.cit.; cf. amongst others RGRK [-*Steffen*], BGB[12], § 677, no. 4; Erman [-*Ehmann*], BGB I[10], § 677, no. 5; Staudinger [-*Wittmann*], BGB[13], § 677, no. 5). The existence of such a duty to continue the intervention is established where continuation is possible and not difficult for the intervener, but an abandonment by the intervention would severely aggravate the situation of the principal (RG 21 November 1921, WarnRspr. 1922 no. 12: a person who takes up an object left by another

has to keep it in safe custody). Furthermore, a duty to continue may also exist where the intervention has prevented a third party from acting on behalf of the principal or if the principal is likely to suffer a damage from the intervention being discontinued which would not have occurred if the intervener had taken no action at all (Mot. II, 480; see also RG 5 December 1929, RGZ 126, 287, 292: duty to maintain a loan). The infringement of such a duty will result in liability for damages, but it cannot be enforced by means of a claim for performance (Soergel [-*Beuthien*], BGB[12], § 677, no. 20). Following the death of the intervener his rights and duties devolve to his heirs.

33. The duty to continue an intervention once commenced is also not expressly provided for in GREEK law. It is therefore presumed that the intervener is not generally obliged to continue an intervention he has begun. As in Germany, however, such a duty may arise in exceptional circumstances by virtue of the principle of good faith. This may occur in particular where the continuation would not be an unjust burden for the intervener, but discontinuation would result in damage for the principal (Georgiades and Stathopoulos [-*Papanikolaou*], Art. 730, no. 42). *Filios*, Enochiko Dikaio I/2, 201 argues in favour of an application of CC art. 725 (2) by analogy.

34. PORTUGUESE CC art. 466 (1) to a large extent corresponds with Article 2:101(2). Under this provision "the intervener is liable" only "for damages which he has caused by an unjustified interruption (*interrupção injustificada*)." In that regard there is a marked difference in comparison to French and Italian law (*Menezes Cordeiro*, Obrigações II, 20; *Vaz Serra*, Gestão de negócios, 114-115). Where a duty to continue exists, it cannot be specifically enforced under Portuguese law; the only available remedy in case of failure of performance is a claim for damages (*Menezes Cordeiro*, loc.cit.). The intervention may be aborted if there is a specific justification. Such justification can arise in particular from conduct of the principal.

35. Under AUSTRIAN CC § 1039 too the intervener will be obliged to continue his intervention until the task undertaken is concluded. This duty to continue – this follows from CC § 1312 – does not apply in the case of intervention in an emergency under CC § 1036 (OGH 26 November 1981, SZ 54/176; *Meissel*, GoA, 154). It arises only in the case of 'useful' benevolent intervention under CC § 1037. It is understood as a mere standard of care as opposed to a duty to perform which would be enforceable by a separate claim (*Meissel*, loc.cit. 162 et seq.; Rummel [-*Rummel*], ABGB I[3], § 1039 no. 2, Schwimann [-*Apathy*], ABGB V[2], §§ 1036-1040 no. 16; but possibly a different view in OGH 20 January 1977, MietSlg. 29.128=RIS-Justiz RS0013779). The limits of the duty to continue are reached where further action would appear to be useless (CC § 1038; Rummel [-*Rummel*], ABGB I[3], § 1039 no. 6).

36. BELGIAN, FRENCH and LUXEMBOURGIAN CC art. 1372 (1) obliges the intervener to continue and to complete the intervention until the principal is once more in a position to attend to his own affairs. If the principal is in that position, then the intervention may be terminated by notice that the intervener does not intend to continue the intervention (JClCiv [-*Bout*], arts. 1372-1375, Fasc. 20 no. 10). CC art. 1373 enhances the duty to continue by imposing the obligation that the intervener continue the intervention after the death of the principal until the heir is able to take over the management of the affair. The view is expressed, going beyond the literal wording of that article, that this rule should also be applied where the principal is either incapacitated or declared bankrupt: in such cases the intervention cannot be

discontinued before the representative or administrator is capable of attending to the matter (*Bout* loc.cit. no. 12; *Paulus*, Zaakwaarneming, no. 62 p. 45). If the principal has disappeared, the intervener may apply to the guardianship court under FRENCH CC art. 112 et seq. for the appointment of a representative to take over the management (*Bout*, loc.cit.). The same applies to an intervention which requires an extraordinary long attendance to the matter (*Bout* loc.cit. no. 14). Force majeure will constitute a reason for justified termination. In addition French legal literature has suggested the analogous application of CC art. 2007 (which forms part of the law of mandate), so that danger to the intervener or the threat of substantial disadvantage to the intervener may constitutes reasons for termination (*le Tourneau*, Rép.Dr.Civ., VI, v° Gestion d'affaires (2002), no. 70). The BELGIAN perception, by contrast, it that CC art. 1373 remains applicable also in the case where the principal has disappeared (*De Page*, Droit Civil Belge II[3], no. 1082 p. 1147). That the intervener may terminate the intervention if continuation is impossible for him is only stated in general terms (*RPDB*, v° Quasi-contrat, no. 58). One explanation for this strict duty to continue an intervention which has sometimes been offered is that a perfunctory or aborted intervention may prevent other more qualified persons from undertaking the necessary measures for the protection of the principal's interests (*Carbonnier*, Les obligations[21], no. 301 p. 501). An elaborate regulation of the duty to continue an intervention may also be found in MALTESE CC arts. 1013 and 1014.

37. According to the opinion of one SPANISH author the duty to continue the intervention pursuant to CC art. 1888 represents the main duty of the intervener because without the continuation of the intervention there would be no room for the duty of care (*Sánchez Jordán*, loc.cit. 410). Other authors hold the order of priority to be the other way round (e. g. Albaladejo [-*Santos Briz*], Código Civil y compilaciones forales, XXIV, 445). CC art. 1888 prevents the intervener from discontinuing the intervention *ad libitum* because otherwise more severe damage may occur than that which the intervention was intended to prevent (Paz-Ares/Díez-Picazo/Bercovitz/Salvador [-*Díez-Picazo*], Código Civil II, 1945). The duty to continue is said to serve two purposes: to prevent damage and to prevent the thoughtless interference with another's affairs (*Lacruz Berdejo*, Rev.Crít.Der.Inm. 1975, 264). Pursuant to CC art. 1888 the duty to continue an intervention once begun concerns both 'the affair' and the 'auxiliary matters'. If the intervener is no longer willing or no longer in the position to continue the intervention, then CC art. 1888 permits the intervener "to call upon the principal to replace him in the conduct of the intervention provided that he is in the position to conduct that intervention on his own". In the law of mandate (CC art. 1736), by contrast, the agent may "resign by giving the principal notice thereof. If the latter suffers damage as a consequence of such resignation, the agent must make reparation for that loss, unless he can justify the termination because it has become impossible to complete the mandate without severe harm to his own interests". Thus according to the wording of the CC the contractual agent can give up his mandate under less strict conditions than an intervener without authority. This has repeatedly prompted scholars to argue in favour of an analogous application of the provision of the law of mandate to benevolent intervention (e. g. *Sánchez Jordán*, loc.cit. 428). If the intervener in accordance with CC art. 1888 calls upon the principal to replace him in the management of the affair, the mere request will not as such terminate the duty to continue the intervention. Termination will not occur before the principal attends

to the affair himself; if he is not in a position to do so (for which the ability to instruct a third party would suffice) then the duty to continue persists. *Fuero Nuevo de* NAVARRA Ley 560 likewise obliges the intervener "to complete an intervention begun".

38. Under SLOVENIAN Code of Obligations art. 200 the intervention must be continued provided this is reasonable and as long as the principal is not in a position to attend to his own affairs again. POLISH CC art. 753 (1) also obliges an intervener to continue an intervention until such time as the principal is in a position 'to attend to the business himself'. By contrast CZECH and SLOVAKIAN CC do not provide for a duty to continue an intervention. The same holds true for the ESTONIAN and the HUNGARIAN CC.

39. Under ITALIAN CC art 2028 the intervener is obliged to continue an intervention and to bring it to an end until the principal is in a position to attend to his own affairs. This duty to continue also exists where the principal dies before the intervener has completed the task undertaken for the principal. It will persist until the heirs can take care of the affair. The duty to continue an intervention will cease if the management has become impossible due to a reason for which the intervener is not responsible (Cass. 11 November 1958, no. 3692, Rep.Giur.it. 1958, voce Gestione d'affari, no. 6-8) or useless or even dangerous.

40. Under DUTCH CC art. 6:199 (1) the intervener must "continue the management of another's affair he has begun ... to the extent that this can reasonably be required of him". From this it follows that the intervener may not discontinue at an improper time. The particulars will depend on the circumstances of the individual case – in particular whether or not the principal is in the position to act himself and the balance between the interest of the principal in the continuation of the management of his affairs and the effort and expenditure which continuation would entail for the intervener (T. M. Parlementaire Geschiedenis VI, 793; Asser [-*Hartkamp*], Verbintenissenrecht III[11], no. 308 p. 319-320).

41. In SCOTLAND the duty to continue and to complete the intervention is one of the main duties of the intervener. This was recognised by the institutional writers (*Bell* § 541; *Stair*, Institutions, Book I, 8, 5) and remains the law today (*Walker*, Principles of Scottish Private Law, II[4], 513). The duty to continue terminates only when it would result in management of a new affair; it does not end automatically with the death of the principal or the intervener (Stair [-*Whitty*], The Laws of Scotland, vol. 15, para 130; *Stair*, Institutions, Book I, 8, 3; *Erskine*, Book III, Volume II, 53). Legal literature in the NORDIC COUNTRIES has not elaborated on the obligation to continue. In ENGLISH law a question of a duty to continue an intervention rarely poses itself in that form. Agency of necessity largely operates in the context of an existing relationship and an agent is regarded as not merely being authorised to intervene, but actually bound to take reasonable measures in order to protect the principal's interests: for authority asserting an obligation on the part of a ship's captain in a case of necessity, see *The Gratitudine* (1801) 3 C. Rob 240 at 259, 165 ER 450 at 457 (Sir *W. Scott*); *Tronson v. Dent* (1853) 8 Moore PC 419, 449 (Sir *John Patteson*); *The Hamburg* (1863) 2 Moore PC (N. S.) 289, 302 (Dr *Lushington*); *Australasian SN Co v. Morse* (1872) LR 4 PC 222, 228; *Gaudet v. Brown* (1872) LR 5 PC 134, 165 (Sir *Montague Smith*); *Hingston v. Wendt* (1876) 1 QBD 367, 372 (*Blackburn* J); *Metcalfe v. Britannia Ironworks Co* (1876) 1 QBD 613, 625 (*Cockburn* CJ). The question of when the agent may abandon the intervention is simply subsumed within the broader question of the scope of the duty to act in

the principal's interests: intervention is required so long as the necessity requires a solution to the unforeseen problem and a response can reasonably be expected of the agent. In the case of a gratuitous agent, this will often mean there is no duty to act: cf *Fridman*, Agency[5], 138. However, a duty of an intervener who acts gratuitously or is not an agent of necessity to continue their intervention may arise under tort law on the basis that their interference (if now followed by an omission to improve matters) would cause damage for which he would be liable as a tortfeasor on the basis of negligence: cf. *Gomer v. Pitt & Scott* (1922) 12 Ll L Rep 115, 116 (*Warrington* LJ).

Illustration 1 is taken from BGH 4 December 1975, BGHZ 65, 354; **illustration 5** from TS 2 February 1954, RAJ 1954 no. 322 p. 198.

Article 2:102: Duties after Intervention

(1) After intervening the intervener must without undue delay report and account to the principal and hand over anything obtained as a result of the intervention.
(2) If at the time of intervening the intervener lacks full legal capacity, the duty to hand over is subject to the defences which would be available in the law of unjustified enrichment (PEL Unjust.Enr.).

Comments

A. General

1. **Three duties after intervention** Article 2:102(1) sets out the duties which the party acting encounters after his activity: the duty to report, to account and to hand over anything obtained as a result of the intervention. Among these, the duty to hand over may be the most important in the practical application of the law. The *gestor*'s duty to deliver up extends to everything which he has received by managing the principal's affairs. He is additionally obliged to the principal to give information and an account. The main purpose of these duties is to support the principal's claim for surrender. The duty to report, however, is also effective in cases where a claim for surrender is not in consideration. Its purpose is to protect the principal against loss which he may sustain if he has no knowledge of the intermeddling with his affairs and therefore refrains from taking necessary decisions or himself undertakes activity which in the changed circumstances will be wrong or useless. Para (2) limits the claim for surrender vis-à-vis an intervener who lacks full legal capacity to the enrichment which they still have in possession (see D below).

2. **"After intervening"** It will depend on the circumstances of the individual case at what point in time the management of the affair is completed. Frequently the intervention will be terminated as soon as the intervener discharges his duty to inform under Article 2:101 (Duties during Intervention) with the result that the principal can himself

attend to his affairs. The duty to inform under Article 2:102 may coincide in such cases with the duty under Article 2:101 and may be discharged by the same act. In other cases the intervention will be completed if the dangerous situation which prompted the intervener to take action has been eliminated at least temporarily. Cessation of the intervention also occurs where the intervener of his own accord ceases his management of the affair, be it for other good cause or in breach of his duty to continue under Article 2:101(2).

3. **"Without undue delay"** All three duties arising under Article 2:102 have to be discharged by the intervener without undue delay. It will not infrequently be the case that the intervener has no knowledge of the principal's identity and reasonable inquiry has been made to no avail, those duties cannot be discharged before the intervener learns of the principal's identity (name and address).

4. **Duties and rights** These Principles set out the duties (and in Chapter 3 the rights) of an intervener. They thereby define at the same time the rights (and in Chapter 3 the duties) of the principal. The principal's rights which arise under Article 2:102 are susceptible to claims for performance and may be enforced independently because their counterpart on the side of the intervener does not merely represent a duty of care (as is the case in Article 2:101 (Duties during Intervention)). The discharge of the latter is not specifically enforceable; as with breach of the duties arising from Article 2:102 non-performance results in a liability for damages (see Article 2:103 (Reparation for Damage Caused by Breach of Duty)).

B. The Duties to Report and to Account

5. **The duty to report** The intervener is obliged to make every reasonable effort to contact the principal and to give an account of the management of the affair – both after the intervention as well as during it. Thus the intervener is obliged to act on his own initiative. If the principal learns of the intervention, the intervener will have to provide information on request. If the intervener has not obtained any proceeds from the intervention, his duties subsequent to the completion of the intervention will be limited to the duty to provide information. The scope of this duty will mirror its purpose of making the principal sufficiently aware of the situation so that he can resume the management of the affair in question. The duty to provide information is not dependent on the existence of a claim for delivery up; it may be, for example, that the intervener has to disclose the account books or files and allow inspection of them, but is not obliged to hand them over to the principal.

6. **The duty to account** The duty to account in essence serves the purpose that the principal may obtain the information necessary to specify his claim for surrender of proceeds of the intervention. From a procedural perspective he may have to bring an action against the intervener by stages. The latter's duty to account to the principal includes the duty to provide an orderly and comprehensive overview of the separate expenses incurred and profits obtained which if needs be can be checked. To what extent and by what means this is to be carried out will depend on the circumstances of

the case. Moreover the principal's request to account is also subject to the general reservation of the principle of good faith (which in the context of contract law has been set out in PECL Article 1:201(1)). In a case of spontaneous assistance, such as between persons living in the same house or neighbours, much less may be demanded than in the case of management without authority of another's substantial assets or business. Here, depending on the circumstances, the duty to account may perhaps only be discharged by supplying accounts satisfying professional standards.

Illustration 1
I, the daughter-in-law of a mentally disabled elderly man who has been admitted to a psychiatric institution for that reason, takes care of her father-in-law for a period of several years. His insurance company has remitted to her account the insurance payments which were owed to him. Out of this money I has made small expenditures for her father-in-law's benefit (clean bed linen, fruit, chocolate, cigarettes, taxi fares, replacement of glasses and alarm-clocks which he regularly breaks, etc.) until the death of the latter's wife, who consented to the expenditure. On the death of the father-in-law his heirs claim surrender of the insurance payments subject to a deduction of the expenses – specified precisely. The daughter-in-law cannot provide an account for these various minor expenses which in their entirety add up to a considerable sum, the more so, as she will not have received a receipt for the majority of these purchases. It would be contrary to the principle of good faith to request an account with a detailed list of all expenses. A rough estimation will suffice.

C. The Duty to Deliver Up

7. **The most important economic duty of the intervener** The duty to deliver up to the principal all that he has achieved as a result of his activities is in practice the most important duty of the intervener. It is recognised in all jurisdictions of the European Union and follows from the nature of benevolent intervention as management of another's affairs with the intention of benefiting another. It is part of its character that the intervener may neither enrich himself nor suffer a disadvantage. He acts on behalf of another; as a general rule his own financial situation should not be altered either positively or negatively. Thus the duty to hand over all proceeds of the intervention finds its counterpart in the claim for compensation for expenses incurred under Article 3:101 (Right to Indemnification or Reimbursement).

Illustration 2
A person who collects the rent for the absent owner of a house must deliver up the money received.

8. **Content and extent of the duty to surrender** The principal's claim for surrender (the duty of the intervener to deliver up) typically relates to the payment of monies received. More often than not it concerns the collection of receivables or the proceeds from the sales of another's goods (e. g. from the forced sale of perishable goods) or other assets (management of a bank deposit or sale of stocks). However, it may also occur that

the intervener is obliged to hand over specific objects or documents. An example of the former is where the intervener has purchased a thing for the principal, but in his own name, and the latter has subsequently ratified the intervention (cf. illustration 30 at Article 1:101 (Intervention to Benefit Another)); the second situation may occur where the intervener has received a debtor's bond from the creditor, who in the meantime has been paid. The intervener may offset his claim for reparation against the principal's claim to deliver up proceeds or, as the case may be, withhold delivery up until such time as the principal offers payment of the compensation he owes the intervener.

Illustration 3
I in the course of a benevolent intervention purchases goods at a bargain price from X for P. For this transaction I has accepted a promise of a premium from X. If P pays the purchase price to I, then I must assign his claim for the premium vis-à-vis X to P and transfer ownership of the goods to P.

9. **Interest** The intervener has to deliver up "anything" obtained as a result of the intervention. Consequently this also includes interest on the monies received. If the *gestor* in the course of his *negotiorum gestio* has received money and deposited it in an interest-bearing account, the claim for delivery up encompasses the interest as well as the money because the interest was received as a result of the conduct of the principal's affairs. If, however, the *gestor* has not deposited the money to earn interest, the question will arise whether the failure to do so was a breach of the duty of care under Article 2:101(1)(a) and (b). If there is no breach (because, for example, the *gestor* could not reasonably risk tying up the money for a long time in a savings account, though it later emerges that the *gestor* was only able to discover the principal's identity some six months later), then the principal has no claim for the interest foregone. On the other hand, if the *gestor* employs the money for his own purposes, he appropriates this enrichment for himself. The intention to benefit the *gestor* having at this point in time exhausted itself, the interest-earning deposit is not an act pursuant to the *negotiorum gestio*. The basis for the principal's claim in that case is not one of damages for breach of the duty of care, but rather under the law of unjustified enrichment, or, as the case may be, under tort law.

D. Protection of Interveners without Full Legal Capacity

10. **Para (2)** Although interventions by persons who lack full legal capacity are rare, they still occur. Children and mentally disabled adults may not be capable of binding themselves by way of contract, but they may nonetheless act as benevolent interveners if they can command sufficient capacity in fact to form the intention to look after the interests of another. They therefore enjoy the full legal protection of the law of *negotiorum gestio*; they can look not merely to the rights conferred by Article 3:101, but also to the protective mechanism of para (2) which circumscribes their potential liability. This group of persons is only liable to the extent they are still enriched by the intervention. They are able to invoke all those defences which are available in the law of unjustified enrichment. That principle is the subject matter of para (2). In substance it is primarily a pointer to the defence based on change of position (disenrichment in good faith).

11. Lack of full legal capacity The prerequisites for a person to enjoy full legal capacity and the different shades of less than full legal capacity do not form the subject-matter of these Principles. The only statement which can be made in this respect is that para (2) applies in any event to interventions which consist of physical acts. No statement can be made as to which conditions enable a minor himself or with the consent of his legal representative to effect or conclude juridical acts. For the time being the text assumes that every minor may rely on the defence of change of position. This includes a minor who has acted with the consent of his parents. It may well be the case that this principle will require re-consideration if at some future date European Principles on liability of minors and other persons lacking full legal capacity are formulated.

Notes

I. *Duty to Inform and Duty to Render an Account*

1. The above mentioned duties are recognised in all jurisdictions of the European Union which provide for a distinct law of benevolent intervention. Where they are not already provided for in the text of the Civil Codes themselves, they have been developed by case law and supported in legal literature.
2. GERMAN CC § 681 sentence 2 refers to the law of mandate, where the same duties may be found in CC § 666. The intervener is obliged to inform the principal of the particulars of the intervention in accordance with generally acknowledged standards and to provide an overview of what he has undertaken, even where those activities do not lead to a duty to surrender under CC § 681 in conjunction with § 667 (BGH 30 November 1989, BGHZ 109, 260, 266). The duty to give an account arises as a rule after the completion of the intervention; in a case of incomplete execution it arises immediately after termination. The duty to account includes – beyond mere information – a duty to substantiate the information by providing an orderly account of receipts and expenses. The intervener has the burden of proving the accuracy of the account and in particular the whereabouts of funds received and that he has disposed of assets in accordance with the principal's instructions or in the latter's interest (Palandt [-*Sprau*], BGB^{63}, § 666, no. 2-4). HUNGARIAN CC art. 486 (1) (for details see *Ujlaki*, Gazdaság és Jog 10/2001, 24-25), POLISH CC art. 753 (2) as well as CZECH and SLOVAKIAN CC art. 746 are based on very similar concepts.
3. Similarly, GREEK CC art. 734 imposes on the justified intervener accessory duties derived from the law of mandate. The latter provides for a duty to render an account and thereby refers impliedly to CC art. 303 (Georgiades/Stathopoulos [-*Papanikolaou*], Art. 718, no. 2). Under that provision the management of another's affair (which has since finished) must result in income or expenditure (Georgiades/Stathopoulos [-*Papanikolaou*], Art. 719, no. 2). Otherwise a duty to provide an account will not arise.
4. PORTUGUESE CC regulates the duty to provide information about the intervention undertaken in art. 465 limb d and the duty to render an account in art. 465 limb c.
5. AUSTRIAN CC § 1039 obliges the intervener to give an account just as an agent is obliged to (CC § 1012). The claim enables the principal to check the management undertaken and the expenses incurred (Rummel [-*Rummel*], ABGB I^{3}, § 1039 no. 3). The duty to render an account applies to all types of benevolent intervention (Schwi-

mann [-*Apathy*], ABGB V², §§ 1036-1040 no. 17; *Meissel*, GoA, 164 et seq., Rummel [-*Rummel*], ABGB I³, § 1039 no. 7), including merely negligent unjustified intervention in another's affairs (OGH 11 May 1976, SZ 49/63; OGH 14 October 1986, RdW 1987, 51; see, however, OGH 22 November 1994, SZ 67/207).

6. Under BELGIAN, FRENCH and LUXEMBOURG law the *obligation de rendre compte* is conceived as one of the main duties of the intervener (*Carbonnier*, Les obligations[21], no. 299 p. 498). It is derived from CC art. 1372 (2) and the corresponding application of the rules on the contract of *mandat* (CC art. 1993) (JClCiv [-*Bout*], Art. 1372-1375, Fasc. 20 no. 40; *RPDB*, v° Quasi-contrat, no. 61 p. 16). The intervener has to inform the principal comprehensively about the management of the affair (*le Tourneau*, Rép. Dr. Civ., Bd. VI, v° Gestion d'affaires [2002], no. 81; CA Mons 27 February 1995, Rev. not. b. 1996, 33). Furthermore, under CC art. 1993 there is an obligation on the intervener to hand over all that he has received in the course of the management (*le Tourneau*, loc.cit.). The only exception from this *obligation de rendre compte* granted to an intervener is *force majeure*; otherwise he will be liable in a case of non-performance for damages (*Bout*, loc.cit. nos. 41-42). The form in which the account is provided will be determined by the particular circumstances of the individual case; in a long-term management concerning the private affairs of another, an oral report of the separate measures taken, giving the principal the opportunity to request further particulars, may suffice (CA Mons 2 March 2004, JT 2004, 555).

7. SPANISH CC (as opposed to Ley 560 of the *Nueva Compilación* of the law of NAVARRA) likewise does not contain an explicit provision on the duty to render an account. Here again this duty has been repeatedly confirmed by the case law (*inter alia* by TS 13 June 1956, RAJ 1956 (1) no. 1948 p. 1312). The duty to provide an account applies to all persons who manage the affairs of another (whether or not on a contractual basis). The intervener has to recount the measures undertaken and to provide information in an orderly account of all receipts and expenses. Under ITALIAN law too it is undisputed that after completion of the management of the affair the intervener is subject to the duty to render an account as provided for in the law of mandate (CC art. 1713 (1)) (*Breccia*, La gestione d'affari², 897; Cass. 7 June 1993, no. 6358, Giust. Civ. Mass. 1993, 998).

8. DUTCH CC art. 6:199 (2) contains both a general duty of information and the duty to render an account. The intervener must provide information as soon as reasonably possible and if he has either received monies or incurred expenses he must also give an account of these transactions (T. M. Parlementaire Geschiedenis VI, 793-794; Asser [-*Hartkamp*], Verbintenissenrecht III[10], no. 309 p. 320).

9. The *gestor*'s 'duty to account for intromissions' in SCOTLAND is considered to be self-evident (*Bell* § 541; *Stair*, Institutions, Book I, 8, 4; *Erskine*, Book III, Volume II, 52; Stair [-*Whitty*], The Laws of Scotland, vol. 15, para 132). It corresponds to the intervener's claim for reimbursement of expenditure. Where there are multiple interveners, each intervener will only have to render an account on the share which he took in the intervention (*Whitty*, loc.cit.).

10. A duty to provide an account is unknown under SWEDISH law. Under the Swedish Interest Act [*räntelag* (1975:635)] § 3 (2) (cf. on this HD 16 September 1997, NJA 1997, 612) the duty to pay default interest begins the same day as an account would have had to be provided. Legal literature argues in favour of a corresponding application of the law of mandate to the management of another's affair without authority

(*Håstad*, Tjänster utan uppdrag, 57). This points to ComC ch. 18 § 9, a rule which concerns the law of limitation and is itself a highly contentious rule (*Lindskog*, Preskription[2], 161 et seq.). According to this provision the principal's claims are subject to a one year limitation period which starts to run from the day the mandate was completed and the account rendered (for details see HD 14 September 1998, NJA 1998, 520; *Lindskog*, loc.cit. 163; *Millqvist*, JT 1998-99 p. 387-390 and *Kleineman*, Festskrift Walin, 207-225).

11. In ENGLISH LAW an equitable jurisdiction to order an agent to give an account to his principal is of long-standing: see Snell (-*Baker/Langan*), Equity[29], pp. 637-638. Even a self-appointed agent is under a duty to give an account: see, for example, *Brown v. Litton* (1711) 1 P Wms 140, 24 ER 329; 10 Mod 20, 88 ER 606 (Harcourt LK).

II. The Duty to Surrender

12. The intervener's duty to surrender is of considerable importance. GERMAN CC provides for this duty in §§ 681 (sentence 2) and 667. The intervener has to deliver up all that he has received in the course of the intervention, including the entire profits realized (MünchKomm [-*Seiler*], BGB[3], § 681, no. 7; Staudinger [-*Wittmann*], BGB[13], § 681, no. 3; Erman [-*Ehmann*], BGB I[10], § 681, no. 3). By CC § 687 (2) the scope of application of the duty to deliver up is extended to the cases of disbursements out of profits in cases of arrogated management of another's affair, which are of particular practical relevance (for details see MünchKomm [-*Seiler*], BGB[3], § 687, no. 10, 21). POLISH CC art. 753 (2) sets out in one breath both the duty to deliver up proceeds and the duty to render an account. ESTONIAN CC § 1021 (1) corresponds to the rule provided for in Article 2:102 (1).
13. In GREECE it is also assumed that the intervener's duty to surrender also includes profits which he has made (Georgiades and Stathopoulos [-*Papanikolaou*], Art. 734, no. 3). In the case of impure *negotiorum gestio*, however, the balance of interests is thought to lead to a different result: it is suggested that the intervener may keep the profit which he has brought about by his own personal expertise (*Papanikolaou* loc.cit. Art. 739, no. 10; *Kallimopoulos*, I mi gnisia dioikisi allotrion, 189).
14. Under PORTUGUESE CC art. 465 limb (e) the intervener is obliged to deliver up all that he has received from third parties in the course of the management of the *gestão* or the balance of the account. The intervener also has to surrender proceeds obtained by legal transactions he has conducted in his own name or the name of the principal. The intervener must return not only the *lucrum ex re*, but also the *lucum propter negotiationem perteptum* (*Antunes Varela*, Obrigações em Geral I[10], 464).
15. The AUSTRIAN CC does not explicitly provide for the intervener's duty to surrender. However, that duty is recognised and is derived by an analogy with the law governing the contract of mandate (CC § 1009) (Rummel [-*Rummel*], ABGB I[3], § 1039 no. 4). If the intervener disputes the fact that he intended to act in another's interest, the principal's claim for surrender will be derived from the intrusion into the legal sphere of the person who has suffered damage or whose rights have been infringed. The claim for surrender in that cases arises out of unjustified enrichment (*Meissel*, GoA, 168; Rummel [-*Rummel*], ABGB I[3], § 1039 nos. 4 and 7).
16. In both the FRENCH and the BELGIAN legal systems the duty to surrender is conceived as a sub-category of the duty to render an account (CC art. 1372 (2) in con-

junction with art. 1993). Under this provisions the intervener is obliged to deliver up to the principal all that he has received in the course of the intervention (*le Tourneau*, Rép.Dr.Civ. VI, v° Gestion d'affaires (2002), no. 81; *Paulus*, Zaakwaarneming, no. 74 p. 47-48).

17. The SPANISH CC only provides for a duty to surrender proceeds obtained in the context of the law of mandate and not in the rules on benevolent intervention. Under CC art. 1720 the intervener is obliged to deliver up to the principal all that he has received as a consequence of the mandate, whether or not the benefits received were due to the principal. Legal literature considers it to be self-evident that this duty to surrender also applies to the regime of benevolent intervention, but to date can only rely on case law concerning the law of mandate (amongst other cases TS 19 December 1983, RAJ 1983 (3) no. 6967 p. 5355; TS 6 October 1994, RAJ 1994 (4) no. 7459 p. 9703). The duty to surrender profits is placed in the context of the duty to render an account and in part even is deduced from it (for details see *Lacruz Berdejo*, Rev.Crít.Der.Inm. 1975, 267; *Sánchez Jordán*, Gestión de negocios, 489; *Pasquau Liaño*, La gestión de negocios ajenos, 135). A distinction is drawn between the duty to return what the intervener has obtained from the principal and the duty to deliver up what the intervener has received from third parties or has been created in the course of the intervention. Both duties, some authors maintain, are intended to prevent an unjustified enrichment of the intervener (*Sánchez Jordán*, loc.cit. 489). However, the particulars are barely explained and it is an open question whether the rules of the law on the owner-possessor-relationship are to be applied to the duty to make restitution by analogy (this is supported by *Sánchez Jordán*, loc.cit. 492). A further provision which is regarded as applicable by analogy is CC art. 1730. It provides that the agent may retain the assets, which are the object of the mandate, as a security until the principal discharges his duty to compensate (*Sánchez Jordán*, loc.cit. 1730).

18. The intervener is also obliged under ITALIAN law to deliver up to the principal all he has obtained on the occasion of the intervention. If the intervention concerned the purchase of movable goods, the intervener is obliged to hand over the profit obtained (which need not necessarily match the value of the asset): see Cass. 16 February 1949, no. 255, Rep.Giur.it. 1949, voce Gestione d'affari, no. 2- 11; voce Obbligazioni e contratti no. 110. This conforms to the rule on the law of mandate in CC art. 1713.

19. Under DUTCH law the duty to deliver up is derived from the general duty of care under CC art. 6:199 (1). If the intervener takes control of assets which belong to the principal then the intervener is obliged to take care of them and to return them to the principal at the completion of the action, including any profits realized. If the intervention was unjustified the duty to surrender is not subject to a corresponding right of retention with regard to expenses incurred (Verbintenissenrecht [-*Scheltema*], Art. 6:199, no. 2. 2). More generally it may be said that the legislature considered the duty to surrender to be self-evident and has therefore not provided for further rules on the matter. The scope of the duty to surrender falls to be determined in the particular circumstances of each individual case (MvA. II Parlementaire Geschiedenis VI, 794).

20. Similarly under SCOTS law the "*gestor*'s duty to surrender all fruits and profits earned from the gestio" is beyond question (*Bell*, § 541; *Stair*, Institutions, Book I, 8, 4; *Erskine*, Book III, Volume II, 52). It includes the duty to surrender interest actually obtained or which according to commercial usage could have been obtained (*Erskine* loc.cit.; Stair [-*Whitty*], The Laws of Scotland, vol. 15, para 133).

21. Under SWEDISH law it is stated (as in Spain) that the duty to render an account will also encompass a duty to deliver up what the *gestor* has in possession for the principal. In this respect an analogous application of the law of mandate is supported (*Håstad*, Tjänster utan uppdrag, 57). As regards his counterclaim against the principal, the intervener has at most a right of retention which operates against the principal alone and not (as under the DANISH [cf. further CFI 4 March 1959, UfR 1959, 678 and CA 28 June 1973, UfR 1973, 696] and SWEDISH Commission Act § 32 in the case of the commission agent) a right of retention by operation of law effective also against third parties (HD 19 March 1985, NJA 1985, 205; cf. amongst others *Håstad*, Sakrätt avseende lös egendom[6], 350). The same must apply to the intervener without authority (*Håstad*, loc.cit.).

22. In ENGLISH law an agent, whether authorised or merely self-appointed, is liable to surrender any profit obtained if it belongs at law or in equity to the principal or is obtained by use of property of the principal or his position and opportunities as agent (unless its retention is authorised by the principal): see, for example, *De Bussche v. Alt* (1878) 8 Ch D 286, 304 (*Hall* VC, affirmed by CA); for an older authority more closely concerned with necessitous intervention, see *Brown v. Litton* (1711) 1 P Wms 140, 24 ER 329; 10 Mod 20, 88 ER 606 (*Harcourt* LK), where on the death of the ship's captain in the course of a voyage a mate took it upon himself to invest money which the captain had taken with him for that purpose (notifying the widow to that effect) and was compelled to surrender the profits, subject to an allowance for his labour and skill in managing the property, his liability not being limited as he argued to a repayment plus interest. The principle even applies where the agent has entered into transaction which the principal himself could not have entered into: *Boston Deep Sea Fishing and Ice Co v. Farnham* [1957] 1 WLR 1051, 1058 (*Harman* J); *Boardman v. Phipps* [1967] 2 AC 46 (agents of a trust making investments outside the trustees' powers). This follows from (or in cases perhaps extends) the principle that a fiduciary is not entitled to make an unauthorised profit from assets belonging to or held for the person on whose behalf the fiduciary acts: the fiduciary is liable to surrender it (less appropriate deductions for his personal contribution to the profit in the form of expertise and work). See *Hugh Stevenson and Sons Ltd v. AG für Carton-Nagen-Industrie* [1918] AC 239, 250 (Lord *Atkinson*) (a case concerning a partnership, but see p. 256 for explicit confirmation that the principle applies to agents). However, where the agent has a right to reimbursement from the principal, the agent will have a right of retention in the form of a possessory lien to protect that claim: *Petrinovic & co Ltd v. Mission Francaise des Transports des Maritimes* (1941) 71 Ll L R 208, 222 (Atkinson J) and see also *Tetley & Co. v. British Trade Corporation* (1922) 10 Ll.L.Rep. 678 (where the claim for reimbursement of the cost of transporting the principal's goods could be set off against the proceeds of sale which the agent was otherwise liable to deliver up to the principal).

III. *In Particular: The Duty to Pay Interest on Monies Received*

23. If the intervener in the course of his intervention has collected money for the principal then in the majority of the jurisdictions he will have to pay interest on the monies if and only if he has actually obtained that interest. GERMAN CC § 681 (sentence 2) in conjunction with § 668, however, places on a par with that case the situation where

the intervener has used monies received for his own purposes (in particular: spent it) despite his duty to deliver it up to the principal or use it for the principal's purposes. The fact that the intervener has merely delayed his handing over of the money, or its application for the principal's purposes, does not by itself trigger a duty to pay interest. Moreover, the duty to pay interest as a rule depends on neither fault, delay nor the occurrence of any damage for the principal. The duty to pay interest arises from the date the intervener has used the monies for his own purpose and in a case of mixing the funds with his own monies from the time the combined monies were spent. The interest rate will be determined by CC § 246 (4%) and Ccom § 352 (5%).

24. The legal situation in GREECE is similar. An intervener who has not himself obtained interest is only obliged to pay it if he has self-interestedly used the principal's monies for his own purposes (Georgiades and Stathopoulos [-*Papanikolaou*], Art. 734, no. 1; *Filios*, Enochiko Dikaio I/2, 201). Only sporadically is it maintained that the intervener is also obliged to pay interest if (on the basis of general practice and the actual or presumed wishes of the principal) the omission to profitably invest the money was culpable (so ErmAK [-*Saketas*], Art. 734 no. 4).

25. PORTUGUESE CC art. 465 limb e sets out the duty to pay interest in express terms: "The intervener must surrender all that he has obtained from third parties as a result of the intervention or the balance of the corresponding accounts and in the case of money together with statutory interest from the time when the claim for surrender has fallen due." Statutory interest (CC art. 559 (1)) thus accrues from the time the delivery up should have taken place and not merely from the time the court determines the balance (*Antunes Varela*, Obrigações em Geral I^{10}, 465). A corresponding rule is provided for in POLISH CC art. 753 (2), which likewise obliges the intervener to pay statutory interest.

26. Under AUSTRIAN law the duty to surrender (which has been developed by case law to go beyond the wording of the ABGB) undisputedly also encompasses the interest actually obtained and capital gains (Schwimann [-*Apathy*], ABGB V^2, § 1009 no. 17 with further references). Although the case law mostly concerns the law of mandate (OGH 12 January 1926, SZ 8/18; OGH 11 March 1924 SZ 6/103; OGH 29 October 1952, SZ 25/286), it may arguably be inferred from OGH 26 November 1981, SZ 54/176, that the claim for surrender of proceeds in the law of benevolent intervention is limited to the surplus actually generated.

27. In FRENCH and BELGIAN law CC art. 1996 may be applied to the law of benevolent intervention by way of analogy (JClCiv (-*Bout*], Art. 1372-1375, Fasc. 20 no. 30; *Paulus*, Zaakwaarneming, no. 75 p. 48). Under this provision the *mandataire* has to pay interest on the sums which he has applied for his own benefit from the day he has made use of them. For all other amounts he will only be obliged to pay interest from the day of default. Thus interest on money which he has applied for the benefit of the principal will only accrue from the time of delay in performance, whereas interest on the money he used for his own benefit will accrue immediately (*Bout*, loc.cit.).

28. The starting point of SPANISH law is the general principle that the principal is entitled to all benefits arising from an intervention (*Pasquau Liaño*, La gestión de negocios ajenos, 162). Thus the intervener will also have to deliver up all interest he has obtained on monies collected. Legal literature in explaining this principle refers to the rules on the owner-possessor-relationship (*Sánchez Jordán*, Gestión de negocios,

492). Under CC art. 455 a possessor in bad faith must deliver up all profits and all benefits obtained which the person entitled could have acquired. This too encompasses interest. Other authors rely for the same result on a reference to CC art. 354 (3), which provides that the owner is also entitled to the civil fruits (*Pasquau Liaño,* loc.cit. 163).

29. The rules of ITALIAN law are that the intervener has to deliver up interest actually obtained and must do so even if these are higher than the statutory interest rate; if the intervener has only kept the monies safe without investing it profitably, he is not obliged to pay interest on it; if, by contrast, he has disposed of the amounts in his own interest, statutory interest becomes due from that point of time onwards (*Aru*, Gestione d'affari, 37).

30. In DUTCH law the question of whether or not the intervener is obliged to pay interest has attracted scant attention. In the Parlamentaire Geschiedenis only the opposite situation is expressly considered, namely whether the intervener who has spent his own assets or money may also claim interest foregone (T. M. Parlementaire Geschiedenis VI, 795). The question discussed is considered as one aspect of the intervener's general duty of care regarding the monies collected. It is held that depending on the circumstances he may be obliged to invest the money profitably (*Schoordijk*, Het algemeen gedeelte van het verbintenissenrecht naar het nieuw BW, 417; Verbintenissenrecht [-*Scheltema*], art. 6:199 BW, no. 2. 2).

31. In SCOTLAND the duty to surrender profits includes interest actually gained and interest which according to commercial usage in general are achieved (*Erskine*, Book III, Volume II, 52; Stair [-*Whitty*], The Laws of Scotland, vol. 15, para 133).

32. The legal situation in the NORDIC COUNTRIES is rather difficult to ascertain. Express rules on the law of benevolent intervention are lacking. The application of the 'general principles of mandate law' which relate to the duty to render an account would lead to the result that the *gestor* is obliged to pay interest on the monies collected (*Lindskog*, Lagen om handelsbolag och enkla bolag. 418). A duty of the agent to pay interest, for instance, may be found in the SWEDISH Act on Floating of Timber [*lag* (1919:426) *om flottning i allmän flottled*] § 20 (3) and similarly in the Swedish Act regarding Factors [*lag* (1991:981) *om värdepappersrörelse*] Ch. 3 § 5). It is considered part of the duty to account that, firstly, the sums may not be mixed with the assets of the agent and, secondly, that they must be placed in a manner which serves the interests of the principal (*Hellner*, Speciell Avtalsrätt II: Kontraktsrätt. 1. volume: Särskilda avtal[3], 209). Where the monies have been kept separate and invested with due diligence, the duty to surrender profits will be limited to the interest actually obtained. Whether or not the 'general principles of mandate law' may be applied without restriction to benevolent intervention in another's affair has not yet been decided by case law. Arguments supporting that solution may be found in the Swedish Interest Act § 3 (2), which provides that interest is due on "a claim which is founded on the fact that an agent or another has to render an account with respect to sums he has received from the principal or from a third party" from the day that the account has been rendered or, as the case may be, ought to have been rendered. An example for this is where a person sells a thing for another and subsequently to the sale collects the purchase price for the former owner (HD 16 September 1997, NJA 1997, 612, 621, where it is expressly stated that the duty to render an account does not depend on the existence of a contract).

33. In ENGLISH LAW an agent will have to account for interest which has actually accrued if the money in his hands is regarded as belonging at law or in equity to his principal (except in so far as a right to retain interest has been agreed): see Bowstead (*-Reynolds/Graziadei*), Agency[1], Article 54. Moreover, an agent may also be liable for interest which, by prudent investment, he would have obtained if he in retaining the money improperly or failing to invest it he has committed a breach of an equitable duty: cf. *Re Waterman's W. T.* [1952] 2 All ER 1054 (*Harman J*) (breach of duty as trustee); *Wallersteiner v. Moir (No. 2)* [1975] QB 373 (company director misusing company funds).

IV. *Intervener without Full Legal Capacity*

34. GERMAN CC § 682 contains a particular provision for the protection of an intervener who does not possess full legal capacity. It has also been the model for Article 2:102 of these Principles. If the intervener lacks legal capacity or is restricted in his legal capacity, then under § 682 he is only held liable according to the provisions on compensation for torts and the rules on the surrender of unjustified enrichment. However, as far as unjustified enrichment law is concerned the reference made is a reference to the legal basis of a claim (Palandt [*-Sprau*], BGB[63], § 682, no. 2). Thus the provision does not state that CC §§ 677 et seq. are only applicable to persons over the age of majority (Soergel [*-Beuthien*], BGB[12], § 682, no. 1). However, in the legal literature (there is no case law on this point) it is disputed whether CC § 682 is also applicable to legal transactions effected by an underage person if the legal representative has granted consent (or if it should only be applied to physical acts of benevolent intervention or legal transactions which lack the consent of the statutory representative), cf. MünchKomm (*-Seiler*), BGB[3], § 682, no. 2 et seq.

35. Provisions corresponding to CC § 682 may be found in ESTONIAN CC § 1021 (2) and in GREEK CC art. 735. Under these provisions the person lacking legal capacity (in the former case) and a minor (in the latter) will similarly be liable only according to the provisions of unjustified enrichment law. Again the statutory reference is confined to a reference to the legal basis of the claim (Georgiades and Stathopoulos [*-Papanikolaou*], Art. 735, no. 7). It only relates the liability of the intervener; it does not prevent a relationship of benevolent intervention involving a person lacking full legal capacity from arising in the first place (*Papanikolaou* loc.cit. no. 1). Where the activity undertaken takes the form of the conclusion of a legal transaction, the want of legal capacity implies no benevolent intervention can subsist (*Papanikolaou* loc.cit. no. 2). The scope of application of CC art. 735 is thus restricted to purely physical acts. An intervener who is a minor is not afforded the protection of this rule if his parents have ratified the legal transaction he has conducted (*Papanikolaou* loc.cit. no. 5).

36. A provision similar to German CC § 682 is not known in the PORTUGUESE CC. Under AUSTRIAN law an intervener lacking full legal capacity is only obliged to deliver up in accordance with the provisions of unjustified enrichment law. (The only point in dispute is whether the same also applies with regard to a minor's claim for reimbursement of expenditure: cf. Klang [*-Stanzl*], ABGB IV/1[2], 893.) A person lacking full legal capacity is not obliged to continue an intervention once commenced (Schwimann [*-Apathy*], ABGB V[2], § 1035 no. 4). Many further details (determination of the intention to act on another's behalf, duty to render an account, possibility of ratifica-

tion by a legal representative) are a matter of dispute (for details see Rummel [-*Rummel*], ABGB I[3], § 1035 no. 7).

37. According to BELGIAN legal literature if the intervener lacks full legal capacity the benevolent intervention will be a *nullité*. The *nullité*, however, is relative: only the person lacking full legal capacity may rely on this defect. If he does so the law of benevolent intervention is rendered inapplicable with retroactive effect; it will then be supplanted by CC arts. 1310 and 1312. Thus the person lacking full legal capacity will only be liable in accordance with tort law and unjustified enrichment law. If the person lacking full legal capacity does not invoke the *nullité relative* the relationship between him and the principal will be governed by the rules of benevolent intervention (*Paulus*, Zaakwaarneming, no. 76 p. 48-49). In FRENCH legal literature a majority opinion is that the intervener's lack of full legal capacity will only be relevant if the intervener concludes the juridical act in his own name; in the case of a mere *acte matériel* or an *acte juridique* concluded in the name of the principal the intervener's *capacité juridique* will be irrelevant (only in the latter case is it of importance that the principal has full legal capacity). A juridical act conducted in his own name may by contrast be declared void; in this case no benevolent intervention arises (*Marty and Raynaud*, Les obligations I[2]. Les sources, no. 384 p. 398-399). To the extent that intervention without authority by a person lacking full legal capacity remains possible they do not enjoy any special protection (*Marty and Raynaud*, loc.cit., fn. 1).

38. Nor does the SPANISH CC contain an explicit protection for underage interveners. Legal literature opts for the analogous application of the provisions on formation of contracts (Albaladejo [-*Santos Briz*], Código Civil y compilaciones forales, XXIV, 57). Some authors even consider an intervention by a person lacking full legal capacity to be impossible; such persons, it is argued, cannot bind themselves either by a contrat or by a quasi-contractual act (*Lacruz Berdejo*, Rev.Crít.Der.Inm. 1975, 254). An approach similar to that of Article 2:102 (2), however, is afforded by CC art. 1304, which provides that "if the nullity (of the contract) is a result of the intervener's lack of legal capacity the person lacking legal capacity is only obliged to surrender the asset or monies he has received in so far as he is enriched." This is considered to afford sufficient protection to a person lacking full legal capacity (*Lacruz Berdejo*, loc.cit.).

39. Under ITALIAN CC art. 2029 (which on this point has a corresponding rule in MALTESE CC art. 1013) the intervener as a general rule must have the capacity to conclude contracts; as regards mere physical acts, however, accountability for one's actions is sufficient. Juridical acts concluded by a person lacking legal capacity are ineffective vis-à-vis the principal. Moreover, juridical acts concluded in his name cannot bind him in relation to third parties (*Bianca*, Diritto civile, Il contratto[2], 142). In the case of an intervention which benefits the principal, the law of unjustified enrichment applies; in the case of a detrimental intervention, tort law will apply (*Aru*, Gestione d'affari, 27).

40. DUTCH Law does also not have a special provision on the protection of minors or other interveners lacking full legal capacity. However, it is recognised that a person lacking full legal capacity can undertake as a benevolent intervention both physical acts and such legal acts as he effects in the name of the principal. Juridical acts which the person lacking legal capacity effects in his own name are voidable under CC art. 3:32 (2) (Asser [-*Hartkamp*], Verbintenissenrecht III[11], no. 304 p. 316; Verbintenissenrecht [-*Heisterkamp*], Art. 6:198 BW, no. 15).

41. Under SCOTS law the liability of minors and mentally disabled persons arising from quasi-contract is restricted to the surrender of an unjustified enrichment, and thus also the liability incurred by benevolent intervention (Stair [-Whitty], The Laws of Scotland, vol. 15, para 141). The NORDIC countries do not provide for specific rules on an intervener lacking full legal capacity. In ENGLISH law a minor and other persons without full capacity to contract on their own behalf may nonetheless act as an agent unless lacking sufficient mental capacity (cf. Bowstead (-*Reynolds/Graziadei*), Agency[17], article 5) and in principle may act as an agent of necessity. Even where such agency is non-contractual, an agent remains in principle subject to the duty to hand over the principal's money and to surrender any unauthorised profit. Where no agency can be established, the intervener's liability will in any case be governed by the law of restitution (unjustified enrichment).

Illustration 1 is taken from CA Mons 2 March 2004, JT 2004, 555, and **illustration 3** from RG 14 November 1919, Das Recht 1920 no. 628.

Article 2:103: Reparation for Damage Caused by Breach of Duty

(1) The intervener is liable to make reparation to the principal for damage caused by breach of a duty set out in this Book if the damage resulted from a risk which the intervener created, increased or intentionally perpetuated.

(2) The intervener's liability is reduced or excluded in so far as this is fair and reasonable, having regard to, among other things, the intervener's reasons for acting.

(3) An intervener who at the time of intervening lacks full legal capacity is liable to make reparation only in so far as that intervener is also liable to make reparation under the law of non-contractual obligations arising out of damage caused to another (PEL Liab.Dam.).

Comments

A. Liability to make Reparation for Breach of Duty

1. **The duty to make reparation under the law of benevolent intervention in another's affairs** Para (1) establishes the intervener's liability for damages and thus at the same time the basis for a claim of the principal. Such provision appears necessary firstly because there should not be any discussion at the outset whether the principal's claim to damages arising out of the culpable execution of a benevolent intervention is in its nature a tortious one or is a claim which must be derived from an analogous application of the contract law provisions. It is neither the one nor the other. Rather it takes the form of a claim to damages under the law of *negotiorum gestio* itself. Secondly, para (1) is required to give expression in a general rule to the specific limits of this claim to reparation.

2. **Reparation** In agreement with the legal terminology being used in the law of extra-contractual liability in respect of a damage – in particular in keeping with the European Principles of Non-Contractual Liability Arising out of Damage Caused to Another (PEL Liab.Dam.) – the concept of 'reparation' embraces every form of making good a damage. Usually this will take the form of 'compensation' (monetary reparation; damages), but it may also assume another form of indemnification of the damage – in particular the restoration of the *status quo ante* by reparation in kind.

3. **Damage** As in tort law (in the concept of "legally relevant damage") and the law of contract, the expression "damage" also encompasses here economic as well as non-economic losses. The provisions on the law of tort regarding compensation for damage suffered by close relations are applicable here too by analogy where the facts of the case call for it. The crucial point is always that the damage must be the consequence of a breach of a duty which is imposed by Articles 2:101 and 2:102 upon a *gestor* whose intervention is justified in the sense prescribed by Articles 1:101 and 1:102. Someone who intermeddles in the affairs of another without reasonable ground is liable for any damage which results not under the law of benevolent intervention, but under other provisions – in particular those of the law of tort.

B. General Limits to Liability for Defective Execution of a Benevolent Intervention (Para (1))

4. **Causation** The duty to make reparation for a breach of duty imposed on the *gestor qua gestor* is limited by various requirements, first and foremost from the perspective of causation. Damage which has occurred does not generate a claim to reparation if it is attributable to a risk which gave cause for the intervener's measure or, to formulate the same proposition in positive terms, damage is reparable only if it results from the intervention of the *gestor*. The *gestor* must have either created or increased the relevant danger, or else he must have deliberately allowed it to continue.

5. **Three situations** It is not enough as regards the required limitation of liability simply to point to the general instrumentality of causation. Rather what is needed is a specific connection between the breach of duty of the intervener and the damage which has occurred. That is because there is a host of cases in which the damage would not have occurred if the intervener had acted in accordance with his duties, but the damage would have occurred anyway if the intervener had not interfered at all. In situations of this type there has to be an exact examination of attributability of the damage to the intervention. Liability ought to be incurred in only three basic situations: (i) where the *gestor* has created the risk of damage by his intervention; (ii) where, though he has not created that risk, the *gestor* has increased it; and (iii) where he has terminated his intervention prematurely without reasonable ground and in the conscious assumption of the risk that damage will follow.

6. **Liability for the realisation of a risk created by the gestor** An intervener is liable for the realisation of a risk of damage which he has brought about. The mere omission to intervene to break a chain of causation which is already in progress does not generate

any liability to compensate – even if a reasonable intervener would have behaved differently.

Illustration 1
As a result of heavy and sustained rainfall, an entire region is flooded. As the house owner is on holiday and has left no contact address, a neighbour takes it upon himself to enter the house and rescue a suite of Chippendale chairs. The neighbour is not liable for his negligence in failing to see that in the adjoining room there are other Chippendale chairs; nor is he liable for negligently failing to appreciate that it would have been more important to remove from the house a considerably more valuable Persian rug.

7. **Liability for the realisation of a risk increased by the gestor** The intervener need not have created the risk; it suffices that he has enhanced it by his intervention.

Illustration 2
Customers in a supermarket find a handbag and hand this in at one of the tills. The cashier announces over the loudspeaker that the bag has been found and asks the owner, whose name is read from the identity card contained in the bag, to retrieve it. Since nobody comes to claim it, the cashier hands it back to the customers who found it, as they lead her to believe that they know the owner and will bring it to her. In fact they keep the bag and the money which it contained. The supermarket is liable for the loss because it increased the risk of the ultimate loss of the bag and contents in handing the bag back out, it being secure in the custody of the supermarket's employee following the *negotiorum gestio* in taking possession. The case would be correspondingly the same in Illustration 1 if after rescuing the chairs the neighbour stores them so carelessly that they sustain damage while in his possession. That damage is attributable to his breach of duty.

8. **The gestor intentionally perpetuated the risk** The third basic situation is a premature termination of the intervention in breach of duty (Article 2:101 (2) (Duties during Intervention)). This breach of duty too ought not to lead to liability for all damage which results. In addition to the requirement of causation it must be established that the *gestor* has caused the perpetuation of the risk intentionally.

Illustration 3
Intervener I negligently supposes that he has finished necessary repairs and thus leaves the scene of action. In fact the problem has not been remedied: a short time later water starts once again to pour out of the damaged pipe. I is not liable to the principal.

Illustration 4
The facts are the same as in illustration 1, except that in this case the neighbour has carried the chairs out of the adjoining room into the hall, where he leaves them because it has suddenly become a matter of indifference to him what happens to the chairs. He has intentionally perpetuated the risk.

9. **Intention** The meaning of the term "intention" follows the definition in PEL Liab.Dam. Article 3:101.

C. Liability for Others; Multiple *Gestors*

10. **No general liability for other gestors** The text contains neither special rules on liability for the defaults of others nor particular provisions on situations in which several benevolent interveners become active. Liability of the intervener for a failure to choose with care a person to render assistance is already provided for by para (1) in conjunction with Article 1:201(1)(a). Since there is no contract between the intervener and the principal governing the measure being undertaken and the intervener is therefore not obliged to the principal to undertake it, a genuine liability for the default of others fundamentally cannot be regarded as justified. The act of engaging another may, of course, be an act of *negotiorum gestio* in itself, from which it follows that the intervener is obliged to surrender to the principal all the rights which he acquires under the contract he makes with the engaged third party. The risk of the third party's insolvency is thus borne by the principal and not the intervener. The situation is otherwise where the intervener engages a third party in order to discharge a duty which is already imposed on the intervener himself, such as the duty to deliver up and account. In that case the intervener is liable according to general principles for the non-performance of his duty if he has delegated performance to a third party who fails in that undertaking.

11. **No joint liability of multiple interveners as a general rule** For the same reasons it did not appear to be justified to include a provision according to which multiple interveners would be jointly they and severally liable. Such joint liability may generally only be considered where several interveners are under the duty to undertake the same activity – a situation, however, which will be a rare exception.

D. Reduction of Liability (Para (2))

12. **General** The provision in para (2) is a means of protecting persons who take care of others or their interests for especially commendable reasons. Para (2) will typically (but not necessarily) operate in favour of emergency rescuers. The policy consideration behind para (2) is therefore tied to one very specific aspect of *negotiorum gestio*: the existence and extent of the (required) element of intention to benefit another. The fundamental belief that helpers who render assistance to another for altruistic reasons should be privileged as regards liability is familiar to all European jurisdictions. Only the means by which this fundamental belief is implemented differ. Some legal systems reduce the applicable standard of care to gross negligence, only granting this privilege to helpers acting in an emergency, whereas other jurisdictions engage a more open reasonableness test without altering the standard of care. Para (2) adheres to the latter model. The fact that in urgent situations of emergency non-professional helpers may easily misreact due to fear or precipitance is already taken into account in the context of the assessment under Article 2:101(1)(a): see the comments thereon. Para (2) therefore does not concern the basis of liability, but relates instead exclusively to the extent of the

compensation. It is not confined to cases where the context to the *negotiorum gestio* is the presence of a situation of imminent danger to another's body or health.

13. **The fairness test** Liability may be either reduced or completely excluded under para (2). Whether and to what extent such a reduction of liability (which in a suitable case may be a reduction to nil) applies will depend on a general fairness test ("fair and reasonable"). It must be determined according to the circumstances of the individual case and in particular depend on the altruistic motive of the acting party.

Illustration 5
Mrs A looks after the estate of Mr X after he has died. She was due to inherit under a will, but has disclaimed the heritance. A dispute arises between Mrs A and Mr X's relatives concerning some animals which Mrs A has entrusted to the care of third parties. With regard to the majority of the animals Mrs A has acted exemplary, whereas she has not timeously discharged her duty of information with respect to a goat and a sheep. The liability for damage may be reduced in the light of the altruistic motive of the intervener and the slightness of her oversight.

Illustration 6
Using his tractor Farmer F tows away to the roadside a tree which had been uprooted by a storm; the removal was the responsibility of the local authority. Four months later the local authority has not taken any steps. At night an accident occurs. F has committed a fault as he did not completely remove the tree from the street and, together with the local authority, is liable to the road user as a joint debtor. However, inter partes his share in the liability is to be reduced considerably below 50%.

E. Gestors without full Legal Capacity (Para (3))

14. **General liability under the law of tort also required** The rule in para (2) alone, however, does not offer the class of persons named in para (3) adequate protection. Such persons ought only to be liable to make reparation if neither the law of *negotiorum gestio* nor the law of tort provides a protection against liability. The most important practical case is to be found in the law relating to protection of minors and the rules on the minimum age for tortious liability (see PEL Liab.Dam. Article 3:103). Comparatively less important (but also to be considered) are the cases in which for other reasons there is liability in the law of *negotiorum gestio*, but not in the law of tort. That may come about because the *gestor* has infringed the duty imposed on him by Article 2:101(1)(b) to comply with the wishes of the principal, or the duty to continue an intervention (Article 2:101(2)) (which as a rule will be alien to the law of tort), or because he has caused a damage which is not legally relevant within the concept of the law of tort.

Notes

I. The Basis of the Claim for Damages

1. The GERMAN CC does not provide for an independant claim for damages within the law of benevolent intervention. If the intervener is in breach of his duties under CC §§ 677 and 681, the principal may claim damages subject to the general requirements of CC § 280, which applies to all breaches of duty. As regards fault, CC § 280 (1) sentence 2 provides for a reversal of the burden of proof in favour of the creditor (in this case the principal). A claim for damages is excluded if an approval by the principal covers the particular mode of managing the affair (Palandt [-*Sprau*], BGB[63], § 677, no. 15; § 681, no. 4; § 684, no. 2). The lack of success does not necessarily imply the conclusion that the intervention has been mismanaged (RGRK [-*Steffen*], BGB[12], § 677, no. 11). A breach of the duty arising under CC § 681 does not result in a loss of the intervener's claim for reimbursement of expenses incurred (BGH 4 December 1975, BGHZ 65, 354, 356) since the benevolent intervention remains a justified intervention. Although the claim for damages pursuant to CC § 280 includes the 'positive' interest and thus all direct and indirect disadvantages which are the result of the harmful conduct, the liability will only extend to such damage as results from carrying out the intervention. Disadvantages which result from a reasonable though unsuccessful management of the affair are not taken into consideration, because the unauthorized intervener is not under an obligation to achieve a successful intervention (Soergel [-*Beuthien*], BGB[12], § 677, no. 20). The principal is to be placed in the position he would have occupied if the intervener had given notice to the principal timeously, abstained from action or informed the principal (BGH loc.cit. 357).
2. A similar legal situation may be found in GREECE. The sole matter of dispute is whether the legal basis for the claim for damages is to be found in the general provisions on non-performance (CC arts. 335 et seq.; *Filios*, Enochiko Dikaio I/2, 201) or may be derived directly from the provisions of CC arts. 730, 731 (in favour of this solution *Kavkas and Kavkas*, Enochikon Dikaion II/2, 25). Despite a breach of duty the intervener will retain his claims against the principal (Georgiades and Stathopoulos [-*Papanikolaou*], Art. 730, no. 40).
3. PORTUGUESE CC art. 466 (1) by contrast provides for a separate basis for liability of the intervener for damages: "The intervener is liable to the principal for damage which he causes by defective execution of the management or by an unjustified interruption of the management". CC art. 466 (2) spells out that an intervener acts negligently if he does not act in accordance with the interest and the wishes of the principal. This is in line with CC art. 465 limb (a). Furthermore, the general provisions on liability for damages also apply in the context of the law of benevolent intervention (*Menezes Leitão*, Responsabilidade do gestor, 273 ff). The liability of a lawyer who has conducted proceedings without authority is expressly stated in CCP art. 41 (2).
4. AUSTRIAN law also distinguishes between the different types of benevolent intervention with respect to the question of the intervener's liability for damages (*Koziol*, Haftpflichtrecht I[3], no. 4/96, p. 185). CC § 1312 limits the intervener's liability in a case of intervention in an emergency (CC § 1036); he will not be held responsible for the want of a successful outcome to his intervention. This will only be otherwise under CC § 1312 if the intervener has "by his fault prevented another from acting who would

have achieved a better result". CC § 1312 sentence 2 grants the intervener the possibility to set off the profits gained against the damage sustained. This is considered as a particular case of equalisation of benefits (Rummel [-*Reischauer*], ABGB II², § 1312 no. 2). The intervener in a case of emergency is also subject to a duty of care; he is liable for damage negligently caused (Schwimann [-*Apathy*], ABGB V², §§ 1036-1040 no. 18), though the urgency of the intervention and the extent of the impending danger will be taken into consideration (*Meissel*, GoA, 140). As far as 'useful benevolent intervention' is concerned (CC § 1037) CC § 1311 (sentence 2, third alternative) applies. According to this provision the intervener "who without urgency intermeddles with another's affairs" will be liable for all disadvantages which would not have occurred but for his intervention (*v. Zeiller*, Commentar III § 1311 no. 9 p. 739, gives the example of an intervener who stores the fruit which he has harvested on behalf of the owner at a place where the owner would not have put them and where they are subsequently destroyed by a fire). A fault in venturing the intervention will suffice and the damage need not have been foreseeable (*Karollus*, Schutzgesetzverletzung, 63; Schwimann [-*Apathy*], ABGB V², §§ 1036-1040 no. 19). The intervener may set off against his own counterclaims. However CC § 1312 sentence 2 (see above) is not applicable. If the damage caused by the intervener exceeds the benefit brought about this will constitute a case under CC § 1038. Under that provision, in contrast to CC § 1324, the intervener will also be liable (even if only slightly negligent) for 'full satisfaction' and thus also for lost profits (Rummel [-*Rummel*], ABGB I³, § 1038 no. 5; *Meissel*, GoA, 140 et seq.; the details are, however, a matter of dispute).

5. Under BELGIAN and FRENCH law the principle that the intervener who has breached his duties will be liable for the damage arising as a result is undisputed. However the wording of CC arts. 1372-1375 (apart from the reduction clause in CC art. 1374 (2)) do not further specify either the legal nature or the exact structure of liability. The majority of FRENCH authors hold the opinion that the liability of the intervener is in its nature a tortious one (*Viney*, Introduction à la responsabilité², no. 191 p. 348-349), others argue in favour of a concept of a contractual nature (*Acquarone*, D. 1986 chron. 21-26), while a yet third group consider it to be *sui generis* (*Starck/Roland/Boyer*, Les Obligations⁶, no. 2045 p. 713). In BELGIAN legal literature, by contrast, the nearly unanimous view is that the intervener's liability is extra-contractual and thus tortious in nature (*Dalcq*, Traité de la responsabilité civile, I², no. 116 p. 131). The *travaux préparatoires* on the Belgian Limitation Act, however, reveal that the limitation of actions arising from quasi-contracts are subject to the general provisions on limitation of contractual claims (Parl. St., Kamer, 1997-98, no. 1087/1, p. 8 and 11).

6. Under SPANISH law the liability of the intervener for damages for the breach of duty of care is based on CC art. 1889. The duty to pay compensation will cover all damage which has been caused by the defective management without regard to its nature. CC art. 1106 (which in its wording actually only concerns liability for breach of contract and provides that lost profits are compensable) is applied correspondingly (Paz-Ares/Díez-Picazo/Bercovitz/Salvador (-*Díez-Picazo*), Código Civil II, 1946; *Sánchez Jordán*, Gestión de negocios, 453; see also *Cavanillas Múgica and Tapia Fernández*, Concurrencia de responsabilidad, 9). CC art. 1889 requires that the intervener has not acted in accordance with the care of a *bonus paterfamilias*. Yet his liability is not regarded as tortious, but rather as (quasi-)contractual (*Díez-Picazo*, loc.cit., *Pasquau Liaño*, La gestión de negocios ajenos, 130; *Sánchez Jordán*, loc.cit.). It is disputed whether liability

will also arise in a case of slight or the slightest negligence (*culpa leve* and *culpa levissima*) (this is answered in the negative by Albaladejo [-*Santos Briz*], Código Civil y compilaciones forales, XXIV, 58; *Lacruz Berdejo*, Rev.Crít.Der.Inm. 1975, 266). As regards liability for breach of the duty to continue the intervention, it has been suggested (so far as this question is at all discussed) that the provisions of tort law apply (*Pasquau Liaño*, La gestión de negocios ajenos, 129).

7. According to the ITALIAN legal approach the liability of an intervener for the malperformance of his duties follows the principles of contract law (*Franzoni*, Dei fatti illeciti, in Commentario del c.c. Scialoja Branca, IV, Delle obbligazioni, arts. 2043-2059, p. 14). As the principal has no right to claim performance by the intervener it is assumed that only the negative interest will be compensated (i. e. the interest not to suffer any damage from another's interference in one's own sphere of legal interests).

8. Under DUTCH CC the intervener's liability for a breach of his duty of care (CC art. 6:199) is derived from CC arts. 6:74 et seq., i. e. the provisions on liability for non-performance of an obligation. The extent of liability is determined according to the general rules on damages contained in CC arts. 6:95 et seq. (Asser [-*Hartkamp*], Verbintenissenrecht III[11], no. 299, p. 312-313 and nos. 310-312, p. 320-321; *Schrage*, Verbintenissen uit andere bron, no. 23, p. 16; Verbintenissenrecht [-*Scheltema*], Art. 6:199 BW, no. 3).

9. In SCOTLAND the intervener's liability for damages (which is generally acknowledged) is apparently of delictual nature (*Harloff*, Tartan & Torts, 51; Stair [-*Whitty*], vol. 15, para 90). No details as to liability for breach of the duty to inform or the duty of care are to be found in the SCANDINAVIAN jurisdictions. Both the legal basis and the extent of such liability may apparently similarly arise out of tort law.

10. In the COMMON LAW liability of the intervener for breach of the duty of care will be a matter of tort law (negligence), though a (concurrent) liability in contract law is possible in those cases of agency of necessity which are based on contract where necessity has operated to impose a duty and confer an authority to act in the unforeseen circumstances. The intervener attempting a rescue (and whose intereference is justified by necessity) is only liable in tort if he makes matters worse: *East Suffolk Rivers Catchment Board v. Kent* [1941] AC 74 (no liability in negligently repairing sea will since under no duty to do so and damage no worse than if not had repaired at all), and contrast *Capital and Counties plc v. Hampshire* CC [1997] QB 1004 (where the fire service was liable because in negligently turning off a sprinkler system it enabled the fire to spread more quickly). The burden of proving that negligence has not increased the damage rests on the intervener: *Capital and Counties plc v. Hampshire* CC loc. cit. at 1034 (*Stuart-Smith* LJ). However, an assumption of responsibility on the part of the intervener may be regarded as creating an affirmative duty to act, in which case the intervener will be liable for the negligent discharge of that duty to assist: cf. *Kent v. Griffiths* [2000] 2 WLR 1158 – where, however, there was in any case a public law duty to act.

II. *Liability for Others; Multiple Gestors*

11. Under GERMAN law several interveners will be liable as joint and several debtors (CC § 427 applied correspondingly) if together they have managed the same affair for the principal (Soergel [-*Beuthien*], BGB[12], Vor § 677, no. 11; Staudinger [-*Wittmann*],

BGB[13], Introd. to §§ 677 et seq., no. 58). A person who has merely acted as an assistant of the intervener, on the other hand, will naturally not be considered as a joint debtor (RGRK [-*Steffen*], BGB[12], Vor § 677, no. 103). Interveners acting independently are debtors liable for their own share of the debts (CC § 420; *Wittmann*, loc.cit.). An example for joint liability of interveners as regards an unjustified intervention (CC § 687 (2)) may be found in BGH 30 January 1959, MDR 1959, 635 (liability of publisher and author for surrender of profits in the case of an infringement of a copyright).

12. Under GREEK law several interveners are jointly liable if they have undertaken common action for the principal (CC art. 926 (1); *Kavkas and Kavkas*, Enochiko Dikaio II, 14). Interveners who act independently will be jointly liable if (and only if) it is impossible to ascertain whose action has caused the damage (CC art. 926 (2); *Kavkas and Kavkas* loc.cit.). An intervener is liable for the acts of his assistant according to the rules of CC arts. 330 and 334 (Georgiades/Stathopoulos [-*Papanikolaou*], Art. 731, no. 1).

13. In contrast to the German and Greek Civil Codes the PORTUGUESE CC art. 467 expressly provides for the case where "two or more interveners have acted solidarily". If so they are jointly liable to the principal (CC arts. 512 et seq., 518 et seq.; *Pires de Lima and Antunes Varela*, Código Civil Anotado I[4], 449, note 1 under art. 467). Under CC art. 512 (1) "a legal relationship is a solidary relationship if every debtor is liable for the entire performance and such performance discharges the debt with respect to all debtors or if each creditor may request the entire performance and such performance discharges the debtor's duty to all creditors." CC art. 524 then provides for the usual rights of recourse in a case of joint debtors.

14. Under AUSTRIAN Law it must be ascertained as a first step whether in fact several interveners have acted or whether one of the active parties has only acted as an assistant to the true intervener. An intervener will be liable for his assistant under CC § 1313a (*Meissel*, GoA, 150 et seq.). By contrast in the case of several interveners CC § 1011 is thought to apply *mutatis mutandis:* Klang (-*Stanzl*), ABGB IV/1[2], 896 CC § 1011 (collective representation). In consequence only the particular intervener who is at fault will be liable.

15. For cases involving a plurality of interveners BELGIAN and FRENCH legal literature as a general rule reject the creation of a *responsabilité solidaire*. In France this result is reached by analogous application of CC art. 1995. However a judgment holding several interveners liable *in solidum* is conceivable if the activities of the various interveners cannot be distinguished and thus their exact participation cannot be ascertained (JClCiv [-*Bout*], Art. 1372-1375, Fasc. 20 no. 33; RPDB, v° Quasi-contrat, no. 114).

16. Under SPANISH law (in contrast to the position under the law of mandate, cf. CC art. 1723) several interveners without authority will in general be jointly liable (CC art. 1890 (2)). This does not apply, however, if there were different activities which lack an inherent interrelationship (Paz-Ares/Díez-Picazo/Bercovitz/Salvador [-*Díez-Picazo*], Código Civil II, 1948; *Puig Brutau*, Compendio II, 602). If the intervener assigns tasks to third parties he will nonetheless remain liable for correct performance – even though the third parties will also be liable to the principal as if they themselves were interveners (CC art. 1890 (1); *Díez-Picazo*, loc.cit. 1946). Thus the principal may choose against whom he wishes to make his demands; both the actual intervener and the agents the latter has instructed will be liable as joint debtors.

17. The ITALIAN CC does not elaborate on the liability of multiple interveners. CC art. 1716 in para (3) in the context of the law of mandate provides for joint liability in respect of multiple agents, but it is considered not to be applicable to the law of benevolent intervention (*Rescigno*, Codice civile, sub Art. 2030 CC).

18. Under DUTCH law the intervener may appoint assistants both in his own name and in the name of the principal. This will be relevant in particular if the intervener does not personally possess the expertise necessary for the execution of the measure to be undertaken. Liability for culpable acts of the appointed assistants arises in the context of the duty to continue the intervention (CC art. 6:199 (1)) from CC art. 6:76, though a reduction of liability under CC art. 6:109 is conceivable (*Verburg*, De vrijwillige zaakwaarneming, no. 66 p. 97; no. 73 p. 109; *Schoordijk*, Het algemeen gedeelte van het verbintenissenrecht naar het nieuw BW, 417-418). However, it has also been held that an intervener who for good reason leaves the entire intervention to a third party will be freed from the duty to continue the intervention. In this case the intervener is only liable if he makes a poor choice of the third party; he is not liable as such for the latter's defective execution. The third party in such cases assumes the position of the actual intervener (Verbintenissenrecht [-*Scheltema*], Art. 6:199 BW, note 2.1).

19. No clear-cut statement of the law could be divined for SCOTS law. The legal position within the SCANDINAVIAN jurisdictions is likewise not free from doubts. Several tortfeasors and several contract debtors according to the different statutes will in general be jointly liable. However there is no elaboration as to whether and, if so, in which cases this general principle may also be applied to multiple interveners. In the COMMON LAW too, where necessitous intervention is in any case fragmented into the law of agency, bailment and resitution, the matter depends on the applicable regime governing liability and is not susceptible of a precise general statement.

III. *Reduction of Liability*

20. Most legal systems afford special measures of protection against liability to the intervener. Where such rules exist they consist of a provision which either excludes liability for slight negligence in emergency situations or corresponds to Article 2:103(2). Moreover, general mechanisms for reduction of liability in a case of contributory fault on the part of the person entitled to redress of course also play a role within the law of benevolent intervention.

21. GERMAN CC § 680 provides that the intervener who has acted in order to avert an imminent danger threatening the principal will only be liable for loss caused intentionally or by gross negligence. This reduction of liability only applies inter partes between the intervener and the principal. It relates to both assumption of the intervention and its execution (BGH 30 November 1971, NJW 1972, 475; BGH 16 March 1965, BGHZ 43, 188, 193; CA Hamburg 5 January 1984, VersR 1984, 758), and it modifies the standard of fault under CC § 276 which is generally applicable to claims for damages under CC § 280 (BGH 30 November 1971, NJW 1972, 475). CC § 680 extends to the principal's claims for damages arising under tort law (BGH 20 December 1966, BGHZ 46, 313, 316; BGH 23 March 1966, BGHZ 46, 140, 145). Apart from this a reduction of the intervener's liability may only be considered under the aspect of contributory negligence (CC § 254).

22. Rules corresponding to German CC § 680 may be found in ESTONIAN CC § 1022 (2), POLISH CC art. 757 and GREEK CC art. 732. Under these provisions the intervener who acts to avert imminent danger is likewise only liable for loss caused intentionally or by gross negligence. The precondition is an immediate danger to the person or property of the principal or one of his relatives (Georgiades and Stathopoulos [-*Papanikolaou*], Art. 732, no. 2; ErmAK [-*Sakketas*], Art. 732, no. 2). Greek CC art. 732 is thought to apply if the intervener has assumed erroneously but without gross negligence that a situation of imminent danger has arisen (*Papanikolaou*, loc.cit. no. 3; *Sakketas*, loc.cit. no. 4). CC art. 732 also has an impact on the claim arising from a tort, but it will not be applied if the intervener has acted contrary to the principal's wishes, which he knew or, had he not been grossly negligent, would have known (*Papanikolaou*, loc.cit. nos. 4-5).

23. The drafters of the PORTUGUESE Civil Code decided not to adopt a provision corresponding to German CC § 680 (*Vieira Gomes*, Gestão de negócios, 184 et seq.). They considered the French and Italian model to be preferable (*Vaz Serra*, Gestão de negócios, 135), but did not implement it specifically in the law of benevolent intervention, adopting instead a general tort law reduction clause in CC art. 294, which is of significance to all obligations to make reparation (*Menezes Leitão*, Responsabilidade do gestor, 280-281, 290). Accordingly the duty to compensate for damages in a case of *mera culpa* may be reduced on grounds of fairness and reasonableness. Those grounds include the economic position of the participants and the presence of a situation of imminent danger. Moreover, a reduction or exclusions of liability may arise in a case of contributory negligence on the part of the principal (CC art. 570). It is likewise possible under HUNGARIAN law to apply the tort law reduction clause (CC § 339 (2)) *mutatis mutandis* within the law of benevolent intervention.

24. AUSTRIAN CC law does not contain a reduction clause for the intervener's liability to the principal to make reparation. CC § 1312 merely clarifies that a person who has rendered assistance to another in a case of emergency will not be liable merely because he has not succeeded in averting the damage. The case is otherwise only if the active party has prevented a third party who was better qualified to manage the affair from acting. Finally, CC § 1299 provides that an intervener in an emergency will not be subject to an elevated standard of care even if such care was actually required for the management of the affair.

25. FRENCH, BELGIAN and LUXEMBOURGIAN CC art. 1374 (2) grant the judge discretion to reduce the quantum of reparation according to the circumstances which induced the intervener to intervene – a rule which is described in France as *très exceptionnelle* because it deviates from the overall principle of full restitution (*Mazeaud and Chabas*, Obligations[9], no. 687 p. 814). However, there is no explicit discussion of whether CC art. 1374 (2) relates to all types of breach of duty or whether it is restricted to the breach of the general duty of care. Only in Belgium has it been argued (*Paulus*, Zaakwaarneming, no. 69 p. 46) that CC art. 1374 (2) should apply also to claims for damages arising from the infringement of specific duties (such as the duty to render an account). A reduction clause similar to that of French law may also be found in MALTESE CC art. 1017.

26. SPANISH CC art. 1889 (2) allows the courts to reduce the amount of liability according to the circumstances of the particular case or even to reduce it to nothing (*Sánchez Jordán*, Gestión de negocios, 455). A restriction to liability for intentional conduct and

gross negligence (as in all Romance legal systems) is unknown. Typical reasons for a reduction of liability are the urgent character of the necessity to intervene, the intention to avert impending damage bound up with it, as well as the difficulty to correctly assess the situation (*Sánchez Jordán*, loc.cit. 456; Paz-Ares/Díez-Picazo/Bercovitz/Salvador [-*Díez-Picazo*], Código Civil II, 1947). All these aspects, however, – in contrast to the systems under Germanic influence – have no impact on the determination of the severity of fault; they are taken into consideration in the context of the assessment of the amount of damages owed (*Pasquau Liaño*, La gestión de negocios ajenos, 133; of different opinion however *Díez-Picazo*, loc.cit.). The legal notion underlying CC art. 1889 (2) is reiterated in CC art. 1103 with regard to all cases of contractual liability (*Pasquau Liaño*, loc.cit.).

27. A court under ITALIAN CC art. 2030 (2) may likewise take into account all aspects which have prompted the intervener to undertake the management of the affair and accordingly reduce the amount of damages. On the other hand, CC art. 1710 (1), under which "liability for negligence is to be judged less severely" in case of a gratuitous mandate is not applicable within the law of benevolent intervention (Cass. 4 October 1956, no. 3336, Rep. Giur. It. 1956, voce Gestione d'affari, nos. 8, 9, 12 and 13; Cass. 20 May 1953, no. 1472, Rep.Giur.it. 1953, voce Gestione d'affari, no. 5). It is, however, emphasized that the claim for damages may be reduced in a case of contributory negligence (CC art. 1227 (1)) if the principal has neglected to attend to his own affairs in an unreasonable manner (*Bianca*, Diritto civile III, Il contratto², 149-150).

28. As regards DUTCH law the rule is that malperformance or non-performance by the intervener of a duty set out in CC 6:199 will give rise to liability for damages under the general rules of CC arts. 6:74 et seq. The fact that the intervener has acted on another's behalf and not in pursuit of his own interests is, though, a factor which the court may take into account in the assessment of the quantum of damages and may thus lead to a reduction on equitable grounds (CC art. 6:109). This may be the case, for example, if an intervener seeks to save the life of another, but by an incautious measure contributes to that person's injury or death. The case is otherwise where an intervener within the meaning of CC art. 6:200 (2) acts in exercise of his profession or trade (M. v.A II, Parlementaire Geschiedenis VI, 449 and 793; Asser [-*Hartkamp*], Verbintenissenrecht I¹², no. 496, p. 458-459; *Schrage*, Mon. Nieuw BW, no. 23 p. 16). The Code does not provide for a special standard of care privileging an intervener. It merely leaves a scope of appreciation to the judge with regard to the assessment of the content of the duty of care in the sense of CC art. 6:199 (1) (Asser [-*Hartkamp*], Verbintenissenrecht III¹¹, no. 307 p. 318-319; *Schrage*, loc.cit.).

29. Since the decision in AS *Kolbin & Sons v. William Kinnear & Co.* (SC(HL) 1931, 128) the general standard of care of a reasonable person applied to his own affairs will be decisive in SCOTLAND. The particulars of the individual case are to be taken into account, which may include the fact that the intervention concerned an emergency (*Walker*, Principles of Scottish Private Law, II⁴,513-514; *Leslie*, Jur.Rev. 1983, 27). The Institutional Writers intended the intervener's liability in such cases to require gross negligence (*Bell*, § 541; *Erskine*, Book III, Volume II, 53), which, judged by the practical results, hardly deviates from the current situation.

30. The solution of German CC § 680 is discussed within SWEDISH legal literature and it has been stated that a comparable solution may be reached *inter alia* by introducing into the determination of negligence the fact that an emergency situation exists

(*Håstad*, Tjänster utan uppdrag, 142). As regards DENMARK *Vinding Kruse* has included a provision similar to German CC § 680 into his draft of a common civil code for the Nordic countries (*Vinding Kruse*, En nordisk lovbog, 6-14-2 p. 272 et. seq. and 599; *idem*. A Nordic Draft Code, § 1438 p. 379).

31. ENGLISH law does not address damage caused by interveners on any special basis, the supposition being that the general tort law rules of negligence take sufficient account of the particular circumstances and the difficulties faced by a rescuer: cf. *Harrison v. British Railways Board* [1981] 3 All ER 679, 686 (finding of contributory negligence on the part of a rescuer rarely appropriate). The Trustee Act 1925, sec. 61, enables a court to wholly or partly relieve from liability a trustee who has "acted honestly and reasonably, and ought fairly to be excused", but this anomalous provision (which, according to the case law, is seldom satisfied) is explicable as providing protection for a trustee in respect of (inadvertent) breach of those trust law duties which result in strict liability.

IV. *Intervener without Full Legal Capacity*

32. GERMAN Law in CC § 682 provides that an intervener lacking full legal capacity will be responsible only under the provisions relating to compensation for torts. This provision has the character of a reference to the legal basis of a tort law claim, which in particular results in the application of CC arts. 827-829 (Palandt [-*Sprau*], BGB[63], § 682, no. 2). The provision does not state, however, that CC §§ 677 et seq. are only applicable to interveners who have attained full age (Soergel [-*Beuthien*], BGB[12], § 682, no. 1). A similar provision is contained in ESTONIAN CC § 1022 (5).

33. The legal situation arising under GREEK CC art. 735 is virtually identical. Again there is a statutory reference to the legal basis of a tort law claim (Georgiades/Stathopoulos [-*Papanikolaou*], Art. 735, no. 7), which ends in CC arts. 915 et seq. (*Kavkas and Kavkas*, Enochiko Dikaio II, 23). Again CC art. 735 only concerns the question whether an intervener may be held liable; it does not touch upon the possibility of an underage intervener asserting rights provided for under CC art. 736 (*Papanikolaou*, loc.cit. no. 6).

34. In PORTUGAL the liability of an intervener lacking full legal capacity will be determined by the specific rules on tort law contained in CC arts. 488, 489 and 491 (*Almeida Costa*, Obrigações[9], 440; *Pires de Lima and Antunes Varela*, Código Civil Anotado I[4], 449, note 5 under Art. 466). Under CC art. 489 (1) a person lacking full legal capacity is liable on equitable grounds but only subsidiarily, i. e. in the event that the intervener is unable to obtain compensation from the person who was obliged to take charge of the person underage. CC art. 489 (2) only imposes a duty to pay such damages as that person can economically afford without putting his own reasonable livelihood at risk. CC art. 491 effects a liability for presumed defective supervision on the part of the supervisor. The person under supervision has a right of recourse against the supervisor, which may be of value if at a later point in time the latter again comes into money. CC art. 488 (1) provides that no one "who at the instant the act was undertaken for whatever reason was unable to understand or to wilfully act" will be accountable for the consequences of a damaging act "unless he has himself culpably brought about such condition of a merely temporary nature." Under CC art. 488 (2) the absence of accountability is presumed with respect to minors under the age of seven and persons which are completely incapacitated due to mental illness. A minor

is a person under the age of 18 (CC art. 122); minors between the age of 7 and 18 have limited legal capacity (CC art. 123).

35. The liability for damages of an intervener lacking full legal capacity under AUSTRIAN law is likewise restricted to his liability for tortious acts (CC § 1310) (Klang [-*Stanzl*], ABGB IV/1[2], 893). Differing opinions are held on the issue of the intention to act on another's behalf and the duty to render an account where the intervener lacks full legal capacity and the possibility of ratification by the legal representative (see further Rummel [-*Rummel*], ABGB I[3], § 1035 no. 7).

36. Under BELGIAN and FRENCH law the rules of benevolent intervention are applicable to the relationship between the intervener and the principal without restrictions, unless the one of the parties' lack of full legal capacity excludes the application of the law of benevolent intervention altogether (*Marty and Raynaud*, Les obligations. I[2]. Les sources, no. 384 p. 398-399, fn. 1; *Paulus*, Zaakwaarneming, no. 76 p. 48-49). The prevailing opinion characterises liability for damage arising as a result of a breach of duty by an intervener lacking full legal capacity as tortious in nature (*Viney*, Introduction à la responsabilité[2], no. 191 p. 348-349; *Dalcq*, Traité de la responsabilité civile I[2], no. 116 p. 131). In the French legal system this leads to the result that the intervener lacking full legal capacity cannot rely on the defence of *absence de discernement* in order to escape (tortious) liability for an established *faute* (for references see *Flour/Aubert/Savaux*, Le fait juridique[10], no. 101 p. 98-99). By contrast, the rule under BELGIAN law is that it is impossible to assert that a person lacking full legal capacity has acted with tortious *faute* if at the material time that person lacked the ability to distinguish between good and evil (*Van Gerven*, Verbintenissenrecht II[7], 302).

37. SPANISH legal literature (provisions on this point are lacking) is locked in a controversial discussion. Many authors arrive at the conclusion that the general rules on the capacity to conclude legal transactions should be applied (Albaladejo [-*Santos Briz*], Código Civil y compilaciones forales, XXIV, 57), whereas others consider an intervention by a person lacking full legal capacity to be impossible (*Lacruz Berdejo*, Rev.Crít.Der.Inm. 1975, 254).

38. Under ITALIAN CC art. 2029 the intervener must have capacity to conclude legal transactions, whereas the ability to be accountable is sufficient in the case of merely physical acts. Where there is accountability, any liability will be tortious (CC art. 2043) (*Aru*, Gestione d'affari, 27).

39. It appears the issue of liability of an intervener lacking full legal capacity is not discussed in DUTCH law. The solution must be derived from the general rules. Most likely only a tortious liability comes into question since the application *mutatis mutandis* to the law of benevolent intervention of CC art. 3:32 (which provides that legal transactions conducted by a person lacking full legal capacity are voidable) would lead to the result that liability for non-performance of an obligation (CC art. 6:74) is excluded. On the other hand, the act of a child who has not yet turned 14 pursuant to CC art. 6:174 cannot be characterised as a tort. A child's liability for his own actions is replaced by a parental strict liability (CC art. 6:169).

40. In SCOTS law the liability of minors and persons under a disability apparently falls to be decided by the law of delict. Illustrative case law, however, is naturally lacking, because the personal liability of minors will as a general rule be overridden by their parents' liability in respect of supervision (see further *Walker*, The Law of Delict in Scotland, 86).

41. In SWEDISH law both an intervener lacking full legal capacity, including infants, may be subject to tortious liability if their acts are covered by liability insurance (Damages Liability Act [*skadeståndslag* (1972:207)] Ch. 2 § 4). Moreover (this issue is not dealt with by legal literature) the general rules seem to be applicable. Thus tortious liability is imposed on a person lacking full legal capacity with regard to physical acts (in particular for criminal offences, see HD 22 March 1901, NJA 1901, 129) whereas juridical acts will only come into consideration if the legal representative has ratified such acts. As a general rule a person under the age of 18 will lack full legal capacity and is therefore unable to dispose of his own assets or to bind himself (Parents Act [*föräldrabalk* (1949:381) Ch. 9 § 1). As regards tortious liability under FINNISH and DANISH law see the Finnish Act on Liability for Damages (*skadeståndslag*) ch. 2 § 2 and the Danish Act on Liability for Damages (*EAL*) § 24a. Insurance solutions too are of considerable importance for these countries (*von Eyben/Isager*, Lærebog i erstatningsret[5], Ch. 5).

42. In ENGLISH law a minor may be an agent or a bailee, since these arrangements do not depend on the existence of a contract; his minority will not affect his liabilities in tort (arising out of the bailment or gratuitous agency): cf. Clerk and Lindsell (*-Jones*), Torts[18], para. 4-58. The liability of a person of unsound mind will similarly sound in tort (as to which see Clerk and Lindsell (*-Jones*), Torts[18], paras. 4-67- 4-68).

Illustration 2 is taken from Cass. civ. 3 January 1985, Bull. civ. 1985 I, no. 5 p. 4; Gaz. Pal. 1985 pan. 90, obs. *Piedelièvre*; RTD civ. 1985, 575, obs. *Mestre*; **illustration 5** from CA Mons 27 February 1995, Rev. not. b. 1996, 33; and **illustration 6** from CFI Zinnik 10 June 1992, TAgrR 1993, 202.

Chapter 3: Rights and Authority of Intervener

Article 3:101: Right to Indemnification or Reimbursement

The intervener has a right against the principal for indemnification or, as the case may be, reimbursement in respect of an obligation or expenditure (whether of money or other assets) in so far as reasonably incurred for the purposes of the intervention.

Comments

A. Two Core Elements of *negotiorum gestio*

1. **Chapter 3 in overview** The subject-matter of Chapter 3 consists of the rights of the intervener and his authority to act in the name of the principal (Article 3:106). Art. 3:102 concerns the right to remuneration of interveners who act in the course of their profession or trade, Article 3:103 concerns the right to reparation of an intervener who has himself suffered personal injury in the course of a dangerous intervention, Art. 3:104 the reduction or exclusion of the intervener's rights for compensation and Art. 3:105 the principal's right to indemnification against a third party, who is accountable for the causation of damage which the intervener has intended to avert. In practice the most important of the intervener's rights, however, seems to be the right to claim indemnification and reimbursement. These therefore are to be found at the head of the Chapter on the rights of the intervener. These rights in turn are the mirror image of the duties of the principal. If the latter breaches his duties he will have to make reparation for the ensuing damage according to the general rules (PECL chapter 9 section 2). Of course all rules which depend on the existence of a contract between the parties, i. e. PECL arts. 9:503 (Foreseeability), 9:506 (Substitute Transactions) and 9:507 (Current Price), will remain inapplicable.

2. **Reimbursement and indemnification** Article 3:101 contains two core elements of the law of *negotiorum gestio* – as understood at any rate in the continental European legal systems: the claim of the intervener to reimbursement of expenditure, and for indemnification of liabilities incurred. Article 3:101 thus distinguishes between the claim to reimbursement of outlays or other disbursements (reimbursement claims), on the one hand, and the claim for indemnification on the other. In this way the claim to reimbursement is flanked by a claim for indemnification. The intervener can also secure these rights in accordance with general rules by exercising a right of retention: until the principal offers to indemnify the intervener (in respect of his liability to a third party) or reimburse him, the intervener may refuse to deliver up to the principal that which he has obtained in the course of his intervention. PECL art. 7:104 can be applied correspondingly.

B. The Claim for Indemnification

3. **Indemnification** The claim for an indemnification has as its operand the relief of the intervener from any liability he properly incurred. Where possible, he is to be saved having to discharge the liability to a third party from out of his own funds.

> *Illustration 1*
> If A engages B in his own name, in order that B will render benefit to C, then A has a claim against C for C to settle his (A's) liability to B directly or at least to put him (A) in funds in order that he can himself discharge the liability he incurred to B.

4. **Mode of indemnification** The claim to indemnification may be satisfied by the principal in one of two ways according to the principal's election: the principal can make a direct payment to the third party (the intervener's creditor), or he can put the intervener in funds sufficient to enable him in turn to pay the third party. So far as possible and reasonable, the intervener must alert the principal to the existence of the debt before he (the intervener) discharges it himself. If in the circumstances the intervener had to pay before the principal could have an opportunity of doing so himself, then the intervener of course has a claim to reimbursement of the outlay. That claim may be asserted even in the case where the intervener discharged the debt without a compelling ground to do so before the principal's election. However, if in such a case the principal suffers damage because of that, he can set off against the intervener's claim a corresponding claim for damages.

C. The Claim for Reimbursement

5. **Reimbursement** The second remedy is a right to reimbursement. In the context of a claim to reimbursement for burdens the latter may take the form of disbursements of money or the disposal of goods of value ("expenditure (whether of money or other assets)"). A liability incurred is also a "burden", but in that case, for the period before liability is satisfied by a monetary payment, the redress which the intervener is entitled to from the principal is indemnification.

D. General Requirements Applicable to Both Claims

6. **The intervention must be reasonable but need not be successful** The main purpose of the law of benevolent intervention in another's affairs is the protection of the intervener's performance. His remedies are therefore not dependent on an "enrichment" of the principal and thus also not on whether the intervention is in the end successful. It suffices that there was a reasonable ground to attempt the venture. It may be assumed that the principal would likewise have chanced an attempt, had he himself been in the position to make a decision personally.

7. **No restriction to situations of emergency** Article 3:101 does not differentiate between help in a case of emergency and all other manifestations of *negotiorum gestio*. It is enough that it was reasonable to seek to advance or safeguard the principal's interests; it is not possible to draw out different degrees of lesser or greater reasonableness within this test.

8. **Reasonable expenditure** An intervener is entitled in relation to a principal to demand from him the amount of a debt which he, the intervener, incurred in his own name *vis-à-vis* a third party. This claim to indemnification of course only touches upon the internal relationship between the intervener and the principal. Moreover, this claim is subject to the same restrictions to which the reimbursement claim is subject: the obligation incurred must have been reasonable according to its nature and extent. The claims to indemnification and reimbursement are limited to such expenditure as the acting party was entitled to consider reasonable in his situation. In this regard the matter again turns on all the circumstances of the particular case – in particular the special difficulty of forming a view and decision-making in a situation of emergency.

Illustration 2
After damage caused by a storm to the roof on the property of his neighbour Y, the intervener X, on being asked by the roofing contractor he has instructed as to which roof tiles are to be used, indicates roof tiles which are considerably more expensive than those which need replacement. Even if the new roof tiles are of a better quality, the expenses incurred will be unreasonable. X may only demand the (notional) costs of roof tiles which would have matched those which were replaced. Of course it would be different if the old roof tiles are no longer obtainable on the market and X thus had no other choice than to accept the offer made by the contractor. But the expenses would also be unreasonable if under the prevailing and forecast weather conditions a provisional repair would have been possible and it had been known that the principal would soon return. In such a case the decision on a lasting solution should have been left to the principal.

Illustration 3
After a traffic accident a vehicle has to be towed away. The company instructed tows the car to a storage place which belongs to the company but is far away and where further costs are incurred. It would have been possible to bring the vehicle to the owner's place of residence. The company could have easily ascertained the address by asking the police. The costs so far as they exceed the expenses which would have been incurred had the vehicle been towed to the owner's residence are not recoverable.

9. **Interest on expenditure** The draft does not envisage an independent claim to interest on expenditure. The reason for that is that an intervener should be entitled to receive reimbursement only for the disadvantages which he has actually sustained by managing another's affairs and those disadvantages are already covered by the rule. The text proceeds on the footing that an intervener may obtain reimbursement of debt interest which he has paid as much as for interest on his funds in credit which in the concrete circumstances of the case he has had to forego and which he can prove he has

actually foregone; but the intervener is not entitled to a claim for interest foregone in the "abstract" (that is to say, by irrebutable presumption of loss). Hence also it is not necessary to lay down a rule governing the quantum of such an "abstract" claim to interest. The right to interest on expenditure from the point in time at which it is incurred is parasitic on the right to reimbursement. Hence, most obviously, the intervener is entitled to interest only on that expenditure for which he is in law entitled to have reimbursed because it was reasonable for it to be expended; it does not apply to expenditure which was in fact incurred, but which, for the purposes of the right of reimbursement, is disallowed. However, the possibility of claiming compensation for damage caused by the principal's default in reimbursing expenditure incurred or in indemnifying the intervener for liabilities incurred – by resort to a corresponding application of PECL art. 8:106(2) for delay of performance – remains unaffected.

> *Illustration 4*
> The roof of X's historic mansion is severely damaged in a storm while X is on his yacht somewhere in the Atlantic ocean and Y, his helpful neighbour, cannot contact him. Emergency repairs to X's roof must be sensitive to the heritage of its construction (something which to Y's knowledge X sets great store by). There are also paintings and furniture in the endangered upper storey which must be moved to protect them from the elements. All of this is beyond Y's meagre budget, so he obtains a loan from a bank at the going rate. Y is not merely entitled to reimbursement of the loan received from the bank which he has used to pay for the necessary repairs and removals. The interest which he pays to the bank, discharging an obligation which was properly incurred in order to perform the act benefiting the principal, is also expenditure which must be reimbursed and which is subject to interest from the time of payment. The same principle would apply in the case of a hire-purchase. However, Y would not be entitled to any interest on his expenditure if the sum owed by him to the contractors was rather small so that Y could pay it in cash with money that he would not have paid into an interest-bearing account anyway.

10. **Expenditure, whether of money or other assets** If the intervener has paid out money, his claim to reimbursement is in respect of this form of "expenditure." "Expenditure of other assets" encompasses by contrast all patrimonial detriments which are voluntarily sustained, but do not take the form of an outlay of money. "Expenditure" is the umbrella term for obligations incurred, outlays and other contributions. Hence, "expenditure" for the purposes of the intervener's right of reimbursement under Article 3:101 covers not only out of pocket expenses. It extends to any form of wilful disposition out of the intervener's own patrimony responsibly devoted to the cause of the principal's benefit. Thus it will include, for example, the intervener's loss of property when he intentionally disposes of this or when he voluntarily acts to cause its destruction as part of his performance in the principal's interest. (*Involuntary* damage to property may fall to be compensated under Article 3:103 (Right to Reparation)).

Illustration 5
A person who employs his own motor vehicle for the benefit of another may not only claim compensation for the fuel used, but also a compensation for the fact that he could not otherwise make use of his car during the material time.

11. **Services** However, "expenditure" does not extend to investment of labour, for which only professional or commercial interveners may make a claim within the limits provided for in Article 3:102 (Right to Remuneration). This does not mean that the non-professional intervener can never make a claim for remuneration for his labour. He will be able to do so if he can show he has enriched the principal and the enrichment gives rise to a claim under the law of unjustified enrichment.

12. **Loss of income** "Expenditure" likewise excludes any claim for loss of income which the intervener sustains because he was preoccupied with the interests of the principal. That is a matter of damage and not of expenditure in this sense of an outlay or contribution.

Notes

I. *The Right to Indemnification*

1. GERMAN CC § 257 provides that a person who is entitled to claim compensation for expenses may also claim indemnification from liabilities incurred. This rule is also applicable in the law of benevolent intervention (MünchKomm [-*Krüger*], BGB[4], § 257, no. 2). As a rule the debtor obliged to indemnify – in this case the principal – has a right to choose by which means he wants to discharge his duty to indemnify (BGH 8 October 1964, NJW 1965, 249, 251; BGH 11 April 1984, BGHZ 91, 73, 77). He may perform as a third party (CC § 267), may conclude a contract with the creditor on cancellation of the debt in favour of the debtor, may persuade him to waive his claim or agree with him that he (the principal) will assume the obligation and that the intervener be released from the obligation (CC §§ 414, 415). The decisive factor will be that the result which the principal is bound to bring about is realized, namely the intervener's release from the obligation. This result, however, does not occur simply because the party obliged to indemnify another places the amount necessary to discharge the debt to the party claiming indemnification – in the present case the intervener – at the latter's disposal. The principal will be held not to have satisfied the claim for indemnification as long as the money paid to the intervener has not yet been used to discharge the latter's debt. This result is justified on the basis that it is not the person entitled to indemnification but rather the person obliged to indemnify who should bear the risk that the liability is not (completely) discharged, whether because other creditors seize the money or other difficulties arise. The claim for indemnification thus in general focuses exclusively on the liability incurred; the principle of restitution in kind applies (Staudinger [-*Bittner*], BGB[13], § 257, no. 7; Soergel [-M. *Wolf*], BGB[12], § 257, no. 5; Erman [-*Kuckuk*], BGB I[10], § 257, no. 2). As an exception a claim for payment (to him) by the person entitled to indemnification can be made if the claim by the third party is definitely forthcoming (RG 2 December 1911, RGZ 78,

26, 34; RG 12 January 1934, JW 1934, 685). Similar exceptions exist where the party entitled to indemnification has set a deadline (BGH 11 June 1986, NJW-RR 1987, 43), where the third party has assigned its claim to the party entitled to indemnification (BGH 20 March 1978, BGHZ 71, 167, 170) and where the party to be indemnified has been declared bankrupt (BGH 22 September 1971, BGHZ 57, 78, 81; BGH 16 September 1993, NJW 1994, 49). In such situations the claim for indemnification according to prevailing opinion is transformed into a claim for payment (*Krüger*, loc.cit. no. 4 ff; *Bittner, loc.cit.* no. 7 et seq.). However, BGH 8 October 1964, NJW 1965, 249, 251 has held that the claim for indemnification of a commission agent against the principal may also be discharged by the principal making "the purchase money available [to the agent] for the purpose of discharging the seller". According to CA Karlsruhe 11 February 1993, NJW-RR 1994, 1157, 1159 the party obliged to indemnify discharges that obligation by payment only if the party entitled has given consent. POLISH CC art. 753 (2) and ESTONIAN CC § 1023 (1) similarly provide explicitly for the intervener's claim for indemnification.

2. Under GREEK Law the intervener's claim for compensation against the principal may also take the form of a claim for indemnification, if the intervener has incurred a liability to a third party (Georgiades and Stathopoulos [-*Papanikolaou*], Art. 736, no. 9). (By contrast in the law of mandate the claim for indemnification is considered a specification of the claim for reimbursement of expenses: Georgiades and Stathopoulos [-*Karassis*], Art. 722, no. 3.) The indemnification will be effected either by performance of the principal to the third party or by assumption of the obligation pursuant to CC art. 471 (*Karassis*, loc.cit.).

3. Under PORTUGUESE Law the claim for indemnification arises from a synthesis of CC arts. 471, 1182 and 595 (1). The intervener who conducts legal transactions for the principal in his own name acts as a "*gestão não representative*". In such a case CC art. 471 refers to the provisions of CC arts. 1180 to 1184. The intervener is obliged to assign the rights obtained to the principal (CC art. 1181 (1)) and the principal may assert the claims which the intervener has acquired (CC art. 1181 (2)). On the other hand the principal has to assume the obligations the intervener has incurred (CC art. 1182). This assumption of liability may be effected either by a contract between the old and the new debtor and the corresponding consent of the creditor (CC art. 595 (1)(a)) or by means of a contract between the new debtor and the creditor, which does not require the consent of the old debtor (CC art. 595 (1)(b)). If the principal is unable to assume the obligation then he will have to provide the intervener with the necessary funds to discharge the debt in advance or refund such costs (CC art. 1182). If the creditor refuses consent to the assumption of the obligation by the principal, then intervener and principal will be jointly liable to the creditor (CC art. 595(2)).

4. A claim for indemnification likewise arises under AUSTRIAN Law (Rummel [-*Rummel*] ABGB I^3 § 1035 no. 2). In the commentaries – the Code is silent on this question – it is argued that an obligation incurred may constitute compensable expenditure (Klang [-*Stanzl*], ABGB $IV/1^2$, 898). This in turn would mean that the intervener has a claim for the amount due under the obligation he has incurred but not yet discharged. A right of the intervener to request payment in advance of his outlay, however, is apparently not accepted in the case law (OGH 4 June 1987, SZ 60/100 [which, however, concerns a case within the scope of CC § 1037]; Schwimann [-*Apathy*], ABGB V^2, § 1036-1040 no. 10).

5. FRENCH, BELGIAN and LUXEMBOURGIAN CC art. 1375 oblige the principal to 'compensate' the intervener for obligations incurred by the latter in his own name and which therefore only bind the intervener. Thus the principal has to refund the costs incurred by the intervener who has already discharged his obligations (JClCiv [-*Bout*], Art. 1372 à 1375, Fasc. 20 no. 68). If the intervener has not yet discharged his obligations then according to French legal literature the principal has to exonerate him from his liability. To this end the principal may directly discharge the obligation or propose to the third party an assumption of obligation with the effect of releasing the intervener from his debt (which of course will only take effect if the third party agrees to the proposal) (*Bout*, loc.cit.). As regards Belgian academic analysis it is merely stated that the principal has to exonerate the intervener from the liabilities, compensate him in respect of them and release him from his obligations. The intervener may request the principal either present a receipt made out by the third party or prove that the third party has agreed to an assumption of liability (*De Page*, Droit Civil Belge II[3], no. 1091 p. 1153). MALTESE CC art. 1018 provides for both the intervener's right to indemnification and his right to reparation for expenses incurred.

6. Under SPANISH CC art. 1893 (1) the principal is liable to the intervener "for obligations which have been incurred in the interest of the principal". This is a consequence of the principal's duty to compensate for damages which includes a duty to exonerate the intervener from all liabilities to third parties independent of their particular legal basis (*Pasquau Liaño*, La gestión de negocios ajenos, 154). If the intervener acts in his own name then of course the principal is only obliged vis-à-vis the intervener (*Pasquau Liaño*, loc.cit. 155). A third party in this case may not assert a claim directly against the principal (*Sánchez Jordán*, Gestión de negocios, 615; TS 9 February 1957, RAJ 1957 no. 701 p. 448).

7. Subject to the condition that the intervention has been commenced profitably ITALIAN CC art. 2031 imposes the duty on the principal to discharge the obligations the intervener has incurred in the principal's name and to indemnify the intervener for all liabilities incurred to which the intervener has committed himself. In the latter case the principal will have to provide such funds to the intervener as are necessary in order that all liabilities can be discharged (*Bianca*, Diritto civile, 3, Il contratto[2], 150).

8. Under DUTCH Law the intervener may likewise act in his own name or in the name of the principal (CC arts. 6:198 and 6:201). The intervener will most likely choose the first alternative, so it is said, in a case of minor outlay or if his contract partner insists on concluding the contract with the intervener and not with a principal he does not know. (Asser [-*Hartkamp*], Verbintenissenrecht III[10], no. 305, p. 317). The new CC no longer expressly provides for a right to indemnification. (By contrast CC art. 1393 in force until the end of 1991 did provide such rule, though details were disputed.) The current CC art. 6:200 (1) obliges the principal to compensate the intervener for 'damage' sustained, whereby the term 'damage' covers both expenses sustained and the outlays which he has incurred. Whether or not incurring an obligation may in itself be regarded as 'damage' for these purposes seems to be unresolved.

9. SCOTS law obliges the principal to discharge the intervener from all obligations which the latter has incurred in the course of the intervention (*Bell*, § 541; *Erkine*, Volume II, 52; Stair [-*Whitty*], The Laws of Scotland, XV, para 127). In SCANDINAVIAN legal literature the question of a right to indemnification has not been discussed in the context of benevolent intervention. In the context of the law of mandate the rule is

that the principal will only be obliged to make advance payment if this has been contractually agreed or is to be inferred in the circumstances (*Hellner*, Speciell Avtalsrätt. II (1): Kontraktsrätt. Särskilda avtal[3], 211). For some specific areas, such as insolvency law, there are particular provisions on the right to request advance payment. However, a general right to indemnification is apparently unknown in Nordic patrimonial law.

10. The COMMON LAW likewise recognises a right on the part of an agent of necessity to call upon the principal to discharge an obligation which, by virtue of the authority conferred by the necessituous situation, the agent has incurred to a third party: cf. *Stoljar*, Agency, 155. Where he has control of the principal's property, he may have a lien over or a right to recoup from that property: cf. *Selby v. Jackson* (1843) 6 Beav 192 at 202-203, 49 ER 799 at 803 (Lord *Langdale* MR). Of course, where the agent has concluded the contract in the principal's name, the principal is bound directly to the third party: see, for instance, *Gunn v. Roberts* (1874) LR 9 CP 331, 335 (*Brett* J: obligation to pay for supplies or repay money advanced). An equitable right to indemnification, even if the intervener is not formally a trustee, exists in favour of a person who with good cause takes upon himself the management of the property of a person who is incapable of making decisions for themselves: cf. *Selby v. Jackson*, loc. cit. at 202-203 (803) (Lord *Langdale* MR), affirmed (1844) unreported (Lord *Lyndhurst* LC). By statute (when it comes into force) an intervener acting in connection with the care or treatment of a person who is reasonably believed to lack capacity, reasonably believing it to be in that person's best interests to act, and incurring expenditure as a result will have a right under English law to reimburse himself from money in that person's possession or be otherwise indemnified: Mental Capacity Act 2005, sec. 8(2).

II. *Claim for Reimbursement*

11. The claim for reimbursement is less problematic in all jurisdictions. GERMAN CC provides for a claim in §§ 683, 677, 670, according to which the justified intervener may demand reimbursement of his expenditure like an agent. Expenditure within the meaning of CC § 670 encompasses the voluntary sacrifice of valuable assets (BGH 10 November 1988, NJW 1989, 1284, 1285; Soergel [-*Beuthien*], BGB[12], § 670, no. 2). Expenses need not necessarily take the form of disbursement of money. They may also be of a legal nature (e. g. incurring an obligation: BGH 23 February 1981, NJW 1981, 1502, 1503) or physical (e. g. excessive overuse of a thing) (*Beuthien* loc.cit. 2). Only expenditure which the intervener was entitled to regard as necessary is compensable, but the matter will not depend on whether or not it was (in the end) beneficial (BGH 12 July 1993, NJW-RR 1994, 87). The principal has to bear the risk of expenditure where the outcome is not a success (Staudinger [-*Wittmann*], BGB[13], § 670, no. 2). Under CC §§ 256 and 246 the principal is obliged to pay 4% interest on the intervener's expenditure from the point in time the intervener incurred it; default is not a requirement.

12. Under ESTONIAN CC § 1023 (1) and GREEK CC art. 736 too the intervener enjoys a claim, like an agent under the law of mandate, to compensation for expenditure which he properly held to be necessary; this will not depend on whether or not the intervention has turned out to be successful (Georgiades and Stathopoulos [-*Papanikolaou*], Art. 736, no. 2). Thus expenditure without success is compensable if the intervener

was entitled to regard them as reasonable in view of the aim to which he aspired. The claim encompasses statutory interest form the point in time the expenditure is incurred (CC art. 301; for details see also CA Thessaloniki 1139/1992, Arm 46/1992, 712). The claim for reimbursement is independent of whether the intervener has invested his own money or has merely managed another's funds (A. P. 580/1953, NoB 2/1954, 168).

13. PORTUGUESE CC art. 468 (1) obliges the principal to reimburse necessary expenditure which an intervener has incurred in the course of a lawful act, including interest thereon from the day the expenditure was incurred. According to the wording of the provision all expenses are compensable "which the intervener held to be necessary". It is not required that the expenses were indispensable (*indispensáveis*); it will suffice that for good reason the intervener considered them to be necessary (*necessárias*). Thus it is possible that the principal may be obliged to reimburse expenses which from an objective perspective have not had a beneficial impact (*Menezes Leitão*, Obrigações I[3], 497). The claim for reimbursement also arises in a case of an intervention which was originally unlawful but has subsequently been ratified by the principal (CC art. 469 in conjunction with CC art. 468 (1)).

14. Under AUSTRIAN law the intervener's claim for reimbursement of expenditure will be allowed in a case of intervention in an emergency (CC § 1036) as in a case of beneficial intervention within the meaning of CC § 1037, together with interest (OGH 5 March 1963 EvBl 1963/309). In the case of CC § 1036 necessary and purposive expenditure must be reimbursed, even if the intervention has proved unsuccessful. Whether expenditure was necessary and purposive will be determined by means of an objective test according to the presumed view of a diligent third party who is hypothetically placed in the intervener's shoes at the material time of action (Schwimann [-*Apathy*], ABGB V[2], § 1036-1040 no. 11; Rummel [-*Rummel*], ABGB I[3], § 1036 no. 3; *Koziol and Welser*, Grundriss II[12], 365; *Meissel*, GoA, 170). As regards the rescue of things, besides the reimbursement of expenditure the intervener may also claim under CC § 403 a reward in the maximum amount of 10% of the value of the asset secured, though this claim is almost irrelevant in practice (*Rummel*, loc.cit. no. 5, *Meissel*, loc.cit. 39). In cases within the scope of CC § 1037 a claim for reimbursement of expenditure is only granted if a clear and predominant benefit of the principal was achieved. CC § 1037 resembles an unjustified enrichment claim (*Meissel*, loc.cit. 14, 172). The intervener bears the risk that the intervention remains unsuccessful; in addition he has to prove the benefit achieved (*Apathy* loc.cit. no. 12). POLISH CC arts. 754, 755 and 757 similarly draw a distinction in relation to the requirements for reimbursement of expenditure between the different emanations of benevolent intervention and in particular between prevention of damage in a case of emergency and an act which was not based on "compelling necessity" (CC art. 755).

15. BELGIAN, FRENCH and LUXEMBOURGIAN CC art. 1375 oblige the principal to reimburse to the intervener all expenses which were useful or necessary; the intervener should not have to shoulder disadvantages arising from his altruistic intervention (JClCiv [-*Bout*], Art. 1372 à 1375, Fasc. 20 no. 51). Expenses are necessary if they serve the 'preservation of the affair'; they are useful if they serve its 'improvement' (JClCiv [-*Bout*], Art. 1372 à 1375, Fasc. 20 no. 52); the category of useful expenses encompasses necessary expenses (*Bout*, loc.cit.; *Paulus*, Zaakwaarneming no. 83 p. 51). In FRANCE too expenses are compensable although they have proved to be useless (Cass. req. 28 February 1910, D. 1911, I, 137, note *Dupuich*), whereas in BELGIUM such

expenses are apparently not covered (*Paulus*, loc.cit.; *RPDB*, v° Quasi-contrat, no. 74). In French legal literature it is asserted that only expenses actually incurred are compensable. An intervener who discharges a debt by transfer of negotiable instruments which at the time of transfer have a market value below their nominal value may only claim reimbursement of the market value (*Bout*, loc.cit. no. 55). In both countries by means of analogous application of CC art. 2001 the courts grant the intervener a claim for interest on the funds disbursed (Cass. civ. 12 June 1979, Bull. civ. 1979, I, no. 173 p. 140; D. 1979 IR 539; Defrénois 1980, art. 32421, p. 1215, obs. *Aubert*; CA Brussel 7 February 1964, Pas. belge 1965, II, 70). The interest rate is that of statutory interest (*Malaurie/Aynès/Stoffel-Munck*, Droit civil. Les obligations, no. 1033 p. 537).

16. Under SPANISH CC art. 1893 the principal is obliged to reimburse the intervener for necessary and useful expenses. There does not seem to be case law elaborating on what expenses are considered to be necessary and useful. Academic commentaries refer to the corresponding terminology to be found in the law of possession in CC arts. 453 and 454 (Paz-Ares/Diez-Picazo/Bercovitz/Salvador [-*Lasarte*], Código Civil II, 1951). From this it follows that payment for the reasonable preservation and storage of goods are compensable as are costs which have served in a suitable manner to improve or increase the value of an asset (Paz-Ares/Diez-Picazo/Bercovitz/Salvador [-*Miquel González*], Código Civil I, 452-453).

17. ITALIAN CC art. 2031 provides *inter alia* that the principal has to reimburse the intervener for all necessary or useful expenditure (together with statutory interest form the day the expenditure was incurred). The intervener's claim for reimbursement of expenses is secured by means of a right of retention (*Aru*, Gestione d'affari, 54). This claim for reimbursement goes beyond the claim arising from the law of unjustified enrichment under CC art. 2041. Usefulness and necessity of the expenditure are assessed according to the standard of a *bonus paterfamilias*. The principal's obligation is a 'real value' obligation because it imposes a duty to compensate (*Breccia*, La gestione d'affari[2], 898).

18. Under DUTCH CC art. 6:200 (1) the principal is obliged to compensate the intervener for any damage which the latter has sustained in managing the principal's affair if the intervener has attended to the principal's interests properly. The concept of 'damage' (which must be interpreted in a wide sense) enompasses costs and expenses as well as the value of spent goods and interest foregone. In contrast to the law of unjustified enrichment it is not a requirement that the principal has obtained any real benefit. It will suffice that the intervention has been undertaken properly, i. e. that the intervener was entitled to assume that the expenses would contribute to the principal's benefit. The extent of the damage will be assessed according to the general rules of CC arts. 6:95 et seq. (T. M. Parlementaire Geschiedenis VI, 795; Asser [-*Hartkamp*], Verbintenissenrecht III[11], no. 311, p. 320-321).

19. The justified intervener is likewise granted a claim for reimbursement of expenditure against the principal under SCOTS law. This claim will cover all necessary useful expenditure, which the intervener has incurred in the course of the intervention. The intervener is also entitled to interest on his outlay on a commercial basis (*Bell*, § 541; *Erskine*, Book III, Vol. II, 52; Stair [-*Whitty*], The Laws of Scotland, XV, para 126).

20. The intervener's claim for reimbursement in general is also acknowledged in the NORDIC countries even though there is hardly any case law on this issue (for an extraordinary case see Danish HD 24 May 1937, UfR 1937, 697: reimbursement of

postal charges of 70 øre). Whether the claim for reimbursement includes a claim for interest cannot be stated beyond doubt because in the cases already decided only interest payable from commencement of proceedings has apparently been claimed (interest as from service of process) (Danish HD 3 December 1936, UfR 1937, 357; 26 October 1906, UfR 1907, 54). Swedish HD 29 March 1978, NJA 1978, 144 concerned a claim for recourse in respect of child maintenance (governed by superseded family law rules) between the husband of the mother and the biological father; interest was granted from the time of service of process in respect of the claim and not from the time the judgment declaring fatherhood (out of wedlock) became res iudicata. Whether or not a general principle may be inferred from this judgment, however, has yet to be resolved.

21. In ENGLISH law too a person who acts as agent of necessity and reasonably incurs expenses has a right to reimbursement: *Gaudet v. Brown* (1872) LR 5 PC 134, 165 (Sir *Montague Smith*, for the PC); *Petrinovic & Co Ltd v. Mission Francaise des Transports des Maritimes* (1941) 71 Ll L R 208, 222 (*Atkinson* J); *China Pacific SA v. Food Corpn of India* [1982] AC 939, 965D-F (Lord *Simon*). Thus a carrier of an animal who is forced to provide it with food and shelter because it is not collected at its destination will have a claim for reimbursement of the costs: *Great Northern Ry Co v. Swafield* (1874) LR 9 Ex 132. The right to reimbursement extends to the costs of contacting the principal in order to ascertain his instructions: see *Pocahontas Fuel Co (Incorporated) v. Ambatielos* (1922) 27 Com Cas 148, 156 (*McCardie* J), and contrast the earlier position impliedly stated by Sir *Robert Phillimore* in *The St. Lawrence* (1880) 5 PD 250, 253. The right to reimbursement of expenses reasonably incurred is a manifestation of a broader principle applicable to all agents acting within the scope of their authority: *Leigh v. Dickeson* (1884) 15 QBD 60, 64 (*Brett* MR: "If a person is employed in a business which requires an expenditure in order that it may be carried on, [...] the principal must indemnify his agent for the expenditure which he incurs"), and see also *Fridman*, Agency[5], 47, and specifically in relation to the claim in equity of fiduciary agents *Wallersteiner v. Moir (No. 2)* [1975] QB 373, 391G-H (Lord *Denning* MR), 403F (*Buckley* LJ) and 407B-C (*Scarman* LJ). This holds even if the agent has acted in error and the intervention has not resulted in benefit to the principal, provided the measure taken was reasonable and justified in the circumstances: *Tetley & Co. v. British Trade Corporation* (1922) 10 Ll. L.Rep. 678; *John Koch Ltd v. C & H Products Ltd* [1956] 2 Lloyd's Rep 59). Where the agent is also liable to surrender to the principal benefits obtained as a result of the agency, the agent will have a right of retention in the form of a possessory lien to protect his claim to reimbursement: see Chapter 2, Art. 2:102, Notes I, 22. The main difficulty, however, is that a right to reimbursement or recompense in cases of necessitous intervention outside the recognised categories of agency of necessity is not wholeheartedly assured by the existing case law. According to one *dictum* even a person who procures medical assistance for an unconscious person found lying in the street (e.g, by driving them to hospital) has apparently no common law right to reimbursement for the expenses incurred (*Schneider v Eisovitch* [1960] 2 QB 430, 438 (*Paull* J)), though a clearer case of supply of a necessary to a person incapable of contracting for themselves could hardly be envisaged.

Illustration 2 is taken from *Paulus*, Zaakwaarneming no. 83 p. 51; **illustration 3** from OGH 21 April 1982, JBl 1984, 256; **illustration 5** from BGH 15 December 1975, BGHZ 65, 384.

Article 3:102: Right to Remuneration

(1) The intervener has a right to remuneration in so far as the intervention is reasonable and undertaken in the course of the intervener's profession or trade.
(2) The remuneration due is the amount, so far as reasonable, which is ordinarily paid at the time and place of intervention in order to obtain a performance of the kind undertaken.

Comments

A. Remuneration of Professionals (Para (1))

1. **Should there be a right to remuneration?** Para (1) confers on persons who intervene in the course of their profession or trade a claim to remuneration. That they should have such a claim is by no means self-evident. The substantive appropriateness of such a rule, which can be found in many, but certainly not all legal systems of the European Union, can indeed be disputed in terms of legal policy. Is it at all possible to maintain that someone who demands remuneration for his action predominantly advances another's interests? Is it not a contradiction of the "spirit" of the law of benevolent intervention in another's affairs to allow a claim to remuneration? And why should a lay person not have the same rights as someone who undertakes the intervention in the course of his or her trade or profession?

2. **Underlying policy considerations of the rule** The first question can doubtless be answered affirmatively. All that the intervener has to demonstrate is that the conditions of Article 1:101 (Intervention to Benefit Another) are met. A doctor helping someone who lies unconscious or a breakdown recovery service salvaging a car which has been involved in an accident and whose owner has already been admitted to hospital are capable of acting predominantly with the intention of helping the person concerned. That they ultimately submit a bill for their service does not change their state of mind at the time of acting. The matter only becomes problematic when the active party mentally inverts the relationship between the reason for and the consequences of his action – in other words, when he acts predominantly for the purposes of acquiring a right to remuneration. Such persons are not *gestors* and consequently are assigned to the law of unjustified enrichment (including its restrictive rules on unsolicited enrichments).

> *Illustration 1*
> X, a genealogist, earns a considerable part of his income by professionally 'searching for heirs'. He reacts to public announcements of estates of persons who according to the knowledge of the authority in charge do not have any relatives and thus no successors. At the expiration of the time-limit indicated in the announcement the intestate estate will devolve to the state. X succeeds in tracing a relative (Y) of a deceased person and offers to disclose to him the necessary information for a consideration of 20% of the inheritance. In order to indicate the reliability of the offer X discloses some vague information. Y declines the contract

offered. However the information provided suffices to locate the authority concerned and to accept the inheritance. Y is not indebted to X.

The claim to remuneration under para (1) is thus conceived as a claim consequential on an undertaking which was *not* rendered with a view to an expected counter-performance. Such a claim, however, does not in any way contradict the 'spirit' of the law of benevolent intervention in another's affairs.

Illustration 2
I, a professional shipping agent by means of a justified benevolent intervention in the course of an auction purchases three tank ships for F. P is obliged to pay to I the usual remuneration for such action.

3. **Remuneration only for professionals** There are good reasons of legal policy for treating private individuals differently from persons who intervene in the course of their profession or trade. Firstly, a "pro" gives a greater input than an amateur so that the former's performance from the perspective of the benefited party is as a rule simply more valuable than the latter's. In this respect the rule supports both core elements of *negotiorum gestio*: the protection of the performance of the intervener and (albeit on a lower plane) the aspect of usefulness of the undertaking anticipated at the time of its commencement. Related to this is the further argument that remuneration is justified for provision of a professional level of performance as a correlative of the higher (professional) standard of care to which an intervener who acts as a professional will be implicitly subject under Article 2:101(1)(a) (see comment B6 under that provision). Additionally the law of benevolent intervention in another's affairs aims to establish incentives for humane action. For professional providers of services the incentives to act must be more pronounced than for private individuals.

4. **The main policy consideration** One can of course muster against the rule the fact that it may make no difference to the aspect of the intention to benefit another, which is at the same time constitutive of *negotiorum gestio*, whether the action falls within the intervener's professional or commercial field of activity. The argument would then run that a *gestor* always acts "privately". However, this objection too is not convincing: a *gestor* who, from lack of time, expertise or ability, does not trust himself to do what is required may naturally commission a professional to undertake it and he can then pass the bill to the principal. Assuming this starting position it makes no sense to cut off from the possibility of billing for his services a *gestor* who himself becomes active in the context of his profession. That is probably the strongest policy consideration in favour of the rule. Furthermore, the criterion of reasonableness ensures that the intervener as a rule is only authorised to undertake provisional measures.

5. **"undertaken in the course of the intervener's profession or trade"** Moreover, it must always be examined whether assistance is actually rendered "in the course of the intervener's profession or trade". Falling under that rubric, for example, would be a doctor who while on holiday gives aid at the hotel to a fellow guest who has fallen unconscious beside the swimming pool, but it would not cover someone who at the

point in time when he undertakes the relevant activity no longer practises his profession or has ceased to pursue his trade (for example, a doctor who has retired).

6. **Non-profit organisations** The formula "profession or trade" includes not-for-profit organisations. If such organisations, constituted as legal persons, intervene, they will often equate to "trade" on account of the legal form which their organisation takes, irrespective of the fact that they are not orientated towards making a (distributable) profit. Where the applicable national law does not allow for that outcome, such organisations are encompassed by the expression "profession" if and to the extent that they have been formed for the purpose of rendering assistance, they have rendered that assistance to a professional standard and the intervention in question stems from their activity in that area.

7. **Reasonableness** The claim to remuneration – just like the claims under Article 3:101 (Right to Indemnification or Reimbursement) – requires that the measure undertaken was reasonable according to its nature and extent. More often than not it will only be reasonable to undertake provisional measures and thus all services rendered beyond this will, if at all, only confer a claim for compensation according to the rules of unjustified enrichment. In any case no claim for remuneration will arise under the law of benevolent intervention.

B. Quantum of Remuneration (Para (2))

8. **The usual price** With regard to the quantum of remuneration, the basic principle is that the principal must pay for that breadth of performance which the principal himself, had he been in a position to do so, would reasonably have had to commission. To make this notion more concrete the Article takes as the fundamental benchmark the usual price at the time and place of the intervention. Where tables of fees exist (e. g. for the services of self-employed persons), these are to be adopted.

9. **"so far as reasonable"** The economic activities of life are, however, so multifarious that this rule too must be subject to the general test of reasonableness. It may be that the intervener must act at a multitude of different places, but it is not sensible to ascertain an individual customary price for each of them. One can contemplate cases in which a *gestor* was overqualified for the performance which he rendered, but there was nobody else available who could have rendered it. Other cases which can be imagined include those for which no bearable expenditure would yield a local market price. In such cases the judge is left with no other choice than to make a general evaluation of all the circumstances of the particular case. Where assistance is rendered to someone who lacks full legal capacity, that may likewise be a relevant factor for the purposes of para (2). Had a person (in the language of *negotiorum gestio*: the principal) himself been able to conclude a contract for the assistance rendered to him – exceptionally so, precisely because it was aid in an emergency situation – no further considerations are required. On the other hand, had the principal not been in a position legally to conclude a contract, the case in this special situation resolves according to its nature into an

unjustified enrichment claim and that must be taken into consideration in calculating the quantum of the claim.

Notes

I. *The Foundation of the Claim to Remuneration*

1. The basic rule of the law of benevolent intervention more or less everywhere is that the intervener will not be remunerated for his activity. However, there are a number of exceptions from this basic rule which exactly concern the group of persons which Article 3:102 has in view. Some of them have been developed by case law and are therefore not provided for in the wording of the Codes. As regards GERMAN law the principle (i. e. no remuneration) is inferred from the reference contained in CC § 683 to mandate law, which according to CC 662 is a gratuitous contract for services. Case law (BGH 15 December 1975, BGHZ 65, 384, 390; BGH 7 March 1989, NJW-RR 1989, 970; BGH 21 October 1999, BGHZ 143, 9, 16) and legal literature (e. g. *Medicus*, Schuldrecht II BT[12], no. 626) maintain by contrast that a right to remuneration is appropriate if the benevolent intervention is within the scope of the intervener's profession or trade, as in the case of a doctor who renders assistance to a person lying unconscious or a breakdown recovery service which tows away a car in order to clear the road. This result is founded on an analogous application of CC § 1835 (3) under which compensable expenses of a guardian also include such services "which fall within his trade or profession", (cf. Staudinger (-*Wittmann*)[13], § 683 no. 3 and *Medicus* loc.cit.).
2. The same result is arrived at in GREECE. The intervener has a claim to remuneration if the activity undertaken as benevolent intervention belongs to his trade or profession (Georgiades and Stathopoulos [-*Papanikolaou*], Art. 736, no. 11; *Filios*, Enochiko Dikaio I/2, 203; but taking a different view, *Kavkas and Kavkas*, Enochiko Dikaio II, 25). The *travaux preperatoire* to the Greek CC (Schedion Astikou Kodikos, II: Enochikon Dikaion, 232: doctor attending to an injured person) and the case law (CA Athen 6980/1987, EllDik 30/1989, 805) have confirmed this approach. ESTONIAN CC § 1023 (2) has codified this concept; the rule corresponds in all its material parts with Article 3:102. HUNGARIAN CC § 486 (2) contains a reference to the law of mandate, which in CC § 478 (2) makes it clear that "the agent shall be entitled to demand remuneration even if his actions brought no results. The principal shall be entitled to reduce the remuneration or refuse to pay it if he is able to prove that success was not achieved in part or in whole for a reason for which the agent is responsible" (Official Translation, Hungarian Legal Regulations in Force in three Languages, CompLex CD HMJ, 2004).
3. PORTUGUESE CC art. 470 (1) in conjunction with CC art. 1158 (2) only provides for a right to remuneration where the intervention was undertaken in the course of a profession. The prime examples for such *gestão mista* concerns assistance rendered by lawyers (see also CCP art. 41 (1)) and doctors (*Almeida Costa*, Obrigações[9], 441). Non-professional interveners are not entitled to remuneration. This is criticized in part on policy grounds; the rule is considered to be out-dated because it should be presumed now that any service is provided in return for payment. Notwithstanding its sponta-

neous nature a *gestão de negócios* constitutes a provision of services (*Menezes Leitão*, Obrigações I[3], 497).

4. AUSTRIAN law on the face of the CC likewise does not grant the intervener any claim to remuneration (*v. Zeiller*, Commentar III § 1039 no. 3 p. 324). The only exception provided for may be found in CC § 403 (salvage award in a case of a successful intervention), a provision to which CC § 1036 makes reference. According to recent settled case law a claim for compensation for the loss of time will be granted if (and only if) the intervener has undertaken the intervention in the course of his profession or trade (OGH 26 November 1981, SZ 54/176; further references in RIS-Justiz RS 0019940). As a rationale for this position it is asserted that although also in the case of professional services the claim is confined as such to reimbursement of expenditure, the professional intervener has a right to compensation for loss of earnings. A loss of earnings will be presumed, which as a result leads to a claim to remuneration (Rummel [-*Rummel*], ABGB I[3], § 1036 no. 4; Schwimann [-*Apathy*], ABGB V[2], § 1036-1040 no. 10) at any rate if, as in the case law, the loss of earnings is irrebuttably presumed (OGH 3 October 1996, RdW 1997, 275; see further *Fötschl*, ERPL 2002, 550, 553).

5. As regards FRANCE the legal situation seems to be in a state of flux. Until recently case law has adhered to the principle of CC art. 1375, whereby the intervener only has a claim for compensation and no claim for either remuneration or fees (CA Paris 7 July 1989, Juris Data 1989-023369; Cass.civ. 15 December 1992, Bull.civ. 1992, IV, no. 415 p. 293). For costs incurred even the exact amount has to be verified; a judgment for payment of a lump sum which would result in the granting of a remuneration is unlawful (Cass.civ. 19 February 2002, Juris Data 2002-013264). Cass. req. 10 January 1910, D. 1911, I, 370 (which affirmed a claim to remuneration) has thus long ceased to good law. On the hand, recent case law on the concept of *gestion d'affaires intéressée* must be taken into account. It is possible that Cass. civ. 18 April 2000, Bull. civ. 2000, I, no. 113 p. 76 has established that a *rémunération* for the intervener in the context of this sub-category of *gestion d'affaires* may be conceivable. The official headnote states that an undertaking which has rendered services as *gérant d'affaires* for the account of another undertaking may as a rule only claim compensation for expenditure "unless the undertaking has also acted in its own interest".

6. In BELGIUM the prevailing opinion is that the principal as a general rule is obliged to pay remuneration to the intervener. Such remuneration should not be regarded as real remuneration, but rather as a monetary compensation for the time, the knowledge and professional skills which the intervener has contributed. A remuneration is due in particular where the intervener has acted in the course of his profession (*B. H.Verb.* [-*Roodhooft*], December 2003, Hdst. V, De quasi-contracten, no. 2249).

7. SPANISH CC does not provide for a right to remuneration. The case law has even on one occasion stated that a person who requests remuneration may not even qualify as an intervener because they have no intention to benefit another (TS 15 June 1925, cited, inter alia, by *Pasquau Liaño*, La gestión de negocios ajenos, 158). Thus any claims must be based on the law of unjustified enrichment; the law of benevolent intervention does not even confer a right to remuneration on interveners who act in the course of their profession. However, this solution is almost unanimously criticized (*Lacruz Berdejo*, Rev.Crít.Der.Inm. 1975, 269; *Sánchez Jordán*, Gestión de negocios, 550; *Lete del Río*, Obligaciones II[3], 128; *Pasquau Liaño*, loc.cit. 411; *Lasarte*, Principios

II5, 309) and an effort is made to find a basis for its rectification, *inter alia* by means of reference to CC art. 1711 or an extension of the concept of damage under CC art. 1893 (Paz-Ares/Diez-Picazo/Bercovitz/Salvador [-*Lasarte*], Código Civil II, 1952). It may be that TS 23 July 1999, RAJ 1999 (4) no. 6355 p. 9958 has signalled a change in the case law. In its judgment the *Tribunal Supremo* dismissed a claim for remuneration made by an architect who had acted without authority, but it based this decision on the fact that the requirements of CC art. 1893 were not satisfied; there was no reference to the principle that a claim for remuneration is unknown in the law of benevolent intervention. (As this did not concern an emergency, it would have been a prerequisite that the intervener had made use of the plans, which was not the case.) CA Barcelona 12 February 2004, Aranzadi Civil 6/2004 no. 434 p. 832 likewise heads in this direction, as in that case the plaintiff had undertaken the bookkeeping for a condominium association without authority and a remuneration was granted for this activity.

8. Similarly the prevailing opinion in ITALY maintains that the intervener has no claim for remuneration against the principal because CC art. 1709 is not applicable in the law of benevolent intervention (*Breccia*, La gestione d'affari2, 899). A principal who pays the intervener effects a so-called rewarding gift (CC art. 770; *Aru*, Gestione d'affari, 55). However, a right to remuneration has been granted in one case where the principal had ratified the intervention (CFI Firenze 31 May 1948, Mon.Trib. 1949, 90, cited by *Breccia*, loc.cit. 899, fn. 12).
9. Notwithstanding that a claim for damages under DUTCH CC arts. 6:95 et seq. may also include lost profits and loss of earnings (CC art. 6:96), the law of benevolent intervention only exceptionally provides for a claim to remuneration. One such exception is set out in CC art. 6:200 (2), which reads: "Where a manager of another's affair has acted in the conduct of a business or profession, he has, to the extent that this is reasonable, the further right to be paid for his activities in accordance with the prices usually charged for such activities at the time of his management of another's affairs". A second exception may be found in the law concerning lost property (CC art. 5:10 (2)).
10. In SCOTS law the view has become accepted that an intervener who has acted for altruistic reasons may not claim remuneration (Stair [-*Whitty*], The Laws of Scotland, XV, para 126 with reference to the Institutional Writers, of which only *Stair* favours a claim for remuneration of services).
11. The legal position of the NORDIC countries is not easily ascertained. With regard to DANISH case law it may perhaps be inferred from HD 24 May 1937, UfR 1937, 697 that a claim to remuneration is rejected (see *Håstad*, Tjänster utan uppdrag, 70, cautiously arguing in this direction). However, it is possible that this decision was predicated by curious facts and too much may be read into it. There does not appear to be further case law in point. Within SWEDISH legal literature (again there is no case law) it is argued there is a claim to remuneration subject to the condition that the activity undertaken was not a (physical) act pure and simple or an act of friendship. Claims to remuneration may be considered in a case involving extensive measures or if the *gestor* acts in the course of his profession or trade (*Håstad*, loc.cit. 68 et seq.).
12. In the COMMON LAW systems a right to remuneration must ordinarily be based either on contractual agreement or a restitutionary claim such as *quantum meruit* based on unjustified enrichment. Unless provided for in a contract between them, the mere discharge of duties as an agent of necessity does not as a rule entitle the agent to

remuneration from the principal. However, at any rate where the intervention has proved beneficial to the principal and the intervener is under a duty to surrender profits, Equity will make an allowance for the labour and skill which the intervener has invested if what has been done goes beyond fulfilment of basic duties: see, for instance, *Brown v. Litton* (1711) 1 P Wms 140, 24 ER 329; 10 Mod 20, 88 ER 606 (*Harcourt* LK) (investment of deceased's money on behalf of executrix in trade). There is less than overwhelming authority in favour of a restitutionary claim to remuneration (e. g. for the value of pure services rendered) in a case of necessituous intervention, even though it is recognised that (in conrast to salvage) *quantum meruit* does not depend on the success of the venture: cf. *Aitchison v. Lohre* (1879) 4 App Cas 755 at 766-767 (Lord *Cairns* LC) and at 765 (Lord *Blackburn*, implicitly). There is a reluctance to recognise exceptions to the principle that a stranger cannot compel a person to pay for a benefit bestowed without his consent: *China Pacific SA v. Food Corpn of India* [1982] AC 939, 961E-F (Lord *Diplock*). In part this seems to be based on a deeply-rooted (though erroneous) assumption that any intervention by a stranger without request is a mere impertinence (cf. *Re Leslie* (1883) 23 Ch D 552, 561 (*Fry* LJ)) – which disregards questions of necessity (though in *Pontypridd Union v. Drew* [1927] 1 KB 214 *Atkin* LJ went so far as to assert "[t]here is no principle of law which compels a man to repay expenses necessarily incurred for his benefit"). In addition there is a tendency to regard exceptions as justified only where this is needed as an encouragement to dangerous services involving a risk to the intervener's person (in contrast to the acts of someone who merely finds and safeguards another's property): cf. *Nicholson v. Chapman* (1793) 2 H Bl 254 at 257, 126 ER 536 at 538 (*Eyre* LCJ). A further reason may be a false analogy with salvage: cf. *Sorrell v. Paget* [1950] 1 KB 252, 260 (*Bucknill* LJ: "salvage on land is not a recognized head of claim in the common law"), 265 (*Asquith* LJ: "slavage by land is a legal chimera"). The failure of claims raised by interveners in leading cases can, however, be explained on the basis that the claimant was averring not a mere claim to recompense, but a right in the nature of salvage or a security right (lien or charge), though it must be conceded that generally (a) the tenor of the judgments is critical in wider terms and (b) the assumption or conclusion seems to have been also that that there was no underlying claim to support proprietary rights: see in particular *Binstead v. Buck* (1777) 2 Black W 1117, 96 ER 660 (no defence to trover in respect of dog taken into care by the defendant that he had maintained it and retained it until the costs incurred were paid because those expenses were not capable of supporting a particular common law lien); *Nicholson v. Chapman*, loc. cit. (no lien and no salvage where lost timber retrieved, though the court envisaged a possible (unsecured) personal claim); *Re Leslie*, loc. cit. (payment by husband of premiums to keep up wife's insurance policy not establishing lien in favour of former's personal representatives, where it was also assumed there would be no personal claim unless the payment was by request); *The Gas Float Whitton No. 2.* [1895] P 301, reversed [1896] P 42 (CA); *sub nom. Wells v. Owners of the Gas Float Whitton No. 2* [1897] AC 337 (HL upholding CA) (salvage does not extend to all constructions on the sea). Whatever the limitations of those authorities, they have repeatedly been regarded as laying down a wider general rule which precludes even a mere personal claim to recompense for the service rendered: *Aitchison v. Lohre*, loc. cit., 760 (Lord *Blackburn*: "No claim for remuneration from the owner is given by the Common Law to those who preserve goods on shore, unless they interfered at the request of the owner:"); *The Gas Float Whitton No. 2*, loc. cit. at 311 (*Jeune*

P: "[F]or services rendered in preserving property astray [...] no payment is legally due."). Nonetheless, there is case law on claims to remuneration for funeral undertakers (see Chapter 1, Art. 1:102, Notes, II, 16) and solicitors and other professionals providing necessaries to persons without full legal capacity (see Chapter 1, Art. 1:101, Notes, V, 59 and Art. 1:103, Notes, V, 38). Moreover, in *White v. J. D. Troups Transport* [1976] CLY 33 (Stockton-on-Tees County Court) a business hiring out equipment had a claim for hire costs when, at the request of the police, it employed its equipment to remove the defendant's vehicle from the road under a bridge which it was blocking and so acted as the defendant's agency of necessity – though the claim was reduced because the claimant had could have employed smaller and thus cheaper equipment and the use of the excessively large and more expensive machine resulted from a failure to make precise inquiry beforehand. A claim to the value of care services may also arise where the person assisted was in need of care (which the intervener has provided) as a result of injuries for which a third party is liable in tort, conditional on the injured person making a claim against the third party in respect of those services: see Chapter 3, Art. 3:105, Notes, 1. Statutory provisions (which also apply in SCOTLAND) provide for a special regime where emergency medical treatment is given by a qualified medical practitioner or a hospital to a person injured as a result of a road traffic accident: see Road Traffic Act 1988, secs. 158-159. The claim under sec. 158 falls short of being fully comparable to remuneration of a *gestor* along the lines of Art. 3:102 not least because (a) the remuneration is on a fixed scale without regard to the precise (extent of the) services rendered and (b) remuneration is due not from the person injured (or, where the injuries are fatal, his estate), but from the person using the vehicle causing the accident. In the case of a claim by a hospital there are further limitations confining its scope to private non-profit-making organisations: see sec. 161(1). Sec. 157 of the Act imposes on an insurer who is liable to pay in respect of the accident a liability to pay towards expenses incurred by such a hospital (subject to maximum amounts). Though the context is undoubtedly that of compulsory insurance, this may also reflect, perhaps, an approach articulated on the bench that if there is to be a right to remuneration for services rendered in cases of this type this is best addressed by public law or arrangement with public authorities responsible for such services in the public interest: cf. *Wells v. Owners of the Gas Float Whitton No. 2* [1897] AC 337, 349 (Lord *Macnaghten*).

II. *Quantum of Remuneration*

10. Provisions or case law on the quantum of remuneration are naturally only to be found in jurisdictions which provide for a claim to remuneration (under the conditions set out under I. above). As regards GERMANY remuneration is quantified as the usual remuneration (BGH 7 January 1971, NJW 1971, 609, 612; BGH 15 December 1975, BGHZ 65, 384, 390; BGH 7 March 1989, NJW-RR 1989, 970). GREEK case law refers to remuneration "which is usually owed" (CA Athens 6980/1987, EllDik 30/1989, 805). There does not appear to be reported BELGIAN (and FRENCH) case law dealing with the quantum of remuneration.

11. PORTUGUESE CC art. 470 (2) refers to the provision of mandate law in CC art. 1158 (2). According to that provision the quantum of remuneration will be determined, unless the parties have agreed otherwise, by the fees of the relevant occupational group

or alternatively customs and practice, or if such benchmarks are not available then according to what is fair and reasonable.

12. The solution of Article 3:102 also corresponds with DUTCH CC art. 6:200 (2), which reads: "Where a manager of another's affair has acted in the conduct of a business or profession, he has, to the extent that this is reasonable, the further right to be paid for his activities in accordance with the prices usually charged for such activities at the time of his management of another's affairs" (translation by *Haanappel* et. al., Legislation).

Illustration 1 is taken from BGH 23 September 1999, NJW 2000, 72; OGH 3 October 1996, RdW 1997, 275 and from Cass.civ. 31 January 1995, Bull.civ. 1995, I, no. 59; **illustration 2** from CA Athens 6980/1987, EllDik 30/1989, 805.

Article 3:103: Right to Reparation

An intervener who acts to protect the principal, or the principal's property or interests, against danger has a right against the principal for reparation for loss caused as a result of personal injury or property damage, suffered in acting, if:
(a) the intervention created or significantly increased the risk of such injury or damage; and
(b) that risk, so far as foreseeable, was in reasonable proportion to the risk to the principal.

Comments

A. The Claim to Reparation for Concomitant Damage

1. **Policy considerations** Article 3:103 is based on a simple consideration of justice. If a person undertakes an intervention to protect another or such person's property against damage but in the course of this act himself sustains damage then a decision must be made as to who is to bear such damage: the intervener or the principal. This Article, in line with the overwhelming majority of European legal systems, has decided to choose the second alternative. Only this solution corresponds to one of the main objectives of the law of benevolent intervention: the protection of the justified intervener.

2. **Need for regulation** Article 3:103 is indispensable because Article 3:101 only secures that the principal will discharge the obligations the intervener has committed himself to and will reimburse expenditure incurred. Thus Article 3:101 concerns patrimonial detriments which are voluntarily sustained by the principal. Involuntary patrimonial detriment ("damage") does not come within the scope of the regime provided for by Article 3:101. This will be dealt with by Article 3:103.

3. **Consideration of the principal's interests** The decision of general principle in favour of the intervener in some respects requires further specification. Article 3:103 subjects the claim for damages to the condition that the damage in question is a typical

realization of the risk incurred. The realization of the general risks of life will not give rise to a claim. Additional provisions in Articles 3:104 (Reduction or Exclusion of Intervener's Rights) and 3:105 (Obligation of Third Person to Indemnify or Reimburse the Principal) further alleviate the burden on the principal. If and to the extent that state insurance schemes or insurance schemes prescribed by law provide for compensation of the intervener this may, depending on the circumstances, operate to relieve the principal under Article 3:104(2). See the comments on that principle.

4. **Relationship to tort law** Article 3:103 adds an independent concurrent claim to those provided by tort law. If the principal is also liable to the intervener under the provisions on tortious liability the intervener may rely on the compensation scheme which is more favourable to him.

B. The Individual Requirements of the Claim

5. **A strict liability outside the law of tort** Article 3:103 amounts to a strict liability (i. e. a liability without intention or negligence on the part of the principal) in damages to the intervener. If, by contrast, the principal's liability for damage depended on wrongful conduct or fault on his part, then the rule would more often than not prove to be superfluous. For in these cases the principal's liability would already arise under the provisions of the law on extra-contractual liability (PEL Liab.Dam.).

Illustration 1
A car driver is badly injured because he steers his car into a field in order to avoid a person who has suddenly rushed out in front of his car. According to the rule in Article 3:103, liability is imposed on that person, even though he might not, for some special reason, be liable in tort law for the accident. The person may for instance be a bicyclist who has suffered a hornet-sting and in consequence has lost control over his bike for an instant and thus swerved into the oncoming lane.

6. **Reparable damage** Damage which can give rise to a claim for reparation consists of injury to the person and damage to property and the damage which arises consequential on those (extending to economic as well as non-economic consequential losses). In contrast, so-called pure economic losses (meaning, here, losses which are not the consequence of bodily injury or damage to property) do not support a claim to reparation under the law of benevolent intervention in another's affairs. That is connected with the special nature of that economic damage and with the fact that fundamentally there should be no compensation for an expenditure of time (i. e. what the *gestor* might otherwise have earned during the time he devoted to the *negotiorum gestio* and therefore forewent in order to act). Personal injury is defined in PEL Liab.Dam. Article 2:201, as is damage to property in PEL Liab.Dam. Article 2:206(2)(b). According to the latter provision "property damage" will only cover damage to the physical integrity of a thing.

Illustration 2
If A rushes into B's burning house in order to save B, stranded in a smoke-filled bedroom, and sustains severe burns as well as ruining his clothing, B may be liable

to compensate A for his personal injury, the lingering pain and discomfort associated with the damaged tissue, the loss of income while he is under treatment and recovering his health and the more trivial damage to his property. However, if A, in order to rescue B, must forego a business appointment, B will not be liable for A's economic loss consequential on the missed appointment. In order to avoid all argument about whether such items of damage are attributable to the risks generated by the *negotiorum gestio*, pure economic losses have been removed at the outset from the protective sphere of the claim to reparation.

7. **Damage suffered by third parties in consequence of the intervener's death** With regard to personal injury, however, liability under this provision may be as extensive as liability would have been in tort law in a case of liability independent of breach of duty. Hence, if the intervener has suffered a fatal injury in attempting to protect the principal, the principal will be liable to the intervener's successors and dependants in a manner analogous to the corresponding provisions in tort law (see PEL Liab.Dam. Article 2:203).

8. **General limits of the principal's liability** Since the liability provided for in Article 3:103 is strict (see *B5* above), some further limitation to its scope seems to be appropriate in order to ensure that a just balance is struck between the conflicting interests of two innocent parties.

9. **Protection against danger** Under the rule a claim to damages only comes into consideration if, firstly, it is a case of emergency which is in issue. There must be a damage which the intervener sustained because he strove to protect the person, property or other interests of the principal "against danger". A danger is understood to exist where the situation will in all likelihood take a turn for the worse.

Illustration 3
After his graduation ceremony P, who is completely drunk, gets behind the wheel of his car. I takes away the key from P, who refuses to listen to reason, and himself gets behind the wheel. I acts to rescue P from danger. P's protest is irrelevant as he is in a state which renders him incapable of forming a legally relevant will.

10. **Questions of causation** Article 3:103 also makes it clear that in order to make the principal liable for the realisation of a danger in the form of damage of the specified type, a particularly close causal connection is required between the intervention and the endangerment of the intervener. Not every damage which is causally connected to the act of the intervener will fall within the provision.

11. **Damage suffered in acting** Firstly, damage must be suffered "in acting", and hence in the course of an undertaking to protect the person, property or other interests of the principal. The field of potential liability is opened up only from the point in time when the *gestor* commences the protective act – that is to say, the act which in fact provides protection or, were it not frustrated by nature or the intervention of third parties, would have rendered protection.

Illustration 4
In illustration 2, A is entitled to claim from B's estate for his damage even if A is unfortunately beaten back by the heat and B cannot be rescued. This point in time arises only when the *gestor* confronts and engages with the danger surrounding B or his interests because an act of rendering protection is the process of eliminating the danger. Hence, if, in racing to reach B's burning house, A has rushed from his shop leaving it unlocked and it is looted in his absence or A has been knocked down by a passing vehicle while crossing the road then, quite apart from considerations of A's contributory want of care or the tortious role of third parties in causing A's damage, A could not have a claim against B under this Article because such losses are not sustained "in acting" to render protection. They are losses sustained by A merely in placing himself in a position from which he is then able to render or attempt to render protection. The same is true where A trips on a loose flagstone in the path to B's house, breaks a bone and never reaches the burning front door. Any redress which A might have against B in such a case lies in tort.

Illustration 5
For one evening and one morning I attends to the animals of his unmarried neighbour who is also a farmer and had to be taken to hospital suddenly due to a heart attack. An infectious animal disease has broken out. Without the fault of any party, since it could not yet be known that P's animals have been infected, I transmits the virus to his own flock. The damage is a mere consequential loss and thus does not qualify as damage which I has suffered "in acting".

12. **Created or significantly increased risk (limb (a))** Secondly, the risk that such damage would be incurred must be "created or significantly increased" by rendering the specific protection. By contrast, all other risks will (even in the case of an emergency) fall within the ordinary hazards to which a helper is exposed.

Illustration 6
The proprietor of a business sees an accident occur in the immediate vicinity of his premises. He shuts his corner shop in order to help. (The loss of income is not a compensable damage.) Should the grocer drive the victim to hospital and in the course of the journey a further accident occur in which the grocer's car is damaged, this damage too is only sufficiently closely bound up with the act of rendering assistance if in the circumstances it was necessary to adopt a particularly risky approach to making the journey by car.

13. **Reasonable proportion between the danger to the principal and the risk incurred by the gestor (limb (b))** Secondly, a claim for the intervener to reparation only arises if he has not incurred an unreasonable risk. Ultimately this follows simply from the general principles as it cannot be in the principal's interest that the intervener assume an unreasonable risk. In a normal case it might be unreasonable, for example, knowingly to endanger one's own life or health in order to save the property of others. This principle of proportionality may also be conceptualized in categories of causation. If a reasonable person in the circumstances would not have felt called upon to act in the

manner in which the intervention was undertaken, then the risk realized should not be qualified as a consequence of the danger threatening the principal.

Illustration 7
The intervener's risk could be defined as the product of the probability of loss occurring and the extent of probable damage. If, as an example, there is a high probability (50%), that the intervener by his intervention would incur a comparably low property damage (he ruins his suit which has a value of 1.000 €) in order to preserve another's property of high value (a painting or a laptop computer containing important data of which no other backup copy exists), then he incurs a reasonable risk even if the danger that the painting or the computer (value 10.000,- €) would be lost were comparatively low (10%).

14. **"so far as foreseeable"** The disproportionality between the danger to be prevented and the risk incurred however must have been observable for the intervener in the circumstances of the case. The risk of a reasonable but inaccurate estimation of the actual situation will again have to be borne by the principal.

Illustration 8
This may be illustrated by the example of a person entering a building in which the principal has stored dangerous substances of which the intervener could not have any knowledge and which endanger his lungs. Had he known, or ought to have known, of the danger it would have been unreasonable to even attempt to rescue valuables in such circumstances.

15. **Intervener's contributory fault** The contributory fault of the intervener (for example, A runs into the neighbour's burning house in highly inflammable plastic clothing) will result – in accordance with general principles – in a commensurate reduction of the quantum of the claim to reparation. It does not, as a matter of principle, lead to elimination of the claim to reparation. A complete exclusion of the claim to reparation by reason of contributory fault only comes into play if the damage is really entirely attributable to the *gestor* because he behaved in a way which is beyond all bounds of reasonable conduct. In assessing whether the intervener is contributorily at fault, however, all the circumstances of the particular case have to be taken into account and, in particular, the fact that in a case of emergency not much time is left for consideration. In a panic situation, it cannot be expected that someone who is not specially trained to cope with such predicaments will proceed with the same care and consider the matter with the same level-headed deliberation as would be demanded in normal circumstances.

Notes

1. The general principle of Article 3:103 is broadly established in Europe; the result it achieves is in substance, however, reached by different methodological approaches and on the basis of legal texts with markedly different wording. According to the literal terms of GERMAN CC § 670 only 'expenditure' is compensable thus excluding 'dam-

age'. Yet case law has gone on to treat such damage as equivalent to 'expenditure' which the intervener incurs in the course of an effort to avert damage which has generated a substantial risk for himself (inter alia BGH 7 November 1960, BGHZ 33, 251, 257; BGH 27 November 1962, BGHZ 38, 270, 277; see further MünchKomm [-*Seiler*], BGB[3], § 683, no. 18 et seq.). In order to demarcate further damage which is compensable recourse is had to the notion of concomitant damage which is a typical realization of the risk concerned. Only damage which appears to be a realization of the typical risk of the assumed activity will be held to be compensable (*Medicus*, Bürgerliches Recht[19], no. 428; BGH 4 May 1993, NJW 1993, 2234). In cases of 'self-sacrifice' on the roads (by means of a manoeuvre a driver of a motor vehicle prevents a collision with another road user, the principal, but thereby himself sustains damage) case law recognises a claim not for full compensation but rather for a reasonable reparation (BGH 27 November 1962 loc.cit.). In a case of contributory fault by the intervener CC § 254 will be applied analogously to the claim for damages which is based on CC § 670 (Palandt [-*Heinrichs*], BGB[63], § 254, no. 6; BGH 27 November 1962, loc.cit.; *Larenz*, Schuldrecht BT II/1[13], 450). The claim for damages in a case of personal injury will also encompass non-economic losses (CC § 253). In a case of fatal injury CC §§ 844 and 845 will be applied by means of analogy (Staudinger [-*Wittmann*], BGB[13], § 683, no. 5; RG 7 May 1941, RGZ 167, 85, 89; Soergel [-*Beuthien*], BGB[12], § 683, no. 8).

2. As regards GREEK Law the starting point is more transparent as CC art. 736 explicitly provides for both a claim to compensation for expenses incurred independent of fault and a claim for damages. All damage which has been sustained during and as a result of the intervention will be compensated (ErmAK [-*Sakketas*], Art. 736 no. 12), though no compensation for pain and suffering is granted because the law of mandate does not provide for such a claim either (*Kavkas and Kavkas*, Enochikon Dikaion, 26). By contrast damage suffered by relatives will be compensated for by means of a corresponding application of CC arts. 928 and 929 (Georgiades and Stathopoulos [-*Karassis*], note under Art. 723). In a case of intervention in an emergency (CC art. 732) slight negligence on the part of the intervener will not result in a reduction of the claim (*Papanikolaou*, loc.cit. no. 7). In a case of self-sacrifice in a road traffic accident the reparation is quantified according to what is fair and reasonable (CC arts. 300 and 918) (*Papanikolaou*, loc.cit. no. 10 and Art. 730 no. 11). ESTONIAN CC § 1025 (1) too corresponds in all material points to the rule in Article 3:103.

3. PORTUGUESE CC provides for two legal bases for a claim for compensation of a rescuer. The tort law provision of CC art. 495 (2) grants any person who (whether or not he was obliged by law) renders assistance to a person injured or fatally injured and thereby has himself sustained physical injury a claim for compensation against the person who is accountable for the injury of the primary victim (for details see *Vieira Gomes*, Gestão de negócios, 210). Derived from general principles of justice CC art. 468 (1) in addition grants a justified intervener a claim independent of fault against the principal (the primary victim) for 'losses sustained'. Where there is contributory fault on the side of the intervener, his claim will be reduced by corresponding application of CC art. 570 (*Antunes Varela*, Obrigações em Geral I[10], p. 468, fn. 2). By means of an *aprovação* of the intervention the principal acknowledges his liability for damages (CC art. 469).

4. It has been a long-standing dispute under AUSTRIAN law whether the intervener should be granted a claim for damages against the principal (*Meissel*, GoA, 185 et

seq.). Recent case law grants a claim for appropriate compensation in a case of damage sustained in the course of rendering emergency assistance. This claim is characterised as a liability on grounds of equity which will be determined according to the circumstances of the individual case (OGH 24 August 1995, SZ 68/142; OGH 18 June 1997, SZ 70/113; Rummel [*-Rummel*], ABGB I^3, § 1036 no. 4). CC § 1014 is not applicable either directly or by analogy because it only confers a claim on a contractual agent. The principle is instead a manifestation of the underlying ethos of appropriate compensation (CC §§ 1015, 1043 and 967). That in turn allows for a corresponding application of CC §§ 1306a, 1310 (Liability for equitable reasons without culpability).

5. FRENCH CC remains similarly silent on the question whether the intervener who has suffered damage as a consequence of his intervention may claim compensation from the principal, but case law has always recognised such a claim independent of fault, both for *dommages pécuniaires* and for personal injury (JClCiv [*-Bout*], Art. 1372 à 1375, Fasc. 20, nos. 63-64). Legal literature holds this to be founded on an analogous application of CC art. 2000 (*Flour/Aubert/Savaux*, Le fait juridique[10], no. 15 p. 17). Fault on the part of the intervener may reduce the claim or even exclude it altogether, but the matter is dealt with in generous terms for the intervener if he has taken a wrong decision in an emergency which left little time for deliberation (*Bout* loc.cit. no. 65; *le Tourneau*, Rép. Dr. Civ., VI, v° Gestion d'affaires (2002), no. 91). Likewise BELGIAN case law on principle awards the intervener a claim for compensation of damage which he has sustained in the course of his intervention (*Paulus*, Zaakwaarneming, no. 85 p. 51). No distinction is drawn between property damage and personal injury sustained by the intervener; reference is likewise made to CC art. 2000 (*RPDB*, v° Quasi-contrat, no. 77). A distinctive feature of FRENCH law is the case law on the so-called contracts of assistance. French courts have recognised a contractual claim for damages in favour of persons who, without being obliged to, answered the request of others and rendered assistance to them. A contract between the rescuer and the person assisted arises which confers a duty on the person accepting assistance to compensate the rescuer for any personal injury suffered (leading case Cass.civ. 27 May 1959, JCP 1959 no. 11187). This concept of a *convention* (or a *contrat*) *d'assistance* has met with opposition in legal literature (e. g. *Viney*, JCP 1998 éd. G, I. 144, no. 7, p. 1096), but case law adheres to this concept. LUXEMBOURGIAN case law has adopted the French solution (CA Luxembourg 27 June 2001, Pas. lux. 2002, 154). In BELGIUM the French approach has not been adopted (*Glansdorff* and *Legros*, RCJB 28 [1974], 82-85). Instead the rules on benevolent intervention (by which nearly the same result may be achieved) are held to be sufficient.

6. SPANISH CC art. 1893 (1) explicitly states: "[T]he principal compensates the intervener ... for such damage, as he has sustained during the management of his task." Consequently the intervener has a claim to compensation for all damage which he has not caused himself and for which he is not legally responsible (CC art. 1729) (*Sánchez Jordán*, Gestión de negocios, 517; *Lacruz Berdejo*, Rev.Crít.Der.Inm. 1975, 267). The principal's liability is independent of fault; he will be liable in a case of accidental loss (*Sánchez Jordán*, loc.cit. 518.). Interest and earnings which are foregone qualify as compensable damage (Paz-Ares/Diez-Picazo/Bercovitz/Salvador (*-Lasarte*), Código Civil II, 1952.).

7. The legal basis of a an intervener's claim for damage he has sustained is unresolved under ITALIAN law. Under the old *Codice civile* it was undisputed that such a claim

existed. Currently recourse is predominantly had to the notion that damage suffered in the course of giving assistance in an emergency may be qualified as necessary or useful expenditure (*Pane*, Solidarietà sociale e gestione di affari altrui, 124-125; for the analogous application of CC art. 1720 (2) (law of mandate) in favour of an executive director of a corporate entity also Cass. 14 December 1994, no. 10680, Rep. Foro it. 1994, voce Mandato, no. 27). However, it is still a matter of dispute whether this claim can really be based on CC art. 1720 (2) (*Sirena*, Gestione di affari, 35-37).

8. DUTCH CC art. 200 (1) imposes a duty on the principal not only to compensate the intervener for expenditure incurred, but also to compensate for damage. The quantum of this claim for damages will be determined according to CC arts. 6:95 et seq. From these provisions it follows in turn that the principal as a rule may also be liable for personal injury or as the case may be fatal injury of the intervener (Asser [-*Hartkamp*], Verbintenissenrecht III[11], no. 311 p. 320-321). The case of intervention in an emergency for the benefit of the principal may serve as an example in which compensation has been held to be appropriate (Parlamentaire Geschiedenis VI, 796). In legal literature (*Hartkamp*, loc.cit. no. 312, p. 321-322) it has however been indicated that a too generous application of the law of benevolent intervention may lead to a dysfunction with tort law – for instance, where an intervener is under age, cf. CC art. 6:164. Under CC art. 6:106, according to the circumstances of the particular case, the judge may grant an intervener who has sustained personal injury compensation for non-economic damage.

9. In SCOTLAND a claim of the *gestor* for compensation for damage sustained by him in the course of the intervention as distinct from the claim for reimbursement is not discussed.

10. As regards SWEDISH law it has been suggested that a distinction should be drawn between measures for the protection of a person and measures for the protection of property (*Håstad*, Tjänster utan uppdrag, 215). In the last mentioned case a claim for compensation should only be conferred on the intervener if the value of the asset sacrificed is significantly below the value of the property protected. If the intervener hazards the consequences of damage to his own interests, he should similarly be granted a claim for compensation subject to the condition that the loss is proportionate, independently of whether or not the measure is successful (*Håstad* loc.cit. 164, 168 and 215). The legal consequences if the intervener has not accepted the possibility of injury to himself or damage to his property, however, are uncertain. If the intervener suffers damage in order to save the principal's person, the consequences are similarly uncertain. Theses cases ought at any rate to produce a different outcome, it is argued, because they do not in the main concern the preservation or improvement of the principal's solvency. A solution might be to compensate for minor damage involuntarily incurred and in a case of severe damage to operate on the basis of an equitable reduction of damages (*Håstad*, loc.cit. 216). Under DANISH law a separate claim for damages by the person rendering emergency assistance does not apparently exist, and a concept similar to the *contrat d'assistance* is unknown, cf. HD 2 May 1960, UfR 1960, 851: the plaintiff together with the defendant loaded tree trunks on to a lorry. The plaintiff had not properly secured the crane and in consequence suffered damage. In the course of the effort to come to the defendant's assistance the plaintiff was similarly injured. His claim based exclusively on tort law was dismissed for lack of causation.

11. In ENGLISH LAW, where there is no independent *negotiorum gestio* liability, a strict liability to compensate for loss could ordinarily only arise on the basis of contract (where the agency is contractual). Tortious liability follows ordinary principles which as a rule require negligence on the part of the principal in creating the danger tackled by the intervener in order to vest in the intervener a claim to compensation: see Clerk and Lindsell (*-Dugdale*), Torts[18], paras. 7-27 – 7-29. However, an extra-contractual strict liability to compensate for pecuniary loss may arise in the law of restitution – at any rate if old authority is to be relied on: see, for example, *Shallcross v. Wright* (1850) 12 Beav 558, 50 ER 1174 (Lord *Langdale* MR) where an ill person moved into a friend's home in order that he might obtain better medical treatment, but died shortly afterwards and, on account of the infectious nature of the fatal illness, the home had to be evacuated, fumigated and cleaned, and it was held that (on the basis of an 'implied contract') the home owner had a right to payment of the hotel costs for him and his family and compensation for loss of furniture which had to be burned (and consequently the executors of the deceased lawfully disposed of assets of the deceased when they made such payments).

Illustration 1 is taken from *Carmarthenshire County Council v. Lewis* [1955] AC 549 and BGH 27 November 1962, BGHZ 38, 270**; illustration 3** from BGH 30 November 1971, NJW 1972, 475.

Article 3:104: Reduction or Exclusion of Intervener's Rights

(1) The intervener's rights are reduced or excluded in so far as the intervener at the time of acting did not want to demand indemnification, reimbursement, remuneration or reparation, as the case may be.

(2) These rights are also reduced or excluded in so far as this is fair and reasonable, having regard among other things to whether the intervener acted to protect the principal in a situation of joint danger, whether the liability of the principal would be excessive and whether the intervener could reasonably be expected to obtain appropriate redress from another.

Comments

A. Acting with *animus donandi* and Related Cases (Para (1))

1. **Legal certainty** Article 3:104(1) has been prompted by reasons of legal certainty. The provision is a clarification which is found in the same or a similar form in statutory rules on *negotiorum gestio* and, beyond that, is a generally accepted principle. One who acts with *animus donandi* (to use the older terminology) has no claim to compensation. In an individual instance it may of course be the case that the acting party has acted with *animus donandi* only with respect to particular rights and not all of them. A case in which it is particularly advisable to examine whether the intervener was looking to the

principal for reimbursement of his expenditure at the time of performance is where maintenance is paid to close relatives. In a case of doubt one would proceed on the footing that the intervener certainly intended to have recourse against the person obliged to provide the maintenance, but acted with a donative intent in relation to the recipients.

Illustration 1
A man and a woman cohabit for three years without being married. During this period the woman has improved the apartment by her good taste and style and in consequence increased its value. She is not entitled to claim monetary compensation for the services she has provided as an expression of her affection. This was done merely out of friendship.

2. **No waiver of rights** It may also be noted, at a more general level, that we are not concerned here with estoppel or waiver; instead the intervener has no claim from the outset (and there is thus nothing which he can disclaim). Para (1) does not allow for any doubt about that because it takes as the decisive point in time the moment when the intervener acts; a later change of mind is not material. Whether the intervener at the time of acting had the intention of intervening without a given recompense and, if so, which recompense that intention concerned are questions which in the absence of express statement by the intervener are to be answered by employing the same criteria as are to be found in PECL Articles 5:101 and 5:102.

3. **The other rules of the law of benevolent intervention remain applicable** Article 3:104 and in particular its para (1) does not alter the starting point that a person acting with "*animus donandi*" may still be a (justified) intervener within the meaning of this Book. The principle set out above merely grants the principal a defence and does not constitute a (negative) pre-condition for the application of the law of benevolent intervention. This can already be deduced from Article 1:103 (Exclusions), which does not mention '*animus donandi*'. Thus the intervener will remain under the duty to act carefully, provide information and surrender proceeds.

4. **The scope of para (1)** Para (1) is not limited to the claim to reimbursement of expenditure or the pre-emptive claim to indemnification. It equally embraces the claim to remuneration and the claim to reparation. That follows from the unqualified language of the article.

Illustration 2
During a privately organised football match among friends, a player is injured. Another player who happens to be a doctor provides makeshift aid to the injured party on the spot. It is to be presumed in the circumstances that there is no scope for a claim to remuneration: the incentive for rendering first aid is predominantly friendship and the joint activity. This is irreconcilable with a claim for reimbursement.

Illustration 3
In P's apartment a quarrel between the father P and his son X turns violent. I, the other son, comes to his father's assistance but in the course of the events is injured at his wrist by a blow X delivers with a plate. I (or rather his health insurance which wants to assert a claim against the father on the basis of subrogated rights) does not have a claim against P. The assistance provided to P by I arose from family commitment and was based on the bond of affection between father and son.

B. Reduction of Liability on Grounds of Equity (Para (2))

5. **General** Para (2) provides for a reduction of the intervener's claims on grounds of equity. In litigation this grants a discretionary power to the court. At the same time para (2), without claiming to be exhaustive, sets out the most important reasons, which may give rise to a reduction of the claim.

6. **Scope** Para (2) primarily has the claim for reparation under Article 3:103 (Right to Reparation) in focus, but it is not restricted to this claim. In fact it also concerns the intervener's rights to indemnification, reimbursement and remuneration.

Illustration 4
An example for the reduction of the claim for reimbursement of expenditures in a situation of joint danger has already been given in illustration 17 under Article 1:101 (Intervention to Benefit Another).

7. **Reasons to reduce or exclude the principal's liability** The liability of the principal is subject to the general restriction that it must not be inequitable in the circumstances of the particular case. Para (2) specifies a number of aspects which might make it justifiable to reduce or even exclude liability. However, the reasons which the provision offers for a possible reduction of liability are not exhaustive. The provision merely makes explicit the most important cases.

8. **Joint danger** Expressly mentioned is the situation of common danger, an aspect which originates in the law of general average. In a situation of common danger for which neither the *gestor* nor the principal are accountable the rule will generally be that liability must be divided.

Illustration 5
The case of a driver of a motor vehicle who avoids hitting a teenage pedestrian, who suddenly appears in his lane but is not responsible for this mishap, may serve as an example. A further example may be found in illustration 4.

9. **The principal's economic capacity** However, the economic capacity of the principal also calls for consideration. A measure undertaken in benevolent intervention in another's affairs can easily lead to costs and damage whose indemnification may lie beyond the financial capabilities of the principal (especially if the principal is a child).

Of course it is impossible to frame a rule which will suit all cases; ultimately the decisive question will always be whether or not it is fair and reasonable to reduce liability in the particular circumstances. In general such reduction will be considered more in relation to the intervener's claim for reparation than with regard to his claim for reimbursement: expenditures in general result to the principal's benefit, whereas damage sustained by the intervener naturally does not afford any benefit to the principal. Thus the claim for reimbursement of expenditures which have contributed to the successful outcome should only be reduced in rare and exceptional cases, as for instance if the costs of financing a measure are concerned, which the principal had he been asked would have declined for economic reasons.

10. **The intervener can reasonably obtain redress from another** The principal ought generally only to be liable in a subsidiary way if it is reasonable for the *gestor* to look to another to obtain redress. This applies in particular to compensation for damage caused by a third party in a tortiously relevant manner. If such a third party can be identified as a tortfeasor who clearly has assets sufficient to satisfy the intervener's claim, then the intervener must look to the third party tortfeasor. The risk of the tortfeasor's inability to pay, however, must be placed on the principal rather than the intervener (see Article 3:105 (Obligation of Third Party to Indemnify or Reimburse the Principal)).

Illustration 6
A hotel keeper asks one of his guests to assist him in the apprehension of a robber. The guest acts on the request, but in the course of events is wounded by a gunshot from the robber. As a rule the hotel keeper will be liable to the guest under Article 3:103 (Right to Reparation). However, his liability will be reduced in so far as the guest can actually obtain compensation from the robber.

11. **Rights against an insurer** It is fair to oblige the principal to ensure the *gestor* is protected against damage when the latter must otherwise personally carry the risk of endangering himself. However, if the *gestor* has a viable claim against an insurance, then the question may arise whether the insurance should be entitled to recourse against the principal. This will be relevant in particular with regard to personal injury of persons rendering assistance in an emergency. As the latter for practical reasons will turn first to their insurance the problem is ultimately whether or not the insurance should be granted a right of recourse (against the principal whose insurance cover will usually not extend to his duty to compensate arising from the law of benevolent intervention) by means of an assignment by operation of law. This question too cannot be answered by a comprehensive rule appropriate to all cases. The decision should turn on considerations such as the basis of the insurance cover and the extent and the funding of the insurance. For example, many Member States of the European Union have established a public insurance body, which compensates persons who have injured themselves in the course of rendering assistance to another. As far as such (state-run) health insurance for the benefit of emergency rescuers is funded by public tax revenues, the principal should not be burdened with liability for the intervener's personal injury: as everyone pays, everyone should profit. This is even more so where the reason for insurance cover may also be the fact that the legislator has imposed a sanction on failure to render aid.

Where the insurance cover is not funded by taxes, but instead secured by contributions of (for example) either only employees or only employers, then it is not plausible why third parties who have not made any contribution (in this case: the principal) should profit from such payments, i. e. why they should not be subject to the insurer's recourse. Of course the principal's liability will be a precondition for such recourse; without his liability to the intervener there is nothing which can be subrogated to the insurance company.

Illustration 7
A is a witness of an attack on a tourist at an underground station. He comes to the tourist's aid, but is himself injured. To the extent that A benefits from statutory non-contributory insurance, his claim against the tourist is correspondingly reduced by the amount received from the insurer. The operator of the insurance scheme acquires A's claim in tort against the tortfeasors, but not A's claim against the tourist under the law of *negotiorum gestio*. That is because A has no claim which is capable of transfer to the insurer.

12. Burden of proof The burden of proof lies with the principal. He must assert and in a contested case prove that the requirements of the clause enabling a reduction of liability are satisfied.

Notes

I. Acting with animus donandi

1. GERMAN CC § 685 (1) denies the intervener any claim if at the time of intervention he did not intend to demand compensation. This fact constitutes an exclusionary defence (CA Karlsruhe 18 May 2004, FamRZ 2004, 1870, 1871), precluding the intervener's claim for reimbursement of expenditure (CC § 683) and surrender of enrichment (CC § 684) to which regard must be had *ex officio*. As the law does not provide for a claim for compensation or for remuneration these are not explicitly addressed in CC § 685 (1). While the intention to waive need not be expressly declared, it must be evident to third parties; the onus of proof lies with the principal. The intention of the intervener not to demand compensation from a particular person who is assumed to be the principal does not automatically exclude the liability of the actual principal (Palandt [-*Sprau*], BGB[63], § 685, nos. 1-2, § 686, no. 2). CC § 685 (2) provides a presumption of law (BGH 5 November 1997, NJW 1998, 978, 979), that payments of maintenance made without a statutory obligation between persons who are related in the direct line have been made with *animus donandi* (unless the principal proves the contrary). However, this only concerns the relationship to the immediate payee (example: grandfather furnishes maintenance to the grandchild because the father does not pay; the possibility to take recourse against the father remains unaffected).
2. The intervener will likewise not be entitled to a claim under ESTONIAN CC § 1023 (3) and GREEK CC art. 738 if at the time of acting the intervener did not have the intention to demand reimbursement of expenditure or compensation for damage. This rule is interpreted as an application of the prohibition of inconsistent conduct (*venire*

contra factum proprium) (Georgiades and Stathopoulos [-*Papanikolaou*], Art. 738, no. 1). It will suffice that the intention of the principal not to demand compensation may be inferred from the circumstances – for example where the son protects the father against an attack from a third party and thereby suffers damage himself (*Papanikolaou*, loc.cit. no. 2). CC art. 738 (2) adds a rule of interpretation which goes beyond the German CC § 685 (2) as it applies to benefits provided to siblings. This apart, the provisions are congruent. Under Greek law too the principal will have to prove that the intervener has acted with *animus donandi*; only within the scope of CC art. 738 (2) does the intervener have to prove he furnished maintenance without such intention (*Papanikolaou*, loc.cit. no. 6-7).

3. PORTUGUESE CC does not contain a provision similar to German CC § 685 and Estonian CC § 1023 (3) or Greek CC art. 738; nor does a particular rule exist on maintenance furnished to relatives without an underlying obligation. A proposal to that effect (*Vaz Serra*, Gestão de negócios, 228, 278 et seq.) has not been adopted onto the statute book. Nor does the case law seem to accept the defence that the intervener has acted with the intention of making a transfer by way of donation (STJ 29 February 2000, CJ(ST) VIII [2000-1] 116).

4. The AUSTRIAN CC similarly does not mention the defence of *animus donandi*. Academic writing (in contrast to Article 3:104 (1)) considers that animus donandi can only concern expenditure and thus does not apply to the other claims (*Meissel*, GoA, 82). The discharge of another's duty to furnish maintenance falls within the scope of CC § 1042 – a provision forming part of unjustified enrichment law (Schwimann [-*Apathy*], ABGB V², § 1042 no. 5). It is presumed that the person rendering payment does not intend thereby to release the debtor from his obligation (Rummel [-*Rummel*], ABGB I³, § 1042 no. 6).

5. In FRANCE it is questionable whether an *animus donandi* on the part of the intervener does not inherently rule out a relationship of benevolent intervention; case law has not yet entirely resolved this question. *Douchy*, La notion de quasi-contrat en droit positif français, no. 46 p. 112-113 considers that a person who acts with *animus donandi* does not act as an intervener. However, the prevailing view tends to the approach that the *intention libérale* merely constitutes a particularly altruistic form of an *intention de gérer* and thus is not inconsistent with benevolent intervention (JClCiv [-*Bout*], Art. 1372 à 1375, Fasc. 10, no. 39). However, an *animus donandi* implies the intervener's waiver of (all) his claims against the principal. It gives rise to an offer of a *remise de dette*, which if the principal accepts operates to exclude benevolent intervention after all (*Bout*, loc.cit. Fasc. 20, no. 48). Both prior approval and subsequent acceptance (in the latter case by means of a *ratification*) lead to the conclusion of a contract (*Bout*, loc.cit., Fasc. 10 nos. 40-41). These cases apart an *intention libérale* will not be presumed; it must be proven (CA Paris 14 October 1997, JurisData 1997-023144). In BELGIUM it is said that an *intention libérale* on the part of the intervener will as a general rule exclude the formation of a legal relationship of benevolent intervention (*Stijns/Van Gerven/Wéry*, JT 1996, 689 no. 17). The case is considered instead as a donation. As in France, an *intention libérale* must be proven in Belgium (B. H.Verb. [-*Roodhooft*], II.5, p. 15 no. 2236-2237).

6. In SPAIN too the absence of an *animus donandi* is interpreted as a (negative) requirement of a benevolent intervention. An intervener is assumed to be defined by the very fact that he acts neither with the intention to gain profit nor to make a donation (*Puig*

Brutau, Compendio II, 599). The existence of an *animus donandi* will prevent the formation of a claim for reimbursement of expenditures because in such cases the conduct does not qualify from the onset as benevolent intervention (TS 15 June 1925, cited by *Pasquau Liaño*, La gestión de negocios ajenos, 158, and TS 2 February 1954, RAJ 1954 no. 322 p. 198). CC art. 1894 on benevolent intervention, however, states that an 'outsider' who without knowledge of the person liable to provide maintenance pays to those due maintenance has a claim for reimbursement unless it is certain that he acted 'out of sympathy' and without the intention to demand reimbursement. The burden of proof is reversed if a blood relationship exists between intervener and principal (TS 25 September 1968, RAJ 1968 (2) no. 3959 p. 2657). The Foral law of NAVARRA Ley 560 *in fine* contains an elaborate provision on the defence of *animus donandi*. Under that law the principal's liability requires in general (i. e. not only with respect to provision of maintenance) that "the intervener has acted without munificence". Such munificence will in turn be presumed if intervener and principal are related to each other (*Sánchez Jordán*, Gestión de negocios, 318).

7. In ITALIAN law a subtle distinction is drawn between cases of pure munificence (in which it is assumed that the requirement of *animus negotia aliena gerendi* is not met, cf. Cass. 29 March 2001, no. 4623, Riv. Notariato 2001, 1423) and cases in which the intervener acts with the intention not to demand reimbursement of his expenditure and thus acts with *animus donandi*. The desire to receive reimbursement is not considered to be a necessary requirement of benevolent intervention (*Aru*, Gestione d'affari, 14-15). Against this background difficult and in part unresolved questions of demarcation arise as far as maintenance payments within a family are concerned; for details see Cass. 17 July 1969, no. 2636, Foro it. 1970, I, 260 with note *Pisu*, Foro it. 1971, I, 713.

8. The problem referred to in Article 3:104 has not played any role in the development of the DUTCH CC; consequently the law does not address this problem. Yet in the case law of the appellate courts the aspect of munificence has repeatedly led to the dismissal of a claim based on benevolent intervention and sometimes on the ground that the intervener must have the intention to act for the account and expense of the principal (e. g. CFI Roermond 15 April 1915, NedJur 1915, p. 992; CFI Amsterdam 4 April 1939, NedJur 1939, no. 628 p. 978; CFI Haarlem 8 January 1954, NedJur 1954, no. 615 p. 1143). This reasoning has been criticized by commentators, because the existence of munificence need not lead to the result that the intervener is released from his regular duties, such as, inter alia, his duty to continue the intervention. Rather the case actually concerns the necessity to prevent the intervener from *venire contra factum proprium* (*Verburg*, De vrijwillige zaakwaarneming, nos. 60-62, p. 90-92). In recent case law it has been stated that friendly acts done for the benefit of a person with whom the active party lives in extra-marital cohabitation may not be qualified as benevolent intervention (CFI s'Gravenhage 28 February 2001, LJN-number AB1265, www.rechtspraak.nl).

9. Similarly it holds true for SCOTS Law that "there can be no claim for expenses where the *gestor* has acted *animo donandi*" (*Leslie*, Jur.Rev. 1983, 33). If the intervener is a close relative of the principal such *animus donandi* will be presumed (Stair [-*Whitty*], The Laws of Scotland, XV, paras 95 and 116).

10. In accordance with Article 3:104 (1) SWEDISH academic writing has stated that a *gestor* who acts with the intention of making a donation is neither entitled to a claim

for remuneration nor for reimbursement of expenditure (*Hellner*, Om obehörig vinst, 362). Such acts are mere acts of friendship (*Håstad*, Tjänster utan uppdrag, 68).

11. Where there is a recognised legal relationship of agency in the COMMON LAW (whether by agreement, necessity or ratification) or bailment, the terms of that relationship will determine the scope of the intervener's rights. In that context, where the intervener's generous state of mind is formed too late to help fix in advance the terms of the relationship, the principles of waiver and estoppel may come into operation to control the rights of the intervener against the principal. Any other benevolent intervener acting with *animus donandi* will have no claim to the extent to which the service or benefits are freely provided. For authorities confirming that a person supporting someone without full legal capacity has no claim if they did not intend to be reimbursed see *Wentworth v. Tubb* (1841) 1 Y & C CC 171 at 174, 62 ER 840 at 842 (*Knight Bruce* VC); *Re Rhodes* (1890) 44 Ch D 94, 102 (*Kay* J: absence of intention to claim reimbursement could be inferred in the circumstances from fact neither payer had made a claim before the recipient's death or bothered with book-keeping), and on appeal (where the decision was affirmed) loc. cit at 106 (*Cotton* LJ), 107 (*Lindley* LJ: "[I]n order to raise an obligation to repay, the money must have been expended with the intention on the part of that person providing it that it should be repaid."), 103-104 and 108 (*Lopes* LJ); see also *Carter v. Beard* (1839) 10 Sim 7 at 8, 59 ER 514 at 515 (*Shadwell* VC), which decision if correct (notwithstanding the doubts of *Cotton* und *Lopes* LJJ on that point in *Re Rhodes* loc. cit., 103) is explicable on the basis that there was an "act of bounty" for which the claimant did not intend to be reimbursed. This exclusion of a restitutionary claim follows from the fact that the exceptional liability to a stranger for a benefit conferred is based on necessity for the intervention providing an unjust factor establishing a restitutionary claim and the intervener's free consent to the enrichment of the principal precludes redress on that basis. Indeed the position is more restrictive than this: the intervener has no restitutionary claim for remuneration if the intervener did not intend such a claim against the recipient of the benefit because the intervener intended to obtain reimbursement or a benefit in return through other channels. See, for example, *Wentworth v. Tubb*, loc. cit. (no claim for reimbursement for necessaries provided to a person without full capacity if intended to be reimbursed by a third party); *Shallcross v. Wright* (1850) 12 Beav 558, 50 ER 1174 (Lord *Langdale* MR), where the doctor provided medical assistance supposedly not on the basis of a contract with the patient, but in the expectation of receiving a legacy in the latter's will, and was thus denied a claim to remuneration. The latter decision, however, is open to some doubt not least because of its association with the broader but now moribund proposition that a doctor and a barrister have no legal claim to remuneration for their professional services (*Chorley v. Bolcott* (1791) 4 TR 317, 100 ER 1040) and the recognition of claims on the footing of constructive trusts and proprietary estoppel where services are freely rendered on a non-contractual basis, but in the expectation of a reward. Where a claim is being made in respect of medical treatment provided in respect of a road traffic accident under secs. 157-158 of the Road Traffic Act 1988, that claim must be made either at the time of treatment or in writing within seven days. This may serve in effect to exclude claims where there was no intention to seek recompense contemporaneous with provision of the service, but the purpose of the rule is presumably a different one and related to liability of and settlement by a driver's or owner's insurers.

II. *Reduction of Liability on Grounds of Equity*

12. GERMAN CC does not provide for a rule corresponding to Article 3:104(2). However, in a case in which the driver of a motor vehicle avoided hitting a cyclist, who suddenly appeared in his lane but was not responsible for this mishap, and thereby sustained severe personal injury, the BGH reduced the motorist's claim for compensation to 50% and in doing so relied on an argument by analogy with the provisions on general average contained in maritime law; it was considered to be a case of common danger (BGH 27 November 1962, BGHZ 38, 270, 277). Many further details are as yet unresolved. It is predominantly emphasized that the compensation of damage is strongly influenced by considerations of equity. In this context benefits provided under a social insurance scheme to a person who has rendered assistance are to be taken into consideration as far as appropriate (Palandt [-*Sprau*], BGB^{63}, § 683, no. 9; RGRK [-*Steffen*], BGB^{12}, § 683, no. 11; MünchKomm [-*Seiler*], BGB^{3}, § 683, no. 20). In the case of 'affairs of one's own which are also those of another' (i.e. coincidence of management of an affair on another's behalf and in pursuit of one's own interests) the intervener will as a rule only be entitled to reimbursement of expenditure corresponding to the share of the intervention which was on another's behalf (*Sprau*, loc.cit. no. 8). If the proportion cannot be determined in such a way, then the importance of responsibility, interests and benefits will be decisive (BGH 15 December 1954, BGHZ 16, 12, 16; BGH 18 September 1986, BGHZ 98, 235, 242; BGH 8 March 1990, BGHZ 110, 313).
13. ESTONIAN CC § 1025 (1) (ii) states that compensation may not be demanded from the principal if the employer, mandator of the intervener, provider of social security or health insurer of the intervener has the obligation to compensate for the loss sustained.
14. In PORTUGUESE law the question of a reduction of the intervener's claim for damages against the principal has apparently not been an issue of discussion. It only seems to be recognised (for the opposite case) that CC art. 570 (the reduction clause provided for by tort law) may be applied if the intervener has contributed by his own fault to an aggravation of the principal's damage (*Antunes Varela*, Obrigações em Geral I^{10}, p. 468, fn. 2.).
15. In AUSTRIA both case law (OGH 24 August 1995, SZ 68/142) and academic writing (*Meissel*, GoA, 190) emphasize that in accordance with CC § 967 sentence 2 "appropriate compensation" must be afforded. If and to what extent an intervener who has rendered emergency assistance is entitled to such appropriate compensation will depend on the circumstances of the particular case. The factors calling for consideration will be the balance between the danger impending for the principal and the risk incurred by the intervener, the type and extent of the intervener's damage, the latter's contribution to the dangerous situation (if any) and financial capacity (cf. *Fitz*, Risikozurechnung, 100). The proportionality of danger and damage is assessed from an *ex post* perspective (Rummel [-*Reischauer*], ABGB II^{2}, § 1306a no. 12). Existing insurance cover is in general taken into account (*Reischauer*, loc.cit. § 1310 no. 9). However, the social security accident insurer of an emergency helper is not supposed to release the principal from his obligation; thus the insurer may have recourse to the principal (OGH 24 August 1995, SZ 68/142). This may perhaps rely on the fact that the insurance cover draws on funds which are exclusively contributed by employers.

16. The BELGIAN, FRENCH and LUXEMBOURGIAN *Code civil* do not provide for a reduction of the principal's liability on grounds of equity. Academic writing has not advanced an opinion on this topic. The same holds true for MALTA.
17. SPANISH CC art. 1890 (2) only contains a reduction clause with regard to the intervener's liability for damages – not with regard to the principal's liability for damages. Given that the general provisions of contract law may be applied to the principal's liability, it is to be expected against this background that the general rule of CC art. 1103 is similarly applicable. Accordingly liability in a case of negligence can be reduced by the courts according to the circumstances of the particular case; this will result in a proportionate reduction of the creditor's claims (e. g. TS 18 July 1994, RAJ 1994 (4) no. 6446 p. 8274 and TS 29 November 1993, RAJ 1993 (5) no. 9145 p. 11800). Case law bearing out this assumption that the principal's liability may similarly be reduced (and the circumstances on which such reduction would depend) does not apparently exist.
18. In ITALY the situation is as in Spain. CC art. 2030 (2) only concerns the intervener's liability; the law does not provide for the opposite situation which is of interest in this context.
19. DUTCH CC art. 6:200 (1) in conjunction with art. 6:109 permits not only a reduction of liability but also the reduction of the intervener's claim for compensation. A typical example would be the altruistic effort to rescue another in the course of which the intervener harms himself (T. M. Parlementaire Geschiedenis VI, 795; MvA II, Parlementaire Geschiedenis VI, 449-450; *Schoordijk*, Het algemeen gedeelte van het verbintenissenrecht naar het nieuw BW, 279).
20. A reduction of liability on grounds of equity is unknown under SCOTS law.
21. In DENMARK (*Lov om arbejdskadesikring* § 4 Nr. 3 and 4 [Act on Labour Insurance Employment Accidents of 20 May 1992 no. 390]; cf. on the preceding statute HD 8 February 1961, UfR 1961, 344) and in FINLAND (*Lag om skadestånd för olycksfall vid räddning av människoliv* § 1 [Act on Damages for Accidents by Saving Another Person's Life of 12 April 1935/158]) rescuers who render assistance after an accident are protected by state insurance cover (for details see Karnov and Hansen [*- Preben/RasmussenKolbjørn*], Arbejdsskadesikringsloven § 2 no. 11). The SWEDISH Act on Insurance for Accidents at Work [*lag* (1976:380) *om arbetsskadeförsäkring*] by contrast only applies to employees. The insurer (governed by public law) is not entitled to seek recourse from the tortfeasor (National Insurance Act [*lag* (1962:381) *om allmän försäkring*] Ch. 20 § 7 (2); for details see *Wendel*, Sweden, in Magnus (ed.), The Impact of Social Security Law on Tort Law, 183), which apparently indicates that the insurer may not have take recourse against a principal either.
22. ENGLISH law does not provide for any general judicial discretionary reduction in liability in private law, though where a claimant is seeking an equitable remedy principles involving discretionary elements (including a consideration of hardship to the defendant) may apply so as in effect to diminish liability.

Illustration 1 is taken from CFI 's-Gravenhage 28 February 2001, LJN-number AB1265, www.rechtspraak.nl**; illustration 3** from BGH 6 December 1962, BGHZ 38, 302; **illustration 5** from *Carmarthenshire County Council v. Lewis* [1955] AC 549; **illustration 6** from BGH 19 May 1969, BGHZ 52, 115.

Article 3:105: Obligation of Third Party to Indemnify or Reimburse the Principal

If the intervener acts to protect the principal from damage, a person who would be accountable under PEL Liab.Dam. for the causation of such damage to the principal is obliged to indemnify or, as the case may be, reimburse the principal's liability to the intervener.

Comments

I. **Purpose of the rule** Article 3:105 concerns the situation in which the intervener prevents damage for which, had it occurred, a third party would have been liable to the principal according to the rules on tort law. In other words the intervention has prevented impending damage to the principal or his interests. But it has resulted in detriment to the intervener: for instance, he has incurred expenditure or himself sustained damage. If and in so far as the principal is liable to the intervener in respect of such detriment he (the principal) is entitled to recourse against the third party (the potential tortfeasor). The third party is not to be relieved from liability by the fact that another (the intervener) has prevented the damaging event. Thus the principal is freed from the burden of establishing that *his liability to the intervener* constitutes in relation to the third party "legally relevant damage" and that with respect to *this* damage (which in fact is a 'pure economic loss') the other requirements of tortious liability (causation and accountability) are met.

Illustration 1
Miscreants let a yacht off the line and it threatens to drift away. The owner of another yacht motors up alongside it, but in heading back to the quay damages his own engine. In such a case the owner of the drifting yacht can be looked upon as the benefited party (the principal). Consequently, the owner of the second yacht will have a claim for damages to the value of the costs of repairing his engine. The owner of the rescued yacht will in turn have a claim for redress against the miscreants under Article 3:105, but he will bear the risk of their ascertainment and of their ability to pay when successfully sued. However, Article 3:105 at least relieves the principal from the difficulty that a court could deem the intervention of the *gestor* for the purposes of liability in tort to be a *novus actus interveniens* or that an action for recourse based in tort law may fail for other reasons.

Illustration 2
For inexplicable reasons a toddler disappears from protected premises and runs on to the road. In order to avoid hitting the child, who suddenly appears in front of his vehicle, A steers away, but as a result of the consequent accident suffers injury. The child remains unharmed. A on principle has a claim against the child under Article 3:103 (Right to Reparation). However, this claim will be reduced under Article 3:104(2) (Reduction or Exclusion of Intervener's Rights), if and to the extent that A has a claim for reparation of damages vis-à-vis the nursery. Whether A in fact has such a claim is left to tort law to decide. If there is no such claim, the child will have a claim for recourse against the nursery school arising from Article

3:105, if the nursery school would have been liable vis-à-vis *the child* if the latter had been hit by A's vehicle.

2. **Rights in *negotiorum gestio* and in tort law** The provision proceeds therefore on the basis that the *gestor* has direct redress against the principal, to whom passes in turn the burden of identifying the appropriate wrongdoer. This provides the necessary protection for the *gestor*, commensurate with his sustaining damage for altruistic reasons, because the principal rather than the *gestor* will carry the risk that the tortfeasor who is ultimately responsible for the *gestor*'s damage is unable to satisfy the liability to compensate.

3. **Tortfeasor and gestor** The person responsible for the danger – the potential tortfeasor – might be the party rendering aid himself rather than a third party. As noted earlier, the tortfeasor who has injured another and then sets about reparation of the harm caused cannot act as *gestor* in relation to the victim because, by the rules of tort law, he is obliged to compensate the victim for the damage he wrongfully caused. His act of 'healing' the damage is a performance of the private law obligation he owes to the victim and is thus excluded from *negotiorum gestio* by Article 1:103(a) (Exclusions).

Notes

1. The subject-matter of this Article has only rarely been a point of discussion in the various legal systems. If it is considered at all, then more often than not the issue treated is restricted to the question whether or not the rescuer has a direct claim against the tortfeasor, which in turn is often answered in the affirmative, cf. for SPANISH law CP art. 113; for DUTCH law Asser (*-Hartkamp*), Verbintenissenrecht III[11], no. 312 p. 321-322; for DANISH and SWEDISH law *Andersson*, Skyddsändamål och adekvans, 437 et seq. (who though in this respect also points towards insurance solutions which may often render the question of recourse irrelevant); and for ENGLISH Law *Carmarthenshire County Council v. Lewis* [1955] AC 549, and see also the Road Traffic Act, sec. 158(4), where liabiltiy of a car user to pay in respect of medical treatment given to a person injured in a road accident is damage recoverable from the person responsible in tort. Also of note as regards ENGLISH law is the possibility that one who provides gratuitous but necessary care services to a person injured as a result of the tort of a third party may recover from the injured person (on the basis of a trust of the damages) the value of those services or reimbursement of travelling expenses if the injured person sues the third party and recovers damages in respect of them: see *Hunt v. Severs* [1994] 2 AC 350 (where, however, the services were provided by the tortfeasor himself and the principle was inapplicable on the facts), approving *Cunningham v. Harrison* [1973] QB 942, 952A-C (Lord *Denning* MR). SCOTS law makes similar arrangements (expressly restricted to relatives) in the Administration of Justice Act 1982, sec. 8 (injured person under an obligation to account).
2. AUSTRIAN Law apparently addresses the question whether or not the principal is entitled to recourse in the context of tort law. Compensable damage may also consist of monetary expenditure of the aggrieved party which served to prevent further damage (*Koziol*, Haftpflichtrecht I[3], no. 2/66 p. 53). In addition incurring an obligation to a third party may likewise qualify as damage (*Koziol* loc.cit.; OGH 10 October 1979, SZ

52/146). For details on the claim of the rescuer against the person who caused the dangerous situation see *Koziol* loc.cit. no. 8/43, p. 261.

3. The lack of discussion on the problem addressed by Article 3:105 also holds true for FRENCH and BELGIAN academic writing. However, in terms of outcome it seems to be considered as self-evident that the principal is entitled to an independent claim under tort law against the third party who would have been accountable had the damage occurred. The principal may claim the amount which he (the principal) was obliged to pay to the intervener as compensation for the latter's damage. CAA Lyon 22 September 1993, RTD civ. 1994, 101, obs. *Mestre,* concerned a customer who – following the armed robbery of a store – pursued the robbers. One of them dropped the spoils, but another fired at the customer and injured him. The *Cour de Cassation* allowed a claim for damages based on benevolent intervention of the customer against the keeper of the shop (Cass. civ. 26 January 1988, Bull. Civ. 1988, I, no. 25 p. 16; JCP 1989 éd. G, no. 21217, obs. *Dagorne-Labbe*; *RTD civ.* 1988, 539, obs. *Mestre*; D. 1989 Jur., 405, note *Martin*). Subsequently the CAA Lyon upheld the claim for recourse made by the store operator's insurer against the state. The customer was held to have acted as a *collaborateur bénévole d'un service public*. For damage to the latter strict liability is imposed on the state. For BELGIAN law Cass. 30 November 1977, Pas. belge 1978, I, 351 has held that the expenses incurred by a third party rendering emergency assistance on which the victim is dependent will constitute a damage of the victim compensable under tort law, even if the assistance was provided gratuitously. Furthermore, an injured *gestor* (who acted gratuitously) may take legal action directly against the person responsible for the accident (Cass. 6 November 2001, Pas. belge 2001, 1790, conclusions *du Jardin*; for details see *Lindenbergh*, TPR 2002, no. 27 p. 1437-1438).
4. As regards SPANISH law attention should be drawn to CC art. 1729. According to this provision the principal will have to compensate a (contractual) agent for all damage and detriment which he has sustained as a result of the performance of the mandate. If a third party is responsible for the causation of such damage the principal is entitled to recourse against that third party (Paz-Ares/Diez-Picazo/Bercovitz/Salvador [*-Górdillo Cañas*], Código Civil II, 1575). It may be possible indeed to apply this provision accordingly to cases of benevolent intervention.
5. With regard to ITALIAN Law *Sirena*, Gestione di affari, 291-292 has argued that the rescuer may also be seen as an intervener on behalf of the tortfeasor, which in turn would lead to the result that two principals (the victim and the tortfeasor) have to be dealt with, at least in so far as the rescuer renders assistance going beyond the duties imposed by law. *Inter partes* the person who has received assistance is entitled to recourse against the tortfeasor. The claim will cover all payments that he (the victim) has made to the intervener.

Illustration 2 is taken from *Carmarthenshire County Council v. Lewis* [1955] AC 549.

Article 3:106: Authority of Intervener to Act in the Name of the Principal

(1) The intervener may conclude legal transactions or perform other juridical acts in the name of the principal in so far as this is reasonable to benefit the principal.

(2) However, a unilateral act by the intervener in the name of the principal has no effect if a third person to whom it is addressed rejects the act without undue delay.

Comments

A. Third Party Relations

1. **Three different situations** Where third parties are engaged there are three situations to be differentiated which are legally distinguishable, though in terms of everyday life they are relatively proximate. Firstly, there is the situation where someone intends himself to be active as *gestor*, but – for example because he personally lacks the necessary expertise – leaves the actual carrying out of the work to another, such as an employee or an independent contractor. The second basic situation is where one person (A) merely alerts another (B) to the fact that the principal (C) is in danger or otherwise needs help, A leaving it up to B whether he (B) will intervene or not for the benefit of C. Finally, in the third basic situation A again turns to B, but this time concludes a contract with him (or effects a unilateral juridical act vis-à-vis B), but in the name of and on behalf of C and without being authorised by C to do so. Article 3:106 is only concerned with the last of these three situations.

2. **Conclusion of a contract in the gestor's own name** In the first mentioned situation (where A concludes a contract with B in his own name, though for the purpose of benefiting C) only A (i. e. the person who gives the commission) is a *gestor*. The party taking up the commission (in our example, the employee or independent contractor) does not satisfy the conditions of Article 1:101 (Intervention to Benefit Another) (see further Article 1:103(c) (Exclusions)) and is accordingly not a *gestor* – not even in relation to the benefited party. In that regard the outcome is no different if the contract between A and B is so constituted that as a genuine contract for the benefit of a third party it confers rights on C against B. If the contract is so constituted as a genuine contract for the benefit of a third party, this merely furnishes a further reason for excluding B from the law of benevolent intervention, namely Article 1:103(a). However, the *gestor* (the party giving the commission) for his part of course remains obliged in relation to the principal, though he has made use of another in order to fulfil his own duties.

3. **Engagement of third parties without conclusion of a contract** There is no need for further rules either for the (second) case where someone, who has become aware of a danger threatening the principal, alerts a third party (once again, as a rule an independent operator) to the situation and abdicates to him the decision whether or not he wants to intervene at his own risk. If the third person steps in, then we are faced with two different measures taken (the invitation to act, on the one hand, and the actual

carrying out of the preventative measures, on the other) and therefore with two *gestors* who are completely independent of one another and two independent acts of benevolent intervention.

4. **Conclusion of a contract in the principal's name** Finally, the third question looks to whether a *gestor* may conclude a contract with a third party on behalf of the principal. This question is addressed in Article 3:106(1) and is answered here in the affirmative. The *gestor* may conclude contracts with third parties in the name of the principal if in doing so the *gestor* is advancing the principal's interest appropriately. The *gestor* in this situation, incidentally, is only the person who concludes the contract (A) and not the third party (B), because B will provide his service to the principal (C) on the basis of a valid contract subsisting between him (B) and C.

B. The Intervener's Power of Representation

5. **Considerations of legal policy** The European jurisdictions disagree on whether or not a power of legal representation should be conferred on the *gestor* (cf. above Introduction *B25*, and the following notes). Article 3:106(1), which answers this question in the affirmative, proceeds from the basic idea that such authority does not impose an undue burden on the principal, but at the same time appropriately accommodates the interests of the intervener as well as those of third parties. The intervener who concludes in his own name a contract with a third party is entitled to demand indemnification and reimbursement of expenditure from the principal (Article 3:101 (Right to Indemnification or Reimbursement)). Thus the principal will already have to bear the economic consequences: he will have to pay to the intervener the amount the latter is obliged to pay the third party. Thus from an economic perspective it does not make any difference whether a duty is imposed on the principal to perform directly to the third party. His position is by no means weakened. On the other hand the position of the intervener is improved in so far as he does not incur any liability from the conclusion of the contract with the third party provided he acts within the scope of his representative authority. The third party in turn must take action against the principal which results in a reallocation of the risk of insolvency. Yet exactly this reallocation on policy considerations seems both appropriate and desirable since the third party knows that the intervener acts in the name of the principal and he leaves it to his (the third party's) decision whether or not to accept the offer to conclude a contract with the principal.

6. **Relation to the PECL Rules on representative authority** As regards the relationship between the agency rules of PECL and Article 3:106 see the notes above in the Introduction under *L93*. Article 3:106 only substitutes for a lack of authority conferred by contract. The general requirement of representation – namely that the intervener has to disclose that he acts in the name of person represented (in this case the principal) – remains unaffected. A juridical act effected in his own name will only bind the intervener in relation to the third party. If he acts in another's name, but in excess of the scope of authority conferred by Article 3:106, the intervener will likewise be personally liable by corresponding application of PECL art. 3:204(2), namely as a *falsus procurator*.

7. **Transactions covered** Article 3:106(1) embraces legal transactions of all types. In particular it is not limited to the conclusion of a contract by way of offer and acceptance; it also covers unilateral declarations of the principal's will (e. g. a notice to quit). However, Article 3:106(2) provides for a special rule in the case of unilateral acts. Self-evident (and therefore not mentioned as such) is the proposition that there can be no agency for strictly personal acts (see Comment *B15* under Article 1:101 (Intervention to Benefit Another)). Whether and to what extent an intervener may undertake the conduct of litigation is, as already stressed in Comment *B16* under Article 1:101, a matter for the law of procedure and begs no decision here.

8. **"in so far as this is reasonable to benefit the principal"** A valid representation of the principal by the intervener may naturally only be considered if the general requirements set out in the first Chapter of this Book are met. Moreover Article 3:106(1) requires that the course of action chosen by the intervener, namely the making of an offer or other statement of intention *in the name of the principal* must have been reasonable in order to benefit the latter. As may already be inferred from the general rules, conclusion of a contract by the *gestor* will as a rule only be considered justified for the purpose of temporarily stabilising a critical situation. Article 3:106 in addition demands that it must have been reasonable to commit the principal to the third party. This also applies to cases in which an agent appointed by contract is forced in the circumstances to act in excess of his contractual authority in order to advance the interests of the principal.

Illustration 1
A, a celebrated public character, observes that B is in need of help. A wants to ensure that assistance is provided but does not himself want to be associated with this matter in public. This may be a sufficient reason to appoint a third party in B's name to render the necessary assistance.

Illustration 2
In this case not A, but B, the principal, is a celebrated public character, who visits another city incognito. As A knows, B suffers from a cerebral disease, which B has consistently concealed from the public due to reasonable concern for his career. Furthermore, B has good reason to conceal his presence in the city from the public. B is suddenly in urgent need of a hotel room for a few hours. A books this hotel room. It would be inappropriate to conclude the contract in the name of B.

C. Unilateral Acts (Para (2))

9. **Third party protection** With respect to unilateral acts which the intervener conducts in the name of the principal a further provision is necessary in order to protect the third party. It is contained in Article 3:106(2). In contrast to a conventional offer with a view to conclusion of a contract, a third party cannot simply ignore a declaration of termination, rescission of a contact, avoidance, a measure interrupting the period of limitation or a declaration by which an option is exercised or any comparable declaration which the *gestor* may effect in the name of the principal. Such declarations, if they

are valid, modify the legal situation by themselves. Consequently the third party must know where he stands. Thus para (2) provides for the possibility to reject unilateral legal acts which the *gestor* effects in the principal's name, provided the repudiation is done without undue delay. It would be inequitable to impose on him the risk entailed in the fact that within a short space of time it may not be clarified whether the requirements of Article 1:101 for a valid *negotiorum gestio* (and consequently a power of representation under Article 3:106(1)) were actually satisfied or not.

Notes

1. As mentioned above the European jurisdictions are divided with regard to the question whether or not the intervener's authority should also include the possibility to act in the name of the principal and thus to represent him. CZECH, ESTONIAN, GERMAN, HUNGARIAN and POLISH law answer this question in the negative. Unless particular statutory rules provide otherwise – which rules may incidentally be found in the context of emergency assistance – an intervener cannot directly bind the principal nor dispose of the latter's property in his name. If such acts occur they fall within the scope of the rules on representation without authority (BGH 4 October 1977, BGHZ 69, 323, 327; BGH 4 May 1955, BGHZ 17, 181, 188; BGH 8 July 1953, LM § 683 no. 2). However, in the exceptional case that the intervener discharges a duty of the principal the performance of which is required as a matter of overriding public interest (CC § 679) a duty to ratify is contemplated (BGH 9 February 1951, NJW 1951, 398, *obiter*). This apart, the intervener has to rely on his claim for indemnification against the principal (MünchKomm [-*Seiler*], BGB[3], Introduction to § 677, no. 6 and § 683, no. 27; Staudinger [-*Wittmann*], BGB[13], Introduction to § 677 et seq., no. 60; RGRK [-*Steffen*], BGB[12], Introduction to § 677, no. 83; a contrary view is only advanced by *Baur*, JZ 1952, 328).
2. GREEK law likewise only imposes duties on the intervener *inter partes*, i. e. in relation to the principal; no provision is made for a power of representation. Legal transactions which the intervener effects in the name of the principal come within the rules on representation without authority. In consequence they will only be valid if the principal ratifies them according to CC arts. 229 et seq. (Georgiades/Stathopoulos [-*Papanikolaou*], Introduction to Arts. 730-740, no. 13; ErmAK [-*Sakketas*], Art. 737, no. 13).
3. PORTUGUESE CC art. 471 also excludes a representative authority for the intervener (for details see *Menezes Leitão*, Responsabilidade do gestor, 210). If, despite this rule, the intervener concludes legal transactions with third parties in the name of the principal (and thus gives rise to a *gestão representativa*), CC art. 471 refers to CC art. 268, according to which such legal transactions will only have a binding effect on the principal if he ratifies them. The legal position of third parties is comparatively weak. The only possible means for a third party to protect himself against the invalidity of a legal transaction pursuant to CC art. 260 (1) is in general to request his contracting party to provide evidence of his representative authority (cf. CA Evora 1 June 1999, CJ XXIV [1993-3] 270). Moreover, under CC art. 268 (4) the third party is only granted a power of revocation if that party did not know that the intervener acted without authority.

4. AUSTRIAN law similarly proceeds on the basis that the intervener is not the principal's representative (Schwimann [-*Apathy*], ABGB V^2, § 1035 no. 4; Rummel [-*Rummel*], ABGB I^3, § 1035 no. 2, *Meissel*, GoA, 73). The law of benevolent intervention provides solely for the internal relationship between intervener and principal (OGH 17 May 1950, SZ 23/159).

5. By contrast the legal position in FRANCE, BELGIUM and LUXEMBOURG is completely different. Here the creation of representative authority is regarded as a statutory consequence of benevolent intervention (JClCiv [-*Bout*], Art. 1372 à 1375, Fasc. 20 no. 90; *De Page*, Droit Civil Belge II^3, no. 1090 p. 1153). In order to bind the principal it will be sufficient that the intervener points to the benevolent intervention and discloses that he acts in the name of the principal (Cass. civ. 14 January 1959, D. 1959 Jur. 106; RTD civ. 1959, 334, note *Henri* and *Léon Mazeaud*). The third party may of course make it a condition of the conclusion of the contract that the *gestor* personally binds himself too (Cass.civ. 14 January 1959 loc.cit.). In this case the result will be that the third party will have rights against both the intervener and the principal (*Starck/Roland/Boyer*, Droit Civil. Les Obligations, II^6, no. 2172 p. 762). Moreover the intervener may be liable to the third party under tort law – for instance if he has made a false statement with respect to the principal's solvency (Planiol/Ripert [-*Esmein/Radouant/Gabolde*], Droit civil français VII^2, no. 732 p. 19). The representative authority of a *gestor* may exceed that of a *mandataire* because the former can also bring about a contractual obligation of a principal who lacks full legal capacity (*Bout*, loc.cit. no. 93; *Paulus*, Zaakwaarneming, no. 100 p. 57-58).

6. Although SPANISH CC art. 1893 merely states that "the owner of property or the principal of the affairs is liable for the obligations, which have been incurred in his interest", it is accepted in academic writing that the intervener may act both in his own name and in the name of the principal. In the latter case the principal will be bound directly vis-à-vis the third party (*Pasquau Liaño*, La gestión de negocios ajenos, 198; *Sánchez Jordán*, Gestión de negocios, 603; *Lacruz Berdejo*, Rev.Crít.Der.Inm. 1975, 267, Albaladejo [-*Santos Briz*], Código Civil y compilaciones forales, XXIV, 67). Of course the general requirements of a justified intervention on another's behalf (CC arts. 1892 and 1893) have to be met. If this is not the case (for instance, because the intervention does not qualify as useful or because the principal has not ratified the intervention), then according to the view advanced by some authors the contract is not void under CC art. 1259 but instead binds the intervener (*Lacruz Berdejo* loc.cit.; *Sánchez Jordán*, loc.cit. 606). However, it is difficult to find support for this opinion in the wording of the Code. The reference to CC art. 1259 *in fine* seems to be important, according to which a contract which has been concluded in the name of another who was neither granted a power of representation nor in possession of a statutory power of representation will be void unless the person in whose name the contract was concluded has "ratified, prior to the other contracting party's revocation". *Lacruz*, Elementos II (1), 524 considers that it is for exactly those cases in which the intervener has acted in another's name that provision has been made for the possibility to revoke. Until the contract is ratified its validity will be in suspense; if the third party revokes the contract prior to a ratification, it will be a dead letter. In this case the intervener will not be liable either.

7. Under ITALIAN Law the intervener may even conclude contracts which are subject to formality requirements (Cass. 20 March 1995, no. 3225, Foro it. 1996, I, 203, note F.

Loria). That a statutory representative authority is conferred on the intervener which enables the latter to act in the name and for the account of the principal is nearly undisputed (a contrary opinion has apparently only been advances by *Biondo*, Foro it. 1954, I, 98). The statutory authority arises from CC art. 2031 and encompasses both agreements creating obligations and transactions disposing of rights (*Breccia*, La gestione d'affari[2], 893).

8. Under DUTCH Law the intervener may conduct legal transactions both in his own name and in the name of the principal (T. M. Parlementaire Geschiedenis VI, 790; Asser [*-Hartkamp*], Verbintenissenrecht III[11], no. 295, p. 309; *Schrage*, Verbintenissen uit andere bron dan onrechtmatige daad of overeenkomst, no. 5, p. 5). The authority to act in another's name is explicitly provided for in CC art. 6:201. To the extent that the intervener by his acts conducted in the principal's name properly looks after the latter's interests the principal will be directly bound and entitled by such contract. CC art. 3:78 provides for the applicability of some mandate law provisions, which is set out in detail in CC arts. 3:60 et seq. (T. M. Parlementaire Geschiedenis VI, 797 et seq.; Hartkamp loc.cit. no. 305, p. 316-317; *Vriesendorp*, Verbintenissen uit de wet en schadevergoeding, no. 283, p. 269-270). See also CFI Arnhem 19 May 2004, LJN-number AP6938, www.rechtspraak.nl.

9. Whether SCOTS Law confers representative authority on the intervener is apparently still unresolved. Although *SMT Sales and Services Co. Ltd. v. Motor and General Finance Co. Ltd.* 1954 S. L. T. (Sh CT) 107 (where the police as *gestor* appointed a breakdown recovery service which subsequently succeeded in its direct action for costs against the principal) may be taken as an indicator that such representative authority is recognised, there is no express statement to that end. The basis of this direct claim is still a matter of debate (for details see Stair [*-Whitty*], The Laws of Scotland, XV, paras 101 and 143).

10. In SWEDISH law it seems to be acknowledged that a *gestor* may interrupt a limitation period on behalf of the principal (*Håstad*, Tjänster utan uppdrag, 275; *Lindskog*, Preskription[2], 298; cf. also HD 11 October 1966, NJA 1966, 489, where the interruption of the limitation period was denied on the facts and not on the ground of legal principle). One who acts in his own name as a rule also binds himself (exceptions arise in 'man of straw' cases). *Håstad*, loc.cit. 230 et seq., following an elaborate discussion on the protection of the involved parties, has advanced the opinion that a representative authority of the *gestor* should be endorsed if the *gestor*, had he acted in his own name, would have been entitled to recourse against the principal. However there is no apparent case law which adopts this approach yet. Nevertheless (and in addition to the former Commercial Code Ch. 18 § 10) some recent statutory provisions have been adopted which permit a person to act in another's name, e. g. Contract Act § 24 (although a declaration of bankruptcy generally terminates all powers of authority, an emergency representative power for the protection of the principal's assets will remain effective until the appointment of an administrator in bankruptcy: *Grönfors*, Avtalslagen[3], 155); Maritime Code Ch. 6 § 8 [*sjölag* (1994:1009)] (concerning the captain's authority to conclude contracts for the preservation of the vessel, passengers and the cargo, which bind the ship-owner); Commission Act § 8 [*lag* (1914:45) *om kommission*] of 15. September 1986 no. 636 (commission agent's authority to act in excess of his mandate if the principal's interests so require); Commission Act § 48 (entitlement and duty of the commission agent to take certain protective measures prior to the expiry of

the contract); Marriage Act Ch. 6 § 4 [*äktenskapsbalk* (1987:230)] (emergency power of representation between spouses). With regard to DANISH law see also HD 12 November 1917, UfR 1918, 42 and HD 12 November 1917, UfR 1918, 45 (emergency authority of a shipping company vis-à-vis the bearer of a bill of lading).

11. As the COMMON LAW operates in this field primarily with the instrument of agency of necessity and agency in the strict sense presupposes representation so as to change the principal's legal position vis-à-vis third parties, it is unsurprising that English law recognises that in appropriate cases (i.e, where the transaction is necessary and in the best interests of the principal) an agent of necessity has a power to conclude a transaction binding the principal. See, for example, *Wolff v. Horncastle* (1798) 1 Bos & Pul 316 at 323, 126 ER 924 at 928 (principal sending goods by sea and instructing agents to send bill of lading to defendant so that the defendant might insure the goods; defendant refusing to accept bill; agents procured insurance and notified principal; insurance valid and principal liable to pay premiums even if the acts of the agents had not been ratified). Indeed, English law sees the necessity for such intervention equally in terms of a *duty* of the agent to undertake the transaction: see, for example, *Metcalfe v. Britannia Ironworks Co* (1876) 1 QBD 613, 626 (*Cockburn* CJ: if the cargo is damaged, the damage cannot be eradicated by reasonable expenditure, and the cargo will deteriorate if transport continues, he is obliged to sell it). A holder or carrier of perishable goods which are not collected may have authority from necessity to sell them: *Sims v. Midland Ry Co Ltd* [1913] 1 KB 103, and compare *Springer v. Great Western Ry Co* [1921] 1 KB 257. Unsurprisingly there are voluminous authorities to the effect that in order to enable the ship's safe onward journey a ship's captain may enter into a loan in his principal's name and, if necessary, secure it in respect of his principal's ship in favour of creditors in a case of necessity (be it to finance essential repairs to a damaged ship, to pay fees and taxes at the port, or to pay the cost of repairs already incurred or pay the crew's wages or make payments to other creditors of the principal in respect of outstanding debts who are in a position to hold the ship in port or seize it): *Corset v. Husely* (1689) Comb 135, 90 ER 389; *Watkinson v. Bernadiston* (1726) 2 P Wms 367, 367-368, 24 ER 769 (*Jekyll* MR); *Hayman v. Molton* (1803) 5 Esp. 65 at 67, 170 ER 739 at 739-740 (Lord *Ellenborough* CJ); *Hussey v. Christie* (1808) 9 East 426, 432 (Lord *Ellenborough* CJ); *Arthur v. Barton* (1840) 6 M & W 138, 143-144 (Lord *Abinger* CB); *The Lord Cochrane* (1844) 2 W Rob 320, at 165 ER 775 (Dr *Lushington*); *Beldon v. Campbell* (1851) 6 Exch 886, 889-890 (*Parke* B) (where, however, the court did not accept there was any necessity); *The Royal Arch* (1857) Swab 269 at 275, 166 ER 1131 at 1135 (Dr *Lushington*); *The Karnak* (1868) LR 2 A & E 289, 300 (Sir *Robert Phillimore*), affirmed by the PC (1869) LR 2 PC 505. See also the IRISH case *The Staffordshire* (1871) 25 LT (N. S.) 137, 140 (*Townsend* J), affirmed *sub nom. Smith v. Bank of New South Wales*. The same applies in any other case where pledging the principal's credit is the best solution for the principal in the circumstances of the case: *Robinson v. Lyall* (1819) 7 Price 592, 146 ER 1071. Cf. *Miller & Co v. Potter, Wilson & Co* (1875) R 105, 111 (Lord *Gifford*), where the comparable SCOTS law was expounded ("The captain of a ship at a foreign port who is without the means of communicating with his owners or employers, and where repairs or supplies to the vessel are indispensable, is entitled to get such necessary repairs executed or necessary supplies made, and to pledge therefor the credit of his owners or employers [...] .") In that case it is suggested (loc. cit., 111 (Lord *Gifford*) and 115 (Lord Justice-Clerk *Moncrieff*)) the

power to create a proprietary security exists only if an unsecured loan is unavailable. See also in this regard *The Gaetano and Maria* (1882) 7 PD 137, 143-144 (*Brett* LJ) (where, however, the CA held that English law was not applicable). It may be doubted whether that restriction is still good law. The assumption on which it was based (that an unsecured loan would be cheaper) may be counter-factual (a security reducing risk to the lender potentially enables a lower interest rate, though that might be off-set by higher transaction fees). The better view must be a more flexible test of whether a security is reasonably necessary in the circumstances. Similarly, in appropriately necessitous circumstances a captain has a power to conclude in the name of the principal a contract of salvage: *The Renpor* (1883) 8 PD 115; *The Unique Mariner* [1978] 1 Lloyd's Rep 438. In appropriately dire circumstances the captain even has a power of sale: see, for example, *The Victor* (1865) 13 L. T. (N. S.) 21 (Dr *Lushington*), a case of sale by public auction where the master had no credit and was unable to effect even temporary repairs, and the ship was under threat of arrest from creditors and in any case deteriorating daily, and see also *The Australia* (1859) 13 Moore PC 132 (the cost of repair of the ship – for which the captain had no funds, for which a secured loan could not easily be obtained, but without which a continuation of the journey was impossible – would have exceeded the value of the ship). See further *Read v. Bonham* (1821) 3 Brod & B 147, where the captain likewise had no funds to finance the substantial repairs needed, even on the basis of a secured loan, although in the minority view of *Richardson* J there was no necessity for a sale because the captain could have offered the cargo as additional security and thus had not exhausted all opportunity to obtain a loan for the repairs; *Idle v. Royal Exchange Assurance Co* (1819) 8 Taunt 755 at 772, 129 ER 577 at 584 (*Dallas* CJ); *Freeman v. East India Co* (1822) 5 B & Ald 617 at 621, 106 ER 1316 at 1318 (*Bayley* J); *Robertson v. Clark* (1824) 1 Bing 445, 450 (Lord *Gifford* CJ) (where the prospective cost of repairs exceeded the ship's value); *Hunter v. Parker* (1840) 7 M & W 322, 342 (*Parke* B) (where, however, it was held there was ratification so that the question of authority by virtue of necessity did not have to be answered); *The Segredo* (1853) 1 Spinks Ecc & Ad 36 at 46-47, 164 ER 22 at 28 (Dr *Lushington*), where, however, necessity was not made out; *The Glasgow* (1856) Swab 145, 166 ER 1065 (Dr *Lushington*); *The Victor*, loc. cit. (Dr *Lushington*). As the above authorities indicate, however, the proposition has been more voiced than applied by the courts and it seems that to justify such a drastic step the circumstances must be extreme: *Hayman v. Molton* (1803) 5 Esp. 65 at 67-68, 170 ER 739 at 740 (Lord *Ellenborough* CJ: "extreme necessity" not proven); *The Lord Cochrane*, loc. cit., 334-335 (781) (Dr *Lushington*: "very extreme"). Authority denying a power of sale seems to be of no real weight. The assertion of *Holt* CJ in *Johnson v. Shippen* (1703) 2 Ld Raym 982 at 984, 92 ER 154 at 155 that a captain may pledge a ship but not sell it was dismissed in *Idle v. Royal Exchange Assurance Co*, loc. cit., 771 (584) by *Dallas* CJ on the basis that in that case a mortgage would have sufficed and so in the circumstances of the case there was no necessity and accordingly no authority for a sale. Similarly criticism may be launched at Lord *Ellenborough* CJ's assertion in *Reid v. Derby* (1808) 10 East 143 at 157, 103 ER 730 at 735, as as it was based on the *dictum* in *Johnson v. Shippen*, loc. cit., while in *Reid v. Derby* the sale was invalid independently of the captain's authority because the transfer of title failed to comply with statutory requirements of form. Moreover, *Dallas* CJ in *Idle v. Royal Exchange Assurance Co* (1819) 8 Taunt 755 at 773, 129 ER 577 at 584, considered that no necessity was made out in *Reid v. Derby* – an explanation of the decision which, however, does not have any clear point of reference in the court's judgment. Equally, a ship's captain has a power in a case of necessity to pledge all or part of the cargo so as to bind the owners of the cargo: *The Gratitudine* (1801) 3 C. Rob 240 at 263, 165 ER 450 at 458 (Sir *W. Scott*); *Freeman v. East India* Co, loc. cit. at 621 (1318) (*Bayley* J). See also *Miller & Co v. Potter, Wilson & Co*, loc. cit., 111 (Lord *Gifford*), where the comparable SCOTS law is set out. Likewise, where circumstances render it appropriate, the captain has a a power to sell cargo: *Australasian SN Co v. Morse* (1872) LR 4 PC 222, 228 (Sir *Montague Smith*) (wool which was in bad condition as a result of a shipping accident could not be dried out in port and stored and thus had to be sold). See also *The Gratitudine*, loc. cit., 259 (457) (Sir *W. Scott*, giving the example of cargo which threatens to deteriorate and cannot be transported further); *Freeman v. East India Co*, loc. cit. at 621 (1318) (*Bayley* J, giving the same example), at 622-623 (1318) (*Holroyd* J, giving the same example and the further example of sale of part in order to finance the onward transport of the remainder); *Atkinson v. Stephens* (1852) 7 Ex 567, 155 ER 1074 at 574 (1077) *per Martin* B and 576-577 (1078) *per Pollock* CB (sale of part of the cargo was a lawful method of borrowing money to finance necessary repairs). A captain likewise has a power in a case of necessity to commission another to salvage cargo (*Hingston v. Wendt* (1876) 1 QBD 367, 371 (*Blackburn* J); *China Pacific SA v. Food Corpn of India* [1982] AC 939 (HL)), to bail it to another (creating a bailment between cargo owners and bailee) (*China Pacific SA v. Food Corpn of India*, loc. cit.), or to commission an agent (e. g. a legal adviser, where there is a dispute with a salvor) who will safeguard the cargo owners' interests (*The Soblomsten* (1866) LR 1 A & E 293, 299-300 (Dr *Lushington*)). In all of these cases the authority to transact and bind the principal rests on the fundamental requirement of a necessity for the transaction. Thus money borrowed or goods procured must be needed (*Gunn v. Roberts* (1874) LR 9 CP 331, 335 (*Brett* J: reasonably necessary according to the usual course of careful conduct) and applied to necessary ends or expenditure (*The Karnak*, loc. cit., 300 (Sir *Robert Phillimore*)). Money cannot be obtained by means of a (secured) loan if funds are already there (e. g. because provided for the purpose by the principal) or available from other (more advantageous) sources: cf. *Soares v. Rahn* (1838) 3 Moore PC 1 at 9, 13 ER 1 at 4 (Dr *Lushington* for the PC); *The Hebe* (1843) 2 W Rob 146 at 150-151, 166 ER 710 at 712 (possibility of obtaining payment from principal's debtor); *Smith v. Bank of New South Wales* (1872) LR 4 PC 194, 202 (*Mellish* LJ for the PC, implicitly); *Gunn v. Roberts* loc. cit., 333 and 337 (Brett J), and see also *The Lochiel* (1843) 2 W Rob 34 at 48, 166 ER 668 at 673 (Dr *Lushington*). Equally the transaction concluded must be proportionate to the problem. A sale of cargo by a ship's captain will not be authorised unless reasonable efforts to arrange onward transportation have been made and failed or there are no resources available to that end or it would be uneconomic because the expenditure involved would exceed the value of the goods themselves or, as a result of deterioration during transportation, they would lose further value: cf. *Hunter v. Prinsep* (1808) 10 East 378, 394-395 (Lord *Ellenborough* CJ); *Atlantic Mutual Insurance Co v. Huth* (1880) 16 Ch D 474, 481 (*Cotton* LJ), where the captain did not try to commission a salvor or obtain funds to conduct a rescue attempt. Correspondingly, a sale by a captain of a damaged ship will not be authorised if it can be economically repaired and funds are available or can be obtained on economic terms: *Somes v. Sugrue* (1830) 4 Car & P 276 at 283-284, 172 ER 703 at 706 (*Tindal* CJ); *The Segredo*, loc. cit., 48 (28-29) and 55 (32) (Dr *Lushington*). If the agent has conducted himself reasonably and properly when assessing the situation as apparent to him and concluding that in the circumstances a transaction is necessary, the matter cannot be impeached, and the agent is not accountable to the principal for the loss, if it subsequently emerges that it was not strictly necessary – for example, because, despite all the indications, a ship could in fact be repaired economically and need not have been sold: *Robertson v. Caruthers* (1819) 2 Stark 571 at 572, 171 ER 739 (*Abbott* LCJ); *Lindsay v. Leathley* (1863) 3 F & F 902 at 937, 176 ER 410 at 427 (*Cockburn* CJ). By statute (when it comes into force) an intervener acting in connection with the care or treatment of a person who is reasonably believed to lack capacity, reasonably believing it to be in that person's best interests, may pledge that person's credit or apply money of that person in that person's possession in order to meet expenditure: Mental Capacity Act 2005, sec. 8(1).

Annexes

Abbreviations

AA	Ars Aequi Juridisch Studentenblad (Zwolle [later Nijmegen], 1. 1951/1952 ff., cited by year and page)
AB	Wet algemeene bepalingen. Act of 15 May 1829 on the general provisions for the legislation of the kingdom (Stb. 28, The Netherlands)
ABGB	Allgemeines Bürgerliches Gesetzbuch, 1 June 1811 (JGS 946) (Civil Code, Austria)
AC	Law Reports, Appeal Cases (House of Lords) (London, 1. 1875/76 ff.; the older part of the collection up to 1890 cited as Appeal Cases; from 1891 the abbreviation A. C. is used; cited by year, book, and page)
AC	Actualidad Civil (Madrid 1. 2004 ff., cited by year and page)
ACLR	Australian Current Law Review (Sydney, 1969-1971)
AcP	Archiv für die civilistische Praxis (Tübingen, 1. 1818-50. 1867; N. F. 1 = 51. 1868-49 = 99. 1906; 100. 1906-120. 1922; N. F. [= 3.F.] 1. = 121. 1923-29. = 149. 1944; 30 = 150. 1948/49-53 = 173. 1973; 174. 1974 ff.); incorporating Archiv für bürgerliches Recht; cited by volume, year and page
A & E	Admiralty and Ecclesiastical Cases (London 1865-1875; cited by year, book, and page; see L. R.)
affd	affirmed
AfP	Archiv für Presserecht (Düsseldorf 1. 1953 ff.; cited by year and page)
AG	Amtsgericht (Local Court, Germany and Austria); Aktiengesellschaft (joint-stock company, plc)
A-G	Advocaat-Generaal (Netherlands); Attorney-General (England); Avocat-Général (Belgium; France)
AGBG	Gesetz v. 9.12.1976 zur Regelung des Rechts der Allgemeinen Geschäftsbedingungen (Act on General Contract Terms, 9 Dec. 1976; BGBl. 1976 I S. 3317, Germany) repealed [01. 01. 2002] by the Schuldrechtsmodernisierungsgesetz and inserted into the BGB
AID	Archeion Idiotiku Dikaiu (Triminiaia nomiki epitheorisis; Athens 1. 1934-17. 1954/59; cited by volume, year, and page)
AK	Astikos Kodikas (Civil Code, Greece, 23.2.1946 [A. N. 2250/1940; FEK A 91/1940 S. 597])
ALJR	Australian Law Journal Reports (Sydney, 1958-, cited by vol. and page)
AllER	All England Law Reports (London, 1. 1936 ff.; cited by year, book, and page)
Alm.Del	Almindelig Del (general part)
ALR	Allgemeines Landrecht für die preußischen Staaten, 1 June 1794 (Civil Code, Prussia)
A. L. R.	The Australian Law Reports (Sydney 1. 1973 ff.; cited by volume, year, and page)
alt.	alternative

AMG	Arzneimittelgesetz. Gesetz zur Neurordnung des Arzneimittelrechts v. 24.08.1976 (Act on Medication Reform, 24 Aug. 1976; BGBl. 1976 I p. 2995, Germany)
AmJCompL	The American Journal of Comparative Law (Baltimore 1. 1952 ff.; cited by volume, year, and page)
AN	Anagastikos Nomos (Emergency Laws, Greece)
AnDerCiv.	Anuario de Derecho Civil (Madrid 1. 1948 ff.; cited by volume, year, and page)
AnfO	Anfechtungsordnung v. 10.12.1914 (Contesting Act, RGBl 1914/337, Austria)
AngG	Angestelltengesetz v. 11.5.1921 (Employees' Act, BGBl 1921/292, Austria)
Annal.prop. industr.	Annales de la propriété industrielle, artistique et littéraire (Paris 1. 1855 ff.; cited by year and page)
Ann.Dr.Liège	Actualités du droit: Revue de la Faculté de droit de Liège (Luik 1. 1956 ff., since 1986 Brussels; until 1990 Annales de droit de Liège; cited by year and page)
Ann. Louv.	Annales de Droit de Louvain (Brussels 41. 1981 ff.; previously Annales de droit et de sciences politiques; cited by year and page)
Anst	Anstruther's Exchequer Reports (145 ER) (London 1792-1797; cited by year, volume and page)
A. P.	Areios Pagos (Greek Supreme Court in Civil Matters)
AP	Audiencia Provincial (Court of Appeal, Spain)
App	Corte d'Appello (Court of Appeal, Italy)
App.Cas.	see AC
APR	Annual percentage of rate
Apygardu teismai	Regional Court, Lithuania
Apylinkiu teismai	Local Court, Lithuania
AR	Arrêté Royal (Royal decree, Belgium)
Aranzadi Civil	Repertorio Aranzadi de Jurisprudencia Civil (Navarra 1. 1992 ff.; cited by year, volume, number and page)
Arch.civ.	Archivio civile (Piacenza, 4th Series 1. 1958 ff.; cited by year and page)
Arch.Giur. circolaz.	Archivio Giuridico della circolazione e dei sinistri stradali (Piacenza, 4th Series 1. 1955-22. 1976 ff.; cited by year and page)
ArchN	Archeion Nomologicas (Athens 1. 1949 ff.; cited by volume, year, and page)
Arch.resp.civ.	Archivio della responsabilità civile e dei problemi del danno (Piacenza 1. 1958 ff.; cited by year and page)
ARIL	Annual Review of Irish Law (Byrne and Binchy, eds.) (Dublin and London; 1. 1987 [1988])
Arm	Armenopoulos miniaia nomiki epitheorisis (Thessalonika 1. 1946/47 ff.; cited by year and page)
Arr.Cass.	Arresten van het Hof van Cassatie (Brussel 1967 ff.; from 1937-1961 published as "Arresten van het Hof van Verbreking"; the collection did not appear 1962-1966)
art(s).	article(s)
ASA	Advertising Standards Authority

ASVG	Allgemeines Sozialversicherungsrecht (General Social Insurance Act) (BGBl. 1955/189, Austria)
AT	Audiencia Territorial (Court of First Instance, Spain)
AtomG	Gesetz über die friedliche Verwendung der Kernenergie und den Schutz gegen ihre Gefahren (Atomgesetz), 31. Oct. 1976 (BGBl I 3035) (Germany)
AtomHG	Atomhaftpflichtgesetz (Nuclear Liability Act) (BGBl. 1964/117, Austria)
A & V	Aansprakelijkheid en Verzekering (Deventer 1.1993 ff.; cited by year and page)
Avd	Avdeling (Part)
Avv. e proc.	Avvocato e procuratore
AWSt-A	Reference term used in the publications of the BfAI; see BfAI
B	Baron
B & Ad	Barnewall & Adolphus' King's Bench Reports (ER 109-110) (London 1.1830-11.1840; cited by volume and page)
BAG	Bundesarbeitsgericht (Federal Labour Court, Germany)
BAGE	Entscheidungen des Bundesarbeitsgericht (Decisions of the Federal Labour Court) (Berlin 1.1955 ff.; cited by volume and page)
B & Ald	Barnewall and Alderson's Reports, Kings Bench (ER 106) (London 1817-1822)
BankFin	Bank- en Financiewezen/Revue de la banque (Brussels, 1.1936/37 ff.)
Banque	Revue banque (Paris, 1926-1998)
BAnz	Bundesanzeiger (42.1990, 186 (5.Okt.); Cologne: 1990-)
BB	Der Betriebs-Berater (Heidelberg, 1.1946 ff.; cited by year and page)
BBTC	Banca, borsa e titoli di credito = rivista di dottrina e giurisprudenza (Milan 1.1934-8.1941, 11.1948 ff.; cited by year book, and column)
B & C	Barnewall & Cresswell's King's Bench Reports (ER 107-109) (London 1822-1830, cited by year, volume and page)
BCLC	Butterworths Company Law Cases (London 1.1983 ff.; cited by year, book, and page)
BD	Byretsdom (Local Court judgment, Denmark)
Beav	Beaven's Rolls Court Reports (ER 48-55) (London 1838-1866, cited by year, volume and page)
BfAI	Bundesstelle für Außenhandelsinformation (Federal Information Centre on Foreign Trade Law; Cologne, Germany)
BFD	Universidade de Coimbra. Boletim da Faculdade de Direito (Coimbra 1.1914/15 – 9.1925/26 = no.1 – 90; 10.1926/28 – ; cited by volume, year and page)
BG	Bundesgericht (Supreme Court, Switzerland); Bezirksgericht (Court of Appeal, former GDR; partly also Germany); Bezirksgericht (Court of First Instance, general jurisdiction, Austria)
BGB	Bürgerliches Gesetzbuch, 18 Aug. 1896 (RGBl. 195) (Civil Code, Germany)
BGBl.	Bundesgesetzblatt (Official Gazette, Germany) 1950; then in parts: BGBl. part I (1951 ff.) BGBl. part II (1951 ff.) BGBl. part III = Sammlung des Bundesrechts (Collection of Federal Statutes; Cologne, Bonn 1.1958 ff.); Official Gazette, Austria 1920-1938; 1945 ff., form 2004 distributed Online www.ris.bka.gv.at

BGE	Entscheidungen des schweizerischen Bundesgerichtes (Decisions of the Swiss Supreme Court; can also be referred to as Arrêts du Tribunal Fédéral Suisse) (Lausanne 1. 1875 ff.; from 23. 1897 2 books without special titles; separation from 40. 1914; cited by volume, book, and page)
BGH	Bundesgerichtshof (Federal Supreme Court, Germany – before 1990 only for West Germany)
BGHR	BGH-Rechtsprechung Zivilsachen (Cologne 1987, CD-ROM; cited by § and keyword)
BGHZ	Amtliche Sammlung der Entscheidungen des Bundesgerichtshofes in Zivilsachen (decisions of the German Supreme Court in civil matters) (Cologne, Berlin 1. 1951 ff.; cited by volume and page)
Bing	Bingham's Reports, Common Pleas (ER 130-131) (London 1822-1834; cited by year, volume and page)
BinnSchG	Binnenschiffahrtsgesetz (Inland Waterways Act, Austria) (RGBl. 1898, 369, 868); Gesetz über den gewerblichen Binnenschiffsverkehr (Act on Industrial Inland Waterway Traffic, Germany) (as amended on 8 Jan. 1969) (BGBl. I 66)
BJagdG	Bundesjagdgesetz (Federal Hunting Act, Germany) (as amended on 29 Sep. 1976) (BGBl. I 2849)
BJC	Boletín de Jurisprudencia Constitucional (Bulletin of the Constitutional Court, Spain) (Madrid 1. 1981 ff.; cited by volume, year, and page)
BJIB & FL	Butterworths Journal of International Banking and Financial Law (London, 1986-, cited by year and page)
Bligh NS	Bligh's Reports, New Series (ER 4-6) (London 1827-1837; cited by year, volume and page)
BOE	Boletín Oficial del Estado (Official Gazette, Spain) (Madrid 1. 1936 ff.; cited by year, number, and date)
BolMinJus	Boletim do Ministério da Justiça (Bulletin of the Ministry of Justice) (Lisbon 1. 1940/41 ff.; cited by volume, year, and page)
BRats-Drucks	Bundesratsdrucksachen. Verhandlungen des Bundesrates (Proceedings of the 2nd Chamber of the German Federal Parliament; Bonn 1949 ff.; cited by volume, year and, if necessary, by page)
BrB	Brottsbalk (Criminal Code of 21 Dec. 1962, SFS 1962:700, Sweden)
B. R. H.	Belgische Rechtspraak in Handelszaken/Jurisprudence commerciale de Belgique (Antwerp, 1968-1982)
Brussels Convention	Brussels Convention. Convention on Jurisdiction and the Enforcement of Judgments in Civil and Commercial Matters, 27 Sep. 1968 (OJ 1978 L304, p. 77)
B & S	Best & Smith Queen's Bench Reports (London 1. 1861-5. 1865; cited by year, volume and page)
BS	Belgisch Staatsblad; see Monit. belge
BT-Drucks.	Bundestagsdrucksachen. Verhandlungen des Bundestages (Proceedings of the 1st Chamber of the German Federal Parliament; Bonn 1949 ff.; cited by volume, year, and if necessary, by page)
Build LR	Building Law Reports (London, 1976-1998, cited by volume and page)
Bull.Ass.	Bulletin des Assurances (Brussels 1. 1921 ff.; cited by year and page)

Bull.civ.	Bulletin des arrêts de la Cour de Cassation rendus en matière civile (Bulletin of the decisions of the Court of Cassation in civil matters, France) (Paris 12.1804/05, 128.1926 ff.; cited by year, book, and number)
Bull.com.	Bulletin des arrêts de la Cour de Cassation rendus en matière commerciale (= Book IV [formerly Book III] of Bull.civ.)
Bull.crim.	Bulletin des arrêts de la Cour de Cassation rendus en matière criminelle (Bulletin of the decisions of the Court of Cassation in criminal matters, France) (Paris 9.1804 ff.; cited by year, book and number)
BullEU	Bulletin of the European Union; (before 1993, Bulletin of the European Communities) (Luxemburg 1.1968 ff.; cited by year and number)
Burr	Burrow's King's Bench Reports tempore Mansfield (97-98 ER) (London 1757-1771; cited by year, volume and page)
BVerfG	Bundesverfassungsgericht (Federal Constitutional Court, Germany)
BVerfGE	Amtliche Sammlung der Entscheidungen des Bundesverfassungsgerichts (Decisions of the Federal Constitutional Court, Germany) (Tübingen 1952 ff.; cited by volume and page)
BVerfGG	Bundesverfassungsgerichtsgesetz (Statute of the Constitutional Court of the Federal Republic of Germany) as amended on the announcement of 12 Dec. 1985 (BGBl. I 2229)
BW	Burgerlijk Wetboek (The Netherlands) (Boek 1: Stb. 1969, no. 167 in conjunction with Stb. 1969 no. 259, in force since 1 Jan. 1970; Boek 2: Stb. 1976 no. 228 in conjunction with Stb. 1976 no. 342, in force since 26 July 1976; Boek 3, 5, 6 and 7: Stb. 1991 no. 600 in conjunction with Stb. 1989 no. 616 and 290, in force since 1 Jan. 1992; Boek 4: Stb. 1999 no. 300, in force since 1 Jan. 2003; Book 7A, Stb. 1989 no. 378, in force as Book 4 of the old BW since 18 Oct. 1838; Book 8 Stb. 1991 no. 126, in force since 1 Apr. 1991)
BW (old)	Burgerlijk Wetboek, 1 Sep. 1838 (Stb. 1831 nos. 1 and 6 in conjunction with KB, 10 Apr. 1838, Stb. 1838 no. 12) (Civil Code, The Netherlands)
CA	Audiencia Provincial (Spain); Corte d'Appello (Italy); Cour d'Appel (Belgium, France); Court of Appeal (England); Efeteion (Greece); High Court (Ireland) (in its appellate jurisdiction); Hof (The Netherlands); Hovrätt (Finland, Sweden); Inner House (Court of Session, Scotland); Kammergericht (Berlin, Germany); Krajsky sùd (Slovakia); Lietuvos apeliacinis teismas (Lithuania), Megyei birosàg (Hungary); Oberlandesgericht (Austria, Germany); Østre Landsret (Denmark); Relação (Portugal); Ringkonnakohus (Estonia); Sadem pierwszej instancji (Poland) Søndre Landsret (Denmark), Vestre Landsret (Denmark); Visje Sodisce (Slovenia); Vrnchi soud (Czech Republic)
CAA	Cour d'appel administratif (France)
Cal 3d	California Reports, Third Series (San Francisco, 1974-, cited by volume, year and page)
CAP	British Code of Advertising and Sales Promotion
Cass.	Hof van Cassatie/Cour de Cassation (Belgium); Cour de Cassation (France), Corte Suprema di Cassazione (Italy, when none other specified: sezione civile) (Court of Cassation)

Cass.ass.plén.	Cour de cassation, Assemblée Plénière (France)
Cass.ch.mixte	Cour de cassation, Chambre Mixte (France)
Cass.ch.réun.	Cour de Cassation, Chambres Réunies (France)
Cass.civ.	Cour de cassation, Chambre Civile (France)
Cass.com.	Cour de cassation, Chambre Commerciale et financière (France)
Cass.crim.	Cour de cassation, Chambre criminelle (France)
Cass.pén.	Cour de cassation, Chambre pénale (France); see Cass.crim.
Cass.req.	Cour de cassation, Chambre des Requêtes (abolished) (France)
Cass.sez.lav.	Corte di Cassazione, sezione lavoro (Italy)
Cass.sez.pen.	Corte di Cassazione, sezione penale (Italy)
Cass.sez.un.	Corte di Cassazione, sezione unite (Italy)
Cass.soc.	Cour de cassation, Chambre Sociale (France)
CB	Common Bench Reports (ER 135-139) (London 1845-1856)
CB (N. S.)	Common Bench Reports, New Series (ER 140-144) (London 1857-1866)
CBR Jaarboek	Centrum voor Beroepsvervolmaking in de Rechten. Universiteit Antwerpen. Jaarboek (Antwerp and Apeldoorn 1. 1996/97 ff.; cited by year and page)
CC	Civil Code Civil Code (Malta), 22 Jan. 1874 (Ordinance VII of 1868); Code Civil (France, Luxembourg), 21 Mar. 1804; Burgerlijk Wetboek/Code Civil (Belgium); Codice Civile (Italy) (Gaz.Uff., 4 Apr. 1942, no. 79 and 79bis; edizione straordinaria); Código Civil (Spain) 24 July 1889 (Gaceta de Madrid no. 206, 25 July 1889); Código Civil (Portugal) (Decreto-Lei no. 47-344, 25 Nov. 1966) See also ABGB, AK, BGB, BW, CK, EOA/VÕS, KC, ObcZ, OZ, Ptk
CCC	Contrats, concurrence et consommation (Paris, 1. 1991 ff.)
CC Introd.Act	Civil Code Introductory Act (Eisagogikos nomos, Greece; AN 2783/1941 FEK A 29/1941 p. 145); (Einführungsgesetz zum Bürgerlichen Gesetzbuch, Germany, see EGBGB)
CCLT	Canadian Cases on the Law of Torts (Toronto, 1976-, cited by volume and page)
Ccom	Commercial Code Código comercial (Portugal), 28 June 1888 (Diário do Governo no. 203, 6 Sep. 1888); Código de comercio (Spain) 22 Aug. 1885 (Gaceta de Madrid no. 289-328, 16 Oct. – 24 Nov. 1885); Code de commerce (France) 1808; Wetboek van Koophandel/Code de commerce (Belgium, 10 Sep. 1807); Handelsbalken (Sweden) 1734 See also HGB
CCP	Code on Civil Procedure Act 1/2000 on Civil Procedure (Spain), 7 January 2000 (BOE no. 7, 8 January 2000) See further Code jud.; CPC; C.proc.civ., GerW, KpolDik, Rv, ZPO
CDP	Cadernos de Direito Privado (Braga 1. 2003 ff.; cited by year, number and page)
CE	Consticución Española (Constitution, Spain) 27 Dec. 1987, altered 27 Aug. 1992 (BOE no. 311. 1., 29 Dec. 1978)
cf.	confer

CFI	Court of First Instance, general jurisdiction See further AG, Apygardu teismai, Apylinkiu teismai, AT, BD, BG, Civ., Conc., Corr, HC, Helyi birosàg, JP, Kerülti birosàg, KS, Ktg, LG, Linnakohus, Maakohus, MPr, OH, Okj, Okz, ØL, OS, PPr, Pr, Pret., Rb, Sady grodzkie, Sad okregowny, SH, Sh.Ct., TGI, TI, Trib., Trib.com., Trib.Corr., Trib.enfants, Varosi birosàg, VL, Vred
Ch	The Law Reports. Chancery (London 1.1891 ff.; cited by year, volume and page)
chap.	chapter
ChApp	Chancery Appeals (London 1865-1875; cited by year, volume and page; see L. R.)
ChD	The Law Reports, Chancery Division (London 1.1875/76-1890; cited by year, volume and page; see L. R.)
CICR	Comitato interministeriale per il credito e il consumo (the Interministerial Committee for Credit and Savings, referred also as the Credit Committee, Italy)
CIM	Convention internationale concernant le transport des marchandises par chemins de fer. International Agreement of 7 Feb. 1970 on Rail Freight (BGB1. 1974 II 381).
Cir.	Circuit
CISG	Vienna UN-Convention on the International Sale of Goods of 11.4.1980 (http://www.uncitral.org/en-index.htm)
Civ.	Tribunal de première instance (Chambre civile, Belgium)
CJ	Colectânea de Jurisprudência (Coimbra 1.1976 ff. cited by year, volume and page)
CJ (ST)	Colectânea de Jurisprudência. Acórdãos do Supremo Tribunal de Justiça (Coimbra 1.1993 ff.; cited by year, volume, and page)
C. J.	Lord Chief Justice (England)
CK	Lietuvos civilinis kodeksas (The Lithuanian Civil Code)
CLC	Commercial Law Cases (London, 2002 ff.)
CLJ	The Cambridge Law Journal (Cambridge 1.1921/23 ff., parts without volume numbers; cited, as far as possible, by volume, year, and page)
CLR	Commonwealth Law Reports (Melbourne 1.1903 ff.; cited by volume, year and page)
CLY	Current Law Yearbook (London 1.1947 ff.; cited by year and issue)
CMLR	Common Market Law Reports (London 1.1963 ff.; cited by volume, year and page)
Cmnd	Command Papers (London, cited by year and page)
CMR	Convention relative au Contrat de transport international de marchandises par route. Convention on the Contract for the International Carriage of Goods by Road, 19 May 1956 (UNTS vol. 399 p. 189)
Code jud.	Code judiciaire (Code of civil procedure, Belgium), 10 Oct. 1967 (Monit. belge, 31 Oct. 1967)
col	colona
Coll. Arb.	Collegio Arbitrale (Italy)
Col.Leg.Esp.	Colección Legislativa de España. First series, third part: Jurisprudencia civil (Madrid 1.1889 ff.; cited by volume, year, book, number and page)

COM	Publications of the European Commission (Brussels 1.1968 ff.)
CompLYB	Comparative Law Yearbook ('s-Gravenhage 1.1977 ff.; cited by year and page)
Conc.	Conciliatore (Justice of the Peace, Italy)
ConsC	Code de la consommation, Loi n° 93-949 du 26 juillet 1993, relative au code de la consommation (partie Législative) (Journal officiel de la République Française of 27 July 1993, 10538) (Consumer Code, France)
ConsCredA	Consumer Credit Act (Belgium: law of 12 June 1991 as amended in 2003 "Loi relative au crédit à la consummation/Wet op het consumentenkrediet", BS 9 July and 6 Aug. 1991; England/Scotland 1974 c. 1939; Germany: law of 17 Dec. 1990 "Verbraucherkreditgesetz", BGBl III 402-6; Portugal: DL 359/91 of 21 September 1991 "Establece normas relatives ao credito ao consumo", DR 3,2 no. 218, Serie I-A of 21 Sept. 1991, 4998-5003; Spain: law no. 7/1995 of 23 March 1995 "Ley de credito al consumo", BOE no. 72 of 25 March and no. 113 of 12 May 1995; Sweden: "Konsumentkreditlag", SFS 1992:830)
ConsProtA	Consumer Protection Act (Austria: law of 8 March 1979 "Konsumentenschutzgesetz", as amended in 1983, 1984, 1985, 1993, 1996, 1997 and 2001, BGBl 1979 no. 140; England/Scotland: Consumer Protection Act 1987 c. 43; Finland; Greece: (former) law no. 1961/1991 and law no. 2251/1994 on Consumer Protection "Prostasia ton Katanaloton", Official Gazette 191 as amended in 1999, 2000, 2002; Luxembourg: law of 25 Aug 1983 "Loi relative à la protection du consommateur", Memorial 1983, 1494, as amended in 1986, 1987, 1993, 1997 and 2000; Portugal: Law no. 24/96 of 31 July 1996 "Estabelece o regime legal aplicável à defesa dos consumidores. Revoga a Lei n° 29/81 do 22.8.1981" commonly called "Lei de Defesa do Consumidor", DR no. 176, Serie I-A of 31 July 1996, 2184-2189; Spain: law 26/1984 of 19 July 1984 "General Ley para la Defensa de los Consumidores y Usuarios", BOE no. 176 of 24 July 1984)
Const LJ	Construction Law Journal (London, 1984-, cited by volume and page)
Const LR	Construction Law Reports (London, 1984-, cited by volume and page)
ContrA	Contract Act (Denmark: Aftaleloven, n. 242 of 8 May 1917, lovbekendtgørelse om aftaler og andre retshandler på formuerettens område no. 781 of 26 Aug. 1996; Finland: Lag om rättshandlingar på förmögenhetsrättens område of 13 June 1929 no. 228; Sweden: Lag om avtal och andra rättshandlingar på förmögenhetsrättens område, SFS 1915:218)
Contratto e Impresa	Contratto e Impresa (Padova 1.1985 ff.; cited by year and page)
Corr	Correctionnel (Court of First Instance in Criminal Matters, Belgium)
Corr.giur.	Corriere giuridico (Milan 1.1984 ff.; cited by year and page)
Corte Cost.	Corte Costituzionale (Constitutional Court, Italy)
Cost.	Costituzione of 27 Dec. 1947 (Constitution Italy; Gaz.Uff. no. 298, edizione straordinaria)
COTIF	Convention relative aux transports internationaux ferroviaires of 9 May 1980
Cour	Cour Supérieure de Justice (in its function as Cour d'assises, Cour de cassation or Cour d'appel, Luxembourg)
Cox Eq Cas	Cox's Equity Cases (London, 1745-1797, cited by year, vol. and page)

CP	Code Pénal (Penal Code, France, Luxembourg), 16 June 1879 (Mémorial 1879 p. 589); Code Pénal / Strafwetboek (Penal Code, Belgium), 8 June 1867 (Monit.belge 9 June 1867); Codice Penale (Penal Code, Italy), n. 1938, 19 Sep. 1930 (Gaz.Uff. no. 253 suppl. 28 Sep. 1930); Código Penal (Penal Code Spain), 14 Sep. 1973 (BOE no. 297-300, 12-15 Dec. 1973); Código Penal (Penal Code, Portugal), Decreto 16 Sep. 1886
C. P.	Common Pleas Cases (London 1865-1875; cited by year, volume and page; see L. R.)
C & P	Carrington and Payne's Reports (ER 171-173), 1823-1841
CPC	Codice di procedura civile (Italy)
CPD	Common Pleas Division (London 1875/76-1890; cited by year, volume and page; see L. R.)
CPR	Civil Procedure Rules 1998 (SI 1998/3132) (England)
C.proc.civ.	(Nouveau) Code de Procédure Civile of 1.1.1976 (Code of Civil Procedure, France) (décret n° 75-1123, 5.12.1975); Codice di procedura civile of 21 Apr. 1942 (Code of Civil Procedure, Italy) (R. D., 28 Oct. 1940, no. 1443 Gaz.Uff. no. 253, 28 Oct. 1940); Código do Processo Civil of 28.12.1961 (Code of Civil Procedure, Portugal) (Decreto Lei Nr. 44129)
C.proc.crim.	Code d'instruction criminelle (Wetboek van Strafvordering, Belgium) (17 Apr. 1878 [Monit.belge, 25 Apr. 1878])
C.proc.pen.	Codice di procedura penate (Italy, 1 July 1931 [RD, 19 Oct. 1930 no. 1399: Gaz.Uff. 28 Oct. 1930 no. 253 Suppl.]); Código de processo penal (Portugal [Decreto Lei no. 16489, 15 Feb. 1929 Diário do Governo]). (Code of Criminal Procedure)
C.proc.pén.	Code de procédure pénale (Code of Criminal Procedure, France)
CrimLR	Criminal Law Review (London 1. 1954 ff.; cited by volume, year and page)
CRvB	Centrale Raad van Beroep (Administrative Court, The Netherlands)
ctr.	contra
CuadCivJur.	Cuadernos Civitas de Jurisprudencia Civil (Madrid 1. 1983 ff.; cited by year and page)
CurrLegProbl.	Current Legal Problems (London 1. 1948 ff.; cited by volume, year and page)
D.	Recueil de jurisprudence Dalloz (Paris; with different forms and titles: D. A. (Recueil analytique Dalloz [1941-1944]); D. C. (Recueil critique Dalloz [1941-1944]); D. H. (Recueil hebdomadaire Dalloz [1924-1940]); D. P. (Recueil périodique et critique mensuel Dalloz [1924-1940]); Recueil Dalloz, Recueil Sirey, combined since 1955; Recueil Dalloz et Recueil Sirey; from 1965: Recueil Dalloz-Sirey; appearing in sections: D. Chron./Jur. [Chronique/Jurisprudence], D. I. R./Légis. [Informations Rapides/Législation], D. Somm.Comm. [Sommaires Commentés]; cited by year, book, and page) (older forms and titles omitted)
D	décret (decree, France)
D	Digesten

D	Dunlop's Session Cases (1838-1862)
Danske Lov	Kong Christian den Femtes Danske Lov af 15. Apr. 1683 (Danish Code of King Christian the fifth of 15 Apr. 1683)
Danno e resp.	Danno e responsabilità. Problemi di responsabilitá civile e assicurazioni (Milan 1.1996 ff.; cited by year and page)
DAOR	Le droit des affaires/Het ondernemingsrecht (Gent 1.2000/01 ff.)
DAR	Deutsches Autorecht (München 1.1926 ff.; cited by year and page)
DB	Der Betrieb. Wochenschrift für Betriebswirtschaft, Steuerrecht, Wirtschaftsrecht, Arbeitsrecht (Düsseldorf, 1.1948 ff.; cited by year and page)
D, B & M Rep.	Dunlop, Bell & Murray's Reports, Session Cases, Second Series (Scotland) (1838-1862)
D. C.	see D.
DDike	Dioikitiki Dike (Athens 1.1989 ff.; cited by year and page)
DEE	Dikaio Epicheiriseon kai Etairion (Enterprises and Company Law; 1.1995, Athens)
De G. F. & J.	De Gex, Fisher and Jones's Reports, Chancery (ER 45) (London 1859-1862
De Verz	Tijdschrift voor Verzekering (formerly De Verzekering)/Bulletin des Assurances (Brussels 1.1921 ff.; cited by year and page)
D. H.	see D.
DHG	Dienstnehmerhaftpflichtgesetz. Bundesgesetz v. 31.3.1965 über die Beschränkung der Schadensersatzpflicht der Dienstnehmer (Federal Law on the Limitation of Personal Liability of Employees, Austria, 31 Mar. 1965; BGBl. 1965/80)
Diário Rep	Diário da República. Portugese government gazette (Lisbon 1.1976 ff.; cited by year and number)
Dir.fam.pers.	Il diritto di famiglia e delle persone (Milan 1.1972 ff.; cited by year, and if necessary, by part and page)
Dir.inf.	Diritto dell'informazione e dell'informatica (Milan 1.1985 ff.; cited by year and page)
Dir.just.	Direito e justicia (Lisbon 1.1980 ff.; cited by year and page)
diss.	dissertation
DJ	Deutsche Justiz (Berlin 1.1933-13.1945; cited by year and page)
DJT	Deutscher Juristentag (German Lawyers' Association)
DL	Decreto legge, decreto ley (Decree-law, Greece, Italy, Portugal)
DLgs	Decreto legislativo (Legislative Decree, Italy)
DLR	Dominion Law Reports (Aurora, Ontario: First Series 1.1912-70.1922; 1923-1955; Second Series 1.1956-70.1968; Third Series: 1.1969-150.1984; Fourth Series 1.1984 ff.; cited by year, volume and page)
DNotZ	Deutsche Notarzeitschrift (Munich, Berlin 1.1901-33..1933 Magazine of the German Association of Public Notaries; 33.1933 ff.; cited by year and page)
Dow	Dow's Reports (England), House of Lords (ER 3), 1812-1818
Dow & RyKB	Dowling and Ryland's Reports, King's Bench (ER 171), 1822-1827
D. P.	see D.
DPR	Decreto Presidente della Repubblica (Presidential decree, Italy)
DR	Diário da República (Official Gazette, Portugal, Lisbon 1.1976 ff.)
Droit soc	Droit social (Paris 1.1938 ff.; cited by year and page)

Dr.prat.com.int.	Droit et pratique du commerce international (Paris 1975-1994; cited by year and page)
DStR	Deutsches Steuerrecht (Munich 1.1962/63 ff.; cited by year and page)
DTI	Department of Trade and Industry (United Kingdom)
DULJ	Dublin University Law Journal (Dublin 1976-1981. New Series from 1982; cited by year, volume and page)
EAL	Erstatningsansvarsloven (Damages Liability Act, no. 228, 23 May 1984; Lovtidende A p. 742; Lovbekendtgørelse om erstatningsansvar, no. 750, 4 Sept. 2002 Denmark)
East	East's Term Reports, King's Bench (102-104 ER) (London 1801-1812; cited by year, volume and page)
E & B	Ellis and Blackburn's Reports (ER 118-120) (London 1852-1858; cited by year, volume and page)
EC	European Community
ECE	Economic Commission for Europe
ECHR	European Court of Human Rights (Strasbourg)
ECJ	European Court of Justice (Luxembourg)
ECLR	European Competition Law Review (Oxford 1.1980 ff.; cited by volume, year, and page)
ecolex	Fachzeitschrift für Wirtschaftsrecht (Vienna 1.1990 ff.; cited by year and page)
ECR	European court reports. Reports of cases before the Court of Justice and the Court of First Instance (Luxembourg 1.1954 ff.) (until 1989 Reports of cases before the Court) (cited by volume, year, and page)
ed.	edition, editor(s)
Edinburgh LRev	The Edinburgh Law Review (Edinburgh 1.1997 ff.; quoted by volume, year and page)
EEC	European Economic Community
EED	Epitheorissis Egatikou Dikaiou (Review of Commercial Law) (Athens 1.1941 ff.; cited by volume, year, and page)
EEN	Ephimeris Ellinon Nomikon (Journal of Greek Jurists) (Athens 1.1934 ff.; cited by volume, year, and page)
Ef	Efeteion (Court of Appeals, Greece)
EFSlg	Ehe- und familienrechtliche Entscheidungen (Decisions on Marriage and Family Law) (Vienna 1.1965 ff.; cited by the number of the decision)
e. g.	exempli gratia (for example)
EGBGB	Einführungsgesetz zum Bürgerlichen Gesetzbuche (BGB Introductory Act, 18 Aug. 1896; RGBl. 604) (Germany)
Eis.	Eisagogi (introduction)
EKHG	Eisenbahn- und Kraftfahrzeughaftpflicht-Gesetz (Rail and Road Traffic Liability Act of 21 Jan. 1959; BGBl. 1959/48, Austria)
El.Bl. & El.	Ellis, Blackburn & Ellis' Queen's Bench Reports (120 ER) (London 1858; cited by year, volume, and page)
EllDik	Elliniki Dikeosini (Athens 1.1960 ff.; cited by volume, year, and page)
EMLR	Entertainment and Media Law Reports (London 1998-, cited by year and page)

EOA	see VÕS
EPA	Employment Protection Act 1990 (United Kingdom)
EpTrD	Epitheoresis Trapeziku Dikaiou (Review of Banking Law, Greece)
EpTrAksXrD	Epitheoresis Trapeziku Aksiografiku kai Xrimatistiriakou Dikaiou (Review of Banking, Negotiable Instruments and Capital Market, Greece)
ER	The English Reports (London 1.1900-178.1932; cited by volume and page)
ErmAK	Ermineia tou Astikou Kodikos (Commentary to the Greek Civil Code)
ERPL	European Review of Private Law (Deventer 1.1994 ff.; cited by volume, year, and page)
et. al.	et alii (and others)
ETS	European Treaty Series of Agreements and Conventions of the Council of Europe (Strasbourg 1.1949-3.1949, 4.1950 ff./61.1971 ff.; cited by volume and number)
EU	European Union
EuGRZ	Europäische Grundrechte-Zeitschrift (Strasbourg 1.1974 ff.; cited by year and page)
Eur.Conv. Hum.Rt	European Convention on the Protection of Human Rights, 4 Nov. 1950
Eur.Transp. L.	European Transport Law (Antwerp 1.1966 ff.; cited by volume, year, and page)
EuZW	Europäische Zeitschrift für Wirtschaftsrecht (Munich, Frankfurt/Main 1.1990 ff.; cited by year and page)
EvBl	Evidenzblatt der Rechtsmittelentscheidungen (Vienna 1.1934 ff.; included in the ÖJZ [since 1946]; see there; cited by year and page)
EWCA Civ	Approved Judgment of the Court of Appeal, Civil Division, England and Wales
EWHC	Approved Judgment of the High Court, England and Wales
EWiR	Entscheidungen zum Wirtschaftsrecht (Cologne 1.1985 ff.; cited by §, number, year, and page)
EWS	Europäisches Wirtschafts- und Steuerrecht (Munich 1.1990 ff.; cited by year and page)
Ex	Exchequer Cases (London 1865-1875; cited by volume, year, and page; see L. R.)
Exchq	Court of the Exchequer
ExchqCh	Exchequer Chamber
ExD	Exchequer Division (London 1876-1880 cited by volume, year, and page; see L. R.)
F	Fraser's Session Cases, 5th Series (Scotland) (1898-1906)
f(f)	following page(s)
FAL	Forsikringsaftaleloven (Denmark: Law on Insurance Contracts; no. 129, 15 Apr. 1930, lovbekendtgørelse om forsikringsaftaler n. 726 of 24 Oct. 1986; Finland: Lag om Försäkringsavtal of 28 June 1994 no. 543; Sweden: Lag om Försäkringsavtal (Law on Insurance Contracts, SFS 1927:77)
Fallim	Fallimento e le altre procedure concorsuali (Milan 1.1979 ff)

Fam	The Law Reports, Family Division (London 1972 ff.; formerly: The Law Reports, Probate, Divorce and Admiralty Division 1.1865/1869 ff.; cited by year and page)
FamRZ	Zeitschrift für das gesamte Familienrecht (Bielefeld 1.1954 ff.; until 9.1962: Ehe und Familie im privaten und öffentlichen Recht [Marriage and Family within Private and Public Law]; cited by year and page)
fasc.	fascicule
FED	Forsikrings- og Erstatningsretlig Domssamling (Copenhagen 1.1994 ff.; cited by year and page)
FEK	Fyllo Ephimeridas Kyberniseos (Government Gazette, Greece; Athens 1.1833; cited by year, volume, and if necessary, book, and number)
f(f)	following page(s)
F & F	Foster & Finlason's Nisi Prius Reports (ER 175-176) (London 1856-1867; cited by year, volume and page)
FFR	Försäkringsjuridiska föreningens rättsfallsamling (Stockholm 1939-1984; cited by year, volume and page)
FFS	Finlands Författningssamling (Official Gazette; Finland) (Helsinki 1.1860 ff.; cited by year, number, and page)
Fin LR	Financial Law Reports (Brentford 1982-, cited by volume, year and page)
FL	Færdselsloven, Act no. 149 on Road Traffic, Denmark, 20 Mar. 1918 (Lovtidende A 1918 pp. 578-592)
fn.	footnote
Foro it.	Il Foro italiano: raccolta di giurisprudenza civile, commerciale, penale, amministrativa (Rome, 1.1876 ff.; cited by year, book, and column)
Foro it.Mass.	Massimario del Foro italiano (Rome 1.1930 ff.; cited by volume, year, number, and column)
Foro pad.	Il Foro padano (Milan 1.1946 ff.; cited by year, book, and column)
FP6	Sixth Framework Programme on Research
FS	Festschrift
FSA	Financial Services Authority
FSMA	Financial Services and Markets Act 2000 (United Kingdom)
FSR	Fleet Street Patent Law Reports (London 1.1963 ff.; cited by year and page)
FSupp	Federal Supplement (St. Paul/Minnesota 1.1932/33 ff.; cited by volume and page)
FTLR	Financial Times Law Reports (Brentford 1982, 1986-1988)
FuR	Familie und Recht (Neuwied 1.1990 ff.; cited by year and page)
GazPal	La gazette du palais: feuille officielle d'annonces légales (Paris 1.1886 ff.; cited by year, book, and page)
GazUff	Gazzetta Ufficiale della Repubblica Italiana (Official Gazette; Italy) (Rome 1.1860 ff.; cited by year, number and page)
GenTG	Gentechnikgesetz. Gesetz zur Regelung der Gentechnik v. 20.6.1990 (Act on the Regulation of Genetic Engineering, 20 June 1990, Germany) (BGB1. I 1080)
GerW	Gerechtelijk Wetboek (Code of Civil Procedure, Belgium)
GG	Grundgesetz (Basic Law, Constitution, Germany)

GGSt	Gefahrgutbeförderungsgesetz. Bundesgesetz v. 23.2.1979 über die Beförderung gefährlicher Güter auf der Straße und über eine Änderung des Kraftfahrgesetzes 1967 und der Straßenverkehrsordnung (Federal Act on the Transportation of Dangerous Goods, 23 Feb. 1979; BGBl. 209/1979, Austria)
GlU	Sammlung von Civilrechtlichen Entscheidungen des kk Obersten Gerichtshofes, begründet von Glaser und Unger (Collection of Civil Law cases, established by Glaser and Unger) (Vienna 1898-1915; cited by the number of the decision)
GlUNF	Neue Folge der Sammlung von Civilrechtlichen Entscheidungen des kk Obersten Gerichtshofes, begründet von Glaser und Unger (New Series of Civil Law Cases, established by Glaser and Unger) (Vienna 1898-1915; cited by the number of the decision)
Giff	Giffard's Chancery Reports (ER 65-66) (London, 1857-1865)
giur. civ. comm.	La Nuova giurisprudenza civile commentata: rivista bimestrale delle nuove leggi civili commentate, Padova: Cedam, 1. 1985-
Giur.cost.	Giurisprudenza costituzionale (Milan 1. 1956-20. 1975; then: Parte 1 = Corte costituzionale 21. 1976 ff.; Parte 2 = Ordinanza di rinivio ed i ricorsi 21. 1976 ff.; Parte 3 = Quaderni della giurisprudenza costituzionale 1. 1964-7. 1968; new series 1. 1972 ff.)
Giur.it.	Giurisprudenza italiana (Torino 14. 1862-25. 1873; 3rd series 26. 1874-32. 1880, 4th series 33. 1881-43. 1891, 5th series 44. 1892-64. 1912, 110. 1958 ff.; cited by year, part, and if necessary, section and column)
Giur.it.Mass.	Massimario della Giurisprudenza italiana (Torino 1. 1931 ff.; cited by year, number and page)
Giur.mer.	Giurisprudenza di merito (Milan 1. 1969 ff.; cited by year, book and page)
Giur.tosc.	Giurisprudenza toscana (Milan et al. 1. 1950 ff.; cited by year and page)
Giust.civ.	Giustizia civile. Rivista bimestrale di giurisprudenza (Milan 1. 1951 ff.; cited by year, book and page)
Giust.civ.Mass.	Massimario annotato della cassazione Milan: Giuffrè, 5. 1955(1955/56)-7. 1957(1957/58); [8.]1958-[31.]1981; 32. 1983 – (Giustizia civile)
Giust. Pen.	Giustizia penale. Rivista critica di dottrina, giurisprudenza, legislazione (Rome 1. 1895 ff.; cited by year, book and page)
GmbH	Gesellschaft mit beschränkter Haftung (private company limited by shares)
GmbHR	GmbH-Report. Gesellschafts- und Steuerrecht der GmbH und GmbH & Co (Cologne 1. 1963 ff., until 75. 1985: GmbH-Rundschau; cited by year and page)
GRUR	Gewerblicher Rechtsschutz und Urheberrecht (Weinheim 1. 1896-49. 1944, 50. 1948 ff.; cited by year and page)
GRUR Int	Gewerblicher Rechtsschutz und Urheberrecht, Internationaler Teil (Weinheim 1. 1980 ff.; from 1966 to 1980 Auslands- und internationaler Teil; cited by year and page)
GrW	Grondwet (Constitution, The Netherlands, 17 Feb. 1983) (Stb. p. 70)
GWB	Gesetz gegen Wettbewerbsbeschränkungen (Act against Restrictions to Competition, Germany), 27 July 1957 (BGBl. I 1081)

H	Danish Højesteret (Supreme Court)
HaftPflG	Haftpflichtgesetz, 4 Jan. 1978 (BGBl I 145) (Liability Act, Germany)
HBl	Henry Blackstone's Common Pleas Reports (126 ER) (London 1788-96)
HC	High Court (Court of Appeal, Ireland)
HD	Redogörelser och meddelanden angående högsta domstolens avgöranden (Collection of Judgments by the Finnish Supreme Court) (Helsinki 1. 1926 ff.; cited by year, number and page)
HD	Højesteretsdom (Denmark); Høyesterettsdom (Norway); Högsta domstolens domar (Sweden, Finland) (Judgment of the Supreme Court)
Hdst.	Hoofdstuk
Helyi biroság	Local Court (Court of First Instance), Hungary
HGB	Handelsgesetzbuch (Commercial Code, Germany 10 May 1897; RGBl. p. 219, BGBl III 4100-1); Austria (March 1939, RGBl I 1938/1999)
HK	Højesterets kendelse (Supreme Court Decisions, Denmark)
HKLR	Hong Kong Law Reports (1. 1905/06 – 40. 1956; 1957-1995)
HL	House of Lords (United Kingdom)
HLC	Clark's House of Lords Cases (ER 9-11) (London 1. 1847-10. 1866; cited by volume, year and page)
HL(Ir)	See LR
HLR	Housing Law Reports (London 1. 1967 ff.; cited by year, volume, and page)
HL(Sc)	See LR
H & N	Hurlstone and Norman's Reports (ER 156-158) (London 1856-1862, cited by volume, year and page)
Hof	Gerechtshof (Court of Appeal, The Netherlands)
HovR	Hovrätt (Court of Appeal, Finland, Sweden)
HPflG	Haftpflichtgesetz (Liability Act, Germany, 4 Jan. 1978; BGBl. I 145)
HR	Hoge Raad (Supreme Court, The Netherlands)
HRR	Höchstrichterliche Rechtsprechung (Berlin, book. 4 [1928]-book. 18 [1942]; formerly: Juristische Rundschau [Suppl.], Die Rechtsprechung der Oberlandesgerichte and Höchstrichterliche Rechtsprechung auf dem Gebiet des Strafrechts; cited by year and number)
H & Tw	Hall & Twell's Chancery Reports (ER 47) (London 1849-1850; cited by volume, year and page)
ICC	International Chamber of Commerce
ICCLR	International Company and Commercial Law Review (London, 1990-, cited by year and page)
ICLQ	International and Comparative Law Quarterly (London, 1952-, cited by year, number and page)
ICR	Industrial Cases Reports (London 1. 1975 ff.; cited by year and page)
ICSTIS	Independent Committee for the Supervision of Telefone Information Services (United Kingdom)
i. e.	id est (that is to say)
IECL	The International Encyclopedia of Comparative Law (Tübingen, New York 1. 1970 ff.; cited by volume, chapter and margin number)
IEHC	Approved Judgment of the High Court, Republic of Ireland
Inner House	Inner House (Court of Session, Scotland)

IHR	Internationales Handelsrecht, Zeitschrift für das Recht des internationalen Warenkaufs und -vertriebs (Munich 1999-, cited by year and page)
ILRM	Irish Law Reports Monthly (Dublin 1. 1981 ff.; cited by year and page)
ILT	Irish Law Times (New Series, Dublin 1. 1983 ff.; cited by year and page)
ILTR	Irish Law Times Reports (Dublin 1. 1867 ff.; cited by year, book, and page)
Incoterms	International Commercial Terms
Inf AuslR	Informationsbrief Ausländerrecht (Frankfurt/Main 1. 1979 ff.; cited by year and page)
Inf. prev.	Informazione e previdenziale. Rivista bimestriale dell'avvocatura dell'Istituto Nazionale delle Previdenza Sociale (Rome 1. 1985 ff; cited by year and page)
IntBusLawyer	International Business Lawyer (London 1. 1973 ff.; cited by year and page)
IPRax	Praxis des Internationalen Privat- und Verfahrensrechts (Bielefeld 1. 1981 ff; cited by year and page)
IPRE	IPR-Entscheidungen 1-3, Österreichische Entscheidungen zum Internationalen Privatrecht bis 1993, ed. by Schwimann
IPRG	Bundesgesetz über das Internationale Privatrecht, 15.6.1978 (BGBl 304) (Act on Private International Law, Austria)
I. R.	Informations rapides du recueil Dalloz, France; see D.
IR	The Irish Reports (Dublin 1. 1894 ff.; including the sub-series Common Law Series [1. 1867 (1868)-11. 1877 (1878)] as well as Equity Series [1. 1867 (1868) ff.]; cited by year, book and page)
IrEqR	Irish Equity Reports (Dublin 1838-1850; cited by year and page)
Ir.Jurist	Irish Jurist (Dublin 1. 1935 ff.; cited by year and page)
Ir.Jurist R.	Irish Jurist Reports (Dublin 1. 1935 ff.; cited by volume, year and page)
IRLR	Industrial Relations Law Reports (London 1. 1972 ff.; cited by year and page)
IrLR	Irish Law Reports, 1st series (Dublin 1. 1838-12. 1850; cited by year, book and page)
IT-law	The law related to Information Technology
J	Juristen (Copenhagen 1. 1919 ff.; cited by year and page)
J.	Judge (High Court, UK)
JA	Juristische Arbeitsblätter (Bielefeld 1. 1969 ff.; cited by year and page)
Jahrb. f.ital. R.	Jahrbuch für italienisches Recht (Heidelberg 1. 1988 ff.; cited by volume, year and page)
JAR	Jurisprudentie arbeidsrecht ('s-Gravenhage 1. 1992 ff.; cited by year and page)
JBl	Juristische Blätter (Vienna 1. 1872 ff.; cited by year and page)
JbOstR	Jahrbuch für Ostrecht (Munich 1. 1960 ff.; cited by volume, year and page)
JClCiv	Collection des Juris-Classeurs. Juris-Classeur Civil. Directeurs à partir de 1980 Pierre Catala and Philippe Simler. (Paris 1962 ff.)
JCP	Juris-Classeur périodique; see Sem.Jur.
JCP E	Semaine Juridique édition entreprise (France); see Sem.Jur.
JCP G	Semaine Juridique édition générale (France); see Sem.Jur.
JCP N	Semaine Juridique éditions nouvelles (France); see Sem.Jur.
JDI	Journal du droit international (Paris, 1874-, citec by year and page) (also known as Clunet)
J.Environ. L.	Journal of Environmental Law (New York 1. 1974/75 ff; cited by volume, year and page)

JFT	Tidskrift utgiven av Juridiska Föreningen i Finland (Helsingfors 1.1936 ff.; cited by year and page)
JGG	Jugendgerichtsgesetz (Juvenile Court Act, Germany), 4 Aug. 1953 (BGBl. I 751)
JGS	Justizgesetzsammlung. Gesetze und Verordnungen in Justizsachen (Collection of Statutes on the Administration of Justice, Austria) (Vienna 1780-1848; cited by year and number)
JhJb	Jherings Jahrbücher für die Dogmatik des bürgerlichen Rechts (Jena 1.1857-90.1943; until 37.1897 Jahrbuch für die Dogmatik des heutigen römischen Rechts und deutschen Privatrechts; cited by volume, year and page)
JIBFL	Butterworths Journal of International Banking and Financial Law, London 1986 ff.
J. Int'l Fin. Mkt.	Journal of International Financial Markets (Amsterdam, 1994-, cited by year, volume and page)
JL	Jurisprudence de Liège (83.1978, Oct. – 93.1986, afterwards published as JLMB [see JLMB])
JLMB	Revue de jurisprudence de Liège, Mons et Bruxelles (Liége, 94.1987 ff)
JO	Journal Officiel de la République Française. Lois et Décrets. Official gazette of the French Republic. Acts and Decrees (Paris 1.1869 ff.; cited by date of issue)
JöR	Jahrbuch des öffentlichen Rechts der Gegenwart (Tübingen 1.1907-25.1938; NS 1.1951 ff.; cited by volume, year, and page)
John	Johnson's Chancery Reports (ER 70) (London 1859)
JP	Juge de Paix (Luxembourg); Juge de Paix (Belgium) (Justice of the Peace)
JR	Juristische Rundschau (Berlin 1.1947 ff.; cited by year and page)
JT	Juridisk tidskrift vid Stockholms universitet (Stockholm 1.1989/90 ff.; cited by year and page)
JT	Journal des Tribunaux (Brussels 1.1881-96.1981; 101.1982 ff; 97-100 not produced; cited by year and page)
JT (Lausanne)	Journal des Tribunaux (Lausanne 1.1929 ff.; cited by year and page)
Jur.	Jurisprudence
Jura	Jura. Juristische Ausbildung (Berlin et al 1.1979 ff.; cited by year and page)
JuridRev	The Juridical Review (Edingburgh, London 1.1889-67.1955; new series 1.1956 ff.; cited by year and page)
JuS	Juristische Schulung (Munich, Frankfurt am Main 1.1961 ff.; cited by year and page)
JUS	Rivista di scienze giuridiche (Milan 1.1940-4.1943; NS 1.1950-20.1969; 21.1974 ff.; cited by year and page)
JW	Juristische Wochenschrift. Organ des Deutschen Anwaltsvereins (Bulletin of the German Lawyers' Association) (Leipzig 1.1872-68.1939, 1940 merged with Deutsches Recht; cited by year and page)
JZ	Juristenzeitung (Tübingen 1.1945 ff.; Continuation of the German Rechtszeitschrift and the South German Juristenzeitung, volume 6.1951 ff.; cited by year and page)

KB	King's Bench
KB	The Law Reports. King's Bench Division (London, 1. 1875/76 ff.; cited by year, book and page)
KB	Koninklijk Besluit (Royal decree, Belgium and The Netherlands)
KC	Kodeks cywilny (Civil Code, Poland)
Kerülti birosàg	District Court (Court of First Instance), Hungary
KF	Karlsruher Forum. Supplement to VersR (Karlsruhe 1. 1959 ff.; cited by year and page)
KFG	Kraftfahrgesetz (Act on Road Traffic, Austria, BGBl. 1967/267)
KG	Kort Geding (from 1. 1981 contained in Rechtspraak van de Week; see RvdW)
KG	Kammergericht (Berlin, Court of Appeal, Germany)
KIR	Knight's Industrial Reports (London 1. 1966-10. 1975; cited by year, volume and page)
KO	Konkursordnung i. d. F. v. 20.5.1898 (Bankruptcy Act, Austria, RGBl. 369)
KPD	Kodikas Pinikis Dikonomias (Code of Criminal Procedure, Greece) (Act no. 1493, 17 Aug. 1950, FEK 182/1950 pp. 1004-1074)
KPolDik	Kodikas Politikis Dikonomias (Code of Civil Procedure, Greece) (Royal Decree 657/1971 FEK 219/1 Jan. 1971 p. 75)
KritE	Kritiki Epitheorisi (Athens 1. 1994, cited by year and page)
KS	Krajsky soud (District Court, Court of First Instance, Czech Republik); Krajsky sùd (District Court, Court of Appeal, Slovakia)
KSchG	Konsumentenschutzgesetz, 8 March 1979 (BGBl 1979/140) (Consumer Protection Act, Austria)
Ktg	Kantongerecht (Local Court, The Netherlands)
KTS	Konkurs-, Treuhand- und Schiedsgerichtswesen (Cologne et al. 1. 1939-52. 1991; cited by year and page)
KunstUrhG	Gesetz betreffend das Urheberrecht an Werken der bildenden Künste und der Photographie (Act on Copyright on Works of Fine Art and Photography, Germany, 9 Jan. 1907; RGBl. 1907 p. 7)
L	Loi (France); Lov (Denmark); Lag (Finland, Sweden)
La Ley	Revista jurídica española de doctrina, jurisprudencia y bibliografía (Madrid 1. 1980 ff.; cited by year, book and page)
Lavoro 80	Lavoro 80 – Rivista di diritto del lavoro pubblico e privato (Milan 1. 1981 ff.; cited by year and page)
Lav.prev.oggi	Lavoro e previdenza oggi (Milan 1. 1974 ff.; cited by year and page)
Law Com.	Law Commission Report, England and Wales
LC	Lord Chancellor (UK)
LDepGuar	Finnish Law on Dependent Guarantees of 1999 (L om borgen och tredjemanspant 19.3.1999/361)
LEC	Ley de Enjuiciamiento Civil, act 1/2000 of 7.1.2000, put into force 1.1.2001 (Code of Civil Procedure, Spain, BOE n. 7 of 8.1.2000 p. 575, adjusted by BOE n. 90 of 14.4.2000 p. 15278.)
LECr	Ley de Enjuiciamiento Criminal, 14 July 1882 (Code of Criminal Procedure, Spain. Gaceta de Madrid no. 260-283, 17 Sep.-10 Oct. 1882)

Legal Studies	Legal Studies. The Journal of the Society of Public Teachers of Law (London 1. 1947 ff.; cited by volume, year and page)
Legf.Bir.	Legfelsöbb birosàg (Supreme Court of Hungary)
Linnakohus	City Court, Estonia
LFZG	Lohnfortzahlungsgesetz. Gesetz über die Fortzahlung des Arbeitsentgelts im Krankheitsfalle (Act of 27 July 1969 on Continued Payment of Wages for Employees Who are off Sick; Germany, BGBl. 1969 I 946)
LG	Landgericht (Germany); Landesgericht (Court of First Instance, general jurisdiction, also Court of Appeal for Local Courts, Austria)
LGDJ	Librairie Générale de Droit et de Jurisprudence; French publishing company
LGR	Local Government Law Reports (London 1. 1911 ff.; cited by volume, year and page)
Lietuvos apeliacinis teismas	Court of Appeal, Lithuania
Lietuvos Aukscìausiasis Teismas	Supreme Court of Lithuania
Limb. Rechtsl.	Limburgs Rechtsleven (Beringen 1. 1958 ff.; cited by year and page)
Linnakohus	County Court, Estonia
lit.	litera
L. J.	Lord Justice (Court of Appeal judge, UK)
LJAdm(NS), LJCP, LJCh(NS), LJExch(NS), LJKB(NS)	Law Journal Reports, London. Various series 1831-1946, decisions cited with indicator of competent jurisdiction: Adm (Admiralty), CP (Common Pleas), Ch (Chancery), Exch (Exchequer), KB / QB (King's or Queen's Bench) (NS: New Series)
Lloyd's List Law Rep	Lloyd's List Law Reports (London 1. 1919-32. 1950; cited by volume, year and page)
Lloyd's Rep	Lloyd's Law Reports (London 1. 1968 ff.; cited by volume, year and page)
Lloyd's Rep Med	Lloyd's Reports: Medical (London 1. 1968 ff., cited by volume, year and page)
LM	Lindenmaier-Möhring, Nachschlagewerk des Bundesgerichtshofs (in civil cases, Munich 1. 1951 ff.; cited by act, paragraph and number)
LNTS	League of Nations Treaty Series (Geneva 1. 1920-205. 1944/46; cited by volume and page)
loc. cit.	loco citato (the place already cited)
LOTC	Ley Orgánica del Tribunal Consticucional, 3 Oct. 1979 (BOE no. 239, 5 Oct. 1979) (Statute of the Constitutional Court, Spain)
LQR	The Law Quaterly Review (London 1. 1885 ff.; cited by volume, year and page)
LR	Law Reports. Publications of the Incorporated Council of Law Reporting (1865-1875 [the year of foundation of the High Court] in 11 series [here cited with the A & E, Ch.App., the C. P., the Eq., the Ex., the H. L., H. L. (Ir), H. L. (Sc)., P. C. and the Q. B.]; usually L. R. is put at the head of citations of decisions of the series up to 1875. 1875 the 11 series were reduced to 6 [App.Cas., Ch. D., Q. B. D., C. P. D., Ex. D., P. D.]. Since 1881 the Law Reports are published in 4 series [App.Cas., Ch. D., Q. B. D., P. D.]. Since 1890 cited in a different way: the volume does not appear any more, but the

	year, put at the head within brackets; in case the reporting took more than one volume, the volume appears behind the year)
LREx	Law Reports, Exchequer Division (London 1.1875/76-5.1879/80; cited by year, book and page) (see LR)
LRIr	Law Reports, Ireland (Dublin 1878-1893; cited by year, book and page)
LT	Law Times Reports (London 1859-1947; cited by year, book and page)
Ltd	Limited
LuftVG	Luftverkehrsgesetz (Air Traffic Act) 14 Jan. 1981 (BGBl. I 61, Germany); (RGBl. 1936 I p.653, Austria)
M	Macpherson's Session Cases, 3rd series (Scotland) (1862-1873; cited by year, book and page)
Maakohus	County Court, Estonia
Macn & G	Macnaghten & Gordon's Chancery Reports (ER 41-42) (London 1848-1851; cited by year, book and page)
MB	Megyei birosàg (Court of Appeal, Hungary)
McGill LJ	McGill Law Journal (Montreal 1.1952/55 (1954); cited by volume, year and page)
MDR	Monatsschrift für Deutsches Recht: Zeitschrift für die Zivilrechts-Praxis (Cologne, Hamburg 1.1947 ff.; cited by year and page)
MedienG	Mediengesetz (Media Act, Austria) (BGBl. 1981/314)
MJ	Maastricht Journal of European and Comparative Law (Antwerp, Baden-Baden 1.1994; cited by volume, year and page)
ML	Myndighedsloven. Act on Minors and Guardianship, Denmark, 30 June 1922 no. 277 (Lovtidende A p.1379-1389)
MLR	The Modern Law Review (London 1.1937/38 ff.; cited by year and page)
M & M	Moody and Malkin's Nisi Prius Reports (173 ER) (London 1826-1830; cited by year and page)
MonC	Code monétaire (ordonnance relative à la partie législative du code monétaire et financier, France: since government act no. 2000-1223 of 14 Dec. 2000)
Monit belge	Moniteur belge des arrêtés des secrétaires généraux: journal officiel (Official gazette; Belgium) (Brussels 1.1831 ff.; cited by date)
Mon.Trib.	Monitore dei Tribunali, giornale di legislazione e giurisprudenza civile e penale (Milan 1.1859/60-1977; cited by year and page)
Mor	Morison's Dictionary of Decisions, Court of Session (1540-1808)
Mot II	Motive. Explanatory Report on the Draft of a Civil Code for the German Reich. Vol. II: Law of Obligations (Berlin, Leipzig 1888)
MPr	Monomeles Protodikio (One-member First Instance Court, Greece)
MR	Master of the Rolls (Member and President of the Court of Appeal, UK)
M & S	Maule & Selwyn's King's Bench Reports (105 ER) (London 1813-1817; cited by volume and page)
MuSchG	Gesetz zum Schutz der erwerbstätigen Mutter (Act on the Protection of Working Mothers, Germany) (18 Apr. 1968; BGBl. I 315)
MvA	Memorie van Antwoord. Parlementaire Geschiedenis (The Netherlands)
MvT, Parl. Gesch.	Memorie van Toelichting. Parlementaire Geschiedenis (The Netherlands)

M & W	Meeson and Welsby's Reports, Exchequer (ER 150-153) (London 1.1836-16.1847; cited by year, volume and page)
NBW	see BW
NCP	Nuevo Código Penal, 23 Nov. 1995 (New Penal Code, Spain) (Ley Orgánica 10/1995, 23 Nov. 1995, BOE no. 281, 24 Nov. 1995)
NCPC	Nouveau Code de procédure civile. French Code on Procedural Law
ND	Neon Dikaion (New Law, Greece)
NDS	Nordisk Domssamling (Oslo 1.1958 ff.; cited by year and page; in Scandinavia the NDS is often cited by the year of the judgment, which is often one year prior to the year of publication)
NdsRpflege	Niedersächsische Rechtspflege (Celle 1.1947 ff.; cited by year and page)
NedJur	Nederlandse jurisprudentie (Zwolle 1913 ff.; until 1935 cited by year and page, then by year, number and page)
NedJur (kort)	See NedJur (supplementary collection of judgments that have not entered into effect; cited by year and number)
Ned. Rechtspraak	Nederlandsche Rechtspraak of verzameling van arresten en gewijsden van den Hoogen Raad der Nederlanden en verdere rechtscollegien ('s-Gravenhage 1.1838 ff.; cited by volume, year and page)
NedTIR	Nederlands Tijdschrift voor International Recht (Leiden 1.1953/54 with various titles; Nederlands International Law Review 22.1975 ff.; cited by volume, year and page)
New LJ	New Law Journal (London 1.1850 ff.; cited by volume, year, and page)
NFT	Nordisk forsikringstidsskrift (Danish ed.); Nordisk försäkringstidskrift (Swedish ed.) (Copenhagen 1.1921 ff.; cited by year and page)
NGCC	Nuova Giurisprudenza Civile Commentata (Padova 1.1984 ff.; cited by year, book and page)
NILQ	Northern Ireland Legal Quaterly (Belfast 1.1936/37-14.1960/61; NS 1 = 15.1964 ff.; cited by volume, year and page)
NILR	Netherlands International Law Review; see NedTIR
NJA	Nytt Juridiskt Arkiv (Stockholm 1.1874 ff.; as of 1876 separation into two divisions: division 1: Rättsfall från högsta domstolen, cited by year and page; division 2: Tidskrift för lagstiftning, cited by year, division and page)
NJB	Nederlands Juristenblad (Zwolle 1.1926 ff.; 1936-1943; same contents as Weekblad van het recht; cited by year and page)
NJW	Neue Juristische Wochenschrift (Munich et al. 1.1947 ff.; previously: JW; cited by year and page)
NJW-RR	NJW-Rechtsprechungsreport (Munich 1.1986 ff.; cited by year and page)
NoB	Nomiko Bima; miniaion nomikon periodikon (Law Tribune; Athens 1.1953 ff.; cited by volume, year and page)
no(s).	number(s); margin number(s)
Notiziario giur. lav.	Notiziario giuridico. Diritto del lavoro, diritto civile e commerciale, diritto amministrativo e costituzionale, diritto communitario (Torino 1.1970 ff., cited by year and page)
Nov.Dig.it.	Nuovissimo Digesto italiano (Torino 1957 ff.)
NPC	New Property Cases (London 1.1998 ff.; cited by year and page)
NRt	see Rt

NS	New Series; Nejvyssi soud (Supreme Court of the Czech Republic)
NS SR	Najvyssi sùd Slovenskej Republiky (Supreme Court of the Republic of Slovakia)
NSWLR	New South Wales Law Reports (Sydney, 2001 ff.)
NTBR	Nederlands Tijdschrift voor Burgerlijk Recht (Deventer 1. 1984 ff.; cited by year and page)
NuR	Natur und Recht (Hamburg, Berlin 1. 1979 ff.; cited by year and page)
NVwZ	Neue Zeitschrift für Verwaltungsrecht (Munich, Frankfurt/Main 1. 1988 ff.; cited by year and page)
NY	New York Court of Appeals Reports (Albany, NY, 1893-, cited by number, year and page)
NZLR	New Zealand Law Reports (Wellington 1. 1883 ff.; cited by year, section and page)
NZV	Neue Zeitschrift für Verkehrsrecht (Munich and Frankfurt/Main 1. 1988 ff.; cited by year and page)
ObcZ	Obcansky zakonik (Civil Code, Czech Republic)
obs.	observations
ÖBA	Österreichisches Bankarchiv (Vienna 1. 1953 ff.; cited by year and page)
Öbl	Österreichische Blätter für gewerblichen Rechtsschutz und Urheberrecht (Vienna 1. 1952 ff.; cited by year and page)
ÖJZ	Österreichische Juristenzeitung (Vienna 1. 1946 ff.; cited by year and page)
ÖRZ	Österreichische Richterzeitung (Vienna 1. 1908-3. 1909, 7. 1914-12. 1919, 19. 1926-31. 1938, 32. 1954 ff.; cited by year and page)
OGH	Oberster Gerichtshof (Supreme Court, Austria)
OGH BritZ	Oberster Gerichtshof für die Britische Zone (Supreme Court for the British Zone, Germany)
OH	Outer House (Court of Session, Scotland)
OJ	Official Journal of the European Communities (Brussels 1. 1958 ff.; from 11. 1968 ff.: issue C [Communication]: Information and Notice: Issue L [Législation]: Legislation; cited by issue, number, date and page)
Okj	Okrajno sodisce (District Court, Court of First Instance, Slovenia)
Okz	Okrozno sodisce (Regional Court, Court of First Instance, Slovenia)
ØL	Østre Landsret (Eastern High Court; Denmark)
ØLD	Østre Landsrets Dom (Judgments of the Eastern High Court; Denmark)
OLG	Oberlandesgericht (Court of Appeal; Austria, Germany, Greece)
OLGR	OLG-Report. Zivilrechtsprechung der Oberlandesgerichte (Decisions of the Court of Appeal in civil matters, Cologne 1. 1997 ff.: cited by year and page)
OLGZ	Entscheidungen der Oberlandesgerichte in Zivilsachen einschließlich der freiwilligen Gerichtsbarkeit (Decisions of the Court of Appeal in Civil Matters including Jurisdiction over Non-contentious Matters) (Munich, Berlin 1. 1965 ff.; cited by year and page)
ØLK	Østre Landsrets Kendelse (Decisions of the Eastern High Court, Denmark)
Ont HCJ	Ontario High Court of Justice
op. cit.	opere citato (work already cited)

OR	Obligationenrecht (Bundesgesetz betreffend die Ergänzung des Schweizerischen Zivilgesetzbuches: 5th Part: Obligationenrecht, vom 30.3.1911 [SR 220]) (Code of Obligation, Switzerland, 30 Mar. 1911)
OR (2d)	Ontario Reports, Second Series (Toronto, 1882-, cited by year, number and page)
OS	Okrajno sodisce (District Court, Court of First Instance, Slovenia); Okresni soud (District Court, Court of First Instance, Czech Republic); Okresny súd (District Court, Court of First Instance, Slovakia)
OVG	Oberverwaltungsgericht (Administrative Court of Appeal, Germany)
Ow	(Rijks-) Octrooiwet, Netherlands (Patent Act), 7 Nov. 1910 (Stb. 313) and 15 Dec. 1995 (Stb. 51)
OZ	Obcansky zakonik (Civil Code, Czech Republic and Slovakia); Obligacijski zakonik (Law of Obligations, Slovenia)
P	President (official name, United Kingdom)
P	Law Reports. Probate, Divorce and Admiralty Divison (London 1.1891 ff.; cited by year, volume, and page)
p(p).	page(s)
para(s)	paragraph(s)
Parl. St. Kamer	Parlamentaire Stukken Kamer (Publications of the committee of the chamber of the belgian parliament, Brussels)
Pas belge	Pasicrisie belge (Recueil général de la jurisprudence des cours et tribunaux de Belgique. I = Arrêts de la Cour de Cassation 3rd Series 1865-1924; 112.1925 ff.; II = Arrêts de la Cour d'Appel 3rd Series 1865-1924; 112.1925 ff.; III = Jugements des tribunaux 3rd Series 1865-1924; 112.1925 ff.; IV = Jurisprudence étrangère 3rd Series 1893-1924; 112.1925 ff.; v. = Revue de droit belge 3rd Series 1893 ff.; cited by year, book and page)
Pasin belge	Pasinomie belge ou Collection complète des lois, décrets, arrêtés et règlements généraux qui peuvent être invoqués en Belgique (Brussels 1.1788 ff.; cited by year and page)
Pas luxemb	Pasicrisie luxembourgeoise (Recueil de la jurisprudence luxembourgeoise en matière civile, commerciale, criminale, de droit public, fiscal, administratif et notariel; Luxembourg 1.1881 ff.; cited by volume, year and page)
PC	Privy Council (United Kingdom); Privy Council Appeals (London 1865-1875; cited by year, volume and page; see LR)
PD	Probate Division (London 1875/76-1890; cited by year, volume and page; see LR)
PECL	Principles of European Contract Law. Prepared by the Commission on European Contract Law. Parts I and II. Edited by Ole Lando and Hugh Beale (The Hague 2000); Part III. Edited by Ole Lando, Eric Clive, André Prüm and Reinhard Zimmermann (The Hague 2003)
PflVG	Gesetz über die Pflichtversicherung für Kraftfahrzeughalter (Act on Compulsory Insurance for the Keeper of a Motor Vehicle, Germany, 5 Apr. 1965; BGBl. I 213; BGBl. III 925-1)
PHI	Produkthaftung International (Karlsruhe 1.1981 ff.; cited by year and page)
PK	Penikos Kodikas (Criminal Code, Greece. Act no. 1492/1950. FEK 182/1950 pp. 963-1003)

plc	public limited company
PNLR	Professional Negligence and Liability Reports (London, 1. 1999 ff., cited by year and page)
Poder Judicial	Conseijo General del Poder Judicial (Madrid 1. 1981 ff.; cited by year and page)
POS Regulations	The Public Offers of Securities Regulations (United Kingdom)
p(p).	page(s)
PPr	Polymeles Protodikio (Multi-member First Instance Court, Greece)
Pr	Protodikio (First Instance Court, Greece)
pr.	principium
Pret.	Pretura (Local Court, Italy)
Prg	De Praktijkgids. Tijdschrift gewijd aan de rechtspraktijk en aan de jurisprudentie van de kantongerechten (Arnhem 1. 1980 ff.; cited by year and number)
ProdHG	Produkthaftungsgesetz. Gesetz über die Haftung für fehlerhafte Produkte (Product Liability Act, Germany, 15 Dec. 1989; BGBl. I 2198)
Prop	Proposition (Official proposal for a statute, Sweden)
Prot II	Protokolle. Reports of the Commission for the Second Reading of the Draft German Civil Code. Prepared by Order of the Reich Ministry of Justice by Achilles, Gebhard and Spahn. Vol. II: Law of Obligations (Berlin 1898)
Ptk	Polgári Törvényköny (Civil Code, Hungary)
QB (ComCt)	Queen's Bench Division, Commercial Court
QB	The Law Reports. Queen's Bench Division (London 1. 1890 ff.; cited by year, book, and page, additional LR cited: London 1865-1875)
QBD	Queen's Bench Division (London 1875/76-1890; cited by year, book and page); see LR
QC	Queen's Council
R.	Regina or Rex
R	Rettie's Session Cases (Edinburgh 1873-1898)
R.	Règlement (order, France)
RabelsZ	Zeitschrift für ausländisches und internationales Privatrecht (Berlin, Tübingen, 1. 1927 ff.; from vol. 26. 1961: Rabels Zeitschrift für ausländisches und internationales Privatrecht; cited by volume, year and page)
RaDC	Rassegna di diritto civile (Naples 1. 1980 ff.; cited by year and page)
RAJ	Repertorio Aranzadi de Jurisprudencia (Pamplona 1. 1930/31, 2. 1934 ff.; cited by year, number and page)
RAJ (TSJ y AP)	Repertorio Aranzadi de Jurisprudencia. Sentencias de Tribunales Superiores de Justicia y Audiencias Provinciales y otros Tribunales (Pamplona 1. 1996 ff.; cited by year, number and page)
Rass.Avv.Stato	La Rassegna mensile dell' Avvocatura dello Stato (Rome 1. 1948 ff.; cited by year, book and page)
Rass.dir.civ.	Rassegna di diritto civile (Naples 1. 1980 ff.; cited by year and page)
Rb	Arrondissementsrechtbank (District Court, Court of First Instance, general jurisdiction, The Netherlands), Rechtbank van eerste anleg (Court of First Instance, Belgium)

RCJB	Revue critique de jurisprudence belge (1. 1947 ff.; cited by year and page)
RCR	Relazione della Commissione Reale al progetto del libro ›obbligazioni e contratti‹ (see Pandolfelli et al., Codice civile, in the table of literature cited in an abbreviated form)
RD	Regio Decreto (Royal decree, Italy)
RdA	Recht der Arbeit (Munich 1. 1948 ff.; cited by year and page)
RD banc	Revue de droit bancaire et de la bourse (France, 1. 1987 ff.)
RDBB	Revista de derecho bancario y bursatil (Madrid, 1981 ff.)
RDE	Revista de Direito e Economia (Coimbra 1. 1975 ff.; cited by volume, year and page)
RdS	Recht der Schule (Vienna 1. 1979 ff.; cited by year and page)
RdW	Österreichisches Recht der Wirtschaft (Vienna 1. 1983 ff.; cited by year and page)
recht	Recht, Zeitschrift für juristische Ausbildung (Berne 1. 1983 ff.; cited by year and page)
ref.	reference
Rel.Guard.	Relazione del Guardasigilli al progetto ministeriale delle obbligazioni (see Pandolfelli et al., Codice civile, in the table of literature cited in an abbreviated form)
RépDrCiv	Répertoire de droit civil (Paris 1. 1951-5. 1955; 2nd ed. 1. 1970 ff.; see details in the table of literature)
Rep.Foro it.	Repertorio del Foro italiano (legislazione, bibliografia, giurisprudenza; Rome 1. 1878 ff.; previously: Repertorio generale annuale di giurisprudenza, bibliografia e legislazione; cited by volume, year and column)
Rep.gen.	Repertorio generale della Giurisprudenza italiana (Torino 1. 1890 ff.; previously: Repertorio generale annuale della Giurisprudenza italiana; cited by year, and column and number)
Rep.Giur.it.	Repertorio generale della giurisprudenza italiana (Torino 1. 1848 ff.; cited by year, key word and number)
resp.	respectively
Resp.Civ. e Prev.	Responsabilità Civile e Previdenza (Milan 1. 1930 ff.; cited by year and page)
Resp. civ. et assur.	Responsabilité civile et assurances. Revue mensuelle (Paris 1. 1988 ff.; cited by year and page)
Restitution LRev	Restitution Law Review (London 1. 1993 ff.; cited by year and page)
Rev.Crit.Der. Inm.	Revista Crítica de Derecho Inmobiliario (Madrid 1. 1925 ff.; cited by year and page)
Rev.crit.dr.int.pr.	Revue critique de droit international privé (Paris, 1905-, cited by year and page)
Rev.crit.jur.belge	Revue critique de jurisprudence belge (Brussels 1. 1947 ff.; cited by year and page)
Rev.crit.législ. et juris.	Revue critique de législation et de jurisprudence (Paris 1. 1851 ff.; cited by year and page)
Rev.dr.int.dr.-comp.	Revue de droit international et de droit comparé (Brussels 1. 1924 ff.; 1940-48 not published; cited by volume, year and page)
Rev.dr.publ.	Revue de droit public et de la science politique en France et à l'étranger (Paris 1. 1894 ff.; cited by volume, year and page)
Rev.dr.sanit.soc.	Revue de droit sanitaire et social (Paris 1. 1965 ff.; cited by year and page)

Rev.dr.uniforme	Revue de droit uniforme. Uniform Law Review (Rome 1. 1973 ff.; cited by year, part and page)
Rev.gén.dr.	Revue générale du droit, de la législation et de jurisprudence en France et à l'étranger (Paris 1. 1877-62. 1938; cited by year and page)
Rev.Hell.	Revue Hellénique de droit international (Athens 1. 1948 ff.; cited by volume, year and page)
Rev.int.dr.comp.	Revue internationale de droit comparé (1. 1869/72-71. 1947/48; previously: Bulletin de la Société de législation comparée; Paris, 1. 1949 ff.; cited by volume, year and page)
Rev.jur.pol. Ind.Coop.	Revue juridique et politique, Indépendance et Coopération (Paris NS 1. 1946 ff.; cited by volume, year and page)
Rev.not. b.	Revue du notariat belge (Brussels 1. 1896 ff.; until 1970 Revue pratique du notariat belge and Annales du notariat et de l'Enregistrement)
Rev.trim.dr.civ.	Revue trimestrielle de droit civil (Paris 1. 1902-38. 1939, 39/40. 1940/41-78. 1979 = tome 39-77, 79. 1980 ff.; until 1977 by volume, then by year and page)
Rev.trim.dr.com.	Revue trimestrielle de droit commercial (Paris 1. 1948 ff.)
RFDA	Revue Française de Droit Administratif (Paris 1. 1946/47 (1947) ff.; cited by year and page)
RG	Reichsgericht (Supreme Court of the German Reich, Germany)
RGAR	Révue générale des assurances et des responsabilités (Brussels 1. 1927 ff:; cited by year and number)
RGBl	Reichsgesetzblatt (Government Gazette of the German Reich) (Berlin 1871-1945; since 1922 divided into parts I and II); (Government Gazette of the Austro-Hungarion Monarchy) (Vienna, 1848-1918)
RGD	Revista general de derecho (Valencia 1. 1945 ff.)
RGDC	Revue générale de droit civil/Tijdschrift voor Belgisch Burgerlijk Recht (1. 1987-)
RGZ	Amtliche Sammlung der Entscheidungen des Reichsgerichtes in Zivilsachen (Decisions of the German Reichsgericht in civil matters) (Berlin 1. 1872-172. 1945; cited by volume and page)
RH	Rättsfall från Hovrätterna (Decisions of the Swedish Court of Appeal, changing places of publication, usually Stockholm, 1. 1980 ff.; cited by year and number)
RHG	Reichshaftpflichtgesetz (Third Party Liability Act, Austria; RGBl. 1871, 201)
Riigikohus tsiviilkollegium	Supreme Court Civil Chamber, Estonia
Ringkonnakohus	District Court, Court of Appeal, Estonia
RIS-Justiz	Austrian internetpublication of OGH-decisions, www.ris.bka.gv.at/jus/; decisions are cited by date, number of legal subject and keyword
Riv.crit.dir.priv.	Rivista critica del diritto privato (Bologna 1. 1989 ff.; cited by year and page)
Riv.Dir.Civ.	Rivista di Diritto Civile (Padova 1. 1955 ff.; cited by year, book and page)
Riv.Dir.Com.	Rivista del Diritto Commerciale e del Diritto generale delle obbligazioni (Milan 1. 1903 ff.; cited by year, book and page)
Riv.dir.eur.	Rivista di diritto europeo (Rome 1. 1961 ff.; cited by year and page)
Riv.dir.int. priv.proc.	Rivista di diritto internazionale privato e processuale (Padova 1. 1969 ff., cited by year and page)

Riv.dir.lav.	Rivista di diritto del lavoro (Milan 1.1949-32.1980; cited by year and page)
Riv.dir.sport.	Rivista di diritto sportivo (Milan 1.1949 ff.; cited by year and page)
Riv.giur. circ.trasp.	Rivista giuridica della circolazione e dei trasporti (Rome 1.1947 ff.; cited by year and page)
Riv.giur.lav.	Rivista giuridica del lavoro e della previdenza sociale (Rome 1.1954 ff.; part 1: Dottrina; part 2: Giurisprudenza; part 3: Previdenza; part 4: Diritto penale del lavoro; cited by year, book and page)
Riv.it.med.leg.	Rivista italiana di medicina legale (Milan, 1979-, cited by year and page)
Riv.pen.	Rivista penale (Rome 1.1952 ff.; cited by year and page)
Riv.trim. dir.proc.civ.	Rivista trimestrale di diritto e procedura civile (Milan 1.1947 ff.; cited by year and page)
RIW	Recht der Internationalen Wirtschaft (Heidelberg 1954-1957 and 1975 ff.; from 1958 to 1974 Außenwirtschaftdienst des Betriebsberaters [AWD]; cited by year and page)
RJDA	Revue de jurisprudence du droit des affaires (Paris 1.1991 ff.; cited by year and page)
RLJ	Revista de Legislação e Jurisprudência (Coimbra 1.1868/69 ff.; cited by volume, year and page)
RM	Rechtsgeleerd magazijn: tijdschrift voor binnen- en buitenlandsche rechtsstudie (Haarlem 1.1882-58.1939; cited by year and page)
RM-Themis	Rechtsgeleerd magazijn Themis. Tijdschrift voor publiek- en privaatrecht. (Zwolle 1.1939 ff.; cited by year and page)
ROA	Revista da Ordem dos Advogados (Lisbon 1941 ff.)
RP	RP 189/1998 rd – Regeringens proposition till Riksdagen med förslag till lagstiftning om borgen och tredjemanspant (Finland)
RPC	Reports of Patent, Design & Trade Mark Cases (London 1.1884 ff.; cited by year and page)
RPDB	Répertoire pratique du droit belge – Encyclopédie Reeks (Brussels and Paris 1.1928 ff.)
RPL	Retsplejeloven (Rules of Procedure, Denmark, no. 90, 11 Apr. 1916, lovbekendtgørelse no. 815 of 30 Sept. 2003)
RRJ	Revue de la Recherche Juridique. Droit Prospectif (Aix-en-Provence 1.1974/75 ff.; cited by year and page)
r+s	Recht und Schaden. (Kippenheim 1.1974 ff.; cited by year and page)
RSC	Rules of the Supreme Court (England)
RSCOrd	Rules of the Supreme Court, Order (England)
RT	Revista dos Tribunais (Sao Paulo 1912 ff.)
Rt	Retstidende, publishing the decisions of the Norwegian Høyesterett (Supreme Court)
RTD civ	Revue trimestrielle de droit civil (Paris, 1.1902 ff.) ; see Rev.trim.dr.civ.
RTD com	Revue trimestrielle de droit commercial (Paris, 1.1948 ff.) ; see Rev.trim.dr.com.
RTR	Road Traffic Reports (London 1.1970 ff.; cited by year and page)
Rv	Wetboek van Burgerlijke Rechtsvordering (Code of Civil Procedure, The Netherlands) (Stb. 1828 no. 14)
RvdW	Rechtspraak van de Week (Zwolle 1.1939 ff.; cited by year and number)

RvT	Raad van Toezicht op het Verzekeringswezen (Council for the Supervision of the Insurance Sector, The Netherlands)
RW	Rechtskundig Weekblad (Antwerp 1.1931/32 ff.; cited by year and page)
S	Shaw's Session Cases, First Series (Scotland)(1821-1838)
S.	Recueil général des lois et arrêts resp. Recueil Sirey; 1801/02 ff. ; see D.
Sadem pierwszej instancji	Court of Appeal, Poland
Sad Najwyzszy	Supreme Court, Poland
Sad okregowy	Circuit Court (Court of First Instance), Poland
Sady grodzkie	Court of First Instance, Poland
Salk	Salkeld's Reports (ER 91) (London 1689-1712, cited by year, volume and page)
SALR	South Australian Law Reports (Melbourne, 1869-, cited by number and page)
SAP	Sentencia de la Audiencia Provincial (Decision of a Court of Appeal, Spain)
SavZ Rom.Abt.	Zeitschrift der Savigny-Stiftung für Rechtsgeschichte (until volume 31 divided into Germanist.Abt., Rom.Abt. and Kanonist.Abt. Each department has its own system of numbering volumes. Rom.Abt.: 1. = 14. 1880-65 = 78. 1947 ff.; cited by volume, year and page)
SC	Session Cases. New Series. Cases decided in the Court of Session, and also in the Court of Justiciary (J. C.) and the House of Lords (H. L.); Edinburgh 1. 1907 ff.; cited by year and page)
ScanStudL	Scandinavian Studies in Law (Stockholm 1. 1957 ff., cited by volume, year, and page)
sch.	schedule(s)
Scientia jurídica	Scientia jurídica. Revista de direito comparado português e brasileiro (Braga 1. 1951/52 ff.; cited by volume, year and page)
SCLR	Scottish Civil Law Reports (Edinburgh, 1987-, cited by year and page)
Scot.Law Com.	Scottish Law Commission Report (Edinburgh, 1966-, cited by number, year and paras.)
Scot CS	Approved judgment of the Court of Session. Scotland
SDR	Special Drawing Rights
sec., secs.	section, sections
SEK	Reference of the Commission General Secretary's Office and of the Council of the European Union
SemJur	La Semaine Juridique. Edition Entreprise. Cahiers de Droit de l'entreprise (Paris 1. 1966 ff.; cited by year, part and number), Edition Générale. (also Juris Classeur Périodique; Paris 1. 1927 ff.; cited by year, part and number), Edition Nouvelles, Panorama (Pan.), Sommaire (Som.), also quoted as JCP, see there
sent.	sentence(s)
SeuffArch	Seuffert's Archiv für Entscheidungen der obersten Gerichte in den deutschen Staaten (1. 1847-98. 1944; from 1. 1847 – 11. 1857: Archiv für Entscheidungen der obersten Gerichte in den deutschen Staaten; cited by volume, year, number and page)
Sez. giur.	Sezione giurisdizionale
SFS	Svensk författningssamling (Official gazette, Sweden) (Stockholm 1. 1825 ff.; cited by year and number)

SGB	Sozialgesetzbuch (Social Security Code, Germany) 11 Dec. 1975 (BGBl. I 3015)
SGECC	Study Group on a European Civil Code
SH	Sø- og Handelsretten. Maritime and Commercial Court (Copenhagen, Denmark)
ShApp	Shaw's Appeals (Scotland 1821-1824; cited by year, book and page)
Sh.Ct.	Sheriff Court (Court of First Instance in Civil and Criminal Matters; Scotland)
SHD	Sø- og Handelsretsdom (Judgement of the Maritime and Commercial Court Copenhagen, Denmark)
S. I.	Statutory Instrument
SJ	Solicitor's Journal (London 1. 1857 ff.; cited by year and page)
SJZ	Schweizerische Juristenzeitung (Zurich 1. 1904/1905 ff.; cited by year and page)
SKL	Skadeståndslag. Damages Liability Act (Sweden: SFS 1972:207; Finland: 31 May 1974 no. 412)
SLD	Søndre Landsrets Dom (decisions of the Southern Court in Denmark)
SLPQ	Scottish Law and Practice Quarterly (London 1. 1995 ff., cited by year, number and page)
SLR	Scottish Law Reporter (1865-1925)
SLT (Rep)	The Scots Law Times (News and Reports, the latter with separate pagination) (Edinburgh 1. 1893/94 ff.; Sheriff Court Reports 1. 1922 ff., cited by year and page)
SmLC	Smith's Leading Cases in Various Branches of the Law (13th ed. London 1929)
SN	Session Notes (Edinburgh 1925-1948)
SOU	Statens offentliga utredningar (Government gazette, Sweden) (Stockholm 1. 1939 ff.; cited by year, number, title and page)
Sr	Wetboek van Strafrecht (Penal Code, The Netherlands) (Stb. 1881, p. 40 [Nr. 35])
SR	Systematische Sammlung des Bundesrechts (Systematic collection of Swiss Statutes, Switzerland, since 1970; cited by number)
SR NSW	New South Wales, State Reports, (1. 1901 ff.)
s(s).	et sequentia
S & S	Schip en Schade. Beslissingen op het gebiet van zee- en binnenvaartrecht en brandverzekeringsrecht (Zwolle 1. 1957 ff.; cited by year and page)
STA	Supremo Tribunal Administrativo (Supreme Court in Administrative Matters, Portugal)
Stark	Starkie's Nisi Prius Reports (171 ER, London 1814-1823)
StAZ	Das Standesamt. Zeitschrift für Standesamtswesen: Personenstandsrecht, Ehe- und Kindschaftsrecht, Staatsangehörigkeitsrecht (Neue Folge Frankfurt/ Main 1. 1948 ff.; cited by year and page)
Stb	Staatsblad van het Koninkrijk der Nederlanden (Official Gazette; The Netherlands) (Zwolle 1. 1813 ff.; cited by year and page)
StGB	Strafgesetzbuch (Penal Code, Germany) 15 May 1871 (RGBl. p. 127) formulation of the bulletin of 13.11.1998, BGBl I 3322;

	Bundesgesetz vom 23.1.1974 über die mit gerichtlicher Strafe bedrohten Handlungen (Penal Code, Austria, 23 Jan. 1974) (BGB1. no. 60 1974)
STJ	Supremo Tribunal da Justiça (Supreme Court, Portugal)
StPO	Strafprozeßordnung (Code of Criminal Procedure, Germany, as amended by Act of 7 Apr. 1987; BGBl. I 1075)
STRFL	Borgerlig Straffelov (Civil Penal Code, Denmark) (Act no. 126, 15 Apr. 1930 [Lovtidende A 1930, p. 697-752])
STS	Sentencia del Tribunal Supremo (decision of the Supreme Court, Portugal)
StVG	Straßenverkehrsgesetz (Road Traffic Act, Germany, 19 Dec. 1952; BGBl. I 832)
StVO	Straßenverkehrsordnung (Road Traffic Regulation, Germany, 16 Nov. 1970 (BGBl. I 1565)
subs.	subsections
Sup.Ct.	Supreme Court (Ireland)
Suppl.	Supplement
Suppl.ord.	Supplemento ordinario (Part of the government gazette, Italy)
Sv	Wetboek van Strafvordering (Code of Criminal Procedure, The Netherlands; Stb. 15 Jan. 1921, p. 14)
SvJT	Svensk Juristtidning (Stockholm 1. 1916 ff.; cited by year and page)
SZ	Entscheidungen des österreichischen Obersten Gerichtshofs in Zivilsachen (Decisions of the Austrian Supreme Court in Civil Matters) (Vienna 1. 1919-20. 1938; 21. 1946 ff.; with changing titles; until vol. 34. 1961: Entscheidungen des österreichischen obersten Gerichtshofs in Zivil- und Justizverwaltungssachen; cited by volume, number, and page)
SZIER	Schweizerische Zeitschrift für internationales und europäisches Recht (Zurich 1. 1991 ff.; cited by year and page)
tab.	tabulae
TAgrR	Tijdschrift voor agrarisch recht; Revue de droit rural (Brussels 1. 1979 ff.; cited by year and page)
TBBR	Tijdschrift voor Belgisch Burgerlijk Recht; see RGDC
TBH	Tijdschrift voor Belgisch handelsrecht; Revue de droit commercial belge (Antwerp 1. 1967-29. 1996; 103. 1997 ff.; continuation of the Jurisprudence commerciale de Belgique)
TBP	Tijdtschrift voor Bestuurswetenschappen en Publiekrecht (Brussels 1. 1946 ff., from 1. 1946 to 6. 1951 under the title Tijdtschrift voor Bestuurswetenschappen; cited by year and page)
TBR	Tijdschrift voor Brugse rechtspraak (Bruges 1. 1983 ff.; cited by year and page)
TC	Tribunal Constitucional (Constitutional Court; Spain)
Tel Aviv UnivStudL	Tel Aviv University Studies in Law (Tel Aviv 1. 1975 ff.; cited by volume, year and page)
Temi	Il Temi. Rivista di giurisprudenza Italiana (Parma, Milan et al. NS 1 = 22. 1946 ff.; cited by year and page)
Temi nap.	Il Temi napoletana (Milan 1. 1958 ff.; cited by year and page)
Temi rom.	Temi romana (Milan 1. 1929-5. 1933; [n.F.] 1. 1952-40. 1991; cited by year and page)
Term Rep	Dunford & East's Term Reports (ER 99-101) (London 1785-1800)

TfR	Tidsskrift for Rettsvitenskap (Oslo 1. 1888 ff.; cited by year and page)
TGI	Tribunal de grande instance (Court of First Instance, France)
Themis	Hebdomacliaia dikastike ephemeris ekdiclomene en Athenais (Athens 1. 1890/91 (1930)-65. 1954/55; cited by volume, year and page)
TI	Tribunal d'instance (Court of first instance, France)
TLR	Annual Digest of the Times Law Reports (London 1. 1884 ff.; cited by volume, year and page)
TMA	Tweemaandelijks tijdschrift voor milieu aansprakelijkheid. Environmental Liability Law Review (Lelystad 1. 1987 ff.; cited by year and page)
Toσ	To Syntagma (Athens 1. 1975 ff.; cited by volume, year and page)
TPR	Tijdschrift voor Privaatrecht (Gent 1. 1964 ff.; cited by year and page)
TR	Durnford & East's Term Reports, King's Bench (ER 99-101) (London 1785-1800; cited by volume, year and page)
TranspR	Transportrecht (Frankfurt/Main 1. 1978 ff.; cited by year and page)
Trb	Tractatenblad van het Koninkrijk der Nederlanden (Official Gazette recording treaties in force in the Netherlands) (s'Gravenhage 1. 1951 ff.; cited by year and page)
Treaty of Rome	Treaty establishing the European Community, 25 Mar. 1957
Trib.	Tribunale (Court of First Instance, general jurisdiction; Court of Appeal in small claims matters; Italy); Tribunal de première instance (Court of First Instance; Belgium, France); Tribunal d'arrondissement (Court of First Instance, general jurisdiction, Luxembourg)
Trib.com.	Tribunal de Commerce (Commercial Court; Belgium and France)
Trib.Corr.	Tribunal Correctionnel (Criminal Court, Belgium)
Trib. enfants	Tribunal pour enfants (Youth Court, France)
TS	Tribunal Supremo (if not specified: senate for civil matters) (Supreme Court, Spain)
TSJ	Tribunal Superior de Justicia (Supreme Court of the autonomous regions, Spain)
TSL	Trafikskadelag (Traffic Damages Act; SFS 1975: 410, Sweden)
TulCivLaw Forum	Tulane Civil Law Forum (New Orleans, 1. 1973-1977; NS 1. 1987 ff.; cited by volume, year and page)
TulLRev	Tulane Law Review (New Orleans, 1. 1916 ff.; cited by volume, year and page)
TvC	Tijdschrift voor Consumentenrecht (Deventer 1. 1985 ff.; cited by year and page)
UfR	Ugeskrift for Retsvæsen (Copenhagen 1. 1867 ff.; as of 1902 division into: A = Danks domssamling; B = Juridiske afhandlinger, meddelelser; C = Abstracts; cited by year, book and page)
UIC	Ufficio Italiano dei Cambi (Italian Foreign Exchange Office)
UKHL	Approved judgment of the House of Lords (United Kingdom)
Ulp.	Ulpian
UmweltHG	Umwelthaftungsgesetz (Environmental Liability Act, Germany, 10 Dec. 1990; BGBl. I 2634)
UNCITRAL	United Nations Commission for International Trade Law

UnfContTA	Unfair Contract Terms Act (France: Law no. 95-96 of 1 Feb. 1995 art. 1 consolidated in ConsC art. 132-1; United Kingdom: Unfair Contract Terms Act 1977)
UniflRev	Uniform Law Review = Revue de droit uniforme; see Rev.dr.uniforme
UNTS	United Nations Treaty Series. Treaties and international agreements registered or filed and recorded with the Secretariat of the United Nations (Washington DC 1. 1946/47 ff.; cited by volume and page)
UrhG	Gesetz über Urheberrecht und verwandte Schutzrechte v. 9. Sept. 1965 (Act on Copyright and Related Patent Rights, Germany, BGBl I 1273, formulation of 1.9.2000; BGBl I S. 1375); Urheberrechtsgesetz v. 9.4.1914 (Copyright-Act, Austria, BGBl 1936/111)
UTR	Umwelt- und Technikrecht (Düsseldorf 1. 1986 ff.; cited by volume, year and page)
UWG	Gesetz gegen den unlauteren Wettbewerb (Act against Unfair Competition, Germany, 7 June 1909; RGBl. 499; 3 July 2004, BGBl I 1414)
v.	versus
V°	Verbo
V-C	Vice-Chancellor (UK)
Varosi birosàg	City Court (Court of First Instance), Hungary
Vern	Vernon's Chancery Reports (ER 23, London 1680-1719)
VersR	Versicherungsrecht (Juristische Rundschau für die Individualversicherung; Karlsruhe 1. 1950 ff.; cited by year and page)
VersRAI	Versicherungsrecht Beilage Ausland (Karlsruhe 1. 1959/60, 2. 1961 ff.; cited by year and page)
VfGH	Verfassungsgerichtshof (Constitutional Court, Austria)
VfSlg	Verfassungssammlung. Sammlung der Erkenntnisse und wichtigsten Beschlüsse des Verfassungsgerichtshofes (Collection of cases before the Austrian Constitutional Court) (Vienna 1. 1919 ff., New Series 33. 1968 ff.; cited by the 1 fd. no. of the decision)
VG	Verwaltungsgericht (Administrative Court, Germany)
VL	Vestre Landsret (Western High Court, Denmark)
VLD	Vestre Landsrets dom (Judgments of Western High Court, Denmark)
VLK	Vestre Landsrets kendelse (Decisions of Western High Court, Denmark)
vol	Volume
VÕS	Võlaõigusseadus (Estonian Law of Obligations Act of 1 July 2002; Official Journal I 2002, 53, 336)
VR	Verkeersrecht ('s-Gravenhage 1. 1953/54 ff.; cited by year and page)
Vrb	Verzekeringsrechtelijke berichten (Zwolle 1. 1989 ff.; cited by year and page)
Vred	Vredegerecht (Magistrates Court, Belgium)
VS	Visje sodisce (Court of Appeal, Slovenia); Vrnchi soud (Court of Appeal, Czech Republic)
VS RS	Vrhovno sodisce Republike Slovenije (Supreme Court of Slovenia)
V. T.SV.	Voorafgaande Titel Wetboek van Strafvordering. Preliminary Title to the Penal Code (Belgium)
VVDStRL	Veröffentlichungen der Vereinigung Deutscher Staatsrechtslehrer (Berlin 1. 1924 ff.; cited by volume, year and page)

VVG	Gesetz über den Versicherungsvertrag (Act on Insurance Contracts, Germany), 30 May 1908 (RGBl. p. 263)
Vw	Versicherungswirtschaft (Karlsruhe 1.1946 ff.; cited by year and page)
VwGH	Verwaltungsgerichtshof (Supreme Administrative Court, Austria)
W	Weekblad van het Recht (Zwolle et al. 1.1839-105.1943; from 1936 contents the same as Nederlands Juristenblad (NJB); cited by year, number and page)
WAM	Wet betreffende de verplichte aansprakelijkheidsverzekering inzake motorrijtuigen (Act on Compulsory Insurance for Keepers of a Motor Vehicle, Belgium, 1 July 1956; B. S. 15 July 1956; as amended by Act of 21 Nov. 1989; B. S. 8. Dec. 1989)
Warsaw Convention	Warsaw Convention, 12 Oct. 1929. Convention for the Unification of Certain Rules Relating to International Carriage by Air (as amended)
WBl	Wirtschaftsrechtliche Blätter (Vienna, 1.1987 ff.; cited by year and page)
WHG	Wasserhaushaltsgesetz. Gesetz zur Ordnung des Wasserhaushalts (Water Budget Act, Germany, 23 Sep. 1986; BGBl. III 753)
WiB	Wirtschaftsrechtliche Beratung (Munich, Frankfurt/Main 1.1994 ff.; cited by year and page)
WL	West Law
WLR	The Weekly Law Reports (containing decisions in the House of Lords, the Privy Council, the Supreme Court of Case Law, Assize Courts; London 1.1953 ff.; cited by year, book and page)
WM	Wertpapier-Mitteilungen: Zeitschrift für Wirtschafts- und Bankrecht (Frankfurt/Main et al. 1.1947 ff.; cited by year and page)
Wm Bl	Sir William Blackstone's King's Bench Reports (ER 96) (London 1746-1780)
WPNR	Weekblad voor privaatrecht, notariaat en registratie ('s-Gravenhage 1.1870 ff.; cited by year, number and page)
WR	The Weekly Reporter (London 1.1852/53 (1853) – 54.1905/06 (1906))
WRG	Wasserrechtsgesetz (Water Act of 1959, Austria; BGBl. 215)
WRP	Wettbewerb in Recht und Praxis (Frankfurt/Main 1.1955 ff.; cited by year and page)
WVW	Wegenverkeerswet (Road Traffic Act, The Netherlands), 13 Sep. 1935 (Stb. 554) and 21 Apr. 1994 (Stb 475)
WWR	Western Weekly Reports (Calgary 1.1911/12 (1912) – 10.1916; 1917-1950; NS 1.1951 ff.; cited by year, book and page)
YAR	York Antwerp Rules (London 1996)
Y & J	Younge and Jervis' Exchequer Reports (ER 148) (London 1826-30; cited by volume, year and page)
Zacchia	Zacchia. Archivio di medicina legale, sociale e criminologica (Rome 1.1921-13.1934; 2nd series 1.1937 ff.; cited by year and page)
ZBB	Zeitschrift für Bankrecht und Bankwirtschaft (Cologne 1.1989 ff.; cited by year and page)
ZBernJV	Zeitschrift des Bernischen Juristenvereins (Revue de la société des juristes bernois; Berne 1.1864/65 ff.; cited by volume year and page)

ZEuP	Zeitschrift für Europäisches Privatrecht (Munich 1. 1993 ff.; cited by year and page)
ZEV	Zeitschrift für Erbrecht und Vermögensnachfolge (Munich, Frankfurt/Main 1. 1994 ff.; cited by year and page)
ZfRV	Zeitschrift für Rechtsvergleichung (Vienna 1. 1960 ff.; cited by year and page)
ZfS	Zeitschrift für Schadensrecht (Essen 1. 1980 ff.; cited by year and page)
ZfU	Zeitschrift für Umweltpolitik und Umweltrecht. Journal of Environmental Law and Policy. Revue de la politique et du droit d'environnement (Frankfurt/Main 1. 1978 ff.; cited by year and page)
ZfVB	Zeitschrift für Verwaltung; supplement: decisions of the VfGH and VwGH (Vienna 1. 1976 ff.; cited by year and page)
ZHR	Zeitschrift für das gesamte Handels- und Wirtschaftsrecht (Heidelberg 1. 1858-110. 1944, 111. 1948 under different titles: until volume 60: Zeitschrift für das gesamte Handelsrecht, until volume 124 (1962): Zeitschrift für das gesamte Handels- und Wirtschaftsrecht; cited by volume, year, and page)
ZIP	Zeitschrift für Wirtschaftsrecht und Insolvenzpraxis (previously Insolvenzrecht; Cologne 1. 1980 ff.; cited by year and page)
ZPO	Zivilprozeßordnung (Code of Civil Procedure, Germany) 12 Sep. 1950 (BGBl. 1950 I 533); Zivilprozeßordnung (Code of Civil Procedure, Austria) 1 Aug. 1895 (RGBl 1895/113)
ZRP	Zeitschrift für Rechtspolitik (Munich 1. 1968 ff.; cited by year and page)
ZSR	Zeitschrift für Schweizerisches Recht (Basel NS 1. 1882 ff.; cited by volume, year and page)
ZVersWiss	Zeitschrift für die gesamte Versicherungswissenschaft (Karlsruhe 1. 1901 ff.; 43. 1943, 56. 1967 ff.; cited by year and page)
ZVglRWiss	Zeitschrift für vergleichende Rechtswissenschaft (Heidelberg 1. 1878 ff.; cited by volume, year and page)
ZVR	Zeitschrift für Verkehrsrecht (Vienna 1. 1956 ff.; cited by year, number of the decision and page)
ZZP	Zeitschrift für Zivilprozeß (Cologne et al. 63. 1943, 64. 1950/51, 65. 1952 ff.; cited by volume, year and page)

Table of Codes and Statutes

Austria

Civil Code (Allgemeines Bürgerliches Gesetzbuch) 1 June 1811 (JGS 946)

Consumer Protection Act (Konsumentenschutzgesetz) of 8 March 1979 (BGBl 1979/140)

General Social Insurance Act (Allgemeines Sozialversicherungsgesetz, ASVG) of 9 November 1955 (BGBl 1955/189)

Belgium

Act of 1 August 1985 concerning fiscal and other provisions (Wet van 1 augustus 1985 houdende fiscale en andere bepalingen/Loi portant des mesures fiscales et autres) (B. S. 6 August 1985)

Civil Code (Code Civil) 5 March 1803

Czech Republik

Denmark

Act on Commission Agents (Kommissionslov), lovbekendtgørelse 15 September 1986 (no. 636)

§ 7:	Chapter 2, Art. 2:101, Notes, II 19, III 30
§ 8:	Introd. I 56, 56 (71)
§ 32:	Chapter 2, Art. 2:102, Notes, II 21

Contract Act (Aftaleloven (of 8 May 1917 (no. 242)), lovbekendtgørelse om aftaler og andre retshandler på formuerettens område), 26 August 1996 (no. 781)

§ 4 (2):	Chapter 1, Art. 1:103, Notes, I 9
§ 6 (2):	Chapter 1, Art. 1:103, Notes, I 9

Damages Liability Act (Lovbekendtgørelse om erstatningsansvar), 4 September 2002 (no. 750)

§ 24a:	Chapter 2, Art. 2:103, Notes, IV 41

Lease Act (Lejelov), 14 May 2001 (no. 347)

§ 11 (1):	Introd. I 56

Lost Property Act (Lovbekendtgørelse om hittegods), 1 September 1986 (no. 591)

§ 3:	Introd. I 56, 56 (73)

Penal Code (Straffelov), 30 September 2003 (no. 814)

§ 253 CP:	Chapter 1, Art. 1:103, Notes, III 24

Estonia

Law of Obligations Act, 5 June 2002 (RTI I 2001, 81, 487)

§ 1018 CC:	Chapter 1, Art. 1:101, Notes, I 2
§ 1018 (1) CC:	Chapter 1, Art. 1:102, Notes, I 2, Art. 1:103, Notes, I, 2
§ 1018 (1), (2) CC:	Chapter 1, Art. 1:101, Notes, II 27, VII 74
§ 1018 (1) (i) CC:	Chapter 1, Art. 1:101, Notes, IX 98
§ 1018 (1) (iii) CC:	Introd. B 16, Art. 1:102, Notes, II 12
§§ 1018-1023 CC:	Introd. B 11
§ 1019 CC:	Introd. B 15
§§ 1019-1023 CC:	Chapter 1, Art. 1:101, Notes, I 2
§ 1020 CC:	Introd. B 20, Chapter 2, Art. 2:101, Notes, III 23
§ 1021 (1) CC:	Introd. B 21, Chapter 2, Art. 2:102, Notes, II 12
§ 1021 (2) CC:	Introd. B 15, Chapter 2, Art. 1:102, Notes, IV 35
§ 1022 CC:	Chapter 2, Art. 2:101, Notes, I 2
§ 1022 (2) CC:	Introd. F 46, Chapter 2, Art. 2:103, Notes, III 22
§ 1022 (5) CC:	Chapter 2, Art. 2:103, Notes, IV 32
§ 1023 CC:	Introd. B 23
§ 1023 (1) CC:	Introd. B 24, Chapter 3, Art. 3:101, Notes, I 1, II 12
§ 1023 (2) CC:	Introd. B 24, Chapter 3, Art. 3:102, Notes, I 2
§ 1023 (3) CC:	Introd. B 24, Chapter 3, Art. 3:104, Notes, I 2, 3
§ 1024 CC:	Introd. C 27
§ 1025 CC:	Introd. B 24
§ 1025 (1) CC:	Chapter 3, Art. 3:103, Notes, I 2

§ 1025 (1) (ii) CC: Chapter 3, Art. 3:104, Notes, II 13
§ 1026 (1) CC: Introd. C 29
§ 1026 (2) CC: Introd. C 28

Finland

Act on Damages for Accidents by Saving Another Person's Life (Lag om skadestånd för olycksfall vid räddning av människoliv), 12 April 1935 (no. 158)
§ 1: Introd. L 87, 87 (173), Chapter 3, Art. 3:104, Notes, II 21

Act on Renting of Flats (Lag om hyra av bostadslägenhet), 31 March 1995 no. 481
§ 20 (2) (3): Introd. I 56

Act on Certain Joint Property Relations (Lag om vissa samäganderättsförhållanden), 25 April 1958 (no. 180)
§ 4: Introd. I 56, 56 (80)

Code of Inheritance (Ärvdabalk), 5 February 1965 (no. 40)
Ch. 18, §§ 2-4 Introd. I 56

Code of Judicial Procedure (Rättegångsbalk), 31 December 1734 (no. 4)
Ch. 15 § 4: Chapter 1, Art. 1:101, Notes, II 20

Commercial Code (Handelsbalk), 31 December 1734 (no. 3)
Ch. 18 § 10: Introd. I 55, Chapter 1, Art. 1:101, Notes, I 10, II 20, IX 104

Consumer Protection Act (Konsumentskyddslag), 20 January 1978 (no. 38)
Ch. 8, § 6: Introd. I 55, Chapter 1, Art. 1:103, Notes, I 9

Contract Act (Lag om rättshandlingar på förmögenhetsrättens område), 13 June 1929 (no. 228)
§ 4 (2): Chapter 1, Art. 1:103, Notes, I 9
§ 6 (2): Chapter 1, Art. 1:103, Notes, I 9

Damages Liability Act (Skadeståndslag), 31 May 1974 (no. 412)
Ch. 2 § 2: Chapter 2, Art. 2:103, Notes, IV 41

Debt Enforcement Act (Utsökningslag), 3 December 1895 (no. 37)
Ch. 4 § 25: Chapter 1, Art. 1:101, Notes, VI 70,
Chapter 1, Art. 1:103, Notes, IV 29

Gift Promises Act (Lag om gåvoutfästelser), 31 Juli 1947 (no. 625)
§ 4: Chapter 1, Art. 1:101, Notes, II 21

France

Germany

Civil Code (Bürgerliches Gesetzbuch), 18 August 1896 (RGBl. 195)

Commercial Code (Handelsgesetzbuch), 10 May 1857 (RGBl. 219)

Social Security Code, Book VII (Sozialgesetzbuch, SGB, Siebtes Buch), 7 August 1996 (BGBl. I 1996, 1254)

Social Security Code, Book X (Sozialgesetzbuch, SGB, Zehntes Buch), 18 August 1980 (BGBl. I, 1469)

Greece

Civil Code (Astikos Kodikas), 23 February 1946 (A. N. 2250/1940; FEK A 91/1940, 597)

Hungary

Civil Code (1959. évi IV. törvény a Polgári Törvénykönyvről)

Ireland

Succession Act 1965

Italy

Civil Code (Codice Civile), 4 April 1942 (Gazz. Uff. no. 79 and 79bis; edizione straordinaria)

Art. 1711 (2) CC:	Introd. D 36
Art. 1712 CC:	Introd. B 20, Chapter 2, Art. 2:101, Notes, III 27
Art. 1712 (2) CC:	Chapter 1, Art. 1:101, Notes, IX 101
Art. 1713 CC:	Chapter 2, Art. 2:102, Notes, II 18
Art. 1713 (1) CC:	Introd. B 21, Chapter 2, Art. 2:102, Notes, I 7
Art. 1716 (3) CC:	Chapter 2, Art. 2:103, Notes, II 17
Art. 1720 (2) CC:	Chapter 3, Art. 3:103, Notes, I 7
Art. 1727 (1) CC:	Chapter 2, Art. 2:103, Notes, III 27
Art. 1789 (1) CC:	Introd. D 36
Art. 1808 (2) CC:	Introd. D 36
Art. 2028 CC:	Introd. B 14, 19, F 44, L 99, Chapter 1, Art. 1:101, Notes, III 33, Art. 1:103, Notes, I 5, Chapter 2, Art. 2:101, Notes, IV 39
Artt. 2028 ff CC:	Chapter 1, Art. 1:101, Notes, I 3
Artt. 2028-2032 CC:	Introd. B 11
Art. 2029 CC:	Introd. B 15, E 40, Chapter 2, Art. 1:102, Notes, IV 39, Art. 2:103, Notes, IV 38
Art. 2030 CC:	Introd. B 20, Chapter 2, Art. 2:101, Notes, I 4
Art. 2030 (1) CC:	Introd. B 18, 21
Art. 2030 (2) CC:	Introd. B 18, F 46 (58), Chapter 2, Art. 2:103, Notes, III 25, Chapter 3, Art. 3:104, Notes, II 18
Art. 2031 CC:	Introd. B 23, 25, Chapter 1, Art. 1:101, Notes, VII 77, Art. 1:102, Notes, I 7, Chapter 3, Art. 3:101, Notes, I 7, II 17, Art. 3:106, Notes, 7
Art. 2031 (1) CC:	Introd. B 24
Art. 2031 (2) CC:	Introd. B 16, Chapter 1, Art. 1:101, Notes, VII 77, VIII 89
Art. 2032 CC:	Introd. C 29, Chapter 1, Art. 1:101, Notes, IX 101
Art. 2041 CC:	Chapter 3, Art. 3:101, Notes, II 17
Art. 2042 CC:	Introd. F 47 (62)
Art. 2043 CC:	Chapter 2, Art. 2:103, Notes, IV 38
Art. 2697 CC:	Chapter 1, Art. 1:101, Notes, X 112

Penal Code (Codice penale) Regio decreto 19 October 1930, no. 1398

Art. 593 CP:	Chapter 1, Art. 1:103, Notes, III 22

Lithuania

Civil Code, 6 September 2000

Artt. 6:229-6:236:	Introd. B 11

Luxembourg

Civil Code (Code Civil), 5 March 1803

Art. 1372 CC:	Introd. B 14, Chapter 2, Art. 2:101, Notes, I 1
Art. 1372 (1) CC:	Chapter 2, Art. 2:101, Notes, IV 36
Art. 1372 (2) CC:	Introd. B 21, Chapter 2, Art. 2:102, Notes, I 6
Artt. 1372 f CC:	Introd. B 19

Artt. 1372-1375 CC:	Introd. B 11, Chapter 1, Art. 1:101, Notes, I 7
Art. 1373 CC:	Chapter 2, Art. 2:101, Notes, IV 36
Art. 1374 CC:	Introd. F 46 (58)
Art. 1374 (1) CC:	Introd. B 18, Chapter 2, Art. 2:101, Notes, I 1, II 14
Art. 1374 (2) CC:	Introd. B 18, Chapter 2, Art. 2:103, Notes, III 25
Art. 1375 CC:	Introd. B 22, 23, 24, 25, Chapter 3, Art. 3:101, Notes, I 5, II 15
Art. 1947 CC:	Introd. D 36
Art. 1992 (1) CC:	Chapter 2, Art. 2:101, Notes, I 1
Art. 1993 CC:	Introd. B 21, Chapter 2, Art. 2:102, Notes, I 6
Art. 2001 CC:	Chapter 3, Art. 3:101, Notes, II 15

Malta

Civil Code, 22 January 1874

Art. 1013 CC:	Introd. E 40, Chapter 1, Art. 1:101, Notes, I 7, Art. 1:103, Notes, I 5, Chapter 2, Art. 1:102, Notes, IV 39
Artt. 1013 f CC:	Introd. B 19, Chapter 2, Art. 2:101, Notes, IV 36
Artt. 1013-1020 CC:	Introd. B 11
Art. 1015 CC:	Chapter 2, Art. 2:101, Notes, I 1, II 14
Art. 1016 CC:	Chapter 2, Art. 2:101, Notes, I 1, II 14
Art. 1017 CC:	Introd. F 46 (58), Chapter 2, Art. 2:103, Notes, III 25
Art. 1018 CC:	Chapter 3, Art. 3:101, Notes, I 5
Art. 2018 CC:	Introd. B 23
Art. 2019 CC:	Chapter 1, Art. 1:101, Notes, III 31

The Netherlands

New Civil Code (Nieuw Burgerlijk Wetboek), 1 January 1992 (for details see abbreviation list "BW")

Art. 3:32 CC:	Chapter 2, Art. 2:103, Notes, IV 39
Art. 3:32 (2) CC:	Chapter 2, Art. 1:102, Notes, IV 40
Art. 3:53 (2) CC:	Chapter 1, Art. 1:101, Notes, V 56
Artt. 3:60 ff CC:	Chapter 3, Art. 3:106, Notes, 8
Art. 3:78 CC:	Chapter 3, Art. 3:106, Notes, 8
Art. 5:10 (1) CC:	Introd. D 33
Art. 5:10 (2) CC:	Chapter 3, Art. 3:102, Notes, I 9
Art. 6:8 CC:	Chapter 1, Art. 1:103, Notes, II 18
Art. 6:30 CC:	Introd. D 34, Chapter 1, Art. 1:101, Notes, II 18
Art. 6:74 CC:	Chapter 2, Art. 2:103, Notes, IV 39
Artt. 6:74 ff CC:	Chapter 2, Art. 2:103, Notes, I 8, III 28
Art. 6:76 CC:	Chapter 2, Art. 2:103, Notes, II 18
Artt. 6:95 ff CC:	Chapter 2, Art. 2:103, Notes, I 8, Chapter 3, Art. 3:101, Notes, II 18, Art. 3:102, Notes, I 9, Art. 3:103, Notes, I 8
Art. 6:96 CC:	Chapter 3, Art. 3:102, Notes, I 9
Art. 6:104 CC:	Introd. C 28

Poland

Civil Code, 23 April 1964 (Dz. U. 1964, no. 16, Pos. 93)

Portugal

Civil Code (Código Civil), 25 November 1966 (Decreto-Lei no. 47-344)

Code of Advertising (Código da Publicidade), 23 October 1990 (Decreto-Lei no. 330/90), changed by Decreto-Lei no. 275/98 of 9 September 1998

Art. 11:	Introd. L 85 (170)

Code of Civil Procedure (Código do Processo Civil), 28 December 1961 (Decreto-Lei no. 44129), as amended by Decreto-Lei no. 324/2003 of 27 December 2003

Art. 41 (1) CCP:	Chapter 1, Art. 1:101, Notes, IX 97, Chapter 3, Art. 3:102, Notes, I 3
Art. 41 (2) CCP:	Chapter 2, Art. 2:103, Notes, I 3

Regulation of Accidents at Work and Occupational Diseases (Regime jurídico dos acidentes de trabalho e das doenças profissionais), 13 September 1997 (no. 100/97)

	Introd. L 87

Social Security Act (Bases da Segurança Social), 20 December 2002 (Law no. 32/2002)

	Introd. L 87 (177)

Slovakia

Civil Code, 26 February 1964 (no. 40/1964 Sb)

Artt. 742-746 CC:	Introd. B 11
Art. 743 (1) CC:	Chapter 1, Art. 1:101, Notes, VIII 85, Chapter 2, Art. 2:101, Notes, III 23
Art. 746 CC:	Chapter 2, Art. 2:102, Notes, I 2

Slovenia

Code of Obligations, 3 October 2001 (RS no. 83/2001, 8345)

Art. 199:	Introd. B 11, Chapter 1, Art. 1:101, Notes, I 8
Artt. 199-206:	Introd. B 11
Art. 200:	Chapter 2, Art. 2:101, Notes, III 23, IV 38
Art. 201:	Chapter 2, Art. 2:101, Notes, II 13
Art. 204:	Chapter 2, Art. 2:101, Notes, II 13
Art. 210:	Chapter 2, Art. 2:101, Notes, I 5

Spain

Civil Code (Código Civil), 24 July 1889 (Gaceta de Madrid no. 206, 25 July 1889)

Art. 354 (3) CC:	Chapter 2, Art. 1:102, Notes, III 28
Artt. 446 ff CC:	Introd. D 33
Art. 453 CC:	Chapter 3, Art. 3:101, Notes, II 16
Art. 454 CC:	Chapter 3, Art. 3:101, Notes, II 16
Art. 455 CC:	Chapter 2, Art. 1:102, Notes, III 28
Art. 487 CC:	Introd. D 36
Art. 615 CC:	Introd. D 33

Ley 560 and 561 of the Collection of Civil Laws of (the Assembly of) Navarra, adopted by Law 1/1973 (Ley 560 y 561 de la Corepilación del Derecho Civil Foral de Navarra, aprobada por ley 1/1973), 1 March 1973 (BOE 7 March 1973, no. 57)

Introd. B 11, 19, 21, 23, Chapter 1, Art. 1:101, Notes, I 6, IX 100, Art. 1:102, Notes, I 6, Art. 1:103, Notes, I 4, Chapter 2, Art. 2:101, Notes, II 15, IV 37, Art. 2:102, Notes, I 7, Chapter 3, Art. 3:104, Notes, I 6

Penal Code (Código Penal), 14 September 1973 (BOE no. 297-300, 12-15 December 1973)

Art. 195 CP: Chapter 1, Art. 1:103, Notes, III 22
Art. 593 CP: Chapter 1, Art. 1:103, Notes, III 22

Royal Legislative Decree 1/1994, to adopt the Consolidated General Law on Social Security (Real Decreto Legislativo 1/1994, de 20 de junio, por el que se aprueba el Texto Refundido de la Ley General de la Seguridad Social), 20 June 1994 (BOE 29 June 1994, no. 154)

Art. 115: Introd. L 87, 87 (175)
Art. 115 (2) (d): Introd. L 87

Code of Civil Procedure (Código Procesal Civil), Act 1/2000 on Civil Procedure (Ley de Enjuiciamiento Civil), 7 January 2000 (BOE no. 7, 8 January 2000)

Art. 113 CCP: Chapter 3, Art. 3:105, Notes, I 1
Art. 217 CCP: Chapter 1, Art. 1:101, Notes, X 111

Sweden

Act on Certain Stolen Goods etc (Lag om visst stöldgods m. m.), 29 November 1974 (1974:1065)

§ 7: Chapter 1, Art. 1:101, Notes, I 10, II 20

Act on Joint Property (Lag om samäganderätt), 30 September 1904 (1904:48 p. 1)

§ 2: Introd. I 56, 56 (79)

Act on Partnership and Non-registered Partnership (Lag om handelsbolag och enkla bolag), 28 June 1895 (1895:64 p. 1)

§ 5: Introd. I 56, 56 (76)
§ 48: Introd. I 56, 56 (76)

Act on Partnership and Non-registered Partnership (Lag om handelsbolag och enkla bolag), 11 December 1980 (1980:1102)

Ch. 2 § 3: Introd. I 56, 56 (77)
Ch. 4 § 3: Introd. I 56, 56 (77)
Ch. 11 § 3: Introd. I 56
Ch. 12 § 8: Introd. I 56

Act on Proceeding with Abandoned Property and Lost Property etc (Lag om förfarande med förverkad egendom och hittegods m. m.), 29 November 1974 (1974:1066)

Chapter 1, Art. 1:101, Notes, II 22

Interest Act (Räntelag), 5 June 1975 (1975:635)
§ 3 (2): Chapter 2, Art. 2:102, Notes, I 10, III 32

Land Code (Jordabalk), 17 December 1970 (1970:994)
Ch. 5 § 3: Introd. I 56
Ch. 9 § 17 (2), (3): Introd. I 56
Ch. 12 § 11 no. 1: Introd. I 56
Ch. 12 § 17: Introd. I 56

Lost Property Act (Lag om hittegods), 22 April 1938 (1938:121)
§ 3: Introd. I 56, 56 (72)

Maintenance Support Act (Lag om underhållsstöd), 31 October 1996 (1996:1030)
§§ 21-31: Chapter 1, Art. 1:102, Notes, II 15

Maritime Code (Sjölag), 9 June 1994 (1994:1009)
Ch. 6 § 8: Chapter 3, Art. 3:106, Notes, 10
Ch. 13 § 12: Chapter 2, Art. 2:101, Notes, II 19, III 30
Ch. 13 § 16 (3): Chapter 2, Art. 2:101, Notes, III 30

Marriage Code (Äktenskapsbalk), 14 May 1987 (1987:230)
Ch. 6 § 4: Introd. I 57 (82), Chapter 3, Art. 3:106, Notes, 10

Ordinance on Compensation and Reward for someone who helps the Police (Förordning om ersättning och belöning åt den som hjälper polisen), 22 June 1988 (1988:842)
§§ 1 (1), (2), 2,
5 a, 10: Introd. L 87, 87 (176)

Parental Code (Föräldrabalk), 10 June 1949 (1995:974) (1949:381)
Ch. 9 § 1: Chapter 2, Art. 2:103, Notes, IV 41
Ch. 11 § 3: Chapter 1, Art. 1:101, Notes, VI 70

Promissory Notes Act (Lag om skuldebrev), 27 March 1936 (1936:81)
§ 2: Chapter 1, Art. 1:103, Notes, II 19

Registered Partnership Act (Lag om registrerat partnerskap), 23 June 1994 (1994:1117)
Ch. 3 § 1: Introd. I 57 (67)

Sale of Goods Act (Köplag), 6 September 1990 (1990:931)
§§ 72-78: Introd. I 56, Chapter 1, Art. 1:101, Notes, VIII 92

Securities Business Act (Lag om värdepappersrörelse), 13 June 1991 (1991:981)
Ch. 3 § 5: Chapter 2, Art. 1:102, Notes, III 32

United Kingdom

Administration of Estates Act 1925 (15 & 16 Geo. 5 c. 23)

secs. 33(2), 34(3): Chapter 1, Art. 1:102, Notes, II 16

Administration of Justice Act 1982 (1982 c. 53)

sec. 8: Chapter 3, Art. 3:105, Notes, 1

Child Care Act 1980 (1980 c. 5)

sec. 25: Chapter 1, Art. 1:103, Notes, IV 30

Child Support Act 1991 (1991 c. 48)

Chapter 1, Art. 1:102, Notes, II 16

Child Support Act 1995 (1995 c. 34)

Chapter 1, Art. 1:102, Notes, II 16

Child Support, Pensions and Social Security Act 2000 (2000 c. 19)

Part 1: Chapter 1, Art. 1:102, Notes, II 16

Children Act 1989 (1989 c. 41)

sec 3(5): Chapter 1, Art. 1:101, Notes, I 1
sec 29: Chapter 1, Art. 1:102, Notes, II 16
Sch. 2: Chapter 1, Art. 1:102, Notes, II 16; Art. 1:103, Notes, IV, 30

Children and Young Persons Act 1933 (23 Geo. 5 c. 12)

sec. 1: Chapter 1, Art. 1:103, Notes, III 24

Enduring Powers of Attorney Act 1985 (1985 c. 29)

Chapter 1, Art. 1:103, Notes, IV 30

Mental Capacity Act 2005 (2005 c. 9)

Chapter 1, Art. 1:103, Notes, IV 30
secs. 5-6: Chapter 1, Art. 1:102, Notes, I 11
sec. 7: Chapter 1, Art. 1:101, Notes, V 59
sec. 8(1): Chapter 3, Art. 3:106, Notes, 11
sec. 8(2): Chapter 3, Art. 3:101, Notes, I 10

Mental Health Act 1983 (1983 c. 20)

Part VII: Chapter 1, Art. 1:103, Notes, IV 30

National Assistance Act 1948 (11 & 12 Geo. 6 c. 29)

secs. 21-22: Chapter 1, Art. 1:103, Notes, IV 30
sec. 42: Chapter 1, Art. 1:103, Notes, IV 30

Table of UK and Irish Cases

Table of Treaties and Enactments of the European Union

Convention for the Unification of Certain Rules of Law relating to Assistance and Salvage at Sea of September 23rd 1910: Introd. K 78

Directive on Protection of Consumers in Respect of Distance Contracts
(97/7/EC of May 20th 1997), 97/7/EC, OJ L 144,
4/6/1997, p. 19: Introd. L 84 (166)
Art. 9: Introd. K 80 (165), Chapter 1, Art. 1:101, Comments, C 21

London International Convention on Salvage of April 28th 1989
(Text of the Convention in UNTS vol 1954 (1996) No. I-33479, p. 166 and in http://www.jus.uio.no/lm/imo.salvage.convention.1989/doc.html)
Artt. 12, 14: Introd. K 78 (163)

Principles of European Contract Law (PECL)

Table of Literature Cited in Abbreviated Form

Acquarone, D. 1986 chron. 21	*Daniel Acquarone*, La nature juridique de la responsabilité civile du gérant d'affaire dans ses rapports avec le maître de l'affaire, D. 1986 chron. 21-26
Albaladejo, Derecho civil II (2)^{12}	*Manuel Albaladejo*, Derecho civil, vol. II: Derecho de obligaciones, book 2: Los contratos en particular y las obligaciones no contractuales, 12th ed., Barcelona 2004
Albaladejo (*-Santos Briz*), Código Civil y compilaciones forales XXIV	Manuel Albaladejo (ed.), Código Civil y compilaciones forales, vol. XXIV: art. 1887-1929, Madrid 1984, quoted here with the commentaries of arts. 1888-1894 by *Jaime Santos Briz*
Allen, 40 (1931) Yale LJ 331	*Carleton Kemp Allen*, Legal Duties, 40 (1931) Yale LJ 331
Almeida Costa, Obrigações^{9}	*Mário Júlio Almeida Costa*, Direito das Obrigações, 9th ed., Coimbra 2001
Andersson, Skyddsändamål och adekvans	*Håkan Andersson*, Skyddsändamål och adekvans: om skadeståndsansvarets gränser, Uppsala 1993
Andersson/Söderlund, JT 2002-03, 3	*Eilert Andersson and Johan Söderlund*, Entreprenörens rätt till ersättning för ändringar och tilläggsarbeten, JT 2002-03, 3-15
Antunes Varela, Obrigações em Geral I^{10}	*João de Matos Antunes Varela*, Das Obrigações em Geral, vol. I, 10th ed., Coimbra 2000
Aru, Gestione d'affari	Antonio Scialoja and Giuseppe Branca (ed.), Commentario al codice civile, Libro IV, Delle obbligazioni (Artt. 2028-2042), Bologna- Roma 1981, quoted here with the commentaries of arts. 2028-2032 c. c., Della gestione d'affari, by *Luigi Aru*
Ashworth, Principles of Criminal Law^{3}	*Andrew Ashworth*, Principles of Criminal Law, 3rd ed., Oxford 1999
Asser (*-Hartkamp*), Verbintenissenrecht III^{11}	Carel Asser's Handleiding tot de beoefening van het Nederlands burgerlijk recht. Verbintenissenrecht Deel III: De verbintenis uit de wet, by *Arthur S. Hartkamp*, 11th ed., Deventer 2002
Aubert, JCP 1970, II, no. 16445	*Jean-Luc Aubert*, note Cass. civ. 1 December 1969, JCP 1970, II, no. 16445
v. Bar, Festschrift Werner Lorenz	*Christian v. Bar*, Die Äquivalente des Common Law für das kontinentaleuropäische Konzept der berechtigten Geschäftsführung ohne Auftrag, in: Festschrift für Werner Lorenz zum 80. Geburtstag, edited by Thomas Rauscher and Heinz Peter Mansel, 441-461, München 2001
v. Bar, Festschrift Schlechtriem	*Christian v. Bar*, Geschäftsbesorgungen im Sinne des Rechts der Geschäftsführung ohne Auftrag, in: Festschrift für Peter Schlechtriem zum 70. Geburtstag, edited by Ingeborg Schwenzer and Günter Hager, 699-719, Tübingen 2003

v. Bar (*-author*), Sachenrecht in Europa	Christian v. Bar (ed.), Sachenrecht in Europa, Osnabrück 1999-2001. Vol. 1: Dänemark (*Tanya-Caroline Hitchock* and *Malene Stein Poulsen*), Schweden (*Dirk Westermann* and *Reinhard Herrmann*), Finland (*Matias Collan* and *Juha Koivula*), England (*Sean Middleton*), 2000; vol. 2: Polen (*Jerzy Poczobut*), Ungarn (*Lajos Vékás*), Tschechien (*Michaela Zuklinnová*), 2000; vol. 3: Griechenland (*Evlalia Eleftheriadou*), Portugal (*Maria Margarida R. A. C. de Seabra* and *Yanko Marcius de Alencar Xavier*), Niederlande (*Franz Nieper* and *Hendrik Ploeger*), 1999; vol. 4: Belgien/Frankreich (*Erwin Beysen*), Italien (*Lucas Plancker* and *Karl Pfeifer*), Spanien (*Elena Mariscal Rodriguez*), 2001
Baur, JZ 1952, 328	*Fritz Baur*, Zur "dinglichen Seite" der Geschäftsführung ohne Auftrag, JZ 1952, 328-329
Bell	*John Bell*, Principles of the Law of Scotland, Edinburgh 1899
Bell, Personal Property	*Andrew P. Bell*, Modern Law of Personal Property, London 1989
Bengtsson/Victorin, Hyra och annan nyttjanderätt till fast egendom[6]	*Bertil Bengtsson and Anders Victorin*, Hyra och annan nyttjanderätt till fast egendom, 6th ed., Stockholm 2004 (sometimes also quoted from the 5th ed., Stockholm 1997)
Benjamin (*-author*), Sale of Goods[6]	A. G. *Guest and others*, Benjamin's Sale of Goods, 6th ed., London 2002
Bianca, Diritto civile, III[2]	*Massimo Bianca*, Diritto civile. Vol. III: Il contratto, 2nd ed., Milano 2000, reprint Milano 2003
Biondi, Foro it. 1954, I, 98	*Biondo Biondi*, Gestione rappresentativa e ratifica, Foro it. 1954, I, 98-102
Birks, 24 (1971) CurrLegProbl. 110	*Peter Birks*, Negotiorum Gestio and the Common Law, 24 (1971) CurrLegProbl. 110
Bosdas, NoB 18/1970, 769	*Dimitrios Bosdas*, Symvoli eis tin ennolian tis dioikiseos allotrion, NoB 18/1970, 769–779
Bowstead (*-Reynolds/ Graziadei*), Agency[17]	*Francis Martin Baillie Reynolds* with the contribution of *William Bowstead* and *Michele Graziadei*, Bowstead and Reynold on Agency, 17th ed., London 2001, sometimes quoted from the 16th ed., London 1996
Breccia, La gestione di affari[2]	*Umberto Breccia*, La gestione di affari, in: Pietro Rescigno (ed.), Trattato di Diritto Privato. Vol. IX: Obbligazioni e contratti, Tomo primo, 2nd ed., Torino 1999, reprint Torino 2000
Burrows and McKendrick, Cases and Materials	*Andrew S. Burrows and Ewan McKendrick*, Cases and Materials on the Law of Restitution, Oxford 1997
Carbonnier, Les obligations[21]	*Jean Carbonnier*, Droit civil, 4, Les obligations, 21th ed., Paris 1998
Cavanillas Múgica and Tapia Fernández, Concurrencia de responsabilidad	*Santiago Cavanillas Múgica and Isabel Tapia Fernández*, La concurrencia de responsabilidad contractual y extracontractual: tratamiento sustantivo y procesal, Madrid 1992
Cigoj, Komentar II	*Stojan Cigoj*, Komentar obligacijskih razmerij, II. knjiga, Ljubljana 1984
Cigoj, Teorija obligacij	*Stojan Cigoj*, Teorija obligacij, Ljubljana 1998

Clerk and Lindsell (*-author*), Torts^{18}	Clerk and Lindsell on Torts, 18th ed. by *Anthony* M. *Dugdale* and others, London 2000, Ch. 3 – Ch. 4 by M. *Jones*, Ch. 7 by A. M. *Dugdale*
Cornelis, Algemene theorie van de verbintenis	*Ludo Cornelis*, Algemene theorie van de verbintenis, Antwerpen – Groningen 2000
Dalcq, Traité de la responsabilité civile I^{2}	*Roger* O. *Dalcq*, Traité de la responsabilité civile, vol. I: Les causes de responsabilité, 2nd ed., Bruxelles 1967
Diamond, Contract and Tort	*Aubrey* L. *Diamond*, "The Law of Contract and Tort", in: Law Reform Now, edited by Gerald Gardiner and Andrew Martin, London 1964
Díez-Picazo, Fundamentos II^{5}	*Luis Díez-Picazo*, Fundamentos del Derecho civil patrimonial, vol. II: Las relaciones obligatorias, 5th ed., Madrid 1996
Díez-Picazo/Gullón, Sistema II^{9}	*Luis Díez-Picazo and Antonio Gullón*, Sistema de derecho civil, vol. II: El contrato en general, la relación obligatoria, contratos en especial, cuasi contratos, enriquecimiento sin causa, responsabilidad extracontractual, 9th ed., Madrid 2001, sometimes also quoted from earlier editions
Dirix/Van Oevelen, RW 1992-93, 1249	E. *Dirix and* A. *Van Oevelen*, Kroniek van het verbintenissenrecht 1985-1992, RW 1992-93, 1249-1265
Douchy, Notion de quasi-contrat	*Melina Douchy*, La notion de quasi-contrat en droit positif français, Paris 1997
Ehrenzweig, System II (1)^{2}	*Albert* A. *Ehrenzweig*, System des österreichischen allgemeinen Privatrechts, vol. II, 1st part: Das Recht der Schuldverhältnisse, 2nd ed., Vienna 1928
Enciclopedia giuridica Treccani (*-Vela*)	A. *Vela*, Gestione di affari, I, vol. XV, Roma 1992, in: Lucio Lanfranchi, Brunetto Carpino and Pietro Masi (gen. ed.), Enciclopedia giuridica Treccani, 33 vols., Roma 1988-1997
ErmAk (*-Sakketas*)	Ermineia tou Astikou Kodikos, Athens 1949 ff.; quoted here with the commentaries of arts. 730-739 by *Sakketas*
Erman (*-author*) BGB I^{10}	Walter Erman (editor until the 4th. ed.), Harm Peter Westermann (ed.), Handkommentar zum Bürgerlichen Gesetzbuch in zwei Bänden, vol. I, 10th ed., Münster 2000
Erskine	*John Erskine* with the contribution of James Ivory, An institute of the law of Scotland: in four books, in the order of Sir George Mackenzie's Institutions of that law, vol. 2, Edinburgh 1828
Esmein, JCP 1956 II no. 9087	*Paul Esmein*, note Cass. civ. 16. November 1955, JCP 1956, II, no. 9087
Esmein, JCP 1959 II no. 11187	*Paul Esmein*, note Cass. civ. 27. May 1959, JCP 1959, II, no. 11187
v. Eyben/Isager, Lærebog i erstatningsret^{5}	*Bo von Eyben and Helle Isager*, Lærebog i erstatningsret, 5th ed., København 2003
Esser/Weyers, Schuldrecht II(2)^{8}	*Josef Esser and Hans-Leo Weyers*, Schuldrecht, vol. 2: Besonderer Teil, part 2: Gesetzliche Schuldverhältnisse, 8th ed., Heidelberg 2000
Filios, Enochiko Dikaio, I^{2}	*Pavlos Filios*, Enochiko Dikaio, vol. I: Geniko Meros, 2nd ed., Athens 1996
Fitz, Risikozurechnung	*Hanns Fitz*, Risikozurechnung bei Tätigkeit im fremden Interesse, Berlin 1985

Flour/Aubert/Flour/Savaux, Le rapport d'obligation[3]	*Jaques Flour, Jean-Luc Aubert, Yvonne Flour and Éric Savaux*, Droit civil. Les obligations, vol. III: Le rapport d'obligation: la preuve, les effets de l'obligation, la responsabilité contractuelle, transmission, transformation, extinction, 3rd ed., Paris 2004
Flour/Aubert/Savaux, Le fait juridique[10]	*Jaques Flour, Jean-Luc Aubert and Éric Savaux*, Droit civil. Les obligations, vol. II: Le fait juridique, 10th ed., Paris 2003, sometimes also quoted from earlier editions
Fötschl, ÖJZ 2004, 781	*Andreas Fötschl*, Zur Ausgleichsfähigkeit von Kosten eines Vorprozesses, ÖJZ 2004, 781-789
Fötschl, ZVR 2003, 220	*Andreas Fötschl*, Reservehaltungskosten und Geschäftsführung ohne Auftrag, ZVR 2003, 220-234
Fötschl, ERPL 2002, 550	*Andreas Fötschl*, note under BGH, Urteil v. 23. Sept. 1999 – Zum Vergütungsanspruch eines "Erbensuchers" gegen einen ermittelten unbekannten Erben, ERPL 2002, 550–578
Franzoni, Dei fatti illeciti	Antonio Scialoja and Giuseppe Branca (ed.), Commentario al codice civile, Libro IV, Delle obbligazioni (Artt. 2043-2059), Bologna-Roma 1993, quoted here with the commentaries of Arts. 2043-2059, Dei fatti illeciti, by *Massimo Franzoni*
Frenk/Messer, NJB 1993, 45	*Niels Frenk and Ward Messer*, Art. 47 lid 5 jo. Art. v. Wet bodembescherming: 'Much ado about nothing?', NJB 1993, 45-49
Fridman, Agency[5]	G. H. L. *Fridman*, The law of agency, 5th ed., London 1983
Galvão Telles, Obrigações[7]	*Inocêncio Galvão Telles*, Direito das Obrigações, 7th ed., Coimbra 1997
Georgiades/Stathopoulos (*-author*)	Apostolos Georgiades and Michael Stathopoulos, Astikos Kodikas (erminia kat'arthro), vol. III: Eidiko Enochiko, Athenai 1980, quoted here with the commentaries by *Papanikolaou* and *Karassis*
van Gerven, Verbintenissenrecht II[7]	*Walter van Gerven*, Verbintenissenrecht, book 2, 7th ed., Leuven 2000
Glansdorff and Legros, RCJB 28 (1974), 60	*François Glansdorff and Pierre Legros*, La réparation du préjudice subi par l'auteur d'un acte de sauvetage, RCJB 28 (1974) 60-87
Gloag/Henderson, The Law of Scotland[10]	*W. M. Gloag and R. Candlish Henderson*, Introduction to the Law of Scotland, 10th ed. by A. B. Wilkinson and W. A. Wilson assisted by J. A. D. Hope, A. F. Rodger and Ann Paton, Edinburgh 1995
Goff and Jones, Restitution[6]	*Robert Goff and Gareth Jones*, The Law of Restitution, 6th ed., London 2002, sometimes also quoted from the 5th ed., London 1998
Gretton, SLT 1978, 145	*George Gretton*, Reparation and Negotiorum Gestio, SLT 1978, 145
Grönfors, Avtalslagen[3]	*Kurt Grönfors*, Avtalslagen, 3rd ed., Stockholm 1995
Grönfors, Ställningsfullmakt och bulvanskap	*Kurt Grönfors*, Ställningsfullmakt och bulvanskap, Stockholm 1961
Gschnitzer, Schuldrecht, Besonderer Teil[2]	*Franz Gschnitzer*, Österreichisches Schuldrecht. Besonderer Teil und Schadenersatz, 2nd ed. by Christoph Faistenberger, Heinz Barta and Bernhard Eccher, Vienna – New York 1988
Gursky, AcP 185 (1985) 13	*Karl Heinz Gursky*, Der Tatbestand der Geschäftsführung ohne Auftrag, AcP 185 (1985) 13-45
Gursky, Schuldrecht, Besonderer Teil[4]	*Karl Heinz Gursky*, Schuldrecht Besonderer Teil, 4th ed., Heidelberg 2002

Hanbury, Agency[2]	*Harold Greville Hanbury*, The Principles of Agency, 2nd ed., London, 1960
Harloff, Tartan & Torts	*Stephanie Harloff*, Tartan & Torts. Das schottische law of delict im Vergleich zum englischen tort law, Münsteraner Studien zur Rechtsvergleichung, vol. 87, Münster 2002
Håstad, Tjänster utan uppdrag	*Torgny Håstad*, Tjänster utan uppdrag, Stockholm 1973
Håstad, Sakrätt avseende lös egendom[6]	*Torgny Håstad*, Sakrätt avseende lös egendom, 6th ed., Stockholm 2000 (with Supplement 2004)
Hellner, Om obehörig vinst	*Jan Hellner*, Om obehörig vinst, Uppsala 1950
Hellner, Speciell Avtalsrätt, II (2)[3]	*Jan Hellner*, Speciell Avtalsrätt, vol. II: Kontraktsrätt, part 2: Allmänna ämnen, 3rd ed., Stockholm 1996
Hellner/Ramberg, Speciell avtalsrätt I[2]	*Jan Hellner and Jan Ramberg*, Speciell avtalsrätt, vol. I: Köprätt, 2nd ed., Stockholm 1991
Hume, 2 (1956) Sydney L Rev 109	S. G. *Hume*, "Dead Bodies", 2 (1956) Sydney L Rev 109
Jauernig (*-author*)	Othmar Jauernig (ed.), Bürgerliches Gesetzbuch: Kommentar, 11th ed., München 2004
JClCiv (*-Bout*)	Collection des Juris-Classeurs. Juris-Classeur Civil. Directeurs à partir de 1980 Pierre Catala and Philippe Simler. Loose-leaf, Paris 1962 ff (cited by author, keyword, article, and if necessary fasc.); quoted here with the commentaries of Art. 1372-1375, v. Quasi-Contrats. Gestion d'affaires – Conditions d'existence, Fasc. 10 by *Bout*
Jehoram, WPNR 1968, no. 5014, 447	*Herman Cohen Jehoram*, De Zaakwaarneming in het ontwerp nieuw BW, WPNR 1968, no. 5014, S. 446-449
Jørgensen, Kontraktsret II	*Stig Jørgensen*, Kontraktsret, vol. II, København 1973
Kallimopoulos, I mi gnisia dioikisi allotrion (A. K. 739)	*Georgios D. Kallimopoulos*, I mi gnisia dioikisi allotrion (A. K. 739), Symvoli sti theoria tis exodikaiopraktikis evthinis, Athen 1978
Karlgren, TfR 1951, 171	*Hjalmar Karlgren*, Bokanmeldelse: Jan Hellner: Om obehörig vinst särskilt utanför kontraktsförhållanden. Ett civilrättsligt problem i komparativ belysning. Akad. avh. Uppsala 1950, TfR 1951, 171-183
Karnov (*-author*)	Karnov (-author), Bo von Eyben, Jan Pedersen and Thomas Rørdam (ed.), Karnovs lovsamling, København 2004 Karnov (-author), Birgitta Blom, Anders Eriksson, Johan Hirschfeldt and Jan Ramberg (ed.), Karnov. Svensk lagsamling med kommentarer, Stockholm 2002
Karollus, Schutzgesetzverletzung	*Martin Karollus*, Funktion und Dogmatik der Haftung aus Schutzgesetzverletzung: zugleich ein Beitrag zum Deliktssystem des ABGB und zur Haftung für casus mixtus, Vienna 1992
Kavkas and Kavkas, Enochikon Dikaion, II (2)[7]	*Konstantin Kavkas and Dimitrios Kavkas*, Enochikon Dikaion (Erminia kata arthron), Eidiko meros, vol. II (Artt. 730-944 CC), 7th ed., Athens 1993
Klang (*-Stanzl*), ABGB IV, 1[2]	Heinrich Klang, continued by Franz Gschnitzer (ed.), Franz Gschnitzer and Gustav Stanzl, Kommentar zum Allgemeinen

	bürgerlichen Gesetzbuch, vol. IV, book 1, §§ 859-1044, 2nd ed., Vienna 1968, quoted here with the commentaries of §§ 1002-1044 by *Gustav Stanzl*
Kleineman, Festskrift Walin	*Jan Kleineman*, Utomkontraktuella lojalitetsplikter – ett sakrättsligt problem?, in: Festskrift till Gösta Walin, 207-225, Stockholm 2002
Koziol, Österreichisches Haftpflichtrecht I[3]	*Helmut Koziol*, Österreichisches Haftpflichtrecht, vol. I: general part, 3rd ed., Vienna 1997
Koziol and Welser, Grundriss II[12]	*Helmut Koziol and Rudolf Welser*, Grundriss des bürgerlichen Rechts, vol. II, 12th ed., Vienna 2001
Kropholler, Studienkommentar BGB[6]	*Jan Kropholler*, Studienkommentar BGB, 6th ed., Munich 2004
Lacruz Berdejo, Elementos II (2)[2]	*José Luis Lacruz Berdejo et al.*, Elementos de Derecho Civil, vol. II: Derecho de Obligaciones, part 2: Contratos y cuasicontratos, Delito y Cuasidelito, nueva edición, 2nd ed., Barcelona 2002, sometimes quoted from the first ed., Barcelona 1999
Lacruz Berdejo, Rev. Crit. Der. Inm. 1975, 249	*José Luis Lacruz Berdejo*, La gestión de negocios sin mandato, Rev. Crit. Der. Inm. 1975, 249-270
Lando/Beale, PECL I-II	Ole Lando and Huge Beale (ed.), Principles of European Contract Law, Parts I and II combined and revised, The Hague a. o. 2000
Lando/Clive/Prüm/ Zimmermann, PECL III	Ole Lando, Eric Clive, André Prüm and Reinhard Zimmermann (ed.), Principles of European Contract Law Part III, The Hague a. o. 2003
Larenz/Canaris, Schuldrecht Besonderer Teil II[13]	*Karl Larenz*, Lehrbuch des Schuldrechts, 2nd book: Besonderer Teil; continued by *Claus-Wilhelm Canaris*, 13th ed., München 1994
Larroumet D. 1972, 436	*Christian Larroumet*, note under Cass. civ. 1. July 1971, D. 1972, 436-439
Lasarte, Principios II[8]	*Carlos Lasarte Álvarez*, Principios de Derecho Civil, vol. II: 8th ed., Madrid 2003; sometimes also quoted from earlier editions
Lassen, Haandbog i obligationsretten	*Jul. Lassen*, Haandbog i obligationsretten, Speciel del, København 1897
Lassen, Handlinger paa fremmed formueretsomraade i romersk og dansk ret	*Jul. Lassen*, Handlinger paa fremmed formueretsomraade i romersk og dansk ret, København 1880
Lassen, Lærebog i obligationsrettens specielle del	*Jul. Lassen*, Lærebog i obligationsrettens specielle del, København 1912
Lehrberg, Borgen	Bert Lehrberg (ed.), Borgen. Förutsättningsfrågor, regressfrågor, konsumentfrågor, Stockholm 1995
Lennander, Återvinning i konkurs[3]	*Gertrud Lennander*, Återvinning i konkurs, 3rd ed., Stockholm 2004, sometimes also quoted from the 2nd ed., Stockholm 1999
Leslie, SLT 1981, 259	*R. D. Leslie*, Negotiorum Gestio in Scots Law, SLT 1981, 259-261
Leslie, JurRev 1983, 12	*R. D. Leslie*, Negotiorum Gestio in Scots Law: The Claim of the Privileged Gestor, JurRev 1983, 12-35
Lete del Río, Obligaciones II[3]	*José Manuel Lete del Río*, Derecho de Obligaciones, vol. II: El contrato en general. Cuasicontratos. Enriquecimiento sin causa. Responsabilidad extracontractual, 3rd ed., Madrid 1998

le Tourneau/Cadiet, Droit de la responsabilité (1996, 2002/2003, 2004/2005)	*Philippe le Tourneau and Loïc Cadiet*, Droit de la responsabilité. Responsabilités civile et pénale; responsabilités civiles délictuelles et quasi-délictuelles; formation et exécution du contrat; défaillances contractuelles et professionnelles; contrats spéciaux; régimes spéciaux d'indemnisation; accidents de la circulation; actions récursoires, ed. 1996, Paris 1996; Droit de la responsabilité et des contrats, ed. 2002/2003, Paris 2002; ed. 2004/2005, Paris 2004
le Tourneau, v° Gestion d'affaires	*Philippe le Tourneau*, RépDrCiv, vol. VI, v° Gestion d'affaires, Paris 1997 and 2002
Lienhard, D. 2002, 2531	*Alain Lienhard*, note under Cass. ch. mixte 6. Sept. 2002, D. 2002, 2531-2532
Lindenbergh, TPR 2002, 1421	*S. D. Lindenbergh*, Schade van derden door verwonding of overlijden van een naaste, TPR 2002, 1421-1473
Lindskog, Lagen om handelsbolag och enkla bolag	*Stefan Lindskog*, Lagen om handelsbolag och enkla bolag. En kommentar, Stockholm 2001
Lindskog, Preskription[2]	*Stefan Lindskog*, Preskription: om civilrättsliga förpliktelsers upphörande efter viss tid, 2nd ed., Stockholm 2002
Macgregor, Edinburgh LRev 2000, 19	*Laura J. Macgregor*, Illegal Contracts and Unjustified Enrichment, Edinburgh LRev 2000, 19-45
MacQueen, JuridRev 1994, 137	*Hector MacQueen*, Unjustified Enrichment and Breach of Contract, JuridRev 1994, 137-166
Malaurie and Aynès, Contrats et quasi-contrats[11]	*Philippe Malaurie and Laurent Aynès*, Contrats et quasi-contrats, 11th ed., Paris 2001
Malaurie/Aynès/Stoffel-Munck, Les obligations	*Philippe Malaurie, Laurent Aynès and Philippe Stoffel-Munck*, Les obligations, Paris 2003
Malinvaud, Droit des obligations[8]	*Philippe Malinvaud*, Droit des obligations, 8th ed., Paris 2003; sometimes also quoted from the 7th ed., Paris 2001
Marasinghe, 8 (1976) Ottawa L Rev 573	*M. L. Marasinghe*, The Place of Negotiorum Gestio in English Law, 8 (1976) Ottawa L Rev 573
Marshall, General Principles of Scots Law[5]	*Enid Ann Marshall*, General Principles of Scots Law, 5th ed., Edinburgh 1999
Marshall, Scots Mercantile Law[3]	*Enid Ann Marshall*, Scots Mercantile Law, 3rd ed., Edinburgh 1997
Marty and Raynaud, Obligations II (1)[2]	*Gabriel Marty and Pierre Raynaud*, Droit civil. Vol. II: Les obligations. Book 1: Les sources, 2nd ed., Paris 1988
Mazeaud, D. 2002, 2963	*Denis Mazeaud*, note under Cass. ch. mixte 6. Sept. 2002, D. 2002, 2963-2967
Mazeaud, RTD civ 1956, 356	*Henri et Léon Mazeaud*, obs. under Cass. civ. 16. Nov. 1955, RTD civ 1956, 356
Mazeaud and Chabas, Leçons de droit civil II (1)[9]	Established by Henri, Léon and Jean Mazeaud; *François Chabas*, Leçons de droit civil, vol. II, book 1: Obligations, théorie générale, 9th ed., Paris 1998
McBryde, The Law of Contract in Scotland[2]	*William McBryde*, The Law of Contract in Scotland, 2nd ed., Edinburgh 2001

McCamus, 11 (1979) Ottawa L Rev 297	*John D. McCamus*, "Necessitous Intervention: The Altruistic Intermeddler and the Law of Restitution", 11 (1979) Ottawa L Rev 297
Medicus, Schuldrecht II, Besonderer Teil[12]	*Dieter Medicus*, Schuldrecht II: Besonderer Teil, 12th ed., München 2004
Meissel, GoA	*Franz-Stefan Meissel*, Geschäftsführung ohne Auftrag – zwischen Quasikontrakt und aufgedrängter Bereicherung –, Vienna 1993
Menezes Cordeiro, Obrigações II	*António Menezes Cordeiro*, Direito das obrigações, vol. II, Lisboa 1994
Menezes Leitão, Responsabilidade do gestor	*Luís Manuel Teles de Menezes Leitão*, A responsabilidade do gestor perante o dono do negócio no direito civil português, Lisboa 1991
Menezes Leitão, Enriquecimento sem causa	*Luís Manuel Teles de Menezes Leitão*, O enriquecimento sem causa no direito civil, Lisboa 1996
Menezes Leitão, Obrigações I[3]	*Luís Manuel Teles de Menezes Leitão*, Direito das obrigações, Bd. I, 3rd. ed., Coimbra 2003
Mestre/Fages, RTD civ 2003, 94	*Jacques Mestre and Bertrand Fages*, obs. under Cass. ch. mixte 6. September 2002, RTD civ 2003, 94
Mellqvist and Persson, Fordran och skuld[7]	*Mikael Mellqvist and Ingemar Persson*, Fordran och skuld, 7th ed., Uppsala 2004; sometimes quoted also from the 6th ed., Uppsala 2001
Millqvist, JT 1998-99, 387	*Göran Millqvist*, Skadeståndsansvar för panthållare som utlämnar pant till pantsättaren utan panthavarens vetskap, JT 1998-99, 387-390
Muccioli, Riv. dir. comm. 2004, 211	*N. Muccioli*, Un contratto reale senza consenso?, Riv. dir. comm. 2004, 211-240
MünchKomm (*-author*), BGB[4]	Kurt Rebmann, Franz Jürgen Säcker and Roland Rixecker (ed.), Münchener Kommentar zum Bürgerlichen Gesetzbuch, 11 vol., 4th ed., München 1993-2002
Nicholson, Crim LR 1992, 611	*Donald Nicholson*, The Citizen's Duty to Assist the Police, Crim LR 1992, 611
van Ommeslaghe, Droit des obligations II[2]	*Pierre van Ommeslaghe*, Droit des obligations, vol. II, part 1: Les sources des obligations, 2nd ed., Bruxelles 1987
de Page, Droit Civil Belge II[3]	*Henri de Page*, Traité élémentaire de droit civil belge, vol. II: Les incapables, les obligations, 3rd ed., Bruxelles 1964
Palandt (*-Sprau*), BGB[63]	Palandt, Bürgerliches Gesetzbuch, 63rd ed., München 2004; quoted here with the commentaries by *Sprau*
Pane, Solidarietà sociale e gestione di affari altrui	*Rosanna Pane*, Solidarietà sociale e gestione di affari altrui, Napoli 1996
Pasquau Liaño, La gestión de negocios ajenos	*Miguel Pasquau Liaño*, La gestión de negocios ajenos, Madrid 1986
Paulus, Zaakwaarneming	*C. Paulus*, Zaakwaarneming, Bruxelles 1970
Paz-Ares/Díez-Picazo/Bercovitz/Salvador (*-author*), Código Civil, I[2], II[2]	Cándido Paz-Ares Rodríguez, Luis Díez-Picazo Ponce de León, Rodrigo Bercovitz and Pablo Salvador Cordech (ed.), Comentario del Código Civil, 2 vols., published by the Ministerio de Justicia, 2nd ed., Madrid 1993
Pereira Coelho, O enriquecimento e o dano	*Francisco Manuel Pereira Coelho*, O enriquecimento e o dano, Coimbra 1999

Pires de Lima and Antunes Varela, Código civil anotado I^{4}	*Fernando Andrade Pires de Lima and João de Matos Antunes Varela* with the contribution of *Manuel Henrique Mesquita*, Código civil anotado, vol. I, 4th ed., Coimbra 1987
Pochmarski/Strauss, JBl 2002, 353	*Konstantin Pochmarski and Clemens Strauss*, Die Rechtsprechung des OGH zum Regress von Prozesskosten, JBl 2002, 353-374
Puig Brutau, Compendio II^{3}	*José Puig Brutau*, Compendio de Derecho Civil, vol. II: Derecho de obligaciones, contratos y cuasi contratos, Obligaciones derivadas de actos ilícitos, 3rd ed., Barcelona 1997
Reifegerste, JCP G 2002, II, 10173	*Stephan Reifegerste*, note under Cass. ch. mixte 6. Sept. 2002, JCP 2002 éd. G, II, 10173
Rescigno (*-Cercone*), Codice civile^{5}	Pietro Rescigno, Codice civile, 5th ed., Milano 2003; quoted here with the commentaries by *Roberto Cercone*
RGRK (*-Steffen*), BGB^{12}	Das Bürgerliche Gesetzbuch mit besonderer Berücksichtigung der Rechtsprechung des Reichsgerichts und des Bundesgerichtshofs, 12th ed., Berlin 1978, formerly Reichgerichtsrätekommentar; quoted here with the commentaries by *Erich Steffen*
Ribeiro de Faria, Obrigações I	*Jorge Leite Areias Ribeiro de Faria*, Direito das Obrigações, vol. 1, Coimbra 1990
Roodhooft (*-author*), B. H.Verb.	Jan Roodhooft (general ed.), Bestendig Handboek Verbintenissenrecht, V, De quasi-contracten (II.5-1 to II.5-31), Loose-leaf, Antwerpen 2003 ff.
RPDB, v° Quasi-contrat	Emile Brunet, Jean Servais and Charles Resteau (ed.), Répertoire Pratique du Droit Belge. Législation, doctrine et jurisprudence. Cited by key-words; "Quasi contrat", vol. XI, Brussel-Paris 1940, 1-49
Rummel (*-author*), ABGB, I^{3}	Peter Rummel, Kommentar zum Allgemeinen Bürgerlichen Gesetzbuch in zwei Bänden, 3rd ed., Vienna 2000; quoted here with the commentaries by *Welser, Krejci, Gamerith, Strasser, Rummel and Reischauer*
Sacco, Il possesso^{2}	*Rodolfo Sacco*, Il possesso, 2nd ed., Milano 2000
Sánchez Jordán, Gestión de negocios	*María Elena Sánchez Jordán*, La gestión de negocios ajenos, Madrid 2000
Savaux, Def. 2002, 37644	*Eric Savaux*, note under Cass. ch. mixte 6. Sept. 2002, Def. 2002, art. 37644, 1608-1614
Schneiderhan, Der Quasi-Contract im schottischen und englischen Recht	*Peter Schneiderhan*, Der Quasi-Contract im schottischen und englischen Recht, Tübingen 1995
Schoordijk, Zaakwaarneming	*H. C. F. Schoordijk*, Zaakwaarneming: een onderbelichte bron van verbintenis, Deventer – Kluwer 1983
Schoordijk, Het algemeen gedeelte van het verbintenissenrecht	*H. C. F. Schoordijk*, Het algemeen gedeelte van het verbintenissenrecht naar het Nieuw Burgerlijk Wetboek, Deventer 1979
Schrage, Verbintenissen uit andere bron	*E. J. H. Schrage*, Monografieën Nieuw BW, Verbintenissen uit andere bron dan onrechtmatige daad of overeenkomst, Deventer 1998
Schwimann (*-Apathy*), ABGB, V^{2}	Michael Schwimann, Praxiskommentar zum Bürgerlichen Gesetzbuch samt Nebengesetzen in fünf Bänden, 2nd ed.,

	Vienna 1997-1998; quoted here with the commentaries of §§ 1035-1040 by *Apathy*
Seiler, Der Tatbestand der negotiorum gestio im römischen Recht	*Hans Hermann Seiler*, Der Tatbestand der negotiorum gestio im römischen Recht, Köln 1968
Sirena, Gestione di affari	*Pietro Sirena*, La gestione di affari altrui, Ingerenze altruistiche, ingerenze egoistiche e restituzione del profitto, Torino 1999
Snell (*-Baker/Langan*), Equity[29]	*P. V. Baker and P. St. J. Langan*, Snell's Equity, 29th ed., London 1990
Soergel (*-author*), BGB[12]	Bürgerliches Gesetzbuch mit Einführungsgesetz und Nebengesetzen, started by Hs. Th. Soergel, 12th ed., Stuttgart 1999; quoted here with the commentaries by *Beuthien*, *Mühl*, and M. *Wolf*, sometimes quoted from 11th ed., Stuttgart 1980
Spier/Hartlief/Maanen,van/ Vriesendorp, Verbintenissen uit de wet en Schadevergoeding[2]	*J. Spier, T. Hartlief, G.E. van Maanen and R.D. Vriesendorp*, Verbintenissen uit de wet en Schadevergoeding, 2nd ed., Deventer 2000
Stair, Book I	David M. Walker (ed.), *James Dalrymple Viscount of Stair*, The Institutions of the Law of Scotland, deduced from its originals, and collated with the civil canon and feudal laws, and with the customs of neighbouring nations in 4 books, Book I, reprint Edinburgh-Glasgow 1981
Stair (*-author*), The laws of Scotland	Stair, The laws of Scotland: Stair memorial encyclopaedia / The Law Society of Scotland (founded by: James Dalrymple Stair. General ed.: Thomas Smith) Edinburgh 1987 ff. Vol. VII, Criminal Law to Customs and axcise, 1995 by *Christie*; vol. XV, Obligations to parliamentary and other elections, 1996 by *Whitty*
Starck (*-Roland/Boyer*), Les Obligations II[6]	Established by Boris Starck; *Henri Roland and Laurent Boyer*, Droit Civil. Les Obligations. Vol. II: Contrat, 6th ed., Paris 1998
Staudinger (*-author*), BGB[13]	J. v. Staudinger's Kommentar zum Bürgerlichen Gesetzbuch mit Einführungsgesetz und Nebengesetzen, 13th ed., Berlin 2001; quoted here with the commentaries by *Wittmann* and *Bittner*
Stijns/Van Gerven/Wéry, JT 1996, 689	*Sophie Stijns, Dirk Van Gerven and Patrick Wéry*, Chronique de jurisprudence. Les obligations: Les sources (1985-1995), JT 1996, 689-752
Stolfi, Giur. it. 1975, I, 1, 1373	*Giuseppe Stolfi*, note under Cass. 25. Jan. 1974, no. 199, Giur. it. 1975, I, 1, 1373-1375
Stoljar, Agency	*S.J. Stoljar*, The Law of Agency, London, 1961
Stoljar, Negotiorum Gestio	*Samuel Jacob Stoljar*, Negotiorum Gestio, IECL X 17, 141
Stone, Offences against the Person	*Richard Stone*, Offences against the Person, London 1999
T & C Vermogensrecht (*-author*)[4]	J.H. Nieuwenhuis, C.J.J. M. Stolker and W. L. Valk (ed.), Nieuw Burgerlijk Wetboek. Tekst & Commentaar, 4th ed., Deventer 2001; quoted here with the commentaries by *Hijma*
Terré/Simler/Lequette, Les obligations[8]	*François Terré, Philippe Simler and Yves Lequette*, Droit civil. Les Obligations, 8th ed., Paris 2002

Tettenborn, Restitution[3]	*Andrew M. Tettenborn*, Law of Restitution in England and Ireland, 3rd ed., London 2002
Ujlaki, Gazdaság és Jog, 10/2001, p. 24	*László Ujlaki*, Ingatlan sajátjakénti értékesítése megbízás nélküli ügyvivő részéről (Selling a real estate as his own by the intervener), Gazdaság és Jog (Economy and Law [Periodical]), No. 10/2001, 24-25
Vasseur, RTD civ 1954, 405	*Michel Vasseur*, Urgence en droit civil, RTD civ 1954, 405-437
Vaz Serra, Gestão de negócios	*Adriano Paes da Silva Vaz Serra*, Gestão de negócios, BolMinJus 66 (1957) 45-283
Verbintenissenrecht (*-author*)	Ewoud H. Hondius (ed.), Y. G. Blei Weissmann, Willem H. van Boom and others, Verbintenissenrecht, loose leaf; Commentary on the BW, since March 1991-2004; quoted here with the commentaries by *Heisterkamp* and *Scheltema*
Verburg, De vrijwillige zaakwaarneming	G. *Verburg*, De vrijwillige zaakwaarneming, Proefschrift Vrije Universiteit te Amsterdam, Amsterdam 1949
Vieira Gomes, Gestão de negócios	*Júlio Manuel Vieira Gomes*, A gestão de negócios. Um instituto · jurídico numa encruzilhada, Coimbra 1993
Vinding Kruse, Erstatningsretten[5]	*Anders Vinding Kruse*, Erstatningsretten, 5th ed., København 1989
Vinding Kruse, En nordisk lovbog	*Fredrik Vinding Kruse*, En nordisk lovbog, Udkast til en fælles borgerlig lovbog for Danmark, Finland, Island, Norge og Sverrig, København 1949 (*Fredrik Vinding Kruse*. A Nordic Draft Code, A Draft Code for Denmark, Finland, Ireland, Norway and Sweden, København 1963)
Viney, Introduction à la responsabilité[2]	*Geneviève Viney*, Traité de droit civil, [2]: Les obligations, Introduction à la responsabilité, 2nd ed., Paris 1995
Viney, JCP G 1998, I, 144, n° 7	*Geneviève Viney*, La convention d'assistance bénévole, JCP 1998 éd. G, I, 1095-1096
Viney, JCP G 2002, I, 186, n° 1	*Geneviève Viney*, note under Cass. ch. mixte 6. Sept. 2002, JCP 2002 éd. G, I, 186, n° 1
Viney, JCP E 2002, 1869	*Geneviève Viney*, note under Cass. ch. mixte 6. Sept. 2002, JCP 2002 éd. E, 1869-1874
Virgo, Restitution	*Graham Virgo*, The Principles of the Law of Restitution, Oxford 1999
Vriesendorp, Verbintenissen uit de wet en schadevergoeding[2]	*J. Spier, T. Hartlief, G. E. van Maanen and R. D. Vriesendorp*, Verbintenissen uit de wet en schadevergoeding, 2nd ed., Deventer 2000
Walin, Lagen om skuldebrev m. m.[2]	*Gösta Walin*, Lagen om skuldebrev m. m., 2nd ed., Stockholm 1997
Walin, Borgen och tredjemanspant[3]	*Gösta Walin*, Borgen och tredjemanspant, 3rd ed., Stockholm 2002
Walker, Principles of Scottish Private Law II[4]	*David M. Walker*, Principles of Scottish Private Law, Vol. II, Book IV, Law of Obligations, 4th ed., Oxford 1988
Whitty, JuridRev 1994, 200	*Niall R. Whitty*, Indirect Enrichment in Scots Law, Part III: Negotiorum Gestio and Indirect Enrichment, JuridRev 1994, 200-282

Williston, 22 (1944) Can. Bar Rev. 492	*Walter B. Williston*, Agency of Necessity, 22 (1944) Can. Bar Rev. 492
Wittmann, Begriff und Funktionen der Geschäftsführung ohne Auftrag	*Roland Wittmann*, Begriff und Funktionen der Geschäftsführung ohne Auftrag. Eine zivilistisch-dogmengeschichtliche Abhandlung, München 1981
Zackariasson, Direktkrav	*Laila Zackariasson*, Direktkrav: om rätt att rikta anspråk mot gäldenärens gäldenär, Uppsala 1999
v. Zeiller, II/III	*Franz v. Zeiller*, Commentar über das Allgemeine bürgerliche Gesetzbuch für die gesammten Deutschen Erbländer der Oesterreichischen Monarchie, Wien 1811, vols. II and III
Zimmermann, Law of Obligations	*Reinhard Zimmermann*, The Law of Obligations. Roman Foundations of the Civilian Tradition, Cape Town 1990

Index